(continued from front flap)

Jane Ellis is a Senior Researcher and Editor
of *Religion in Communist Lands* at
Keston College, Kent.

*Jacket illustration shows a service in the
Trapezny Church of the Holy Trinity
Monastery of St Sergi in Zagorsk. The priests
prepare to serve Communion to the
faithful. It is lent courtesy of The
Novosti Press Agency.*

THE RUSSIAN ORTHODOX CHURCH

The Russian Orthodox Church

A Contemporary History

JANE ELLIS

87 - 1069

INDIANA UNIVERSITY PRESS
Bloomington and Indianapolis

Library of Congress Cataloging in Publication Data

Ellis, Jane, 1951–
   The Russian Orthodox Church.

   Bibliography: p.
   Includes index.
   1. Russkaia pravoslavnaia tserkov —History—20th
century. 2. Orthodox Eastern Church—Soviet Union—
History—20th century. 3. Soviet Union—Church
history—1917–   . 4. Dissenters, Religious—Soviet
Union—History—20th century. 5. Persecution—Soviet
Union—History—20th century. I. Title.
BX492.E56   1986   281.9′47   85-45884
ISBN 0-253-35029-8

Printed and bound in Great Britain

CONTENTS

ACKNOWLEDGEMENTS

I am very grateful to the many people who have helped me in the writing of this book. There are some, who would prefer not to be named, who have generously spent many hours helping me to gain insights into the complex and sometimes obscure life of the Russian Orthodox Church in the Soviet Union. No doubt my understanding is still deficient in some respects, and I hope they will forgive me for it.

Several people read and made valuable and much appreciated comments upon one or more of my chapters at an early stage. They are: the Very Rev. John Arnold, Archpriest Sergei Hackel, Father Raymond Oppenheim, Father Basil Osborne, Peter Reddaway and Theo van der Voort.

At a later stage, a number of extremely useful observations were made by Bishop Kallistos (Ware), Sir John Lawrence, and the late Professor Leonard Schapiro.

My research assistant for part of the time I was writing this book, Paul Lucey, was enthusiastic and dedicated both in research and in offering constructive criticism. At a later stage, a similar task was performed with like dedication, albeit more briefly, by John Anderson.

I wish to thank Dr Philip Walters, the Research Director of Keston College, for his understanding and support during the final stages of writing; also Malcolm Walker, the librarian and archivist at the college, for his helpful response to my many enquiries about source material.

A special word of thanks is due to those responsible for the lengthy and demanding task of producing the typescript, in particular to Marion Broucher, and also to Alexandra Avaloff, Audrey Anderson, Lorna Forrester and Shirley Harrison.

I was able to take time off from Keston College to undertake the research for the book thanks to a generous grant to Keston College from the Leverhulme Trust.

Jane Ellis

INTRODUCTION

The emergence of the Russian Orthodox Church into the international ecclesiastical arena, which began shortly after Stalin allowed the restoration of the Moscow Patriarchate (the church's administrative centre) in 1943, and gained momentum when the church joined the World Council of Churches in 1961, has continued to gather pace during the last two decades. The stately presence of bearded, black-robed figures at religious forums around the globe has become a familiar sight. The Russian Orthodox Church is currently engaged in a series of continuing discussions with the Roman Catholic Church, the Anglican Church, Lutheran Churches, the non-Chalcedonian Churches of the Middle East, and others. It participates actively in the World Council of Churches, the Council of European Churches, and other international bodies. There has been a marked increase in the number of official overseas visits by delegates of the Moscow Patriarchate and of visits by foreign church leaders to the Soviet Union, where the hospitality of the Russian churchmen is fast becoming legendary. The increased international contacts have doubtless been keenly desired by Russian churchmen, long isolated from their fellow-believers abroad. They are due partly to improved ease of modern communications and travel, partly to the brief flowering of *détente* between the countries of the East European bloc and those of the Western hemisphere during the 1970s, and partly to the desire of the Soviet government to foster abroad the belief that freedom of religion exists in the Soviet Union. (Other religious bodies in the USSR have increased their international contacts in a similar manner.)

Over the same period, and in puzzling contradiction to this apparent freedom, an increasing quantity of documentation (*samizdat*) has been reaching the West concerning the very severe problems which many parishes and individual believers in the Russian Orthodox Church are facing. The same factors have contributed to the increase in such documentation. Greater ease of travel and greater desire for contacts between East and West have provided more opportunities for documents to be sent out of the USSR through unofficial channels. And the documents have for the most part been written for the purpose of counteracting the Soviet government's claim and demonstrating that freedom of religion does *not* exist in the Soviet Union.

The problem of the true status of religious believers in the USSR is by no means a new one, but it does seem to be increasing in intensity. Newly confronted with two authoritative channels of information about the Russian Orthodox Church, the average Christian in a Western country may well feel he has no adequate criterion for deciding which is closer to the truth. The problem lies in the partial nature of the information provided to him and the lack of a context into which to put it. The presence of the church's delegates at international conferences can do little to convey to most Western Christians the richness of its liturgical life and the fervour and piety of its faithful. On the other hand, press reports of protests by 'dissidents' in the church and of 'persecution' of religion very often give little or no explanation of the issues involved. Much of the documentation on the subject remains untranslated and unpublished. In order to understand the situation of Russian Orthodox believers in the Soviet Union, it is necessary to understand something of the nature of Orthodox life and worship, and something of the nature of Soviet society and the life of the Soviet citizen — two widely different areas of rather specialised study.

The Russian Orthodox Church is approaching its millennium, to be celebrated in 1988, and the publicity which it may be expected to attract during that year renders the problem of Western perceptions of it more acute. The purpose of this book is to fill in some of the many gaps in the knowledge of Russian Orthodox Church life which still exist in the West. The spotlight on some areas of the church's life may have intensified, but other areas remain in comparative darkness. In the first part of the book we shall examine the life of the bishops, the priests and the faithful; of the parishes, the monasteries and other church institutions. This section will attempt to describe how the Moscow Patriarchate functions, how worship and administration of church life are organised, and what problems are encountered in the process. (There will not, however, be space for a detailed analysis of the church's foreign relations.) Part 2 chronicles the development of public criticism of the Moscow Patriarchate's policies, which has been swelling during the last two decades, and the great personal hardships which many of the critics have suffered as a consequence. It also looks more closely at the ideals and philosophies which inspire the critics; a heady mixture which indicates that the future of the church in the Soviet period may be no less controversial than its past.

For many years there was no new full-length comprehensive survey of the Russian Orthodox Church since Nikita Struve's *Christians in Contemporary Russia*, issued in French in 1963 and revised in 1966 for the English translation (published by Harvill Press in 1967). This situation was rectified in 1984 by the publication of Dimitri Pospielovsky's *The Russian Church under the Soviet Regime 1917–1982* (St Vladimir's Seminary Press). The present book covers much the same time-span as the excellent final chapter of Pospielovsky's book, entitled 'The Russian Orthodox Church, 1965–1982', but in greater detail and with more attention paid to dissent. The emergence of dissent within the church from the Moscow Patriarchate's policies has been documented in Michael Bourdeaux's *Patriarch and Prophets: Persecution of the Russian Orthodox Church* completed in 1968 (reprinted by Mowbrays in 1975). The purpose of the present book is to describe the situation of the Russian Orthodox Church at the time of writing, up to the end of 1984, and to discuss historical developments which have occurred since the completion of Struve's and Bourdeaux's books in the light of the contribution which they have made to the current state of affairs. (Other treatments of this subject include several by the Very Rev. Dimitry Konstantinow, the most recent of which are *Crown of Thorns* (Zarya, London, Ontario, 1979) and *Stations of the Cross* (Zarya, 1984).)

In attempting this task the writer is faced with the problem of controlling and making selections from a large and ever-increasing quantity of first-hand material. The *samizdat* (unofficially self-published) documents alone run into thousands of pages, which are often closely typed carbon copies. *Patriarch and Prophets* was able to employ the admirable device of 'letting the documents speak for themselves'; it contains translations of virtually every document written by Russian Orthodox believers which had reached the West by 1968. This is no longer possible; the trickle of documents has become a flood, and the present work must adopt a more analytical approach.

Despite this, we still do not possess as much information as we should like about all aspects of religious life in the Soviet Union. The present condition of church–state relations in the USSR means that not all information about church life is freely available, and normal methods of research are not always practicable. One is limited to such information as is made available, and cannot always seek out answers to all the questions which arise. Extensiveness is, unfortunately, not the same as comprehensiveness.

Historical Background

In order to understand developments during the period covered in this book, roughly from the end of the 1960s to the end of 1984, it is necessary to have some basic information about the fate of the Russian Orthodox Church during the Soviet period, especially the post-war period. Some of this historical background will be supplied as necessary during the chapters which follow, but an outline of the main phases may be helpful here.

After the October Revolution in 1917, the church enjoyed a very brief period of relative freedom, while the new Bolshevik government was occupied with more pressing matters. In 1917 it was able to convene a Council to discuss important issues in the life of the church, and to elect a Patriarch. (This had not been possible for over 200 years, since Peter the Great had suppressed the Patriarchate and forbidden the church to function as an independent entity.) However, church property was soon nationalised by the 1918 Decree on the Separation of Church and State. Moreover, the first of many bishops was murdered while the Council was in session, and increasingly during the 1920s and on a massive scale during the 1930s, nearly all the bishops and clergy and incalculably large numbers of faithful perished in the labour camps or were shot.

The Soviet state attempted to neutralise the church by the creation in the early 1920s of a rival body, the so-called 'Renovationist' (*obnovlencheskaya*) Church, also known as the 'Living Church'. It was headed by Orthodox priests, talented in many ways, who gave unstinting support to the socialist cause. Initially, it had some success, and many parishes went over to it. But though it survived into the 1940s, it was a spent force long before. This was because the state had lost interest in promoting it, having discovered that it could achieve its purpose through the Patriarchal church. The state had put strong pressure upon Patriarch Tikhon, who was elected in 1918, to declare his loyalty to the Soviet regime. After a period of imprisonment, he made a statement to this effect, the authenticity of which is still disputed. He died in 1925, and there are still those who believe that he was murdered. His successor, Metropolitan Sergi (Stragorodsky), was not directly appointed by either the Council or Patriarch Tikhon, and his legitimacy as head of the church was (and still is) hotly debated. Sergi was also imprisoned, and after being released, in 1927, he issued a declaration of loyalty to the Soviet state. Since that time the Patriarchal church has been completely subservient to the state. Many thousands of faithful left the church in opposition to Sergi's declaration and went underground; they formed various groups which in time became known as the True Orthodox Church or True Orthodox Christians.

By 1939, after many years of persistent persecution, the Russian Orthodox Church had virtually ceased to exist as an institution. There were only four ruling bishops at liberty and very few of the thousands of churches remained open for worship. Theological education, monasticism and religious publications had long ceased. This situation was reversed due to an unforeseen historical event: Hitler's invasion of the USSR. Stalin found that he needed the support of the church leaders to kindle popular support and patriotic fervour for an unexpected war. The Orthodox faith, though suppressed institutionally, had remained alive in the hearts of the people, and the banner of Orthodoxy had to be lifted aloft in order to rally them to the defence of the nation. Moreover, in the areas under German occupation churches and monasteries were reopened, and people who had lived without them for years flooded back to them. All this made it clear that the people had not abandoned their traditional faith, and after the war the policy was to permit the church a legitimate, though very closely controlled, existence, so that the state could keep it under surveillance, rather than drive it underground, where the state would have difficulty keeping track of it. A further factor was the flourishing church life which existed in the western areas of the present-day USSR which were annexed after the war.

In 1943, the three senior hierarchs of the church were invited to a meeting with Stalin, after which the church was restored to an official and public existence. It continued to give the unstinting support which it had already demonstrated for the war effort. After the war, theological education was resumed, some monasteries reopened, and publication of religious literature, albeit in tiny quantities, recommenced. Overseas contacts grew from 1944 onwards.

This gradual improvement in institutional church life, which continued during the 1950s, was severely disrupted by the anti-religious campaign of 1959–64. This was the initiative of the then leader of the Soviet Union, Khrushchev. It was a marked aberration in what could otherwise have been seen as a reasonably consistent pattern of relations between church and state in the post-war period. Floods of virulently anti-religious literature were published; some Orthodox priests publicly defected to atheism and published statements denouncing their former faith; bishops, priests, monks and nuns were tried and imprisoned on fabricated 'criminal' charges; 10,000 or more Orthodox churches (more than half) were closed and have not since been reopened; and theological education was severely curtailed. The anti-religious campaign ceased abruptly with Khrushchev's sudden removal from power, but many of the losses sustained by the church, above all the closed churches, have never been rectified.

This brief summary brings us almost to the point at which this book commences. Dissent within the church, discussed in Part 2, took its pioneering steps during the anti-religious campaign, as a response to the injustices done to it, broadened in the less restrictive atmosphere following Khrushchev's fall from power, and flowered during the period of East–West *détente* during the late 1970s. State policy towards the official life of the church relaxed quickly after 1964, although close monitoring of every aspect of church life persisted and continues to be the norm.

The Russian Orthodox Church in Context

Two points need to be made here which will be amplified in the ensuing chapters. The first is the position of the Russian Orthodox Church on the religious map of the USSR. It is only one of a number of other churches and religions which, together, amount to a significant proportion of the Soviet population. It is, however, by far the largest of any of these groups, with a membership estimated at not less than 50 million (see Chapter 7). The next-largest religious group is the Muslims, numbering 45–50 million and located in Soviet Central Asia and the Caucasus. The other religious groups are much smaller. There are between 2.5 and 3 million Jews, and about 0.5 million Buddhists in the Soviet Far East. There are an estimated 5.5 million Roman Catholics, mostly in the western borderlands, and an unknown number of outlawed Eastern-rite Catholics (Uniates) in western Ukraine.

Protestants, of whom Baptists are the most numerous, are widely scattered throughout the Soviet Union and number altogether probably between 4 and 5 million. There are an unknown number of members of sects of Orthodox origin. Other very localised groups include Georgian Orthodox in Georgia, the Armenian Church in Armenia, and Lutherans, largely in the Baltic area. (See Chapter 9, especially note 5, for further details.)

As well as being the largest religious body in the Soviet Union, the Russian Orthodox Church has also had the greatest influence on the history and culture of Russia and, to varying degrees, its neighbouring countries. (The Armenian and Georgian Churches are both older than the Russian Church, but have had little influence outside their respective countries.) This is of particular significance in view of the growing Russian nationalist sentiment observable in both official and unofficial circles in the Russian republic of the USSR. Both Catholicism and Protestantism are regarded to some extent as being interlopers from the West. Catholicism is strongest in the western borderlands which did not become part of the USSR until after the Second World War; and Protestantism was not introduced to the indigenous peoples of the Russian Empire until just over a century ago (though German immigrants from the time of Catherine the Great had retained their Lutheran and Mennonite faiths). Buddhism and Islam are the faiths of national minorities (albeit substantial, in the case of the Muslims). Although all these groups, except Buddhists, are vigorous and growing in numbers, none of them remotely threatens the position of the Russian Orthodox Church as the historical church of the majority of the peoples of the Soviet Union, and the bearer of their culture and traditions.

The most troublesome and controversial relationships of the Russian Orthodox Church with other religious groups in the Soviet Union are with the Ukrainians and the Jews. The Ukrainians, in this context, form two distinct groups: Orthodox and Eastern-rite Catholic. Ukrainian Orthodox resent their position as, administratively speaking, merely a part of the Russian Orthodox Church, with no independence or autonomy and little or no concession to their national heritage and traditions. The resentment is all the greater because a very large proportion of members of the Russian Orthodox Church are in fact Ukrainians. Ukraine does have the distinction of being an Exarchate of the Moscow Patriarchate, the only one within the Soviet Union, and the few Ukrainian-language publications of the church are the only non-Russian ones. However, there is no form and no structure for the discussion and resolution of specifically Ukrainian problems within the church: there has been no Synod of all the Ukrainian bishops since the 1920s. Ukrainians view this status of their church as one of many aspects of a Moscow-inspired policy of russification in Ukraine; they regard the Moscow Patriarchate as conniving in this.

The Eastern-rite Catholics (who worship according to the Orthodox rite, but are loyal to the Pope) have been outlawed since 1946, when under pressure from the Soviet authorities they were forcibly obliged to 'rejoin' the Moscow Patriarchate. Many of them depend for occasional religious services, the sacraments and religious instruction, upon the underground or catacomb Eastern-rite Catholic Church. Others, in order to practise their religion regularly and openly, are formally members of the Orthodox Church, but consider themselves Catholics at heart. (This means that, in the following chapters, when figures related to the various church institutions are given, it needs to be borne in mind that an unknown but sizable number of nominal Orthodox in western Ukraine in fact regard themselves as Catholics.) The strong aspirations of the Eastern-rite Catholics to independence have not diminished with the death of their figurehead, Cardinal Slipyj, who died in 1984.

Although formal relations between the Moscow Patriarchate and the small Jewish religious community in the Soviet Union are minimal, the attitude of Russian Orthodox Christians towards the Jews as a national–religious group continues to be a live issue, and all too often a controversial and painful one. The traditional streak of anti-semitism among some of the more nationalistically inclined members of the Russian Orthodox Church is still in evidence. The problem is complicated by the fact that a number of young Jewish intellectuals have converted to Orthodoxy in recent years. Their struggle to combine their Jewish nationality with their Christian faith forms one aspect of the problem; resentment of them by a minority of Russian church members is a second; and controversy between these conservative Russian nationalists and liberal intellectual Russians within the church who have a very positive attitude to the Jews forms a third aspect. (The conversion of some Jews to Orthodox Christianity forms part of a significant move back to the Russian Orthodox Church by young urban intellectuals in recent years. This will be discussed in Part 2. Simultaneously, there has been a growing awareness among Soviet Jews of their national and religious roots and traditions, and a revival of religious Judaism.)

The question of Russian Orthodox relations to Ukrainians and to Jews will be touched upon a number of times in this book, but there will not be space for a detailed treatment of either of these important subjects.

The second point is the legal position of the Russian Orthodox Church. Though its size and its special place in the life of the Russian nation have sometimes necessitated special treatment, the basic legislation which governs it is the same as for all denominations and religions in the Consitution of the Soviet Union, which declares that Soviet citizens have the freedom to 'perform religious rites or to conduct atheist propaganda'. This means in practice that the only legal religious activity is worship, and that the spreading of atheism, including its teaching through the education system, cannot be countered by the churches. The chief legislation regulating church life is the Law on Religious Associations (enacted in 1929 and revised in 1975), which lays down in detail the responsibilities of the churches with regard to conducting worship and maintaining a building for the purpose. The legal situation of the Russian Orthodox Church is described in detail in Chapters 2 and 9.

The Sources

The sources used in writing this book mostly fall into two categories: those made available officially by the Moscow Patriarchate with the tacit approval of the Soviet state, and the *samizdat* documents written by individual Christians referred to above, which circulate unofficially. In addition, use has been made of Soviet and Western press reports, reports of foreign churchmen's visits to the Soviet Union and of reciprocal visits to Western countries, and various secondary sources in the form of articles and books concerned with the Russian Orthodox Church, both Soviet and Western. To return to the first two categories, it may be helpful at the outset to say a few words about some of the sources within them which will be extensively used.

The most important official source is the *Journal of the Moscow Patriarchate* (*JMP*), which appears monthly in both Russian and English editions. Its chief value is in recording the changes and transfers in the episcopate, decisions of the Holy Synod, and developments in the church's international relations. More will be said about *JMP* in Chapter 6.

A second important source falls between the two categories: it is an official report which has been made available unofficially — or 'leaked'. This consists of extracts from reports of the Council for Religious Affairs under the Council of Ministers of the USSR dated 1968–74, apparently from a series of annual reports made to the Central Committee of the Communist Party of the Soviet Union (CPSU). The Council for Religious Affairs (CRA) is reponsible for seeing that Soviet legislation on religion is obeyed and for overseeing the life of the religious bodies in the Soviet Union; we shall have more to say about it in Chapter 9. The CRA Report, as we shall call it, is an extremely revealing and important source for studying aspects of the church's life which are normally hidden, and one which provides firsthand evidence of the attitude of government officials to the church. The fact that it has reached the West through unofficial channels naturally raises questions as to its authenticity, but these are dispelled upon a careful study of the text. What is said there conforms both to what is already known of the functions of the CRA and to what is said by the *samizdat* documents written by Russian Orthodox believers. In fact, it is largely true to say that the CRA Report does not so much provide new information for assiduous students of the Russian Orthodox Church as confirm what had already been pieced together from other sources, or what had been strongly suspected but could not be proved. None the less, the CRA Report has to be handled with great care, and its statements cannot always be taken at face value. The CRA has to perform a rather difficult function in this report to the Central Committee of the CPSU: it has to prove that it is coping efficiently with its task of limiting and controlling church activity, and at the same time it has to prove that religion is still enough of a factor in Soviet life for its own continued existence to be necessary. This leads to some rather tortuous bureaucratic phraseology which has to be disentangled with care.[1]

We have already referred to the *samizdat* (literally, 'self-published') documents which, in order to circumvent the strict censorship laws of the Soviet Union, are typed — sometimes handwritten, occasionally printed, photographed or duplicated — and circulated from hand to hand. The people who write them, or who are found with them in their possession, are liable to be sentenced to terms of imprisonment, and the documents reach the West with great difficulty through clandestine channels. It follows that, if the authors of *samizdat* are prepared to suffer imprisonment in the event of discovery, they are likely to be very strongly convinced of both the truth and the importance of what they are writing. Their only defence in a court of law is that they wrote the truth and nothing but the truth. It is not possible to check every fact which appears in *samizdat*, but where it has been possible to check (by comparison with the Soviet press, by the testimony of *émigrés* from the Soviet Union, by reports of Western visitors to the USSR, by checking for internal consistency with other *samizdat* documents), it has been found that a high standard of accuracy has been maintained.

A particularly important *samizdat* source for this book is the *Documents of the Christian Committee for the Defence of Believers' Rights in the USSR (DCCDBR).*[2] The Christian Committee, which is described in Chapter 12, was founded at the end of 1976 by three Russian Orthodox Christians, with the aim of helping religious believers in the USSR to protect their civil rights. The chief way in which this was done was by painstaking and extensive documentation of the violations of those civil rights. The Committee has compiled and sent to the West more than 1,300 pages of documents. Much of this relates to Russian Orthodox believers, and it provides a great deal of previously unobtainable information about the problems they face at parish level.

Finally, an important *samizdat* report on the situation of the Russian Orthodox Church, dated 15 August 1979, has been compiled by a founder-member of the Christian Committee, Father Gleb Yakunin.[3] The Yakunin Report, as we shall call it, commences with the thesis that the Moscow Patriarchate has grown spiritually weak and is so severely limited by the state in its actions that it is incapable of responding to or giving guidance to the renaissance of Christian faith which is taking place in the USSR. There follows an analysis of different aspects of the church's life to which we shall refer in the chapters of Part 1. In the final section of his report, Yakunin makes recommendations about the future of the church which will be discussed in Part 2. Yakunin himself played a very significant role in the public dissent from the policies of the Moscow Patriarchate which will be examined in Part 2.

PART 1

1   CHURCHES AND DIOCESES

Worship is central to Orthodoxy. Regular attendance at the liturgy, or eucharist, is the most important element in the life of an Orthodox Christian. Other services also constantly attract the devout Orthodox believer to his or her local church: matins, vespers and the other offices; the sacraments of baptism and marriage, burial, and other special services of blessing; the services of hymns, chants and prayers which mark saints' days, feasts of the Mother of God and other landmarks in the church's year; or simply the lighting of a candle and private prayer before one of the many icons which cover the walls of every Orthodox church. It is no exaggeration to say that the life of an Orthodox believer revolves around the church building. A contemporary Orthodox theologian, Georges Florovsky, has written: 'Christianity is a liturgical religion. The Church is first of all a wor-shipping community. Worship comes first, doctrine and discipline second.'[1] In the Orthodox Church, beliefs and teaching are conveyed primarily through worship. Many a modern enquirer into the nature of Orthodoxy has found that the discussion ends, not with a clearly expounded statement of beliefs, but with his Orthodox interlocutor saying simply: 'Come and see. Come and worship with us.'

The central role of worship is as much a feature of the Russian Orthodox Church as of any other branch of Orthodoxy. (Both the Greek-derived word orthodoxy and its Russian translation, *pravoslaviye*, mean 'right worship'.) Orthodoxy was adopted *c*. AD 988 in Kievan Rus, because, among other reasons, its ruler, Prince Vladimir, was so impressed with the accounts of Orthodox worship which his emissaries brought back from Byzantium: they are reported to have said, 'We knew not whether we were in heaven or on earth.' For contemporary Russian Orthodox believers nearly 1,000 years later, the church is still the meeting-point of heaven and earth, and the icons, the priests' sanctuary behind the iconostasis and the sheer beauty and splendour of the worship are all windows through which they hope to catch a glimpse of heaven.

This devotion to the church has impressed many Western visitors, who have marvelled at the long hours Russian Orthodox believers spend there. One wrote:

> The church is always packed to the doors for the liturgy, which may be punctuated by as many as three sermons. The congregation takes a full and active part in the service. Often they do not have room to prostrate themselves properly so that their foreheads touch the ground in front of them, but they cross themselves ceaselessly and join in singing the Lord's

Prayer, the Creed and other parts of the service, though they do not have any books to follow it with. It can take nearly an hour at the end of the service for everyone to communicate. After the liturgy the church does not empty, but remains a hive of activity for most of the rest of the day. A number of priests remain on duty for baptisms, marriages and funerals, these ceremonies often going on at different altars simultaneously.[2]

This was in 1959 in Moscow; a visitor to Leningrad 20 years later produced a remarkably similar description of the life of an urban church. His surprise at so much activity was shrugged off: 'Routine, they said. Normal. You'll find it in many churches in our big towns.'[13]

Number of Churches

It is clear from this that a prime necessity for any Orthodox community in the Soviet Union is to have an open church in which to worship. Without this, it is difficult to hold the liturgy and other services, and therefore virtually impossible to maintain any kind of corporate life. Many Orthodox communities are enduring great difficulties because of the reduction in the number of open churches, or 'working' churches as they are called in the Soviet Union, which has been observable throughout the Soviet period and which has not abated up to the present day. In 1914, according to a report of the Holy Synod, there were 54,147 churches and 25,593 chapels in the Russian Empire (which included Finland and much of Poland but not western Ukraine);[4] when the Russian Orthodox Church entered the World Council of Churches in 1961 it stated that it had 20,000 churches;[5] but this figure is contradicted by two Soviet publications which state that in 1961 the Orthodox Church possessed 11,000 churches.[6] In any event, the years 1959–64 saw a virulent anti-religious campaign waged by Khrushchev, which, according to two sources, reduced the number of Orthodox churches to 10,000.[7] Although the western borders of the Russian Empire differed from those of the Soviet Union today, and although the Soviet western borders have varied since 1917, making precise comparisons impossible, the overall pattern of decline in the number of Orthodox churches is unmistakable.

These figures do not tell the whole story, however; they obscure the fluctuation caused by the Second World War. In the immediate pre-war period, the number of churches had dropped to no more than 4,225, and possibly as few as 100.[8] The post-war increase was largely made up of the churches which existed in the territories incorporated into the USSR at the end of the war. These included both former Soviet territories occupied by the Germans, where closed churches were reopened,[9] and territories newly annexed from Eastern European countries, such as western Ukraine,

Moldavia and the Baltic countries. In addition to these, churches were reopened on Soviet territory during and immediately after the war. Had it not been for this historical accident, the decline in the number of open Orthodox churches would probably have been much swifter.

It is not known how many open Orthodox churches exist in the Soviet Union at the present time. Presumably the Moscow Patriarchate must know how many open churches there are in each of the dioceses in its care, but it has not published any figures. Frequent references are made to named individual churches in the 'From the Dioceses' section of the monthly *Journal of the Moscow Patriarchate*, but a careful analysis of issues from 1965 to the present has not proved helpful in estimating the overall total. The Council for Religious Affairs (CRA), which is responsible to the Council of Ministers of the USSR, must know how many open churches there are, since one of the clauses in its Statute states that the CRA 'keeps a list of religious associations, prayer houses and buildings'.[10] However, it has not divulged this information, and sometimes even seems to mislead foreign visitors. Two Western journalists who visited the USSR at different times in 1979 and had interviews with Mr Pyotr Makartsev, a deputy-chairman of the CRA, came away with quite different impressions. One reported that there were 5,000 Orthodox churches functioning,[11] while the other quoted Makartsev directly as saying there were 11,000.[12]

This gives some idea of the difficulties of obtaining reliable figures. However, estimates are available, from official Soviet sources, from *samizdat* and from *émigrés*, and careful comparison of these enables us to form a rough approximation of the true total of churches. These sources also lead to the view that the decline in the number of open churches has been continuous, albeit more gradual, even since the end of the anti-religious campaign in 1964. A Soviet source in 1966 gave the figure of 7,500 open churches,[13] markedly less than the figure of 10,000 in 1964 quoted above from another official Soviet source. Even Soviet writers on atheistic and anti-religious themes, it appears, cannot always be sure of obtaining reliable statistics: one of them must be wrong. Otherwise the only alternative is that 2,500 churches were closed in less than two years, a rate of closure higher than during the anti-religious campaign. The figure of 7,500 churches is mentioned again by a Soviet writer in 1971,[14] and it is easier to accept that the number may have declined to this level with the passage of a few more years. The CRA Report for 1974 gave the lower, but apparently precise, figure of 7,062 registered churches, but did not state specifically whether or not they were all open for worship.[15] A recent *émigré*, Anatoli Levitin-Krasnov, estimated in 1975 that there were 7,200 working churches.[16] From about 1975 onwards, all the estimates we have been able to find are below 7,000. Levitin-Krasnov, repeating his figure of 7,000 churches a few weeks later, added the qualification: 'it is even supposed that altogether only a little more than 6,000 churches remain'.[17] A *samizdat* author writing in 1976 stated that there were 'about 6,500' Orthodox parishes in the USSR, but without giving any source for this figure.[18] Mrs Irina Ginzburg, shortly after emigrating from the USSR in 1980, gave the same figure of 6,500, again without supporting evidence.[19] These estimates receive some support from the CRA: one of its deputy-chairmen, V. Furov, speaking at a private lecture in 1976, also indicated that there were 6,500 functioning churches. He said that though 7,500 Orthodox churches were registered, 'about 1,000 were formally listed but were not in use'.[20] An inconsistency was introduced by the CRA chairman, Vladimir Kuroyedov, in a book published in 1984, in which he claimed that there were 8,500 Orthodox churches.[21] In the same book, he stated that 33 Orthodox churches had been opened since 1977; if this is so, then it would make his total of 8,500 churches inconsistent with the previous figures given by the CRA. It is therefore probably safest to regard this total as an exaggeration.

On the basis of this evidence, it seems reasonable to assume that the number of functioning Orthodox churches in the USSR had declined to about 6,500 by the end of the 1970s. Moreover, as we shall see in this and following chapters, many functioning churches hold services very infrequently. It is less easy to say whether or not the decline apparent since the mid-1960s has continued, or will continue. As we shall see later in this chapter, a few churches were said to have been opened at the end of the 1970s, but there were also reports of churches being forcibly closed, against the wishes of the local populace. It seems not unlikely that the general pattern of slow decline has been continuing, in which case the present number of churches may be closer to 6,000, but there can be no certainty about this for the present. (Some commentators have suggested that there may be even fewer.[22])

This is a very small number of churches for a country which still numbers many millions of Orthodox believers. In Chapter 7 we shall see that there are probably at least 50 million Orthodox Christians in the USSR, which means that there is approximately one church for every 7,700 worshippers. No doubt some of the larger urban cathedrals which have several weekly services could cope with their share, but it is quite certain that the small village churches could not. These figures suggest that there are many Orthodox who wish to worship but are unable to do so, and information discussed below bears out this assumption.

The situation of the Russian Orthodox Church compares unfavourably with its sister Orthodox churches in Eastern Europe in this respect. The two Eastern European countries where Orthodoxy is the traditional faith of the majority of the population are Bulgaria and Romania. In 1966 Bulgaria was said to have 3,700 churches for 6 million Orthodox believers, or a church for every 1,600 or so worshippers.[23] Romania in 1973 reportedly had 8,185 Orthodox parishes and 11,722 places of worship for 13 million believers (though some put the total of believers higher), which works out at one church for every 1,110 or so worshippers.[24] Bucharest, with a population of 1.5 million, had 250 Orthodox churches,[25] while Moscow, with a population of 7.6 million, had 43 open Orthodox churches.[26] Within the USSR, the Baptist Church, which is much smaller than the Orthodox Church, though growing rapidly, is reported to have 5,000 churches for 545,000 church members.[27] Many non-members habitually attend church, a total of at least 3 million, but even so this means a church for every 600 believers, a far higher ratio than for their Orthodox neighbours. The fast growth of the Baptist Church may account for this, but at the same time it is possible that the Soviet authorities are not averse to encouraging the growth of the officially recognised Baptist Church as a way of diminishing the influence of the far older and larger Orthodox Church.

Distribution of Churches

The churches are very unequally distributed throughout the USSR. Most of them are to be found in the four republics of the USSR where the population is traditionally Orthodox: Russia, Belorussia, Ukraine and Moldavia. There are, however, a number of churches in the predominantly Muslim area of Central Asia, where there is a sizable Russian population, and the largest church in the Soviet Union to have been built since 1917 is in Tashkent. This was the achievement of the then diocesan bishop, Archbishop Yermogen, who is also noted for having resisted the closure of churches in Tashkent diocese during the anti-religious campaign of 1959–64. There are also a good number of open Orthodox churches in the Baltic countries; there are more in Latvia and Estonia than in the predominantly Catholic country of Lithuania. Riga is said to have no less than 14 working Orthodox churches,[28] more than any other Soviet city except Moscow. Leningrad, though much larger, has only ten churches.

Within the traditionally Orthodox areas, the densest concentration of churches is in the more westerly parts. The vast expanse of Siberia is almost devoid of churches: there are only 29 in Irkutsk diocese,[29] which covers most of eastern Siberia, and probably about the same number in Novosibirsk diocese in central Siberia. Although Siberia is far more sparsely populated than the westerly parts of the Russian republic, this seems none the less a small scattering of churches in an area which was in the past a focus of Russian Orthodox missionary endeavour. The cold northerly areas of the European part of Russia also have very few churches. The large diocese of Arkhangelsk is thought to have no more than 20 churches, and the extensive diocese of Vologda to its south (and to the east of Leningrad) has only 17 churches, according to one of its former bishops, who described it as a 'quite insignificant diocese' (see p. 242).[30] The number of churches is greatest in western Ukraine and, generally speaking, diminishes as one goes northwards and eastwards.[31] The effects of the Second World War are seen in the distribution of churches as well as the overall numbers. Though we do not know the precise numbers of churches in each diocese, it is a safe generalisation that the concentration of churches is greatest in the areas which were not incorporated into the Soviet Union until after the Second World War (notably western Ukraine and Moldavia), and next greatest in the areas which came under German occupation during the war, where churches were reopened — for example, southern Ukraine, Belorussia, southwest Russia and the northern Caucasus.[32] In the tiny republic of Moldavia (Kishinyov diocese), the existence of no less than 116 churches has been recorded in the *Journal of the Moscow Patriarchate*, although in about 30 cases there is some doubt as to whether the churches are open for worship. The diocese of Lvov further to the west, which includes the Soviet administrative regions of Lvov and Ternopol, is said to have 950 or more churches or parishes,[33] and the CRA Report for 1974 stated that Lvov region alone had 657 churches.[34] However, the reference was to registered as opposed to functioning churches, and we cannot be sure that all the churches in the diocese are open for worship. This seems even more probable when we compare the case of the neighbouring diocese of Ivano-Frankovsk. In 1974, according to CRA, there were 363 registered churches, but only 182 functioned constantly: 126 held services once or twice a month, 23 churches had services four or five times a year at festivals, and 33 churches did not function at all.[35]

It has been estimated that half of the functioning Russian Orthodox churches in the Soviet Union are in Ukraine, with more than a quarter of the nationwide total in the predominantly Ukrainian Catholic western regions.[36] Ukraine has just under one-fifth of the Soviet population, according to the 1979 census. An additional reason for the greater number of churches here may well be the Soviet authorities' desire to convert Ukrainian Catholics to Orthodoxy. The churches in eastern Ukraine have been described by one Ukrainian commentator as 'a bastion of russification'.[37] (The Moscow Patriarchate is regarded by Ukrainians as a willing instrument of the Soviet government's russification programme, and as such is fiercely resented.)

Belorussia, which was under German occupation during the war, has 370 Orthodox parishes.[38] The German-occupied areas of southern Russia, however, though they have more churches than areas farther to the north, have far fewer churches than the small Ukrainian dioceses. Krasnodar, for example, has about 70 churches,[39] while the large neighbouring diocese of Stavropol has about 100.[40] An exception to the general pattern is Moscow diocese, which, no doubt because of its status as capital and its large number of foreign visitors, has more churches than some of the more northerly neighbouring dioceses: there are 132 churches in Moscow region plus 43 in the city, a total of 175 in the diocese.[41]

Dioceses

There are 73 dioceses of the Russian Orthodox Church in the Soviet Union, 57 of which have ruling diocesan bishops. The remaining 16 have fallen vacant during the Soviet period: 11 of them have been 'temporarily administered' (in most cases for 15 years or more) and five have lapsed and merged with neighbouring dioceses. (The appendix at the end of this chapter lists the dioceses, both occupied and vacant, and the areas they cover.) The dioceses vary very greatly from one another in size, climate and population, stretching as they do from Central Europe to the shores of the Pacific, and from the Arctic Sea down into Central Asia and the Chinese border. The largest diocese is Irkutsk and Chita, whose bishop also has jurisdiction over the vacant diocese of Khabarovsk. The combined dioceses stretch eastwards from Lake Baikal to the Pacific coast, and from the northernmost reaches of Siberia, including the Kamchatka peninsula, down to the Soviet borders with Mongolia and northern China. Bishop Mefodi, who was appointed to the diocese in 1980 at the age of only 31, is responsible for an area of more than 7.5 million square kilometres, larger than the entire mainland of the USA excluding Alaska. The Central Asian dioceses are also vast. The diocese of Tashkent and Central Asia includes four of the five Soviet Central Asian republics: Uzbekistan, Tadzhikistan, Kirgizia and Turkmenia, an area of some 1.25 million square kilometres, or about the same as France, Spain and West Germany combined. The diocese of Alma-Ata and Kazakhstan is more than twice as large again: it corresponds to the boundaries of the Soviet republic of Kazakhstan, an area of about 2.75 million square kilometres. Though these dioceses have few churches, the bishop's task is demanding, as he is obliged to travel long distances to keep in touch with his flock. The smaller dioceses in the western part of the USSR where the number of open churches is greater are still sizable. The diocese of Ivanovo, northeast of Moscow, is bigger than Wales, and Voronezh diocese, some way to the south, is bigger than the whole of Scotland.

Nearly two-thirds of the dioceses which have ruling bishops, 36 altogether, are in the Russian republic of the Soviet Union, the RSFSR. The diocesan boundaries follow Soviet administrative boundaries. In many cases a diocese corresponds to a Soviet region (*oblast*), but it may cover two or more regions or other administrative units. (See the appendix at the end of this chapter.) Fourteen dioceses are within the Ukrainian Exarchate, corresponding to the Soviet republic of Ukraine.[42] The remaining seven dioceses are all coterminous with other Soviet republics: Belorussia, Moldavia on the border with Romania, the three Baltic republics of Latvia, Lithuania and Estonia, and the two dioceses mentioned above which cover the five Central Asian republics. This accounts for 12 of the 15 Soviet republics. The few Russian Orthodox churches in the Azerbaidzhani republic (where Islam predominates) are under the jurisdiction of one of the Russian dioceses, Stavropol and Baku. The two remaining Caucasian republics, Georgia and Armenia, contain no parishes or other institutions of the Russian Orthodox Church. Georgia is under the jurisdiction of the Georgian Orthodox Church, headed by Catholicos Iliya, Patriarch of All Georgia, and Armenia is the preserve of the Armenian Apostolic Church under the Supreme Patriarch-Catholicos of All Armenians, Vazgen I.

It is not entirely clear why the vacant dioceses have remained vacant.[43]

All the dioceses, including the vacant ones, appear to have functioning diocesan cathedrals, although there is some doubt about Chernigov diocese in northeastern Ukraine. The cathedral was reported in 1973 to have been closed.[44] In 1977 a *samizdat* appeal stated that there was only one small church in the town.[45] However, the *Journal of the Moscow Patriarchate* in 1979 reported that services were taking place in the cathedral.[46] The journal's reports do not contain any details about the services, and it is possible that only occasional services are permitted there. A foreigner who visited Chernigov in 1983 reported that the former cathedral had in fact been turned into a museum, so it is probable that a smaller church has been redesignated as the cathedral.[47]

Parishioners in Vladimir feared in 1974 that their twelfth-century Cathedral of the Dormition would be closed for worship. An article in the regional newspaper in April that year proposed that restoration of this unique historical monument should be commenced, and that services should be suspended for the duration of the restoration. The parishioners, fearing there was no guarantee that the cathedral would be returned to them after the restoration, opposed the suspension of services, and some weeks of argument followed.[48] The restoration proceeded, and the main part of the cathedral was not open for worship again until August 1979. We should note that, though the original suggestion had been that the cathedral should be restored as an architectural monument belonging to the country as a whole, not just to the believers, it was the Russian Orthodox Church which paid the costs of the restoration (500,000 roubles).[49] After restoration, services were reportedly being held in the central area of the cathedral and in the side-chapel of St Andrew, while restoration was proceeding in the side-chapel of St Gleb.[50]

Apart from the diocesan cathedrals, there are a few other cathedrals in the older towns. Most of the remaining churches are purpose-built in the traditional style of Russian ecclesiastical architecture (*khram*), but there are also some other premises which have been adapted from other purposes and dedicated for worship: one of these is known as a prayer house (*molitvenny dom*). Some of the churches are former cemetery chapels, which are quite small.

The Background to Recent Church Openings

There are very few reports of Orthodox churches in the Soviet Union being opened or reopened. Their number has increased towards the end of the 1970s, but even so they are few and far between. Kuroyedov, as noted above, claimed that 33 new churches had been opened between 1977 and 1984; elsewhere, and consistently with this, he gave the figure of 30 new churches between 1977 and 1982.[51] However, he gave no details of where these churches were. In 1977 a church in Yefremov, Tula region, was reported to have been reopened after members of the parish had been pleading with the authorities for 30 years.[52] Three churches were opened in Irkutsk diocese in the mid-1970s, in Sovetskaya Gavan, Komsomolsk-on-Amur and Arsenyev (the latter a prayer house), bringing the total up from 26 to 29,[53] and it is possible that another has been opened more recently.[54] The Cathedral of the Ascension in Novosibirsk has been enlarged and modernised, according to a journalist who visited it in 1978 and spoke to parishioners who were voluntarily undertaking rebuilding work: a photograph shows young men carrying bricks and elderly ladies working away with shovels.[55] Patriarch Pimen announced the opening of new churches in a report in May 1978. He stated that churches had been opened 'in recent months' in Asino, Tomsk region; Slavgorod, Altai territory; Morozovka, Rostov region; Kattakurgan, Uzbek SSR; and Balkhash, Makinsk and Ekibastuz, Kazakh SSR. The Patriarch also reported the building of new stone churches in Vladivostok and in Novokuznetsk, Novosibirsk diocese. The stone church of St Nikolai was currently being built in Novgorod, and the wooden church of the Icon of Our Lady of Kazan, also in Novgorod, had been rebuilt.[56]

However, the Yakunin Report points out that the Patriarch's list paints too rosy a picture:

> The Patriarch's report contains inaccuracies. One could mistakenly conclude from the report that, for example, the stone church of St Nikolai in Vladivostok has been built in a place where there had been no church. In fact this church has been built in place of a wooden church where services were held. The *JMP* also published inaccurate statistics in No. 4, 1979 (pp. 11–14), which reported the consecration of a new church dedicated to St Nikolai the Miracle-Worker. In fact it was only a side-chapel (*pridel*) that was consecrated, built alongside the Church of St Filipp, the only one in Novgorod, which has been functioning for a long time. No new church community (*obshchina*) was registered.[57]

The bone of contention here is over the definition of a 'new church'. There is no doubt that additional space has been made available for worship, but Yakunin is correct in pointing out that there is no new possibility for worship where none existed before, and it is in this sense that the report in the *Journal of the Moscow Patriarchate* is misleading. However, it is easier for the church to manage the opening of a new space for worship than the opening of a new church.

Yakunin also makes an interesting observation about the other newly opened churches in 1978:

With the exception of Morozovka, Rostov region, all the other newly-opened parishes enumerated in the Patriarch's report are in direct or strategic proximity to China. Evidently, by their more liberal policy towards the Russian Orthodox Church, the authorities want to use religion in these geographic zones as one of the strengthening factors of stability in areas close to the border with a potential enemy.[58]

A comparison with the map shows this statement to be true. It is also true of one of the new churches recorded in issues of the *Journal of the Moscow Patriarchate* for 1980, that in Prokopevsk in Novosibirsk diocese. However, Yakunin's observation does not apply to other new churches and church buildings in 1980. A new church was opened in Drakino, Penza diocese; in Moscow diocese a domestic chapel was consecrated in newly opened workshops of the Moscow Patriarchate in Sofrino; new church buildings were erected in place of old ones in Pavlysh and Salkovo, Kirovograd diocese, and in Obilnoye, Izobilny and Alexandriya in Stavropol diocese.[59] It is too early yet to see whether Father Gleb's theory about the area bordering on China has any continuing validity.

Some interesting background to one of the churches mentioned in the Patriarch's list was given in a *samizdat* source in 1981. Parishioners in the town of Asino, Tomsk region, described the lengthy struggle they had had with the local CRA commissioner, G. P. Dobrynin, before they were able to register a church at all — it had taken over 20 years. They then applied for permission to enlarge the house which they used for worship, which was 64 square metres in area, by a further 80 square metres. However, the authorities would permit an extension of only 56 square metres. At the time of writing, the dispute over the extra 24 square metres had been going on for nearly six years.[60]

It is too early to say whether or not the few churches opened at the end of the 1970s represent a new trend, but even if they do, they are a drop in the ocean. It will be a very long time before the opening of half a dozen churches a year, if that, can increase the overall total to even the 1965 level of 10,000. The shortage of churches, which is a problem experienced by all denominations in the USSR, is particularly acute for the Orthodox. The centre of Orthodox life and worship is the liturgy, which must be performed by a priest in a consecrated church. (In fact, the liturgy may be celebrated anywhere, provided there is a priest and an *antimnis* (communion cloth). In practice, however, in the USSR, a consecrated, registered church is necessary for a congregation to gather regularly for the eucharist.) No other form of worship or religious observation can replace it. Baptists deprived of church buildings can (and do) meet in private homes, or even outdoors, for informal prayer, Bible study and worship. For an Orthodox believer, this is insufficient, but if he is able to attend the liturgy in a church, the centre of his religious life remains intact. The closure of a church is therefore a matter of critical importance to an Orthodox community.

What then can be the reason for the closure of so many churches in a country with a predominantly Orthodox population? The reasons usually put forward, by church leaders and official Soviet spokesmen, are that increasing secularisation means that fewer people wish to worship, or that the apathy towards religion of the population in a given place has led to the closure of the local church. There is no doubt some truth in the first of these reasons, as in other industrialised countries, but it is not sufficient to account for the scale and speed of church closures. It is hard to conceive of a process of secularisation so abrupt and rapid as that which closed 10,000 churches between 1959 and 1964. The second reason is invariably advanced without citing specific examples, and moreover it is belied by documentation from the parishioners of many closed churches, indicating that the closures were against their will. These documents, which we shall discuss in some detail, allege that Soviet government agencies have closed many churches in direct defiance of the known wishes of their members.

The procedures used to do this during 1959 to 1964 have been described by an authoritative source, the late Metropolitan Nikolai (Yarushevich) of Krutitsy and Kolomna, who died in 1961. Shortly before his death he was able to have a private conversation with Archbishop Vasili of Brussels, in which the latter later reported him as saying:

'A good and zealous priest is serving in a certain church. He preaches and organises processions (*krestnye khody*) . . . the commissioner [of the CRA][61] deregisters him or demands his transfer to another parish under threat of deregistration. The bishop is obliged to submit and appoint another priest to the parish. But the commissioner stubbornly refuses to register him or any other priest whom the bishop attempts to appoint to the parish. As a result no services are performed in the church for more than six months, and the authorities close it, as being a non-functioning church. But there are harsher ways of closing a church. On a day appointed by the authorities, usually Sunday, after the service is over and the people about to disperse, a crowd of several hundred people gathers around the church, Communists, members of the Young Communist League (*Komsomol*), all the so-called active element, with the necessary instruments, and during the course of a few hours they physically destroy and annihilate the church. The church utensils, books, vestments and so on, are loaded on to a lorry and taken off goodness knows where.' 'But presumably this happens only in the villages?' I asked, shaken by *Vladyka* Nikolai's story [*Vladyka*, which originally meant 'master' or 'sovereign' is the form of address used in conversation with Russian Orthodox bishops]. 'Certainly not only in the villages, but even in quite large towns', replied Metropolitan Nikolai.[62]

For 10,000 churches to be closed in five years, an average of five or six must have been closed every day; and even if the majority were closed by the 'peaceful' method, acts of violence such as those described above must have been quite frequent throughout the USSR. The closed churches are used for a variety of purposes, often as warehouses and stores, sometimes as clubs for young people, and in a number of cases as anti-religious museums, which is insulting to believers' feelings.[63] The mass closure of churches appears to have affected all parts of the Soviet Union, with one or two notable exceptions. Archbishop Yermogen, as we have mentioned, was renowned for his determined resistance to church closures and Metropolitan Ioann of Pskov is also referred to (by Father Gleb Yakunin) as resisting the closure of churches.[64]

The effects of the mass closure of churches during 1959–64 are still being keenly felt by Orthodox believers today. Since 1977 a number of documents have reached the West from Orthodox believers who have been trying, unsuccessfully, to reopen churches forcibly closed at that time.

Attempts to Reopen Closed Churches

In order for a church to be opened in the Soviet Union, 20 religious believers of the same denomination and living in the same place (*dvadtsatka*) must apply in writing to the district (*raion*) executive committee (in rural areas) or to the city executive committee (in cities) of the local Soviet of Workers' Deputies. Before the 1975 revisions of the law these bodies could take some independent decisions on matters of church registration, but now the decision has to be passed upwards to the regional (*oblast*) executive committee, then to republican level, and finally to the CRA in Moscow.[65] The new procedure means that the CRA alone is responsible for deciding on the opening and closing of churches throughout the whole of the Soviet Union. If the CRA rejects an application to open a church, believers have no other court of appeal. As well as dealing with local executive committees, believers are supervised by CRA commissioners who exist at republican and regional level throughout the USSR. Both the CRA and the executive committees of *soviets* are ultimately responsible to the Council of Ministers of the USSR, a government body. There are two separate administrative procedures involved in registering a church for worship: first, the 20 believers must be registered as a religious association (*obyedinyeniye*) after which they may lease and register a suitable building for worship.[66] As we have seen from Metropolitan Nikolai, the registering of a priest to conduct worship is a third separate administrative procedure.

Possibly the longest-running campaign to reopen closed churches was begun by citizens of Gorky in 1967.[67] With its population of 1,200,000 it was the third-largest city in the Russian republic, but it had only three open churches, and they were all small village churches that had latterly been absorbed into the city limits. In 1977, the campaign was revived, the city's population having risen to 1,500,000 in the meantime. In August 1977 about 2,000 signatures had been gathered on petitions which had been forwarded to five district executive committees in different quarters of the city.[68] In September Veniamin Kozulin, the leader of the campaign, wrote to Soviet leaders Brezhnev and Kosygin to ask for their help in view of the unsatisfactory response of all five executive committees.[69] His letter was backed up by an appeal signed by 1,600 citizens, who wrote:

On Sundays and on other Orthodox festivals the [three small] churches are packed solid and cannot accommodate all the worshippers. In wintertime and in bad weather people of advanced years stand under the open sky, risking their health. The stuffiness in the overcrowded churches has more than once led to fatalities. And this is happening when within the limits of the old Nizhni Novgorod [as Gorky was named until 1932] and Sormov a number of huge church buildings are empty, each of them capable of accommodating more than all the three presently functioning churches together.[70]

This appeal met with no response. By now the believers had exhausted all the legal possibilities open to them: after being turned down by the five district executive committees, they had appealed to city and regional committees, and finally to the CRA in Moscow, only to meet with further refusals. Not only did the CRA refuse to lease the believers churches, it even refused to register them as religious communities. In January 1978 the believers sent a letter explaining their plight to the Belgrade Conference then taking place,[71] but so far as is known the conference was unable to take any action to help the citizens of Gorky.[72]

In September 1977 Kozulin was reported as saying in an interview with Western journalists that nine people who had taken part in the earlier campaign to open a church had lost their jobs, and he himself had been threatened with incarceration in a mental asylum.[73] On 2 July 1978 an article appeared in the local paper, *Gorkovskaya pravda (Gorky Truth)*, about the campaign to open churches. It made a number of offensive assertions about Kozulin, stating among other things that he was indifferent to religion. Believers who knew him well wrote an indignant, detailed letter

rebutting these accusations,[74] and five people quoted in the article wrote
signed statements to the newspaper saying that they had been misquoted,[75]
but they were not published, and so the paper's readers were left in
ignorance regarding the true state of affairs. The element of hostility to
believers by local institutions is one which we shall find repeated in other
cases.

As far as is known at present, no new church has been opened in Gorky.

We could quote a number of similar stories of believers who have been
trying for many years to have their churches reopened since they were closed
during the 1959–64 anti-religious campaign. The detailed documentation
which these believers have supplied shows that many of the problems of the
Gorky believers are repeated in many different places all over the USSR. In
most of these cases there are church buildings perfectly suitable for worship, so the question of lack of satisfactory premises does not arise. The
documents tell a sad story of vain appeals to a succession of Soviet officials;
of believers being endlessly passed on from one office to another without
any effort being made to help them; of fruitless appeals to the CRA chairman, Vladimir Kuroyedov, to Patriarch Pimen, and even to Mr Brezhnev;
and of the invariably unhelpful, often hostile, attitude of officials responsible for registering churches. In several cases believers have travelled long
distances to Moscow at their own expense to plead their cases to CRA
officials. The believers have persisted for many years in their attempts,
despite total lack of encouragement. We know of no case where such efforts
have been successful.

The most detailed reports of these unsuccessful attempts to reregister
closed churches come from, in the Russian republic: Sitskoye village,
Chkalovsk district, Gorky region; Bolshoi Khomutets village, Dobroye district, Lipetsk region; Kotovo town, Volgograd region; in the Ukrainian
republic: Lozovaya town, Kharkov region; Balashovka village, Berezno
district, Rovno region; Velikiye Zagaitsy village, Shumskoye district,
Ternopol region; Budki village, Kremenets district, Ternopol region;
Khotovitsa village, Kremenets district, Ternopol region; and Naberezhnye
Chelny (now renamed Brezhnev) in the Tatar ASSR.[76]

In some cases the authorities have stooped to trickery to stop the
believers' efforts to reopen their churches. In the village of Balashovka, for
example:

> The chairman of the village *soviet*, Maxim Cherebaka, thought of a way
> to solve the matter. He gave the villagers a paper to sign, allegedly an
> undertaking that they would not let their pigs off their farmsteads, but
> above the signatures he secretly placed a statement to the effect that a
> church was not needed. After this the district executive committee would
> not accept a new declaration from the *dvadtsatka* requesting that the
> church be opened.[77]

In most cases the efforts to reopen the church seem to be carried on by a dedicated nucleus of the believers, but, so far as we can tell, they appear to be able to call upon more general support from fellow-villagers. In Kotovo, a list of more than 1,000 people who wanted the church reopened was compiled.[78] Furthermore, those in favour of reopening churches sometimes include people who are acknowledged to have served their country well and are honoured members of Soviet society. This is so in the village of Velikiye Zagaitsy, where efforts to reopen the church were supported by 59 villages who had received the award of the Order of Veterans of Labour, 17 of whom were invalids of the Second World War. They wrote of this in a bitter vein:

> We have a lot of awards for victory over the fascists and awards for labour, but we don't have the right to believe in God and worship in church. The majority of us are pensioners and veterans of labour, but we work, we help the state to grow bread for all the people, so on what grounds have we been deprived of the right to spend our spare time from labour in church? After all, they write and say on television that our state is very concerned about simple labourers. But we see [word unclear] the atheists are forcing their leisure — the club — which is to their liking, on us, but it's not to our liking . . . After all, we fought for freedom for ourselves too, not just for the atheists.[79]

It is possible that these refusals to open churches in different areas of the USSR are influenced by the attitudes of local CRA commissioners. Some commissioners are no doubt more belligerent towards believers — because of ingrained anti-religious views, or a desire to succeed in their careers, or simply a bureaucratic distaste for contact with determined members of the public — while others may be more easygoing personalities with a greater inclination to leniency. However, while the attitudes of commissioners can make or mar relations with believers, they have not been decisive since 1975, when the power to make decisions on the registering of churches was transferred from local authorities to the CRA in Moscow.[80] It is true that local authorities do not have a time limit for passing on applications for registration to the CRA, and can therefore use delaying tactics, but the fact remains that the decisions on opening (or not opening) churches are ultimately taken in Moscow and not locally. The continued refusals to reopen closed churches since 1975, even in cases where believers have travelled to Moscow to visit the CRA headquarters, indicate that this is a nationwide policy.

Several of the parishes where believers have been unsuccessful in reopening closed churches are in Ukraine, where, as we have seen, the number of churches is relatively high compared with other parts of the country. Even here, however, it is clear that there are not enough churches for all the believers who wish to worship.

Continuing Church Closures

It is not only the consequences of the mass closure of churches in 1959–64 which are causing problems for Orthodox believers. Closures are continuing to occur. A report from Ukraine compiled in spring 1974 states that now it is rare to see a church open for worship, whereas previously there used to be one in every village, and gives examples of churches which have been closed or destroyed.[81] The Church of the Dormition in Istomino village, Kaluga region, effectively ceased to operate after the parish priest was unexpectedly transferred in 1974, and persistent efforts by parishioners to keep it open met with an unco-operative, even obstructive, attitude from Soviet officials.[82]

Parishioners in Rechitsa, Gomel region, in Belorussia, came to grief when they carried out repairs on their prayer house in 1979. At first everything seemed to go smoothly, according to their report. The church building was old and far too small for all who wished to worship, leading to over-crowding: 'often a few old ladies would even lose consciousness'. The church council asked the local authorities for permission to carry out repairs; this was granted and the people bought building materials and set to work 'with joy and with prayer' in July 1979. The repairs were completed 'in a surprisingly short time', which 'greatly astonished the city building organisations'. However, when the believers came joyfully to church on 1 September, they found a lock on the church door and a notice from the city fire inspector stating that the building had been closed because of 'gross violation of fire safety regulations'. This seems strange, since the whole rebuilding operation had evidently been carried out in co-operation with the local authorities, who presumably would have been responsible for ensuring that fire regulations and other planning requirements were observed. The believers travelled to Minsk to see the CRA commissioner for the republic, but without result. The local authorities, according to the parishioners, 'are continuing as before their campaign to close the Rechitsa church; they are intimidating members of the church council. There is a 24-hour militia guard on the church. They are planning to make a warehouse in the building.' Judging by the parishioners' account, the only one available, it does seem that they have been unfairly treated. No effort appears to have been made to help them alter the building to comply with fire regulations, or to inspect the building during the course of repairs when such measures could have been taken in good time. The suddenness of the building's closure, with no forewarning, and the presence of an armed militia guard, suggest that the state has simply decided to requisition the building by *force majeure*. Furthermore, it appears that no alternative provision for worship has been made by the requisitioning authorities: 'the believers gather at the gates of the church and, sobbing, sing church hymns'.[83]

In the case of the Church of the Epiphany, Zhitomir, officials went so far as to destroy the church completely, despite anguished appeals from the parishioners. The church was closed in November 1973, and parishioners petitioned for a year and nine months to have it reopened. However,

> On 13 August 1975 the local communist authorities wrecked and demolished the Church of the Epiphany. A fence was set up around the church and around the fence were stationed many militiamen, who did not admit anyone, not a single person, close to the church. There was wailing, sobbing and crying for the Mother Church; everyone looked with horror on the Soviet freedom guaranteed by the Constitution.[84]

We could quote many more instances of church closures during the last ten years or so, sufficient to indicate that, although churches are not being closed on such a large scale as during 1959–64, the same methods that were used then are continuing to be used now. The opening of new churches in a very few places, which we have mentioned, is an indication that the situation may vary slightly from one area to another, possibly influenced by the disposition of the local CRA commissioner. The overall conclusion from the documents we have examined, however, is that the nationwide policy remains the same as it was in the 1960s: to resist the opening of new churches and to close existing churches when suitable opportunities to do so present themselves. The documents lead to a second conclusion: that this policy is being put into effect in opposition to the known and clearly expressed wishes of the believing population. It is clear that in many places parishioners have followed all the correct procedures for opening or averting the closure of a church and have been repeatedly rebuffed by several different authorities. The tone of the documents leaves little doubt that people genuinely wish to worship in a local church, and that being unable to do so causes them great anguish and distress. The church *samizdat* writer Anatoli Levitin-Krasnov reminds us of the trauma suffered by believers whose church has been closed:

> The believers have never been reconciled and never will be reconciled to the closure of churches, for one needs to understand what a church is for a believer. A church is not simply a building, it is not even like one's own (*rodnoi*) home. Every church is the most precious thing in the whole world, it is washed with the believer's tears, with the tears of his fathers and grandfathers. Here he brings his loftiest feelings; he was carried here as a baby and he will be carried out from here into the churchyard; his parents and all those closest to him were carried from here to their eternal rest. And now insolent, thick-skinned, coarse people have forced their way in here, and coarseness, vulgarity and blasphemy reign supreme. Every believer who passes by a closed, desecrated church feels as though someone had spit, not in his face (that is easy to wipe away), but into his

soul, into everything he holds most dear and sacred.[85]

The sight of closed church buildings being used for other purposes is an additional affliction for believers. This distress has been well expressed in a letter to Patriarch Pimen from layman Yuri Belov (who now lives in West Germany, and has become a Catholic)

> Travelling about Russia, one cannot fail to notice hundreds of churches, raised by our work-loving and God-fearing forefathers, and now in a state of neglect, or used for other purposes. The heart is wrung even more by the sight of beautiful churches turned into museums. The most holy place for the whole Orthodox people, the complex of churches in the Moscow Kremlin, has been turned into a tourist bazaar . . . It is even more deplorable to observe the spectacle of an atheist museum housed in the Cathedral of the Icon of Our Lady of Kazan [in Leningrad]. Could not the atheists have built a completely new building for their own amusement, of non-ecclesiastical architecture?[86]

We should note also that towards the end of the 1970s laments over closed and neglected churches appeared in officially published Soviet magazines and newspapers. Usually their loss was regretted on aesthetic grounds, because particular churches and cathedrals were valuable pieces of architecture or symbols of Russia's historical past. This was one manifestation of a growing Russian nationalist tendency, found both in official publications and in *samizdat*, which cherished cultural, moral and religious values from the Russian past, and which we shall discuss in Part 2. There was some reference even to the moral, as opposed to purely aesthetic, influence of churches.[88]

Such protests were no doubt chiefly due to the All-Russian Society for the Preservation of Historical and Cultural Monuments (known by its Russian acronym, VOOPIK), which was founded in 1966. The growth of the organisation has been impressive: it had more than 7 million members by January 1972, and more than 12 million by January 1977. This demonstrates very considerable concern among Russians to preserve monuments of their past, including churches. The Society has undertaken an extensive campaign of lectures and article-writing in support of its aims, and has the support of leading writers and other figures in Soviet public life. It is not easy, however, to assess its overall success as far as restoring or preventing the destruction of ancient churches is concerned. A number of churches have indeed been saved from either misuse or planned demolition, and in some cases local officials have been disciplined for irresponsible behaviour.[89] But reports of endangered churches continue to be made. In 1983, for example, it was reported that the church in the village of Podmoklovo, Kursk region, was decaying despite the fact that professional specialists and representatives of the public had tried many times to raise the issue. The church is one of the earliest extant examples of Russian architecture in the round, and has an unusual Baroque rotunda surrounded by an arcade bearing 16 statues of the apostles (12 disciples and 4 evangelists, John and Matthew each being represented twice). The cornice is reportedly crumbling, and this had resulted in the fall and breakage of four of the statues by the end of 1981. An article about the church was published in the journal *Decorative Art in the USSR*, but even this failed to achieve any result.[90] Even in cases where VOOPIK has been successful in saving churches of architectural value, it does not seem that they are reopened for worship; at any rate, there have been no reports of this to date.

Worship without Churches

What do Orthodox believers do when they have no church to worship in? Our information on this point is very scarce. The documents record that villagers in Bolshoi Khomutets met for prayers in a private house, and that parishioners of the Rechitsa church met at its gate to sing hymns. Another example of such activity has been documented in an article on atheist work in Voronezh region, which includes an account of how local atheists dealt with Orthodox believers in Ivanovka village:

> There is no church here, but there are Orthodox believers. The most zealous of them attempted to organise a kind of 'house-church'. When these facts were made known to the district committee of the CPSU, an atheist agitation-brigade was formed . . . Members of the brigade told the believers about the bases of Soviet legislation on cults, and that the creation of a 'house-church' is an illegal act.[91]

This incident not only points to the difficulties of finding alternatives to worship in church, it also demonstrates another element which believers have to deal with, that of active proselytisation by atheists. Soviet literature on atheist work is extensive, and contains numerous accounts of the efforts made by local atheists, with state backing, to win over religious believers to atheism. Religious believers are prohibited by law from similar proselytisation, and find themselves therefore in an unequal relationship with their atheist neighbours.[92] Moreover, overt hostility is sometimes shown to believers trying to open churches, as we have seen in the case of Kozulin in Gorky. This is important, because it means that attempts to secure the right to worship in a church do not take place in a neutral, impartial atmosphere, but in one which is ideologically weighted against religious believers.

However, these few examples of worship outside churches are an insufficient basis for generalisation. Reports of unofficially sanctioned meetings for worship among Baptists and Pentecostals who are unable to meet in churches are extensive, but in the case of the Orthodox we have no precise information as to what most of them do when they are unable to worship in church. Their need for worship can to some extent be met by saying the traditional Orthodox prayers before icons kept in the home, by commemorating saints' days and festivals and by keeping fasts. Many also make a special effort to visit a distant church on the great festivals, especially at Easter, when churches are regularly reported to be overflowing. Believers also make pilgrimages to the few remaining monasteries (as we shall see in Chapter 5), perhaps endeavouring by a period of intense prayer and veneration to make up for the deficiencies of previous months or years.

Churchless Areas

There are, however, some areas of the USSR where there are no Orthodox churches at all for many hundreds of miles, and travel on a special occasion to the nearest open church would represent a major undertaking. There are no churches of any denomination in the region of Kaliningrad. This is an anomaly, since it is the westernmost outpost of the USSR, in the area where there is the greatest concentration of churches of all denominations. Kaliningrad region belongs to the Russian republic but it is entirely separated from it by Lithuania; it juts into Poland. According to a *samizdat* source, this area, formerly East Prussia, was annexed by the Russian republic after it 'lost its local inhabitants when they fled the Red Army, were driven out or died from starvation' during the Second World War.[93] In 1975 a Catholic priest from Lithuania visited the region at the request of the faithful and began to minister to them; he baptised Orthodox as well as Catholic children. However, he began to be followed by agents of the authorities, and a believer whom he visited had her home searched and was questioned.[94] Another source states that many Orthodox live in the region, and that there are many church buildings in the city of Kaliningrad which are in good condition or in only slight disrepair. The believers go to the cemetery to pray, at Easter and possibly at other times.[95] The reason for Kaliningrad's dearth of churches would appear to be that, unlike the other territories annexed by the USSR after the war, it did not already possess strong church communities, due to its population having fled. The Soviet government seems to have adopted a policy of keeping the region totally without churches.

Thousands of miles away the eastern extremity of the USSR, the Kamchatka peninsula, is in the same condition. Fr Gleb Yakunin in his report writes that a representative of the Orthodox believers there came to visit him in Moscow, and told him that believers of Petropavlovsk, the capital of Kamchatka, have been trying fruitlessly for many years to have a church opened. Kamchatka is a closed zone, and travellers need a special pass to enter it, so it is only once every few years that a priest is allowed to go there from Vladivostok, at the petitioning of the believers, to give communion, administer extreme unction and perform baptisms. As Yakunin points out, the whole vast area of eastern Siberia and the Soviet Far East is almost without churches, even though this was formerly an area of active evangelism and church-building in the time of Metropolitan Innokenti, whose life's work had been extolled in a series of articles recently published in the *Journal of the Moscow Patriarchate*.[96] Yakunin's point is that the Moscow Patriarchate is making no effort to counteract the problem of church closures and to provide for the needs of those who live far away from any church; the church leadership venerates Metropolitan Innokenti but makes no attempt to follow his example.

On the face of it, this assessment seems to be correct, for the whole of the Soviet Union, not just Siberia. We do not know what efforts may have been made privately by the Holy Synod or by diocesan bishops, but they have met with no success up to the present. The opening of the few churches mentioned above will alleviate the situation of local believers, but the numbers are so small as to make little difference to the overall situation of the church.

That overall situation is a very critical one. The evidence we have studied has shown that the number of Orthodox churches in the Soviet Union has been reduced drastically since 1959 and is possibly continuing to decline; that the Orthodox have proportionately very many fewer churches than Soviet Baptists and other Orthodox churches in Eastern Europe; that the small number of churches appears to be a matter of state policy; and that closure of churches is causing great distress to Orthodox believers. The state's total control over the opening and closure of churches, exercised through the CRA and through local government agencies, means that the situation is unlikely to alter unless there is a radical change in government policy towards the Orthodox Church. The provision, or lack of provision, of churches represents an important means by which state control over the church's activity throughout the USSR can be, and is, exercised.

Appendix: Dioceses

The diocesan boundaries follow Soviet administrative boundaries and use Soviet place-names in their designations (which means that some of them have changed their names as Soviet place-names have changed). There is a total of 73 dioceses, according to an official list published in 1958 (see note 97), but some have since lapsed. The Russian republic has 42 dioceses, 36 occupied and 6 vacant; Ukraine has 14 occupied and 4 vacant dioceses, a total of 18; and the remaining 7 dioceses are identical with other Soviet republics. This leaves 6 dioceses which have lapsed altogether and been absorbed into neighbouring dioceses. The vacant and lapsed dioceses are listed separately on p. 36.

The Dioceses and the Administrative Area they Cover

The Siberian dioceses (in the RSFSR) are:

Irkutsk and Chita (Irkutsk obl. (obl. = *oblast* or region), Chita obl., Amur obl., Yakut ASSR (ASSR = Autonomous Republic) and Buryat ASSR), temporarily administering Khabarovsk diocese (Khabarovsk krai (krai = territory) and Primorsky krai): presumably these combined dioceses also include Magadan obl., Kamchatka obl. (peninsula), and Sakhalin obl. (island), but as there are no churches there this is unclear: *Novosibirsk and Barnaul* (Novosibirsk obl., Kemerovo obl., Tomsk obl., and Altai krai), temporarily administering Krasnoyarsk diocese (Krasnoyarsk krai and probably the Tuvin ASSR, but there are no churches there);
Omsk and Tyumen (Omsk obl. and Tyumen obl.).

The remaining Russian dioceses are:

Arkhangelsk and Kholmogory (Arkhangelsk obl., Murmansk obl., and Komi ASSR);
Astrakhan and Yenotayevka (Astrakhan obl.);
Cheboksary and Chuvashia (Chuvash ASSR);
Gorky and Arzamas (Gorky obl.);
Ivanovo and Kineshema (Ivanovo obl.);
Kalinin and Kashin (Kalinin obl.);
Kaluga and Borovsk (Kaluga obl.);
Kazan and Mari (Tatar ASSR and Mari ASSR), temporarily administering Izhevsk diocese (Udmurt ASSR);
Kirov and Slobodskoi (Kirov obl.);
Kostroma and Galich (Kostroma obl.);
Krasnodar and Kuban (Krasnodar krai);
Kuibyshev and Syzran (Kuibyshev obl.), temporarily administering Ulyanovsk diocese (Ulyanovsk obl.);
Kursk and Belgorod (Kursk obl. and Belgorod obl.);
Leningrad and Novgorod (Leningrad obl. and Novgorod obl.), temporarily administering Olonets diocese (Karelian ASSR);
Moscow (Moscow obl.);
Oryol and Bryansk (Oryol obl. and Bryansk obl.);
Orenburg and Buzuluk (Orenburg obl.);
Penza and Saransk (Penza obl. and Mordovian ASSR);

Perm and Solikamsk (Perm obl.);
Pskov and Porkhov (Pskov obl.);
Rostov and Novocherkassk (Rostov obl.);
Ryazan and Kasimov (Ryazan obl.);
Saratov and Volgograd (Saratov obl. and Volgograd obl.);
Smolensk and Vyazma (Smolensk obl.);
Stavropol and Baku (Stavropol krai, Checheno-Ingush ASSR, Dagestan ASSR, Kabardino-Balkarskaya ASSR, Kalmyk ASSR, Severo-Osetinskaya ASSR, Azerbaidzhani republic);
Sverdlovsk and Kurgan (Sverdlovsk obl. and Kurgan obl.), temporarily administering Chelyabinsk diocese (Chelyabinsk obl.);
Tambov and Michurinsk (Tambov obl.);
Tula and Belev (Tula obl.);
Ufa and Sterlitamak (Bashkir ASSR);
Vladimir and Suzdal (Vladimir obl.);
Vologda and Veliki Ustyug (Vologda obl.);
Voronezh and Lipetsk (Voronezh obl. and Lipetsk obl.);
Yaroslavl and Rostov (Yaroslavl obl.).

This leaves one area of the RSFSR unaccounted for: Kaliningrad obl. It is not clear which diocese it comes under, but as there are no churches there, the question is purely academic.

The Ukrainian dioceses are:

Chernigov and Nezhin (Chernigov obl.), temporarily administering Sumy diocese (Sumy obl.);
Chernovtsy and Bukovina (Chernovtsy obl.);
Ivano-Frankovsk (formerly Stanislavsky) *and Kolymyya* (Ivano-Frankovsk obl.);
Kharkov and Bogodukhov (Kharkov obl.);
Kiev and Galicia (Kiev obl. and Cherkassy obl.);
Kirovograd and Nikolayev (Kirovograd obl. and Nikolayev obl.);
Lvov and Ternopol (Lvov obl. and Ternopol obl.);
Mukhachevo and Uzhgorod (Zakarpatskaya obl.);
Odessa and Kherson (Odessa obl. and Kherson obl.), temporarily administering Voroshilovgrad (formerly Lugansk) diocese (Voroshilovgrad obl. and Donetsk obl.);
Poltava and Kremenchug (Poltava obl.);
Simferopol and Crimea (Krymskaya obl.), temporarily administering Dnepropetrovsk diocese (Dnepropetrovsk obl. and Zaporozhe obl.);
Vinnitsa and Bratslav (Vinnitsa obl.), temporarily administering Khmelnitsky diocese (Khmelnitsky obl.);
Volhynia and Rovno (Volhynia obl. and Rovno obl.);
Zhitomir and Ovruch (Zhitomir obl.).

The remaining seven dioceses are:

Minsk and Belorussia (Belorussian SSR);
Kishinyov and Moldavia (Moldavian SSR);
Tallinn and Estonia (Estonian SSR);
Riga and Latvia (Latvian SSR);
Vilnius and Lithuania (Lithuanian SSR);
Alma-Ata and Kazakhstan (Kazakh SSR);
Tashkent and Central Asia (Uzbek SSR, Kirgiz SSR, Tadzhik SSR, Turkmen SSR).

(The administrative areas covered by each diocese have been ascertained by reference to the 'From the Dioceses' section of the *Journal of the Moscow Patriarchate* since 1965.)
The vacant dioceses (16) are:

Krasnoyarsk, vacant since 1948, under the jurisdiction of Novosibirsk;
Khabarovsk, vacant since 1949 and since then referred to as 'the Khabarovsk deanery (*blagochiniye*) of Irkutsk diocese';
Olonets, vacant since 1949, under the jurisdiction of Leningrad;
Izhevsk, vacant since 1959, under the jurisdiction of Kazan;
Semipalatinsk, vacant since 1959, under the jurisdiction of Alma-Ata;
Sumy, vacant since 1959, under the jurisdiction of Chernigov;
Ulyanovsk, vacant since 1959, under the jurisdiction of Kuibyshev;
Chelyabinsk, vacant since 1961, under the jurisdiction of Sverdlovsk;
Khmelnitsky, vacant since 1962, under the jurisdiction of Vinnitsa;
Dnepropetrovsk, vacant since 1965, under the jurisdiction of Simferopol;
Voroshilovgrad, vacant since 1965, under the jurisdiction of Odessa;
Petropavlovsk, apparently absorbed into the diocese of Alma-Ata in 1961;
Novgorod, which in 1967 became part of the diocese of Leningrad and Ladoga, renamed Leningrad and Novgorod;
Pinsk, vacant since 1950 (now restored in 1980, with the consecration of Bishop Afanasi, but not with diocesan status);
Grodno, vacant since 1946;
Drogobych and Sambor, vacant since 1959.

(This information is taken from *Religiya i ateizm v SSSR*, nos 9–10 (September–October 1972), pp. 59–60, which is based on *The Russian Orthodox Church: Organisation, Situation, Activity*, published by the Moscow Patriarchate in 1958, and on issues of the *Journal of the Moscow Patriarchate* and the *Information Bulletin* of the Department of External Church Relations of the Moscow Patriarchate.)
Overseas dioceses are:

Argentina and South America (Exarchate);
Berlin and Central Europe (Exarchate);
Baden-Baden and Bavaria, which in 1982 was divided into two dioceses:
Baden-Baden and Bavaria, and Düsseldorf. The former was comprised of
Bavaria and Baden-Wüttemburg. The latter consisted of: Bremen,
Hamburg, Hesse, Lower Saxony, Rheinland-Pfalz, Saarland, northern
Rhein-Westphalia and Schleswig-Holstein (*JMP*, no. 8 (1982), p. 9);
Brussels and Belgium;
The Hague and The Netherlands;
Sourozh (*London*);
Vienna and Austria;
Zurich.

These dioceses have bishops either permanently serving abroad or sent temporarily from the Soviet Union. There are other overseas bishops, but they
are suffragans, not diocesans. For details, see the appendix to Chapter 8.

Official References to the Number of Dioceses

Spokesmen for the Moscow Patriarchate have at different times given
different figures for the number of dioceses, which can be confusing. The
discrepancies appear to depend on whether they are counting some, all or
none of the overseas dioceses and the vacant dioceses, but as the sources do
not list the dioceses they are referring to, it is hard to be sure. There has
been no list of dioceses published since 1958, when an official source[97] listed
73 dioceses within the Soviet Union. These are the same as the 57 occupied
dioceses and 16 vacant dioceses we have listed above (though some dioceses
have changed their titles due to changes in Soviet place-names).

In November 1980 Archbishop Pitirim, on a visit to the Vatican, repeated
this figure of 73 dioceses within the USSR.[98]

In 1977 another official source stated that there were 76 dioceses in the
church as a whole.[99] This total appears to be made up of the 57 occupied
dioceses in the USSR, 8 overseas dioceses, and 11 of the vacant dioceses.
The 11 vacant dioceses counted are evidently those being temporarily
administered by other dioceses; this would mean that the remaining 5 have
ceased to be counted altogether. This figure of 76 dioceses was repeated in
the Church Calendar for 1980.[100]

In 1980 Archbishop Khrizostom was quoted as saying there were 62
dioceses in the church.[101] He must have been referring to the 57 occupied
dioceses in the USSR and 5 overseas ones. They are presumably Sourozh
(London), The Hague, Vienna, Baden-Baden and Brussels, leaving out
Zurich, which he could be counting as a vicariate of the West European
Exarchate, and Berlin and Argentina, which he could be counting as
Exarchates rather than as dioceses. If this is so, then his counting of the
dioceses is inconsistent with that in the Church Calendar.

Finally, the CRA Report for 1974 stated that there were then 67 dioceses in the USSR, and that at the beginning of the 1960s there had been 73.[102] This can be explained only by their method of counting the vacant dioceses. If they started with the original total of 73 which they state existed at the beginning of the 1960s, and subtracted the 6 dioceses which fell vacant since then (Chelyabinsk, Khmelnitsky, Dnepropetrovsk, Voroshilovgrad, Petropavlovsk and Novgorod) they would be left with 67 dioceses, 57 occupied and 10 having fallen vacant earlier. This seems rather an odd way to count them: they are simultaneously crossing off 6 newly vacant dioceses from their list and continuing to count 10 which have been vacant for some time. However, we can see no other way of arriving at their figure of 67 dioceses within the USSR. The wording of the passage in the CRA Report suggests that they may wish to impress their political masters with their zeal in closing down 6 dioceses, which would explain this odd method of counting them.

2 PARISH LIFE

Each of the 6,000—6,500 functioning Orthodox churches in the Soviet Union has its own parish community which worships together and also has to fulfil certain financial and administrative obligations under Soviet law. In this chapter we shall attempt to describe how parish life is organised and examine the experiences of a few specific parishes. First of all, here is a general impression of parish life and worship from a foreigner who studied for the priesthood in Leningrad:

> In the very first months of my study in the Theological Academy I was struck by the religious state of the people who surrounded me, and as time went on I became more deeply convinced of it . . . The more than half a century's history of Orthodox Christians in Soviet Russia has yet again affirmed the truth of Christianity that lies in the power of prayer. Here I involuntarily recall the impression made on Monsignor Poupard [Pro-President of the Vatican's Secretariat for Non-Believers] by a Russian church overflowing with believing people: 'Anything could happen here, even an earthquake, but the church would remain unharmed because of the prayer of the people.' . . .
>
> Imagine for a moment that you are in, for example, the overflowing church of the Leningrad Theological Academy. The deacon intones: 'Let us love one another and let us confess in unity of mind . . .' and the whole congregation sings the rest of the Eucharistic canon. It is impossible to convey the spiritual mood of the people which 'with one mouth and one heart' glorifies the name of God, and I am convinced that someone dropping into church for the first time will remain in it for that moment, so majestic and powerful are those minutes . . .
>
> A typical picture in the Academy are the young people who can be seen in the vestibule, on the street and in front of the academy gates, conversing with the students. I often took part in such conversations, practically every day one of the bystanders would ask me something about the faith, and it was clear that this was not simply curiosity but a deep, well-considered interest in the Church.[1]

This impression of overflowing churches and of deeply felt, prayerful worship has been recorded many a time by foreign visitors to the larger cities of the USSR, especially Moscow and Leningrad. Most speak of their visits to Russian Orthodox church services as a moving and memorable experience. We do not know whether such experiences of worship are typical throughout the USSR, as accounts of worship in village churches, or even smaller towns, are rare. It does seem, generally speaking, that young people are not so much in evidence in village churches as they are in city ones, and in this respect the impressions quoted above are probably not typical of all churches. However, the piety and prayerfulness of congregations are described by most observers both as being typically Russian and as resulting from the sufferings which the faithful have endured during the Soviet period, and it therefore seems reasonable to assume that these characteristics are to be found in rural congregations also.

The weekly round of worship in a cathedral, with interesting glimpses of the life in rural churches, is described as follows by a believer, A. Udodov, who attended Minsk Cathedral for a time in the early 1970s before emigrating to the West:

in Minsk two churches continue to function. The cemetery is closed. In the Cathedral there are two liturgies every day: the early one at 7 a.m. and the later one at 9 a.m. In addition, rites are performed in the side chapel, mostly burial services. At 6 p.m. there is Vespers. The Cathedral has several priests. On Mondays, if it is not a festival day, the Cathedral is closed. On Sundays (and festivals) the late liturgy is at 10 a.m., not 9 a.m. Usually it is the bishop — the Archbishop of Minsk and Belorussia — who officiates. Sermons are given only on Sundays and festivals, but they are preached intelligibly and with feeling, and often move the hearts of the believers. They behave unrestrainedly in church, spontaneously and sincerely, and one feels that for many the church is like their own home. But they prefer not to enter into conversation, fearing the numerous agents of the KGB. These agents, however, evidently have instructions to confine themselves to observation and information-gathering. No arrests, brawls or disturbances took place in the Minsk Cathedral while I was there, though in the depths of the Russian provinces, so they say, these are a most common occurrence.

On non-festival days there's plenty of room in church. Usually it accommodates no more than 500 people, but 1,000 can cram in. It is generally elderly people who attend church (every day, if they can), but there are also middle-aged people, and young people who are fervent churchgoers, though they are few.

On Saturdays [in the Orthodox Church the main weekly services are on Saturday evening and Sunday morning] the church is full 'as normal'; on Sundays it's overflowing. The local inhabitants, who live closest, try to attend the early liturgy in order not to get in the way of those who come from a distance. It is crowded in church, and there would be a real crush if people did not try to make room for others (in contrast to the usual Soviet crowd, where one can be trampled underfoot).

At festivals, especially the big ones, it's impossible to get closer than a hundred metres to the church: thousands of people surround it in the hope of making their way through to the church doors for even a few minutes or of receiving the bishop's blessing.

. . . It's characteristic that on non-working days many people travel to the Cathedral from far away, often in their own cars or in taxis (which wait for them for hours at the church gates), in other words, even among the Soviet privileged class seriously believing people are met with. The KGB agents do not have such facilities to travel to their observation posts! But the fact of their presence is well known, and parishioners prefer not to enter into conversation around the church. People dressed in the well-known uniforms of the militia [MVD: Ministry of Internal Affairs] or the KGB did not show themselves around Minsk Cathedral when I was there.

Once again, as I was told, this was in contrast to more remote provincial localities, where the terror of the Bolshevik administration was not constrained by the presence of foreigners.[2]

This account gives us an idea of the functioning of a particular Orthodox community, but it also introduces an 'unchurchly' and therefore perhaps unexpected element, the almost casual allusion to the presence of 'numerous' agents of the secret police among the congregation. Since church services are entirely within the bounds of the law, it appears that (as in other areas of Soviet life) the KGB agents are assigned to watch ordinary citizens: to report who goes to church and what they say and do when they are there. This is surely an infringement of the Soviet citizen's constitutional right to freedom of worship: one is not entirely *free* to worship if the fact of one's doing so is reported, without one's knowledge, to the secret police. The 'well-known' presence of KGB agents in churches is evidently a barrier to true Christian community, since it renders believers reluctant to talk freely to one another and obviously inhibits their approach to strangers whom they would otherwise wish to welcome into the church.

The Yakunin Report, which takes a pessimistic view of parish life and worship, has this to say:

In the modern Orthodox parish, as in no other communities of no other denominations, the sense of Christian brotherhood is weakened. In big cities paradoxical cases are encountered. People who have stood side by side in worship and have taken Communion from the same chalice for decades, seeing as bystanders their children and grandchildren growing up and themselves growing older, turn out to be unacquainted with one another.[3]

This may be partly due to the fear of KGB agents mentioned by Udodov, but it cannot be the whole explanation, since Yakunin states that the unfriendly relations he has observed are to be found only in Orthodox churches and not in other Christian communities. He ascribed this coldness to the lack of a true sense of Christian community in Orthodox churches, and attributes this to lack of proper Christian teaching and to the Moscow Patriarchate's unwillingness or inability to provide elementary Christian teaching or to do anything to engender a true community spirit in the parishes. A similar comment was made by a young man converted to Christianity who found that parish life did not meet his expectations or his needs:

in the Russian Church, the parish is not like a brotherly community where Christian love to one's neighbour becomes a reality. The State persecutes every manifestation of church life, except for the performance of 'a religious cult'. Our thirst for spiritual communion, religious education and missionary service runs up against all the might of the State's repressive machinery.[4]

Anyone who has experienced Orthodox worship in the USSR may find it strange that such densely packed, united, devout congregations should be charged with coldness to one another and lack of community spirit, but we cannot ignore such charges when they are made by two people who are clearly speaking from personal experience. It seems to us that in many cases Soviet citizens may attend Orthodox churches out of personal needs, rather than because they identify themselves with the Christian community as a whole. Church attendance is often probably thought of more in terms of an individual relationship between the worshipper and the church, or the worshipper and God, rather than as the worshipper's being fully integrated into the church, the Body of Christ. This means that the Russian Orthodox Church, though by far the largest in the USSR, is less cohesive and unified than the smaller Christian communities. As the oldest and largest Christian community in the land, the Orthodox Church is the natural place for any citizen with even a slight, awakening interest in religion to turn, or for anyone who wants to attend church for cultural or aesthetic reasons. This carries the corresponding disadvantage that such people see the church as a place for satisfying their personal needs, rather than as a community of which they are an integral part and to which they feel committed.

The comments quoted above all relate to urban churches. As stated above, our knowledge of the weekly round of worship in rural churches is almost non-existent, and we do not know what relations are like between the members of worshipping communities.

Parish Adminstration

Our knowledge concerning the administration of parishes, both urban and rural, is very much clearer. Both Soviet laws and church regulations provide detailed information on what parishes may and may not do. There is only one permitted activity — holding services of worship and performing sacraments within a building registered for that purpose. We saw in Chapter 1 that a religious association containing at least 20 members must register, that is, obtain official permission to exist, then seek permission to register a suitable building for worship, and then obtain the services of a priest, appointed by the bishop and registered, that is, given permission to exercise his priestly ministry in a given place, by the local CRA commissioner. If it proves possible to complete all these arrangements, the only activity the parish may then legally engage in is holding services within the registered building. Any other activities within the church are illegal, and any worship-related activities outside the building are also illegal. (Processions (*krestnye khody*) around the exterior walls of the church, which are an integral part of Easter and other services, are permitted 'provided they do not disturb normal street traffic'.)[5]

The list of what parishes may not do is much longer:

Religious associations may not: (a) create mutual undertakings, or in general use property at their disposal other than for the satisfaction of religious needs; (b) give material support to their members; (c) organise special prayer or other meetings for children, young people and women, nor general Bible, literary, handicraft, work, catechetical and other similar meetings, groups, circles and departments, nor organise excursions and children's playgrounds, nor open libraries and reading rooms, nor organise sanatoria and medical help. Only books necessary for the performance of the relevant cult may be kept in the prayer buildings and premises.[6]

These words have since 1929 made it impossible for Christians in the USSR to engage in activities which are regarded as a normal part of parish life by most churches in most countries of the world. Without entering into a long discussion on the balance between worship and social action in the Christian life (itself an important and controversial issue), we feel it is safe to assert that most Christians would regard as an integral part of their faith two aspects mentioned in this law: teaching young people and new converts about the nature of the Christian faith, and giving assistance to the needy, whether members of the church community or outsiders. Certainly it has always been customary in the Orthodox Church for instruction about the faith to be given to newcomers, and Orthodox charitable giving to the poor and needy is a striking characteristic of the faith — many are the stories of holy men and women who have given away everything they possessed to those in need. True, individual Christians can still give to the poor, and newcomers can learn about the faith by attending church, but none the less the church as a body is prevented from communally ministering to needs which Orthodox and other Christians would generally regard as a concern of the church as a whole. Worship in church is, as we have said, the central, most important aspect of Orthodox corporate life, but this does not mean that that life is confined only to worship. There is no doubt that this law makes it difficult for Christians to live out the totality of their faith in their daily lives.

The administration of parish life is governed by civil legislation and by ecclesiastical regulations which have been enacted under the supervision of the Council for Religious Affairs (or, before 1965, the Council for Russian Orthodox Church Affairs: CROCA). The civil legislation is the Law on Religious Associations of 1929, amended in 1932 and revised in 1975, together with government commentaries on its application. The fundamental ecclesiastical regulation governing the organisation of the Russian Orthodox Church as a whole, including its parishes, is the Statute on the Administration of the Russian Orthodox Church adopted by the Local Council of 1945.[7] The Statute has four parts, devoted to the Patriarch, the Holy Synod, the dioceses and the parishes. The fourth section, on the parishes, was almost entirely altered by a Council of Bishops which met in 1961.[8] The amendments were confirmed by the Local Council (*Pomestny Sobor*) of the Russian Orthodox Church in 1971.

The terminology of the various bodies concerned with the administration of parishes is rather complicated. We have already seen that a religious community (of any denomination) must consist of at least 20 people of the same denomination living in the same place, and that they must be officially registered before they are able to lease a building for worship. (All church buildings are leased from the state, not owned by the church.) These 20 founder-members are known as a 'group of 20' (*dvadtsatka*). After the founding of the community, other local believers may obtain equal status in it with the founders by signing the registration agreement. They then form a body referred to in civil legislation as a religious association (*obedineniye*). Religious associations may in theory be of two types: those with less than 20 members, who may form a 'group of believers', and those with 20 or more members, who may form a religious society. In practice, the existence of groups of believers is virtually unknown, and we shall therefore be concerned with what the law calls a religious society (*obshchestvo*).[9] This collection of believers in a given locality is also commonly referred to in both Soviet secular literature and church literature as a community (*obshchina*), a term which is used in a general sense and not a specific legal sense. In church literature, this community is also referred to in general terms as a parish (*prikhod*). This clearly refers to the believers worshipping in a particular church[10] and not to the territorial area for which that church and its priest have pastoral responsibility, which is its normal usage in most churches throughout the world.

As church activities are limited by law to worship only, there can clearly be no question of a church or priest having even a self-imposed responsibility for the cure of souls of the local population. Decisions on the running of the parish are made by a general assembly (*sobraniye*) of the religious society, which may be held periodically as required, but for which permission must be obtained in advance from the local state authorities each time.[11] The day-to-day affairs of the parish are in the hands of an executive committee (*ispolnitelny komitet*), whose members are elected by the general assembly of the religious society,[12] but whose election is subject to a veto by the state registration agencies.[13] This executive committee consists of three members: in the Orthodox Church they are a churchwarden or elder (*starosta*), his or her assistant (*pomoshchnik starosty*), and a treasurer (*kaznachei*).

The income of the religious society, consisting of voluntary donations only,[14] is paid into the State Bank, into an account in the name of the religious society, from which withdrawals are made by cheques signed by the churchwarden and treasurer.[15] The financial affairs of the religious society are subject to the periodical scrutiny of an auditing commission (*revizionnaya kommissiya*) of three people, also elected by the general assembly of the religious society.[16] This auditing commission submits its findings to the general assembly of the parish, but if it finds any malpractices or absence of property or money, it reports this, not to the parish or higher church authorities, but to the local town or village *soviet*.[17] The executive committee and the auditing commission do not require the permission of the local state authorities for their meetings.[18]

It will be clear from this outline that the system of parish administration vests a great deal of power directly in the hands of the executive committee, and indirectly in the hands of the local state authorities. Although the general assembly of the religious society is legally responsible for the church building and the running of the parish, it may meet only with permission from local state authorities. This gives the state a very effective means of control over the parish: it can virtually paralyse it simply by refusing to allow the believers to meet together. Although the general assembly elects the executive committee, the local authorities can, as stated above, veto its choice. This gives the state organs a means of ensuring that only people favourable to the state's line on church affairs have the opportunity to exercise control over parish life. That they have made active use of the means available to them is indicated in a secret circular of the CROCA sent to local state executive committees, which instructed them: 'It is desirable that you take part in the selection of members for the executive organ and select those persons who adhere to our line'.[19] Neither the civil laws nor the church regulations make any reference to a procedure for removing a member or members of the executive body who discharge their duties unsatisfactorily in the opinion of the general assembly. The church regulations state that 'the executive organ of the parish community of believers is responsible for its activity to the general parish assembly',[20] which may imply the assembly's right to censure or remove members of the executive committee, but as no mechanism for this is mentioned it is not possible to be clear on this point. No term of office for members of the executive committee is mentioned in the civil or church sources, and the implication is that their appointments are permanent.

Once installed, the executive committee has quite considerable powers. Its members alone can sign cheques, as mentioned above, and therefore they alone have ultimate control over the money given to the church by believers. The law holds the members of the religious society as a whole liable for the maintenance of the building and property leased to the church, but the church Statute points out that it is the executive committee which 'is responsible for the protection of the buildings and the property of the church, conducts church management, concerns itself with maintenance, heating, lighting and repairs of the church and utensils . . . the executive committee is the reponsible manager of the monetary resources of the parish'.[21]

This means that the most important aspects of the financial and administrative side of parish life are in the hands of three people approved by the state, possibly not removable from office by other believers, and (since the general assembly of the religious society may meet only with state permission) subject to only tenuous control by the religious society as a whole. The only limit on the activities of the executive committee is that exercised by the auditing commission. This appears to be limited to the financial, not the administrative side of the executive committee's activities: the auditing commission's task is to see that accounts are kept properly and that there is no embezzlement but it does not appear to have any power to control the use to which the church's money is put, which remains at the sole discretion of the executive committee, with the general assembly of believers able to exercise control over it only with the permission of the state. Furthermore, as noted above, any malpractices the auditing commission may discover are to be reported to the local state authorities, not to the church. This effectively removes any ultimate control over parish affairs from the general assembly of believers and the higher church organs, and transfers it to the state organs. They can then take whatever action they consider to be necessary, and the church is given no opportunity to right any wrongs which may have occurred.

The Law on Religious Associations makes quite detailed provision for the regulation of the financial side of religious communities. The state gives no financial assistance of any kind to the church,[22] which exists entirely on worshippers' offerings at collections taken during church services[23] and on proceeds from the sale of candles and prosphora.[24] Income from the sale of candles, which are manufactured in the workshops belonging to the Moscow Patriarchate, is said to constitute a substantial proportion of total income. The religious associations do not pay income tax on this income.[25] All donations must be entered in the account book, and any donations in kind must be entered in the inventory of church property.[26] However, on the closure of a place of worship, valuable or cultural items revert to the state.[27] The income of a religious association may be spent only on the maintenance of the church building and on objects necessary for worship, on salaries for priests and for workers such as cleaners, watchmen, book-keepers, etc. (who pay income tax), and on donations to the diocesan and patriarchal administrations.[28] (Church buildings are considered to be public buildings on a par with, for example, cinemas, and so electricity is sold to them at 25 kopeks a kilowatt instead of the normal rate of 4 kopeks.)[29] The religious associations are responsible for the maintenance of their buildings, even though they are owned by the state. However, the state sometimes gives financial assistance for the restoration of especially old or beautiful churches, though not so far as is known, working churches. On the other hand, the church sometimes helps to maintain or restore churches even when they are not registered for worship, for example, the church at Fili near Moscow.[30]

Two points should be made about expenditure. First, it is known that religious associations make donations, apparently quite substantial ones, to the state-run Peace Fund. References to such donations are made in the *Journal of the Moscow Patriarchate* and the Soviet press from time to time, and the possibility for such donations appears to be provided for in the 1961 amendments to the Church's Statute under the term 'patriotic needs'. However, rather oddly, the Law on Religious Associations does not make provision for donations to the Peace Fund, and the wording of Article 54 would seem to indicate that such donations are not legal. ('Religious communities . . . may pool their resources and collect voluntary donations in the worship building among members of the religious association concerned, *solely* [emphasis added] for purposes of maintaining the worship building and the property of the cult, of hiring the ministers of the cult, and of meeting the costs of the cult's executive organs.') The reason for this anomaly is unclear.

The second comment concerns the maintenance of church buildings and property. Although believers are legally responsible for this, there have been cases where the local authorities have made it difficult or impossible for them to carry out necessary repairs. Some of these cases are described in detail in a letter sent to Mr Brezhnev in 1977 by a diocesan bishop, Bishop Feodosi of Poltava and Kremenchug, in Ukraine.[31] (He was subsequently transferred — see Chapter 8, p. 243.) In Globino district, there is one small (33 square metres) church for 26 villages. It had walls of *pisé* (clay mixed with straw, gravel, etc.), which were old and friable, and a roof of straw, which had rotted. In 1971 the church members decided to face the walls with brick. However, it took months of applications to various offices,

right up to Moscow itself, before permission for this was received, and then
it was only verbal permission. When work had commenced, a midnight
'raid' occurred on the night of 30–31 July 1971. The chairman of the village
soviet, S. S. Kirilenko, accompanied by a militiamen and 20 Komsomol
(Young Communist League) members, destroyed the brick walls which had
already been built and made holes in the original walls. Despite this setback,
and with some help from the bishop, the task was eventually completed.
Then slate was acquired for the roof, but before it could be used, the authorities came and removed it in the absence of the believers. It was not until
the end of 1973 that the parishioners were finally able to acquire roofing
iron and complete their repairs. The bishop concluded: 'It took the Globino
religious community three long and agonising years to do something which
under normal circumstances would have been accomplished in three days.'[32]
The bishop cited similar instances in the prayer house in Belotserkovka,
Velikaya Bagachka district; Polivyanoye village, Mirgorod district; and
Veprik village, Gadyach district.[33] In the latter parish, the believers decided
to paint the roof, but the local authorities refused permission, so they
painted it without permission. The bishop wrote:

> Who in this instance broke the law: the church community, which, in
> repairing the building, was trying to preserve it for the state and for
> posterity, or the local authorities, who were acting contrary to all
> commonsense logic and even to the leasing agreement itself?

Bishop Feodosi himself supplied the answer for the authorities' illogical
behaviour:

> It seems to me that the meaning of their actions is as follows: to deny the
> believers opportunities to repair church buildings, to reduce them to
> partial ruin, and then to declare them dangerous and close them down
> with a clear conscience.

He added:

> During the ten years I have been in Poltava I have never once seen a
> resolution by a [CRA] commissioner giving permission to repair a
> church.[34]

As we shall see later in this chapter, similar intervention by local authorities in other areas has also sometimes prevented believers maintaining their
churches. This may have been due to an uncooperative or even malicious
attitude on the part of the CRA commissioner concerned. However, there
seems little doubt that the chief reason for such actions is that suggested by
Bishop Feodosi: the desire to close down the church.

Finance

Although it is possible to build up a reasonably clear picture of the administration of church finances, little is known of the sums of money involved. The Russian Orthodox Church's income is unknown. We have been able to discover very few statistics relating to the income of individual parishes, but none the less those that are available throw some light on the subject. They come from parishes whose financial situations differ very greatly from one another. According to three foreigners who made separate visits to the large Cathedral of St Nicholas in Leningrad, its income grew from 1 million to 1.3 million roubles a year between 1977 and 1981.[35] Forty per cent of this was reported to come from the sale of candles.[36] The cathedral had a paid staff of 100 in 1981,[37] which, rather surprisingly in view of its increased income, represented a decrease from 120 staff in 1977.[38] It gave 15 per cent of its income to the Peace Fund, a figure which this source reported to be general for the several churches he visited in 1981.[39]

The Holy Trinity Church in the St Alexander Nevsky Lavra in Leningrad is also well-off, according to a journalist who visited it in 1979. He reported that its income was 600,000 roubles a year, derived from donations, the sale of candles and fees for special rites. The church had 64 paid employees, and gave 15 per cent of its income to the Peace Fund. He was told that a small rural parish would have an income of about 50,000 roubles a year.[40]

The cathedral in Odessa, according to a British journalist, has an income of 300,000 roubles per year; this supports six priests and four deacons. This source also (and consistently with the figure given by our previous source for a small rural parish) states that the church in the village of Ostyol, 50 miles from Kiev, has an income of 50,000 roubles per year; the parish priest there estimates 5,000 believers in his flock.[41]

According to a *samizdat* source, the parishioners of the Dormition Church in the provincial Ukrainian town of Pavlograd stated in 1977 that their gross income was 116,000 roubles per year.[42] Their bishop told them that their income was the third-highest in the region,[43] so the average income for smaller congregations in rural churches would be less than this. This suggests that the figure of 50,000 roubles income for a small rural church, quoted above, is plausible. The Pavlograd parishioners stated that they gave 37,000 roubles a year, or just under one-third of their total income, to the Peace Fund.[44]

However, a rather different picture is given by Bishop Feodosi of Poltava, whose letter to Mr Brezhnev we cited above. He stated that the tiny prayer house in the village of Polivyanoye, Velikaya Bagachka district, had an income of 3,500 roubles per year, and found it difficult to make ends meet. He added that 'many' churches in Poltava diocese were financially weak.[45] Furthermore, he complained that the CRA commissioner, I. Ya. Nechitailo, was obliging churches to make larger and larger donations to state funds. Feodosi stated:

> Beginning in 1968, the parishes of the Russian Orthodox Church took the noble initiative of donating sums of money within their means to state needs — to the 'Peace Fund' and for 'maintenance of monuments of the past'.
>
> For these purposes the churches of Poltava diocese transferred at first five, then ten, fifteen and twenty per cent of their annual monetary turnover. But recently the commissioner has begun to insist that some parishes, at times to their own detriment, should give thirty or even forty per cent.

Feodosi then gave figures demonstrating that if the Polivyanoye parish gave 30 per cent of its income to the state funds, it would be unable to pay for ground rent and insurance, and would therefore be liable to closure.[46] He also gave the total amounts contributed to state funds by the parishes of Poltava diocese every year since 1968: the sum had risen from 36,210 roubles in 1968 to 161,328 roubles in 1976.[47]

It is difficult to say to what extent Poltava diocese may differ from others. It is clear from Bishop Feodosi's letter that Commissioner Nechitailo has a rather aggressive attitude to believers, including the bishop, and that the attempts to raise donations to the state funds are his personal initiative. However, it is likely that there are CRA officials with similar attitudes in other dioceses, though we cannot say how many. It is also clear from Feodosi's letter that the situation varies very greatly not only between urban and rural parishes, but also among rural parishes. His figure of 3,500 roubles annual income for a small village church is substantially less than the figure suggested above of 50,000 roubles annual income for a small rural parish. However, the fact that he singles out the Polivyanoye parish for special mention suggests that it may be particularly poor.

Although the dangers of taking such a small sample are obvious, it does not seem unreasonable to use these figures to attempt to estimate a very approximate figure for the total income of the Russian Orthodox Church. Assuming that there are just over 6,000 functioning churches, which can be divided into the listed categories, we may venture to assume an income pattern approximating to that set out in Table 2.1. The chief difficulty in making this estimate lies in knowing what proportion of the assumed number of small rural parishes are in financial difficulties. Our estimate here is arbitrary, in the absence of further evidence. Moreover, in view of the different amounts contributed by parishes to state funds, principally the Peace Fund, we cannot be sure how much of the church's total income remains for its own use. If the large, rich parishes in the capitals are giving 15 per cent of their income to the Peace Fund, and the smaller provincial parishes are giving about 30 per cent, the total must be roughly between

Table 2.1: Estimated Church Income

Assume 10 cathedrals with an income of 1.3 million roubles p.a. (e.g. St Nicholas Cathedral, Leningrad)	13,000,000 r.
Assume 20 large urban churches with an income of 600,000 roubles p.a. (e.g. Holy Trinity Church, Leningrad)	12,000,000 r.
Assume 30 large urban churches with an income of 300,000 roubles p.a. (e.g. the Odessa Cathedral)	9,000,000 r.
Assume 500 medium urban churches with an income in excess of 100,000 roubles p.a. (e.g. the Dormition Church, Pavlograd)	50,000,000 r.
Assume 4,500 small rural parishes with an income of 50,000 roubles p.a.	225,000,000 r.
Assume 1,000 small rural parishes which are financially weak and have an income of about 5,000 roubles p.a. (e.g. Polivyanoye prayer house)	5,000,000 r.
Total annual income of church	314,000,000 r.

20 per cent (62.8 million roubles) and 25 per cent (78.5 million roubles). This would leave the church with about 250 million roubles a year, or slightly less, for its own needs.

If we approach the putative income of 314 million roubles a year from another angle, it represents, say, nearly 32 million regular worshippers giving 10 roubles or so a year, or about 20 kopeks a week each, to the church in the form of offerings, purchase of candles and fees for special services. In fact, there are probably more than 32 million regular worshippers (as we shall see in Chapter 7), and many people would probably give much more than 20 kopeks a week for offerings and candles, so it may be that our estimated total is too low.

It has never been suggested that the church's income is insufficient for its needs. The putative income we have suggested would seem to be quite adequate for the purposes on which the church is allowed to spend its money, described by Metropolitan Alexi as follows:

> The donations are sufficient to maintain the church buildings, to restore icons, frescoes, to keep church choirs and service personnel, and to do everything necessary for the sublime beauty of the churches and divine services. Every parish makes voluntary donations to its diocese, and the dioceses, for their part, donate money to the Moscow Patriarchate for the needs of the entire Church. This money is used to maintain theological schools, to pay pensions to old clergymen and other church workers, their widows and orphans, and to cover the expenditure linked with the ecumenical and peace-making activities.[48]

(The financial affairs of the monasteries and convents, which are discussed in Chapter 5, are quite separate from the rest of the church.) However, though the church appears to have an adequate overall income, this does not alter the fact that some rural churches, such as those mentioned by Bishop Feodosi, have financial problems. As we have seen, neither other Orthodox religious communities, nor the diocese, are allowed to transfer funds to help them.

One reason for the Soviet state's retaining very firm control over religious associations is probably the fact that such large sums of money are involved. In a country where all aspects of life are under the control of the state and the Communist Party, it would be anomalous for any one entity to have a sum in the region of 300 million roubles at its sole disposal. Many documents, especially the CRA Report, indicate that the state is concerned about the sums of money at the church's disposal and the uses to which it is put, and often suspects that people involved in church activities — bishops, clergy and laity — are motivated by a desire to get their hands on the church's money. We shall see this in our discussion of the 1961 reforms of the church's Statute, and also in our study of the clergy in Chapter 3.

Membership

Although the most important aspects of the financial and administrative life of the parish are under the control of the executive committee, the broad base of believers in the parish are, in theory, able to exercise control over it through the general assembly of the religious society. As stated above, this control is subject to state permission for the assembly to take place. Any believer of the appropriate denomination living in the locality may join the original 20 founding-members by signing the registration documents. Upon doing so, he or she receives the right to participate in parish life equally with the founders, and undertakes the same responsibility to the state for the maintenance of the prayer building and its contents. Although the right to join the *dvadtsatka* is clearly stated in the 1929 Law on Religious Associations and its 1975 amendment, it is in practice sometimes denied to believers. (We shall discuss one particular example, in the town of Pavlograd, which we have already mentioned, later in this chapter.) Moreover, at one time it was state policy to restrict membership of the *dvadtsatka* to no more than 20 people, a policy not legally enacted, but outlined in a secret CRA circular sent to regional commissioners.[49] This change led one Western commentator to observe that 'a broad base of believers lost the right to participate in church activities'.[50] In practice, however, this policy appears to have lapsed. The CRA circular was issued during Khrushchev's anti-religious campaign in the early 1960s, and appears to have been revoked, or lapsed, after the campaign ended in 1964.

However, although the broad base of believers now do have the right to participate in church activities, the legal right to join the *dvadtsatka* can also have deleterious consequences for the church. This has been pointed out by Father Gleb Yakunin in his report:

> in recent years there have been more and more cases of people becoming members of *dvadtsatki* and executive committees who have nothing at all to do with the parish, or who are not even believers at all, but are simply trying to get 'a bite of the Church's cake' or who are penetrating the Church so that the anti-religious workers can control the lives of the communities more firmly, or even destroy them entirely from within.[51]

Yakunin points out that there is no definition of what a believer is, either in the law or in church regulations, and therefore anyone at all can join a religious society simply by stating themselves to be Orthodox. Whether they are in fact Christians, and whether or not they worship regularly, is a matter not considered by the law. There is therefore nothing to prevent unbelieving outsiders from joining the religious society and obtaining equal rights with the original *dvadtsatka*, and neither is there anything to prevent such people electing one of their number to the executive committee with the approval of the local state authorities. This gives considerable scope to state officials to undermine religious societies from within.

Thus far we have said nothing about the position of the priest in the regulation of parish life. A consideration of the role of the clergy in general is to be the subject of Chapter 3, but here we must consider their involvement in parish administration. This is defined by the ecclesiastical regulations: the state legislation does not mention priests. A major change in the position of the parish priest was brought about by reforms introduced by the Holy Synod and confirmed by the Council of Bishops in 1961. The effect of the reforms was to remove the parish priest from all involvement in financial and administrative matters and restrict him solely to the spiritual side of the life of the parish community. These reforms, which still affect parishes substantially, generated no little controversy, and the manner in which they were enacted is very instructive. Because of the importance of its reforms, and because it has never been fully described elsewhere, we shall make an excursus to consider in some detail the Council of Bishops of 1961. This event reveals a good deal about the relations between the episcopate and the state, a subject to which we shall return in Chapter 8.

Excursus: The Council of Bishops of 1961

There are two firsthand sources which give a detailed account of the 1961

Council of Bishops. First, there is a lengthy report of the occasion in the *Journal of the Moscow Patriarchate*.[52] Second, there is a *samizdat* report, anonymous and undated, which gives an eyewitness report of the proceedings.[53] This report is extremely interesting. The author is evidently a practised writer, whose style encompasses wit, subtlety and humour, and gives the reader a clear insight into the proceedings of the Council. It is evident from the content of the report that the author was either a bishop present at the Council or a confidant of a bishop. The 'inside information' contained in the report could have been obtained in no other way, since the author makes it quite clear that (apart from specified exceptions which we shall mention later) no one but bishops was present. Furthermore, the account of the proceedings and the descriptions of bishops who were present are remarkably vivid and fresh, and it is hard to conceive that anyone but an eyewitness could have written them. The author records that his motive in writing his report was to enable future historians to know the truth about the Council of Bishops:

> We shall try to tell the truth about this Council, and hope that this truth will reach all Orthodox people, if these lines do not perish. We shall hope that they will be preserved until such time as they fall into the hands of honest historians of the Russian Orthodox Church.[54]

The Council of Bishops was held on 18 July 1961 in the Holy Trinity Monastery of St Sergius at Zagorsk. It lasted one day only. The report that appeared in the *Journal of the Moscow Patriarchate* does not give a list of the bishops who attended, but the eyewitness report states that:

> Altogether there were about 50 bishops at the Council. Almost all the hierarchs were there with the exception of a few who were absent through illness. Also, of course, the retired bishops were absent. As is known, it is always the least 'retiring' bishops who are sent into 'retirement'. [There is a play on words in the Russian text: ' *"Na pokoi" otpravlyayut vsegda "bespokoinykh" yepiskopov'*.] There were none of the less 'retiring' bishops among those present. The only courageous hierarch, who would undoubtedly have come out in opposition, was Yermogen of Tashkent, who had already been retired in September of the previous year. There was no one to be feared.[55]

These words introduce us to one of the main themes of the eyewitness report, which was that the whole proceedings had been carefully prepared beforehand by CROCA, and that the Council of Bishops was merely a rubber stamp. The exclusion of hierarchs expected to express opposition was just one way in which this was effected, and, as we shall see in Chapter 8, the same measure was to be used again at the Local Council of 1971.

Patriarch Alexi's opening speech to the Council, rather revealingly for an official church announcement, confirmed that the Council had been summoned at the suggestion of CROCA.[56]

The most surprising fact about the 1961 Council of Bishops is that no one in the church, including the bishops who participated, knew beforehand that a Council was to take place. The report published in the *Journal of the Moscow Patriarchate* makes no mention of the manner in which the Council was convened, but the eyewitness report gives the following account:

> The bishops who had been summoned to the monastery for St Sergius's Day did not know, right up to the very eve of its opening, that they were to attend a Council. Arriving at the monastery in response to the Patriarch's invitation, few, if any, knew why they had been summoned from their dioceses. This, let it be said, is unprecedented in the entire history of the Christian Church. How many Councils had there been in the 2,000-year history of the Church: ecumenical and national, orthodox and heretical — but not one where, on the eve of its meeting, the bishops did not know that the next day they would have to take part in a Council . . . Since their arrival was timed to coincide with St Sergius's Day, when many bishops traditionally liked to visit the monastery, each could suppose that he alone had been invited — perhaps to discuss some personal matter. Arriving at the monastery, and finding their colleagues present in large numbers, the bishops made the sudden discovery (even then, not from an official announcement but from one another) that 'they were to be hanged tomorrow'.[57]

Archbishop Yermogen, himself excluded from the Council of Bishops, later made the following comment on the manner of its convening:

> It was not summoned, as it should have been, by a letter from the Patriarch, but by telegrams from the Patriarchate to the diocesan bishops. These contained invitations to participate in the services at the monastery in honour of St Sergius, but there was not a single mention of the Council. The bishops who arrived were informed of the intention to hold it only late in the evening after vespers on the eve of the memorial day. They thus had less than 24 hours' notice. Such a way of convening a Council is unusual and cannot, of course, be justified from the canonical standpoint.[58]

Even when they knew there was to be a Council, the bishops had no chance to prepare for it, or to discuss it among themselves, according to the eyewitness. He states that the bishops arrived at the monastery in the afternoon, and after dinner a series of long church services began. After these, 'barely able to remain upright from weariness, the hierarchs crossed them-selves and lay down to rest'. In the morning there was a festal liturgy followed by blessings and an abundant repast, lasting until 3 p.m. Then they were given the agenda for the Council, but 'the bishops had only just begun to come to their senses after the Mass and the heavy meal, and, putting on their spectacles, to look at the agenda, when they were at once summoned to the Patriarchal residence to be photographed . . . There was no time to talk even briefly to one another about the agenda.'[59]

This was an ominous beginning to the Council. The way it was convened was highly irregular but obviously carefully stage-managed, and the bishops must have entered the Patriarchal residence at the monastery with gloomy forebodings.

There were four items on the Council's agenda.[60] The first was the increase in the number of permanent members of the Holy Synod to include the chancellor for the Moscow Patriarchate and the chairman of the Department of External Church Relations, both of whom would hence-forward be of episcopal rank. The third item concerned the entry of the Russian Orthodox Church into the World Council of Churches; the fourth dealt with its participation in the World Christian Congress for the defence of peace (the Congress was based in Prague and became the Christian Peace Conference). These last two important matters, which relate to the external relations of the Russian Orthodox Church, are beyond the scope of the present book. We need only record here that the first, third and fourth items on the agenda were passed unanimously and without incident.

The second item on the agenda was entitled 'Alterations in the Statute on the Administration of the Russian Orthodox Church concerning Section IV — "The Parishes"'. In his speech to the Council, Patriarch Alexi stated that the reason for the proposed alterations was as follows:

In April this year the Council for Russian Orthodox Church Affairs informed us that the Council of Ministers of the USSR had once again taken note of the numerous cases of violations by the clergy of Soviet legislation on cults, and had pointed out the necessity of bringing proper order into the lives of the parishes, and namely, of restoring the rights of executive committees of church communities in the area of financial and administrative activities, [to bring them] into conformity with the legisla-tion on cults.[61]

Two points here deserve comment. First, it seems rather odd that the Council of Ministers of the USSR should suggest that church regulations should be altered to conform with civil legislation when the church regula-tions in question, the Statute of 1945, were clearly passed with state approval. It certainly can be argued that there was a lack of correspondence between church and state as far as the priest's position was concerned.

While the 1929 Law on Religious Associations does not specifically exclude a priest from participation in the administration of a religious society, it makes no provision for the leading, supervisory role in parish life accorded to him by the 1945 Statute. A Western scholar, Bogolepov, has commented:

> There unquestionably was a lack of correspondence between them. But the statutes of the Russian Orthodox Church had been adopted only with the prior agreement and approval of the State. Their lack of correspondence with existing law was allowed by the Council of People's Commissars of the RSFSR as a special reward for the wartime services of the Russian Church.[62]

If this is so, then it is clear that the state was content to let the anomalous situation continue unchallenged for 16 years. That raises the question of why it was precisely in 1961 that it was decided to alter the church Statute. Here we must note that the Council of Bishops occurred during the nationwide anti-religious campaign of 1959–64. In Chapter 1 we discussed the mass closure of churches which took place during those years, and we shall see how the decisions of the Council of Bishops facilitated the closures. It is logical to see the state's instruction to the church to alter its regulations as part of the package of measures designed to restrict church life.[63]

The eyewitness report bears out this view by giving a sharp reminder of the circumstances in which the Council of Bishops met:

> assembled in the luxurious chambers of the Patriarch's residence they [the bishops] were not at all disturbed by the mass closure of churches and the dissolution of monasteries all over the country, by the imposition of unbearable taxes on the clergy which forced them to sell their personal possessions (or, if they were stubborn, have them distrained). Or by the fact that since the spring choirs had been broken up in very many churches, that several seminaries had already been closed and others were threatened with closure in the autumn, and that any uncircumspect priest, innocently agreeing to recommend some churchgoing lad for admission to a seminary, would instantly be deprived of his registration, which is to say prevented by the civil authorities from pursuing his calling as a priest.[64]

The eyewitness report also gives some interesting background information which provides a valuable commentary on the second noteworthy point in Patriarch Alexi's speech, his reference to 'numerous cases of violations by the clergy of Soviet legislation on cults'. In a brief historical excursus, the eyewitness reminds us that 'from the first years of the revolution, the priest was a person without rights'.[65] Bogolepov enlarges on this:

The clergy, though deprived of civil rights, were forced to pay totally unreasonable taxes in comparison with those paid by other members of the so-called 'free professions'. Moreover, clergy were not permitted to be employed in state institutions or to occupy quarters in nationalised residences. Their children were not allowed to enrol in educational institutions.[66]

This status of a virtual outlaw could hardly be in greater contrast with the parish priest's position after 1945, when, in the words of the eyewitness, he became 'the unchecked master and manager of all church monies, which came into the church almost without accounting'.[67] Perhaps it was not surprising if this turned the heads of some priests after the years of deprivation they and their families had endured. The eyewitness records that some of them began to enjoy a life of luxury — 'they acquired country cottages, cars and expensive furniture' — and that the contrast with poorer members of society, the intelligentsia included, could not fail to give rise to envy. And so they began to complain:

From the provinces began to arrive complaints not only that the clergy were living in luxury, but also that they were appropriating church money. Complaints from believers poured into the dioceses, the Patriarchate, even to the newspapers. A fair part of these complaints were perhaps unfounded, and resulted from the envy or vengefulness of people removed by priests from the administration of church income. But there is no doubt that a large part of them reflected the true state of affairs.[68]

Patriarch Alexi also made reference to the complaints in his opening speech to the members of the Council:

You, as diocesan bishops, know better than anyone of such an abnormal situation; but you cannot imagine what a flood of complaints from the provinces is descending not only upon the Patriarchate and the Council for Russian Orthodox Church Affairs, but also upon our higher government establishments — the Council of Ministers of the USSR. People are complaining about disorders in the parishes. Members of the church clergy are complaining about the executive bodies of the parishes; members of these executive bodies — about the incumbents of parishes and the parish clergy; and both one and the other are complaining to the Patriarchate and the Holy Synod, who are allegedly paying no attention at all to the complaints.[69]

Both our sources, then, are agreed that there was a wave of complaints about parish life, but they disagree on the measures which should be adopted to control the problem. The official proposal made at the Council was that more authority in financial and administrative matters should be given to the laity. It fell to the present Patriarch, then Archbishop Pimen of Tula and Belev, to make this proposal. In a brief historical survey, he pointed out that the issue of lay involvement in parish life had exercised previous Councils of the Russian Orthodox Church, but maintained that the canonical arguments advanced against such involvement were not well grounded. He continued:

> The defence of episcopal authority as the only one canonically competent to manage the property of parish communities was also debatable. Such an order in no way corresponded to the canonical order of the ancient Church. Nor did it correspond to the order existing in the parishes in ancient Russia.

His speech continued with a disquisition on the parishes of medieval Russia, and then referred to 'broad democratic transformations' in the country, as a result of which 'the role of the labourers themselves in the social life of the country is growing'. It was therefore illogical that in the church the priests should have full control of parish life and eliminate the laity from positions of responsibility. He concluded by asking the Council to approve the resolution of the Holy Synod of 18 April, with the aim that

> the members of the executive bodies . . . should enjoy their rights in financial and economic matters, and the incumbents of the churches should be challenged to direct their chief attention to the spiritual and liturgical side of church life and display more concern about the spiritual nourishment of their flock.[70]

(It is perhaps worth noting that Pimen has consistently stuck to his espousal of the 1961 reforms and has referred to them publicly with approval more than once since they were adopted. He has maintained this view privately as well, according to the secret CRA Report, which quotes him as saying, during a private conversation with the CRA in 1967, that 'The past years had clearly shown . . . the correctness of the resolution of the Bishops' Council on freeing the clergy from monetary affairs in the churches. Now things had become more peaceful.')[71]

The eyewitness's reaction to the proposal given in the speeches of Pimen and of the Patriarch is a sharp one. He points to the inconsistencies in the proposed reforms:

> Nothing was said about the hierarchs. As it turned out, they were now assembled to deal with a matter which until then had been entirely outside the sphere of their activities. The priests were exceeding their rights, exceeding their powers and breaking canon law. And if priests break the

law, the only answer is to change this law . . .

Usually in such cases, when someone or other breaks the law, the first consideration is how to call him to order. Only then, if it is found that those who break the law are innocent, and that the fault lies with the law itself which is harmful and impossible to obey, does the question of whether to change or repeal the law arise. But on this occasion the question was not put like that. It was stated, simply, that the law was being violated and therefore must be changed.[72]

There is certainly nothing in the official record of the proceedings to show that any consideration was given to what the bishops might do to regularise matters in the parishes. Having pointed out this omission, the eyewitness draws the conclusion:

if deficiencies in the parishes are reported, and for some reason nothing is said about how the bishops have reacted to the deficiences, the implication is that the bishops have no real power, and therefore the episcopate is in fact superfluous.[73]

But the omission of any mention of the bishops' role did not in fact reflect the true state of affairs, as the eyewitness points out with subtle irony:

It was odd that nothing was said about what the bishops were doing to remedy the deficiencies. It would seem that there were deficiencies in the parishes and everyone was complaining to the civil authorities and to the Patriarch — but not to the bishops, who apparently only learned of the complaints from the Patriarch at the Council, or from the newspapers.[74]

It was of course inconceivable that the bishops did not know what was going on: we have already quoted the eyewitness as saying that complaints 'poured into the dioceses' (i.e. the diocesan administrations), as well as to 'the Patriarchate, even to the newspapers'. No doubt some bishops would have tried to take measures to deal with the problem posed by some of their clergy. The deliberate exclusion from the Council of any mention of episcopal involvement in parish life can only be attributed to the fact that another solution to the problem had already been found which was thought to be preferable. As the eyewitness writes:

the Patriarch himself is . . . saying that the Church is gripped by an incurable disease and can only be saved by . . . the laity! In other words, the Patriarch himself at the Council of Bishops declared publicly that the clergy was in a wretchedly bad state, and that there could be no question of the bishops being able to put matters to rights. Not one word, not even one brief hint, of what the bishops should do to improve church life! The situation is grave, the clergy is unfit, as the number of complaints shows, therefore . . . therefore all parish administration must be put into the hands of laymen.[75]

The eyewitness records that the bishops at the Council knew very well what kind of lay people would be put in control of the parishes. He summarises the effect of the reforms as follows:

From among these *dvadtsatki* was elected, or in fact was not elected, but was appointed by someone, an executive committee . . . God alone knew what kind of people they were. There were some good people, and there were also patently bad ones. There were believers, and there were obvious unbelievers . . .

According to the new statute, the bishop no longer appointed a priest to a parish by his own authority, but merely 'recommended' that he should be accepted. The 'parish', that is, we repeat, in fact two or three people, in whose hands rested all power in the church, could refuse to accept the priest suggested by the bishop.

Moreover, if for some reason they did not like the priest who was already in the parish, they could remove him. Now, according to the new statute, the parish authority had to conclude an agreement (*dogovor*) with the priest, defining his conditions of work and pay; in fact, they hired the priest. If they wished, the parish authority could annul the agreement. Then the priest was quite simply thrown out into the street, and could go to the bishop to ask whether he could find some possibility of offering him to some other place.[76]

This summary by the eyewitness of the new situation seems to us to be accurate. Though made within three or four years of the reforms being enacted, its gloomy assessment continues to be borne out in practice, as we shall see. The parish priest has in fact become an employee of the parish executive committee, and can be dismissed by it at will. Since churches are expressly forbidden to engage in any activities except liturgical and sacramental ones, the division between the financial and spiritual sides of parish life referred to by the proposers of the reforms seems exaggerated. In being removed from the financial activities of the parish, the parish priest was being moved solely from financial activities necessary to guarantee the continuation of worship and the maintenance of the worship building. He was put in a very difficult position by being assigned responsibility for worship activities while being totally dependent on a committee of three laymen for the financial provision necessary for worship to continue. The priest's position as head of the parish was undermined by the reforms, though they did not and could not affect his spiritual relationship to his flock. As celebrant of the divine liturgy he remains the head of the parish in the institutional church's eyes, no matter what the law says. However, it would seem that even his freedom to exercise his spiritual authority must have been diminished by making him liable to summary dismissal by lay people whose relationship to the Russian Orthodox Church is not clearly defined and who may be unbelievers. This difficulty could clearly be overcome provided there was good will towards the priest on the part of the executive committee and the *dvadtsatka*, but if disputes arose the priest would be in a tricky and embarrassing situation.

There were two important practical consequences of the 1961 reforms. The first and most obvious was that the mass closure of churches was made much easier because the parish priest was no longer able to offer practical opposition to the closure of his church. The executive committee was under no obligation to heed any objections he might make. As the eyewitness states:

> Now these people [the executive committee], having been given total use of the church, independently of both the priest and the bishop, could at any moment close the church by declaring that they no longer needed it, and neither the priest nor the bishop could save the church from closure.[77]

The second consequence was that, as the eyewitness suggests, the priest and the bishop lost all control over both the church building and the activities of the parish. Notwithstanding the views of Archbishop Pimen, which we quoted above, the eyewitness and a number of other commentators thought that the church's canonical procedure for controlling parish life had been disrupted. According to Apostolic Canon Number 38: 'The bishop has care of all church belongings and is in charge of them.' Apostolic Canon Number 41 adds: 'We command the bishop to have authority over church property. For if precious human souls must be entrusted to him, how much more reason is there why he should be in charge of money, so that he can make arrangements by his own authority.'[78] The reform of 1961 meant that, as the priest had no control over parish property and funds, neither did the bishop set over him. The reformed Statute made it clear that the executive committee now controlled the monies which were (or were not) paid to the diocesan administration and to the Patriarchate for the upkeep of church institutions. The 1945 Statute had said:

> The executive body . . . pays *the necessary amounts* [emphasis added] for support of the diocesan hierarch and his administration, for diocesan theological–pastoral courses, and for general church needs such as the Patriarchal Administration and for the support of the Theological Educational Institutes of the Patriarchate.

The 1961 amendments altered this to:

The executive body . . . contributes *voluntary amounts* [emphasis added] for the support of the diocesan hierarch and his administration and for the Patriarchal Administration.[79]

Funds for the work of the dioceses and the Patriarchate were thus made — and still are — largely dependent on the decision of parish executive committees throughout the USSR, the members of which, as we have seen, may or may not be believers. The 1961 reforms meant that, in the eyes of the law and the state, the church consists of a number of fragmented communities which have no legal relation to one another. The legal and administrative structure of the Russian Orthodox Church was atomised.

The Nature of the Proceedings

We now return to a discussion of the manner in which the Council of Bishops passed this reform. The amendments to the 1945 Statute had been proposed by Patriarch Alexi and Archbishop Pimen. The assembled bishops were being asked to approve them. Patriarch Alexi had made clear what was expected of them in his opening speech: 'We have assembled . . . to decide imminent questions of current church life, or rather, to confirm decisions made by the Holy Synod.'[80] It is not clear whether or not the bishops meeting in July 1961 knew that the Holy Synod had passed a resolution on the parishes, amending the 1945 Statute, in April. The resolution was not recorded in the *Journal of the Moscow Patriarchate*. We do not know whether the bishops might have been informed of it by other means before the Council, giving them time to consider the implications and consequences of the reforms. However, we have seen that the eyewitness understood very well what the consequences were for the parishes, and it is safe to assume that many, if not all, of the bishops sitting on the Council would have reached similar conclusions. Now they were being given a clear lead by the Patriarch to approve the reforms without debate. The eyewitness writes:

'We are gathered here,' said the Patriarch, 'not to argue and discuss at great length, but to make a unanimous decision . . .'
   In these words, the Patriarch invited the bishops to keep silent. It was self-evident — there was nothing to argue about, nothing to debate. All that was required was a unanimous vote of approval, to put a seal on the proposal, as there could be no alternative to it.[81]

In fact, none of the bishops did speak out against the reforms. After Archbishop Pimen had proposed their adoption, several of the senior hierarchs spoke up enthusiastically in their favour. The eyewitness comments sardonically:

Metropolitan Pitirim of Krutitsy and Kolomna commenced his speech in an exalted tone. It was as though he himself and his entire flock had been waiting only for this joyful day, when, at last, this long-awaited new statute would come into force. The old man's voice trembled and it seemed that any moment he would burst into sobs of enthusiasm.[82]

The following speeches were similar in tone.

However, despite the fact that no opposition to the reforms was expressed at the crucial moment, we know that some, perhaps many, of the bishops did oppose them. The eyewitness was himself obviously opposed to them, but he did not say anything. We shall see that some bishops tried to have the reforms reversed at the Local Council of 1971 (though we do not know whether any of the later dissenters were present at the 1961 Council). Finally, Patriarch Alexi himself made a reference to opposition to the reforms expressed before the 1961 Council by three bishops.[83] It is highly probable that these three, whom the Patriarch did not name, were among those excluded from the 1961 Council by illness or retirement. The eyewitness mentions only one hierarch present who might have been expected to oppose the reforms, Archbishop Manuil (Lemeshevsky) of Kuibyshev. He had spent many years in prison and exile; he 'was imprisoned also at the end of the 1940s, when almost none of the clergy were imprisoned any longer'[84] and this had earned him the reputation of being a courageous and independent man. Because of this, the eyewitness continues: 'Before the opening of the Council several people thought that he would express opposition to the new statute, but, having seen the prospects, the archpastor preferred to keep silence.'[85] The 'several people' who expected Archbishop Manuil to speak out can only have been other bishops, since the eyewitness has already told us that no one else knew that a Council was taking place. Perhaps they would have followed his lead, had he given one? What were the 'prospects' which dissuaded him from doing so?

At this point we have to describe an important element of the Council's proceedings, recorded by the eyewitness, which we have not yet mentioned. In describing the photograph of the bishops taken as a record of the Council,[86] the eyewitness's use of irony comes into full play:

Not a single outsider was included in this photograph — there were only the princes of the Church by themselves — the bishops who guide the ship of the Church. Only the bishops and no one else besides! This vividly demonstrated their freedom in administrative matters and the absence of any persons who might have somehow influenced their will, influenced the course of the council of hierarchs of the Russian Orthodox Church. The reverend fathers posed confidently before the camera and as it were ignored those people who, none the less, did exist, but for the present remained in one of the neighbouring rooms. There were three of them. Three people with well-fed, clever faces, on which strong will and confidence were written. These people were not photographed.[87]

These three people were present throughout the deliberations of the Council. The hierarchs sat, in order of rank and seniority, around three sides of an oblong, with the Patriarch and senior Metropolitans facing them, seated along a short end of the oblong. The three civilians sat at a small table by the wall, so that the Patriarch could see them but so that most of the bishops had their backs to them. The eyewitness remarks that the bishops felt uncomfortable with this arrangement. All the bishops were aware that the three civilians represented the Council for Russian Orthodox Church Affairs, the state body appointed to supervise church life:

They were well known to every hierarch. In the provinces, in every diocese, sat the assistants of these men, special commissioners for church affairs. These commissioners in the dioceses were terrible and implacable. They had the power 'to bind and to loose', to forbid a priest to serve and to deprive him of priesthood. And if these commissioners were terrible, how much more terrible were these three, sitting quietly behind the bishops! They were sitting behind them, but their eyes bored through the bishops' backs like drills. They were silent, and apparently had no intention of saying anything, but their silence was eloquent.[88]

This, then, is the reason for the bishops' silence. However, the eyewitness's heavy irony at this point is equivocal; it is directed as much towards the bishops' timorousness in being inhibited by three silent men as it is towards the entirely inappropriate presence of these undoubtedly powerful civilians. He sums up his feelings in a sad analogy which is scornful of both the civilians and the bishops:

They [the three civilians] sat in silence and their faces were tense. It was the tenseness of a trainer in a circus watching the animal he has tamed. Will it do everything it has been ordered, or will it let him down and spoil the act?[89]

Pessimistic as he is about the moral courage of the bishops, the eyewitness also gives a practical reason for their silence:

And moreover, each one knew that, even if he did gather up courage and come out in opposition, he would not find general support and would only risk his own neck and let down the Patriarch.[90]

This is presumably the consideration that led Archbishop Manuil to remain silent: the wholly pragmatic view that if he did say anything, it would achieve nothing. Even if he were sure that other bishops agreed with him, he could not be certain that they would speak up; this was evidently why the bishops were given no chance to consult one another before the proceedings commenced. One is left wondering what would have happened if one bishop *had* summoned up the courage to express opposition — but this is to enter the realm of speculation.

There is, however, one other consideration advanced by the eyewitness. Having witnessed the closures of churches, monasteries and seminaries and arrests of believers during the two or three years of the anti-religious campaign to date, the bishops might well have formed the view that the state was bent on total eradication of church life. If so, they would feel that the reforms proposed at the Council did at least mean that church life was going to continue in some shape or form:

> After all, if some new system, however draconian, is proposed, it implies that a complete eradication has not yet been decided upon. There would be some sort of respite, however brief, and then — what God might grant.[91]

It appears to have been this consideration which influenced the Patriarch, at least in the opinion of the eyewitness:

> Everyone knew very well that in the previous year, when the Patriarch had been asked to reorganise parish administration, he had at first refused, even falling ill from nervous strain, and was not himself for two weeks. But then, seeing that there was nothing to be done, he reconciled himself to it, deciding that this concession might be a chance to delay the approaching end.[92]

After the Council proceedings had ended, the Patriarch went to exchange a few words with the three civilians: 'He stood opposite the three serious people and smiled. And they smiled too, and shook his hand. It was as though a weight had been lifted from both his and their shoulders.'[93] The eyewitness is however at pains to state that he does not feel the Patriarch should be blamed for the role he adopted at the Council. In his opinion, Patriarch Alexi was doing no more than guiding the church along the course laid down by his two predecessors, Patriarchs Tikhon and Sergi. It would have required 'desperate efforts, someone's unbelievably strong arms' to halt the course of concessions, and Patriarch Alexi simply did not possess such strength. He had:

> passed his whole life without struggle. During the years of his patriarchate he had lived as though wrapped in cotton wool, surrounded by the concern and tending of his favourites, lulled by greetings, treated with affection by his friends and his enemies. Why ask him for a feat beyond his powers, if he was not born a hero?[94]

It may seem harsh to say that Alexi had 'passed his whole life without struggle', when he had in fact endured the blockade of Leningrad. Doubtless the eyewitness had in mind sufferings inflicted by the Soviet authorities, not those inflicted from outside and common to all the Soviet people.

So the inglorious Council of Bishops of 1961 came to an end. Whether or not the bishops were to blame in their own eyes, they clearly realised the consequences of their action — or inaction:

The bishops took out their fountain-pens and signed — marking their decision now and for ever. 'The unlawful has been made law,' they muttered afterwards in the corridors. 'The unlawful has been made law,' whispered the monks of the monastery, discussing the bishops' decision that evening. 'The unlawful has been made law,' sighed the parish priests in the provinces, sensing what it was to be dependent on churchwardens. 'The unlawful has been made law,' repeated the hierarchs again and again, as in the autumn of that year they saw the fruits of their decision: the parish *dvadtsatki* ceased to pay them any attention at all, and in time refused to give even the customary dues.[95]

Throughout the report of the eyewitness, his emotional involvement with the events he is describing is evident. The reader can sense that he is constantly grappling with the questions: How *could* the bishops have remained silent? How *could* they have failed to come to the support of their church? On one level he provides an answer, by revealing the intimidating presence of the three civilians, but on another level, the level of the moral responsibility of the hierarchs involved, he does not come to any clear-cut conclusion. He says some harsh and cutting things about the bishops' timidity, but from time to time retracts them, reminding himself and the reader that one cannot really blame them. Clearly the writer was unable to resolve the matter to his own satisfaction. And given that the source of the information must have been one of the participating bishops (whether he wrote it down himself or, conceivably, confided his views to someone else) this is not surprising. He clearly suffered no little anguish of mind over his failure to speak out. The decision to reveal what happened at the Council appears to be a making of amends, an appeasing of his conscience for not having spoken up at the time.

The Canonicity of the Reform

The final point to be discussed with regard to the Council of Bishops of 1961 is the controversial one of whether it itself and the reforms it enacted were or were not canonical. Orthodox canon law is a complicated and esoteric subject, and it would be rash to make sweeping statements. The canons of the Orthodox Church, the oldest of which date from the third century, though most are more recent, form a huge body of material, and in any age there are never more than a few people who master it in detail. The canons are of general validity throughout the Orthodox Church, and, once accepted, cannot be changed. A distinction must be drawn between canons and what are usually called Statutes, the rules according to which a Local Church is administered, which may be altered and superseded. These are the result of each autocephalous church's attempt to apply the canons in its own particular situation. The word 'canon' does not mean 'rule' or 'law', but rather 'standard' or 'norm'. The canons embody general principles, and express an ideal. A church in any given period of history constantly struggles to regulate its life in accordance with the letter, and — more important — with the spirit of the canons, but due to the fallen nature of its members, and to pressures from society, from which it is never entirely independent, it fails to reach the ideal. In a sense, then, church life is always to some extent 'uncanonical', although a departure from the canons, if covered by the principle of 'economy', is not in itself uncanonical.[96]

The Council of Bishops itself as an instrument of ecclesiastical government was specifically authorised by the Statute of 1945.[97] However, it does not have the authority to alter a decision by a Local Council: only another Local Council (i.e. one with the participation of clergy and laity as well as bishops) is competent to do that. The adoption of the reformed Statute by the Council of Bishops was therefore declared to be 'until the convocation of the next Local Council of the Russian Orthodox Church'.[98] This meant that, because the church was unable to convene a Local Council until 1971, it had to live with an improperly revised Statute for ten years.

The singular irregularities of the means of convening the Council of Bishops — the fact that no one, including the participants, knew in advance that there was to be a Council — have already been discussed above (pp. 54–6). As we saw, Archbishop Yermogen (who was a specialist in legal matters), did not declare outright that the method of convening the Council was uncanonical, though he did say that it 'cannot be justified from a canonical point of view', a slightly different and more cautious wording. Presumably he had in mind the Apostolic Canon Number 34, which emphasises that the senior bishop of an autocephalous area must act in concord with the rest of the episcopate. The Patriarch was clearly prevented from doing so in this instance. The Statute of 1945 did not say anything about the procedure for convening a Council of Bishops, so that the means used cannot be said to have been illegal in the strict sense of the word. However, they were certainly irregular, and against the spirit of the canons.

There remains the question of the canonical nature, or otherwise, of the reforms themselves. We have demonstrated above that the effect of the reforms was to disrupt the canonically ordained hierarchical structure of the church by depriving the bishop of control over the economic side of parish life. This would seem to be sufficient to indicate that the reforms were essentially contrary to the spirit and the letter of the canons. Furthermore, many church members openly doubted the canonicity of the reforms. We shall see in our discussion of the 1971 Local Council in Chapter 8 that some of the bishops said on that occasion that they believed the reforms to have been uncanonical. Also, Archbishop Yermogen has explained at some length why he believed the reforms to have been uncanonical. Lastly, we should note that objections to the uncanonical spirit of the reforms were prominent in the open letter to Patriarch Alexi written in 1965 by two Moscow priests, Fathers Nikolai Eshliman and Gleb Yakunin. Their letter was the springboard for dissent within the church, as we shall see in Chapter 10.[99]

The Effects of the Reform: Up to 1971

Returning now to our description of parish life, we shall see that the reforms of 1961 have continued to have a profound effect on church life since they were enacted. The negative forebodings voiced at the time of the Council of Bishops are largely borne out by the observers whom we shall quote below. We shall divide our discussion of the consequences of the reforms over two nearly equal periods: up to and including the Local Council of 1971 and from then to the present. We shall discuss in Chapter 8 the efforts made by some bishops to have the 1961 reforms amended at the Local Council of 1971. Here we shall confine ourselves to examining the nature of their objections to the reforms, concentrating on those raised by Archbishop Veniamin (Novitsky) of Irkutsk. He formulated his views in two letters to Metropolitan Pimen, the chairman of the Commission for the Preparation of the Local Council, and even went so far as to draft a proposed alternative for Section IV of the church's Statute, on the parishes.[100] The other two chief episcopal objectors were Archbishop Pavel (Golyshev) of Novosibirsk, who, so far as we know, did not commit his views to writing, and Archbishop Yermogen, whose comments on the 1961 reforms we have already mentioned, and which are treated at length elsewhere.[101]

The documents written by Archbishop Veniamin summarise nine or ten years' experience of the reforms in his diocese and give a number of instances of the abuses which have resulted from them. The archbishop's chief objection is that the priest is excluded from the running of the parish. He makes it clear that it is not merely a question of the parish priest being reduced to the position of a layman, of the clergy and laity having equal rights in the disposition of parish affairs; it is a question of the priest being reduced to a status lower than that of the laity and being totally dependent on them not only for running the parish but also for his own livelihood. In his letter to Metropolitan Pimen of December 1970, Veniamin also recalled the canonical position, that the spiritual head of the church in a given area, whether priest or bishop, should be head of the whole of church life there.

He gave instances of specific violations of this order:

> There have been instances in the diocese entrusted to me when it has not been thought necessary to invite the incumbent to a general meeting of the *dvadtsatka* (in the city of Chita). In some instances when an incumbent has been present at a meeting, advice given by him has been interpreted as interference in the affairs of the parish executive body, as a result of which he has had to leave the diocese.[102]

Archbishop Veniamin also states that the reforms have led 'not to improving the structure of parish life, but to even greater disorder' in that there is 'an absence of a sense of ecclesiastical law and order in people elected [to the executive committee], as a consequence of which they expand their right of administration beyond the bounds of the possible, to the extent of total arbitrariness (sometimes to the extent of criminality)'.[103]

In his second letter to Metropolitan Pimen, in April 1971, Archbishop Veniamin pointed out that there was nothing at all in Soviet law to forbid the priest being a member of the religious society and that the 1961 resolution of the Council of Bishops was therefore a legal anomaly. Going beyond the experience of his own diocese, he asserted that:

> One may say with confidence that in every diocese there are glaring instances of undeserved humilation of the rank of pastor and total lack of interest in the well-being of the parish.[104]

In the draft revised version of Section IV of the Statute which he submitted to Metropolitan Pimen, Archbishop Veniamin preserved the wording of the 1961 version almost in its entirety, adding a few brief phrases to effect the changes he desired.[105] The effect of these was, chiefly, to reassert the authority of the priest and the bishop in parish life. The amendments suggested by Veniamin include: the right of the bishop to appoint a priest to a parish, taking into account as he does so any candidates who may be suggested by the church community (as opposed to his right merely to give his blessing to a priest elected by the community); the accountability of the executive committee to the general parish meeting together with the incumbent (as opposed to the meeting without him); and a whole new clause stating that the incumbent of the parish and members of the clergy have the right to membership of the *dvadtsatka* and to be elected to the executive committee and the auditing commission. The other two important additions are: that the religious society should not be limited in number to the original 20 founders; and that the auditing commission, if it finds any irregularities, should report them to the diocesan authorities as well as to the local state authorities. We have already discussed these points above, and so the effect of their proposed restoration should be clear. The only point we have commented on above which is not amended by Archbishop Veniamin is the voluntary nature of the financial contributions by the parish to the work of the diocese and the Patriarch. Veniamin left this clause unchanged. He appears to have considered that the restoration of the priest to his former position as head of the parish would resolve this particular issue.

Metropolitan Pimen was sent another letter describing the adverse effects of the 1961 reforms on parish life from a very different person, a church cleaner from Leningrad region named Tatyana Drozdova. Drozdova stated that the *dvadtsatka* in the church where she worked had not met for six years, that the chairman of the auditing commission was appointed by the churchwarden and was insufficiently educated to be capable of conducting an audit even if he were allowed to do so, and that the executive committee was running the church on its own. It consisted of a churchwarden who was dying, an assistant churchwarden who was not properly elected, and a treasurer who was not even baptised. They were not at all concerned with worship, but only with the 'organised misappropriation of the church's resources'. They themselves admitted that they were 'appointed by the [local state] executive committee' and that they were 'guided by the [CRA] commissioner'. Drozdova wrote that she had complained about the embezzlement to the diocesan bishop, Metropolitan Nikodim of Leningrad, to the deputy CRA commissioner and to other officials, but without result. During an interview she had with the CRA commissioner, Zharinov, he warned her to stop making complaints, on the grounds that 'Your episcopate itself abdicated from church administration at the Council of 1961.'[106] Whatever the rationale behind the 1961 reforms, this is a striking instance of how they were viewed at local level. Drozdova appealed to Patriarch Pimen to authorise a proper audit in the parish. Her experiences had convinced her that the diocesan bishop, Metropolitan Nikodim, had no real authority in the churches in his charge, and that this authority had been usurped by the state in the shape of CRA commissioners and a parish executive committee that was under their control.

By the time of the 1971 Local Council, then, we know that its chairman, Metropolitan Pimen, had received at least two strongly worded, urgent complaints about the adverse effects of the 1961 reforms on parish life. The bishop from the eastern reaches of the Soviet Union and the church cleaner from the Leningrad parish, though widely separated by distance and status, were at one in pointing to the disruption of parish life they had witnessed. However, as we shall see, there was no proper discussion of such complaints at the 1971 Council, and attempts to initiate such a discussion were firmly crushed. The objections were ignored, the 1961 reforms were upheld, and remain in force to this day. They can now be altered only by another Local Council of the Russian Orthodox Church.

The Effects of the Reform: After 1971

Since 1971 complaints about irregularities in parish life have continued to be made by Orthodox believers all over the USSR. They are mostly allegations of unwarranted interference in parish life by CRA and other state officials, and of embezzlement of parish funds by corrupt executive committees, usually with the connivance of these same officials. These complaints are not specifically related to the 1961 reforms, but it is clear that those reforms created a basis for the increasing state control over parish life which is evident in the churches from which these complaints emanate. In 1974 a report from the Church of St Sergi in Fergana, Uzbekistan, revealed how the regional CRA commissioner had prevented the registration of new members of the *dvadtsatka* who were not to his liking and had finally announced the appointment of a new *dvadtsatka*, executive committee and auditing commission without elections being held.[107] A complaint from the parish council of St Barbara's Church in Nikolayev region revealed that the deputy CRA commissioner had prevented the *dvadtsatka* from removing the churchwarden, who was known to have embezzled church funds.[108] In 1977 the CRA commissioner for Moscow city, Plekhanov, was reported to have telephoned churches in the capital warning that no one under the age of 40 should be permitted to sing in a church choir.[109] In the Church of St Pimen in Moscow, it was reported that the district executive committee had compelled the church council to dismiss three choir members under 40.[110]

In 1978 a woman described as a known KGB agent, Ye B. Zagryazkina, was appointed book-keeper in the Moscow Church of the Icon of Our Lady of the Sign. Father Gleb Yakunin, in a complaint about her appointment, stated that she had been instrumental in bringing about the arrest of the Orthodox writer Alexander Petrov-Agatov. She had no book-keeping qualifications. Yakunin concluded that the state authorities, alarmed by the fact that this church was one of the most popular in Moscow, attended by many young people, had decided to try to undermine it from within.[111] (Zagryazkina was later to play an unexpected role in Yakunin's own life, as we shall see in Chapter 13.)

We could quote many more instances of state interference in parish life. There is one case on which detailed information is available, the attempt of parishioners of the Church of the Dormition in Pavlograd, Dnepropetrovsk region, Ukraine, to join the *dvadtsatka*.[112] They made repeated approaches to the local CRA commissioner, Shendrik, and to the secretary of the city executive committee, Stanishevskaya. Meeting with no success, they approached the CRA chairman, Kuroyedov, and their bishop, who was initially helpful, and also appealed to Patriarch Pimen and to Mr Brezhnev. Their attempt to become members of the *dvadtsatka* was entirely proper and lawful, as we saw in our discussion of the legislation on religion above, and eventually they obtained a written admission from Shendrik that this was so.[113] Despite this, Shendrik and Stanishevskaya continued to use every possible means to prevent them joining the *dvadtsatka*, and by March 1979 (the date of the last document in the series), after a year and a half of continued approaches to officials, they were no nearer achieving their aim than when they began. Moreover, pressure had been put on the diocesan bishop, Archbishop Leonti of Crimea and Simferopol, who suspended five of the most active parishioners from Holy Communion for three years. Shendrik was quite frank in explaining to the parishioners that he was blocking their attempt to join the *dvadtsatka* because his purposes were better suited by the existing elderly, ailing members, who refused to carry out necessary repairs on the church building, and some of whom embezzled church funds for drinking sessions. He told the would-be reformers: 'Even if they take everything from the church, even if they are flooded in vodka and drunken men climb up on to the cupola — we'll just say thank-you to them.'[114]

Although not all our sources of information are as frank as Shendrik, it seems clear that among the unbelievers whom the CRA infiltrates on to parish executive committees are not a few who embezzle church funds and others who hold drinking sessions on the proceeds, sometimes on church premises. This is not only a means of weakening the institutional church from within, but is also used by the state as propaganda against the church. A recurrent theme in Soviet newspaper articles is the suggestion that drunkenness and embezzlement are practised by ordinary church members — that is, by religious believers — implying that the churches are places where such vices can flourish unchecked. Such articles state that ordinary churchgoers trustingly give their money to church collections, unaware that the church, in the form of some church councils, is squandering their money on drink. A typical article in 1976 described how in the Church of the Resurrection in Frunze the collection each day was divided between the church and a 'far from holy trinity' consisting of two members of the executive committee and the chairman of the auditing commission. In August 1975 alone they were said to have appropriated 272 roubles from the collection, and they also made money by reselling candles.[115] The impression conveyed by such articles is that innocent churchgoers are being defrauded by believers, or at any rate by people who hold their positions solely because churches are permitted to exist. So the Russian Orthodox Church is doubly disadvantaged: by the loss of revenue due to embezzlement by unbelievers and by the propaganda which the state makes out of this situation.

This is not the only apparently contradictory state of affairs we have had occasion to examine in this chapter. We have seen that the state permits services of worship, often magnificent and moving, to take place week by week, while at the same time creating enormous obstacles for the believers responsible for the buildings in which they take place. We have seen that foreigners are able to visit churches in major cities without hindrance, but that KGB informers are present among the congregations or even the church's staff. We shall have more to say about the often paradoxical nature of relations between the Soviet state and the Russian Orthodox Church in Chapter 9. It now seems appropriate to sum up the contradictions inherent in Orthodox parish life in the USSR by examining the point where they are most clearly present, the climax of the church year — Easter.

Easter

Easter, the celebration of the resurrection from the dead of Jesus Christ, is the greatest festival in the year in the Russian Orthodox Church. The contrast between the solemnity of Good Friday and the overwhelming surge of joy on Easter Day is especially poignant in a church which has known so much suffering and death throughout its history, but especially during the last 70 years. Easter Day is ushered in with a service which begins late on Saturday evening and continues until the early hours of Sunday; it is an occasion of great emotion and drama, as numerous accounts testify. The procession around the church in symbolic search for the body of Christ; the ill-suppressed emotion of the densely packed crowd; the pitch darkness in the church at midnight, illumined by the pale glow of one candle and then quenched altogether as candle after candle all over the church is lit one from the next; the celebrant's triumphant shout 'Christ is risen!' answered by the crowd's oft-repeated 'He is risen indeed!' — all this has been vividly described by many visitors to the USSR. Small wonder then that even unbelievers are attracted by the spectacle and that Orthodox churches throughout the land are reported overflowing every Easter.

In 1976 a commentator on Radio Moscow, who hastened to identify himself as an atheist, announced that he 'never missed' Easter festivities because he took 'a serious interest in the history of religion, something that has had a strong influence on human development'. At the church he bumped into an American couple who were amazed because they 'had always thought that there was no freedom of religion in this country'. The commentator was at pains to assure them and his listeners that this was far from the truth. He emphasised that 'there's no doubt whatever that the onlookers outnumbered by far the believers. For most people the Easter ceremony is a kind of theatre. There is a pageantry to it . . . for most people it is just human interest.' The commentator concluded his talk with the remark that 'there's always plenty of law around to protect the believers, although I've never seen or heard of any disturbances'.[116]

Two points in this commentary begin to seem somewhat disingenuous when compared with other accounts of Easter services. The first is the view that the majority present are onlookers at a dramatic but outdated ceremony while only the minority are worshipping. Other accounts suggest that, while there certainly are a number of indifferent onlookers, it is the majority present who are attempting to participate in the religious ceremony. This was stated to be the case by another Soviet journalist a few years later, in an apparent shift of journalistic policy. L. Demidovich, reporting on the crowds at an Orthodox church in Kishinyov, Moldavia, at Easter 1982, noted that, though the curious and the inebriated were present, there were more genuine believers than curious onlookers. He also remarked upon the presence of young and educated people:

Here was a microcosm representing all age groups . . . Of course, most of all there were old people. Middle-aged were fewer. Even fewer were the young people. But the word 'fewer' does not indicate a quantity. It only indicates a comparison. Very many young people stood there holding their Easter cakes . . . Among those who left home on this evening to follow their religious convictions, there were two of my acquaintances, an engineer and a pedagogue.[117]

The second dubious point in Radio Moscow's 1976 commentary is the assertion that 'the law' (which all accounts agree is undoubtedly present) is there 'to protect the believers'. Numerous reports indicate that, on the contrary, the militia and civilian volunteer vigilantes (*druzhinniki*) present on these occasions are there to cause difficulties for the worshippers and to prevent young people from entering the churches. The presence of young rowdies, who jostle and mock the worshippers, and whom the militia do nothing to discourage, is frequently remarked upon. There are also reports of physical violence being used against would-be worshippers. For example, a report from Moscow in 1973 stated:

People aged under 50 were dragged right out of church and crammed into vehicles. Many were beaten up in sight of everyone right in the church grounds. Whole bands of young mongrels in red armbands [worn by vigilantes, i.e. these are the people officially there for the protection of the believers] gave a concert of catcalls to the procession around the church.[118]

Such measures are reported only at churches where foreigners are not present. Where they are, police action is much milder, as a foreign correspondent's report of Easter 1981 in Moscow makes clear:

a crowd of mainly young people waited expectantly by the temporary police barriers. Anyone without the necessary permit was told politely that he or she could not pass. The mood was good humoured, and some of the police chatted back to the crowd . . . Suddenly the barriers were opened enough for one person to pass at a time. Some started running up the middle of the traffic-free road towards the church. A police officer with a megaphone enjoined the comrades to proceed in an orderly manner . . . Close to the church, the police suddenly became assertive, and having allowed part of the crowd in, they stopped the rest and started pushing them back down the road again. Some youths argued with a fair degree of defiance before strolling off through the barriers and going to celebrate Easter elsewhere.[119]

This report concerns the Patriarchal Cathedral, to which many foreigners in Moscow would naturally gravitate, and it describes a far more amicable atmosphere between the police and the worshippers than is the case in most other accounts of Easter in the USSR. Its chief point of similarity with incidents at other churches is the emphasis on the police's concern to keep young people above all out of the churches. As part of its overall policy of inculcating atheism and discouraging religion, the state tries to ensure that young people grow up in an areligious atmosphere. The aesthetic and emotional impact of the Easter liturgy on a person with little or no previous experience of religious worship is considerable, and could well inspire a lively interest in religion. The Soviet state is evidently prepared to go to great lengths, including the deployment of large numbers of police and the use of physical force, to discourage this.

The fact that it is overwhelmingly young people who are excluded from Easter services was underlined by a foreigner who happened to be passing through Novosibirsk at Easter 1976 and who spent some time carefully observing the scene outside an Orthodox church there:

I walked back to where the picketers and a few policemen were filtering the crowd. I stood as close as possible. It was plain that all men and women under about 40 were not being permitted to proceed to the entrance or to approach the railings with the exception of some mature women who were accompanying old people. Several times I witnessed some determined efforts by women to get by with young daughters of about 11 years or more of age and in one case with a boy of about 11. They protested volubly but were firmly separated from their old folk . . . Young couples in their 20s or 30s generally protested slightly and then moved along the line and tried to get in at another spot. A few young men persisted until they were forced roughly away by groups of picketers and policemen . . . Out of the steady trickle of tiny, black-clothed old women one seemed to be involved in a slanging match with a policeman which ended in her being thrown away from the entrance, where she collided with me and just managed to keep her feet . . .

I looked carefully at the age of people being directed away from the church and confirmed to my own satisfaction that the dividing line was about 35−40 unless accompanied by an elderly person.[120]

Many reports of this nature make it clear that the religious significance and the dramatic nature of the Easter celebrations heighten passions and determination on both sides. For believers, whether deeply committed or with only a tenuous link to the church, Easter is the one time of year when they will make every effort to go to church. For the authorities, eager to stamp out religious practices among the population, such demonstrations of religious allegiance can only be seen as a failure, and Easter is therefore the time when they too are at their most resolute. Easter, more than any other time of the year, vividly conveys the attraction of religion for broad masses of the people and the deep fervour of the committed believers, and also the lengths to which the Soviet authorities are prepared to go to suppress these sentiments.

3 THE CLERGY

The Priest's Role

The role of the parish priest is an almost entirely spiritual one, as has been made clear in Chapter 2. His chief tasks are to take divine services, which includes preaching, to administer sacraments — baptism, marriage, confessions, etc. — and to take funerals in the registered church to which he is assigned.[1] He is also enjoined to see to the development of good morals within the parish, and to this end to give a good example by his own personal behaviour, and to give good advice on spiritual matters to members of the congregation.[2] This side of parish life is completely independent of the parish executive committee, which, if it finds any abnormalities, is supposed to refer them to the bishop.[3] Otherwise, the parish priest has no formal role to play at all outside the liturgical and sacramental one. He may *not* engage in any kind of teaching, organise special-interest groups, undertake charitable activity, or visit needy or ill people in the locality where his church is situated. The effect of this is to cut him off entirely from the surrounding populace; the church is a place which people may choose to visit 'for satisfaction of their religious needs',[4] but it is not a part of the community where it is situated and the priest may not try to exert any influence on that community. The priest's permitted activities are confined to his own church; he may not visit other churches to preach or to take services.[5] The only exception to this is that he may perform religious rites in hospitals[6] or in private homes[7] at the request of 'dying or seriously ill persons', provided permission is received from the local authorities. It appears that such permission is difficult to obtain, or is obtained only after lengthy delay (rendering it worthless), but such cases have not been documented.

It has been known for infringements of these regulations to be dealt with strictly by the authorities. In the village of Romodan in Poltava diocese, Father Panteleimon Misyarenko held a funeral out of doors in a yard instead of indoors in a private home because the corpse had begun to decompose, owing to a delay while waiting for a son of the family to return home from the far north. The executive committee of the village *soviet* fined him and the churchwarden 50 roubles each.[8] Another priest of Poltava diocese, Father V. Bondarenko, was asked by Bishop Feodosi to take a service in a church other than his own because the priest there had suddenly fallen ill while people were already gathering for worship. The bishop was unable to obtain the agreement of the CRA commissioner because it was the latter's day off. Later the CRA commissioner summoned the bishop and the priest separately for interviews and angrily accused them of breaking the law. He at first withdrew the priest's registration in his own parish, though he later returned it.[9] There clearly were technical infringements of the law in both these cases, but the extenuating circumstances were strong ones, and a co-operative attitude on the part of the authorities would surely have made light of the incidents. These examples suggest that, in some if not all areas, the regulations on priests' activity are interpreted quite rigidly by the authorities.

One commentator has pointed out that the priest might not have time for other activities beyond liturgical and sacramental ones even if they were permitted, since the shortage of open churches means that he is overwhelmed with liturgical and sacramental functions — particularly in urban churches:

> The priest sees thousands of unknown people process past. He becomes a mere dispenser of the liturgy, completely consumed, not only by the regular performance of the liturgy itself, but also by the interminable string of private ceremonies requested by the faithful (blessing of water, baptism, absolution, prayers for the dead). This professional life, which in practice makes the priest a prisoner of the rites, leaves its mark on his conscience and his psychology; it becomes difficult or almost impossible for him to pass beyond the horizon of a professional cleric, to see the Church's relation to society with the eyes of a secularised person and to find a language to address him.[10]

This is the view of a person well able to judge the situation, and may well be true for the majority of priests. However, we do know that there are some who have risen above these difficulties, and who have shown themselves able to attract people, especially young people, to their churches and to guide them in Christian life. Information about such priests' activity is fragmentary, and is best not published, since some priests have been made to suffer for involvement in youth work, as we shall see later in this chapter. So far as is known, priests involved in work with young people are careful to keep on the right side of the law, but it is not always easy to do so as this is something of a grey area. It is not entirely clear whether guiding young people in this way is teaching, which is forbidden, or giving advice on personal spiritual life, which is allowed. For example, Metropolitan Filaret of Minsk has stated that he advises his priests to gather all the children preparing for confession and communion into one group before the liturgy, and to hold a discussion with them.[11] Judging by his remarks, made at a meeting in London, this practice has not been censured by the CRA, perhaps because it takes place within a church in the context of a service. In practice, however, many young people do benefit from the spiritual guidance of a few of the bolder priests in informal discussions outside the church building, but the authorities are liable to take repressive measures against these priests if they consider that matters are getting out of hand. This is an area in which a resolute but circumspect priest can achieve a great deal for the institutional church and the Gospel, provided he treads very carefully. The young people in question have generally sought out a priest's guidance on their own initiative, after being attracted to Christianity through attending church services or through independent reading and reflection. It could indeed hardly be otherwise, as the church is so effectively prevented from any form of proselytism. However, Soviet atheist and anti-religious literature often makes it appear that priests are going out of their way to attract young people to church by illegal means and to encourage them to engage in activities which are also illegal. One source comments:

> A group of distinctive activists (*svoyeobrazny aktiv*) forms around some priests, concerned not so much with religious activity as with original organisational work — retyping, compilation and distribution of religious literature, charitable work, missionary activity, and so on.[12]

This quotation sums up the position of the Soviet authorities, so far as we can tell: it is not so much the formation of groups of young people which is objected to as their engaging in any kind of activity which could have an influence beyond their own small circle. Thus the reproduction of religious literature essential to the development of a mature spiritual life is frowned upon because it may be 'distributed', i.e. given to people not previously influenced by religion.

Preaching

Preaching sermons is an integral part of Orthodox church services. Their primary purpose, as in any church, is to preach the Gospel, but in theory they could also be a vehicle, again as in any church, for giving the church's views on a range of issues and for guiding the congregation in their participation as Christians in the life of society as a whole. In practice, however, priests are firmly encouraged by the CRA to restrict their sermons to an exposition of the Gospel and to avoid any reference to political and social issues. An exception to this rule is the exhortation to priests to instil 'Soviet patriotism' by preaching as well as by example. This has been apparent in reports of diocesan meetings of clergy with CRA officials in recent issues of the *Journal of the Moscow Patriarchate*.

However, it is clear that the clergy are being asked to propagate views already formulated by the state (with which individual priests may or may not agree), and that the ban on independent reflection on political and social issues by the church remains in force. Neither the law nor church regulations have anything to say about the content of sermons, which is the responsibility of the diocesan bishop and also of the CRA commissioner. The CRA Report for 1970 notes that preaching in a given diocese depends upon the bishop's attitude to it.[13] The CRA therefore works with bishops as well as priests to ensure that sermons are of what it regards as an acceptable nature. The report quotes a circular to parish priests in Moscow diocese from the then Metropolitan of Krutitsy and Kolomna, Serafim, which says that sermons should be on Gospel or apostolic themes, without references to political or social issues.[14] This is of course an issue which exercises many churches around the world, since the balance between preaching on individual piety and on social issues is a controversial matter. The difference in the case of the Russian Orthodox Church (and of other churches in the USSR) is that the church is not free to solve this controversial issue for itself, but is prohibited by the state from preaching on social issues.

The CRA Report contains some interesting examples of ways in which priests in 1970 had attempted to modernise the content of their sermons and make them more attractive to the people. A similar observation was made in 1980 in *Komsomolskaya pravda* (the newspaper of the Young Communist League), where it was claimed that priests in the Chuvash ASSR were directing their preaching at young people.[15] The fact that their attempts are noted by the CRA, however, presumably means that measures would have been taken to discourage them from doing so in the future. The CRA's claim that it carefully monitors church sermons is backed up by occasional references in *samizdat* to criticism by CRA commissioners of priests' preaching. There have been occasional reports of sermons being censored in advance by CRA commissioners. This is mentioned in the Yakunin Report,[16] but it is difficult to ascertain whether or not it happens on a regular or frequent basis. It seems that it may be an occasional practice.

The Yakunin Report has a low opinion in general of sermons given by Moscow priests:

> The sermons preached in the churches are lifeless, removed from the actual issues of real life today. In the best cases they set forth an interpretation of Holy Scripture by the Church Fathers, but in a light far from modern life.[17]

This is unfair to some of the priests well known as good preachers, but may well be true in the majority of cases. However, Father Yakunin also notes that

> there have been cases when zealous priests have been summoned to the patriarchal administration, where they have been reprimanded, with the aim of curtailing their preaching activity.[18]

If this is so, it would furnish a good reason for the lack-lustre character of much of the preaching. Yakunin's criticism is directed as much against the Patriarchate for discouraging priests as it is against the priests themselves.

Numbers of Priests

As in other areas, we do not have reliable figures on the number of Orthodox priests in the USSR, and the figures we do have conflict. In 1961, upon joining the World Council of Churches, the Russian Orthodox Church claimed to have 30,000 priests.[19] A French journalist in 1978 reported 'about 15,000' priests,[20] but this is clearly excessive, as a *Time* article in 1980 stated that there were 10,000 priests,[21] and a Catholic priest studying in the USSR in 1980 thought that there were 'less than 10,000' priests.[22] The 1961 figure is widely thought to be exaggerated, but even so it would seem that there has been a considerable thinning of the clerical ranks, due chiefly to the anti-religious campaign of 1959–64. Australian visitors to Ukraine in 1976 were told that there were 4,500 priests in the 18 Ukrainian dioceses:[23] it seems reasonable that nearly half the priests should be in Ukraine, where there is such a concentration of open churches. This figure is consistent with that reported by a British visitor in 1973, Rev. O. Fielding-Clarke, who stated that there were 500 clergy, not including deacons, in two of the Ukrainian dioceses.[24]

However, a very different picture is given by the CRA Report for 1974, which states that there were 5,994 priests in that year.[25] In a private lecture given in 1976, V. Furov, a deputy CRA chairman, said that there were 5,900 priests.[26] The decrease may be accounted for by the pattern of decline in numbers which is outlined in the 1974 CRA Report. This states that the total has declined by nearly 30 per cent since 1961 (8,252 in 1961, 6,694 in 1967, 6,234 in 1971, 5,994 in 1974).[27] There has been a similar decline in the number of deacons (from 809 in 1961 to 594 in 1974), making an overall decline of 2,473 persons in 13 years, an average of 190 per year, or nearly 30 per cent overall. The rate of decline, however, has slackened: in the four years 1971–4 the reduction was 240 men, or 60 a year. It is to be expected that the rate of decline would have been steeper during the anti-religious campaign in the early 1960s. These figures are quite compatible with a reduction of 94 priests between the writing of the CRA Report at the end of 1974 and Furov's private lecture in May 1976. The CRA Report makes two further points: that the church is not only failing to increase the number of priests but is even failing to maintain it; and that there are fewer priests (5,994) than churches (7,062) and therefore (as noted in Chapter 1) not all registered churches are able to function. The fact that some priests are responsible for two or even three churches is not sufficient to remedy this situation, according to the CRA Report.

The only explanation for the discrepancy between Furov's figures and the rest is that the latter must be including retired priests, or 'supernumerary' (*zashtatny*) priests as they are usually called. These are certainly part and parcel of the church in that it provides them with old age or disability pensions, and sometimes calls upon them to take services if there is no full-time priest available, but they cannot really be considered part of the full-time, active priesthood. It is possible that some of the figures quoted included deacons (only Fielding-Clarke specifically excludes them from his total), but if Furov's figure of less than 600 deacons is correct this would not greatly affect the overall total.

The CRA Report for 1974 concludes from these figures that there is 'a shortage of cadres',[28] and gives some examples of this from different areas. In Kherson region the CRA commissioner reports 'an acute shortage of cadres', even though all retired clergy have been drawn into taking services.[29] The CRA commissioner for Chernigov reports that Archbishop Antoni was trying to get priests to take responsibility for two parishes each, but they were very reluctant, pleading age and illness.[30] (The 1970 CRA Report also has information on the shortage of priests.) Other sources too speak of the dearth of Orthodox priests. The then Archbishop of Canterbury, Dr Donald Coggan, on a visit to the USSR in 1977, said that he was impressed by the large number of believers, but felt that there was a need for more priests.[31] Archbishop Vladimir of Dmitrov, rector of the Moscow Theological Schools, in an interview with a Western correspondent in 1974, also spoke of a shortage of priests. He described how diocesan bishops coped with the shortage:

> The bishops select good, young men without a stain on their characters and ordain them — even if they have no theological education, provided that they come from a suitable family, are true Christians and have a good general education. Then they enrol them with us [i.e. in the theological seminary] for an educational correspondence course. They fulfil written assignments and three or four times a year come for teaching sessions and tests. This is the only method of overcoming the very serious shortage of Orthodox clergy.[32]

(The correspondence course is discussed in more detail in Chapter 4.) Unfortunately, none of the figures quoted above indicates whether these new recruits are included in the total number of priests, and if so, what proportion they form. However, the CRA Report notes that in 1974 only 20.3 per cent of the clergy were aged under 40 (see below, p. 84), so it seems that the proportion of new young recruits was small at that time.

The CRA Report also mentions this method of combating the shortage, pointing out that deacons are used as a 'reserve' for increasing the number of priests. According to the CRA, some bishops openly admit that they would rather have a bad priest in a parish than none at all, since the church will at least remain open.[33] In 1974, when Archbishop Vladimir and the CRA made these comments, this measure was not retrieving the situation, since the rate of natural wastage of priests through death and retirement was greater than the rate of ordinations. In the three years 1972–4, 297 priests and 141 deacons and psalm-readers, a total of 438 men, were ordained, but in the same period 537 priests died or retired.[34] However, it seems likely that the situation has subsequently stabilised, since, as we shall see in Chapter 4, the number of theological students has increased.

The CRA also gives information on the ages and educational level of the clergy. In 1974, 20.3 per cent were under 40, 31.2 per cent were aged 42 to 60, and 48.5 per cent were aged over 60. It is clear from this that the proportion of elderly priests was extremely high. Of the then 5,994 priests, 1,098 (18 per cent) had higher theological education and 2,375 (36.9 per cent) had primary theological education; that is, just over half fell into these two categories. We do not know how many of the remainder had studied by correspondence. Only 139 priests had higher secular education.[35] The picture which emerges is of an ageing clergy with a low level of theological education. However, this will have been changing gradually since 1974, and will continue to change, as the theological schools produce new, young priests. The CRA notes this in its report, where, despite the gloomy picture it has painted, it sounds a note of warning:

> the crisis of cadres can in no wise reassure us. The Church is very hardy. It receives support from the believers and the activists. And its highest authority, the episcopate, is not slumbering. Everything is done to halt the curtailment of services in churches, to find people who can perform rites and conduct services.[36]

Evidence that the CRA has continued to try to combat this state of affairs since 1974 is provided by Bishop Feodosi of Poltava, who states that the shortage of priests was still keenly felt everywhere in 1977, especially in Ukraine, where 'dozens of religious communities have remained without spiritual nourishment for years'. He describes how the situation has worsened in his own personal experience:

> When I arrived here in 1967, I was allowed to accept clergy from other dioceses, from other regions, and also to look for suitable candidates and ordain them to the rank of priest. Then I was forbidden to accept clergy from other dioceses, but I was not deprived of the right to ordain. A little while later, I was told: 'Ordain men from Poltava, but not anyone else.' A short time after that they told me: 'You may ordain only psalm-readers from your own diocese.' After a while, I was ordered to ordain only

psalm-readers who had been at their posts for not less than ten years. And now I am forbidden to ordain anyone at all. No, here I must make a small reservation. The [CRA] commissioner for Poltava region has graciously granted me the right to ordain all those who graduate from the theological seminary. He knows very well that I am virtually unable to make use of this right, since at present I have three men studying at the seminary, who, if they do not go on to study in the academy, will graduate two or three years from now.[37]

We should note that, although a CRA official presumably cannot physically prevent a bishop ordaining a man, he can refuse to register any priest in a parish unless he has been officially ordained with the consent of the CRA. Possibly not all dioceses experience such great difficulties as Poltava, and Bishop Feodosi himself noted that the situation was especially difficult in Ukraine. It is probable that, although the increase in the number of theological students may be sufficient to maintain a stable number of priests throughout the church as a whole, some dioceses continue to suffer a shortage because of an especially intransigent stance adopted by the local CRA official.

Salaries and Taxation

The parish priest is employed by the executive committee of a parish, as we saw in Chapter 2. He has to be assigned to a parish by a diocesan bishop, and must then conclude a contract or agreement (*dogovor*) with the executive committee. The executive committee has the right to veto a bishop's nominee, but we do not know how often this right is exercised in practice. There may be more than one priest in a parish, in which case the senior of them is called the incumbent (*nastoyatel*) and the other or others simply priest (*svyashchennik*), but, due to the shortage of priests, this is rather rare, and seems to be confined to cathedrals and large city churches. A priest is eligible for retirement at 60 and receives a church pension of 50 roubles a month plus one rouble for every year of service.[38] There is no standard salary for priests, since this is a matter for negotiation between the priest and the executive committee in each parish. Since the higher church authorities have no control over the money received at parish level, they are clearly not in a position to impose a standard salary for priests throughout the country. Most commentators have concluded that priests' salaries are quite high. The Australian Anglican report already referred to states that 'Priests receive as much as 240 roubles a month'.[39] A British correspondent noted that 'The average priest's starting salary of 200 roubles a month is already higher than the average income for a middle-aged man.'[40] Mervyn Matthews states that 'A handful of leading clergymen are said to get up to

2,000 roubles, and priests about 600, a month. These sums, however, must be reduced to about 600 and 280 roubles respectively by income tax, for church employment ranks as private practice.'[41] These sums make sense only if the first two sources are quoting figures for salaries after tax, which is not made clear in either case. If they are, then we have a range of salaries from 200 to 280 roubles a month, which seems quite reasonable given the wide variation in ages and experience of priests, from seminary graduates to men over 60. The figure of 2,000 roubles per month for a few hierarchs, which is given only tentatively by Matthews and which cannot be verified, does not seem improbable: it is quite often said, usually unattributably, that some senior clergymen earn very large sums of money. It is also true that the starting salary of 200 roubles a month is higher than the average Soviet salary: Matthews states that this was 141 roubles in 1974, and it had risen to 180 roubles by 1985.[42]

Nevertheless, by no means all clergy earn these relatively high salaries. Priests in senior positions or those serving in parishes with a high income might earn a salary within this range; these are of course the priests most likely to meet foreigners, giving the impression that such salaries are standard. However, priests working in small village churches would receive much less. We saw in Chapter 2 that some rural parishes have very small incomes, and many are unable to support a priest. This is one reason why priests in rural areas are sometimes responsible for two, three or sometimes four parishes. For example, Bishop Feodosi, in his letter to Mr Brezhnev, stated that the church in the village of Polivyanoye was able to pay only 1,500 roubles a year as salary for both the priest and the psalm-reader.[43] If we assume that the priest would receive two-thirds of this amount, 1,000 roubles, that would mean an income of just over 80 roubles a month. Such a priest would need to have two or three parishes altogether, making his total income somewhere between 200 and 300 roubles a month, and he would still have to pay a high level of tax. (An additional factor is that priests traditionally receive gifts, in kind and in money, from parishioners. These are impossible to quantify, and may well vary greatly between one priest and another. However, they do seem to form an important source of income.)

The figures Matthews gives for pre-tax and after-tax salaries indicate that the rate of taxation is very high, because clergy are taxed as private practitioners. Until quite recently 'servants of the cult' were taxed under Article 19 of the tax law, whereas people who worked for a religious association in a non-religious capacity, under agreements concluded with a trade union, such as cleaners, yardmen and stokers, paid a lower rate of tax under Article 5. However, the lower rate of taxation applies to such people only if 'they are not simultaneously members of executive committees of religious societies or representatives of groups of believers, and also do not take part in the performance of religious rites and services'.[44] There is thus a clear distinction made between those who belong to the church and those who do not with regard to the rate of tax paid. Tax paid under Article 5 is that levied on workers in the socialist sector of the economy, that is, the vast majority of Soviet workers. This income tax band has an overall maximum of 13 per cent of taxable salary. (Soviet workers pay a set amount of tax, dependent on their income level, plus a percentage on anything over that level. The percentage mentioned here refers to the additional amount.) Priests, however, and others involved in worship (e.g. altar-servers, choir directors and choir members) paid, under Article 19, income tax ranging from 24 per cent to 81 per cent of taxable salary, depending on their income level.[45]

There are other categories of income tax for people not employed in the socialist sector of the economy: writers and artists (Article 16); doctors, medical assistants, lecturers and others (Article 18); and workers in cottage industries (Article 19a). All of these, however, had minimum and maximum tax rates much lower than those paid by 'servants of the cult' (together with those who hire out property or have other sources of income) under Article 19. Father Gleb Yakunin, in a report[46] on the taxation of the clergy, pointed out that the high income tax levied on them is of considerable benefit to the state: in order to ensure that priests (many of whom have several children) have a reasonable standard of living, the religious associations are obliged to pay them very high salaries so that they are left with a reasonable income after tax. A priest earning 600 roubles a month would have paid about 55 per cent of this in income tax, so the benefit to the state was substantial.[47]

However, the income tax payable by the clergy was reduced from January 1981, when they were transferred from the highest tax band under Article 19, to the next highest, under Article 18.[48] One commentator noted that for clergy on a monthly salary of 300 roubles this would mean a tax cut of about 20 per cent, that is, from 130.8 roubles to 104.7 roubles. On a higher income of 600 roubles, the reduction would be about 17 per cent.[49] Although this represents a considerable concession, the clergy still pay a far higher rate of taxation than most Soviet citizens. For example, a blue-collar worker earning 300 roubles per month would pay about 30 roubles tax. Nevertheless, this reduction, and also some social security benefits announced simultaneously (the government would pay social security for church workers and administrative officials, and they would be allowed to join trade unions) were precisely the measures to end discrimination requested by Yakunin in his report on clergy taxation and in an accompanying letter to Mr Brezhnev from the Christian Committee for the Defence of Believers' Rights.[50] We have no way of knowing what connection, if any, there was between the two events, but this is none the less one of the rare instances of requests made by believers in *samizdat* documents being granted by the Soviet authorities.

We saw in Chapter 2 that in 1945 the clergy were suddenly restored from the status of virtual outlaws to their position as head of the parish, with unlimited access to church funds, and that some of them abused this position. The decision to tax them at the highest rate, taken in 1946 (see note 45) was no doubt intended as a restraint. If so, it was inconsistent to maintain the same tax rate after the 1961 reforms totally altered the clergy's financial situation. The 1981 reduction in income tax may be a very belated attempt to regularise the situation.

Leaving the question of tax aside, however, it still seems that the clergy's after-tax pay is, with some exceptions, higher than the national average in the Soviet Union. It is probable that the state does not object to this; if it did, it could no doubt put pressure on the executive committee of parishes to reduce it. There are two reasons why the state may prefer this privileged position for some of the clergy. First, the higher a priest's pay, the higher the amount the state takes in income tax from the money donated to religious associations. This is in fact a rather simple way for the state to raise revenue. (We should also note that the clergy make substantial donations to the Soviet Peace Fund; see below, p. 94.) Second, a relatively well-paid clergy is distanced from the population at large by being seen as a special, privileged caste, against which it is easy to foster resentment and jealousy. In the Russian mind it instantly raises associations with the popular image of the clergy in the late Tsarist period: wealthy, indolent, and living off the fat of the land in the midst of starving peasantry — as they are still frequently portrayed in Soviet anti-religious propaganda. Indeed, the British correspondent we quoted as saying that a priest's salary was higher than that of an average middle-aged man goes on to say that this is 'certainly a relic of feudalism, and unlike the Western position where most priests earn less than their congregation'.[51] All 'relics of feudalism' in the situation of the Orthodox clergy in the USSR were eliminated when they were totally dispossessed and disfranchised during the 1920s and 1930s, and if any have crept back since 1945, it seems likely that this is a matter of state policy. It is probable that the state wants Soviet citizens, and foreigners, to see the clergy as a 'relic of feudalism', since this will help to undermine any authority or respect they may enjoy among the population.

The Official Soviet View of the Clergy

The subject of the Orthodox clergy and money in fact provides an inexhaustible theme for Soviet anti-religious writers. Building on the popular image of the late-nineteenth-century Russian priest, the Soviet press frequently portrays priests in the Soviet Union as avaricious, money-grubbing, irreligious people who have joined the church solely for what they can get out of it. This is certainly true in the case of a few priests (as we shall see below), but in other cases is clearly libellous. The average Soviet reader, however, has no means of making an independent judgement. In 1973 a priest and cantor in Novosibirsk diocese were reported in the newspaper *Sovetskaya Rossiya* to have been sentenced for embezzlement, together with a tax inspector.[52] In 1977 a report in *Kommunist Tadzhikistana* about the Orthodox Church in Leninabad, Tadzhikistan, gave details of the misuse of church funds and the money-grubbing habits of three successive priests.[53] It is not possible to tell from either report whether these were in fact venal priests justly censured, or innocent men victimised without right of reply. What is clear is that the state displays a great deal of concern over the long-standing issue of money and the clergy.

This concern amounts almost to an obsession in the CRA Reports. The extracts from both the 1968 and the 1974 Reports contain long sections on alleged misuse of church funds by the clergy, with numerous examples of ways in which priests are said to have filched money. The 1968 Report contains a curious mixture of examples. In some cases it seems to be fairly clear, as far as we can ascertain from the facts presented, that venal or immoral clergyman have in fact embezzled money. There are some isolated cases where clergy have taken church money to buy drink or for other illegitimate activities, and in Astrakhan a priest was reported to have organised drinking sessions at the church's expense, and to have run off one night with the collection box.[54] These, however, make up a small number of the incidents reported, the majority of which seem to have more obvious motivations than desire for money. Bishop Bogolep of Kirovograd reportedly tried to encourage parish executive committees to increase the number of clergy and clergy salaries,[55] which seems far more likely to have been motivated by a desire to counteract the shortage of priests and improve their material position than by the venal motives imputed by the CRA. Oryol diocese sent a letter to all executive committees asking for money to repair the cathedral, and Archbishop Pavel of Novosibirsk asked for money to repair the building of the diocesan administration:[56] a reasonable enough course of action when dioceses have no source of finance other than parish executive committees. The CRA also reports cases of what it refers to as charitable activity (which is illegal): Archbishop Antoni of Vilnius wanted to make grants to churches which could not afford their own repairs, and one executive committee gave gifts to people who had lost their belongings in a fire.[57] Both these actions are surely motivated far more by charity than by a desire to siphon off money from the Russian Orthodox Church, as the CRA seems to think.

This section of the CRA Report unintentionally gives a very clear illustration of the continuing difficulties which parish priests face as a result of the 1961 reforms. Many of the numerous cases of alleged misuse of church funds listed here are not in fact cases of misuse by priests, but by executive committees. They are said often to make free with church collection boxes, and to resell small objects, such as decorative cloths or embroidered items, which believers have given to the church. Two citizens in a Kharkov church amassed large sums and lived beyond their means, and in a church in Volgograd region the accountant and his cronies filched large sums of money and destroyed documents to cover up their theft.[58] The CRA records that in 1968 180 members of executive committees were dismissed for such malpractices, but complains that miscreants are not always obliged to make restitution. There is no indication in any of these cases as to whether the culprits were thought to be believers or unbelievers, who, as we saw in Chapter 2, can easily become members of executive committees. It seems quite likely that the latter is the case, and that embezzlement of church funds by unbelievers is a means of undermining church life from within. The CRA, however, does not take this into account: stolen money recovered from the homes of embezzlers in a church in Voronezh was transferred to the accounts of local state district executive committees, not to the church from which it had been stolen.[59] Many similar cases of malpractices and alleged interference by priests are given in the 1974 CRA Report.[60]

One charge frequently levelled at priests, in the CRA Report and elsewhere, is that they perform baptisms without notifying the state authorities or the parish executive committee. The motive imputed to them by the CRA and the Soviet press is that they want to pocket the fee quietly, in addition to their monthly salary and without paying income tax. While this may be true in some cases, there is another much more compelling reason for secret baptisms. Before a baptism can be performed in an Orthodox church in the USSR, the parents of the child being baptised (or the person to be baptised if it is an adult baptism) are required to fill out a form giving their names, addresses, place of work, etc. It is known that in many cases the CRA commissioner, who has access to these records, informs the authorities at the parents' place of work or study, as a result of which they may suffer discrimination. (Examples of this will be given in Chapter 7.) Priests therefore frequently baptise children secretly — either in church without records being kept, or in some other place — in order to avoid unpleasant consequences for the parents. The practice of recording baptisms is nowhere mentioned in Soviet law, but is an instruction of the CRA. Many believers, quite justifiably, consider that it represents a serious violation of the separation of church and state which has existed, in theory, since 1918. The CRA Report for 1968 (which reached the West in 1979) confirmed the already widely-held view that registering of baptisms had been authorised by a CRA instruction, and made a reference to the appropriate 'notification' (*kvitantsiya*) by which this was to be done.[61]

Dismissed Priests

The difficulties of the parish priest are reflected in a circular to area deans (*blagochinniye*) of Moscow diocese issued by Metropolitan Serafim of

Krutitsy in 1974.[62] He refers to violations of Soviet legislation and church discipline by individual priests which are continuing to occur, and reports that complaints about the violations by believers and parish executive committees have been made to him, to the CRA commissioner for Moscow region, A. A. Trushin, and to the Moscow Patriarchate. The Metropolitan states that the most serious violations stem from the 'aspiration by some incumbents of churches to interfere in the economic and financial activity of parish executive committees'. Referring to what he considers the beneficial effects of the 1961 reforms, Serafim states that there have none the less been some attempts by priests to 'be the complete masters in the parish and obtain the opportunity to manage the church's monetary resources personally'. Serafim then gives three examples, naming the priests concerned and stating what they are supposed to have done. However, his version of events in each of the three cases is challenged by Father Gleb Yakunin, in a critical commentary on the circular.[63] Yakunin gives a completely different explanation of the conduct of the priests in each case. We have not space here to recount the alternative versions, and in any case it would be pointless, as we have no means of telling which is closer to the truth. It is, however, not possible to take Serafim's strictures at face value in the light of the fact that a totally different version of events is available. The three priests were all removed from their parishes (one was retired and two transferred to other parishes). So far as one can tell from the conflicting accounts given by Metropolitan Serafim and Yakunin, the priests in question did have the good interests of their churches at heart, and were struggling against executive committees who did not.

A careful reader of Metropolitan Serafim's circular at the time it was issued might well have suspected that he had issued it not of his own volition, but under state pressure. Such suspicions would have been confirmed by reading the CRA Report for 1974, which states clearly that Metropolitan Serafim was invited to visit the CRA office, where the situation was explained to him and 'recommendations' for improving matters were made.[64]

The position of a priest dismissed from his parish is an unhappy one. If he is retired in the normal way, through old age or ill-health, he becomes a supernumerary (*zashtatny*) priest of a given diocese and receives a pension. However, if he is dismissed for alleged misbehaviour, and is not transferred to another parish, he is without a place of residence as well as without employment. As Meerson-Aksyonov has pointed out,[65] a parish priest is bound like other Soviet citizens by the requirement to have a residence permit for every place he may live in. A residence permit, however, can be granted only once a person has obtained permanent employment in a given area. A priest dismissed from his parish loses his right to live in the area, and cannot be given a residence permit for that or any other area until he has been assigned to another parish. It is not easy for a dismissed priest to be appointed to another parish: Patriarch Pimen has issued warnings to diocesan bishops not to appoint priests who come to them from other dioceses and ask to be assigned to parishes.[66] Even if a diocesan bishop does accept him, he still has to be registered with the local authorities (as we saw in Chapter 2) before he can be confirmed in his post and receive a residence permit. A priest who does not succeed in obtaining an appointment to another parish, or some other job, and is therefore without gainful employment, for more than one month, is liable to arrest and imprisonment for 'parasitism', or being without employment, which is a crime under Soviet law.[67] There is some evidence that some priests are imprisoned in this way — though it is not known how many. Former prisoners have reported meeting Orthodox priests in labour camp — for example, A. Udodov, an *émigré* Orthodox layman, who has stated: 'I met Orthodox priests deprived of their parishes, very honest and steadfast men, in the Mordovia concentration camps.'[68]

The story of Father Yevgeni Solodki illustrates something of the difficulties, and the anguish of mind, suffered by priests deprived of their parishes. In 1980 Father Yevgeni sent an appeal to the Orthodox Church of America and other organisations asking for help in emigrating from the USSR, since he was unable to continue his calling as a parish priest there.[69] Father Yevgeni provided a brief history of his priestly ministry. Ordained priest in 1967, at the age of 30, he had served in parishes in Moscow and Moscow region until 1971. He had then been dismissed 'under pressure from the commissioner for religious affairs for Moscow region, A. A. Trushin' because he had sided with his parishioners in an attempt to remove the churchwarden, who was 'completely compromised in the eyes of all the parishioners' and 'a protégé of the godless authorities'. He was unable to obtain another parish until 1977, despite 'continual and persistent appeals to various high Party and state organs of authority'. During this time, Father Yevgeni worked as a lathe operator and then a refuse collector. After informing the CRA's chairman, Vladimir Kuroyedov, in 1976 that he had finally decided to emigrate, an instruction was passed to Metropolitan Serafim of Krutitsy that Father Yevgeni should be given a parish. When Father Yevgeni was appointed to his new parish in June 1977 by Metropolitan Yuvenali (who had succeeded the late Metropolitan Serafim), he was warned that he would be kept under surveillance. His watcher was another priest, Archpriest Yevgeni Sidorychev, who, according to Father Yevgeni, had been responsible for having many priests dismissed from parishes as a result of his reports to the authorities. This was Father Yevgeni's fate also, after two years' work in his parish. Since then his 'numerous written appeals' to Metropolitan Yuvenali have been met with silence, even though 'in many parishes of Moscow region there is an acute need for priests'.

Solodki's experience exemplifies a number of important points: the ease with which a priest can be dismissed from his parish and the difficulty of obtaining a new one; the power of the CRA and the relative helplessness of the higher church authorities in the appointment of priests; and not least the distress suffered by a man barred from priestly ministry for which he has spent years training and to which he feels a vocation.

Deanery and Diocesan Meetings

There is an intermediate level between the parish and the diocese in the form of an area deanery (*blagochiniye*) ruled by an area dean, who is simultaneously a parish priest. The function of the area deans is to 'help the bishop in his administration, supervising the life of the parishes. Through them the bishop gives his instructions to the archpriests and pastors of the churches and sends pastoral messages to his flock.'[70] We have already seen how Metropolitan Serafim's circular to Moscow clergy was issued to the area deans, who were instructed to pass it on to the priests in their charge. There is also a practice of holding periodical meetings for the clergy of an area deanery, which at one time lapsed, but has now been revived. The Yakunin Report contains some interesting information about deanery meetings, and diocesan meetings, which are similar in content:

> During the church 'renaissance' after the Second World War, in the period 1946–9, in some dioceses diocesan and deanery congresses were once more held. Apart from political issues . . . issues of internal church life were still examined at these congresses. [Yakunin quotes from congresses at which priests were encouraged to read the Bible daily and revitalise preaching.]
>
> . . . From the beginning of the 1950s diocesan congresses were no longer convened. But now recently, after a 30-year-break, the practice of such congresses has once again been restored. The traditional prayers — 'O King of Heaven' at the beginning and 'It Is Meet' at the end — are only to observe ecclesiastical form. The main theme of the gathering is a political lecture, for example, 'The International Situation', or 'True and Imaginary Human Rights'. The lecturer is from the 'Knowledge' (*Znaniye*) society (which publishes the anti-religious journal *Science and Religion*). The central figure at the congress is the commissioner of the CRA, who is unfailingly present . . . The commissioner makes a speech, or sometimes gives a lecture himself, for example on 'The New Constitution, Freedom of Conscience and Soviet Legislation on Religious Cults'.[71]

An examination of reports of diocesan and deanery meetings in the *Journal of the Moscow Patriarchate* confirms Father Gleb's view that their content is political rather than religious. In addition to the lectures he mentions, other common topics for the CRA or 'Knowledge' society lecturers are the need to support the Soviet Peace Fund and the economic development of the given locality. These issues formed almost the sole subject-matter of congresses during 1979 and 1980 in the dioceses of Perm, Simferopol, Smolensk,[72] Minsk, Perm again,[73] Leningrad,[74] Kalinin, Kishinyov, Kuibyshev,[75] and Minsk again.[76] The only other speeches were the introductory remarks made by the bishop, who generally reviewed the work of the deanery or diocese and the church as a whole, emphasising international events and work for peace, and urged the clergy to be zealous and patriotic. However, at a meeting of clergy in Mogilev deanery, Minsk diocese, Metropolitan Filaret 'clarified numerous religious and practical problems that arise in parishes', although no details are given;[77] and at a diocesan meeting in Kalinin, Archbishop Alexi 'pointed out that the work of the clergy in the parishes must be based on Holy Scriptures and the canons of the Holy Orthodox Church . . . Every priest and deacon, he said, should observe the age-old religious traditions of the Russian Orthodox Church and her ancient liturgical customs.'[78] Such references to spiritual matters, however, seem to be brief and infrequent.

Enthusiastic support for the Soviet Peace Fund is an invariable feature of such congresses. Often an official from the Peace Fund is in attendance to thank the clergy warmly for their contributions, in response to which it is customary for a member of the clergy to propose a motion urging even greater efforts in the future. Such a motion is invariably passed unanimously. For example, in the Smolensk congress mentioned above, the assembled clergy unanimously approved a suggestion that they should all 'continue, according to the example of the past year, [their] modest but sincere patriotic initiative' by giving to the Soviet Peace Fund 'a donation from their personal savings approximately equivalent to a month's pay'. This sum has also been voted at other congresses. The unanimity of the clergy in agreeing to give up a month's salary is no doubt due to the fact that the vote takes place under the eagle eye of the CRA commissioner. This forms yet another means by which the church is virtually obliged to give substantial sums of money to the state.

Corrupt Priests

We have said above that in some cases — for example, those of alleged embezzlement — it is not possible, on the basis of the evidence available to us, to know whether the priests in question are actually dishonest, or are honest men being libelled. There are, however, other well-documented cases pointing clearly to corrupt and immoral behaviour by priests. We shall first examine the cases of two Orthodox parish priests who are said on all sides to be immoral and corrupt men.

Twelve parishioners of the Church of the Archangel Michael in the town of Osh, Kirghizia, in Tashkent diocese, wrote to Patriarch Pimen to complain about the behaviour of their priest, Father Leonid Demyanovich Alexenko, who was appointed to the church in 1969.[79] The catalogue of Alexenko's misdeeds is truly appalling. He is said to behave coarsely to parishioners and physically rebuke altar boys and even elderly women; he has twice spilt the Holy Sacrament during communion; he takes sums of 100 or 200 roubles as payment for saying prayers for the sick or the dead but does not do so; he is an inveterate drunkard, a wife-beater and the father of two illegitimate children; and if parishioners comment on his behaviour he holds the cross out of reach above their heads when they go up to kiss it after liturgy, and scolds them publicly. People have been driven away from the church by his behaviour, and believers in the town have begun to go to other churches at festivals, one 45 kilometres away and one at 50 kilometres' distance. The parishioners, not surprisingly, ask Patriarch Pimen to have Alexenko unfrocked. There is some support for their description of their priest in a Soviet newspaper article, which describes how one night a militia patrol intervened upon sighting a drunken man beating up his wife in the street; the man was Alexenko.[80]

The obvious question is why such a man is allowed to remain as a parish priest. The answer is clear from the parishioners' letter: 'All the commissioners, the regional and the town ones, are his comrades and friends.'[81] The CRA commissioners are among the guests at his drunken birthday party every year. The inference is that a priest of this kind is quite acceptable to the CRA and to the local authorities, and that they have no wish to see him removed to make way for a sober and honest pastor.

It may appear that Father Leonid could scarcely be surpassed for immoral behaviour, but in fact he has been outdone in this respect by the priest of St Nicholas's Church in Nikolayev, Ukraine, Father Pyotr Stryzhik.[82] He is clearly under the protection of the CRA commissioner, Chunikhin, who is his friend. A letter signed by 119 parishioners complains that Father Pyotr makes parishioners give him money for the rites he performs and pockets it, instead of giving it to the church, and also that he peforms some rites illegally, which Chunikhin allows him, but not the other priests in the church, to do. More seriously, he makes improper advances to women parishioners, in the baptistry and elsewhere, and has raped some of them. A particularly distressing incident occurred while he was serving in another parish, when he raped a young girl while she was unconscious. He promised her and her parents that he would marry her, but when they discovered that he was already married and had children, the mother twice tried to commit suicide and eventually died, the father went blind from shock and is ill and also likely to die, and the girl has left home in a state of deep shock. The parishioners write indignantly: 'The whole family has perished, there is no family, but the criminal lives and flourishes, and under the protection of Chunikhin he continues his crimes'.[83]

A group of parishioners visited their bishop, Archbishop Bogolep of Kirovograd, and asked him to remove Stryzhik. He asked to see the girl, and when he had done so, he suspended Stryzhik from his ministry, on 4 August 1975.[84] After this, Chunikhin, in the parishioners' words, 'declared war on us', and threatened to close down the church if Stryzhik were not reinstated. There is a detailed account of moves and counter-moves over the next two years, during which Chunikhin suspended the *dvadtsatka*, church-warden and deputy-churchwarden and attempted to impose people more to his liking, and the parishioners tried to resist him, so that there were in effect two *dvadtsatki*. The conflict culminated in the local militia cutting the church's locks and opening the safe on 11 November 1976.[85] The effect of this was to give the *dvadtsatka* appointed by Chunikhin control over the church and its money. The parishioners appealed in court against this action, but the court of appeal ruled that the locks had been cut legally, with the permission of the city executive committee.[86] Some of the most active women parishioners were sentenced to hard labour. Although Stryzhik was not reinstated, Archbishop Bogolep was sent into retirement.[87] Stryzhik and his family lived for two years at the church's expense, with money provided by the *dvadtsatka* appointed by Chunikhin, and at the point where the document ends, May 1977, the parishioners feared that the new bishop would reinstate Stryzhik.

Although we do not know of many priests like Alexenko and Stryzhik, it seems that in a few cases local CRA commissioners have decided to keep immoral priests in parishes against the wishes of the parishioners in order to disrupt parish life and give religious communities a bad name among the local populace. Moreover, keeping a bad priest in a parish means that he is occupying a place of a good priest who might have a positive influence on the congregation. What is not clear is at what point in their priestly careers Alexenko and Stryzhik, and other priests who act against the interests of the Russian Orthodox Church in a less spectacular manner, first began to behave immorally. It is possible that in some cases a parish priest may after many years of pressure from the CRA and local officials become too worn down to resist temptation to wrongdoing, and having once committed some error it is possible for him to be pressured, or even blackmailed, into further ones. However, there is also some evidence that the state infiltrates men into the priesthood with the aim of sowing discord in the church; we shall see this in the following chapter when we discuss the admission of candidates to the theological seminaries.

Victimised Priests

The corrupt priests, however, appear to be a fairly small minority. At the other extreme, we know of some outstandingly gifted and dedicated pastors who are held in great esteem by those they serve. We mentioned at the beginning of this chapter that some of them are able to conduct a discreet and valuable ministry among young people, and therefore it would clearly do them no service to draw further attention to them here. However, our information about the majority of priests, who are neither corrupt nor outstandingly gifted, is minimal. It is only the extreme cases which are recorded in writing. The majority of parish priests appear to be honest and religious men, but we do not know enough about them to be able to say in general terms how they are regarded by their parishioners, which no doubt depends largely on the individual priest's character and behaviour, as in any church. On the other hand, we do know something about a few zealous parish priests who have been more indiscreet, or perhaps simply more unlucky, than the others, and have had to pay for their pastoral zeal with dismissal or even imprisonment.

Father Antoni (Vorozhbit) is a monk who has served in a number of different parishes. According to *samizdat* reports, he is a good and popular preacher who attracted many young people. In Vologda, under the influence of his preaching, a number of Young Communist League couples were married in church. Because of his popularity, the authorities kept moving him from one place to another. During Khrushchev's anti-religious campaign he was taxed for a very high (but unknown) amount which he was unable to pay, and although believers helped him, he was obliged to work in factories afterwards. However, he continued to preach to young people and to speak out against the oppression of religious believers. In 1971 he was mugged and spent a long time in hospital, an incident which his friends suspected of being an attempt by the authorities to silence him. In 1975 Father Antoni wrote to Metropolitan Nikodim of Leningrad urging him to speak out against persecution of religion, and in September that year he was arrested in the street. A charge of theft was brought against him, on the grounds that two pieces of aluminium tubing were found in his briefcase at the time of his arrest. This seems to be a rather flimsy ground for such a charge, but the treatment which followed was out of all proportion for an act of alleged petty theft. Father Antoni was not brought to trial, but was committed to Leningrad Psychiatric Hospital Number 5. He was held there for two years, and was injected with a powerful drug, moditen depo, which seriously impaired his internal organs and virtually paralysed his legs. The hospital's head doctor, Kurakina, told him that he would never be allowed to leave, and that 'The place for all believers is in psychiatric hospitals.' The fact that such treatment bears no relation to the charge, coupled with Kurakina's remark, and taking into account the timing of Father Antoni's arrest, strongly suggests that the real motive for his incarceration was his letter to Metropolitan Nikodim. Father Antoni was eventually released in October 1977, but there has been no news of him since then.[88]

There are several other known cases of priests dismissed or imprisoned for their activities. Father Iosif Mikhailov was committed to the Kazan Special Psychiatric Hospital in 1972 and charged under Article 70 of the Criminal Code ('anti-Soviet agitation and propaganda') for writing to the United Nations to complain of interference by the local authorities in his parish in Ufa.[89] Priest–monk Father Savva (Kolchugin) was arrested on 13 June 1980, and his subsequent fate is unknown. He had been banned from serving in the church in the town of Vetluga, Gorky region, more than a year previously, and had been forcibly interned in Gorky Psychiatric Hospital in 1979 and imprisoned for a month in 1980. The brief *samizdat* report containing this information says only that he was arrested for 'conscientious fulfilment of pastoral duties'.[90] Father Pyotr Zdrilyuk was ordained and appointed to the Church of the Ascension in Kiev in 1978, where he soon became known as an exceptionally good preacher. People came to hear him from other Kiev parishes and even from other parts of Ukraine, and this attracted the attention of the CRA and the KGB. In August 1981 his home was searched and a total of 57 religious books, some *samizdat* or printed in the West, described as 'anti-Soviet' were confiscated: they included a Bible, New Testament, a five-volume *Philokalia*, and books by or about Kierkegaard, St Serafim of Sarov, Metropolitan Antony (Bloom) and Father Dimitri Dudko. At an interview with the CRA commissioner for Kiev, M. T. Donchenko, on 15 January 1982, Father Pyotr refused to say who had given him the books, or to answer other questions about his acquaintances, and was then informed that he had been dismissed from his parish.[91] Another Kiev priest, Father Vitali Boiko, who organised a choir of 30 young people in his church, was dismissed from his parish in August 1980. He was unable to serve in a church until January 1981, when he began working as a choirmaster in Irpen, 20 kilometres from Kiev.[92]

The number of cases of state action against Orthodox priests has been rising during the 1980s. This has coincided with increasingly severe repression of active lay dissenters within the church (see Chapters 12 and 13). Father Kirill Chernetsky, who offered prayers for Father Gleb Yakunin before the congregation of his church during the latter's trial in August 1980 (see pp. 439–41), was soon afterwards transferred to a church on the outskirts of Moscow region.[93] Father V. Lapovsky appealed to the Ministry of Internal Affairs in Kerch, Crimea region, in March 1982, because he had been refused permission to register for residence in his mother's house there. He had applied to join the clergy of more than 20 dioceses, but had been turned down either because there were said to be no vacancies, or because the local CRA commissioner had objected.[94] In March 1983 a priest from Siberia, Father Alexander Pivovarov, was arrested: he was sentenced in autumn that year to three and a half years' strict regime labour camp on a charge of distributing unofficially produced religious literature. In fact, the literature in question reportedly consisted of legally published prayer books, service books and other Orthodox literature which had been unofficially photocopied (further details are given in Chapter 6, pp. 165–7). Pivovarov, widely known for his exceptional preaching and deep faith, was popularly called 'the light of Siberia'; from 1975 to April 1982 he was secretary to the Archbishop of Novosibirsk.[95] Deacon Vladimir Rusak was dismissed from parish work and threatened with 'parasitism' (Article 209 of the RSFSR Criminal Code) after an outspoken sermon which he preached in his church in Vitebsk, Belorussia,[96] and after it became known that he was writing a history of the Russian Orthodox Church from 1917. (Details were given in Rusak's appeal to the World Council of Churches Assembly in Vancouver in 1983; see Chapter 13, pp. 450–1, for an account of this.)[97]

Conclusion

We may conclude that the current conditions in the Soviet Union mean that the ministry of a parish is almost entirely confined to the liturgical and sacramental, with some opportunities for pastoral counselling of church members. Although some priests go beyond this and engage in youth work, discussion groups and *samizdat* activities, they are risking dismissal or imprisonment, as the examples above show. Some succeed, none the less — but only if they act with great care and discretion when exceeding the bare minimum of priestly activity which the state regards as desirable. Even within the narrow bounds of activity permitted by the state, parish priests are beset by difficulties caused by state financial policy, the infiltration of immoral priests, and the obstructions of CRA commissioners and parish executive committees. Lastly, the shortage of priests means that those there are are extremely hard pressed, and that old and ill retired priests have to be called upon to take services.

4 THEOLOGICAL EDUCATION

The expansion of theological education in the Russian Orthodox Church during the last decade or so is frequently spoken of as a considerable success for the church. In marked contrast to other areas of church life, statistics and information about the numbers of theological students and the life of the theological schools are available (although the numbers of students are not disclosed in the *Journal of the Moscow Patriarchate*). However, church leaders respond readily to questions about theological education and eagerly give the figures for the increasing numbers of students.

The continuance of theological education is of course crucial for the future of the church. The seminaries provide the parish priests, and the academies the theologians, teachers and specialists in foreign relations, without whom the church would find it very difficult to continue. The numbers of graduates from the theological schools, and the quality of the teaching they receive there, have the utmost importance for the future of the church. The dearth of religious literature in the Soviet Union means that it is extremely difficult for a priest or aspiring priest to study independently of the state-recognised theological schools.

Formal theological education in the Soviet Union was almost totally eliminated from the early 1920s until after the Second World War. (Some theological lectures were kept going with great difficulty in Leningrad until nearly the end of the 1920s.) This meant that when the theological schools did reopen they had much lost ground to make up: the intellectual life of the church had been totally disrupted, and many of its best brains had perished in Stalin's labour camps. The fact that eight seminaries and two academies were functioning by 1947 testifies both to the priority which the Moscow Patriarchate devoted to this area of its reconstruction and to the dedication of those involved in the work.[1] By 1955 an estimated 1,500 students, including correspondence students, were receiving theological education.[2] However, the anti-religious campaign of 1959—64 caused a serious setback. Five of the seminaries were closed down: those in Kiev, Minsk, Saratov (on the Volga), Stavropol (in the northern Caucasus) and Lutsk (in Volynia, Ukraine).[3] The much vaunted expansion of recent years has taken place at the institutions which remained after these closures. These are the Moscow Theological Seminary and Academy, based at Zagorsk, the Leningrad Theological Seminary and Academy, and the Odessa Theological Seminary.

Numbers of Theological Students

Although there are many statistics quoted regarding the numbers of theological students, they are not always entirely compatible with one another, and caution must be exercised when making use of them. The appendix at the end of this chapter lists figures quoted by different sources over the last decade. Discrepancies between them indicate that information given to foreigners on different occasions can vary. Overall, however, Table 4.1 (pp. 120–1) shows a clear rise in the numbers of both residential and correspondence students. We should note that it was not until some time between 1975 and 1977 that the estimated 1955 level of 1,500 students was regained.

We saw in Chapter 3 that it was crucial for the church to make good the severe shortage of parish priests by increasing the number of theological students, and Table 4.1 shows this increase has in fact come about. The question is whether the increase is sufficient to meet the need, given the high age level of the clergy (48.5 per cent were over 60 years of age in 1974, according to the CRA Report). To answer this question we shall need to look a little more closely at the ways in which the increase in the number of students has occurred, and the proportion of students destined for parish work. The increase in the number of students has taken place in two ways. First, the number of forms in each year of the seminaries was doubled, so that by the end of the 1970s there were eight forms in each of the three seminaries, a total of 24. Subsequently, a third parallel class was added at Zagorsk. This was no doubt a simpler expedient for the church than pressing for the reopening of the five closed seminaries, which would have necessitated a change in government policy, and possibly administrative problems as well. Second, the correspondence course was instituted in 1959. This means that not all the students currently being trained will eventually swell the ranks of the clergy, since nearly half of them are already ordained and working in parishes while receiving their theological education. However, if the correspondence course is working as planned, these students, plus those who have already graduated, must be additional to the numbers of clergy a few years ago given in Chapter 3. We see from this that the increase in numbers has taken place among the two sections of the student body, residential seminary students and correspondence students, who are nearly all destined for parish work. This is not the case with the third main section of the student body, the academy students. Most of them will eventually work in the Department of External Church Relations, the teaching staff of the theological schools, and the episcopate. A fair number of academy students will serve in parishes, usually in large cities, but they are cancelled out by the number of seminary graduates who enter the academies each year. Table 4.1 does not make it clear how many of the current number of students are in the two academies, but an estimate can be arrived at in the following manner. There is one form in each year of the two academies, a total of eight. Each form contains about three-quarters of the number of students in a seminary form. This means that the academy students equal the number of students in six seminary forms, or one-quarter of the total number of seminarians. If we assume that in the academic year 1982–3 there was a total of 1,200 or so residential students, then the number of academicians is about one-fifth of this number, or roughly 240 men. This represents an increase over the number of academy students in earlier years shown in Table 4.1: a total of 174 in 1973–4 — according to Oppenheim, and 158 in 1974–5 according to the CRA Report. However, the increase is not as great as the increase in seminarians and correspondence students, suggesting that the need for more senior, better-qualified clergy has not grown as rapidly as the need for more parish priests.

Can the number of graduates each year meet the needs in the parishes? Leaving aside the academy students, there are approximately 2,000 seminarians and correspondence students on four-year courses, which means about 500 graduates each year, 250 new priests and 250 already working in parishes. Some of these are foreigners who will serve overseas, but there should be about three or four new priests for each diocese in the Soviet Union. This level has been reach gradually over the last ten years. Table 4.1 shows that in 1974–5 there were 408 seminary students and over 510 correspondence students. One-quarter of this total, roughly 230 men, would have graduated in 1975. If we assume a gradual increase each year up to the level of 500 graduates assumed in summer 1983, that gives a rough total of about 3,300 graduates over eight years. Returning to the CRA Report's figures for clergy in 1974, which we cited in Chapter 3, we recall that in that year there were just under 6,000 clergy, of whom nearly half were over 60 years of age. In theory, then, the number of new graduates has been more than sufficient to replace them. (In practice, not all graduates are able to obtain registration in a parish, as we shall see later in this chapter.)

These figures and estimates suggest that the expansion in the number of theological students in recent years has been theoretically sufficient to stabilise the numbers of parish clergy below retirement age. It remains to be seen whether the numbers of students will be maintained at this level, or even expanded, to permit an increase in the numbers of parish priests. Much depends upon the correspondence course. It is not yet clear whether it is seen as a temporary measure intended to compensate for an acute shortage of clergy at a particular time, or whether it is a permanent measure designed to increase the strength of the clergy in the long term.

Impressive though the growth in the number of theological students has been, it does not mean that theological education is available for all who want it. Church leaders have stated more than once that there are four or five applicants for every available place. For example, Archbishop Vladimir, rector of the Moscow Theological Schools, stated in an interview in 1974 that in the previous year three-quarters of the 200 applicants had been turned away because there was no room for them.[4] There can be little doubt that the church would like to accept many of these students, were it permitted the facilities to do so.

Life in the Theological Schools

Much of the information which follows derives from two excellent articles by foreigners who have been able to observe the theological schools of the Russian Orthodox Church at close quarters. A most informative and thorough account was written in 1974 by Rev. Raymond Oppenheim, who served as Episcopalian chaplain at the American Embassy in Moscow. Mr Theo van der Voort, a Dutchman who studied at the Leningrad Theological Academy during 1974–7, has written a very full and lively account of it based on his own experience.[5]

The courses at the three seminaries last four years each. The best seminary students may enter the academy course, which also lasts four years. In addition, there is a postgraduate course (*aspirantura*) at the Moscow Academy, after one year of which students are allowed to teach at the Academy.[6] The correspondence course is also based at the Moscow Theological Schools (from 1948 to 1968 it was based in Leningrad).[7] Courses for choir directors or precentors (*regenty*) were opened at all three theological schools in 1969, available to musically gifted students in addition to their other subjects of study. However, this did not solve the problem of increasing the number of precentors, since most students on courses became priests. In 1979, therefore, the precentors' courses were opened to young lay people, most of whom are women. They study theological and ecclesiastical subjects in addition to their musical training.[8] This was the first time in the history of the Russian Orthodox Church that women had been able to study in the theological schools. In 1979 there were reported to be about 20 girls on the precentors' course in Leningrad,[9] one of whom was from Paraguay.[10] The Moscow precentors' course had seven graduates in 1980, making a total of 57 graduates in the eleven years the course had been running. The first woman graduated from the Moscow course in 1981.[11] A woman graduate of the course, speaking at the Vancouver Assembly of the World Council of Churches in 1983, said that the previous year there had been 100 young women applicants for the 20 places available.[12]

Foreign students have attended the Leningrad Theological Schools for many years. Van der Voort states that there were usually 10 to 15,[13] but Oppenheim records that earlier, in 1973–4, there were 23.[14] (The drop in numbers may be due to the fact that a number of Ethiopian students had graduated in 1974 and were not replaced.) The foreign students all go to

Leningrad, not Moscow, although there are a few students from Eastern European countries at Moscow.[15] In 1979–80 there were 48 foreign students at Leningrad,[16] from countries including Greece, Yugoslavia, France, Argentina, Paraguay, the USA and Ethiopia.[17] An official church publication in 1982 stated that members of the Eastern churches of Armenia, India and Egypt, as well as Ethiopia, 'now' study at both Moscow and Leningrad. This source adds Bulgaria, Hungary and Japan to the list of countries from which students come.[18]

Soviet students from the two academies are sent abroad for periods of study at Orthodox, Catholic and Protestant educational institutions. According to a church source, these include the Faculty of Theology of Athens University, the Eastern Institute at the Vatican in Rome, the Catholic Institute of Paris, the Department of Catholic Theology of Regensburg University in West Germany, and the Ecumenical Institute in Bossey in Switzerland.[19] However, another commentator has noted that there have been no Orthodox students from the Soviet Union in Regensburg since 1979, and none at the Vatican since 1981.[20]

Each of the theological schools has its own rector, but the syllabus, courses of study, etc., are decided by the Education Committee of the Moscow Patriarchate, headed by Metropolitan Alexi of Tallinn. The three diocesan bishops in whose dioceses the theological schools are situated — Patriarch Pimen, the Metropolitan of Leningrad and the Metropolitan of Odessa — take a close interest in the life of the theological schools and visit them frequently. The Metropolitan of Leningrad resides on the premises of the Leningrad Theological Schools.[21] The non-academic side of daily life is in charge of the inspector (*inspektor*) and his assistants.[22]

In 1973–4 there were 46 lecturers at Moscow, plus 7 special instructors in fields such as art and music, 31 lecturers at Leningrad, and 16 at Odessa.[23] In 1979 there were reported to be 22 lecturers at Odessa,[24] in 1981 there were 70 at Zagorsk,[25] and in 1982 there were 60 at Leningrad.[26] This would indicate that the teaching staff has increased to keep pace with the growth in the number of students. Admittedly, a 1984 visitor reported 'about 60' teaching staff at Zagorsk, suggesting a decline from the 1981 figure, but it is possible that the imprecision of this figure means that any decline is not serious, and may be only a temporary fluctuation.[27] A few of the teaching staff are theologians who are well known in international ecumenical circles, but the chequered career of the theological schools has meant that it has not been possible for the Russian Orthodox Church to develop any original creative theology. An official church source has stated that a growing number of mathematicians, physicists, doctors, lawyers, biologists, engineers and philologists have joined the teaching staffs of the theological schools. They have all taken holy orders, and about half of them have also taken monastic vows.[28]

The higher degrees awarded by the academies are of three levels:

candidate's, master's and doctor's (in line with the general Soviet higher educational system). Quite large numbers of academy students have taken the candidate's degree (which is similar to a PhD degree, though somewhat less demanding). Students then go out into the world and work for some years before obtaining a master's degree. Doctorates are awarded only after extensive academic work, and often late in life. A church source stated that by 1982 the theological schools had awarded about 1,000 candidate's degrees, 60 Master of Theology degrees, and 15 doctorates.[29]

Most of the seminary students, 90 per cent, according to Oppenheim, take holy orders before the end of the four-year course.[30] They are ordained first deacon, then priest. After their first two years at the seminary, students may serve in parishes as readers or deacons while completing their courses.[31] Some students do not in fact complete their seminary or academy course, because bishops desperately short of parish priests ordain them and appoint them to parishes beforehand.[32] A seminarist must decide whether or not to marry before ordination as deacon. A man who is married may be ordained, but a man who is ordained may not marry. Widowed priests, therefore, may not remarry. It is customary in the Russian Church for unmarried priests to take monastic vows, though it is not absolutely obligatory and not all do so. According to Archbishop Vladimir of the Moscow Theological Schools, most students choose to marry.[33] Less than 20 per cent remain unmarried, and therefore eligible for the episcopate, which is chosen exclusively from the monastic ranks.

The ages of students appear on the whole to be quite low, even though men up to the age of 50 may apply for admission. A visitor to the Moscow Theological Schools in 1979 estimated that the majority of students were aged 20 to 22 years of age, with about 10−15 per cent of them being in the 25−30 age range. Some of them are therefore obliged to undertake the two years' military service which is compulsory for young men in the Soviet Union, unlike other students, who are exempt. Oppenheim states that it 'appears to be a general practice' that ordained students are not drafted, but this is a matter for officials in the student's home town to determine. Military service for students in the academy is deferred, and they usually do not serve if they are ordained. He notes that 'virtually 100 per cent' return from military service to complete their courses.[34] Van der Voort, however, writing at a later date, notes that many students enter the theological schools after their military service. This was repeated by an official church source in 1982.[35]

Students at the theological schools receive a stipend, which is given by the church, not the state, from its Scholarship Fund.[36] The stipend increases as the student passes through the seminary and then on to the academy, and also according to the standard of his work.[37] The increase can be as much as 25−50 per cent for those who study well.[38] This is in line with the situation of all Soviet students, the most able of whom receive an increased stipend.

According to Van der Voort, seminarists received 15 roubles a month and academy students 20 roubles a month. Foreign students also received a stipend from the church, of 30 roubles per month, in addition to which their fares home at least once a year were paid.[39]

The Moscow Theological Schools are situated at the Holy Trinity Monastery of St Sergi, one of the greatest of the Russian shrines and a place of pilgrimage for foreigners and for people from all over the Soviet Union. The schools benefit from the presence of the monastic community and from the powerful historical associations of the place, which has been loved by the Orthodox people since St Sergi founded his monastery there in the fourteenth century.

The Odessa Theological Seminary also benefits from the influence of a monastic community. In fact, this seminary was able to survive the threat of closure at the beginning of the 1960s only by finding new quarters in the Monastery of the Dormition.[40] The Patriarch's summer residence is also located here. Foreign visitors are invited to the seminary, though not as many as to Moscow and Leningrad, but there are no foreign students. Having no academy or graduate students and no special courses, the Odessa seminary is rather eclipsed by Moscow and Leningrad. Little is known of its rector, Archpriest Alexander Kravchenko. According to Oppenheim, the student body is drawn almost entirely from Ukraine[41] and the purpose of this seminary is evidently to provide parish priests for the area of the country where the largest concentration of functioning churches is found. There has been a steady increase in the number of students, and a second storey has been built to accommodate them.[42] According to Archbishop Pitirim, this meant that the seminary could accommodate 100 more students.[43]

The Leningrad Theological Schools differ from the others by being housed in the middle of a large city. They are situated next to the former Monastery of St Alexander Nevsky (where there is no longer a monastic community), but Van der Voort points out that they are flanked by a lunatic asylum and an abortion clinic, and that three storeys on the left of the building are occupied by a military office, though these premises were expected to be vacated and made available to the Leningrad Theological Schools by about 1983.[44] The buildings of the Leningrad Theological Schools were expanded in 1977.[45] The situation of the theological schools, and perhaps also the presence of foreign students, distinguishes the atmosphere of the Leningrad schools from that of Moscow: Oppenheim says that the former have a 'more worldly atmosphere' and that 'the outlook is somewhat more Western', and Van der Voort characterises the atmosphere at Zagorsk as 'more conservative'.[46] The 1974 CRA Report mentions this. It quotes the then Bishop Yermogen of Kalinin as saying:

The composition of our clergy is divided into two categories — representatives of the Zagorsk and the Leningrad Theological Schools. Among the first, unfortunately, there are many obscurantists, fools and fanatics. Among the latter sober-thinking people predominate . . . A stay of four years, or, for some, eight years, within the walls of a monastery cannot but have its effect on a man's psychology.

The CRA commissioner to whom he was speaking agreed with this assessment. However, the CRA Report points out that Bishop Yermogen probably wanted to shed a good light on the Leningrad schools where he himself had studied, and remarked that Moscow graduates say exactly the opposite.[47]

The Moscow and Leningrad Theological Schools both have extensive libraries. According to Oppenheim, in 1974 the library in Moscow contained 270,000 volumes, of which roughly half were pre-revolutionary and 15 per cent in languages other than Russian. In Leningrad there were 117,307 books in Russian and 30,501 in other languages, of which about 75 per cent were pre-revolutionary. In Odessa the library was reported to contain 25,000 books in 1976.[48] It is clear from this that a very large proportion of the books are old and possibly out of date. Van der Voort disputes these figures: he records that in 1977 there were 'about 200,000 books' in Leningrad, and later quoted Archbishop Kirill as saying that the Leningrad library was larger than the one at Zagorsk.[49] An official church source in 1982 suggested a slight increase over these earlier figures (which one would expect): 'about 200,000' volumes in Leningrad and 'close to 300,000' volumes in Moscow.[50] This evidently refutes Archbishop Kirill's assertion that the Leningrad Library was the larger of the two. However, van der Voort has this to say of their quality:

The books in Russian as far as they concern theology are in general pre-revolutionary. Books which have appeared in Russian in the West after 1917 are rare in the library. Soviet books which have a bearing on theology appear now and then, but are of course always at least slightly anti-religious or atheistic. Books on subjects in history are still the best ones, especially if they are about long-distant times. Most of the foreign books received in the library are in German, and can be used by the staff and the few students who know enough of the languages . . . In the reading room the number of theology journals is restricted. The newest copies are always more than one month old. The newspapers on the reading-table are almost all from the so-called socialist countries. Text-books in Russian are either pre-revolutionary or do not exist. With great zeal and love text-books are replaced by hard-covered bound sheets, typed (with some sheets of carbon paper one can make three or four copies, the last one of course of a terrible quality) by typists in the academy. This is the way knowledge has to be transmitted in the last quarter of the twentieth century'![59]

Oppenheim also mentions this problem:

> The greatest complaint from the students is the lack of study materials. Lecture notes, prepared by the faculty members, are distributed in type-written copies. There are rarely enough, however, to go round, and students must share books.[52]

A student's day is divided between the church, the classroom and the refectory. After morning prayer and breakfast, lessons begin at 9 a.m. There are six lessons a day, lasting 45 minutes each with a ten-minute interval between them. Lessons are given six days a week. There are refreshments after the third lesson, and then lunch at 2.30 or 2.40 p.m., which is eaten in silence to a reading from the lives of the saints. Then there is free time until 6. p.m., when there is tea, followed by study until 8 p.m., when supper is served. There is free time until 10.30 p.m., when everyone goes to church for evening prayer, and then is supposed to retire for the night.[53] In practice, van der Voort found that students did not always adhere to this programme: the afternoon free time is 'officially until six o'clock, but nothing is heard if you are absent until 10.30'. Even this rule is sometimes broken, but a culprit is not punished 'if you don't have the misfortune to meet Metropolitan Nikodim, who likes to take some fresh air near the academy before going to bed'.[54] This probably does not occur at Zagorsk and Odessa, which do not have the attractions of a large city on their doorsteps. Van der Voort discovered that retiring at 10.30 p.m. was not observed either:

> one is supposed to go to bed, but sometimes there is an occasion to celebrate, a saint's day, anniversary or something like that, and that can last until after midnight. If one is silent enough, it is hardly probable that the company will be disturbed by one of the assistant inspectors. Students from adjacent rooms are offered a seat when they put their head in to see what is going on, and are also given a drink, which may be tea, wine or vodka.[55]

Van der Voort concluded that 'the discipline in the academy is not very strict', and that though plenty of rules and regulations were hung upon the walls, 'they are there more as a kind of decoration than as a way of checking up on one's behaviour'. However, he discovered that there was no serious disorder because 'almost everybody tries to behave well'. He observed none the less that:

> The only serious problem is drunkenness. It is a plague in the Soviet Union, which has affected the clergy and the students as well. After a couple of serious warnings, some students are expelled because of this problem every year.[56]

Daily attendance at church services forms an important part of a student's life. 'Experience has shown that the daily services (morning and evening), with compulsory attendance of the students as readers, singers or attendants at the altar, are the best practical school for future clerics.'[57] Van der Voort records that the students are divided into groups which take turns at having responsibility for the morning and evening services. There are two choirs for the services on Sundays and feast days which everybody attends, and when the church is filled to overflowing by the local populace. Weddings, tonsurings of monks and ordinations are celebrated in the academy church. During the first week of Great Lent and in the week before Easter there are no lectures, and morning and evening services are celebrated at monastic length. Van der Voort concludes: 'it is no exaggeration to say that the church is the centre of the life of the academy'.[58]

The Selection of Candidates

Rules for admission to the theological seminaries and academies, the correspondence course at Moscow and the choir directors' classes are published annually in the *Journal of the Moscow Patriarchate*. Candidates are required to submit their birth certificate, baptism certificate and various other documents, and must have a letter of recommendation from their diocesan bishop or parish priest. Men are admitted to the seminary between the ages of 18 and 35, and to the academy and the correspondence course between the ages of 18 and 50. Men and women may apply for the choir directors' course on the same conditions as candidates for the seminaries. Candidates may apply to enter directly into the second, third or fourth year of a course, or to enter the academy without attending the seminary, but they must pass the necessary examinations before admission. Applications are accepted up to 1 August, qualifying examinations commence on 20 August, and the term begins on 1 September. Candidates for the seminary must have secondary education, know certain prayers by heart, and be able to read well in Church Slavonic. Candidates for the academy must also have secondary education, and have passed all the seminary examinations. Entrance to the correspondence course is on the same conditions.[59]

We have already mentioned that there are four or five candidates for every place, and it is clear that a rigorous selection process must be carried out. The rector of the Moscow academy, Archbishop Vladimir, stated in an interview with a foreign journalist that the Soviet government plays no role in selecting students for the Zagorsk schools. He said, however, that the Soviet militia are given the names of men accepted for admission so they can be given permission to live in Zagorsk, as a Soviet citizen must receive a pass to live in a city other than his native town.[60] However, many commentators with close knowledge of seminary life have maintained that the

Soviet state agencies do in fact play an important part in selecting candidates for the seminaries. In 1976 a leading Russian Orthodox churchman admitted to a Westerner in a private conversation that the church does not make the first selection of students from among applicants.[61] Various *samizdat* documents have asserted that the CRA and the local authorities in the applicant's home play a significant role in deciding whether or not his application should be accepted, and some have indicated that often the most highly educated candidates are rejected, leaving the church with the less able men. These assertions find confirmation in the CRA Report for 1974, which states: 'Commissioners of the Council, in close contact with local authorities, as in previous years have taken measures to exclude from the theological schools fanatics, extremists and mentally ill people.'[62] This clearly indicates that the CRA and local authorities are in fact involved in the selection process. However, while the exclusion of 'fanatics, extremists and mentally ill people' would appear to be for the good of the theological schools, the examples of such excluded people which the CRA then gives shows that their criteria in these matters are probably not the same as those of the church. The excluded candidates in 1974 included one who had 'expressed anti-Soviet sentiments and in 1971 had been detained near the American Embassy in Moscow, to which he was trying to obtain entrance'; another who was a member of the Young Communist League; a third who 'had contacts abroad'; and a fourth who was a deputy of a village *soviet*.[63] These factors alone would probably not make any of the candidates unacceptable to the church, but the CRA evidently thought otherwise. Presumably the CRA would have regarded the first and third candidates as possible trouble-makers, and the second and fourth as useful members of Soviet society whom it did not wish to 'lose' to religion.

The CRA pays particular attention to candidates from western Ukraine, where, as we have seen, there is a high concentration of Orthodox life. The CRA Report states that it tries to limit the number of students from this region. This may be partly because it hopes to lessen the intensity of religious life there, but it is probably also because citizens of western Ukraine are often thought to have strongly nationalistic views which are anathema to the Soviet government, and because believers from that area are often strongly influenced by the now outlawed Eastern-rite Catholics (Uniates), or perhaps secretly are Eastern-rite Catholics who can obtain theological education only by pretending to be Orthodox. The CRA Report notes that some men from western Ukraine try to evade the limits placed on western Ukrainians by moving to eastern Ukraine and making their application from there.[64] It appears that the CRA may not be altogether successful in limiting the numbers of western Ukrainians, as van der Voort noted that 'a considerable number of students' at Leningrad were from western Ukraine.[65]

Van der Voort also discovered that young men known to have put in an application to the seminary often came under strong pressure from state agencies:

> I heard several times that boys who wanted to enter the seminary were advised by other students to conceal themselves somewhere as soon as they had officially applied to the theological schools. It has happened more than once that candidates for the seminary were arrested on a charge of hooliganism, theft, rape, arson, etc., and were in preventive detention for several weeks. They were released on the day of the admission exams, because of 'lack of proof', but of course could not pass the exam that year and had to wait for the next year. Quite a lot of applicants stayed during the weeks before the admission examination in the Caves Monastery near Pskov, but now that the abbot there has died and been replaced by a pro-Soviet one [see chapter 5, pp. 142−3], this place can hardly be regarded as a real possibility for escaping this kind of problem.[66]

Anatoli Levitin has also provided evidence of the pressures put upon applicants to the seminaries, whether they are successful or not. He states that in 1974 there was an unexpected wave of applicants for the Moscow seminary, seven for every place, and that 'the KGB interfered and rejected the most gifted'.[67] According to Levitin, the KGB, or secret police, as well as the CRA, helps to control the intake of seminary students. Levitin gives an example of the fate of a rejected candidate personally known to him:

> one of those who wished to enter the seminary, Alexi Averyanov, was employed as an altar-server at the Church of the Unexpected Joy in Moscow. He was dismissed from his work in the church for having wished to study at the seminary . . . The KGB ordered the representative of the believers to get rid of the young man, in order to make him a 'parasite' . . . When I left [the Soviet Union], the young man, whose wife had just given birth to a son, had been thrown into the street and was struggling like a fish thrown on to the bank. Nowhere was there anyone who would give him work, and the militia and the secret police were pursuing him in order to charge him with 'parasitism', with all the consequences that that involves.[68]

Averyanov's subsequent fate is unknown.

A candidate accepted for a seminary or academy, therefore, has not only passed the requirements and examinations laid down by the theological schools themselves, but has also been vetted by the CRA, which liaises with the local *soviet* in his home, the militia, which checks up on his past record before giving him a residence permit, and the KGB. The majority of those who are accepted, therefore, are probably sincerely religious young men whose commitment to the church is deep enough for them to face the hardships attendant upon applicants to the theological schools; who have no criminal record, including convictions for political offences, which would lead the militia to refuse them a residence permit; and who are probably not among the best educated or most gifted of the applicants, whose talents the state does not wish to see enriching and strengthening the church.

Recruitment of Informers

The control exercised by state agencies over students does not end once they have been admitted to a course of study. Many *samizdat* documents affirm that the authorities recruit informers in the theological schools, who regularly report on the life there and denounce any student whose views are considered politically or ideologically unacceptable. The informers appear to be of two kinds: those who are deliberately placed there by the Soviet authorities, and who may have little or no religious vocation; and those who are sincerely religious but are pressurised into informing once they arrive at the theological schools. Our information about the former is very slight: we do not know how many of them there are, how they are trained, or precisely what their assigned tasks are. It is possible that priests like Alexenko and Stryzhik, whom we mentioned in Chapter 3, come into this category, in which case their task is clearly to undermine the church from within. We have no way of knowing how many of such people have succeeded in entering the episcopate or other positions of influence in the church. However, their presence in the theological schools seems to be an open secret, as even a foreign student like van der Voort quickly realised. He indicates how such people may be infiltrated:

> The State . . . has a list of persons it wants to be placed. It is even said that a kind of deal is made. 'If you really want this student,' the State says, 'you must take that one (of ours) as well.' So the State knows that always a certain number of students will keep watch on events in the academy and will warn the State if something is going to happen.[69]

The people infiltrated by the state, so far as we can tell, are probably not KGB 'agents', i.e. paid professional secret policemen, but rather people over whom the KGB has some kind of hold, and who can be bullied, blackmailed or intimidated into compliance with its plans.

The second category of informers is those who are pressurised after their enrolment in the theological schools. Anatoli Levitin has written in detail about this.[70] In a lecture in 1974, he stated that the KGB uses three main methods: exploitation of political ignorance, promises of advancement, and threats. The first method can be effectively used against young and inexperienced peasant lads, who are told that helping the KGB is their patriotic duty, and may even have verses of Scripture quoted at them in support of this argument. Using the second approach, the KGB officers, according to Levitin, 'promise literally everything: an ecclesiastical career, aid for studies, foreign travel (this is especially emphasised), and assistance in improving daily life (the right to live in Moscow, help in obtaining accommodation, etc.)'. Finally, there are threats 'of expulsion from the seminary, of long delays in ordination . . . And if there is the slightest pretext, there are threats of a criminal trial.'[71] Van der Voort describes how easy it is for a student to become an informer almost without realising what is happening. After entering the seminary, students have to visit the military registration office, as they are liable for call-up to the army. Some of them

are sent to a room where a nice, friendly, fatherly person starts a talk with him, and asks how he likes the city, the museums and the academy, and how the study is going. When the student feels at ease, suddenly the question is put: 'Are you a citizen of the Soviet Union?' As answering 'No' cannot be recommended in these cases, the answer, 'Yes, of course' is given. The friendly person continues by saying that therefore it is his duty to help his country. As he may know, the Soviet State has many enemies. Of course, the State is not against the Church, the academy and so forth, but there are unfortunately some elements in the academy who are against the Soviet State. Don't forget there are foreign students as well! If he happens to hear something, he should phone or write a report about it. If the student is not very careful, he'll leave that room with a phone number or address, and he is told that a report is expected in a couple of weeks. Sometimes pressure is used, or promises made to get the student's cooperation. There are even cases when a career is started. A paper with the appointment, signed by the church authorities, is shown to the flabbergasted person. If he says 'Yes' to the proposal the KGB is making, everything will be arranged. Many students who are not prepared or accustomed to this treatment, fall into the trap and are forced to cooperate. How many students regularly write reports is not known, of course. But in general, it is said that about 50% voluntarily or involuntarily cooperate. Of course, this strongly affects the atmosphere in the academy, but it does not ruin relationships completely. Many students know how difficult it is to stay out of reach of the tentacles of the KGB, and are more likely to feel sorry for the poor fellows than to accuse them because they fell into the trap.[72]

Although van der Voort and Levitin both speak of the KGB rather than the CRA as the recruiter of informers, it seems that the CRA plays a part in arranging for the friendly chats with students. However, the CRA Report makes no mention of recruiting informers in its section on the theological schools.

A former student at Zagorsk, Hierodeacon Varsonofi (Khaibulin), comments sardonically that the informers are of different kinds:

> It's almost like it was in labour camp: there the local secret police, the camp administration and the KGB all have their own informers, and there are also all-rounders who service all three 'intelligence services' at once. In the Zagorsk seminary, some pious youths reported only to the inspector or the rector, and others directly to the KGB in Nizhnaya Street. And the inspector himself considered it his honourable civic duty to give exhaustive information about his pupils to the town authorities the moment they telephoned.[73]

Some men refuse to co-operate with the KGB, though we have no means of knowing how many. Levitin states that a refusal to co-operate leaves a permanent black mark on a seminarist's record which affects his career:

> It harms his career, it does not permit him to live a normal life. I know the case of a man who finished his studies at the Theological Academy a few years ago as first in his class, and none the less he has been kept for nearly four years now in the rank of deacon in the provinces, and this despite the terrible shortage of priests in the diocese where he is working. This is an act of vengeance: he is being punished for his moral steadfastness in face of efforts to make him a KGB agent.[74]

It would seem from these accounts, especially van der Voort's, that the presence of informers in the seminaries and academies is fairly generally known, and that students would therefore take appropriate precautions in their words and actions. One former student, however, records that he was unaware of the presence of informers:

> I have always been a very trusting person, and I paid no attention at all to warnings that seminary was swarming with informers. I conversed completely openly in the seminary, considering the institution as the only island of freedom in a country of general lawlessness.[75]

This student, Father Lev Konin, was eventually told that a denunciation had been made against him to the effect that he had been receiving religious literature from foreigners. He was allowed to complete the remaining month of his academy course, and to receive his degree, but he lost his post as priest in a Leningrad parish church and was unable to obtain another, in Leningrad or in any of the neighbouring dioceses. (He subsequently emigrated to France.)

The fact that so many candidates continue to present themselves despite all these obstacles testifies that there is no lack of young men earnestly desiring to devote their lives to the church. Levitin calls it 'one of the testimonies to a great revival of religious feeling among young people',[76] which we shall discuss in more detail in Part II. The little we know about the motivation of these young people indicates that their desire to enter the priesthood generally comes about through independent reading and reflection. A British journalist who interviewed Leningrad students in 1979 wrote:

Alexander Zhilyayev is 24 and comes from an atheist family in Moscow. His mother is a retired meterologist, his father was a pilot. He says he decided to become a priest when he was about 19 or 20. He was at a special school for advanced children, concentrating on chemistry and mathematics, and began to believe in God when he was about 15. 'It's difficult to explain it rationally. But I always felt there must be some higher powers, and I got interested in religion. My mother knew what I felt, but probably she did not take it seriously at first. I started to read about religion. I came up to my teachers after school and asked them about it. They answered, but their answers did not affect me, I suppose. When I finished school I applied for the academy.'[77]

Tatyana Burdina, one of the first girls to be accepted for the choir directors' course, had had no thought of working in the church, though her father was a priest. However, she said: 'The Lord's way brought me here. My father always wanted me to go into the Church, and he made me think and understand that it was necessary.'[78] According to the rector of the Moscow Theological Schools, Archbishop Vladimir:

Many . . . have come to religion by means of reading . . . anti-religious literature and reflecting on what they have read. When we ask them how they became believers, it turns out that they have been systematically reading the atheist journal *Science and Religion*.[79]

This rather surprising remark is explained by the fact that religious literature is virtually unobtainable in the USSR, and anyone desirous of finding out about religion has to read carefully between the lines of atheist literature. The monthly *Science and Religion* has a number of interesting articles about various religions, in historical times and in the present, and although they all have an atheistic slant, a discerning reader can distinguish the facts from the ideological interpretation put upon them.

The Courses of Study

The publications of the Moscow Patriarchate do not give a great deal of information about the subjects included in the syllabus of the theological schools, apart from a list of subjects studied published in 1958. There are 25 subjects for seminarians: biblical history (Old and New Testament), the Holy Scriptures (Old and New Testament), catechism, dogmatic theology, moral theology, apologetics, comparative theology, practical guidance for priests, homiletics, church regulations, ritual, general church history, history of the Russian Church, analysis of the doctrines of the Russian schisms and sects, Constitution of the USSR, Church Slavonic, Greek, Latin, a choice of English, French or German, church singing, and Russian (optional), this last presumably for those who are not native Russian speakers. The 24 academy subjects are: the Old Testament, the New Testament, patrology, apologetics, dogmatic theology, moral theology, pastoral theology and ascetics, homiletics, liturgics, church archaeology in connection with the history of Christian art, history of the Ancient Church, history of the Russian Church, Byzantology and the history of the Slav Churches, history and analysis of Western confessions, history and analysis of the doctrines of the Russian schisms and sects, canon law, Constitution of the USSR, church singing, Hebrew, Greek, Latin, and a choice of English, French or German.[80] The list of subjects in the academy is virtually the same as that given by van der Voort in 1977,[81] so there would seem to have been little or no change over a period of 20 years, except for the addition of one subject, stylistics. (The stylistics course requires the students to read about 30 books by Russian authors of the eighteenth, nineteenth and twentieth centuries and to compare their styles. Foreign students are exempt.)

As various observers have pointed out,[82] these are subjects which equip a priest for the basic tasks of parish life, but they do not develop creative thought or enable the future priest to grapple with the problems of society at large and the possible solutions to them which the church might offer. There is no psychology, philosophy or sociology. The student is given a basic knowledge of Holy Scripture, theology, church history, preaching and church singing, liturgy and church practice. This is almost certainly enough to prepare a priest for a life which, as we saw in Chapter 3, consists mainly of sacramental and liturgical activity. It might well be superfluous to teach future priests subjects which they will never have time to make use of in later life. However, it is undeniable that the subjects mentioned, together with the ancient and modern languages and the course in the Constitution of the USSR which complete their syllabus, are all ones which require passive absorption of knowledge rather than a critical or creative approach. As Oppenheim states: 'The Church clearly desires to produce priests who will throw themselves completely into their huge tasks, rather than sit pondering.'[83] To put it another way, the curriculum is clearly designed to produce priests who will continue church life along the lines laid down, rather than attempting any reforms or endeavouring to see beyond the church walls to the spiritual needs of society as a whole.

Van der Voort recorded that a good deal of time was spent on study. The students had to write two long essays a year, and in the first and second year of the academy they had to preach two sermons a year in the church. In the fourth year, lectures were given only on three days, and the other three were devoted to the writing of a thesis. He considered that 'Too much is built upon old-fashioned, rather ineffective lectures.' However, he noted that improvements were in progress, and that seminars, for which the students had to prepare more actively, had been introduced. He remarked that 'the lessons in modern languages are almost completely ineffective', and that the examinations, which were all oral according to the usual Russian pattern, were conducted in a lax manner. Again, however, improvements were being made 'because of stricter control by the professors at the instigation of the new rector, Archbishop Kirill'. In fact, van der Voort's time at the Leningrad academy, 1974–7, saw the rectorship pass from the elderly Bishop Meliton, who did not have an academic background, to Archbishop Kirill, a gifted scholar. It seems probable that Kirill, as the protégé of Metropolitan Nikodim, who always took the greatest interest in the theological schools, has been brought in to improve the academic standards of the schools. Van der Voort also noted that at this time a decision was taken that not all fourth-year academy students would be eligible to write a thesis for the degree of candidate in theology, as previously, but only those whose essays during the previous three years had been of a satisfactory standard, in order to raise the standards of the academy.[84]

Archbishop Kirill certainly seems aware of the need for change:

It was Metropolitan Nikodim's achievement to begin the process of change, to attract new colleagues, to open wider the doors of our institutes. Today a quarter of the students here are mature students, holder of university diplomas, doctors, mathematicians, and electronic specialists. This has greatly raised the level of discussions and of teaching. This allows us to form new theologians capable of beginning the spiritual renewal of the Church, in such a way that it will be open to the world, that it will not be a ghetto or a museum.[85]

It is not yet clear to what extent these radical ideas have been implemented. The proportion of well-educated Soviet students is higher than indicated in earlier sources, and if Archbishop Kirill's statement is true, there must have been some relaxation in the control of incoming students by the KGB and the CRA. No doubt Kirill will have to struggle against the CRA if he intends to stop the church being a 'ghetto or a museum', as the CRA's comments below on the theological schools' syllabus indicate. However, foreign visitors have been impressed with the increasingly lively atmosphere at the Leningrad Theological Schools.

However, this promising situation was ended rather abruptly in

December 1984, when he was transferred from Leningrad to be bishop of Smolensk diocese.[86] This was part of a transferral of several bishops (see Chapter 8, pp. 246–50, for further details). Archbishop Kirill's successor was not nominated at the time of his transfer.

Less is known of the methods of teaching and the standards attained at the Moscow Theological Schools. Archbishop Vladimir, the rector from 1973 to 1982, was said to be a scholarly man.[87] His successor was Archmandrite Alexander Timofeyev, previously the assistant rector, of whom little is known. The only comments we have on the student's ability date from 1965, when Anatoli Levitin wrote with the most scathing contempt of the student's utter ignorance of basic religious knowledge.[88] It is probable that standards have improved since then, but we do not know to what extent.

The fact that two able and academically gifted rectors of the two largest theological schools have been replaced recently by two less distinguished persons has given rise to disquiet. It suggests that the CRA has observed determination to improve this aspect of church life (as evidenced by Kirill's comments quoted above) and has decided to curtail it.

A criticism made in the Yakunin Report concerns the compulsory lectures to students given by professional atheist workers, usually from the *Znaniye* (Knowledge) society. Referring in particular to lectures given to those on the postgraduate course (*aspirantura*), he writes:

> The ideological content of these lectures is that of Marxist–Leninist ideology. As a result of mastering this material, the students experience an erosion of their religious consciousness, a reduction of their religious activism, a spiritual disarming in the face of their ideological opponents. In this way the ground is prepared for making use of the student for activity contrary to his religious conscience.[89]

These are students whose minds the state is particularly anxious to form because they will be working in important posts such as the foreign relations department of the church. It is not difficult to see that constant exposure to lectures with a subtle ideological slant could imperceptibly work their way into a student's thinking, and it is clear from the CRA Report that this is what is intended. However, it may be that the compulsory lectures given by *Znaniye* society lectures do not always have the desired effect. Van der Voort wrote of these occasions:

> waves of Soviet patriotism clash against the walls and drown the innocent listeners. Still, the effect of these efforts is minimal. At the end, when the lecturer asks if there are any questions, deep silence dominates the hall. Once, even, a voice was heard: 'Everything is clear. Let's go to dinner.'[90]

The CRA Report for 1974 states that such lectures, and also films and other means, are one of the methods it adopts to ensure the 'patriotic upbringing of future pastors'. To this end, the CRA commissioners and local authorities 'carry on systematic political work among the lecturers and students of the theological schools', which also includes 'individual and confidential conversations'.[91] The CRA also concerns itself with the content of the syllabus. It claims that it participates in the selection of lecturers, reviews text-books on 'a series of church subjects' in 'the interests of the State', has examined the text-book used for the course on the Constitution of the USSR, and was responsible for introducing a course on the history of the USSR.[92] The Report gives as an example of its work some new topics which were introduced into the moral theology course by Metropolitan Alexi. In December 1974 he visited the CRA office to show them what he proposed, and they approved, noting that 'The programme pays great attention to explaining the duties of believers with regard to the people and the State'. The CRA summarises its objectives in influencing the syllabus as being

> to influence the future servant of the cult in the direction which is necessary for us, to enlarge his theoretical and practical knowledge in a materialistic spirit. This, in our view, will undermine the religious and mystical ideals of the future pastor; it may lead, along with other objective and subjective factors, to an understanding of his own useless-ness as a servant of the cult.[93]

This statement indicates that the state, not content with influencing the selection of students and recruiting informers from their midst, is deter-mined to extend its ideological influence even to the knowledge and ideals which will form the basis of the future priest's life. It must be difficult for the students, especially the very young and inexperienced ones, to realise the direction in which they are being led. However, the CRA itself admits that its policy is not totally successful. It quotes two brief speeches, one by Metropolitan Nikodim at Leningrad, and one by Archbishop Vladimir in Zagorsk, in which they urge the students to be firm and steadfast in their faith and to remember that 'as well as the earthly homeland, there is also the Eternal, Heavenly one'. This remark detracts from the primacy which the CRA, and indeed Soviet society as a whole, constantly gives to the virtue of patriotism and love for the Soviet motherland, and the CRA Report does not fail to comment indignantly upon it. It notes that leaders of the theo-logical schools

> aspire to educate pastors in a spirit of 'courageous steadfast faith' and even renunciation of earthly life . . . and to direct their thoughts 'to the eternal, heavenly homeland'. In this way . . . they are pursuing church interests above all. They say they are against mysticism, but in fact they are sowing it constantly.[94]

There is clearly a subtle but powerful ideological struggle constantly taking place within the theological schools, and their leaders have to tread a metaphysical tightrope with skill and care. The setting for this struggle is the minds of committed young men who, wanting only to equip themselves to serve their church, find themselves preyed upon by the state and under the spiritual guidance of men who must make at least the appearance of concessions to the state's ideological requirements. It would not be surprising if at least some of them became hopelessly muddled in this spiritual tug-of-war.

Despite these difficulties, however, both Oppenheim and van der Voort are optimistic about the future of the theological schools. Van der Voort concludes: 'Of course, the situation is far from ideal, but the developments which are taking place are absolutely positive.'[95] This seems to us a reasonable summing-up. While not wishing to minimise the restrictions and state interference which certainly exist, we feel it is clear that the church is making the maximum use of the limited opportunities available to it in this area. The theological schools, beleaguered though they are, are currently the brightest spot on the Moscow Patriarchate's horizon.

Appendix: Numbers of Theological Students in the Russian Orthodox Church

Table 4.1

Year	Source of information	Moscow Sem.	Acad.	Leningrad Sem.	Acad.	Odessa	Corresp. course	Total
1971–2	Hines visit[1]	250		180				
1972–3	Rigby visit[2]	170	90	?250		150	500	1,160
1973–4	*One Church*[3]					120		
	Oppenheim[4]	180	122	125	52	117	600	1,196
	CRA Report[5]					510		
	IHT (Archbishop Vladimir)[6]	300		?300		about 150		(750)
1974–5	CRA Report[7]	171	96	119	62	118		(566)
	Kathpress[8]					150		
1975–6	Australian Anglican visit[9]				130[a]	140		
1977	*Sputnik*[10]	about 200	100				720	
1977	*Pospielovsky*[11]	788					814	1,602
1978–9	*Der Sonntag*[12]	404		300		200	820	1,724

Table 4.1 — continued

Year	Source of information	Moscow		Leningrad		Odessa	Corresp. course	Total
		Sem.	Acad.	Sem.	Acad.			
1979–80	Metropolitan Filaret[13]	1,013					900	1,913
	Sabant[14]	400		300 (+48 foreign)		200	800	1,748
	Confidential source[15]	1,250[b]		333		245	800	(2,628)
	La Libre Belgique[16]	450		350		450[b]	800	(2,050)
	Catholic Herald[17]	500					800	
1980–1	Archbishop Khrizostom[18]	900					1,100	2,000
1981–2	Pospielovsky[19]			400				
	Archbishop Pitirim (*Catholic Herald*)[20]							2,000
	Archbishop Vladimir[21]	360	120				900	
	Ostkirchliche Information[22]	610						
	Archbishop Kirill[23]			438				
1982	*The Orthodox Church in Russia*[24]						900	
1983–4	Rigby visit[25]	500					800	

Notes:

[a] This figure probably refers to the seminary only, although this is unclear in the source cited.

[b] Figure regarded as erroneous.

Note: Some of the sources below give only partial information (for example, a visitor may have visited only one of the three theological schools) and some columns are therefore left blank. Consequently, some of the figures in the totals column are incomplete, and these are in parentheses. Some sources break down the figures for the seminaries and academies, and others composite them.

Sources: (1) From the 'Report of Bishop J. E. Hines' Trip to Moscow', June 1972, pp. 11, 12; copy in KC archive. (2) Professor T. H. Rigby, Australian National University, Canberra, letter to the present author, 14 May 1984; in KC archive. (3) *One Church*, no. 1 (1973), p. 44. (4) *RCL*, vol. 2, no. 3 (1974), pp. 5, 7, 8. (5) *Vestnik RKhD*, no. 130 (1979), pp. 317, 324. (6) Russian Orthodox Seminary Has Too Many Candidates', *International Herald Tribune*, 19 June 1974 (interview with the rector, Archbishop Vladimir). (7) See source 5. (8) *Kathpress*, 12 April 1975. (9) A. Nichols, 'Documentary Record on the Australian Anglican Delegation's Visit to the Soviet Union, Poland and Yugoslavia', 14 June–4 July 1976 (typescript in KC archive), p. 10; and 'The Church in the Soviet Union', *Southern Cross*, August 1976, p. 4. (10) Yuri Trofimov (of Novosti Press Agency), *Sputnik*, August 1977, p. 23. (11) D. Pospielovsky, *The Russian Church under the Soviet Regime* (St Vladimir's Seminary Press, Crestwood, New York, 1984), p. 407. (12) *Der Sonntag* (East German newspaper), 19 November 1978.

(13) Metropolitan Filaret of Minsk and Belorussia, replying to questions during a visit to France, *Russkaya mysl*, 20 December 1979, p. 5. (14) Philippe Sabant, 'Religion in Russia Today', *The Tablet*, 19 January 1980, p. 55. (15) Information supplied confidentially by a visitor to the USSR, report dated 19 November 1979; in KC archive. (16) *La Libre Belgique*, 12 October 1979, p. 12. (17) Frances Gumley, 'In the Heart of Holy Russia', *Catholic Herald*, 17 October 1980. (18) *The Orthodox Church*, February 1981, pp. 1, 5; *KNS*, no. 121 (9 April 1981), p. 8; *Kathpress*, 10 April 1981, Nr. 70/Seite 40. (19) See source 11. (20) *Catholic Herald*, 19 November 1980. (21) Interview while visiting Munich, *Informationsdienst G2W*, no. 16 (5 October 1981), p. 6. (22) *Ostkirchliche Information*, 81−X/7. (23) Television interview, spring 1982, for the film *Candle in the Wind*, Pacem Productions, California; typescript in KC archive. (24) Archbishop Pitirim, *The Orthodox Church in Russia* (Thames & Hudson, London, 1982), p. 245. (25) See source 2.

Comments on Table 4.1

The figures for 1979−80 are rather confusing. The discrepancies in the figures given by the four foreign sources (14−17) show that even the best-informed visitors to the Soviet Union cannot be sure that they will be given reliable information. Sabant appears to have rounded his figures downwards and has come up with a lower total than the others. Sources 15 and 16 contain what must, in the light of the overall pattern exhibited by the other sources, be gross errors (marked with superscript[b] in Table). However, if we take the more plausible figures from these two sources and composite them, i.e. 450 students in Moscow, 333 in Leningrad and 245 in Odessa, we arrive at a total of 1,028 residential students, which is very close to the figure of 1,013 students given by Metropolitan Filaret. It therefore seems reasonable to assume that there were just over 1,000 residential students in 1979−80.

We cannot, however, be sure whether there were 800 or 900 correspondence students during the same year; the unanimity of the four foreign sources (14−17) is striking, but we know of no reason for discounting Metropolitan Filaret's higher figure. A total of 1,800 or 1,900 students for 1979−80 is therefore indicated.

The figures given by Archbishop Khrizostom for 1980−1 continue the overall upward trend by increasing the total to 2,000 students. However, this figure, rather oddly, represents a decrease of about 10 per cent in the number of residential students. If this is accurate, it would represent a reversal in the trend of recent years. Moreover, it is doubtful whether Khrizostom's figure of 1,100 correspondence students can be correct, given that Archbishop Vladimir the following year reverted to the previous, lower figure of 900 correspondence students. Possibly the Western source which quoted Khrizostom got his two figures the wrong way round. The figures given for the following years, though fragmentary, suggest that numbers have continued to rise slightly, though the figures given by the most recent source (25) seem to indicate a decrease. It remains to be seen whether the decrease will continue or not.

However, the uncertain question of the correspondence course students complicates these calculations. Such figures as we have suggest that the numbers of graduates annually may in fact be lower than the figures we have estimated above. Oppenheim (source 4) said that there were 600 correspondence students in 1973–4, all but two of whom were ordained. This means that 598 priests of the 5,994 claimed in the CRA Report would not be new priests upon graduation. Pospielovsky (source 11) states (without giving a source) that there were 276 graduates in 1979, but adds that in addition another nearly 200 'home-educated' men were ordained priests, making a total of at least 426. Presumably by 'home-educated' he refers to the students on the correspondence course; if so, his figures fit in as well as can be expected with the estimated one-quarter of students the appendix lists for 1978–9 (source 12) who would have graduated in summer 1979. However, a visitor to Zagorsk in spring 1984 (source 25) was told that there were about 60–70 graduates from the seminary and 30–40 from the academy each year. Given that the best seminary students go on to the academy, and that the academy students do not all go to parishes, it would seem best to take the number of seminary graduates as the number of new parish priests per year, that is, not more than about 200 a year from the three seminaries. This is much less than the figure of 500 graduates a year we have estimated above. It would appear, therefore, that the figure given to the 1984 visitor was not including correspondence students (if not, the number of graduates would be less than the 276 reported in 1979).

5 MONASTICISM

Monasticism has been an integral part of Russian Orthodox Christianity from the earliest times. The great Russian monks of old sought solitude in Russia's vast forests, where they lived in isolation and hardship for many long years, conquering the flesh and subduing the passions, and, in the words of St Serafim of Sarov, 'acquiring the Holy Spirit of God'.[1] As they grew in spiritual wisdom and insight, the people began to come to them for guidance, and so was born the tradition of the *starets* or elder, the discerning man of God to whom many came for advice, and to whom some entrusted their entire lives. The great monastic saints are still deeply loved among the Russian people, and the monastic communities they founded still attract many thousands of pilgrims on the great feast days. St Feodosi (Theodosius), founder of the first of the monasteries of ancient *Rus*, the Monastery of the Caves in Kiev, St Sergi of Radonezh, who founded the great spiritual centre of Sergievo, now renamed Zagorsk (after an old Bolshevik!), and the humble eighteenth-century hermit, St Serafim of Sarov, belong not only to the church, but are also part of the history and culture of the Russian and Ukrainian nations; princes as well as peasants came to seek their counsel, and their words affected national as well as individual destinies. In later times, *starets* Amvrosi (Ambrose) of the Optina monastery, through his spiritual counselling of several of the great nineteenth-century writers, including Dostoyevsky and Tolstoy, continued the tradition of influencing secular as well as religious life. Today the spiritual achievements and insights of the great monks, saints and elders of the past continue to make a significant contribution to the distinctive nature of Russian spirituality, but monasticism as an institution survives only in a severely attenuated form.

The Russian Orthodox Church currently has six monasteries and ten convents within the Soviet Union. There are communities of nuns accommodated on the premises of two of the monasteries, so that there are twelve communities of nuns altogether. The monasteries are: the Holy Trinity (*Troitsky*) Monastery of St Sergi at Zagorsk; the Monastery of the Caves (*Pechersky*) near Pskov in northern Russia, close to the Estonian border; the Monastery of the Dormition (*Uspensky*) in Pochayev, in western Ukraine; the Monastery of the Dormition in Odessa, on the Black Sea; the Monastery of the Holy Spirit (*Svyato-dukhovsky*) in Vilnius, Lithuania; and the Monastery of the Dormition in Zhirovitsy, Belorussia; the two last accommodate communities of nuns. The convents are: the Convent of the Protecting Veil of Our Lady (*Pokrovsky*) and the Convent of St Florus

(*Florovsky*) in Kiev; the Convent of the Holy Trinity in Korets, Rovno region; the Convent of the Nativity (*Rozhdestvensky*) in Alexandrovka, Odessa region; the Krasnogorsk Convent of the Protecting Veil of Our Lady in Zolotonosha, Cherkassy region; the Convent of St Nikolai in Mukhachevo, in the Trans-Carpathian region; the Convent of the Ascension (*Voznesensky*) in Chumalevo, also in Trans-Carpathia (these seven convents are all in Ukraine); the Convent of the Ascension in Zhabka, near Kishinyov, Moldavia; the Convent of the Dormition in Pühtitsa, Estonia; and the Convent of the Holy Trinity and St Sergi in Riga, Latvia.[2] (There are also a handful of monks and nuns who have gone from the Soviet Union to the Monastery of St Panteleimon on Mount Athos and the Convent in Jerusalem.)

It will be clear from this list that the tradition of specifically Russian monasticism is now limited to the monasteries at Zagorsk and Pskov. There are no monastic communities in the whole of the Soviet Union east of Zagorsk; and there are no nuns at all on Russian soil. (The convent at Pühtitsa, Estonia, is, however, very Russian in atmosphere, and many Russians visit it.) Ukraine, with its two monasteries and seven convents, has become the bulwark of monastic life in the USSR. The concentration of monastic life in the western republics follows the pattern of church distribution, and for the same reason, the revival of church life in areas occupied by the Germans during the Second World War and the continuing church life in the territories acquired after the war. The 1,105 monasteries and convents existing in 1917 had been reduced to 352 only three years later,[3] and had all been closed down by 1929.[4] The present-day monasteries and convents, with the exception of the one at Zagorsk, are all in areas occupied during the war, where monks and nuns were able to revive their communal monastic life.[5] The post-war boundaries of the USSR incorporated 104 monastic institutions, according to the CRA, of which 88 had already existed in the newly acquired territories and 16 had been founded during the war in the territory under German occupation.[6] However, this number declined steadily during the post-war period: there were about 90 monasteries and convents during the 1950s[7] and by 1958 the church itself claimed only 69.[8] This is in contrast to church life in general during the 1950s, when, as we have seen in previous chapters, church institutions were mostly stable after the post-war renaissance of church life. The monasteries and convents were a prime target of the anti-religious campaign which commenced at the end of the decade. The majority of those remaining were closed, sometimes overnight and with great brutality.[9] In 1961, part-way through the anti-religious campaign, the church claimed 40 monastic institutions.[10] By 1977, according to a church source, there were 16 monasteries and convents, including the one in Jerusalem.[11] (This means that one of the 16 monasteries and convents in the USSR which we have listed above is not included in this total, but it is not clear which one was omitted.)

The monasteries and convents are nowhere mentioned in Soviet legislation on religion, and thus have no legal rights. This makes it simple for the Soviet authorities to close them down, should they choose to do so; it is done by administrative *fiat*. There is no central organisation of monastic life through the Moscow Patriarchate: each monastery or convent is the responsibility of the diocese in which it is situated. Diocesan bishops visit them quite frequently, judging by reports in the *Journal of the Moscow Patriarchate*.

The Monastic Communities

Much of the information in the description of the monastic communities which follows is based on firsthand accounts by three foreigners who visited various monasteries (Philippe Sabant, James Moss and Paul Masson), and on a carefully researched article using church and other sources by Marite Sapiets. The disparate figures they give for the numbers of monks and nuns show that even personal visitors cannot be sure of receiving accurate information, and that we cannot be sure how many monks and nuns are still active in the USSR.

The best-known and best-loved of the present monasteries is the one founded by St Sergi at Zagorsk, which attracts up to 15,000 pilgrims on major festivals such as St Sergi's Day on 11 July.[12] There were reported to be 80 or 90 monks a few years ago.[13] In 1983, however, there were said to be 'over a hundred'; most unusually, this figure was given in the official *Journal of the Moscow Patriarchate*.[14] Monastic life here is much more open to public view than at the other monasteries and convents: large numbers of Soviet and foreign tourists are present at the services celebrated regularly at the fine old churches in the monastery grounds. The close association with the theological seminary and academy, whose alumni replenish the monastic community, give it a scholarly atmosphere. The closure of this monastery after the Revolution is poignantly described in a *samizdat* biography of the last monk to live there, Father Zachariah.[15] It is the only monastery not situated on territory occupied during or acquired after the war which has reopened and continued to function: it would seem to be its position as an important tourist centre which has won it this concession.

'The Monastery of the Caves, situated in the town of Pechory, near Pskov, celebrated the five-hundredth anniversary of its founding in 1972. It was attacked at various times by Poles, Swedes and Lithuanians, but was never captured. After the Bolshevik Revolution it was incorporated into the republic of Estonia, formed in 1918, and was thus saved from closure. Though the monastery suffered under the Germans during the war, it never closed down, and is thus the only Russian monastery to have remained continuously open since its foundation. Until recently, visitors were shown the caves and catacombs beneath the monastery buildings, where former monks lie buried. Their bodies have not decomposed, which the monks attribute to the grace of God and Soviet scientists attribute to the low humidity of the caves. The number of monks is variously said to be between 60 and 100.[16] The monks are mostly former workers and labourers, not intellectuals, and the former superior, Archimandrite Alipi, was a firm believer in hard work for everyone.[17] A visitor in 1979 reported that the monks spent their time restoring the medieval buildings and constructing new ones, and that they provided for their needs from their farm and gardens.[18] This monastery also attracts thousands of pilgrims each year, especially at the great feasts.

The third most revered of the monasteries is the one in Pochayev in western Ukraine. Photographs of festivals in the *Journal of the Moscow Patriarchate* show that large crowds of pilgrims attend festivals there, especially the feast of the translation of the relics of St Iov (Job), a former superior, on 10 September. However, the number of monks has been very greatly reduced, and the monastery narrowly escaped closure during the anti-religious campaign of the 1960s. Foreign tourists are not invited to visit this monastery. The Pochayev monastery is formally known by the Greek-derived word 'Laura' (*lavra*) traditionally given to large and especially honoured monasteries. It shares this distinction with the Zagorsk monastery and two others which are now closed: the Caves Monastery in Kiev and the St Alexander Nevsky Monastery in Leningrad.[19]

The Dormition Monastery at Odessa, founded in the early nineteenth century, was reopened after the war, when restoration work was carried out, and in the early 1950s substantial additions were made to the buildings. The Patriarch established his summer residence there in 1946, and the Odessa Theological Seminary has been housed there since 1961.[20] Groups of foreign churchmen are sometimes invited here. One of them described the monastery as a self-managed community comprising a farm, olive grove, cherry and nut orchard, grape vines and wine cellar managed by 40 monks and other lay workers. It has its own well and electricity supply, as well as attendant machinery and outhouses. The monks hold their daily liturgy in their own church. The same visitor also reported that the monastery had its own *starets* or elder, a 91-year-old monk named Pimen. 'He has been a monk for 67 years — through a Revolution and two world wars. His eyes were bright and his handshake firm.'[21]

The Dormition Monastery at Zhirovitsy has reportedly come under pressure from the state regional executive committee, which tried to confiscate the monastery bells, buildings and kitchen-gardens. The monastery buildings also house nuns, transferred there after the closure of the Grodno and Polotsk convents.[22] This is against strict monastic rules, but the authorities refuse to give the nuns a separate building. Metropolitan Filaret of Minsk, on a visit to London in 1981, said that the monastic community here consisted of 33 nuns and 15 monks.[23] The Holy Spirit Monastery in Vilnius is also obliged to share its premises with a community of nuns. The existence of two Orthodox monastic communities in Lithuania, an almost completely Catholic country, is somewhat ironic in view of the fact that no Catholic monasteries are allowed there. (There are no Catholic monasteries at all in the Soviet Union.)[24]

The largest of the convents seem to have far more residents than any of the monasteries, though again the figures given by Western commentators and visitors vary considerably. One of the largest is the Convent of the Protecting Veil of Our Lady in Kiev, which was reported to have 245 nuns in 1958,[25] but has now declined to about 100.[26] In 1982 there were 95 nuns, ranging in age from 25 to 95 years of age.[27] They occupy themselves with sacerdotal embroidery, quilting and icon-painting.[28] They also have gardening and baking teams: the latter make 1,000 communion loaves (*prosfora*) for the Kiev churches every day, and as many as 6,000 on feast days.[29] The working day is preceded by private prayer beginning at 4 a.m., then general prayer at 5.30 a.m., an hour's Scripture reading, and the liturgy celebrated by a priest from 7 to 9 a.m. In the evening there is the vigil service (vespers and matins) from 5 to 8 p.m., and the nuns then study their vows for half an hour before retiring to their cells for individual bedtime prayers.[30] Foreign visitors who attended the Saturday-evening vigil service in 1976 recorded that the three-hour service was conducted by four priests and a deacon. The nuns formed two choirs, and nuns from both choirs and members of the congregation of about 200 took part in the readings.[31] Archbishop Makari of Uman, in a television interview in 1982, said that the convent, which was founded in 1889 by a sister of the Tsar, gave help, especially medical aid, to the poor people of Kiev. During the Second World War, under German occupation, the nuns hid Kiev Jews, and also sheltered wounded Soviet soldiers, which earned them the gratitude of Red Army leaders.[32] The Convent of the Protecting Veil of Our Lady is situated on a hill overlooking Kiev, and its buildings are large and well constructed. The smaller Convent of St Florus, by contrast, consists of rather ramshackle buildings situated at the other end of the city, and appears to have fewer visitors.[33] This convent follows the ancient rule of Constantinople, unchanged since its foundation 800 years ago: the nuns rise at 2.30 a.m. and the offices can last for 16 hours. The nuns here also embroider vestments.[34] The number of nuns at St Florus seems to have dropped from 150 or so to less than 100.[35] In a television interview in 1983, Archbishop Makari said that there were 'approximately up to 200 nuns in both of [the Kiev convents]', which in the light of the figures given above, must be taken to mean a total of up to 200 nuns in Kiev.[36]

The Convent of the Nativity in Odessa diocese is situated near the village of Alexandrovka in Bolgrad district, close to the Moldavian border, quite some distance from the Odessa monastery. It is remarkable for being the only one of the present monastic communities to have been founded since 1917. A monastery was founded here in 1924, and in 1934 it was reorganised as a convent; this was before its post-war incorporation into Soviet territory. It was renovated considerably in 1969. The nuns work in the vineyards and fields of a nearby collective farm. They are of mixed nationalities — Russian, Ukrainians, Moldavians, Bulgarians and Gagauz (a national group from Moldavia) — and church services are held in Church Slavonic, Moldavian and Gagauz. There are said to be 40 or 50 nuns here.[37]

The Convent of St Nikolai in Mukhachevo has about 100 nuns.[38] It is not known how many there are in the other Trans-Carpathian convent, in Chumalevo, nor in the two remaining Ukrainian convents, in Krasnogorsk and Korets. One source has said that these communities have 15–35 nuns each,[39] which, if true, would represent a very significant decline from the numbers in 1970 as given in the CRA Report.[40] The Korets convent has two choirs renowned for their singing, and the nuns divide their activities between making vestments and working on a nearby collective farm.[41]

The Convent of the Dormition in Estonia is situated at Pühtitsa, which means 'Holy Mountain' in Estonian. The convent was founded in 1891 on the site of a church which was built after the Mother of God was said to have appeared there to some peasants and shepherds at the beginning of the eighteenth century. The nuns spend their time farming, in their own grounds and on a neighbouring state farm.[42] There are between 100 and 150 nuns; the number appears to be declining somewhat.[43]

The convent in Riga has a number of churches and chapels, and also contains a *pustyn* (meaning 'wilderness' or 'hermitage') of the Transfiguration. A *pustyn* contains a smaller number of inmates than the monastic community as a whole and they practise a more ascetic way of life. Sometimes they have little or no contact with other religions or with the outside world. (The Riga hermitage is sometimes counted as a separate institution, bringing the total of convents to eleven.) There were said to be 50 nuns aged between 24 and 90 here in 1980.[44] The convent in Zhabka is the only one remaining in Moldavia of the 15 which are said to have existed there before 1959.[45]

In June 1983, the Danilov Monastery in Moscow was handed back to the Patriarchate by the government, according to an announcement by TASS (the Soviet news agency), and was to be used as an administrative centre.[46] Subsequent reports in the *Journal of the Moscow Patriarchate* gave detailed information about the history and architecture of the monastery, and the uses to which it would be put. The monastery, the oldest in Moscow, was founded in the thirteenth century by Grand Prince Daniil Alexandrovich, also the founder of the Moscow Kremlin, who is buried in the monastery. It is situated on the River Moscow, just over three miles from the Kremlin. Restoration and rebuilding at the monastery complex will apparently be very extensive, but it is hoped that it will be completed by 1988, in time for the celebration of the church's millennium. The restoration is the responsibility of the Executive Committee for the Reception and Restoration of the Danilov Monastery, headed by Metropolitan Alexi of Tallinn, the chancellor of the Moscow Patriarchate. In September 1983, he reported to the Holy Synod that restoration had commenced, a group of architects and engineers had been convened for the purpose, and a new bank account had been opened to receive donations to finance the work. Apparently, donations were already being received from 'diocesan bishops, superiors of monasteries and convents, priests, church councils and lay people'. It is intended that the monastery complex will accommodate the official residence of the Patriarch, some institutions of the Holy Synod, and, on an adjacent plot of land, a conference hall for 'religious and peace-making conferences'.[47]

The superior of the Danilov Monastery, Archimandrite Yevlogi, was born in 1937. He has spent much of his life at the Moscow Theological Academy at Zagorsk, where he was awarded a master's degree in 1979 for a dissertation on Orthodox monasticism, and became a professor in 1980. He was responsible for the new building work carried out recently at Zagorsk.[48] It is not yet clear how many other monks there are at the monastery. One report in the *Journal of the Moscow Patriarchate* spoke rather vaguely of other 'residents' of the monastery.[49] Another report described services attended by monks of the monastic community there, without giving any numbers. The English edition of the *Journal of the Moscow Patriarchate* referred to them as 'monks', while the Russian edition described them only as 'residents'.[50] The church describes the Danilov Monastery as a 'spiritual and administrative centre', and so it appears to be; time will show whether or not the putative small number of monks will be expanded to make it a fully fledged monastery.

The CRA Report on the Monastic Communities

It will be clear from the various figures quoted above concerning the numbers of monks and nuns that accurate information is virtually unobtainable. Church sources give no statistical information about the monastic institutions, and no list of them has been published. Although it is possible to compile a list by careful reference to the *Journal of the Moscow Patriarchate* over a period of some years, this source gives no indication of the number of inmates of each institution. It is therefore almost impossible to say whether the number of monks and nuns is stable, increasing or declining. The only figure we have which seems likely to be reliable is the total of 1,275 monks and nuns given in the CRA Report for 1970:[51] over three-quarters were nuns. The same report states that there were 1,273 monastics in 1968.[52] This modest increase over two years in fact involved a decline in numbers at most of the communities, accompanied by an increase of 19 nuns at the Riga convent and one monk at Zagorsk. (It seems likely that the growth in the number of nuns at Riga was linked with the presence of the *starets* Tavrion, a popular holy man, who arrived there in 1968. (See pp. 147–8).) These may have been nuns transferred from other convents rather than new recruits, since the CRA records only one novice at Riga in 1970. It is clear that the CRA was unable to carry out its stated intention of reducing the number of monastics[53] during this two-year period, but neither did it permit any increase. However, the Yakunin Report in 1979 gave an estimated total of about 1,500 monks and nuns, which would represent an increase; but no source is given for this figure.[54] It is possible that the CRA Report gave lower figures than the true ones, but that is unlikely since, as we have seen, the figures it gave in 1970 for each individual institution are generally speaking higher than the current estimates we have quoted (see note 40). (The one exception is Zagorsk, where the number of monks increased from 53 in 1970 to an estimated 80 at present; this means that the community has nearly attained its 1958 size — see p. 133.) This would appear to constitute a general pattern of decline in numbers, in which case the Yakunin Report's estimate may be over-optimistic.

The CRA Report contains an important section on the monasteries as they were at the end of 1970, giving detailed information on the numbers of monks and nuns, their ages, educational levels, etc., and also on the income and expenditure of all the monasteries and convents. The aim of this section of the report is clearly to show that monasticism is on the decline, and that the CRA is actively assisting this decline. The opening paragraphs where this is evident are, however, somewhat ambivalent. After a brief historical introduction which makes it clear that the monasteries were regarded as counter-revolutionary centres, and only exist at all in the Soviet Union as a result of the Second World War, the report continues:

> In our times, the monasteries are thoroughly obsolete (*gluboki perezhitok*). And although they still continue to receive material support from the believers, they do not receive the chief thing — new members of the monastic communities. The monks are a degenerating category, which has no reserves.[55]

This makes it seem that monastic life is dying out because of a dearth of novices, not for any other reason. There are in fact some novices, as the CRA Report itself and a few other sources indicate, although their numbers are not known. However (as we shall see below), there are clearly more novices than the CRA is willing to admit. It would be a mistake to attribute the decrease of monasteries and monastics in the USSR to a decline in the number of novices alone, as a following paragraph of the CRA Report makes clear:

Guided by instructions of the directing bodies significant local work has been carried out in recent years to reduce the network of monasteries. For this purpose, use has been made of the increased influence of the Council for Russian Orthodox Church Affairs on the Patriarchate and the episcopate. Several dozen monasteries were closed by the hands of the churchmen.

One of the closed monasteries was the oldest of all the great monasteries of ancient *Rus*, the Kiev Monastery of the Caves, a great centre of pilgrimage for centuries. The CRA Report has this to say of its closure:

In 1963, the Kiev Monastery of the Caves, which attracted up to 500,000 pilgrims a year, was closed on a specious excuse (*pod blagovidnym predlogom*) (landslips in the caves, the necessity for examining the earth and for restoration).[56]

The CRA sums up by saying that 'as a result of rather complicated and delicate work, the network of monasteries has been sharply reduced',[57] and provides tables demonstrating the decline. These show that between 1939 and 1968, as well as the decline in the number of monasteries which we have already noted, the number of monastics declined from 5,100 to 1,273, and the total number of pilgrims visiting all the monasteries combined at the great feasts declined from more than 100,000 to up to 20,000.[58]

Another table in the CRA Report indicates that the age level of the remaining monastics is high, and higher than it had been ten years previously. The percentages for the age ranges in 1968 are as follows, with the percentages for 1958 in parentheses: up to 40 years: 17 per cent (26.9 per cent); from 40 to 60 years: 29 per cent (27 per cent); over 60 years: 54 per cent (46.1 per cent). The sharp reduction in the percentage of monastics aged under 40 would appear to indicate that younger people have not been applying for admission, or have been refused admission, to convents and monasteries. The CRA indicates that it has played a part in this:

On the recommendations of the Council, the Moscow Patriarchate has forbidden the tonsuring as monks of persons less than 30 years old. Measures have been taken to expel undesirable elements from the monasteries.[59]

The CRA also notes that the educational level of the monastics is generally low: more than 1,000 are barely literate or have primary education; 175 have secondary education, or incomplete secondary education; and only

14 have higher education or incomplete higher education.[60]

The CRA notes, however, that the church is trying to combat the low educational levels and the increasing preponderance of elderly monastics by concentrating its attention on the two monasteries situated close to theological schools:

the Moscow Patriarchate is paying more attention to the male monasteries in Zagorsk and Odessa. Here more than half of the 93 monks have secondary or incomplete secondary education, and rejuvenation is taking place.

A table comparing the age ranges in 1958 and 1968 in these two monasteries shows that in Zagorsk the percentages of monks under 40 increased from 40 to 84 per cent and in Odessa it increased from 25.4 to 41 per cent (though the overall number of monks dropped sharply during the same period: from 85 to 52 in Zagorsk, and from 59 to 41 in Odessa).[61]

The CRA is in two minds as to whether this is or is not a desirable development from its own point of view. On the one hand, it admits that the increasing youth and higher educational level of monks in these two places is useful, because of 'the necessity of attracting them into work with foreigners, for which young, well-prepared cadres who have been examined in the appropriate manner are more suitable.'[62] This is a clear admission that the CRA is involved in selecting people who represent church life to foreigners in a manner of which the state approves. On the other hand, the CRA is uneasy because 'the rejuvenation of the monastic body and its growth by the addition of people who have graduated from the Zagorsk seminary and academy unquestionably strengthens the monasteries.'[63] The report notes that 46 of the 52 monks at Zagorsk are also priests, and 17 of them have achieved the degree of candidate of theology. They all officiate at services in the monastery's six churches, and 15–20 of them daily hear individual confessions of the pilgrims from different parts of the country, 200,000 of whom visit the monastery every year. The CRA is clearly anxious about the opportunities these educated young priests have to influence large numbers of people from all over the USSR. Similarly at Odessa, 26 of the 41 monks are ordained and actively participate in church services.

It is noteworthy that the CRA Report has little or nothing to say about nuns, even though its own figures show that they constitute over three-quarters of all monastics. As its preoccupation with rejuvenation at Zagorsk and Odessa shows, the CRA is worried about the possible growth in influence of young monks, but does not appear to think that the far larger number of nuns will have any influence on society. This is a realistic view in so far as monks are able to become priests, bishops and even *startsy*, while nuns are not, and therefore the role of monks within, and possibly even outside, the church is potentially more significant. However, it seems possible that the CRA's total failure to consider the role of nuns reflects a probably unconscious assumption that the role of women is inherently less significant than that of men. The CRA Report does not reflect the same anxiety over 'losing' women to the convents as it does over 'losing' male members of Soviet society to the monasteries. This view may underlie an error in the CRA Report: in the tabulation of the numbers of monastics at the 16 monastic institutions, the CRA incorrectly lists them as 3 monasteries and 13 convents (instead of 6 monasteries and 10 convents). It is true that two of the monasteries contain communities of nuns, but this is hardly sufficient justification for calling them convents. It appears that the CRA wishes the Central Committee of the CPSU to believe that the number of monks is declining more sharply than the number of nuns.[64]

The CRA Report contains an interesting table giving otherwise unobtainable information on the finances of the monasteries and convents.[65] They receive no financial support from the Moscow Patriarchate or from the administration of the diocese in which they are situated. Their income, according to the CRA Report, consists of revenue from the sale of candles (about half of the total income), and, in roughly equal amounts, fees for performing rituals, revenue from sale of other ritual objects, offerings, and donations received through the post. This means that the monasteries and convents are entirely supported by the believing population who visit them or send gifts. In 1970 the total income of the monasteries and convents was 2,499,913 roubles. This large sum of money would surely have been more than sufficient for the overall needs of the monastic communities, even including the maintenance of ancient buildings. We should note that this income is in addition to the total income of the church which we attempted to estimate in Chapter 2, though the monasteries are clearly not able to pass any of it on to other bodies within the church. However, this income is very unevenly divided between the monasteries and convents. Over a million roubles, more than two-fifths of the total, was received by the Zagorsk monastery. The next-largest amounts went to the two Kiev convents (255,000 and 160,000 roubles). On the whole, the monasteries received more income than the convents. It would seem from these figures that a couple of the convents might have experienced financial difficulties: the Mukhachevo convent received about 47,000 roubles for all its 123 inmates, which is less than 400 roubles a year each, and the Chumalevo convent, with 41 nuns, received only 5,093 roubles. It seems odd that these two convents should receive so little, since they are both situated in Trans-Carpathia in Ukraine, where, as we have seen, the Orthodox population is very strong. It may be that, situated as they are in the most westerly part of the USSR, these convents do not attract many pilgrims: people coming from far away would be more likely to go to Pochayev, and not travel the extra distance across the Carpathian Mountains to Mukhachevo and Chumalevo.

The monasteries and convents additionally receive parcels from believers. In 1970, according to the CRA Report, they received a total of 5,733 parcels weighing 39,548 kilograms. Again, the distribution is very uneven: the Pskov monastery received nearly 2,500 parcels and the Pochayev monastery over 1,000, while seven monastic communities (the monasteries at Zagorsk, Odessa, Vilnius and Zhirovitsy and the convents at Korets, Chumalevo and Riga) received none at all. The CRA offers no explanation as to why this should be so. However, it does state that, between 1969 and 1970, the overall income of the monasteries decreased slightly, while the number of parcels they received doubled.

The expenditure of the monasteries and convents during 1970 was 2,324,648 roubles, slightly less than income, and in the case of most of the institutions expenditure and income were roughly equivalent. Expenditure included the expenses of the monks and nuns, the expenses of the priests who serve them, repairs and maintenance of buildings, and deductions for the Peace Fund and the preservation of monuments. This last item (which is not broken down), representing funds paid to state institutions, totals 88,551 roubles or about 4 per cent of total expenditure, much less than in the case of the parishes' contributions to the Peace Fund. All these items of expenditure, however, form less than half of the total expenditure. Nearly 1.5 million roubles of expenditure is listed under 'other expenses', which are not described. We are therefore unable to get a clear overall picture of the monastic communities' expenses. It is difficult to conjecture what other major expenses than those listed above there could be. Possibly this large and vague item of expenditure does include funds paid to the state. It could, for example, include taxes, though there is no indication of what taxes the communities might be liable for. It is not clear whether monks and nuns are liable for income tax: they do not of course receive a personal income, but the state might consider them liable for their share of the communal income. It is also unclear from this table whether monks and nuns who are eligible for old age pensions receive them from the state.

We do not have enough information to be able to comment in detail on what changes, if any, there may have been since the situation described by the CRA in 1970, apart from our suspicion, mentioned above, that the overall number of monks and nuns has probable declined somewhat since then. However, the general summary of the situation in 1979 given in the Yakunin Report indicates that changes have probably been few, and that the control exercised by the CRA was as great as before, if not greater:

From the financial point of view any monastery could support a fraternity many times larger than the present one, but the authorities do not permit it. Any member of the population, before becoming a monk, goes through a probation not so much from the point of view of his suitability for the monastery from the Church and religious side, as from the side of the Council and the KGB.

Despite the existence of many people wishing to enter monasteries, especially young people, the brotherhoods in the monasteries consist chiefly of elderly monks of pensionable age, unfit for work. The monasteries today have in fact turned into semi-invalid homes . . .

Those monks who begin active religious and educational activity and gather many pilgrims around themselves are as a rule sent out of the monasteries to serve in parishes, or else either expelled from the monastery altogether, or forbidden to preach and confess pilgrims.[66]

These restrictions are fully in conformity with the final paragraph of the CRA Report for 1970 on the monasteries, which left no doubt that it intended to continue exercising strict control over monastic life:

The Council for Religious Affairs is currently studying the activity of the monasteries. According to the results of this work, the convention of a group of commissioners is being prepared, at which new measures for strengthening control over the activity of the monasteries and further restricting them, and for reducing their influence on the population, will be proposed.[67]

The Ethos of the Monastic Communities

In many monastic orders around the world a thoroughgoing reappraisal, and in some cases alteration, of the traditional way of life has been occurring in recent years as the communities have sought to express their vocations in ways which they regard as more appropriate to the demands of twentieth-century life. Worship, dress, way of life, even vows, have all come under the closest scrutiny. There has, however, been no sign whatever of this happening in the Russian Orthodox monastic communities in the Soviet Union. Their way of life remains entirely traditional, and the generally conservative attitude often found in the church as a whole is particularly in evidence here. The sense of tradition, of being the successors of the great monks and saints of the past, has always been strong in the Russian Orthodox Church, and it is not surprising to find this being vigorously reasserted in the monasteries as a reaction to the profound social upheavals of the last 60 or so years. This conservatism is both a strength and a weakness. For some it offers an opportunity to escape from the bleak materialism of everyday Soviet life by immersing themselves in the spiritual treasures that have been built up in the past. On the other hand, it makes it easy for the state to present the monasteries to the Soviet population as a complete irrelevance in modern life — 'thoroughly obsolete', in the words of the CRA. The conservatism and otherworldliness of the monasteries have been criticised more than once by *samizdat* writers — for example, Nikolai Shemetov:

Of course there are some genuine zealots in the monasteries, but they are very few . . . The inhabitants are either invalids or spiritually broken people. They live shut away, and fear more than anything to leave the monastery walls. They cannot adapt to life, and are afraid of the world. For them, the last real spiritual mentor was Bishop Ignati (Bryanchaninov). [Bishop of Caucasus and the Black Sea, noted for skilful management of his diocese, author of ascetic and theological works. 1807–67.] Everything which deviates from the ascetic ideal which he outlined is considered a devilish temptation. 'The world is condemned, the end of the world is nigh. We must pray and wait' — that is their credo. All attempts at innovation frighten them . . . Divine services in the Russian language, cultivated by Metropolitan Nikodim [see p. 228], are considered as blasphemous, even though there is a resolution of the Synod headed by Metropolitan Sergi (Stragorodsky) which permits services in Russian. [Orthodox church services are held in Church Slavonic, an archaic language close to Russian, which an average modern Russian can understand, but only with difficulty.][68]

The Yakunin Report speaks in very similar terms of the attitude to be found in the monasteries:

convinced . . . that any struggle apart from prayer is useless, because the whole world lies in evil; . . . neither understanding nor accepting any of the creative tasks facing a Christian at the present time, the Patriarchate's version of monasticism is paralysing the social activism of believers. It directs them only towards individual asceticism, only towards awaiting the imminent end of the world.[69]

However this may be, there is none the less a continuing number of Soviet citizens wishing to dedicate themselves to the monastic way of life. The number of novices officially accepted is tiny, but they continue to come forward. The previous superior of the Pskov monastery told a Western journalist in 1979 that they received two or three novices every year. The novitiate lasts three years, and the novice is entrusted to a spiritual father who guides him in the monastic and religious life.[70] Archbishop Makari of Uman stated that the Convent of the Protecting Veil of Our Lady in Kiev receives novices between the ages of 20 and 50 for a novitiate lasting between one and five years, but gave no indication of numbers.[71] The superior of this monastery, Mother Margarita, stated that she found 'no shortage' of aspiring novices. However, she said that 'not all entrants prove suitable', and added that some 'could not get residence permits to move from the countryside to live in Kiev'.[72] Shemetov noted that the late superior of the Pskov monastery, Alipi, had tonsured about 30 new young monks, but made it clear that this was highly exceptional.[73] We do not know how many novices there are at other monasteries and convents. It is difficult to tell how many would become novices if they were admitted, but there is some evidence, in addition to Father Gleb Yakunin's statement that 'many . . . especially young people' wish to enter monasteries, that a growing number of people feel called to the monastic way of life, and practise it unofficially if they cannot do so officially. Tatyana Goricheva, a young philosopher from Leningrad who spent some time at convents after her conversion to Christianity, has recorded that 'almost all' the pilgrims (of both sexes) who visited the monasteries and convents wanted to become novices. They therefore were professed, but sent to live 'in the world'. Goricheva said that she knew a teacher who was a secret nun, and a doctor who would shortly become a monk.[74] There continue to be reports of secret monastic communities. One example was provided by a report of the brutal destruction of such a community. In October 1983, it was reported that some 18 members of an unofficial monastic community had taken refuge in a cave 60 kilometres from the city of Sukhumi, in Georgia. An incendiary device was dropped from a helicopter and landed at the mouth of the cave, killing everyone inside.[75]

The motivation of those who do enter what the Soviet system considers to be an anachronistic and useless way of life is impossible to analyse. An idea of what these monks and nuns may be seeking is given in a letter to a friend written by a monk in the Pskov monastery, probably during the last ten years or so:

The isolated, silent, withdrawn, God-centred life of a monk is valuable, rich and made joyful by many minutes of God's gracious illumination, knowledge of God and knowledge of self, constituting all his happiness on earth and a pledge of salvation and future bliss in heaven.

A monk is a son who has come to himself, for whom all the past, present and future have blended into one and turned into an endlessly long moment of the sweetest self-oblivion on the Father's breast . . . Although the very aim of monasticism is the renewal by the Holy Spirit of the person who has become a monk, the Holy Fathers suggest that the way to this aim is by penitence and humility, by reaching the point of weeping for oneself, and praying in affliction, by revealing so much sinfulness in oneself that one's conscience will bear testimony that we are abject servants in need of mercy.

What makes monasticism difficult? It is not that all the pleasures and good things of the vain world are forbidden! . . . It is hard because of the constant dissatisfaction in achieving its positive result — closer contact with the Lord and *the sense* of this contact, *the sensation of the Lord within* oneself! . . .

The merging of all three vows (obedience, chastity and poverty) into one whole creates conditions favourable to the attainment of the chief aim of a monk — absence of passion and pure prayer. The worldly think that monks are a useless kind of person, but they are wrong to think this. They do not know that a monk prays for the whole world; they do not see his prayers and do not know how graciously the Lord receives them.[76]

State Repression: Pochayev

The Soviet authorities have at times gone far beyond administrative means in their attempts to restrict monastic life. As mentioned above, brutality was used during the closure of monasteries and convents between 1959 and 1964, and nowhere more so than at the Pochayev monastery. Detailed documentary accounts of the events there have reached the West. According to these lengthy *samizdat* reports, the monastery's plot of land and ancillary premises were taken from it, buildings were confiscated and used for state purposes, pilgrims were hounded from the town, and some women pilgrims were beaten and raped, the monks were disbanded, and some of them were forcibly comitted to psychiatric hospitals and given harmful injections. A monk named Golovanov was reported to have died at the age of 35 as a result of this treatment. Before long, the numbers of monks had been reduced by violence from 144 to 36. The *samizdat* allegations that exceptional violence was used at Pochayev received some backing from a conversation which took place in 1965, after the end of the anti-religious campaign, between Anatoli Levitin and a number of leading atheists, including the deputy editor of the journal *Nauka i religiya* (*Science and Religion*), B. T. Grigoryan. He told Levitin: 'I heard about these shocking things going on at Pochayev earlier than you and . . . I've done more to stop them than you.' Whether this is true or not, it seems probable that the events at Pochayev must have been significantly worse than other incidents of the anti-religious campaign for a leading Soviet official to have been provoked into such a statement.[77]

There have continued to be sporadic incidents of state interference and brutality at Pochayev. In 1973 the abbot and the secretary of the Spiritual Council wrote to the CRA chairman, Kuroyedov, complaining that monastery buildings were being used for a workers' club and a mental hospital, and that constant noise from both of them disrupted worship. Pilgrims had nowhere to stay since the former hostel had been taken over, and moreover there were plans to open a museum of atheism on the premises.[78] Although the abbot subsequently denied having written the letter in an interview,[79] it is probable that he was pressurised into doing so. In any case, reports of the misuse of monastery premises have continued to be made. In 1976 the new abbot complained to the chairman of the regional executive committee that the state was illegally encroaching on monastery premises, and that the monastery garden had been confiscated but had then been allowed to deteriorate.[80] About the same time an old man who had gone to Pochayev in the hope of passing his old age there complained that he had been harassed by the militia, arrested and fined and refused permission to stay at the monastery.[81] In 1977 it was reported that the monks' cells were being entered by agents who wandered around freely, that monks had been threatened with arrest, and that pilgrims were being sent to Pochayev Psychiatric Hospital.[82] In 1978 there was a report that an anti-religious propaganda office had been opened in the monastery grounds.[83] In August 1980 the local militia were reported to have raided the monastery, confiscating documents from pilgrims and expelling those they found there; this apparently continued for some days.[84] This harrassment was continuing against a background of attempts by the church to carry on normal monastic life. There are occasional reports in the *Journal of the Moscow Patriarchate* of solemn festal services carried out with the participation of various Ukrainian bishops[85] and in 1975 it was reported that restoration work had been carried out: the exterior, the monks' cells and the cave church had been repaired, the Cathedral of the Dormition was being restored, and heating had been installed in the Trinity Cathedral, the bell-tower of which had been repaired.[86]

From early 1981, the measures taken against monks and pilgrims at Pochayev became even more brutal. Father Amvrosi, a monk well known throughout the Soviet Union for his powerful preaching and spiritual integrity, came under great pressure from the authorities, including threats of physical violence, and was finally expelled from the monastery on 1 March. Other monks were subjected to repeated questionings and beatings in connection with this. One of them, Archimandrite Alipi, died after repeated beatings, and another, Pitirim, lost his sanity.[87] Four other monks were subsequently expelled, and two of them, Apelli and Nestor, wrote statements of protest to Patriarch Pimen, apparently without result.[88] Hegumen Apelli wrote a further statement, in which he accused the superior of the monastery, Archimandrite Yakov (Panchuk), of conniving in state persecution of some monks. Apelli himself, he wrote, had been expelled from the monastery after learning that Yakov had given the local KGB chief a gift of a car.[89] (Apelli had already served three terms of imprisonment, the last a two-year sentence imposed in 1964.)[90]

Foreign visitors to the monastery in 1984 recorded their very disturbing impressions of what they saw. At the evening service on 20 May, a number of plainclothes militiamen were present, many in a drunken state; they demanded that worshippers present their identity documents, and kicked some of them as they left. The visitors reported that a farm-worker at the monastery who had been sent to a psychiatric hospital for two weeks was later detained again, had both his arms broken, and was returned to the psychiatric hospital. According to this report, 'several pensioners have actually been seized during the services and removed from the cathedral straight to psychiatric hospital'.[91]

These measures equal the worst excesses of the anti-religious campaign of the early 1960s, in intensity if not in scale. In an evident attempt to counter-act them, the Moscow Patriarchate in 1983 issued a small pamphlet about the Pochayev monastery. The first part was devoted to the founding of the monastery and the life of its founder (St Iov of Pochayev, 1551–1651) and the second part to the life of the monastery today.[92]

Interference by the state has occasionally been reported from other monastic communites (especially, recently, Pskov — see below), but nothing as persistent or as virulent as at Pochayev. It is possible that some local factor is involved, some particular animosity towards monks or especial zeal on the part of local officials. Doubtless the monastery's situation in the heartland of Eastern-rite Catholicism exacerbates the situa-tion. It is also possible that Pochayev may have been singled out for harsh treatment because it is less frequently visited by foreigners than the other major monasteries.

State Interference: Pskov

There have been difficulties at Pskov which until recently were of a less dramatic nature. They relate to the present superior, Archimandrite Gavriil, and his predecessor. Archimandrite Alipi (Voronov) was appointed superior in 1959, at the beginning of the anti-religious campaign. He was tonsured monk at the age of 46, after a varied life in the world. He had worked on the construction of the Moscow Metro; he served during the war with a tank regiment which reached Berlin, for which he received a number of decorations; and then he became a professional artist.[93] During the anti-religious campaign he was criticised in a defamatory book about the Pskov monastery. Anatoli Levitin vigorously defended him and other monks in a *samizdat* article.[94] Interestingly, the official obituary of Alipi published in the *Journal of the Moscow Patriarchate* picks up several of the positive characteristics mentioned by Levitin: evidently the Soviet censor had for-gotten or had decided to compensate for the derogatory material published earlier about Alipi. Alipi appears to have been a good superior, respected by the monks in his charge. The CRA, however, objected to him, and its 1970 Report stated unequivocally: 'Measures are being taken to remove' him from the position of superior.[95] Reading between the lines of the CRA's complaints, it is possible to make out that Alipi appears to have been a seriously religious and independently minded man. The CRA states that in a conversation with foreign tourists, Alipi failed to uphold the Soviet view that Israel was an aggressor, and stated instead that he believed that 'Jerusalem, as a holy city, should belong to Israel.'[96] Another complaint was that Alipi attracted young men and adolescents to the monastery with money. Alipi, questioned about this, maintained to the CRA that he was acting solely according to scriptural precepts: 'give to him who asks you, give to him who wishes to enter into debt with you and do not ask for recompense . . . love your neighbour as yourself, if anyone wishes to be rich, give and do not ask to whom you are giving . . . and you will obtain great joy and happiness'.[97] As we saw in Chapter 3, the CRA is very suspicious about the financial transactions of the clergy, and here again it has put the most mischievous construction upon Alipi's actions. Alipi, in totally refusing to consider this side of the question, and in relying upon Scripture, seems to have left it somewhat baffled.

The CRA was for some reason unable to achieve its stated intention of removing Alipi from his post, but when he died in 1975 he was replaced with a superior much more to the CRA's liking, Archimandrite Gavriil (Steblyuchenko). He had received advanced theological education, was a candidate of theology, and had spent a year at the Russian Spiritual Mission in Jerusalem; he was only 34 when appointed superior of the Pskov monastery and could evidently expect a rewarding career in the church.[98] He was, in fact, the greatest possible contrast to Alipi. Gavriil soon won himself a reputation as a strict disciplinarian who restricted the activities of monks and pilgrims alike. A pilgrim named Anastasiya Kleimenova described what a change she found when she went to the monastery to ask the monks to pray with her for the reopening of her church (in Bolshoi Khomutets, Lipetsk region — see Chapter 1, p. 26):

> I was given to understand that the superior Gavriil here was very severe, that he had driven out all the poor people from the cloister, and that he also behaved very severely to the monks. They were all harassed and nervous. The services were not the same as under the late Alipi.

Kleimenova reported that Gavriil would not let the monks pray with her, and physically stopped them when they tried to do so, that he prevented pilgrims from entering parts of the monastery, including the famous caves, and that he eventually called the militia to remove her from the monastery. 'There is an ocean of grace in the Caves cloister,' Kleimenova concluded, 'but it is held back by a dam.'[99]

The Christian Committee for the Defence of Believers' Rights appealed to Patriarch Pimen to remove Gavriil from the Pskov monastery. They wrote:

Archimandrite Gavriil, appointed superior after the death of Archimandrite Alipi against the will of the monastic fraternity, within a short time aroused widespread dissatisfaction both among the inhabitants of the monastery and among the believing pilgrims . . . The activity of Archimandrite Gavriil is directed to stifling church life in the monastery, to creating a harsh environment for the spiritual life of the brothers, and to dispelling the desire of pilgrims to visit the monastery.[100]

Evidently the CRA, despite its failure to remove Alipi, has finally achieved the appointment of a superior to its liking at the Pskov monastery. While it is true that any superior might have aroused antipathy after the popular Alipi, and also that an energetic disciplinarian at its head may be no bad thing for a monastery, the reports of Gavriil's behaviour indicate that his 'discipline' is far too stringent for his unpopularity to be accounted for by either of these factors.

A *samizdat* report dated April 1983 spoke of outright brutality by Gavriil. After drinking heavily, Gavriil and another senior monk reportedly brutally beat up Hieromonk Valeri (Klimov), who had come to Pskov on a pilgrimage from Zagorsk. A novice monk, Alexi, was beaten up the same day. The ensuing uproar was quelled by a detachment of militia, summoned by Archimandrite Gavriil. When they arrived, he 'ordered them around quite confidently'. Earlier, according to the document, Gavriil had insulted an investigator of the Pskov Regional Procuracy seriously enough for the latter to institute legal proceedings, and, on a separate occasion, he had assaulted an army officer who had come to Pskov on leave after serving in East Germany. In neither case was Gavriil punished: both cases were dropped before they reached court. The writers of the document conclude that if Gavriil can behave like this with impunity, then he obviously has protection in high places. This is borne out by the fact that some of the monks have appealed to Metropolitans and even to the Patriarch, but in vain. Metropolitans Alexi of Tallinn and Ioann of Pskov apparently expressed sympathy with monks who petitioned them, but were powerless to help. Numerous petitions to the Patriarch have not exactly fallen on deaf ears, for at one stage he made a resolution to remove Gavriil — but this remained on paper only.[101] Other sources state that after Pimen's resolution, Vice-Chairman Furov of the CRA paid a visit to the monastery, and upon his return the Patriarch's resolution was revoked.[102] Foreign visitors to Pskov in summer 1983 (some of whom had paid previous visits) reported that the atmosphere there had changed beyond recognition. Access for pilgrims was hindered, the monks were virtually afraid to speak to visitors, and the churches, normally very lively even on weekdays, were locked and deserted except during services of worship.[103]

There seems little doubt that Gavriil is a KGB appointee, infiltrated with the aim of undermining one of the Russian Orthodox Church's leading spiritual centres. It would have been possible for the CRA to influence

Gavriil's appointment because all monastic superiors are appointed by the Patriarch and the Holy Synod, over whose decisions the CRA claims to have full control (as we shall see in Chapter 8). This is pointed out in the Yakunin Report:

> the brothers do not voluntarily elect an authoritative monk from among themselves as leader of the monastery, someone they trust, but a 'superior' — a manager of the monastery — is appointed by the central church authority, the Patriarch and the Holy Synod. His candidature can be confirmed not only against the will of the brotherhood in the monastery, but also against the will of the ruling bishop in whose diocese the monastery is situated.[104]

The convents do not in general seem to suffer as much hardship as do the monasteries, but none the less there are occasional reports of difficulties for the nuns created by the state authorities. In 1978 a report stated that all the gardens and grounds belonging to the Korets convent had been confiscated. Abbess Natalya had been informed that no more novices would be given residence permits.[105] In the convent at Zolotonosha, permission had been refused to repair the church, which was a dangerous state, and the nuns were obliged to hold their services in a cramped hut.[106]

Attempts to Reopen the Kiev Monastery of the Caves

Believers have protested to the authorities about the closed monasteries, as well as about conditions at those which remain open. The greatest indignation has been voiced over the Monastery of the Caves in Kiev, the birthplace of Russian Christianity. As we have seen, the CRA admitted in its secret report that it had been closed only under a 'specious excuse', as a means of limiting monastic life. The monastery, which was founded in 1051, was closed in 1929. Some monks returned when the area came under German occupation in 1941, and the monastery was able to continue its life until 1961, when it was closed again during the anti-religious campaign.[107] The monastery was turned into a state museum, and is occasionally mentioned in the Soviet press as a valuable historical site, an important element of the national heritage. However, an article in the Communist Party newspaper *Pravda* in 1978 stated that the museum was being gravely mismanaged. No less than eight organisations were responsible for servicing the monastery, but they were acting independently of one another, with the result that work was proceeding slowly and in slipshod fashion, buildings were falling into disrepair, restoration plans were not materialising, garbage was littering the site, and the garages built by several organisations meant that vehicles were rattling around filling the air with exhaust fumes.[108]

This state of affairs must no doubt have been a galling sight to the former monks. The previous year, twelve of them had appealed to Mr Brezhnev for permission to return to the monastery. They stated that the Orthodox people had repeatedly requested the local authorities to reopen the monastery, but had been told that 'the monks themselves had left and now there is no one wishing to inhabit the monastery', and so 'the people accused us, the monks, of remaining silent and being indifferent to the fate of the monastery. We, however, have only been praying, weeping and waiting.'[109] The monks were supported by three young Orthodox Christians who also wrote to Mr Brezhnev: their letter expressed the reverence they felt for this 'first Russian monastery, the cradle of Russian spiritual life'. They said that if lack of resources was an obstacle to reopening the monastery, they themselves would be ready to gather up donations and go to Kiev to set to work.[110] The Christian Committee also supported the monks; it organised a press conference for Western correspondents at which their letter to Mr Brezhnev was distributed. One of the signatories, Hegumen Akhilla, stated that he had been forcibly committed to psychiatric hospitals three times since 1952.[111] The Christian Committee issued an appeal to all Orthodox Christians in the USSR, urging them to support the reopening of the monastery, and pointing out that it had been the 'spiritual focus' of the early life of the Russian Orthodox Church, whose millennium in 1988 was approaching.[112]

Thus far there has been no sign of any response to these appeals. It will be interesting to see whether the church's millennium is in fact to be celebrated with its most ancient monastery still a garbage-strewn 'museum'. Some hope is provided by a report that another of Russia's most famous monasteries, Optina Pustyn, is currently being extensively renovated, having been devastated by the Bolsheviks in the 1920s. Founded in the fourteenth century, Optina Pustyn reached the height of its fame in the nineteenth century, when it was visited by such leading literary figures as Dostoyevsky, Tolstoy, Gogol and Turgenev. However, it is apparently not to be revived as a monastery, but will house a literary museum.[113]

The Fate of Expelled Monastics: Sister Valeriya Makeyeva

We have very little idea of the fate of the monks and nuns expelled from monasteries and convents at the beginning of the 1960s, of whom there must be several hundreds. It is evident that the twelve monks from the Kiev Caves Monastery have kept in some form of contact, and, according to one report, the monastery's monastic community is still in existence.[114] Moreover, fragmentary information concerning the fate of disbanded monastics has been provided by the sad story of the nun Valeriya Makeyeva.

Although brought up in a family of communist unbelievers, Valeriya Makeyeva was attracted to the Orthodox faith by her grandmother. Her own mother informed on her, and she was sent to prison for five years. On her release in the early 1950s she entered a convent in Zhitomir in Ukraine, where she remained for over ten years, until the convent was disbanded during the anti-religious campaign. She then returned to the flat of her deceased mother in Moscow. This information is contained in an appeal sent to the West by Makeyeva's friends after her arrest in June 1978.[115] She was charged with engaging in illegal commercial activities. On her return to Moscow, Sister Valeriya had formed a group which produced small religious artefacts in great demand by believers, notably monastic belts embroidered with the words of the 91st Psalm (numbered as the 90th Psalm in the Russian Bible): 'He that dwelleth in the secret place of the Most High . . .' These belts, which are worn crosswise over the chest and shoulders under the cassock, are said to be in great demand by disbanded monks and nuns, and also by Orthodox laymen who have taken to wearing them. Sister Valeriya and her helpers sold them for between 50 kopeks and a rouble each. The *samizdat* reports say that in time they accumulated enough money to purchase accommodation for homeless nuns[116] but no details are given of how this was done. Evidently a very large number of religious artefacts would have to have been sold for this to be possible, indicating that the demand for them was large.

Sister Valeriya was brought to trial in April 1979, charged under Article 162, Part 2, of the Criminal Code of the RSFSR for engaging in the illegal manufacture of handicrafts. The maximum penalty under this article is four years' deprivation of liberty, but the court decided to commit Sister Valeriya to a special psychiatric hospital on the basis of a diagnosis that she was a psychopath.[117] Public appeals were immediately made by Father Gleb Yakunin and by Academician Andrei Sakharov, who said he regarded the sentence as a clear-cut case of politically motivated abuse of psychiatry. In September it was reported that Sister Valeriya had been interned in the Kazan Special Psychiatric Hospital and was being given intensive drug treatment which paralysed her right arm and was causing serious degeneration of her general state of health.[118] Despite publicity and protest in Western countries, Sister Valeriya was detained in the Kazan hospital until May 1981, when it was reported that she had been transferred to an ordinary psychiatric hospital in Moscow.[119] (Ordinary psychiatric hospitals are controlled by the Ministry of Health and exist primarily to provide psychiatric care for the local community. Treatment and conditions are far more severe, even brutal, in the smaller number of special psychiatric hospitals, which are controlled by the Ministry of Internal Affairs and are primarily for the compulsory internment of prisoners diagnosed as mentally ill. See Sidney Bloch and Peter Reddaway, *Russia's Political Hospitals*, Futura, London, 1978, pp. 187–96.)

Sister Valeriya's unhappy fate has given us some insight into the lives of the former monastics. Those who were working with her evidently wished to continue their communal lives, and may perhaps still be doing so. Moreover, the widespread demand for the objects this group made indicates that many former monastics are trying to some extent to adhere to their old way of life. One appeal for support for Sister Valeriya was sent to the British Prime Minister, Margaret Thatcher, by Sister Valeriya's aunt, the abbess of her former community. This appeal referred to 'the nuns of the community in Zhitomir who are carrying on the holy work of Sister Valeriya Makeyeva'.[120] It seems clear that many former monastics are adhering to their monastic vows and attempting to keep up some form of communal life, but it is not possible to say how they support themselves, or whether there are sufficient of them to be able to speak of 'underground' monastic communities.

Survival of the Monastic Tradition: *Starets* Tavrion

At the beginning of this chapter we mentioned the *startsy*, or elders, men of recognised authority to whom people come for spiritual counsel. According to Anatoli Levitin, there are one or more of these elders at each of the major monasteries, and also some living in private houses.[121] Little is known of them in the West because publicity about them might attract unwelcome attention from the Soviet authorities. However, we have recently learned from an eyewitness account[122] something of the long and influential ministry of Archimandrite Tavrion (Batozsky), who died in 1978. Born in 1898, Tavrion ran away from home to the Glinsk hermitage at the age of only 13, and lived all his long life as a monk, even during the 27 years, between 1928 and 1956, which he spent in labour camp or exile. Despite the hardships, Tavrion spoke of these as good times; when he was transported through the immense, primordial forests of the Urals and Siberia, he saw it as the answer to his prayers that he be allowed to labour in the impenetrable forests as St Sergi of Radonezh and St Serafim of Sarov had done. On one occasion in northern Russia he and some others discovered a whole train-load of frozen corpses (probably a prisoner transport). Tavrion sang the funeral service for each one and dug a grave. After this memorable experience, he celebrated the liturgy every single day until the end of his life. Tavrion served in many monasteries and parishes in widely scattered parts of the Soviet Union.

Eventually, in 1968, he was invited to be the father confessor of the Hermitage of the Transfiguration in the Riga convent. (This is an informal, purely spiritual post, carrying no temporal authority.) The eyewitness describes how Tavrion's presence transformed the convent:

The convent, until then little known and in a poor state of repair, able to accommodate barely twenty guests at a meal, was transformed into a place of pilgrimage, bursting with tens of thousands of believers from every part of the country. Drawn by tales of this extraordinary *starets*, they flocked from the spiritual desert of contemporary life as to a fount of 'living waters'; the sick, the old, intellectuals from the big cities, peasants, engineers, hippies, workers, all the suffering people. Today, in summer, there are up to two hundred people a day.

The main themes of Tavrion's teaching were the need to steep oneself in the Bible, the spiritual value of taking Holy Communion every day, and the need for ceaseless prayer. His ministry was attended by many of the signs and gifts traditionally present in a *starets*, but he did not wish this to be known, as the eyewitness remarks:

we must not recount the miracles which took place there, the examples of the clairvoyance of the *starets*, his private dealings with individuals, all the things typical of the picture of a *starets* . . . But I must speak of the feeling of absolute freedom which I had from the first day I assisted at the liturgy, heard his sermons on freedom, and saw it epitomised in the *starets* himself.

At the daily liturgy the young people who came to visit Tavrion were spellbound:

Nowhere have I seen the liturgy celebrated with such humility and gentleness, such conviction and authority, such Paschal joy. Here one can really feel the strength of the prayers of the *starets*, the fire of the Spirit. At every liturgy there is a sermon — often two or three — which is like a torrent of life-giving wisdom, like a judgement before the judgement-seat of God, baring the secrets of the conscience but bathing the heart with the great love and tenderness of the heavenly Father . . . His sermons are splendid. They are evangelical judgement on contemporary reality. They recall every Christian to true penitence. When for the first time I saw the *starets* preaching with his eyes closed and a Gospel in his hands, I felt that such sweetness, humility and power could dwell only in a saint.

It seems that, in *Starets* Tavrion and others, the traditions of Holy Russia are living on, despite the restrictions on monastic life imposed by the state.

6 PUBLICATIONS*

The Publishing Department of the Moscow Patriarchate under the chairmanship of Archbishop Pitirim of Volokolamsk produces religious publications whose frequency and print-runs are very restricted. The regular publications are the monthly *Journal of the Moscow Patriarchate*, the Ukrainian-language *Orthodox Herald* (*Pravoslavni visnik*) and the *Information Bulletin of the Moscow Patriarchate*. The occasional publication *Theological Works* (*Bogoslovskye trudy*) is issued roughly twice a year; there is an annual Church Calendar; occasional small editions of the Bible and New Testament; and occasional editions of liturgical and prayer books. The limiting factor in their production is that the state controls all paper supplies in the Soviet Union and makes only limited amounts available to the church. The state also controls all printing facilities, and the church's publications are all produced on state printing presses. The church was allocated 300 tonnes of paper for all its publications during 1980.[1] As Archbishop Pitirim explained to a Western journalist:

> This year, I published 50,000 copies of the Bible and the same number of the New Testament. We would have liked to produce more, but I have to reserve paper for the monthly journal . . . Every year I have to balance my production like this, in order at one and the same time to serve the faithful and pursue theological education, to educate the people . . . and to deepen the knowledge of servants of the cult.[2] [Although it is doubtful that the Archbishop would have used the phrase 'servants of the cult', this is the translation given in the source quoted.]

The limited paper allocation made to the church is clearly a means by which the state restricts the publication of religious literature. It is difficult to see how there can be a shortage of paper in the Soviet Union, which, with all the forests of northern Russia at its disposal, produced over 5.5 million tonnes of paper in 1978; this had increased to 5.7 million tonnes by 1983. Paper is one of the USSR's chief exports.[3] Furthermore, visitors to the Soviet Union are told that the USSR produces more books annually than any other country in the world. This means that the very low production of Scriptures and other religious literature (and of other works, for example, some of the world-famous classics of Russian literature) is a matter of state policy.

---

*A revised version of this chapter is to be published in *Orthodox Christianity and Politics in the Twentieth Century*, ed. Pedro Ramet (Duke University Press, Virginia, forthcoming).

Further evidence of this is provided by the fact that the churches are restricted in the amount of religious literature they are able to import. If shortage of paper were really the problem, importation would be the obvious way to remedy the dearth of religious literature, although it is true that this might be an embarrassment to the Soviet government, as constituting an admission of its inability to provide for its citizens' needs.

Publication of the Scriptures

Bibles are not officially on sale anywhere in the Soviet Union. They are published, with official permission, only by recognised churches, and may be obtained only through local churches. (Apart from the Russian Orthodox Church, the Baptist Church, the Georgian Orthodox Church and the Armenian Apostolic Church have produced small editions of Scriptures in recent years.)

In addition to the 1979 editions of the Scriptures, the Moscow Patriarchate published editions of the Bible in 1956, 1968 and 1976, the New Testament with Psalter in 1956 and the New Testament in 1976.[4] The 1976 edition marked the hundredth anniversary of the publication of the first Russian Bible. Various figures and estimates have been given at different times for the sizes of these various editions. They quite often conflict, and so it is impossible to provide any reliable estimate of the numbers of Scriptures printed by the church. In particular, figures provided by Deacon Vladimir Rusak, who must be assumed to have more inside knowledge than the other sources quoted, often differ considerably from other figures available. (We mentioned Deacon Rusak at the end of Chapter 3; he is a former employee of the Publishing Department who was dismissed from his parish after it became known that he was writing a history of the Russian Orthodox Church. One section of this history, entitled 'The Problem of Printing' (*'Tipograficheskaya problema'*), supplies the figures given below.) The 1956 editions of the Bible and New Testament had been generally thought to have numbered 50,000 and 25,000 respectively.[5] However, Rusak gave the figure for Bibles as only 25,000 copies. He added that of these, 10,000 were sent abroad; 3,000 were allocated to the theological schools; 2,000 were kept as a reserve; and only 10,000 were left for distribution to churches.[6] Different figures have been quoted for the 1968 edition of the Bible, which appeared to number not more than 30,000 copies, and possibly much less, since a large proportion of the edition was apparently shared with the Baptists.[7] Rusak, surprisingly, gives a much higher figure. He says that 40,000 Bibles were printed in 1968, and that a further 30,000 were run off from the same typesetting in 1970. However, he too says that they were shared with the Baptists. He adds that ten Bibles were distributed to each Moscow church, but that many village churches received none.[8] The 1976 centenary edition, according to a foreign journalist, consisted of 100,000 Bibles and 75,000 New Testaments.[9] Rusak, however, says that there were only 50,000 New Testaments.[10] Archbishop Pitirim, as noted, said that in 1979 he published 50,000 Bibles and 50,000 New Testaments. Rusak, however, gives a figure of 75,000 New Testaments.[11] This discrepancy is difficult to explain, since there is no obvious reason for Pitirim to lower the figure he gave — rather the reverse. It clearly illustrates the difficulty of obtaining reliable statistical information about the Russian Orthodox Church (or other churches in the USSR). In addition to these editions, Archbishop Pitirim announced in November 1983 (while on a visit to Finland) that the church had published 70,000 Bibles that year.[12] This has been widely reported, but there has not been any independent corroboration, so far as is known at present. When the figures are totalled, they show that since 1956 the Moscow Patriarchate has published between 275,000 and 340,000 Bibles, plus 150,000 New Testaments. This is clearly woefully inadequate for a church which numbers many millions. Foreigners have often remarked on the shortage of Bibles, both in the Orthodox Church and among other denominations where study of the Scriptures is much more central to worship and personal devotional life. More than once foreign visitors to the theological schools have met the young men studying for the priesthood who have no Bible of their own.

All the Bibles published by the Russian Orthodox Church since 1917 have been in Russian. This means that many members of the church whose native language is not Russian must either read the Scriptures in a foreign language, or make do with such pre-revolutionary copies as have survived. This particularly affects Ukrainians, who, as we have seen, form the greatest concentration of Orthodox believers in the Soviet Union.

The Russian Orthodox Church has not been permitted to import any Scriptures from abroad (although the Baptist Church was allowed to import 25,000 Bibles at the end of 1978). This has become a sensitive issue, particularly after an incident which occurred in 1978. A commentator on Moscow Radio, in reply to an American listener who wanted to know if he could bring a Bible into the USSR, stated:

> The answer I was looking for [at the office of the Moscow Patriarch] was not long coming. And to be completely frank with you, it was also unexpected. It seems that several years ago the Russian Orthodox Church officially applied to the Soviet authorities requesting that measures be taken to ban the import of Bibles not corresponding to the canonical text accepted by the Russian Orthodox Church. This request was agreed to.[13]

This was an astonishing statement, implying as it did that the Russian Orthodox Church preferred its members to have no Bibles at all rather than to read unauthorised translations. It was widely reported, in tones of indignation and incredulity, in the Western press. At that time Bishop Makari of Uman was representing the Russian Orthodox Church in Geneva, and, evidently unaware of the source of the statement, he reacted strongly to reports of it in the Western press, which he described as 'pure invention, typical of the Western press', adding that the allegation 'was quite idiotic'.[14] Within a very short time, Makari was recalled to the Soviet Union.[15] He has not returned overseas since (except on visits), although he had spent the entire eight years of his episcopal career up to 1978 representing his church abroad.

The sensitivity of the Soviet authorities concerning the importation of Bibles and New Testaments is also shown by the difficulties which tourists have experienced in bringing even quite small numbers of Bibles into the USSR. It is hard to see the justification for this, since there is no law against bringing Bibles into the country. Although there are regulations prohibiting the import of 'anti-Soviet' literature, it is not easy to see how Bibles can come into this category, as they have been officially published in the USSR. However, in practice tourists who have more than one Bible in Russian or another language of the USSR will have the extra copies confiscated, if they are discovered. That it is possible to bring in one Bible is confirmed by the Moscow Radio commentator quoted above:

> you cannot bring in a large number of Bibles, more than one, in fact. But — and this is an important but — no customs official will take away your personal Bible. That is an official fact that I've checked on.[16]

Neither this commentator nor any other Soviet official has to our knowledge provided a satisfactory explanation of why it is not permissible to bring in more than one Bible. The failed attempt to explain the situation by alleging that the Orthodox Church had requested that unauthorised translations should not be imported, which was so quickly exposed by Bishop Makari's statement, shows the weakness of the official Soviet position on this issue. Evidently the state does not wish to declare its position openly by passing a law forbidding the import of Bibles, which would undermine its stance as a self-styled supporter of religious freedom, and so there will presumably continue to be a dichotomy between law and practice.

At present there is no sign that the shortage of Bibles in the Russian Orthodox Church is likely to be remedied. Even the extent of the shortage is hard to estimate. No doubt many Orthodox believers have Bibles surviving from before the Revolution (in which case they will be in the old orthography), or, in the case of the western republics, before the Second World War. It is true that reading and study of the Bible has not played the vital, irreplaceable role in the personal devotional life of Orthodox Christians that it has in the Evangelical churches in the USSR. None the less, there is little doubt that most Orthodox believers would long have to have their own personal Bible if it were possible. In addition, there must be many people on the fringes of church life who would be glad to have a Bible of their own. This adds up to a deficit of millions of Bibles, and it is clear that the small occasional editions which are being authorised at present cannot meet a need on this scale. However, the church is evidently using to the full such opportunities as it has. Printings of the Scriptures have become more frequent and larger in recent years. Moreover, a new translation of the Bible into modern Russian has been undertaken by members of the Leningrad Theological Academy in co-operation with the London-based Bible Societies, who have been working on it for some years. The Gospel of John has been completed, but recent reports suggest that the translation is proceeding only very slowly, if at all.[17]

Liturgical Books

The situation is much the same as regards prayer books and liturgical books: although these have been published more frequently in recent years there is still a great need for more. The Appendix at the end of this chapter lists publications since publishing activity was resumed in 1946. In the first ten years, only a few small service books were produced. From 1956 (the same year as an edition of the Bible was published) the situation improved: a prayer book was published, and in the following years a number of liturgical books were produced. These were chiefly for the use of priests, and were clearly intended to provide them with all the many Orthodox orders of service and instructions on using them: liturgies, sacraments, the many special rites, the daily services — the hours, matins, vespers — and the special services for saints' days and other commemorative occasions, of which there are many.

If the church's activities are confined to worship, it is logical that its publishing programme should concentrate first and foremost on providing the books needed for worship. For some unknown reason, no service books were published between 1965 and 1970, when the *Prayer Book* was published again, but in a longer form than the 1956 edition. More service books were printed during the 1970s. One of them, according to the CRA, was in an edition of 10,000 copies, which means there would have been enough for every active (as opposed to retired) priest to have a copy. In 1979, after some delay, the first two volumes of a projected twelve-volume series of a *Manual for Priests* (*Nastolnaya kniga svyashchennosluzhitelei*) were published. If the CRA's figure of 20,000 copies of the first volume is correct, there are more than enough for all the active priests in the Soviet Union, and it is likely that copies are being sent to priests in the overseas dioceses too. In 1981 there was a burst of publishing activity: the 1970 *Prayer Book* and the 1973 *Psalter* were republished in a joint edition numbering 150,000; the third volume of the *Manual for Priests* was issued; 20,000 copies of the *Book of Hours* were published; and 20,000 copies of the second part of the *Psalter with the Order of Services* appeared (the first part having been published in 1962).[18]

Clearly the scope of the publishing is increasing significantly, with the emphasis on literature for public worship rather than private devotions, as is natural in a church where corporate worship is so central.

Other Publications

The journal *Bogoslovskye trudy* (*Theological Works*) commenced publication in 1960. Only five issues had been published by 1970, but since then it has been issued roughly twice a year. Issues 23 and 24 were published in 1983. The CRA Report, the Yakunin Report, Rusak and other observers agree that its circulation is 3,000 copies. The periodical has an impressive editorial board which includes professors from both theological academies and a few bishops, under the chairmanship of Metropolitan Antoni of Leningrad. However, its contents are rather dull. The majority of the articles so far published have been on liturgical and historical subjects. There is good reason for this: it is clearly important to use the church's only theological publication to transmit basic knowledge about liturgical practice to the clergy, since this is the major part of their ministry. Furthermore, Orthodox liturgics is so deeply traditional and so resistant to change that it would be next to impossible to introduce any new ideological content into it. The state does not appear to have made any attempt to do so, no doubt regarding the subject as an arcane and obsolete one best left to the church. It is therefore in the interests of both church and state to publish articles on a subject in which the church need fear no ideological subversion and which the state regards as irrelevant. The preponderance of historical articles may be explained by the fact that in Orthodoxy, with its great emphasis on Tradition, it is customary to treat current issues and problems in the light of of what the Church Fathers and the great luminaries of the past have said about them. However, it is also true that in Soviet literature and scholarly writing in general authors frequently retreat to historical subjects because of the great ideological difficulties involved in expressing any views on contemporary issues. Not infrequently they use Aesopian language when discussing historical subjects to express views on contemporary issues in a way that an experienced Soviet reader knows how to interpret. This factor has no doubt compelled *Bogoslovskye trudy* to concentrate more on the church's past than on its present. The emphasis on liturgics and history, useful though it may be, has meant that there is almost no evidence of original creative thinking in the church's only theological publication. The other subjects covered have included a series of papers presented at talks with the German Evangelical Church and the Finnish Lutheran Church, which cover the doctrines of both sides on such basic issues as baptism, salvation and the eucharist; a few articles on Orthodox teaching on the Incarnation, the Resurrection and the Dormition of the Mother of God; and articles on the problems of translating the Bible into Russian. The periodical has also published some articles by widely respected Orthodox writers of the recent past, such as Father Pavel Florensky, V. N. Lossky and Bishop Ignati (Bryanchaninov). While opportunities for publishing remain limited, the church is no doubt right to restrict itself to such basic matter, but there is no question that the livelier minds in the church would welcome something more stimulating if only the CRA and the censor would permit it.

The annual Calendar of the Church is in fact a large-format, 80-page illustrated book giving information about feasts and saints' days, the organisation and history of the church, and some facts about other Orthodox Churches. According to Rusak, this desk calendar and a wall calendar were published in editions of 50,000 copies up to 1964, and 40,000 copies thereafter.[19] The CRA Report for 1974 states that 50,000 copies were printed annually, along with 40,000 copies of a wall calendar.[20] In 1979, Archbishop Pitirim stated that a total of 100,000 copies were to be printed the next year,[21] indicating a 10 per cent increase over six years. However, bearing in mind that the calendars supply the overseas dioceses as well as the Soviet ones, this is sufficient for only six or seven calendars per parish in the USSR. In fact, many are not distributed to the parishes, especially those most distant from Moscow, and one reliable source in 1982 said that even Moscow parishes receive only three to six copies each, depending on the size of the parish. The London diocese has difficulty in acquiring copies of the calendar. Rusak noted that in 1979, 1,000 copies of the calendar were sent to the CRA, plus others to district executive committees. He also gives several examples of shortfalls in the number of calendars received from the printers, the largest of which was 3,050 in 1970.[22] A church publication has claimed that a pocket calendar is published, in addition to the desk and wall formats,[23] but no figures concerning it have come to light.

In 1983, for the first time, the Riga diocese published a Church Calendar in Latvian, a brochure of 50 pages.[24]

The overseas publications of the Moscow Patriarchate are: *Messager de l'exarchat du Patriarchate russe en Europe occidentale*, published in Paris in French and Russian; *Stimme der Orthodoxie* (*The Voice of Orthodoxy*), published in East Berlin in German; *Egyhazi kronika* (*Church Chronicle*), published in Budapest in Hungarian; *One Church*, published in New York in English; and *Kanadski pravoslavni visnyk* (*Canadian Orthodox Herald*), published in Edmonton partly in English and partly in Ukrainian.[25] The

CRA Report also mentions a bulletin published in Japanese in Tokyo with which the Moscow Patriarchate has some connection. (There is also the journal *Sourozh*, published by the London diocese). It seems that the Publishing Department does not exercise direct editorial control over the Paris, New York and Edmonton publications, but that the latter restrict themselves to materials provided by the Publishing Department. The ties with *Stimme der Orthodoxie* in East Berlin are much closer, according to the CRA Report, which states that the editors of the *Journal of the Moscow Patriarchate* 'offer their literary and photographic materials every month and pay honoraria for articles published in the bulletin by authors [living in the Soviet Union]'. This section of the CRA Report refers to publications in the Soviet Union not noted elsewhere. It states that the Publishing Department 'maintains relations' with 'an annual Church calendar and arch-pastoral festive and other messages in the Estonian language' and with 'messages for Christmas and Easter and other periodic archpastoral addresses' issued by 'Riga, Ufa and a few other dioceses'.[26] It is not clear what 'maintaining relations' means, but the inference is that these diocesan messages are not subject to direct editorial control by Moscow, and are therefore probably issued after consultation with the local CRA commissioner.

The *Journal of the Moscow Patriarchate*

The *Journal of the Moscow Patriarchate* commenced publication in 1931 but after a few issues it was forced to close down in 1935, and it did not resume publication until 1943,[27] since when it has been published continuously every month. Its editorial offices were located in the Novodevichi Monastery in Moscow, until the opening of a well-equipped, purpose-built office close by in 1981. An English-language edition of the journal has been published since 1971; it consists entirely of translations from the Russian edition, though the items are sometimes shortened slightly, and some are omitted. The translations, according to the CRA, are done by highly qualified people outside the Publishing Department;[28] these appear not to be native English-speakers, and considering this, the translations are generally of a high quality. Both the Russian and English editions have twelve issues a year. An additional special issue was published in 1978 describing the celebrations of the sixtieth anniversary of the restoration of the Moscow Patriarchate in 1977.

In common with other religious publications in the Soviet Union, the print-run (*tirazh*) of the *Journal of the Moscow Patriarchate* is not indicated, although this information is included in all other books and periodicals published in the USSR. This is further evidence of Soviet sensitivity over the amount of officially published religious literature. According to the CRA Report, the print-run in both 1970 and 1974 was 15,000 copies.[29]

The Yakunin Report in 1979 estimated the print-run at about 20,000 copies.[30] However, in an interview with a foreign journalist in 1979, Archbishop Pitirim gave the figure as 25,000 copies.[31] It is strange that Pitirim should suddenly reveal a figure which had been kept secret for so many years, and it seems probable that his figure is exaggerated. This is so because the most recently available figures, those given by Rusak, are much closer to the CRA's 1974 figures. Rusak gives a general figure of just under 14,000 copies a year, and a specific figure of 15,100 copies in 1977. (He notes that the special 1978 jubilee edition was published in 25,000 copies, plus 5,000 copies in English.)

Rusak reports that the Moscow churches each receive ten copies of the journal, and that: 'In a village parish no more than ten people know of the existence of the *Journal of the Moscow Patriarchate*, and apart from the priest, who receives at very best only one copy either for himself or for the church, even fewer read it.'[32]

The print-run of the journal's English edition is given by the CRA and the Yakunin Report as 3,000, but Pitirim, in the above-mentioned interview at a later date, reduces it to 2,500. The English edition makes a financial loss, since copies of it are distributed abroad free of charge. The CRA Report, which points this out, states that copies of the Russian edition are also given away free, and that this adds up to a 'significant deficit'.[33] Rusak, more specifically, says that one-third of the print-run, 4,622 copies, are distributed free of charge: this includes 3,930 abroad and 44 to the CRA and other state institutions. He also states that every edition of the English version costs 8,000 to 10,000 roubles.[34] Given the shortage of religious literature in the USSR, the fact that an English edition of the journal is published at all may seem surprising, since the amount of work involved in translating, editing and printing must be considerable. However, expense is evidently not a limiting factor; it is only the restriction on paper supply that has to be taken into consideration. The fact that the Moscow Patriarchate (with, as always, the approval of the CRA) is willing to expend some of its precious paper on an English edition of its journal is a strong indication of its wish to improve its contacts with churches overseas, and of the state's backing for this. However, it may be going too far in this direction by publishing occasional English-language editions of books about the church. The book about the church's life published on the sixtieth anniversary of the restoration of the Moscow Patriarchate (*The Moscow Patriarchate 1917–1977*), which we have referred to several times, is well produced and has photographs on every page, both black-and-white and colour. The purpose of this and other books is clearly to convey the impression that church life is continuing normally and that no real problems are encountered. Though the book has the merit of bringing the Russian Orthodox Church to the awareness of foreign churchmen, it is simultaneously promoting a one-sided view of the church which is indistinguishable from

Soviet propaganda. It is clearly not in the church's interests to foster such a misconception. An English-language book entitled *The Local Council of 1971* was printed in 3,000 copies.[35] The Yakunin Report, mentioning the great need for religious literature, is probably right to refer to this book as literature 'of an official (*offitsiozny*) type, needed by no one'.[36] It seems that the CRA is leading the church into a misordering of priorities in publishing literature of this kind when, as the Yakunin Report reminds us, 'Religious literature for the general reader [in the Soviet Union] is not published at all.'[37]

Like Bibles, the *Journal of the Moscow Patriarchate* and other religious publications cannot be purchased at bookshops or any other public place in the Soviet Union. They are distributed only through the churches; the method of allocating and distributing copies is not known. The CRA Report states that the journal is distributed through two channels, but at that point the text breaks off and there is a gap, so we do not know what the channels are.[38] The *Journal of the Moscow Patriarchate* is not listed in Soviet catalogues of periodicals, and it is not even possible for individual believers to subscribe to it by post.[39]

Censorship of the *Journal of the Moscow Patriarchate*

The content of the journal comes under close scrutiny from both the CRA and the Soviet censor, to whom all published matter in the Soviet Union is submitted before publication. Anatoli Levitin worked on the journal between 1956 and 1960, and has described how censorship was carried out:

> From the very first few days of my work at the journal I was convinced that an unbelievably harsh censorship prevailed over it. Immediately after an article had been written and accepted by the editors, it went to the Council for Religious Affairs. [*Sic* in the translation quoted; in fact, in the period in question, it would have been the Council for Russian Orthodox Church Affairs (CROCA).] The Council for Religious Affairs has an unlimited power of veto over any article. If it makes use of this right and forbids the article, the conversation is over, the article won't be published. If it makes corrections, the article may appear in a shortened .form.
>
> However, the matter does not end here. When an issue of the journal is made up into pages, it must still be checked by Glavlit [popular acronym for the *Glavnoye upravleniye po delam literatury i izdatelstva* (Chief Administration for Literature and Publishing), responsible for censoring all published matter in the USSR], which for its part may insert any corrections, and this again is an institution against which there is no appeal; there's nowhere to complain to.

Levitin discovered that the censor did not permit articles to contain references to foreign sources: an article he wrote in defence of peace was rejected because, to describe the horrors of war, he quoted from Remarque's *All Quiet on the Western Front*. However, there was more to come:

> the most surprising thing was that it was not allowed to make reference to Soviet sources either. 'What is this? It turns out that we're working for you?' said a representative of the Council. In general, the old principle of 'it will come to no good' lay at the basis of all the censor's work.

The restrictions on subject-matter and its treatment were also strict, as Levitin discovered the hard way:

> In an article on Saint Nikolai I named several Churches of St Nikolai which had existed in Moscow. It was not allowed; those churches didn't exist any more!
>
> In a reportage from Peter [affectionate and popular name for Leningrad, formerly St Petersburg], my home city, on the Monastery of St Alexander Nevsky, occurred the lines: 'Once again, as in years past, the people make their way through the corridors of the Lavra to the Cathedral.' Not allowed — Glavlit cancelled the whole issue! 'As in years past' meant that there had been a break when the monastery had been closed.
>
> At the end of an article about the princess Olga, I spoke of the great role which women had played in the history of the Church. Not allowed: Christianity stifled women.

Levitin soon concluded that the effect of the censorship was that 'the journal was deadly boring and no use to anyone'.[40] He turned to writing in *samizdat* instead.

Deacon Rusak's experience of working for the *Journal of the Moscow Patriarchate* led him to conclusions just as outspoken as Levitin's. He calls the censorship of the journal 'draconian'. Every issue, according to Rusak, is sent to the CRA on the twentieth day of the month, and they spend five days reading it. He notes wryly that the CRA officials 'are the most attentive and the most zealous readers of the church journal'. And this despite the fact that every employee of the Publishing Department already has instructions regarding the content of the journal and the preferred vocabulary. Among many examples he gives, Rusak mentions that the usual Russian word for 'clergy', *dukhovenstvo* (the root of which means 'spirit' or 'spiritual'), should be abandoned in favour of the more neutral, less 'churchly' words *pricht* or *klir*. After giving several examples of items before and after censorship by the CRA, Rusak proceeds to a more central issue:

The Council [CRA] does not merely make certain 'editorial' recommendations. The entire structure of the journal has gradually been
defined by the Council, and at best only one-third of the space has been
made available to purely church historical events. The remainder is peacemaking and ecumenism. The space which is useful to the Church is
bought at the price of that which is useful to the government . . . the
State is simply speculating on the functional duties of the Church. The
State is attempting to reduce the spiritual and salvific activity of the
Church . . . in the mind of the general public to a narrowly social and
public phenomenon . . . and by this, as it were, to justify the very
existence of the Church in an atheistic (anti-religious) State.[41]

Levitin's observations date from before 1960, Rusak's from a later date,
but they are borne out by the CRA Report for 1974, indicating that little or
nothing had changed in the intervening years. The CRA states that it
censors every issue of the *Journal of the Moscow Patriarchate* carefully
because, although it has a small circulation, it has a wide variety of readers,
from ordinary believers and parish priests to 'official services and departments of foreign countries'. This statement makes explicit the fact that the
CRA regards it as part of its duties to influence foreigners' perceptions of
the Russian Orthodox Church. The report continues:

The editorial department of the journal and the authors' collective in
general correctly understand the tasks standing before the journal, but at
the same time there are frequently found among the manuscripts prepared for printing texts whose content does not serve the interests of the
state and the believer, does not promote the formation in the reader of
lofty civil and patriotic qualities, and is in contradiction to the norms of
Soviet legislation on cults . . . a preparatory examination of texts takes
place in the Council, notes and corrections are added.[42]

The material in the journal is divided into sections which, as the CRA
Report notes, 'have already become traditional'.[43] The description of them
given by the CRA in 1974 could be applied almost in its entirety to the 1982
issues. There is an official section giving the texts of messages from the
Patriarch and decisions of the Holy Synod; a section on church life which
includes biographies of new bishops, accounts of important festivals,
reports from the theological schools, news from the dioceses, and obituaries;
a section entitled 'In Defence of Peace' which reports on the church's
activities within the Soviet Peace Fund and with several international
organisations; a section describing the life and history of other Orthodox
Churches; a section on 'Ecumenical Contacts'; a theological section, which,
in the sceptical words of the CRA Report, 'contains reports on different
aspects of the study and propaganda of the Bible, interpretation of its

legends, explanations of some church festivals, materials on the life and activity of many "Holy fathers" of Russian Orthodoxy'.[44] There is also a section explaining aspects of divine services, such as the Creed, and a short bibliographical section describing recent publications of the church or of other Orthodox Churches in socialist countries.

The CRA Report makes one or two interesting comments about the content of the journal. It states that its 'distinguishing characteristic' is 'the optimistic character of the overwhelming majority of its material'. This is owing to the fact that

> in the opinion of many theologians, believers in the USSR have found their place in life among non-Christians (atheists), and that the experience of the last thirty years of the ROC [Russian Orthodox Church] inspires hope and has an exceptional significance for the whole of Christianity and the whole world.[45]

The CRA's own attitude to this is not altogether clear. Presumably it approves of the positive attitude to the situation of the church which it sees reflected in the pages of the journal, but one senses that it may be uneasy at such a wholehearted, even hopeful, embracing of the given situation. However, elsewhere in the report the CRA indicates that it views the church's optimism as misguided:

> The journal is the transmitter of the whole policy of the ROC, its most important platform, by use of which the ideologues of Russian Orthodoxy try to preserve and strengthen the positions of religion and the church, to conceal from the reader the hidden manifestations of crisis which are actually taking place in the ROC, to create for religion the reputation of a socially progressive force, and to raise its prestige in the eyes of believing citizens in our state and abroad.[46]

This is a curious and rather ambiguous comment, since as we have seen, it is primarily the CRA which is responsible for ensuring that the church's problems are not aired publicly and that it presents itself in a good light to the world. Why then should it complain if the church does just that in the pages of its journal? Implicit in this comment by the CRA is an admission that it does in fact regard the church's oft-proclaimed well-being as illusory. However, its attribution of the church's eventual demise to 'hidden manifestations of crisis' (*skrytye krizisnye yavleniya*) rather than to its own efforts, is less than convincing, since it makes no attempt to explain how 'manifestations' can simultaneously be 'hidden'. The tortuous bureaucratic phraseology reveals the basic ambiguity of the comment.

The CRA remarks that with regard to the peace movement the journal 'maintains a realistic position'[47] but is less approbatory of the journal's attitude to the Christian's role in society. It states that the attempt to reconcile Christian and communist ideas in believers' minds 'obliges churchmen to impart a science-like (*naukoobrazny*) form to theology'. It quotes an article by an East German theologian as saying: 'The Gospel contains within itself a tendency to socialism, to a rupture with the class society, to confrontation with the feudal and bourgeois-capitalist form of life.' One might expect that the CRA would approve these words, but in fact it does not, because the passage goes on to claim that the Gospel 'explains the world and simultaneously changes it'. The CRA considers that this is claiming too much for religion: 'Here there is an obvious glimpse of a desire to idealise Christianity, to place it above all other theories, including above the theory and practice of Marxism.'[48] This is surely precisely what one would expect to find in the journal of a Christian church. There is a hint here that the CRA would prefer the journal to give at least equal importance to Marxism, which does not augur well for the Christian integrity of the journal.

The CRA evidently does not wish the *Journal of the Moscow Patriarchate* to say anything which would lead its readers to think that the church has any role to play in society: in the Soviet Union, any beneficial influence in society is the prerogative of the Communist Party. The CRA Report quotes a paragraph from the journal which explains that Christians must be involved in social life, helping to change, renew and transform it; but it is introduced with the comment that the 'ideologues of Orthodoxy' are 'mystifying the role of the church' in this way because they are attempting to 'establish themselves in our conditions, and in doing so guarantee themselves a right to the future'.[49] In this statement the CRA reveals that it sees the church only as an institution attempting to prolong its own existence, not as an organism with any intrinsic merit. The question of whether the church *has* in fact any contribution to make to society is not even raised; it is simply assumed that any influence it could have would inevitably be pernicious, and must be opposed. Once again we see that the CRA's chief concern is to cut the church off from society, to isolate it altogether. This is strikingly shown, perhaps unconsciously, in the phrase quoted above, 'establish themselves in *our* conditions'. This assumes that the whole of Soviet life belongs to 'us' — the Party and the state — and that, though religious believers are recognised to be citizens, they have no part in 'our conditions', but form a kind of unwanted excrescence.

The CRA Report concludes by remarking that there are many articles about saints and holy places in the journal, which aim to give believers examples worthy of imitation in the Christian life and are intended 'to promote the preservation or the revival among believers of the old conceptions, customs and traditions of "holy places" '. The fact that these could inspire believers in their daily lives is a matter for the CRA's disapproval, and it promises to be more vigilant in future: 'Control over them must be strengthened in future, by having a more exacting attitude to manuscripts, and removing from them propaganda about "holy places" and other materials which could activate the church.' The CRA's ideal, evidently, is a journal which would not cause a believer to be in any way inspired, or motivated to any kind of action, by what he reads there. The church is to be made to remain exactly as it is, not changing or influencing anyone or anything. However, the CRA realises that it would be hard for the *Journal of the Moscow Patriarchate* to do anything of the sort, since 'in practice the journal does not reach ordinary believers because of its small print-run'.[50]

Attempts to Meet the Need for Literature

It is clear that the church is prevented from producing even a fraction of the religious literature needed by its members. Many, perhaps, most of its millions of members must pass much of their lives with little or no access to written materials relating to their faith. It is true that the reading of devotional and other materials is not a great feature of the Orthodox way of life, due no doubt to the high rate of illiteracy, until recent times, in Russia. Rather than read a book, a Russian Orthodox believer would be more likely to visit a church, pray before icons, talk to a priest, or journey to see a *starets* in a monastery. However, these traditional activities are becoming more and more difficult to perform due to the great shortage of priests, churches and monasteries. Reading-matter, were it available in sufficient quantities, might provide a substitute for those unable to visit churches or priests. However, the fact that religious literature is distributed only through churches means that only those able to attend church can obtain it — and so those who live far from any open church are doubly deprived.

Rusak indicates very clearly that ordinary Orthodox believers do in fact want Christian reading-matter. He writes:

Hundreds and thousands of letters are addressed to the Patriarch and the Chairman of the Publishing Department of the Moscow Patriarchate, in which people beg tearfully to be sent a Bible, or a church calendar, at their personal expense.

Among several letters he quotes is one which states:

I would like to read the Bible. I have to confess that I have absolutely no idea of its content. I do not know where I can find one to read . . . I would like to own a Bible. I will read it attentively again and again.

Rusak says that the editorial staff of the Publishing Department includes a person whose duties consist solely of replying to such letters — always with a refusal.

Personal visitors to the offices of the Publishing Department, according to Rusak, even if they come from the Far East of the Soviet Union, several days' journey away from Moscow, or from the distant north, are told that the editorial staff cannot make sales.[51]

The Publishing Department appears to be doing its best in a very difficult situation, and is using to the utmost the very limited opportunities available to it. It has recently produced some films about the life of the church, in colour and of quite good quality, which Archbishop Pitirim has shown on his travels to various countries. In 1979 he showed them in Stockholm at a biennial international Christian television festival, the first time that a representative from the Soviet Union had taken part in the festival.[52] Like all the products of the Publishing Department, the films portrayed the life of the church in a purely positive light, making no mention of any problems, but none the less they give a most interesting view of aspects of the church's life.

However, we have to conclude that the need for religious literature of all types — the Scriptures, liturgical and prayer books, the lives of the saints, church history, devotional works, commentaries, dictionaries, teaching materials, to name only those most urgently needed — is very great indeed. It is against this background that *samizdat* has grown up. Anatoli Levitin was not the only person, though he was one of the very first, to realise that the church was unable to provide religious literature, and that believers would have to find ways of remedying the deficiency themselves. *Samizdat* does not consist only of the letters of complaint and protest which we have been quoting, but also of devotional and spiritual materials, sometimes book-length. The fact that people are willing to type out such lengthy texts, knowing that the penalty if they are discovered is at least confiscation and possibly imprisonment, is evidence of a deeply felt need for spiritual literature. *Samizdat* texts sometimes reach the West and are published there: such books are designated as *tamizdat*, or 'publishing over there' (from the words *tam* — 'there'; and *izdat* — 'publish'). If *tamizdat* texts can be conveyed back to the Soviet Union by secret means, they help to supplement the believers' meagre literary diet. In 1977 a periodical called *Nadezhda*, subtitled *Christian Readings*, began to be published in this way. Ten issues had been published in the West by October 1984, and many more prepared for publication in the USSR. *Nadezhda* (*Hope*) includes extracts from the Church Fathers, articles and letters by priests and pastors from both present and former times, poetry and Christian contemporary literature, and works giving a Christian view of the current state of Russia and the Orthodox Church.

Russian Orthodox literature is published in Russian abroad by the YMCA Press in Paris, the Catholic publisher La Vie avec Dieu in Brussels, the Orthodox Monastery of the Holy Trinity at Jordanville in New York State, and by other small Orthodox centres in the USA and Canada. Like other religious literature, these works cannot be officially imported into the USSR, and they are sent by clandestine means as and when possible. These publications are highly valued by Orthodox believers in the Soviet Union. A letter sent to La Vie avec Dieu is typical of many which have reached these Western publishers:

> Dear brothers! Above all I want to thank you with all my heart for the wonderful work which you have taken upon yourselves — the publishing of religious literature in the Russian language . . . These books fill in the almost total absence of modern Russian literature on Biblical studies . . . This is a slender little stream, but it will not allow living faith to dry up, and it is not poisoned by compromises and self-deception.[53]

Appreciative though this letter is, it is undoubtedly right to describe the Orthodox literature coming from the West as no more than a 'slender little stream'. Despite their purely religious, non-political content, such books are liable to be confiscated from tourists and other travellers if discovered at borders. Furthermore, it is common for large quantities of religious literature, belonging to private individuals, to be confiscated during lengthy searches of homes conducted by the militia and/or KGB. Both these practices have intensified during the 1980s. Although the fate of such confiscated literature cannot be established with certainty, the ready availability of Christian books on the black market is highly suggestive. This means that believers can obtain books, but at a price. New Testaments were at one point said to fetch 30 roubles and Bibles 60 roubles, or roughly half a month's average salary. (However, in 1982 these prices had dropped to 16 and 40 roubles respectively, indicating that black market Bibles and New Testaments were more widely available.) Copies of the *Dobrotolyubiye* (*Philokalia*, which consists of five large volumes), were said in 1982 to cost 500 roubles each, or four to five months' salary. The fact that Christians are prepared to pay such large sums is ample evidence both of the scarcity of Christian literature and of the great hunger for it. And, of course, even books acquired on the black market are liable to reconfiscation in a subsequent house-search.

The great demand for religious literature means that, almost inevitably, abuses creep into the informal distribution system. It is clear that some people must be profiting handsomely from black market sales. Moreover, it has been reported that some bishops stockpile religious literature received from the West and use it as an 'alternative currency'. For example, an artist who had restored an entire church was offered as payment either 200 roubles or a copy of the *Philokalia* (worth 500 roubles); being a believer, he chose the latter and was delighted with the bargain, and the church profited by 200 roubles. Another example of possible profiteering came to light when a number of Orthodox believers were arrested in Moscow on 6 April

1982, after lengthy house-searches during which large quantities of religious literature were confiscated. Six thousand prayer books were taken from one address alone. It transpired that these believers had somehow been able to photocopy prayer books and other religious literature, have them bound, and sell them. The profiteering motive was fully represented in the Soviet press.

The newspaper *Sovetskaya Rossiya* devoted articles on two successive days, 8 and 9 July 1982, to criticism of a group of Orthodox Christians who organised the production of large quantities of religious books. They were arrested in April and tried and sentenced in December 1982; they are all now in labour camps. The articles begin by quoting BBC Russian-language broadcasts which assert that they were actively trying to help fellow-believers by providing literature and that such activity was by no means criminal.

The articles attempt to correct this view by stating unequivocally that the men's sole purpose in producing the religious books was to make money. They are denounced as 'speculators', as being 'ready for crime for the sake of easy money', and as having deliberately set out to 'think how, without giving themselves too much trouble, they could make a thousand or two'. No other possible motive is even considered. In addition, one of the group, Alexander Rozanov, is accused of being involved in foreign currency transactions (a serious offence: if true, it is surprising that his sentence was not longer); and Viktor Burdyug, who is regarded as the ringleader, of trying to send 'anti-Soviet' writings abroad for publication. These accusations are, however, subsidiary to the main theme of the articles, and seem to have been brought in to blacken the character of those involved.

The articles give a fair amount of detail about the way the printing operations were carried out. Originally, the 'firm' paid workers in state printing presses to produce religious literature for them, but then they decided to increase their profits by doing the printing themselves. They stole state equipment — a xerox machine, offset litho machine, binding equipment, etc. — and installed it in flats and country houses outside Moscow. The article states that the 'firm' produced 61,500 pieces of literature in two years. It seems that the enterprise was very successful. This is an astonishingly large amount of literature to produce when working clandestinely under difficult conditions.

The question of what happened to the large profits which were allegedly the aim of the whole enterprise is left unclear. The articles simply state that the illegally acquired funds were ordered to be returned to the state. They do not say whether they were in fact returned, what they amounted to, or what the 'entrepreneurs' had done or tried to do with their ill-gotten gains. There are none of the references one might have expected to a luxurious way of life, ostentatious spending or newly acquired possessions. True, Rozanov is said to have brought a Sony stereo system, an expensive National

Panasonic radio and other goods in a Beryozka (foreign-currency shop), but as these were paid for in dollars it is hard to see how they could have been financed by selling religious books to Soviet citizens. All this strongly suggests that receipts from the sale of books were ploughed back into producing more books: it is clear that the whole operation was quite costly and would have had to be self-financing.[54]

Whatever the motives of the people concerned, the arrests and large-scale confiscations in April made it clear that the KGB was still determined to remove religious literature from circulation. Another instance of this was the arrest on 4 August 1982 of Zoya Krakhmalnikova, the compiler of *Nadezhda*. Although her name had appeared on every issue of *Nadezhda* during the six or seven years of its publication, it had never been suggested to her officially that she was doing anything illegal. She was tried on 31 March 1983 and sentenced under Article 70 ('anti-Soviet agitation and propaganda') to one year in labour camp plus five years' internal exile.[55] Her arrest, as well as the other actions mentioned above, make it clear that the Soviet authorities fear the spreading of the production and distribution of religious literature to channels which they cannot observe and control. They are determined to confine all literature production and distribution to the officially recognised channels of the Moscow Patriarchate, where they can regulate it.

It is clear that the amount of religious literature published by the Moscow Patriarchate has been increasing in recent years, and the signs are that this is likely to continue. In September 1981 the Publishing Department moved from its cramped quarters in the Novodevichi Monastery to rooms in a spacious new building close by. Before this, according to Rusak, the Publishing Department had been housed in cramped and inadequate quarters. At first the editorial staff had a small room in the Patriarchate offices in Chisty pereulok, then a room in the Dormition Church in the Novodevichi Convent. The premises then 'expanded', still within Novodevichi, to a room measuring 40 square metres for seven editorial and five administrative staff. The other departments (photographic, tape-recording, production, book-keeping, despatch, library, archive, store-room, copying and typewriting, proof-reading) were all accommodated underground, with no daylight during working hours. The photo laboratory was in a cellar where there was no ventilation to draw off chemical fumes.[56] The new building, said to be lavishly decorated, was built at the expense of the Moscow Patriarchate at a reported cost of 2 million roubles. The Publishing Department's facilities include a darkroom, colour laboratories and a film-editing studio, but not printing presses: its publications will continue to be printed on state presses.[57]

Rusak gives further details about the new building, and different costs. He quotes a resolution of the Supreme Soviet, dated 18 July 1977, to rent the Moscow Patriarchate a 400 square metre, two-storey building in

Pogodinskaya ulitsa because it was 'insufficiently suitable for the further residence of citizens' (nine families). The Publishing Department had to rehouse the families, knock down the building, and then construct new premises for its own needs on the site. This cost 350,000 roubles, but only 70,000 roubles were provided by state funds for the construction of residential accommodation. The Publishing Department provided 138,000 roubles, and the remainder came from the economic department of the Moscow Patriarchate. However, the building remains state property.[58]

Although the Publishing Department now has new premises, there is no indication that the church's paper allocation will be increased in order to enable it to publish more literature. Private sources suggest that the improved facilities have been accompanied by greater state control over the department's work, and more publications destined for overseas use and for foreign visitors than for use of believers in the USSR.

Although it would take many years to make up lost ground, there is no doubt that great strides could be made towards meeting the need for religious literature if the Soviet state would permit religious literature to be officially imported, and if it would increase the church's allocation of paper (or allow it to buy paper abroad). There is no sign that either of these things will happen, and we must conclude that the restrictions on religious literature are a matter of state policy, a further means by which the state is attempting, with some success, to stifle the voice of the Orthodox Church.

Appendix: Service Books Published by the Moscow Patriarchate

1946	*Service to all the Saints who Shone Forth in the Land of Russia*
1947	*Service for the Nativity of Christ*
1948	*Service for the Epiphany*
1950	*Service for the Presentation of Our Lord* *Service for the Dormition of the Mother of God* *Service for St Ioann, Metropolitan of Tobolsk*
1956	*Short Orthodox Prayer Book* (*Kratky pravoslavny Molitvoslov*), 114 pp. (*JMP*, no. 9 (1956), pp. 78–9)
1957	*Typicon* (*Tipikon*), 154 pp. Liturgical manual for priests on orders of service throughout the ecclesiastical year (*JMP*, no. 11 (1958), pp. 71–2)

1958	*Book of Needs*, or *Euchologion* (*Trebnik*), 2 vols, 960 pp. Contains orders of service for sacraments (except the eucharist) and many rites (*JMP*, no. 11 (1958), pp. 72–4)
1960 (dated 1958)	*Service Book* (*Sluzhebnik*) Liturgies of St John Chrysostom, St Basil the Great and of the Presanctified Gifts, also litanies and prayers for vespers and matins and other prayers (*JMP*, no. 3 (1960), pp. 75–6)
1961	*Menaion*, or *Menologion* (*Mineya*) Orders of service for all the fixed days in the year commemorating a historical event or a saint or saints
1962	*Psalter with the Order of Services* (*Psaltyr Sledovannaya*), 507 pp. Psalter, Book of Hours, calendar and various prayers and hymns (*JMP*, no. 12 (1962), p. 71)
1964	*Book of Hours*, or *Horologion* (*Chasoslov*), 322 pp. Contains fixed portions of the ecclesiastical office for the whole year (excluding the liturgy) (*JMP*, no. 12 (1963), p. 70)
1964	*The Book of Eight Tones*, or *Octoechos* (*Oktoikh*), Part 1, tones 1–4 Canons and hymns which form the variable part of the daily services from the first Sunday after Pentecost to the fourth Sunday before Lent (Septuagesima) (*JMP*, no. 6 (1964), p. 79)
1965	*The Book of Eight Tones*, Part 2, tones 5–8
1970	*Orthodox Prayer Book* (*Pravoslavny Molitvoslov*), 192 pp. (*JMP*, no. 1 (1971), p. 73)
1970	*Festal Menaion* (*Mineya prazdnichnaya*) Orders of service for the twelve Great Feasts of the ecclesiastical year (*JMP*, no. 4 (1976), p. 77)
1972	*Lenten Triodion* (*Triod postnaya*) Orders of service from Septuagesima to Easter Saturday (*JMP*, no. 4 (1976), pp. 77–8)

1973   *Psalter (Psaltyr)*, 256 pp.
                     In addition to the Psalter itself, contains many services
                     which include psalms
                     (*JMP*, no. 1(1975), p. 79)

1977   *Festal Triodion*, or *Pentecostarian* (*Triod tsvetnaya*)
(dated 1975)   Orders of service from Easter Day to the first Sunday after
                     Pentecost; 10,000 copies printed (CRA)

1976   *Service Book and Hymn Book* (*Bogosluzhebni sbornik*),
                     352 pp.
                     Orders of the main services, including music; for psalm-
                     reader and choir
                     (*JMP*, no. 9 (1976), p. 78)

1978   *Service Book* (*Sluzhebnik*)
(dated 1977)   Re-edition of the 1958 (1960) *Service Book*, but in two parts,
                     Part I, pp. 1–352, Part II, pp. 353–608; photographic
                     reproduction of the 1903 Synodal edition, with supplemen-
                     tary material
                     (*JMP*, no. 1 (1979), p. 80)
                     Menaion for September
                     (*JMP*, no. 1 (1979), p. 80)

1979   *Manual for Priests* (*Nastolnaya kniga svyashchenno-sluz-*
(dated 1977)   *hitelei*), vol. 1, 768 pp.
                     Orders of chief services and guidance on role of priest;
                     20,000 copies printed (CRA)
                     (*JMP*, no. 1 (1979), pp. 79–80)

1979   *Manual for Priests*, vol. 2
(dated 1978)   Calendar from September to February with the lives of the
                     saints
                     (*JMP*, no. 6 (1979), p. 79)

1980   *Menaion for October*
                     (*JMP*, no. 6 (1981), p. 80)

1981   *Psalter and Prayer Book*
                     Reissued jointly; 150,000 copies printed (*Episkepsis*)
                     (*JMP*, no. 4 (1981), p. 78)
                     Manual for Priests, vol. 3
                     (*JMP*, no. 2 (1984), p. 79)
(dated 1980)   *Book of Hours*
                     20,000 copies printed (*Episkepsis*)
                     (*JMP*, no. 5 (1981), p. 80)

1981   *Psalter with the Order of Services*, 2 vols
(dated 1980) Vol. 1 includes the Psalter and offices for private use; vol. 2
              includes the *Menaion, Horologion* and *Typicon,* as well as
              other chants and prayers; 20,000 copies printed (*Episkepsis*)
              (*JMP*, no. 5 (1981), p. 80)
              Menaions for November and February
              (*JMP*, no. 7 (1982), p. 80)

1982   *All-Night Vigil. Liturgy*
              (*JMP*, no. 12 (1982), p. 80)
              Menaion for December
              (*JMP*, no. 12 (1983), p. 80)
              Orders of Service for Hierarchs (*Chinovnik arkhiyereiskogo
              svyashchennosluzheniya*), vols 1 (252 pp.) and 2
              Vol. 1: hierarch's secret prayers at services and ordination
              services for ranks from deacon to archimandrite; vol. 2:
              services of blessing, consecration service for bishops; pre-
              viously published in other service books but gathered in one
              volume for convenience
              (*JMP*, no. 2 (1983), and no. 11 (1983), p. 80)

Comments on appendix

Dates on the title-pages of books are not always the same as date of publication, due to delays.

Publications before 1976 are listed in *The Moscow Patriarchate 1917–
1977*, p. 26; additional information, and information on subsequent publications, is to be found in the issues of *JMP* indicated.

Numbers of copies printed are taken from the CRA Report for 1974,
Vestnik RKhD, no. 130 (1979), p. 328, and *Episkepsis*, no. 252 (20 May
1981), p. 6.

7 THE LAITY

As the previous chapters have shown, it has been above all the steadfast devotion and piety of untold millions of ordinary believers which has kept the Orthodox faith alive during the Soviet period. Though vast numbers of them suffered and perished in the labour camps during the 1920s and 1930s, alongside most of the clergy and nearly all the bishops, there none the less remained millions who flocked back to the churches and monasteries reopened by the occupying German forces, causing Stalin to recognise belatedly that he needed the support of such a large, and patriotic, sector of the population, and that, from the point of view of political control, it was better to offer them a strictly supervised and limited legal existence than to drive them underground, beyond state surveillance. Today it is still the millions of faithful throughout the Soviet Union who make the Russian Orthodox Church one of the largest, most resilient (and well-financed) churches in the world. They have preserved the faith, the traditions and, latterly, the institutional structures which, in the post-Stalin years, have enabled a constantly growing stream of members of the intelligentsia, both young and old, to embrace Orthodox Christianity. There is a parallel here with nineteenth-century Russia, when in many cases the popular religion of the masses was instrumental in winning back to Orthodoxy sections of the upper classes seduced by the rationalistic, anti-church philosophy of the Western European Enlightenment.[1]

Orthodoxy in Russia has always drawn its spiritual strength from the common people. Princes and bishops have rallied the people in times of national crisis, and members of the intelligentsia have produced the works of theological and philosophical depth which have done so much to enrich Christians of other nations, but it has been the solid bedrock of popular piety which has given the support for the former, and, very often, the inspiration for the latter. The greatest spiritual leaders in the Russian Orthodox Church have always been the simple peasants, the monks and saints, who gave up even the little they had for a life of humility and asceticism, the two hallmarks of the distinctively Russian brand of kenotic Christianity. It has been this self-denial, this uncomplaining acceptance of hardship and suffering, that has kept the church not only alive but vigorous despite the attempts to destroy it totally. Millions of simple but devout believers clung fast to their beliefs despite appalling physical and spiritual deprivation, enabling their church to weather persecution of a scale and intensity never before seen in history. In time this will come to be seen as one of the greatest miracles of the twentieth century.

Numbers of Orthodox Believers

This has long been a vexed question, since no reliable statistical information on the number of members of the Russian Orthodox Church is obtainable. Estimates made by Western observers at different times over the last 20 years or so have ranged from as low as 25 million to as high as 100 million Orthodox believers. Soviet sources, both official and unofficial, have usually given figures of between 30 and 50 million. We shall look more closely at some of these estimates in an attempt to see what lies behind them. We must acknowledge at the outset that any calculations can be only very approximate, but none the less the attempt is worth making. First, however, we should note that, when questioned on the size of the membership of the Russian Orthodox Church, both church leaders and Soviet officials invariably reply that as religion is a private matter in the Soviet Union, Soviet citizens are not expected to declare their religious beliefs, and therefore no statistics are kept. As a Soviet writer on religion has stated: 'There is no way of obtaining exact figures. Official documents do not indicate a citizen's religious affiliation. No official has the right to question anyone about his religious views.'[2] Church leaders who state that they do not keep records of church membership are technically being somewhat disingenuous, since all those baptised into the church are regarded as members, and it is known that records of baptisms are kept — a subject to which we shall return later in this chapter — which could no doubt provide useful statistical information, were they available for inspection. At the same time, however, it is true that baptism records would not be a reliable guide to active church membership, since many children baptised by their parents or grandmothers may not grow up to be believers. For example, Yuri Mashkov (who in later life became a convinced Christian, and subsequently emigrated from the Soviet Union) has noted: 'I was baptised as a child, *of course* [emphasis added], but at school I took off my cross [Orthodox Christians wear a baptismal cross around the neck, and usually under the clothing] and until I was 25 I was a convinced atheist.'[3] However, the continuing practice of infant baptism, which most observers agree is widely observed, does point to the at least latent attachment to Orthodoxy among large numbers of parents and grandparents.

Most commentators during the last decade or so have suggested that the active membership of the Russian Orthodox Church is between 30 and 50 million people, while allowing that this figure might well have to be revised upwards.[4] Church hierarchs have sometimes been quoted to this effect.[5] We can also cite some more precise figures which have been given, though they must be interpreted with care. When the Russian Orthodox Church joined the World Council of Churches in 1961, it gave a figure of 30 million 'regular adult worshippers'.[6] However, this figure may well have been an underestimate. It was produced at the height of the anti-religious campaign, when many believers might have been frightened away from worship, or, more likely, have found their local place of worship suddenly closed. It is even possible that the church leadership knowingly reduced the membership total to avoid attracting even further hostile measures from the Soviet government. (It is likely that the Soviet Baptists have also kept their official membership figures artificially low for the same reason.) Later estimates have been higher than the 1961 figure. For example, Archbishop Khrizostom of Kursk, then a deputy-chairman of the Department of External Church Relations, told a British journalist in 1979:

Secular sources say 12% of the population are believers, which with a Soviet total of 262 million means just over 30 million people . . . We think there are more than that, perhaps 36 to 40 million, but it could be between the two figures.[7]

Anatoli Levitin, shortly after emigrating from the USSR in 1974, stated that he had had the chance, while still in the USSR, to read a secret report by Furov to the Soviet government dated 1971–2, which gave the figure of over 40 million Orthodox Church members, and that he thought this was probably reasonably accurate.[8]

These two figures probably relate to fairly regular worshippers. Both Archbishop Khrizostom, speaking for the Moscow Patriarchate, and Furov, speaking for the CRA, have at their disposal the machinery for obtaining estimates of the sizes of congregations throughout the USSR, whether from information given by priests and bishops to the Patriarchate, or from the reports of local CRA commissioners. Taking their two estimates together, it seems that there are about 40 million regular worshippers. (We have used this estimate in previous chapters, especially Chapter 2.) This is perhaps a higher figure than might have been expected, corresponding to nearly 15 per cent of the population of the USSR (270 million at the beginning of 1983), or to approximately 20 per cent of the traditionally Orthodox republics of Russia, Ukraine, Belorussia and Moldavia.[9] Moreover, in absolute terms this figure represents a large number of people, equivalent to roughly two-thirds of the population of the British Isles. Bearing in mind the strongly atheistic atmosphere of Soviet society, and the fact that the Orthodox Church is one of several churches, not to mention the non-Christian religious communities, this is a significant percentage.[10]

These very approximate figures for church membership do not, however, tell the whole story. Many people who do not attend church regularly (perhaps because there is not a church close enough, perhaps for reasons related to the nature of their faith, perhaps because they are afraid of the consequences of doing so) none the less regard themselves as Orthodox, or will demonstrate allegiance to the church by marrying in an Orthodox church, taking their children there to be baptised or giving their relatives a church funeral. If these people are taken into account, the number of believers is very much higher — though it is a debatable point whether all such people can be called 'believers'. Clearly they have some kind of attachment to Orthodoxy, or they would not have recourse to church sacraments at important junctures in their lives. One might make similar observations with regard to the religious allegiance of people in many Western countries, but in the USSR there is an additional element, namely the strong official discouragement regarding any attachment to religion. Therefore, a Soviet citizen who has a child baptised or a relative buried in church is knowingly incurring a degree of official displeasure, and this argues a stronger attachment to religion than is present in their counterpart in, say, Western Europe. It is difficult to estimate how many there are of these people who, while not committed members of the church, can nevertheless legitimately be referred to as 'Orthodox'. It would probably be impossible to calculate their number accurately even if more comprehensive statistical information were available and there were no reasons for some people to be reticent about their religious convictions. Even under present conditions, however, there are some pointers which helps us to form an idea of the size of latent attachment to Russian Orthodoxy among the Soviet population.

Some light has been thrown on this question by the research conducted by Soviet sociologists of religion. Their findings have been documented by two Western scholars: a British sociologist, Christel Lane; and an American student of religion in the USSR, William C. Fletcher. Lane noted that, during the 1960s, the Orthodox percentage of the Soviet population was estimated by sociologists to be 20−40 per cent in rural areas and 5−16 per cent in urban areas.[11] Figures relating to self-professed allegiance to Orthodoxy showed that 20−25 per cent of the Soviet population regarded themselves as Orthodox.[12] This would have given a figure of between 52 and 65 million people. Fletcher estimated in 1976 that there were approximately 115 million religious believers in the USSR, of whom 'perhaps 50 million' were Orthodox.[13] He subsequently backed up this total of 115 million believers in the USSR, which was much higher than previous estimates, by careful argumentation based on detailed presentation and analysis of the findings of Soviet sociologists of religion.[14] His interpretation of their figures involved making allowances for several important factors: possible ideological influences in the presentation of results; variations in figures by different sociologists at different times; the difficulty of defining a religious believer (Soviet sociologists usually adopt either a cognitive approach, asking simply whether or not a person believes in God, or a behavioural approach, studying evidence of the influence of religious beliefs in a person's life, but as the latter poses a far more complex and difficult task for the researcher, the cognitive approach is more widely used); the difficulty of the use of the concept of 'waverers', employed inconsistently by Soviet sociologists, sometimes to mean waverers between belief and unbelief, and sometimes to mean believers in God who exhibit inconsistencies or doubts; and the varying numbers of categories devised, and inconsistently employed in the corpus of Soviet sociology on religion, to cover the possible ranges of conviction between convinced believers and convinced atheists.[15] Fletcher found that, when all this had been taken into account, an aggregate estimate of 30 per cent of the population as religious believers emerged. However, this applied only to the predominantly Russian areas, where most sociological research projects have taken place, and which form approximately half of the total Soviet population. (This percentage would give a figure of nearly 41 million believers in the RSFSR alone.) Fletcher then produced a rough estimate of approximately 60 per cent of religious believers for the rest of the Soviet population (Ukraine and Belorussia, parts of which were not incorporated into the USSR until after the Second World War, and where the number of open churches is known to be higher than elsewhere; Armenia and Georgia, where religion and nationality are closely linked; Central Asia, where Islam is almost impossible to separate from the culture and way of life; and the Baltic region, where 60 per cent may be a high estimate for Estonia and Latvia, but is certainly too low for Catholic Lithuania). He therefore arrived at an overall estimate for the religious sector of the population of 45 per cent, or 115 million believers.[16]

This figure derived from study of overall levels of religiosity is supported, broadly speaking, by such estimates of denominational and non-Christian affiliation as it has been possible to make. There are currently thought to be 45–50 million Muslims, 2 million or more Jews, and about 0.5 million Buddhists in the USSR. These figures derive as much from national affiliation as from known religious observance, and may therefore need to be slightly reduced, but, in view of the close relationship between culture and religion in these cases, not significantly. Protestants number probably in the region of 5 million: over 3 million Baptists (registered and unregistered), about 0.5 million Pentecostals, and smaller numbers of Lutherans, Methodists and Seventh-Day Adventists. There are about 4 million Catholics, Roman and Uniate, the majority of whom are in Lithuania. Orthodox Christianity is closely allied to national feeling in Georgia, with a population of 5 million, and the same is true of the Armenian Apostolic Church, with its centre in Soviet Armenia, the population of which numbers 3 million. Allowance has to be made when using these estimates for national–religious affiliation, which cannot be a reliable indicator of religious commitment in every case, but they do provide a helpful rough estimate of the proportion of the Soviet population which adheres to one or another religious tradition. The estimates above add up to a total of between 64.5 and 69.5 million believers. However, this figure should be reduced in order to produce a more realistic comparison with the approach adopted by

Soviet sociologists, belief or non-belief in God. Not all of the ethnic Muslims and Jews are religious believers, and many if not all of the 0.5 million Buddhists would call themselves atheists. The figures for Protestants and Catholics are probably as close as it is possible to be, but the figures for Georgia and Armenia should be scaled down, because their entire populations do not belong to the national churches, and even among the high proportion that do some allowance must be made for nominalism. Perhaps we should reduce the totals above to, say, 55–60 million to reach a more realistic notion of the members of non-Russian Orthodox religious traditions who retain personal religious convictions. If we compare this rough total with the admittedly highly approximate estimate of 115 million religious believers in the Soviet Union, we find that the remainder, which must consist very largely of Russian Orthodox,[17] could number 55–60 million.

The inadequacies of these calculations are obvious. However, until such time as we have more reliable information to work with, we can take our estimates no further than this. We can, it seems, use some of the conclusions of Soviet sociologists of religion and generally accepted estimates of the sizes of the chief religious bodies in the USSR to reach the tentative conclusion that as many as 15–20 million Soviet citizens who cannot or do not attend Orthodox worship regularly, none the less retain a sense of themselves as being in some way Orthodox.

Recourse to Orthodox Rituals

Estimates based on the recourse which Soviet citizens have to Orthodox rituals have led to much higher figures than this. Struve, in 1967, assumed that two-thirds of the population of Orthodox origin, 160 million, would have been baptised, and therefore estimated that there were 100 million baptised persons.[18] Other writers, using Soviet sources, agree that the rate of Orthodox baptisms is high. Lane cites Soviet sociologists writing in the 1960s to show that an average of 50 per cent of all those eligible in various regions participate in baptism (and funeral) rites.[19] Fletcher, in a more detailed study of such statistics on baptism as are available, notes that while Soviet sociologists of religion clearly regard baptism as an important area of study, suggesting that its incidence is still sufficiently high to cause concern, they differ, sometimes quite markedly, as to the percentage of the Soviet population which is baptised. Studies in some regions (Latvia, Estonia, Ossetia) cite a low level of baptisms, while others (Voronezh and elsewhere) give a rate of as much as 89 per cent. This comparison would tend to suggest that the baptism rate is higher in at least some traditionally Orthodox areas than elsewhere. Soviet sociologists also differ over the reasons for baptism of children; many suggest that religious motives play a minor role, and that other factors, chiefly pressure from grandmothers and a sense of tradition, predominate. They also point to the small but significant proportion of non-believers, including Party members, who have their children baptised.[20] Binns quotes one Soviet sociologist as saying that baptisms as a proportion of births declined from 40 per cent in 1961 to 20 per cent in 1972 throughout the Soviet Union, without, however, displaying much confidence in this datum.[21] (And even 20 per cent might be considered quite a high rate in view of pressure not to baptise children.) All this does not help very much to indicate what proportion of the Soviet population has recourse to Orthodox baptism, or what proportion may in any meaningful way be termed believers, but it does indicate in very general terms that the rate of Orthodox baptism remains high.

Other non-sociological comments exclusively or partly relating to Orthodox baptism also suggest that there is a high rate of baptism, and throw interesting light on those who practise it and their reasons for doing so. A Moscow priest told foreign visitors that in the 23 years since his ordination he had baptised 15,000 people,[22] an average of ten or eleven every single week. Father Dimitri Dudko kept a diary recording the many people — children and young adults — he baptised between 1960 and 1974, concluding: 'Sometimes I have to baptise two or three adults a day, and one simply can't keep count of the children.'[23] Archbishop Khrizostom of Kursk and Belgorod told a Western journalist that he had baptised the children of captains and colonels in the Soviet army.[24] The atheist writer Duluman (a former priest) stated that the rate of infant baptism in some areas was as high as 50 per cent, and added that this could be explained only by grandparents taking their grandchildren to be baptised without the parents' consent.[25] Archbishop Makari of Uman, interviewed in an American television film in 1982, said that he believed that 50–60 per cent of all newborn Ukrainians were baptised. He said there were 50–60 baptisms a week in his own church in Kiev.[26] A meeting of the Moscow regional Young Communist League early in 1985 heard a report which stated that in Yegorevsk and Pavlovsky Posad districts one in every three newborn babies was baptised, and that instances of school-age children being baptised were not isolated cases.[27] A group of Orthodox Christians in Vladimirets region in Ukraine asserted: 'Rarely do you find a house without icons, or unbaptised children.'[28] While they would doubtless suggest that this proceeds from religious motives, the atheist writer Safronov has a different view: he alleged that in a Belorussian village 22 out of 65 *unbelievers* felt obliged to have their children baptised for fear of ostracism by other villagers or trouble with their relatives.[29] There are clearly differences between urban and rural areas. The general view, however, would be that a significant proportion of the population is baptised, and that Struve's estimate may therefore be fairly realistic. However, while these very general figures enable us to say that the proportion of the Soviet population which regards Orthodox baptism as important is very significant, despite decades of atheist propaganda, they do not indicate how many of these people regard themselves as permanently attached to the Orthodox Church.

Similar inconclusive estimates are obtained from study of recourse to church marriages and funerals. It is generally agreed that while the proportion of church marriages is low, even declining, the rate of church funerals remains high, higher even than baptisms. Binns quotes estimates by Soviet sociologists which suggest that Orthodox marriages constitute less than 3 per cent of all marriages,[30] and Fletcher also quotes figures purporting to show that religious (not necessarily Orthodox) marriages have declined[31] and are not known to have risen significantly above 3 per cent in traditionally Orthodox regions.[32] Lane quoted somewhat higher figures for the 1960s — from 1 to 15 per cent of all those who married had Orthodox weddings — but noted that there had been a 'steady decline' in church weddings and went so far as to say that 'extinction of this rite in the Orthodox Church is becoming a serious possibility'. She pointed, however, to some reasons for the decline in church marriages while the rates of baptisms and church funerals remain high: the central figures in a marriage are likely to be under pressure not to marry in church, which is not true of the central figures in baptisms and funerals, where the decision to opt for a church rite is usually made by a relative; the public nature of the ceremony is more obvious in a wedding, whereas baptisms need not be held in the main church building and funerals can be conducted 'by correspondence' (see below).[33] Moreover, Soviet substitute secular rituals have been more successful in the case of marriages than in the case of funerals or baptisms.[34] However, while it is generally agreed that church weddings, even specifically Orthodox weddings, continue to constitute a small proportion of all weddings, the Soviet press none the less continues to make fairly frequent appeals against them.

By contrast, the proportion of the population which has an Orthodox burial is generally agreed to be high. Clearly there is no danger of reprisals, in this case, to the person undergoing the ceremony, and the relatives who arrange it can appeal to the wishes of the departed one. The high proportion of church funerals is doubtless illustrative of the choices Soviet citizens will make in personal matters concerning religion when there is no danger of reprisals. Binns cites one Soviet sociologist as saying that religious (not Orthodox) funerals declined from 60 per cent in 1961 to 32 per cent in 1972.[35] This is still a high proportion — nearly one-third of all deaths were commemorated in a religious manner. Lane supports this, broadly speaking, when she notes that 50 per cent of those eligible for funerals (and baptisms) performed them according to the Orthodox rite during the 1960s, and that this has 'remained fairly stable or declined only slowly'.[36] She also notes that a significant proportion of funeral rites were conducted 'by correspondence' (*zaochno*), in order to overcome the shortage of priests.

Relatives send some earth from the grave by post to a priest, who blesses it and returns it in the same way. She quotes Soviet sociologists to illustrate that, in some widely separated regions where there are Orthodox communities, funerals 'by correspondence' ranged from 46.8 to 89 per cent during the early to mid-1960s and increased after 1968.[37] These figures, plus those relating to funerals conducted by a layman where the services of a priest are unavailable, probably do not enter the statistics quoted above.[38]

Fletcher, writing at a later date, also gives high figures for funerals 'by correspondence' — between 63 and 89 per cent.[39] He further notes that the decline in the rate of religious funerals has been slight — for example, only 11 per cent in Trans-Carpathia.[40] Fletcher adds, no doubt rightly, that religious funerals are 'the most persistent of all the rites', and that 'attempts to replace them with secular rituals have certainly enjoyed very little success'.[41]

Gleb Rahr, writing in 1973, attempted to estimate the number of people attached to the Russian Orthodox Church through calculations based on the numbers of church baptisms and funerals in Leningrad region during 1970. His figures were obtained from lectures by Soviet propagandists. By this means, he arrived at a figure of 115 million — coincidentally, the same as Fletcher's estimate for the religious population as a whole, and therefore, perhaps, rather higher than might have been expected.[42] Rahr's estimate may illustrate the difference, a fairly large one, between those Soviet citizens who attend church fairly regularly when it is possible to do so, and those who are unable or unwilling to participate in church life on a regular basis, but who none the less have recourse to Orthodox rituals at critical junctures in their lives.

We should also note that the CRA Report for 1974 stated that the Moscow Patriarchate produced 1 million headbands and prayers for the dead every year. These were essential for Orthodox funerals.[43] Some of these could have been for overseas dioceses (although the CRA Report does not explicitly suggest this), but even so this remains a high number of Orthodox funerals.

Here we must add a cautionary note. While the figures and estimates cited above for church attendance and recourse to Orthodox rituals may give us some idea of the support, or potential support, which the Russian Orthodox Church enjoys among the Soviet population, they do not help us to define who an Orthodox believer is. Definitions of any kind in the very sensitive and personal area of religious belief are difficult, if not impossible, to make even in the most favourable circumstances, but here imprecise, even misleading, information can make the task even harder. Regular attendance at worship is no guide to belief in a situation where many committed, even fervent, believers may have no access to a church; and others may attend a nearby church out of curiosity or from aesthetic impulses without having or desiring to have any understanding of the essential truths of Christianity. The Russian Orthodox Church itself, as noted above, claims to have no register of members, and while baptism undoubtedly continues to be the criterion for church membership, as it has always been, the continued widespread practice of infant baptism means that there is no reliable guide to active adult church membership. The cognitive approach to religious belief adopted by most Soviet sociologists of religion can also bedevil any attempt to assess the numbers of Orthodox Christians, or of all Christians, in the Soviet Union. It is perfectly possible to believe in the existence of God, and even to believe in Him within the context of Orthodoxy, without accepting that this belief need make any difference to one's way of life. Furthermore, from a Christian, and Orthodox Christian, point of view, such 'believers' may not necessarily be Christians: a person confronted with a questionnaire may well decide to say that God exists, rather than that He does not, but still have no specifically Christian concept of God, man or the world. Such people may believe in God, even strongly, but have no concept of Christ as the Son of God or of the Holy Spirit; they thus lack the fully developed trinitarian basis which is a central part of Orthodox Christianity. Soviet sociology, then, helps to identify theists rather than Christians. It helps to suggest the extent of varying degrees of support for Orthodox beliefs and way of life, but does little to indicate how many people are what the church itself would regard as fully fledged members.

Sociological Findings on Orthodox Believers

The general impression of members of the Russian Orthodox Church formed by visitors to church services, and in other ways, is that they are predominantly elderly, predominantly female, not particularly well educated and not usually employed in prestigious or important jobs. To most observers, Orthodox (and other) believers appear to exist on the periphery of Soviet society, never in central or leading roles. The findings of Soviet sociologists on religion (which are far from comprehensive) tend to bear out this impression. However, there are some interesting variations among the findings of Soviet sociologists which make it worth while to examine their conclusions a little more closely. There are also other factors to be taken into account, which modify the above impression to some extent.

Lane cites several Soviet sociologists to support the view that 'an overwhelming majority of self-identified Orthodox believers are female and elderly'.[44] However, she adds that her own visits to Orthodox churches in Moscow and Oryol in 1973 confirmed that services 'attracted a noticeable minority of men and young people under forty years of age'.[45] Other foreign visitors to churches in Moscow, Leningrad and other towns would confirm this impression, including the present author. Evidently Orthodoxy (and religion in general) are not without influence among the young. This view is borne out by Fletcher's findings. He begins by quoting several Soviet sociologists who have found a very small proportion of believers among young people, with the percentage of believers increasing in middle age, and, even more markedly, in old age. It is probably safe enough to take these statistics on religion as applying, broadly speaking, to Orthodoxy exclusively. Fletcher suggests that 'the direct relationship between advancing age and an increasing percentage of religiousness in the population is a unanimous finding of Soviet religious sociology'. However, other findings which he quotes modify this view. Soviet sociology has discovered that many young people approve of religion or are indifferent to questions of religion and atheism (25–30 per cent). And surveys conducted by various researchers in various places have recorded rates of religiousness from as low as 5 per cent to as high as 30 per cent. Higher percentages were recorded among the middle-aged, and much higher among the elderly. However, some studies have shown that the elderly constitute less than half the members of religious communities (though few of those cited were Orthodox). By and large, however, the elderly predominate in religious communities.[46] Fletcher notes some reasons for this, not always reflected in Soviet scholarship: there has been a constant supply of religious elderly people throughout the Soviet period, which tends to undermine the official Soviet view that the preponderance of the elderly is symptomatic of the decay of religion; religion generally tends to exercise more influence on people after middle age (and this may be especially true of Russian Orthodoxy); and sanctions against religious young people at work and in education may discourage them from involvement in the church.[47]

Lane's findings that the majority of Orthodox appeared to be female as well as elderly has been noted.[48] Fletcher also supports this view, though citing disparate figures from Soviet researchers which show that the proportion of females attending church services vary from as high as 97 per cent to as low as 65 per cent. However, he also cites figures showing that the proportion of females in the population as a whole is significantly larger than that of males, and therefore the proportion of men attending church is higher than their proportion in the general population. The disparity is largely due to the high rate of male casualties during the Second World War, and will therefore presumably disappear in the course of time.[49]

Soviet sociology of religion has produced numerous figures to illustrate that religious believers are, by and large, not among the best-educated strata of the population. Fletcher quotes several Soviet researchers who have produced results which purport to show that there is 'an inverse correlation between religiousness and educational level in the general population'.[50] Although there are some variations according to the schemes used by researchers and from one place to another, it has not been difficult for Soviet sociology to discover that usually well over half of those educated to secondary level or above are unbelievers; in come cases the figure rises to as high as 80 or 90 per cent. Educational levels among believers themselves have also received a good deal of attention from Soviet researchers. Widely varying results have been recorded. Some scholars found that the proportion of religious believers who were poorly educated was as high as 80 or 90 per cent or more, while others found much lower figures of 50 and even 33 per cent. Moreover, some studies suggested that in at least some groups of believers the poorly educated were few. Fletcher points out that by looking more closely at the categories used by researchers, and even more by allowing for the high levels of the elderly and females (who tend to be less well educated) among believers, it can be shown that in fact the educational levels among believers do not diverge very widely from those of the population as a whole. Educational levels have also been found to be higher among younger believers, which, of course, suggests that educational levels among believers will improve in the future. Fletcher concludes, rightly no doubt, that 'it would not seem that Soviet scholarship has established beyond all question an inverse relationship between religiousness and education level, even though it does indicate that, by and large, the lower levels of education are dominant among religious people'.[51]

Unfortunately for our purposes, neither Fletcher nor his sources indicate denominational affiliation, except occasionally and then usually with reference to Baptists, so that we cannot say how far his findings apply to the Orthodox. On the face of it, however, because the Orthodox form such a large proportion of all believers, and are distributed, albeit unequally, throughout most parts of the Soviet Union, there seems no reason to suppose that their educational levels would differ very widely from those outlined above. Lane's findings, very broadly speaking, support this view. She quotes Soviet sociologists to show that 'around 70 per cent of them are only semi-literate and a mere 1.2 per cent have had secondary education'.[52] However, she does not enquire as closely as Fletcher into the meaning of 'semi-literate'; in fact, as he points out, the term is a technical one indicating that a person has had less than four years' primary education, and does not indicate whether or not they can read.[53] Lane also suggests that the Orthodox are less well educated than the Baptists.

As far as occupation is concerned, it is not surprising to find that religious believers are found predominantly in the non-working category, or in low-paid, non-prestigious jobs. This is a natural consequence of the relatively high levels of the elderly, women and poorly educated among their number. The proportion of those who do not work at all (mostly housekeepers, also the retired and invalids) is high among believers, though the levels reported by different researchers vary very widely: from as high as 99 per cent to as low as 10.3 per cent. One scholar found that 'more than half of the believers of the Orthodox faith were not directly connected with social production'. They included 34 per cent housekeepers, 17 per cent retired people, more than 5 per cent dependants and helpers around the house, and 14 per cent of unskilled people who did odd jobs.[54] Other figures are cited, referring to the religious population as a whole, which show that among the working population, religious believers are found most commonly among collective farmers, less commonly among workers, and very rarely among white-collar workers.[55] Data for one Orthodox village parish were as follows: 55.8 per cent housekeepers and retired, 18.8 per cent employed at odd jobs on a collective farm, 7.8 per cent unskilled labourers, 7 per cent skilled workers (mechanics and the like) and 2.8 per cent office and administrative personnel.[56] Fletcher notes in conclusion that job discrimination against believers may well be responsible to a large extent for their having such a large proportion of low-status occupations.[57] It is certainly true that some Orthodox believers (and many of other denominations) have suffered in this way; we shall discuss this below.

Lane, more briefly, comes to a broadly similar conclusion: she notes that, according to Soviet data, 'members of the technical and cultural intelligentsia are almost completely absent among Orthodox believers'.[58] She then mentions some reports of a revival of interest in Orthodoxy among the intelligentsia, but concludes (writing before 1978) that it was not possible to make generalisations about how significant and widespread the hold of Orthodoxy on members of the elite might be.[59] However, further evidence of the growing interest in and commitment to Orthodoxy has been reaching the West since then, which we shall discuss in Part II, and it is clear by now that the failure of Soviet sociologists to comment upon it must surely be considered a gap in their research. Doubtless few researchers would be willing to tackle research in such an ideologically sensitive area; since the prevailing ideology holds that religiousness should decrease as education (particularly education in a Marxist—Leninist spirit) increases, then (as Fletcher notes) it would be asking for trouble to produce data that demonstrated the opposite.

It appears, then, that the Russian Orthodox Church attracts mostly the least enlightened members of the Soviet population, and those who are on the periphery of society, contributing least to both production and to culture and ideas. In addition, the church attracts a smaller but significant number of the intelligentsia, including some of the best-educated, most gifted people in the land (as we shall show in Part II). It is hard to say to what extent those left on the periphery are there because of their own personal characteristics or because of discrimination. Clearly, both factors contribute. Russian Orthodoxy has always been to a significant extent the religion of the pious but simple masses, and indeed encourages a humble, otherworldly religious attitude. Humility and self-abnegation are among the chief Orthodox virtues, and the devout Orthodox believer has never been encouraged to work for a place of prestige or influence in the affairs of the world. (Which is not to say that some have not achieved one.) Moreover,

Orthodoxy has always had a strong hold upon the rural population, which did not contribute in a significant, active manner to politics, government or culture (although the influence of the peasantry's way of life on many leading members of the intelligentsia, notably Tolstoy and Dostoyevsky, is well known). However, not all the present members of the Russian Orthodox Church come from the peasantry, so this can be only a partial, though important, explanation of their status. Discrimination undoubtedly plays its part, but this is entirely absent from the findings of Soviet sociology of religion, and therefore constitutes an imbalance in them. The ideological framework within which Soviet sociology operates is still strict, and results which run counter to current ideological principles are so rare as to be negligible.

An interesting gloss on the picture presented above is given by Anatoli Levitin-Krasnov, writing on the basis of a lifetime of his own personal experiences in the church. He notes: 'The Russian Orthodox Church attracts both the most educated and the most backward sections of the population. Those who fall between these two groups have mostly left the Church.' Commenting on the predominantly elderly and female membership of the church, Levitin says:

In the 1920s I used to be told that the old folk were dying off and that the Church would also die. Twenty years then passed, and in 1947 a deacon, who was a superficial and ignorant man, said: 'Whatever will happen when the old people die and no one is left in church?' But since then another 30 years have passed and not only are there no fewer churchgoers, there are more . . . Unlike the 1920s, it cannot now be claimed that religion is a survival of the past, since 75 per cent of the old women who go to church today were Komsomol members of the past and went to Soviet schools. It cannot now be asserted that religion is the prop of the ruling classes of the past, since most of these old women come from worker or peasant backgrounds and can remember nothing of pre-revolutionary ways. After all, those who are in the 70s today were only ten at the time of the Revolution, and so have lived most of their lives under Soviet rule.

And he adds: 'But apart from the old women, it is the young people aged between 18 and 30 who are now going to church . . . This milieu of the young Soviet intelligentsia is most receptive to religion.'[60]

It is interesting to speculate why Orthodoxy should attract two strata of the population who are in many ways so far removed from one another — in education, interests, way of life. Perhaps it is the strong element of mysticism in Orthodoxy, the apprehension that this life, the here and now, are only part of a much greater reality. This is attractive both to an intellectual searching for ultimate truth, with time and capacity to think and reflect, and also to someone engaged in hard but mentally undemanding manual labour, also with much time for reflection, closely attached to the earth, the weather and the changing seasons, and so led by their daily work to ponder the mysteries of nature and creation. The intermediate strata of skilled workers, managers and technocrats, by contrast, are generally more orientated towards action than towards reflection. If inclined towards religion at all, they would be more likely to gravitate towards the Baptists than towards Orthodoxy. Levitin-Krasnov comments:

Baptist converts are often young lads from the country or from a small town, they are collective-farm or factory workers, metal-smiths, carpenters or unskilled labourers. They might be white-collar workers, draughtsmen, accountants or technicians . . . An Orthodox church service is incomprehensible to them with its unfamiliar language, rituals, strange clothes, and wailing old women. After five or ten minutes such a person shrugs his shoulders and leaves.[61]

These are of course broad generalisations. At present our information on the social composition of the Russian Orthodox Church is very far from complete.

'Inferior People'

However, despite the strength of the grassroots support for the church, ordinary believers still encounter many serious problems in their daily lives. The following complaint is a particularly vivid example of this:

The whole world believes the word of the government of our country that we have genuine freedom, that there is no religious discrimination and persecution. But in fact, believing people are deprived of the right and the freedom to confess faith and to satisfy their religious needs. We are considered inferior people; believing children are oppressed in schools, we are not admitted to higher educational institutions and to positions of leadership. We live under the constant persecution of the communists and the surveillance of agents of the KGB. Schoolchildren have their crosses torn away from them, and are forced to enrol in the Pioneers and the Komsomol [youth movements attached to the Communist Party, for schoolchildren and teenagers and upwards respectively]. But our entire population, on the whole, are believers. Rarely do you find a house without icons, or unbaptised children. This infuriates the communists, and they descend upon us, destroy, burn and close our churches, so that we shall have nowhere to worship and sustain ourselves spiritually.[62]

Such is the view of 21 Orthodox Christians living in Vladimirets district in Ukraine. Numerous other documents written over the years speak of similar abuses. They suggest that many believers face difficulties not only in participating in the life of the church as an institution, but also in their personal daily lives outside the church.

The previous six chapters have outlined the difficulties which believers encounter as a result of strict state control over the church's institutions. Large numbers of the faithful are unable to worship regularly because there are not enough open churches. Those who attempt to compensate for this by making a pilgrimage to a monastery may have to travel very long distances to one of the few monasteries or convents which remain open, and even there they may encounter rough treatment. A believer with a monastic vocation will find that only very small numbers of novices are admitted. Some believers benefit from the teaching and guidance of a wise and learned priest, but others may have no local parish priest, or one who is too timid, or too overworked, or in a few cases too corrupt, to give adequate pastoral care. In any case, the numbers of clergy are small compared with the numbers of faithful; no doubt they are looking with hope towards the theological schools, wondering if the increase in the numbers of students will eventually lead to an increase in the overall strength of the clergy. It may be possible to make good some of these deficiencies by private reading and study, but the restrictions on publishing of religious literature, and the ban on importing it from abroad, make this very difficult. So the believer is left to private prayers, alone or in a family or group, to observance of the feasts, fasts and saints' days, and to living a Christian way of life day by day. In these circumstances it would not be surprising if erroneous or superstitious ideas did not sometimes make their appearance, but it seems clear none the less that in this quiet way the essentials of the Christian faith are being preserved. The tradition of living in obedience to a spiritual father continues, and a visitor to Moscow in the early 1980s noted that many people there, often whole families, were living in obedience to a monk or *starets*.

The difficulties which Orthodox believers encounter in both personal and institutional religious life, and the exclusion of their point of view from corporate social life, are in clear defiance of the Soviet Constitution, which states that

Citizens of the USSR shall be equal before the law, irrespective of . . . attitude to religion. Equality of rights of citizens of the USSR shall be ensured in all fields of economic, political, social and cultural life [Article 34].

Furthermore,

Incitement of hostility and hatred on religious grounds shall be prohibited [Article 52]

When questioned about religious discrimination in the USSR, official Soviet spokesmen, including church leaders, customarily refer to these provisions of the Constitution as though they were in themselves a guarantee that religious discrimination does not occur. However, the documentary evidence indicates otherwise.

The Vladimirets believers said that they felt themselves to be regarded as 'inferior people'. There are a number of ways in which they and other believers are made to feel this. First and foremost is the view, widely and insistently propagated through all means of communication in the USSR, that a true Soviet citizen is an atheist. Although statements are often made in the Soviet press to the effect that believers have freedom of worship, and that Soviet society provides for their religious needs, the effect is to isolate believers as a separate category of people who have special needs and are not entirely normal citizens. The continual repetition of this viewpoint over many years has its inevitable effect by creating a concept of the 'apartness' of believers which both believers and unbelievers find difficult to overcome. Both must find it difficult to see believers as integral members of society when it is constantly insinuated that the 'best' citizens are always atheists.

This sense of the exclusion of believers from the normal life of society is reinforced by atheist propaganda. Very frequently articles appear in the Soviet press stating that religious life is on the increase in a given area because of the apathy of local atheist activists. The underlying assumption is that religious belief is an undesirable phenomenon which appears the moment right-thinking citizens relax their vigilance. Often atheist and Party activists are publicly exhorted to conduct individual work with believers — that is, get to know them on a personal level and talk to them, aiming to convince them of the error of their ways. Again, there is an underlying assumption, that believers will not persist in their abnormal ideas once they are 'enlightened' by atheists.

Recent examples of this include an article in the Young Communist newspaper *Komsomolskaya pravda* in September 1980. Centring on the Chuvash Autonomous Region, it claimed that, while religion was in a decline in the USSR, Orthodox priests (and sectarians) were attempting to influence the young towards a religious point of view. Many 'non-believers', according to *Komsomolskaya pravda*, marry in church, attend baptisms, celebrate religious holidays and keep religious objects in their homes. The newspaper noted that the greatest hindrance to the effectiveness of atheist education was indifference towards religion. Propagandists, therefore, must be extremely well prepared and tactically aware when approaching children and young people.[63] In March 1981 an article in *Molodyozh Moldavii* (*Youth of Moldavia*) similarly called for improved atheist work, particularly among young people. The author urged all organisations, particularly the Komsomol, to be freshly motivated in the atheist nurturing of youth and to make a concerted effort in the areas of ideological, labour and moral upbringing.[64] In April 1982, *Nauka i religiya* announced a competition launched in the Russian republic for the best publications on atheist upbringing. The aim of the competition was to stimulate publication of materials on atheist upbringing, to assist in overcoming religious prejudices and superstitions and to contribute to the formation of a scientific–materialistic outlook and a positive approach to life in all Soviet citizens.[65]

Assumptions such as these profoundly affect the atmosphere in which believers have to live and work. Despite the fact that on paper they are equal before the law, the whole population is inculcated with the idea that they are misguided people who need to be enlightened before they can become true Soviet citizens. This is most strikingly shown by the fact that there are no publicly identified religious believers in responsible positions in Soviet society. Not only are there no known believers in the ranks of the government and Party, but it is also difficult, if not impossible, for them to become teachers, lawyers or factory managers — in fact, to assume any position in which their beliefs might influence others. As we have seen, there may be 60 to more than 100 million citizens who have some kind of passive attachment to Orthodoxy, and it would clearly be impossible to exclude them all from influential posts. The point is that believers or semi-believers who have attained positions of responsibility find it necessary to keep their faith a secret. Such discrimination contradicts any claim that believers and unbelievers are equal in more than name.

It is likely that in the case of many Orthodox believers, the assumption of their 'inferiority' is the worst they have to suffer. Unlike the much smaller Protestant and Catholic denominations, and the Jews, all of whose active members can expect to endure discrimination, a large proportion of the millions of Orthodox believers may not experience direct discrimination if their expression of their faith is confined to occasional churchgoing. There is, however, no doubt that discrimination is the lot of some Orthodox Christians, and we shall examine the ways in which it occurs.

Discrimination at Work

Some believers experience discrimination at work. One such was a young woman from Poltava district in Ukraine, named Zinaida Girinkova, who wrote to Patriarch Pimen appealing for help:

> The administration at my works, learning that I am a believer and attend God's church, began to mock my religious convictions and force me to

renounce the faith of Christ as the price of my flat and of promotion in my job. Moreover, they accused me of having links 'abroad', which were supposedly financing me. My home was searched . . .

I have worked at this job for seven years and am on the waiting-list for a flat, but I was faced with a choice: either work as an engineer and be given a flat, and renounce the Church, or else leave work. I chose the second, and I shall never return there . . .

Respected Father Pimen! Why do they persecute young believers so cruelly in our country? Why do they try so savagely to burn faith out of our hearts 'with fire and the sword', although it is officially permitted?[66]

While it is possible that the discrimination against Girinkova could have been due to heartless or malicious individuals at her place of work, it is doubtful whether they would have gone so far if pervasive atheist propaganda had not suggested that believers were in some way a legitimate target.

Other examples of discrimination at work against Orthodox Christians have occurred from time to time. A mathematics teacher who was found to have a private chapel in his home was dismissed from his post.[67] A former novice of the Pskov monastery who had also studied at the Leningrad seminary complained that he could not find work and was discriminated against even after he had left: 'What have I done to harm people?' he wrote. 'After all, my faith was in my soul, and did not interfere with anyone.'[68] (His complaint was published in the monthly journal *Nauka i religiya*, and inspired a number of believers and unbelievers to write to the editor expressing sympathy and concern for him.) And an Orthodox woman in Kaluga, after being beaten up at work, complained, and was then committed to a psychiatric hospital for 'treatment'. A doctor told her: 'Admit there is no God, and we will admit that you are healthy'.[69] A very fully documented case of dismissal is that of Tatyana Shchipkova, a lecturer at the Pedagogical Institute in Smolensk, who lost her job after 17 years' teaching there when it became known publicly that she was a practising Christian. (Her case will be discussed in Chapters 12 and 13.) Occasionally, there are reports of people losing their jobs because of the religious activities of their relatives. In 1984, the newspaper *Sovetskaya Rossiya* reported that the First Secretary of the Kirov Communist Party, A. I. Dzyuba, had lost his post because his son-in-law sang in a church choir.[70] Although specific reports of instances of discrimination at work are relatively rare, partly due to the difficulties of conveying them abroad, general allegations of this nature continue to be made by Orthodox believers.

Discrimination in Education

The question of whether or not believers are excluded from higher education is a controversial one. At least two Russian Orthodox bishops are on record as saying that they are not. In 1975 Archbishop Kirill of Vyborg stated:

Christians can qualify just as anyone else. They cannot be discriminated against because of their religion alone. If a person was denied entrance to the university because he was a Christian, the man who denied him would be punished.[71]

This is undoubtedly an accurate reflection of the situation as it should be, according to the Constitution of the USSR, but without any specific examples it is not a complete argument that this is what actually happens in practice. Certainly Christians do study at higher educational institutes — most of the leading independent thinkers in the Orthodox Church have done so — but they almost invariably have to keep their faith a strictly private matter. In 1977 it was reported that one Moscow priest had baptised 13 members of the Soviet Academy of Sciences during one year,[72] but their names were not given, and, so far as is known, they have not identified themselves publicly as believers. Archbishop Pitirim of Volokolamsk commented more specifically on the actual situation in an interview during 1980, in which he stated that there were undoubtedly believers among the students and graduates of higher educational institutes, including priests and 'even' members of the higher Orthodox clergy. He stated that

In my time, I myself studied at the Moscow institute of railway transport engineers. Neither when I entered, nor during my years of study did anyone show any interest in my religious views.[73]

Archbishop Pitirim then named several leading hierarchs of the church who had received higher education; this was before their ordination. It would appear from his remarks that people are not asked about their religious beliefs when applying to higher educational institutes, and that believers who choose to regard their faith as a private matter are able to complete their courses. There are, however, a number of known cases where people who have by chance been discovered to be believers have been expelled from higher educational institutions. One such, curiously enough, is one of the people referred to by Archbishop Pitirim as an example of a priest who had succeeded in obtaining higher education, the Old Believer priest Yevgeni Bobkov. In fact, Bobkov was expelled from Moscow University after he was discovered to be an altar boy at the Old Believer cathedral in Moscow, and was vilified in the Soviet press.[74] Anatoli Levitin-Krasnov defended him vigorously in one of his earliest *samizdat* articles.[75] Evidently Bobkov was permitted to resume his studies after this disruption, which occurred during the anti-religious campaign in 1959. There are more recent examples of discrimination against believers in education.

Sergei Bogdanovsky was a student in the embryology course of the Biology Faculty of Moscow State University. He was expelled after some poems and an article, of a religious nature, were discovered among belongings he had deposited for safekeeping in a storage room at a university hostel. According to the chief deputy-head of administration, who discovered them, they were 'anti-Soviet materials'.[76] Unfortunately, no further description of their content is given, and we therefore have no independent means of assessing this claim. Evidently Bogdanovsky was under suspicion of some kind, if his personal belongings were searched in his absence, and the possibility that he was involved in some kind of political, as well as religious, activity cannot be entirely excluded. According to Bogdanovsky's own account, however (the only one available), it was his religious views which led to his expulsion. In an undated letter to the rector of the university, Bogdanovsky stated that, on 12 May 1978, he had had an interview with the Young Communist League secretary, V. I. Yuzhakov, to whom the discovery had been reported. Bogdanovsky pointed out to him that the confiscation of the written materials was illegal, and that there was no evidence that he had committed any crime. At this, Yuzhakov immediately turned to the issue of his religious convictions, ignoring the question of any possible political involvement: 'V. I. Yuzhakov at once raised the question of my attitude to religion, and the incompatibility of religious convictions with remaining in the ranks of the Komsomol.'[77] This strongly suggests that there was little or no significant political content in the confiscated materials, since this would have been a more serious matter from the Komsomol's point of view than religious beliefs. Bogdanovsky therefore decided to write a voluntary resignation:

> Having come to faith in God, I have become a member of the Russian Orthodox Church. In connection with the fact that remaining in the Young Communist League is incompatible with Christianity, I give notice by this present statement that I am leaving the Young Communist League. I ask that my personal case be heard in my absence. I append the Young Communist League card No. 23395223.[78]

Bogdanovsky's resignation was considered at a meeting of the Moscow State University Committee of the Young Communist League on 15 May, which chose not to accept it, but to expel him from its ranks 'for political immaturity and behaviour unworthy of a Young Communist League member'.[79] The Young Communist League secretary reported this to the dean of the university, who on 18 May signed a statement that Bogdanovsky was to be expelled from his course and evicted from the hostel, 'for behaviour unworthy of a Soviet student'.[80]

It seems possible that Bogdanovsky's expulsion was due to the fact that he had in his possession written religious materials, which he might distribute to others; in other words he was suspected of not keeping his beliefs private but of attempting to influence others. We should note, however, that Yuzhakov did not tax him with this, but referred only to the incompatibility of his beliefs with membership of the Young Communist League.

Another case in which a person's attitude to religion played a part in his expulsion from Moscow State University was that of Alexander Ogorodnikov. His own account of this is as follows:

> In my second year at the All-Union State Cinematography Institute (ASCI) my position was discussed at the Party Office of the Institute. The reason for this was a denunciation by an informer who had seen the cross around my neck. A few days before my expulsion from the Dean's office I was taken to 38 Petrovka Street, to Inspector Spirin of the Moscow Criminal Investigation Department, where my fingerprints were taken. The investigator demanded that I hand over the materials for a film on the religious quest of Soviet youth (*Jesus People*) and announced that my future in ASCI depended on his, Spirin's decision. The Dean of the Institute, V. N. Zhdan, told me in a personal conversation that 'a report on you has come through' and that 'we are forced to expel you'.[81]

In an article about Ogorodnikov published in a Soviet newspaper it was alleged that he had in fact been expelled because he 'was an extremely undisciplined student, systematically missed classes without significant reasons and had not taken examinations in a number of subjects'.[82] However, as none of these alleged misdemeanours was even mentioned until after his attitude to religion was discovered, it is unlikely that this was the true reason for his expulsion.

The cases of Bogdanovsky and Ogorodnikov (plus some members of other denominations) suggests that believers who do not keep their faith to themselves are unlikely to be admitted to, or likely to be expelled from, institutes of higher education. In Ogorodnikov's case, it may well have been his intention to make a film about the 'Jesus people' that caused the authorities to expel him. However, their failure to admit this, and consequent reliance upon 'an informer who had seen a cross around [his] neck' is scarcely a convincing support for their claim that believers are not discriminated against in higher education. Even the apparent practice of the authorities in discriminating only against believers who do not keep their faith private can hardly be said to be altogether even-handed. First, it is obvious that they cannot adopt any attitude towards a person for being a believer if they do not know that that person is one. Second, there is the question of a person influencing others towards religious faith. While at first glance it may seem fair and reasonable to say that a believer should be free to worship but not to attempt to influence others towards religion, this position is in fact a rather weak one. Believers cannot really be considered equal members of society if their points of view on all kinds of questions cannot be put forward and considered equally with those of atheists, agnostics and the indifferent. The intellectual life of a university must surely be diminished by failing even to consider the contribution which educated and intelligent believers have to make. Moreover, if the Soviet authorities were really confident of the ideological and intellectual superiority of Marxim–Leninism, including its atheist content, they would not fear the influence of the religious point of view. Soviet institutes of higher education — and above all Moscow University, from which Bogdanovsky and Ogorodnikov were expelled — admit only the best-educated, most intelligent, and, above all, most ideologically acceptable young people, the *crème de la crème*, and if the authorities could not expect them to view Ogorodnikov's planned film on the 'Jesus people' — surely a subject of at least passing concern from many points of view — without their ideological purity being undermined, then their confidence in their own ideological education system cannot be all that strong.

Admission to and continuance in higher education is conditioned by previous events in a young believer's life. As was seen in the case of Bogdanovsky, membership of the Young Communist League (Komsomol) is an important factor in higher education. Only the most gifted non-Young Communist League members are admitted to the most prestigious institutes of higher education — a corollary of the belief that citizens destined to play a leading role in Soviet society must be politically and ideologically acceptable. However, since known believers are discouraged from joining — or may not wish to join — the Young Communist League, this lowers their chances of admission to higher education. Furthermore, children from religious families, or those who become believers while still at school, are subject to pressure from teachers, who sometimes enlist the support of classmates, to abandon their beliefs. (In some cases involving mostly Baptist and other Protestant children, this has taken the form of bullying, mockery and even violence, though such tactics are not generally reported to any great extent where Orthodox children are concerned.) This must doubtless affect their school performance. Even the fact of being educated in an atmosphere where atheism is all-pervasive must have a deleterious effect upon a religious child, since to be taught one thing at school and another thing at home in a constantly alternating cycle is a classic recipe for producing confusion and disorientation, if not worse. This too may be expected to affect the school performance of all but the most strong-minded children, and therefore to affect their chances of admission to higher education.

A further consequence of the atheistic orientation of all education in the Soviet Union is the consequent difficulties encountered in the religious education of young people (or of older new members of the church). As we noted in Chapter 2, religious education is forbidden by law, except that of children by their parents. (During the 1960s and 1970s there were even some cases of children being removed from their parents and sent to state boarding schools because their parents gave them a religious upbringing, mainly in Protestant families, but few such cases have been reported in recent years, and none concerning Orthodox families.) The church is therefore able to do very little to educate young people. Some efforts have been made: for example, Metropolitan Filaret of Minsk and Belorussia said during a talk in London in 1980 that he advised the priests in his diocese to gather all the children preparing for confession and communion into one group before the liturgy and to hold a discussion with them.[83] Perhaps this happens in other dioceses as well, though a local CRA commissioner who interpreted the law very strictly would doubtless consider such discussions illegal. Father Gleb Yakunin takes a much dimmer view of the church's ability to educate the young. He writes:

In the Orthodox Church, with the very rare exception of some parents who take this feat upon themselves, the issue of the education of the young is allowed to drift. Believing parents, as a rule, do not have the appropriate knowledge and ability for the religious education of their children. The complete absence of modern children's religious literature in Russian has a great negative influence on the question of children's religious education.[84]

Doubtless Father Gleb is right to point to the lack of suitable children's literature as crucial in the question of religious education. While there are many dedicated families able to bring up their children as Orthodox Christians, sometimes with the aid of children's books from the West (none has been published in the Soviet Union, as is evident from Chapter 6), this continues to be a very important problem for the church.

Registration of Baptisms

Another practice which widely affects believing parents is that of registration of baptisms. As indicated above, the rate of baptisms is generally believed to be high. The Soviet authorities have sought to combat this in two ways. One, probably the less effective, is to criticise baptism as harmful to children's health. (Infant baptism in the Orthodox Church is by immersion.) The results of researches published in *Meditsinskaya gazeta* in 1970 alleged that one in every three babies baptised in two churches in Yaroslavl district suffered inflammation of the lungs, and that in Rybinsk baptised babies suffered twice as many illnesses as babies who were not baptised.[85] In Magnitogorsk a baby was said to have choked to death as a result of being immersed in baptismal water.[86] It is not possible to check these assertions but, whether true or not, they do not appear to have discouraged parents from having their children baptised. Much more harmful to parents has been the compulsory registration of baptisms. Before a child can be baptised in church, both parents have to be present and produce their passports — i.e. internal passports, or identity cards, which are carried by all adult Soviet citizens — details from which are entered in a register kept by the church's executive committee. These records are available to CRA commissioners, and enable them to identify local residents as believers. In many cases this fact has been reported to the parents' place of work, and they have suffered discrimination as a result.

Several *samizdat* sources testify to the discriminatory effects of registration of baptisms. Michael Bourdeaux cited some dating from the 1960s: a letter to the Eastern Patriarchs from two Orthodox women,[87] the open letter of Fathers Gleb Yakunin and Nikolai Eshliman to Patriarch Alexi,[88] and articles by Anatoli Levitin-Krasnov on the Moscow parish of Father Vsevolod Shpiller.[89] More recent references show that the practice has continued into the 1970s and 1980s. Father Gleb Yakunin and Father Dimitri Dudko both referred to discrimination against parents who had baptised their children after Father Dimitri had been accused in the Soviet press of baptising children in his home. He responded:

> in church they illegally registered the baptism, and then later, having found out about the people who had been baptised from this record, they forced them out of their place of education or their work.[90]

Father Sergi Zheludkov also referred to sanctions against believers:

> For baptism in a church the child's parents or the person being baptised must yield their passports for registration — which means that they must then live in anxious expectation of extra-legal repression. For a student, for example, this can be expulsion from an educational institution, or for a teacher, dismissal from work and exclusion from his profession for the rest of his life.[91]

Anatoli Levitin-Krasnov discussed the problem again in an article written in 1979: he noted that it had eased in the capital cities but was continuing in the provinces (although, despite this, the number of baptisms was continuing to rise). He also pointed to the problem of single mothers who wished to baptise their children, and who were mocked by officials when they attempted to register for this.[92] In 1980 a newsletter edited by Father Dimitri Dudko mentioned a Moscow church where registration of baptisms was causing particular problems:

> As has become known through the district executive committees, there

are commissions of elderly pensioners (activists with nothing else to do) who copy out the surnames of the parents, find out their places of work and report the baptisms to their employers; then they begin to work on them and torment them.[93]

Bishop Feodosi of Poltava and Kremenchug devoted several pages of his long letter to Mr Brezhnev to the problem of compulsory registration of baptisms. He disclosed that the regional CRA commissioner had demanded that he report the names of all adults who were baptised.[94] Moreover, he questioned the whole basis of the authorities' rationale for registering baptisms:

I totally fail to understand why every person being baptised arouses such great interest, even alarm, among the local authorities. If baptism, as an act, is just as much a private action as eating, taking a walk or relaxing, then it does not need to be registered anywhere and should be a matter of indifference to the authorities; but if the authorities are carrying out intensive surveillance over us, then it must be an act of state importance. But in that case, how are we to understand the principle of separation of the Church from the State and the Leninist doctrine that religion is a private matter?[95]

The practice of registering baptisms was introduced during Khrushchev's anti-religious campaign.[96] It is not mentioned in the Law on Religious Associations or other published legislation on religion. Its official basis appears to be a secret circular issued by the Council for the Affairs of the Russian Orthodox Church (later subsumed into the CRA), which ordered the establishment by regional executive committees of 'public cooperating commissions for controlling the observation of the legislation on cults'. Among their tasks was 'to verify the accuracy of the registering of religious rites, and through verification to stop instances of the baptisms of children without the consent of both parents'.[97] It was emphasised that registering of baptisms was still compulsory after Khrushchev's fall from power in October 1964: a circular from Patriarch Alexi to 'All incumbents of churches in Moscow Diocese' in December that year stated unequivocally that 'the performance of the sacrament of baptism on minors without the appropriate preparatory registration of documents by church executive committees must not take place.'[98] In 1972 a *samizdat* journal reprinted a questionnaire which was being issued in Irkutsk region to parents wishing to baptise their children: it contained 24 questions about the parents' personal lives and attitude to religion.[99] In 1974 Metropolitan Serafim's circular to area deans of Moscow diocese (which we quoted in Chapter 3, pp. 90–1) re-affirmed that it was necessary for all baptisms to be registered:

a priest does not have the right to perform the baptism of a minor in the absence of the mutual consent of the father and mother of the child being baptised. This agreement must be attested by their personal signatures in the church's executive body.[100]

Serafim based his argument on the canons, specifically the 124th rule of the Council of Carthage, which stated that baptism of infants may take place according to the faith of their parents. He also quoted the 59th rule of the Sixth Ecumenical Council, which stated that baptism must take place in a church, not a private house, on pain of excommunication. It is clear from the circular that priests had been frequently performing baptisms outside church premises, or on church premises without registering them, in order to help parents escape the possible unpleasant consequences of registration.

Serafim's point that baptisms should not be performed without the consent of both parents is echoed by the priest-turned-atheist propagandist Duluman, whom we mentioned above. He states that the practice was introduced 'at the demand of believers themselves and in conformity with Soviet law and order in religious communities'.[101] It is clear that church leaders and atheists are united on this point. (In that case, it is legitimate to ask why neither church leaders, nor the CRA, nor atheist propagandists raised the slightest objection to the non-registration of baptisms before the early 1960s.) Furthermore, it is not clear why a written consent is required: why should it not be sufficient for the priest to talk to the parents before the baptism and receive their agreement to it? Presumably something of this nature must have happened before the practice of registration was introduced. As it is, it is clear that many priests are willing to risk the disapproval of their superiors in the church by continuing to perform baptisms without registration.

The fact that registration of baptisms was introduced during a period of vigorous campaigning against the church, and that it is now being used to the detriment of some believers, leads us to conclude that it represents one more way in which the state is attempting to limit the influence of the church, and to discourage ordinary believers from participating in one of the most basic practices of their faith.

Other Sanctions against Orthodox Christians

One of the traditional and greatly loved customs in the Russian Orthodox Church is that of making pilgrimages to so-called 'holy places', sacred because of their association with some great saint or with the appearance of a wonder-working icon. Usually there is an anniversary associated with such places which means that on one day in the year large numbers of believers descend upon it. In some cases, the Soviet authorities have used severe measures, including violence, to prevent such pilgrimages — for example, in the village of Velikoretskoye in Kirov region.

Velikoretskoye has been a place of pilgrimage since 1383, when a wonder-working icon of St Nikolai was discovered there. According to a *samizdat* source,[102] even the cruel persecutions of the 1920s and 1930s did not stop believers coming to Velikoretskoye, although the original icon had disappeared. In the 1950s, priests were forbidden to take part in the ceremonies, but until the mid-1960s 'the Orthodox came with banners and crosses, large icons were carried on horseback, and in the villages the procession was met with bread and salt [a traditional Russian sign of hospitality]'. In the 1960s, however, the authorities began to clamp down:

> In 1967, when the Khrushchev persecution had visibly died down in the capitals, the godless here began a new phase of terror: the church in the village of Velikoretskoye was closed (they made it a grain store, and the grain rots because of the high level of damp), the chapel built over the stream where the icon appeared was razed to its foundations, and the pine-tree where it was found was cut down. The militia prevents the believers from holding prayer-services and makes raids on the paths to Velikoretskoye village, throwing pilgrims into cars like logs and driving them away from the river. After one such 'operation' an elderly woman died.

In 1980, the militia apparently decided to make a special effort to halt the flow of pilgrims, choosing 3 June, when about 1,000 believers arrived in Velikoretskoye. Militiamen were drafted in from surrounding districts and 'The shore was blocked by a chain of militia vehicles, and snarling tractors. An engine had been lowered into the water (it had been brought from the district centre) and was stirring up the water.' Not content with keeping the believers from the river, the militia dispersed them with violence:

> The militiamen, drunk to a man, some of them straight from the river — naked! — fell upon the pilgrims, beating them until the blood flowed. And after all there were old people and women among those who had come. They beat them and they fired blank shots into the air. They shouted ceaselessly through loudspeakers: 'Break up! Don't keep together. Break up and go home!' 'You have no right of assembly in law. You're breaking the law. You have the church.'
>
> When some believers tried to talk peacefully to the representatives of authority and ask what should be done now with the marchers, and who had conferred the right to fire on them, they were answered through the loudspeaker: 'We aren't touching you and no one is firing on you.'
>
> The guardian of order especially tried to seize men, and beat them unmercifully.

A similar incident occurred at Novy Afon in Georgia in 1977, when the militia obstructed pilgrims' access to the cave of a local saint.[103] In reply to a complaint, the Ministry of Internal Affairs upheld the militia's action, stating that they had been right to prevent the performance of 'a service under the open sky, which is categorically forbidden by legislation on religious cults in the USSR'.[104] Another pilgrimage of several hundred Orthodox Christians was halted by militia at Chudinovo, near Pskov, on 3 June 1981. The pilgrims were on their way to church when they were stopped by barbed-wire barriers placed against it due to alleged military manoeuvres in the area.[105]

The Ministry would appear to be correct, since Article 59 of the Law on Religious Associations states:

> Religious processions, performance of religious rites and ceremonies in the open air . . . are allowed only with a special permission, for each separate case, of the executive committee of the district or city Soviet of workers' deputies.

Evidently this permission had not been obtained in Velikoretskoye, and therefore the believers were in violation of the law. However, it would not have been easy, in practical terms, to obtain the required permission. As the church in Velikoretskoye had been closed by the authorities, there was no legally registered body capable of seeking and obtaining permission. Pilgrims coming from long distances would have no means of contacting the local authorities in advance. (The law states that permission must be sought at least two weeks in advance.) No one in the Russian Orthodox Church could be held responsible for co-ordinating the movements of pilgrims from many different places, since the law is specifically intended to atomise church structures and prevent co-ordination beyond the local community. In view of this, the violence used to scatter the pilgrims seems quite excessive.

The treatment meted out to church members who overstep the strict limits imposed by the law in other ways is also severe. The treasurer of an Orthodox church in Lvov was reportedly arrested and sentenced in 1975 for resisting the closure of churches and encouraging young men to study for the priesthood.[106] In Brest region in 1971 a church psalm-reader who held gatherings at which he played tape-recordings of religious music was fined and imprisoned; a journalist from the monthly *Nauka i religiya* who went to look into the matter concluded that, although he had broken the law, he had been too harshly treated.[107] In August 1980 officials disbanded a choir of 30 or so young people in the Church of the Protecting Veil in Kiev, who had expressed a desire to be instructed in liturgical singing. Officials interrupted a rehearsal with the demand that all present should produce their internal passports, and although all those who had their passports with them complied, everyone was made to leave the church. For the next month, carloads of officials arrived at the church every day, demanded to see the passports of anyone attempting to go to the choir stalls, and turned away all young choristers. The priest who directed the choir was moved to another church.[108]

These different incidents indicate that believers can expect disproportionately severe penalties for even the mildest initiatives beyond the narrow circle specifically prescribed by the law. In fact, none of the incidents described above were actually illegal, with the possible exception of the second (although it could be argued that the psalm-reader was not organising unregistered *worship*, merely unauthorised gatherings to listen to religious music). It would be probably wrong to assume that every such action is punished, since in some areas atheist activists may be too lax, or believers too discreet, for them to be detected. However, the fact that detection does normally lead to punishment is evidence of the Soviet authorities' desire to confine the activities of believers well within the prescribed framework.

A recent event which gave offence to many believers in the USSR was the decision of the Soviet government to declare Orthodox Easter Saturday 1975 a working day (*subbotnik*). (Periodically the government declares a Saturday a 'voluntary working day' to boost the economy.) Although Easter Saturday had sometimes been a working day before the Second World War,[109] it had been a free day since the post-war revival of church life, and the 1975 action was seen as an insult to believers. Father Gleb Yakunin wrote a scathing criticism of the decision addressed to the Politburo of the Communist Party (see Chapter 11, p. 353).[110]

Despite this protest, and many others, Easter Saturday in 1982 was also declared a *subbotnik*. This insensitive government action reveals much about the situation of the individual believer. He is accorded certain rights in law, but they are not so much a minimum safeguard of his religious freedom as a definition of the maximum permitted religious activity. And even this is subject to curtailment by administrative action: the legal right to baptise one's child can lead to 'exposure' as a believer, the legal right to celebrate Easter in a registered church can effectively be removed by obliging one to go to work. The much vaunted equality before the law and freedom of religious belief in the Soviet Constitution do not ensure that believers have true parity with unbelievers in practice.

8 THE EPISCOPATE

It is the Holy Spirit who has inducted bishops from the beginning, and He will do so until the end of time. He breathed upon the Apostles with power, like the rushing of a mighty wind, and He breathes still through the uttering of sacramental words upon him who performs a sacrament and him who receives it . . . when you utter sacramental words, when you stretch forth your hands to perform a sacrament, commit yourself as a humble instrument to the Spirit of God with the full force of faith and God-given desire; then you will bring down grace, and you will multiply living fruits of the Spirit of God, and vessels of grace.

These words were spoken to the longest-serving bishop of the Russian Orthodox Church, now Metropolitan Ioann of Pskov and Porkhov, on the day of his consecration as bishop in 1953.[1] Twenty-seven years later, the newest recruit to the church's episcopate in the USSR, Bishop Afanasi of Pinsk, was given this description of his life's work:

The episcopal ministry must in every time and every place be an apostolic ministry, which by its spirit and nature is 'a ministry of reconciliation, a pastoral ministry. To be a pastor means not to live your own life, but the life of your flock, to suffer their pains and their infirmities with the single aim of serving the cause of their salvation, of dying that they may live.'[2]

There are currently (on 15 August 1982, an arbitrarily selected date) 67 Soviet citizens who are devoting their lives to the episcopal ministry thus described (plus others now retired). They are a remarkably diverse body of men. The Russian Orthodox bishops today come from a wide range of backgrounds and differ greatly in their ages, education and personal histories. They are all monks, since the married clergy are not eligible for the episcopate, but this does not mean that they have all experienced life in a monastic community. The 67 men are something of a mystery to the world at large, and usually insufficient account is taken of the variety that exists among them. Even those who appear frequently at international gatherings tend to lose their identities in the black-robed, bearded mass of their brother bishops. In order to gain some insight into their backgrounds, we shall discuss them first of all in terms of age range, and, second, in terms of the offices they hold in the church.

The age range of the Russian Orthodox bishops in the USSR spans just over 50 years: the oldest was born in 1897 and the youngest in 1949.

(Appendix 1 to this chapter, pp. 244–6, lists all the bishops in order of birth.) There is a clearly distinguished group of older bishops, born before the 1917 Revolution. In fact, there is a noticeable gap, the only significant one, in dates of birth between 1914 and 1921. The remaining hierarchs may be divided rather more arbitrarily into a middle group born between 1921 and 1930, and a third group born since 1931 and therefore forming a group of quite young bishops all aged under 50 at the beginning of the 1980s. Nineteen of the 67 bishops, including Patriarch Pimen, belong to the first, pre-revolutionary group. They spent their childhood in a society quite different from that in which they work today, and have lived through the profound social upheavals of the October Revolution, civil war, famine, two world wars, and the Stalinist Terror of the 1930s. As young men, they witnessed the almost total destruction of the Russian Orthodox Church: practically the entire episcopate was executed or perished in labour camps, alongside many thousands of clergy and faithful. By 1939 there were only four ruling bishops of the entire church who remained at liberty. It must have required no little devotion to the church to assume episcopal duties after witnessing this. In view of the fact that the youth of the Russian Orthodox episcopate is often commented upon, it is of interest to note that nearly one-third of them were born before the commencement of the Soviet period. Age, however, does not confer seniority in the church, which is decided by date of episcopal consecration. The oldest member of the episcopate, Archbishop Meliton (Solovyov) of Tikhvin, did not become a bishop until 1970, at the age of 73. There are several other bishops who were consecrated at advanced ages: the drastic curtailment of monastic life and the greatly reduced opportunities for theological education during the Soviet period (which we have discussed in previous chapters) have meant that often the church has had to look for its bishops to widowed parish clergy. (Widowed priests in the Orthodox Church may not remarry.) Metropolitan Ioann (Razumov) of Pskov and Porkhov is, as we have said, the senior bishop of the church by date of consecration. He has spent his entire life in the church: he was a novice in the Smolensk hermitage (now closed) from the age of 18, and was tonsured a monk at 26. He was consecrated bishop in 1953, and has ruled the diocese of Pskov since 1954, except for a three-year break from 1959 to 1962, when he served in Berlin. Having managed to survive the church's great years of trial, he has been able, like several of his contemporaries among the older bishops, to give many years of unbroken pastoral service in one diocese. He is reportedly a great pastoral bishop much loved by his flock, and during the anti-religious campaign of 1959–64 was said to have taken a firm stand and resisted the mass forcible closure of churches.[3]

There are, however, quite a number of very young bishops in the church. The group of 19 older bishops is roughly balanced by the 22 members of the third group, those born since 1931. Three of these are still in their thirties:

Bishop Ilian of Solnechnogorsk, Bishop Mefodi of Irkutsk, and Archbishop Kirill of Vyborg. Despite their youth, they have all been assigned to important positions. Bishop Mefodi, currently the youngest bishop in the church, was given jurisdiction over its largest diocese, Irkutsk, at the age of only 31, and Bishop Ilian was assigned to represent his church abroad, in Czechoslovakia, immediately after his consecration.[4] Archbishop Kirill has had a particularly dazzling career: he was consecrated bishop in 1976, when he was only 29 years old, and by the age of 33 he was an archbishop and rector of the Leningrad Theological Academy. He is also a member of the Central Committee of the World Council of Churches, travels abroad frequently and is often host to foreign visitors in Leningrad. So much responsibility at such an early age cannot fail to recall the similarly meteoric career of the late Metropolitan Nikodim of Leningrad, to whom Kirill was personal secretary from 1970. By this time, at the age of 24, Kirill had completed the eight-year course at the Leningrad seminary and academy in a total of four years, and had received his candidate's degree for a thesis on the church hierarchy.

These three young bishops are typical of the new generation of the Russian episcopate in that, upon completion of advanced theological training, they have immediately been given important and responsible positions. The church has clearly been developing a policy of grooming a new elite of educated and capable young bishops. The majority of the bishops in this younger group have served either overseas or in responsible positions within the Soviet Union. They include Metropolitan Yuvenali of Krutitsy and Kolomna, who is a permanent member of the Holy Synod; all three of the bishops entrusted with the important work of the Department of External Church Relations; and Archbishop Vladimir of Dmitrov, the rector of the Moscow Theological Academy.

The emphasis on theological training and the grooming of future bishops is particularly important for the church in view of the fact that, as we saw in Chapter 4, there was no theological training at all from virtually the beginning of the 1920s until after the Second World War. For a quarter of a century, therefore, the church faced great difficulties in preparing men for episcopal service. This is reflected in the fact that none of the present bishops was born between 1914 and 1921, the only significant gap in the age range. Men born between those dates would have been slightly too old to benefit from the small number of places available for theological students which began to be available from 1944.

This factor has also affected the middle group of bishops, those born between 1921 and 1931, not all of whom were able to avail themselves of the growing, but still limited, opportunities for theological education. In some cases, long years of monastic discipline may have compensated for lack of theological education. The oldest member of this group, Archbishop Nikodim of Kharkov and Bogodukhov, did not graduate from Moscow

Theological Seminary until the rather late age of 37, but he spent 17 years as a monk at the Kreshchatik monastery (now closed); and its youngest member, Bishop Varnava of Cheboksary and Chuvashia, appears to have had no formal theological training at all, but has spent 21 years as a member of the monastic community in the Holy Trinity Monastery of St Sergi at Zagorsk. The small number of men who received their theological training immediately the theological schools reopened after the war include five who have since risen to important posts in the church: Metropolitan Antoni of Leningrad and Novgorod; Metropolitan Filaret of Kiev and Galicia; Metropolitan Alexi of Tallinn and Estonia, the Chancellor of the Moscow Patriarchate; Archbishop Melkhisedek of Berlin, Exarch of Central Europe; and Archbishop Pitirim of Volokolamsk, chairman of the Publishing Department of the Moscow Patriarchate. The remainder of this middle age group, which contains 26 bishops, are all serving in dioceses in the Soviet Union, and the majority of them have spent most of their episcopal careers in this capacity. Only six have served overseas as bishops.[5]

This middle age group is not without its distinguished members, however. Metropolitan Leonid (Polyakov) of Riga studied both medicine and chemistry and practised as a doctor for some years. Although he did not complete his theological training, as an external student, until the age of 39, he then went on to achieve a master's degree in theology and a professorship at Leningrad Theological Academy within six years. Later he became the only bishop of his time to achieve an earned doctorate, an unprecedented feat in the church. He is one of the well-educated men who switched careers and joined the church in middle age, receiving their theological education once it became possible to do so in the post-war years. Another such is Archbishop Mikhail (Chub) of Tambov, who studied as a young man at the Institute of Meteorology and as an external student at the Institute of Foreign Languages, after which he taught languages in schools. He completed a course at the Leningrad Theological Academy after it reopened and then, at the age of 38, became a lecturer in the seminary. He went on to become one of the church's leading theologians and is today a member of the editorial board of the periodical *Theological Works* (*Bogoslovskye trudy*).[6]

By 31 December 1984, the number of bishops remained stable at 67, but there had been a shift within the three age groups. The middle group remained at 26. The number of bishops in the first group, those born before 1917, declined from 19 to 16. The number in the youngest age group grew from 22 to 25. This points to a gradual rejuvenation of the episcopate which is only to be expected.

It is of interest to note that no less than seven of the currently (both in August 1982 and in December 1984) ruling bishops in the USSR — one in ten — were born in 1929. This was at the height of Stalin's persecution of the Russian Orthodox Church, particularly its episcopate, and it is perhaps a comment on the workings of Divine Providence that so many future bishops first saw the light of day in that year.

The Bishops' Duties

The current (15 August 1982) total of 76 bishops of the Moscow Patriarchate is made up of Patriarch Pimen, 54 diocesan bishops, 9 suffragan or titular bishops* serving in the USSR, 2 suffragan or titular bishops and 2 diocesan bishops temporarily serving abroad, and 8 bishops serving permanently abroad who are not Soviet citizens. (Appendix 2 to this chapter, pp. 246—50, lists the bishops serving abroad and the administrative functions of those serving in the Soviet Union who are not simply diocesan bishops.)

The two diocesan bishops temporarily based abroad are in fact Patriarchal Exarchs, responsible for parishes of the Moscow Patriarchate in Argentina and South America, and in Berlin and Central Europe. One of the suffragans serving abroad is based in Canada, where there are Moscow Patriarchate parishes, and one in Damascus, where the Moscow Patriarchate maintains a permanent representative to the Patriarch of Antioch. Together with the bishops permanently based abroad, six in Europe, one in Tokyo and one in San Francisco, they ensure that the Moscow Patriarchate is represented at a number of widely separated points around the globe. (There are also non-episcopal representatives in Jerusalem and Geneva, and some monks on Mount Athos in Greece.)

The chief activities of the 54 diocesan bishops are supervising clergy, ordaining priests and deacons, and making pastoral visits to the dioceses in their care. Their role, like that of the clergy as a whole, is primarily sacramental and liturgical; this is partly a consequence of the fact that the laws of the Soviet Union do not permit the church to engage in non-liturgical activities, but it is also a reflection of the central role which the Orthodox Church has always accorded to liturgical worship. An official publication of the Moscow Patriarchate sums up the bishop's task as follows:

> In his diocese the bishop is the first teacher of faith and morals; he cele-
> brates and administers the sacraments of the Church. In guiding diocesan

---

* We have used the term suffragan or titular bishops for the Russian word *vikari*, sometimes translated as 'vicar-bishop'. Some of these are in fact suffragans in the accepted Western usage — that is, they assist a diocesan bishop in administering the diocese. The titular bishops sometimes have little connection with the places whose names they bear, particularly the overseas ones. The titular bishops in the Soviet Union are attached to a particular diocese, but assigned to a special task, principally in the departments of the Moscow Patriarchate and the theological schools. However, they may also function partially as suffragans, e.g. Archbishop Pitirim of Volokolamsk, who is chairman of the Publishing Department but also regularly takes services in the district of Volokolamsk, north-west of Moscow. The term suffragan is used in the pages which follow as a convenient shorthand term to include all these bishops.

life the bishop is bound to spiritually care for the flock canonically entrusted to him both as a whole and as individuals (2 Tim. 4, 2).[7]

As we noted in our discussion of clergy salaries in Chapter 3 (pp. 85–8), bishops generally receive high salaries, which, even after paying the high rate of income tax, are sufficient to enable them to live very comfortably. This appears to have the approval of the broad masses of ordinary believers, who like to see them as being in the tradition of prince-bishops living in a lordly manner. Some bishops, however, are noted for choosing an ascetic way of life, such as Archbishop Pitirim of Volokolamsk and Metropolitan Leonid of Riga.

Diocesan bishops are called upon periodically to serve on the Holy Synod, the supreme authority in the church between Local Councils. It is chaired by the Patriarch and meets in Moscow. Three places rotate among the diocesan bishops, who serve for six months at a time, during either the autumn–winter or spring–summer sessions. Permanent membership of the Holy Synod belongs to the Metropolitans of Krutitsy and Kolomna, Leningrad and Novgorod, and Kiev and Galicia. The Metropolitan of Krutitsy and Kolomna assists the Patriarch in administering the Moscow diocese; he is thus technically a suffragan, but in fact has the status of a diocesan bishop. He is presently Metropolitan Yuvenali (Poyarkov). Metropolitan Antoni (Melnikov) was appointed to the diocese of Leningrad and Novgorod in 1978, following the sudden death of Metropolitan Nikodim; he is also chairman of the editorial board of the periodical *Theological Works* (*Bogoslovskye trudy*). Metropolitan Filaret of Kiev and Galicia is Exarch of Ukraine, the only one of the church's four exarchates situated within the Soviet Union. He has been a permanent member of the Holy Synod since 1966, and is also chairman of the Holy Synod's Commission on Questions of Christian Unity. In 1961 two further permanent memberships of the Holy Synod were created: the Head of the Department of External Church Relations (DECR) and the Chancellor of the Moscow Patriarchate. It is possible for any of the three other permanent members to hold either of these posts — for example, until April 1981 Metropolitan Yuvenali of Krutitsy was also head of the DECR. The present DECR head, Metropolitan Filaret of Minsk and Belorussia, is also Exarch to Western Europe. The longest-serving member of the Holy Synod (except for the Patriarch) is Metropolitan Alexi of Tallinn and Estonia, who has been chancellor, or administrator (*upravlyayushchi delami*), of the Moscow Patriarchate since 1964. He is also chairman of the Education Committee, which is responsible for the theological schools. As he is the senior permanent member of the Holy Synod by date of episcopal consecration, he will become Locum Tenens on the death of Patriarch Pimen, head of the church until the election of a new Patriarch.

The other departments of the Moscow Patriarchate are the Economic

Management (*khozyaistvennoye upravleniye*), headed by Archpriest Matvei Stadnyuk; the Pensions Committee, headed by Archpriest Dimitri Akinfiev; and the Publishing Department, chaired, as we have seen, by Archbishop Pitirim of Volokolamsk.

Bishops in the Russian Orthodox Church are created, assigned and translated 'by resolution (*postanovleniye*) of His Holiness Patriarch Pimen and the Holy Synod'. This is not in accordance with strict Orthodox practice, according to which a bishop is elected from within the diocese, and, once appointed and consecrated, is irremoveable. The Local Council of 1917–18 strongly reaffirmed this practice, which had lapsed since the time of Peter the Great for political rather than religious reasons, but it was not possible to implement the Council's decision under Soviet conditions, and the practice of frequent translations of bishops has once again become customary.[8] This seems to be true especially of the younger bishops; perhaps it is thought useful for them to have experience of a number of different assignments within the church. Among the older bishops, however, there are some who have served for many years in the same diocese: we have already mentioned Metropolitan Ioann, who has been Bishop of Pskov diocese continuously since 1962, and Metropolitan Filaret, a Ukrainian by birth, who has been Exarch of Ukraine since 1966. Metropolitan Alexi of Tallinn has been assigned to the city of his birth since 1961. There is therefore some evidence that although election within the diocese is not practised, an attempt is made to compensate by assigning bishops to the area of their birth and by leaving them in place where possible.[9] However, as we shall see later in this chapter, the Holy Synod can suddenly transfer a bishop to a remote diocese as a form of punishment.

Appointments to the ranks of Archbishop and Metropolitan are made by an Edict (*Ukaz*) of the Patriarch. They are nowadays chiefly signs of honour and rewards for long and faithful service, and have lost any territorial distinction they formerly possessed.

Relations with the State

The comments of Russian Orthodox hierarchs on the situation of their church and its relations with the Soviet state often attract interest abroad. They invariably speak of the flourishing condition of church life, of good relations with the state, and of the fact that they enjoy complete freedom in their religious life. We may safely assert that no hierarch based in the Soviet Union has publicly made any statement to the contrary. The leading hierarchs of the church are assiduous in proclaiming this point of view. Metropolitan Alexi of Tallinn, for example, said in an interview in 1977:

the church was separated from the State and the schools from the Church

by a decree adopted by the Soviet Government on 23 January 1918 . . .
At present millions of people belong to the Church because they
sincerely, consciously and profoundly believe in God, which could not be
said about the Church in the Russian Empire . . . every citizen has the
right to profess any religion or none at all. The fact that he is a member of
this or that faith never affects his employment, promotion and things like
that . . . The laws of this country forbid persecution of citizens for their
religious beliefs. Those who insult the religious views of the believers are
brought to account. . . . There have been cases when believers or individual religious leaders were brought to account for systematically
violating the laws on religious cults, or for incitement to such violations.
Perhaps it is such cases that are taken in the West as religious
persecution.[10]

Metropolitan Filaret of Kiev and Galicia took the same line in an interview with the Novosti Press Agency:

Q: The radio and press abroad often speak about the need to protect the
persecuted Church and believers in the Soviet Union. What can you say
about this?
A: I am surprised that our Church and believers are considered persecuted. No one is persecuted for religious convictions in the Soviet Union.
Believers and non-believers in our country form one society engaged in
active and creative labour for the good of their Motherland. The attitude
of the Soviet State to the needs of the Church is considerate and understanding. Unfortunately, the Western press disregards the fact that
normal relations exist between the Church and State. Certain news
agencies in the West, on the contrary, make use of slanderous and biased
information to mislead world public opinion.[11]

Metropolitan Yuvenali repeated the criticism of the Western press for
falsifying the situation of the church in a broadcast made on the BBC's
Russian Service during a visit to Britain, in which he spoke of 'the tendency
among some circles in England, supported even by some officials of the
Anglican Church, to present a biased and one-sided picture of Russian
Orthodox Church life'. After expanding on this theme, Metropolitan
Yuvenali concluded:

I would like everyone everywhere to remember that what today exists in
the Russian Orthodox Church — what our friends and brothers in the
West rejoice over, what even those who are perhaps unsympathetic to us
must mention when speaking of religious life — is a spiritual revival; and
that this has been the priceless achievement of the humble and unknown
pastors of the Church who have devoted their whole lives to the service of
Christ and his Church.[12]

The theme of spiritual revival is taken up by Metropolitan Antoni of Leningrad in an interview given to an Italian Christian magazine, though he states that he prefers to speak of stability rather than revival:

Faith in the USSR has never diminished, and, of course, it has not diminished today. There are indeed things which confirm the new interest in religion . . . This gladdens us . . . there are young people who are deciding to dedicate their whole lives to the Gospel and to the Church.[13]

These words of Metropolitans Yuvenali and Antoni contain a logical inconsistency found in very many similar statements: they speak of faith and of persecution as though they were mutually incompatible. Even a passing acquaintance with the history of the universal church shows that the opposite is closer to the truth. Few if any of the observers of Russian Orthodox Church life would doubt the fact of the spiritual growth of which the hierarchs speak (we shall return to this subject in Part II). However, the hierarchs speak of the fervour and piety of large numbers of believers, and of the absence of persecution, as though the former were a proof of the latter.

Such inconsistent statements are often interpreted as being an attempt to evade the issue and simply to pretend that persecution of believers does not exist. This interpretation may be true in part, but it is not the only possible one. It may be that the hierarchs wish to deflect attention from what they see as the sufferings of a small number of people to the situation of the church as a whole. Or it may be that they are anxious to avoid a subject which is deeply painful for their church and to talk instead of the church's blessings. They may also wish to point out that in their view the spiritual growth in the church is due not so much to a few leading spirits who have become well known because of the hardships they have endured, but mostly to the faithful witness of the broad masses of the people and clergy. In addition, there is the strong influence of the history of their church, which has no tradition of opposition to the state, and whose Byzantine theological inheritance does not encourage it to adopt such a position. Criticism of hierarchs for failing to acknowledge the persecution of some members of their flocks is sometimes taken by them as an attempt to make them act in the quite different tradition of Western bishops. All these motivations, both the worthy and the unworthy, play their part in these statements, but their interrelationships are so close that it is impossible to disentangle them.

Rank-and-file bishops are also called upon from time to time to make statements in the press about church–state relations. Here are some brief samples:

Complete religious liberty exists in the Soviet Union . . . The Constitution of the USSR has guaranteed all Soviet citizens a full and unhindered freedom of conscience. I know not a single man who has suffered for his religious beliefs. People of all ages, including children, daily come to our cathedral. All of them freely fulfil their religious needs [Bishop Serapion of Irkutsk].[14]

Knowing the true state of affairs, and from the example of my diocese, I can say with all responsibility and with a clear conscience that freedom of faith has never been suppressed in the Soviet Union . . . From the example of my diocese of Kirov I can say that both priests and parishioners are patriotically inclined. As true sons and daughters of their Fatherland, they rejoice at its successes in all spheres of life, support the policies of the Soviet state, its ceaseless struggle for peace and mutual understanding among peoples, because this reponds to their religious feelings. After all, peace on earth is the ideal of every true Christian [Archbishop Mstislav of Kirov].[15]

The new Constitution of the USSR also guarantees the rights of believing citizens. Any violation of these rights in our country, whether by individual people or by organisations, is forbidden. I do not know of a single instance of believers in the Soviet Union being persecuted for their religious beliefs or for performing church rituals [Archbishop Nikodim of Kharkov].[16]

We could quote a great many more episcopal statements saying much the same things, but have been unable to find any expressing different points of view. The very unanimity of these statements is remarkable. The Russian Orthodox episcopate is, as we have seen, a most diverse body of men, and it is therefore surprising to find that their very different backgrounds have not shaped their views on church–state relations to any significant extent and that the views which they express are so similar — indeed, stereotyped.

The repeated assertions by the hierarchs of the Russian Orthodox Church that complete freedom of religion exists in the Soviet Union have earned them stringent public criticism from some clergy and many lay members of the church who believe almost exactly the opposite. One recent case will serve to illustrate this controversy. A bishop who travels abroad frequently and is often asked for comments by the Western press is Archbishop Pitirim of Volokolamsk, chairman of the Publishing Department of the Moscow Patriarchate. On a visit to West Germany in March 1980 he stuck to the line that he and the other bishops have always maintained: he is reported to have said that the religious situation in the Soviet Union had stabilised and that religious life could develop unhindered under the present legislation on religion. He aroused controversy, however, when, in reply to questions about the many arrests of religious believers in the USSR during previous months, he reportedly said that there was 'no wave of arrests', and that reports to the contrary in the Western press were 'absolutely false'. (Pitirim's remarks are discussed in more detail in Chapter 13, pp. 425–6.) He was sharply criticised by human rights organisations for failing to defend the Christian prisoners.[17] Pitirim has also been criticised by lay members of the church within the Soviet Union, most comprehensively by a recent émigré, Yuri Belov (who has since become a Roman Catholic). Belov wrote an open letter to the archbishop dated just before the latter's trip to West Germany:

> Your Grace,
> My name is Yuri Belov, I am forty years old and I am a Christian. I have spent fourteen years or more in Soviet prisons, labour camps and psychiatric hospitals because of my Christian convictions. After my release I twice visited your residence in Novodevichi Monastery in Moscow, in 1978 and 1979, and you refused to receive me and talk to me. Then I sent messages to you on three occasions, which you also left unanswered . . . Three months ago I emigrated from the USSR to Germany and now I can tell you what you did not want to hear in our homeland.
>
> You have come here in order to talk to strangers, and wish to demonstrate your love for Christ. But why do you not wish to talk to your fellow-countrymen, for whose sake you are serving, at home in your own country? . . . You have shown no sympathy, not only for thousands of non-Orthodox Christians confined in prisons, labour camps and psychiatric hospitals and exiled to Siberia, but have even failed to speak up for the children of your own Russian Orthodox Church and have concurred with their being humiliated by the authorities in prisons, where they are forbidden to wear baptismal crosses, where they are not allowed to keep and to read the Bible, and where prison guards shave priests' heads and do not permit them to grow beards. [Orthodox priests are traditionally obliged to wear their hair shoulder-length and to have beards.] . . .
>
> But you remain silent, you give the impression that there is freedom of religion in the USSR. What a terrible sin you are taking upon your soul — the sin of bearing false witness!

Belov goes on to state that while he was still in the USSR he sent messages to Archbishop Pitirim asking him to defend named Christian prisoners.

> Then in 1979 I was summoned to the KGB, shown the messages I had sent you and threatened with arrest. When I asked them where they had got my letters to you, they replied that your secretary had sent them to the KGB. I want people here to know about these activities of yours. You are deceiving them without any conscience by saying in your interviews that 'reports about the persecution of believers in the USSR have no basis whatever' (interview with *Stern* newspaper, 8 November 1979). I want

people in the whole world to know that in the USSR now more than 2,000 Christians are imprisoned, in exile and in psychiatric hospitals, that old and ill Orthodox, Baptist, Catholic and other priests are enduring mockery in the GULag . . .

In the name of our Saviour Jesus Christ I beg you, speak out in defence of the persecuted and fulfil the command of Christ: 'Blessed are those who are persecuted for righteousness' sake, for theirs is the kingdom of heaven' (Matt. 5,10).

With love in the Lord, Yuri Belov
28 February 1980
Frankfurt-on-Main.[18]

We shall return to the points Belov raises concerning Christian prisoners in the USSR, and religious persecution in general, in Part 2. For the present, we may note that this controversy is much wider than a conflict between two (or more) different points of view about church—state relations in the USSR. Many ordinary believers who have made protests similar to Belov's clearly feel betrayed by those set over them. They are criticising their bishops, not so much for their views, as for failing to care for the flock committed to their charge by the church.

The single occasion on which a bishop based in the Soviet Union has publicly wavered from the general course of official pronouncements was not on a religious issue but on a political one. This was at the February 1980 meeting of the Executive Committee of the World Council of Churches, at which a motion was unanimously passed expressing 'serious concern' about, *inter alia*, 'the military action by the USSR in Afghanistan'. Archbishop Kirill of Vyborg was present at the meeting (as were two other church leaders from Eastern Europe, Patriarch Iliya of Georgia and Bishop Johannes Hempel of East Germany). The fact that these three had supported the motion was widely reported in the Western press, as it was the first time that church leaders from Eastern Europe had voted against, or even failed to support, an action of one of their governments. The fact that all three supported the motion indicates their support was a planned decision and not simply a mistake or a misjudgement. It is possible that they felt it would be futile to protest against the motion in view of the strength of feeling against the invasion of Afghanistan, and that any such protest would only increase negative feelings towards the Soviet Union. If so, they were almost certainly right. They may also have felt that it was worth making a concession on this one point in order to have passed a motion which contained other points in line with Soviet policy, including a criticism of NATO's decision to deploy more than 500 'theatre nuclear weapons' in Europe.[19]

We have said that none of the bishops based in the USSR has dissented publicly from the general view of church—state relations presented by the episcopate, but one of the overseas bishops, Archbishop Vasili of Brussels and Belgium, has done so. He took issue with Archbishop Pitirim over the fact that the Russian Orthodox Church is forbidden to engage in charitable activity and to teach religion to children, which Pitirim had attempted to justify from a Christian standpoint. Vasili demolished Pitirim's case with arguments closely based on Christian doctrine. He pointed out that it would have been a different matter if Pitirim had simply said that Soviet laws did not allow the Church to undertake these activities, 'but it is one thing to submit through necessity and another to justify such a ban, to praise it, to make a virtue of necessity.'[20] Archbishop Vasili apparently spoke out on this occasion because there had been an attempt to distort, or ignore, Christian doctrine in the interests of good relations with the state. Elsewhere, he had pointed out the dangers of making accusations against the Russian episcopate:

> The atheists know . . . that it is thanks to the unity of the bishops, the clergy and the laity . . . that the Church of Russia has been saved from total destruction, and they are trying to destroy this union of love. This is why we must be very careful and not accept lightly accusations against the bishops and the administration of the Moscow Patriarchate in general . . . I am convinced that the bishops of the Russian Orthodox Church in their overwhelming majority accomplish their pastoral work conscientiously and try by all the means in their power to defend the Church and the people of God against their enemies. Unfortunately, their opportunities for doing so are extremely limited . . .[21]

Why do the hierarchs of the Russian Orthodox Church in the USSR continue to make stereotyped pro-government statements to the detriment of their relations with members of their church? Part of the reason lies in the church's strong Caesaro-Papist heritage, as a result of which many bishops firmly believe that it is their patriotic Christian duty to side with the state. This is especially true when their state is criticised by foreigners. However, most observers have concluded that the overwhelming factor is strong state pressure upon them (as upon Soviet citizens in all walks of life) to make such statements. There are two persuasive arguments in support of this view. The first has been mentioned above: it is scarcely conceivable that a large number of such varied personalities should express such unanimous views in the absence of some form of strong pressure from outside. The second is that the unanimous views expressed invariably and fully correspond to the current policies of the Soviet government and the Communist Party of the Soviet Union. The alternative argument to the view that the Soviet bishops are under state pressure is that all of them — continuously, completely and freely — support government and Party policy at all times. This would be too much to expect of any episcopate in any country. No one will deny the deep patriotism of the episcopate (or of the rest of the members of the Russian Orthodox Church), but none the less such a view is quite untenable.

The CRA Report on the Episcopate

These are arguments about possibilities and probabilities. Is there any direct evidence of state pressure upon the bishops of the Russian Orthodox Church? There is: it appears in the 1974 CRA Report, which contains extremely interesting information about the episcopate. The title of the section of the report which is devoted to the episcopate itself speaks volumes: 'The Composition of the Episcopate of the Russian Orthodox Church and the Intensification of Political Work with them in the Interests of the State'.[22] The report acknowledges the influential position of the bishops, but remarks that 'in the new social conditions, a bishop in the Soviet State is deprived of many of his former privileges and his activity is confined within certain limits [imposed by] the law on religious cults'. The report then defines the activities of the bishop in much the same way as we have done above: 'In practice the ruling bishop today performs the ordination and appointment of priests and deacons to parishes', but adds the rider: 'after agreement with the commissioner of the Council [for Religious Affairs] and at the request of the religious association (or parish)'.

The CRA Report then briefly describes the composition of the Holy Synod, correctly describing it as the supreme authority in the church between Local Councils. This being so, the following bald assertion in the report is disturbing:

> The Synod is under the control of the Council [for Religious Affairs]. The question of the selection and placing of its permanent members was and remains completely in the hands of the Council, and the candidature of the non-permanent members is also agreed beforehand with responsible members of the Council. All issues which are to be discussed at the Synod are first discussed by Patriarch Pimen and the permanent members of the Synod with the leaders of the Council and in its departments, and the final 'Decisions (*Opredeleniya*) of the Holy Synod' are also agreed.

Even if we assume that the CRA is exaggerating the situation somewhat in order to impress its political masters with its diligence, this statement still represents very considerable state interference in the affairs of the church — and this in a country where church and state have been officially separated by a decree published almost at the very founding of the state.

There then follows a division of the episcopate into three categories according to their loyalty to the state. It is not entirely clear why the CRA should divide them up in this way, but it is presumably done to help the Central Committee grasp the varying attitudes which exist among the bishops, and to assure them that, while none of the bishops can be considered disloyal, some of them merit the continued exertions of the CRA. The categories are prefaced with the words:

> Many years of observation and profound study of the attitudes of ruling bishops confirm once again that the episcopate is loyal to Soviet power. At the same time it is possible, on the basis of their views on society, on the laws on cults and on the Church today and its mutual relations with the State, and also on their civic obligations, to divide the episcopate, theoretically and very approximately, into the following groups.

The list which follows gives the names of 57 ruling diocesan and suffragan bishops. By reference to reports of the deaths, transfers and appointments of bishops given in reports of the meetings of the Holy Synod contained in the *Journal of the Moscow Patriarchate*, we can date the compilation of this list between 23 October and 26 December 1974.[23] As the report is primarily concerned with the activities of the church within the USSR, it is no surprise to find that 14 bishops are not included on the list because they were abroad, either permanently or temporarily, at the time of its compilation.[24] There are, however, four bishops who are missing from the list for no apparent reason. They are: Archbishop Antoni (Vakarik) of Chernigov, where he remains (at 31 December 1984); Bishop Iov of Ivanovo, who had served a prison sentence from 1960 to 1963 on an apparently trumped-up charge during Khrushchev's anti-religious campaign and who died in December 1977; Archbishop Vladimir (Sabodan) of Dmitrov (from August 1982 Metropolitan of Rostov, and from June 1984 also Exarch to Western Europe); Bishop Varlaam (Ilyushchenko), then of Pereyaslav, now of Chernovtsy. There is no obvious link between these four hierarchs, and it is not at all clear why they are missing from the list.

The CRA Report lists 17 hierarchs in its first category, 23 in the second, and 17 in the third. Many have died or retired since 1974, and we shall list here only those who remain in office at 15 August 1982.

The first category of hierarchs consists of those who, in the words of the CRA Report:

> both in words and deeds affirm not only loyalty but also patriotism towards the socialist society, strictly observe the laws on cults and educate the parish clergy and believers in the same spirit, realistically understand that our state is not interested in proclaiming the role of religion and the church in society and, realising this, do not display any particular activeness in extending the influence of Orthodoxy among the population.

Into this category fall Patriarch Pimen; Metropolitans Alexi of Tallinn,

Yuvenali of Krutitsy and Kolomna (then of Tula), and Sergi of Odessa; Archbishops Nikodim of Kharkov, Pitrim of Volokolamsk, Ionafan of Kishinyov, and Leonti of Simferopol; and Bishop Meliton of Tikhvin, wrongly referred to by the CRA as an archbishop (he was made an archbishop in 1980).[25]

The second category consists of hierarchs who

> maintain a position of loyalty to the state, have a correct attitude to the laws on cults and observe them, but in their everyday administrative and ideological activity strive towards activating servants of 'the cult and active members of the church, stand for the heightening of the role of the church in personal, family and public life with the help of modernistic or traditional concepts, views and activities, and select for priestly office young people who are zealous adherents of Orthodox piety.

This category includes Metropolitans Filaret of Kiev, Ioann of Yaroslavl, Ioann of Pskov, Antoni of Leningrad (then Archbishop of Minsk), Leonid of Riga (then an archbishop) and Alexi of Kalinin (then Archbishop of Krasnodar); Archbishops Varfolomei of Tashkent, Mikhail of Tambov, Leonti of Orenburg, Iosif of Ivano-Frankovsk, Kassian of Kostroma, Damian of Volhynia, Feodosi of Smolensk (then a bishop), Feodosi of Astrakhan (then Bishop of Poltava), Gedeon of Novosibirsk (then a bishop), Simon of Ryazan (then a bishop) and Melkhisedek of Berlin (then Bishop of Penza); and Bishop German of Tula (then of Vilnius).[26]

The third category devised by the CRA consists of:

> The part of the episcopate who at different times have made attempts to evade the laws on cults; some of them are religious conservatives, others are capable of falsifying the position in their dioceses and the attitude which the organs of authority have formed towards them, and in others again attempts to bribe commissioners [of the CRA] and to slander them and officials of the local organs of authority have been observed.

The members of the third category are Metropolitan Nikolai of Lvov; Archbishops Vladimir of Krasnodar (then of Irkutsk, subsequently of Vladimir), Nikon of Kaluga (then of Arkhangelsk), Nikolai of Gorky (then of Vladimir), Mikhail of Vologda (then Bishop of Astrakhan), Pimen of Saratov (then a bishop), Khrizostom of Kursk (then a bishop), Ioann of Kuibyshev (then a bishop); and Bishops Savva of Mukhachevo (then of Chernovtsy), and Damaskin of Poltava (then of Vologda).[27]

It is no surprise to find the first category headed by Patriarch Pimen and Metropolitan Alexi, and from what is known of the other bishops one would expect to find them there too, with the possible exception of Archbishop Ionafan of Kishinyov and Moldavia, who would seem to be a more appropriate candidate for the second category. He is said to have made a good impression during 1967–70 when he served in the USA, and to be a likeable and pastorally minded bishop who does a good job in his diocese and gets along well with other denominations.

There are some surprises in the second category. Judging from comments about them from other sources, one might have expected that some of the bishops who figure here would have been in the first category. On the other hand, some of the bishops in this second classification seem to be natural candidates for the third category, above all Metropolitan Leonid of Riga and Archbishop Mikhail of Tambov, whom we have mentioned above. Mikhail is said to be a very independently minded bishop who would refuse to knuckle under to anyone, and who has the reputation of being a strong, dynamic man. Leonid is said to be gentle, charming and saintly, and at the same time quietly but absolutely fearless. It remains an open question as to whether they and others on this list have latterly been persuaded to be more co-operative towards the state, or whether they are sufficiently adroit and subtle to disguise their true views from the local CRA commissioners on the basis of whose reports this list has been compiled.

Although bishops in the third category merit keen attention from the CRA, even they are not considered so wayward as to be positively objectionable to the state. No effort appears to have been made to remove them, and the CRA Report does not suggest this. Of the 17 bishops listed in 1974, ten were still in office in 1982. (Six had died and one retired.) Some of these ten remained in important dioceses with a relatively large number of churches (notably Metropolitan Nikolai of Lvov); others had been translated from dioceses with few churches to central dioceses with more churches (Archbishop Vladimir from Irkutsk to Vladimir and then Krasnodar; Archbishop Nikon of Arkhangelsk to Kaluga); and three had been promoted from bishop to archbishop.

The CRA's own comments on the categories are very interesting. The report says that they are not concerned with hierarchs' theological or other ideological views, but only with 'the attitude of the episcopate to the Soviet State, its internal and external policies and the laws on cults, and the kind of activity the bishops engage in'. Therefore the divisions into categories are

> quite conditional, the boundaries between the different categories are movable and depend upon a whole series of circumstances, above all on constant political work, based on principles, carried on with the bishops. [We must] conduct a firm course to form patriotic convictions, and not just loyalty to the State, educate them in a spirit of understanding not only the political but also the ideological interests of the State, in both external and internal policy.

There is more than a tinge of bureaucratic self-justification here, and one would like to know more about the content of the indoctrination applied to the bishops and the efficiency of its application before commenting on its effectiveness. One suspects that it may not differ greatly from the content of Soviet ideological propaganda in general, and the efficiency with which it is inculcated, neither of which is high. However, the point here is that, whatever the nature of the indoctrination, bishops are apparently obliged to endure it, the Soviet state thinks it proper for its officials to conduct it, and the Communist Party wishes to be informed about its progress. This surely represents a very high level of state interference in church life. This view is greatly reinforced by the next paragraph of the report:

> The Council and its local representatives pay constant and unremitting attention to studying the episcopate and the activities of not only the members of the Synod but also the wider range of the episcopate. Not a single episcopal consecration, not a single transfer occurs without a painstaking examination of the candidatures by the responsible officials of the Council in close contact with the commissioners, the local authorities and corresponding interested bodies.[28]

It is not easy to know exactly what to make of the CRA's view of the bishops. On the one hand they are saying that they exercise strict control over the episcopate at every level, and on the other hand that, despite this, more than two-thirds of the bishops do not have an entirely desirable attitude to the state, society and the laws on religion. We have already pointed out that, in this report, the CRA is evidently doing two things at once: it is demonstrating that it is fulfilling its duty by maintaining full control over the church, and it is simultaneously trying to justify its continued existence by pointing to problems still to be overcome. This inevitably leads to inconsistencies. However, this is probably not the whole story as far as the episcopate is concerned. Clearly a number of bishops, some more than others, make attempts to conduct a genuine pastoral ministry and to build up the churches in their dioceses — but with the corollary that they are then the objects of increased attention from the CRA commissioner and come under pressure to reduce their activity. There is evidently a complex and constantly shifting pattern of relations between the bishops and the CRA which makes it difficult to categorise many bishops with any finality (as the CRA has pointed out above). It is also clear that degrees of loyalty to the state, from the CRA's viewpoint, cannot be discerned from public utterances: three of the resoundingly loyal statements we quoted above (pp. 209–11) were made by members of the second category (Metropolitans Filaret of Kiev and Antoni of Leningrad, and Archbishop Mstislav of Kirov).

None the less, we should not forget that the range of attitudes under discussion is a narrow one, since the CRA's assertion that all the bishops are loyal to Soviet power and under overall control of the CRA cannot be doubted. The varying attitudes adopted by the bishops, and their shifting relationships with the CRA commissioners, significant though they are, all take place within a quite narrow spectrum.

Further comments by the CRA on the bishops give an idea of the problems bishops face in their diocesan work, and show that they are sometimes not afraid to complain about such difficulties. For example, Comrade Belsky of the CRA writes as follows about Archbishop Pimen of Saratov (listed in the third category):

> Dissatisfaction with the situation of the Church in the USSR is evident from his activities, as is a stubborn desire to create 'grandeur' in the churches and to increase the establishment of priests . . . In personal conversations with commissioners [of the CRA] he has more than once declared his dissatisfaction with the cadres of the priesthood in the Russian Orthodox Church. In his opinion this is the most important issue for the Church at the present time.

Archbishop Khrizostom (also listed in the third category), formerly a deputy-chairman of the Department of External Church Relations (DECR) who frequently met foreigners, was appointed to the diocese of Kursk and Belgorod in September 1974. The CRA Report notes: 'In the first months of his rule information was received from the commissioner of the Council for Belgorod region, Comrade P. F. Shamanov, about the bishop's zealous activities to revitalise religious life.' As a result, the CRA looked into the matter and then held an 'individual conversation' with Khrizostom. During the course of it, Khrizostom reportedly said:

> In my diocese now there are about forty churches which are not functioning because there are no priests. As a deputy chairman of the DECR, and as a bishop, I don't want people to say about me: that bishop is an atheist, that bishop is a *chekist* [i.e. a member of the secret police; the word derives from the name of the Soviet secret police in 1917, the *Cheka*], which is what people do say about us. I want to be a good bishop in the eyes of believers and foreigners. As for the accusation against me by the commissioner about activising religious life, I don't go to the churches suggesting that believers petition for them to be opened. They come to me.
>
> I am a bishop, I am forty years old. I don't intend to leave the Church. I've heard a good many insulting and offensive things from atheists, but these are the times we live in, there's nothing to be done about it.

One final quotation from the CRA Report concerning the episcopate throws an interesting light on the pro-government statements made by bishops, which we examined above:

A certain amount of concern is aroused by the activity of some young ruling bishops who at various times have been recruited for overseas work, but who within the country not infrequently display religious zeal, taking no account of the recommendations of commissioners of the Council and the local authorities. They include the bishops Nikolai of Vladimir [now of Gorky], Vladimir of Irkutsk [now of Krasnodar] Yermogen of Kalinin [since deceased], Damaskin of Vologda [now of Poltava], Khrizostom of Kursk, Savva of Chernigov [now of Mukachevo], Mikhail of Astrakhan [now of Vologda] and some others.

This comment gives grounds for thinking that bishops who are trained by the DECR for work overseas may not be as compliant towards the state as is often supposed. Perhaps these bishops regard the pro-state pronouncements they are obliged to make in this capacity as the price they have to pay in order to maintain a position from which they can improve diocesan life. However, an entirely different point of view is put by Father Gleb Yakunin in his report. His sharply polemical style makes a contrast with the careful bureaucratic prose of the CRA Report. Yakunin notes

the ever-increasing percentage of bishops who have passed through the 'school' of the DECR. In the process of working with the 'external' department, a special type of 'complaisant' hierarch is produced, disciplined, trained in obedience to the Soviet authorities, and moreover adept in relations with foreigners. Some of these hierarchs, by way of exception, are even permitted to display a heightened degree of activity in their diocesan affairs, in order to increase their authority, especially abroad.[29]

In this last sentence, Yakunin is arriving at a conclusion diametrically opposed to the CRA's on the basis of the same observations. He assumes that the CRA is deliberately allowing bishops greater latitude in their dioceses, while the CRA makes it plain that this arouses 'a certain amount of concern' within its ranks. There is no obvious reason why the CRA should attempt to deceive the Central Committee on this issue. This dichotomy appears to point, not to misconceptions or false statements on either side, but to a wide gulf between the two perspectives from which the episcopate is viewed. To the CRA, any variation within the tightly controlled framework of the bishops' actions is a cause for concern, whereas to an outsider within the church, all that is visible is the framework itself.

Yakunin's view of the episcopate is this:

We can no longer expect any kind of initiative, even the most modest, towards improving the situation of the Church from today's episcopate, because as a result of the ever-strengthening artificial selection, only people known to be incapable of opposing state interference in internal church affairs enter the episcopate.[30]

On the face of it, this is rather unfair to bishops such as Archbishop Pimen of Saratov and Archbishop Khrizostom of Kursk, who, according to the CRA Report, seem to be doing their best against heavy odds. However, we have also seen from the CRA Report that it intends to undertake 'constant political work' with the bishops to alter their point of view, and, however strong their faith and their will, they are clearly faced with a major struggle even on the level of bringing about improvements in diocesan life. Father Gleb, in his pessimistic summing-up of the situation of the episcopate, is referring to something on a higher level than this — the situation of the church as a whole, its position in national life. His view that the episcopate is powerless to affect the church's standing at this level because of 'ever-strengthening artificial selection' is borne out by the CRA's statement above that 'not a single episcopal consecration . . . occurs without a painstaking examination of the candidatures by the responsible officials of the Council'. It seems clear that, however many resolute bishops there may be faithfully doing their utmost to improve life in the dioceses, it is well within the capabilities of the CRA to confine their sphere of action within quite narrow bounds.

Metropolitan Iosif of Alma-Ata

Are we to assume from this that all the bishops are frozen and powerless in the bleak embrace of the state? What has happened to the faith, and the love of the church, that led them to join its ranks in the first place, and then impelled them to take on the lonely and unenviable task of episcopal service? The life of Metropolitan Iosif of Alma-Ata, who died in 1975, may serve to illustrate this dilemma. Born Ivan ('Vanya') Chernov in 1983, he displayed devotion to the church from an early age:

His father . . . occasionally took his son to church. As a four-year-old child he grew to love divine service, and with childish curiosity investigated the details of the church services. There was a characteristic incident: one day at the liturgy, during the hymn to the Cherubim, after the Great Entrance when the royal gates are closed and the curtain is drawn, Vanya ran up to the platform in front of them and, kneeling down, tried to peer under the royal gates towards the altar, scrutinising with amazement what was going on there. No one reproved him, but after the service the priest remarked to his father: 'I see your Vanya wants to get to the altar'.[31]

This prophecy was fulfilled: the boy became a novice at 16, a monk at 24, a priest at 27 and a bishop at 39, in 1932. Then came many years of suffering: he was arrested four times and spent a total of 20 years in labour camps and exile. In 1955 he resumed his episcopal ministry. He earned the devotion of his flock and was regarded as one of the great saints of his church. Even the usually restrained and formal style of the *Journal of the Moscow Patriarchate* takes on warmth in its description of his life:

He bore his cross without complaint, often repeating: 'Christianity has special qualities'. Six months before passing away, Father Iosif, recollecting his long and difficult life, emphasised: 'These words can be written on my grave.'

. . . Every service Father Iosif took became a festival for those who worshipped with him, because it communicated true spiritual joy. If he performed the liturgy, it was truly a *divine* liturgy . . .

. . . Father Iosif taught [people] to treat everyone equally — the clever and the foolish, the good and the evil. 'Make the evil good by your example,' he taught, 'and the good, better.' . . . Parishioners not only of the cathedral, but also of other churches where Father Iosif took services, treated their archpastor with the affection of sons and daughters.[32]

Here, evidently, was a deeply spiritual and saintly man who had suffered 20 years of cruel privation and still endured to serve the church he loved. How did he cope with the web of restrictions that the CRA weaves around the bishops under its surveillance? Firsthand evidence is provided by Archbishop Vasili of Brussels, whom we quoted above. Vasili was able to meet and talk to Iosif at the Local Council held in 1971, attended by both the Soviet and the overseas bishops of the Russian Orthodox Church. The previous day, Archbishop Vasili had spoken out on a contentious issue, and Metropolitan Iosif thanked him for doing so:

'All the bishops listened to you yesterday,' he began, 'and agreed with what you said. They all blessed you for it.' . . . 'But in that case why was everyone else silent?' I asked. 'We are cowed. We cannot speak, but you spoke for us all. Thank you,' answered Metropolitan Iosif . . .

'I often ask myself,' he told me, 'are we doing right to remain silent, not exposing what is happening in the Church and the difficulties she is experiencing? Sometimes I get sick of it and I want to throw it all over and retire. And my conscience reproaches me that I don't do it. But then the same conscience tells me that I can't abandon the believers and the Church. After all, to speak up and expose things, or even to criticise church conditions openly, would mean at best being immediately removed from all church activity, and wouldn't change anything anyway. So I try, as long as I have the strength, to work quietly for the Church.'[33]

The CRA evidently regarded Metropolitan Iosif as loyal and co-operative, since they listed him in their first category. Yet behind this cold statistic lay a man whose chief concern was to do all he could for the church. Even the church's most loyal servant, it seems, can find himself manoeuvred into a corner where his freedom of action is extremely limited, and where he may appear to outsiders as nothing more than a complaisant tool of the state.

Contrasts and Controversies

As the CRA Report notes, there are other issues on the basis of which the hierarchs of the Russian Orthodox Church may be distinguished from one another, apart from their attitude to the state: these are their 'theological and ideological' views, with which the CRA says it does not concern itself. No doubt these are as diverse as in any other church, and conditioned by the individual bishop's life experiences, age, nationality and theological education or lack of it, but any substantial information on differing views or schools of thought on theological or other issues is lacking at present. There is, however, known to be controversy between theological progressives and conservatives, discussed below. It is also known that there are tensions and rivalries between some hierarchs, probably no more pronounced than in any other church but exacerbated by the confined and difficult circumstances in which they have to order church life. Here again, information is insubstantial: rumours abound but evidence is scarce. Nevertheless, there is some interesting information about such rivalries at the end of the 1960s contained in the CRA Report. At this time Patriarch Alexi, who died in 1970, was old and ill and took little part in the running of the church. Access to him was controlled by his devoted confidant of many years, Daniil Ostapov, who had a great deal of influence in the Patriarchate. The question of the Patriarch's successor was naturally in the air, and the CRA clearly wanted to know what was being said on the matter. Bishops were questioned on the subject during the regular visits to the CRA office which they were (and are) encouraged to make when in Moscow.

On 9 February 1967 Metropolitan Alexi of Tallinn, the chancellor of the Moscow Patriarchate, visited the CRA and reported on a conversation he had had with Metropolitan Nikodim. He told the CRA that Nikodim wanted to be Metropolitan of Krutitsy and Kolomna, i.e. closer to the Patriarch and in a stronger position to succeed him, and also had his own ideas as to who should occupy other leading positions. Alexi reported a revealing remark Nikodim had made: he had said that if anyone other than himself became Patriarch they [Nikodim and his friends] would receive him with brotherly love but would not 'help him through the CRA as we do now'. What form such 'help' took is unclear, but seems to indicate that, in his conversations with CRA officials, a hierarch could attempt to influence them in making appointments and decisions. In this way the CRA would be drawn into rivalries and alliances between the hierarchs, and was evidently used by them as a means of promoting their interests. It is clear that the CRA was aware of this, and would use rivalries and alliances between hierarchs for its own ends, so that ploys and counter-ploys were — and no doubt are — very complicated.

It is clear from Metropolitan Alexi's conversations with the CRA that he was much closer to Metropolitan Nikodim than to Metropolitan (now Patriarch) Pimen, of whom he seems to have had a rather low opinion. Alexi repeated to the CRA a rumour that Pimen had a family and children in Rostov-on-Don and that he had relationships with women in Moscow. These are extremely serious allegations to make about a monk and a bishop, and it is most remarkable to find one hierarch making them about another to a third party outside the church. Whether personal animosity is involved, or whether it is simply a question of jockeying for position and influence, is unclear. Alexi was asked by the unnamed CRA official conducting the interview for a comparison of Nikodim and Pimen and for a judgement as to which would make a better Patriarch. Alexi considered that Nikodim would be better, since he was firmer, more independent and had more good qualities, but he thought that the Patriarch and the older bishops would support Pimen and oppose Nikodim. As far as we can tell, this was Alexi's true opinion of the situation: it was certainly a perfectly reasonable one to hold in the circumstances.

In the CRA transcripts of these conversations, Alexi comes across as extremely open and forthcoming in his relationship with the CRA officials, ready to give them information (especially about Pimen) which it was perhaps not strictly necessary to give. It is possible that this springs from a genuine desire to keep relations on an amicable footing and to demonstrate to the CRA the church's loyalty and willingness to co-operate with the state. This would fit in with other information about him: he is said to be one of the most pro-state of all the bishops and to maintain this line even in private conversations, and he is also reported to have a bad reputation among lay people in Moscow, who regard him as over-willing to implement decisions which are against the interests of the church.

The only other hierarch whose conversations with the CRA are recorded in the extracts from the CRA Report which have reached the West is Metropolitan Pimen. He appears as rather taciturn compared with Alexi, but this is apparently a genuine characteristic of Pimen's, who in general has a reputation for uncommunicativeness. There was one almost comic incident involving Pimen, Alexi and the CRA which occurred on 26 February 1968.

It concerned the attempt to appoint a new chairman of the financial administration of the Patriarchate. Alexi visited the CRA and informed them that Ostapov had told Pimen that he was to be appointed to the post, but Pimen had refused, saying that he had too much other work and suggesting that Alexi, as chancellor, would be a more suitable person. Alexi informed the CRA that he, too, had too much other work. He was quicker off the mark than Pimen, who arrived later the same day. He reported that Ostapov had spent an hour and a half trying to persuade him to take the job, but Pimen had maintained that the offer was an insult to his dignity as Metropolitan of Krutitsy, since this job had always been done by a suffragan bishop. However, Pimen confided to the CRA, there was another reason he had not revealed to Ostapov, which was that since all financial matters were effectively in his, Ostapov's, hands, no one could have any real influence in the job. Moreover, the Patriarchate was full of all kinds of swindlers, which was a disgrace, and all the chairman did was sign papers.[34]

The spectacle of officials in any organisation, in a church or anywhere else, trying to wriggle out of extra work, is perhaps not all that uncommon; what is so unexpected here is the way the two hierarchs seem to be trying to use the CRA for their own ends. It is as though they regarded the CRA as a kind of safety-valve within the church bureaucratic system. It appears that, from being an outside body appointed to watch over the church, the CRA has become subtly transmuted, at least in the minds of some hierarchs, into being a part of the structure of the church.

Metropolitan Nikodim of Leningrad

As noted above, there has been some controversy within the Russian Orthodox Church between progressives and conservatives. Given the church's inherent conservatism, this debate has not proceeded nearly so far as in many Western churches, and has centred mainly on the question of modernising the language of the liturgy. The main proponent of this was the late Metropolitan Nikodim of Leningrad. He was opposed by many of the older bishops, not least Patriarch Pimen. Nikodim and Pimen were the leading and best-known hierarchs during the 1970s, and both were spoken of as possible successors to Patriarch Alexi. They were strongly contrasting personalities. Nikodim was a brilliantly gifted, highly trained and educated theologian and administrator, able to charm and impress churchmen from many denominations and countries, and determined that his church should be seen to be up to date with modern thinking and concerns in the latter part of the twentieth century. Pimen, however, is a devout but taciturn product of a centuries-old contemplative monastic tradition, preferring to nourish the proven spiritual certainties of the past rather than venture upon the uncertain — and demanding — course of rendering faith more accessible to a modern secularised society. They were representative, therefore, of the two broad tendencies among the episcopate at the present time. Generally speaking, the progressives and conservatives may be distinguished chiefly, though not entirely, by their age. Bishops who, like Pimen, began their service to the church well before the Second World War saw the survival of the Orthodox faith because of its stalwart adherence to tradition, followed by its official restoration. This undoubtedly leads to the view that Orthodoxy cannot be destroyed if it remains faithful to Orthodox tradition. However, bishops who, like Nikodim, rose to prominence in the post-war church, when it was permitted to reopen some of its institutions and make extensive and growing overseas contacts, naturally looked to the opportunities these could bring to establish the church's status in society. They believed (at any rate in the post-Khrushchev period) that an educated, trained episcopate with a web of foreign contacts and friendships would guarantee the church's continued institutional existence — safe from either the terror of a Stalin or the whim of a Khrushchev. Something of the background to these standpoints is conveyed in the necessarily brief biographies which follow.

First, however, we should note one characteristic which they had in common, despite their different attitudes to the modernisation of the liturgy. This was their great devotion to liturgical worship. Several foreign visitors have written feelingly of Metropolitan Nikodim's deep absorption in prayer during church worship and his love of Orthodox services, to which he contributed settings of his own. Pimen's serving of the liturgy is said to be spiritually very impressive, and his piety is generally acknowledged, not least by the Orthodox faithful who regularly flock to the Patriarchal cathedral or to any other church where he is serving.

Metropolitan Nikodim of Leningrad and Novgorod (born Boris Rotov) died in 1978 in the arms of the newly elected Pope John Paul I, soon to die himself of the same cause, a heart attack. The dramatic manner of his passing, though untimely (Nikodim was only 49), somehow seems a fitting climax to a life full of action and controversy. Nikodim imbued with his modernistic ideas a number of young men whom he brought into the episcopate, among them his cousin, Metropolitan Yuvenali of Krutitsy, and Archbishop Kirill, rector of the Leningrad Theological Academy.

We have not space here to do justice to Nikodim's meteoric ascent through the ranks of the church hierarchy, which has in any case been described more than once elsewhere.[35] Suffice it to say that at the age of 31 he was a bishop and the deputy of the Department of External Church Relations, and that by the age of 34 he was Metropolitan of Leningrad. His dynamism and energy have become a byword: it is characteristic that after his death the positions he held — Metropolitan of Leningrad, head of the Department of External Church Relations, Exarch of Western Europe and chairman of the Holy Synod Commission on Christian Unity and Inter-Church Relations had to be shared out among three people.

Nikodim was a fitting person to head the CRA's second category: he was the archetype in modern times of hierarchs who are loyal to the state and at the same time do all they can to build up the church within the sphere of action permitted to it. Theologically, Nikodim's progressiveness expressed itself chiefly through his multifarious ecumenical activities, and particularly through his openness to the Roman Catholic Church. There was clearly a change in his attitude here, as a Western observer has noted.[36] In 1961 he was eager to see the Christian Peace Conference in Prague condemn the 'war-mongering' of the Vatican, but within a year or two he had adopted a more friendly attitude to the Catholic Church after coming to understand the changes which had taken place under Pope John XXIII, on whom Nikodim wrote a master's thesis.[37] It was largely on Nikodim's initiative that some rapprochement between the Russian Orthodox and Roman Catholic Churches occurred, and he is known to have gone even farther than the written agreements allow by giving Holy Communion to Roman Catholic visitors to his cathedral in Leningrad.[38] Nikodim also devoted much energy and enthusiasm over a period of about 20 years to the World Council of Churches, from the Orthodox standpoint an overwhelmingly Protestant body: he led his church into the WCC in 1961 and was one of its presidents at the time of his death.

Perhaps the chief way in which Nikodim's modern attitude expressed itself in his own church was in his desire to translate the services of worship from Church Slavonic into Russian, which he described as 'one of the most important problems of our times'.[39] This aroused considerable opposition from conservatives (whose arguments Nikodim carefully summarised in a report made in 1975),[40] but Nikodim continued to press energetically for its gradual introduction. He stated in the same report:

The use of Russian in divine service is still not very common, but experience has shown that where it is used, our parishioners welcome the practice and even express dissatisfaction if the switch is made back to Church Slavonic.[41]

The conflict between modernism and conservatism exists in many, perhaps even most, of the churches of the world, and in a sense the Russian Orthodox Church is no different from any of them in this respect. We shall not venture more deeply into this controversy here because the arguments on both sides are widely known, having been rehearsed many times in many churches, and a review of them here will not add anything to our knowledge of the Russian Orthodox Church. What needs to be pointed out here is the extent to which analysis of the modernist—conservative debate is clouded by the ever-present factor of the exponents' attitude to the state. Nikodim himself aroused suspicion among many people not only because of his progressive ideas but also by his punctiliously loyal attitude to the Soviet regime; indeed, he was frequently said to be an agent of the KGB.[42] Nikodim himself, according to Dimitri Pospielovsky,

> justified his policies by the need to convince the authorities that the Orthodox Church must remain an organic part of Russian life in all its aspects, being an inseparable expression of Russian spirituality, without which the nation would not be able to last long morally.[43]

This policy (begun in 1927 by the future Patriarch Sergi, of whom Nikodim was a great admirer) has clearly met with some success. As Pospielovsky has pointed out:

> from the point of view of a purely human understanding of the balance of power, the achievement by the Patriarchate of international political prestige has evidently succeeded and today the authorities could not increase persecution of the Church unnoticed and with impunity, as Khrushchev was able to do.[44]

The problem with this kind of policy is that it is so close to what the state itself wants of the church that it is almost impossible for outsiders to distinguish the true motivation of the churchmen concerned. They could be totally sincere in their views, or instruments of the state, or a complicated mixture of the two. Nikodim, with his complex personality and powerful intellect, was certainly the last, but his purposes remain a fascinating but ultimately unsolvable question. There will always be those who think that Nikodim was a full-time member of the KGB infiltrated into the church, just as there will always be those who think that he was totally sincere in following the only policy capable of saving the church from destruction.

In a church where conservative views predominate, which has been somewhat isolated from the rest of Christendom for centuries, and where there has historically been hostility to the Roman Catholic Church, Nikodim's views and actions could hardly fail to arouse hostility. He was opposed by a number of conservative hierarchs, such as Archbishop Pitirim of Volokolamsk, as well as by Patriarch Pimen.

Patriarch Pimen

Patriarch Pimen was born Sergei Mikhailovich Izvekov in 1910 in Moscow region. He became a monk at the age of 17, and much of his life thereafter was spent in various monasteries: from 1946 in the Monastery of St Elijah in Odessa, from 1949 as the superior of the Monastery of the Caves in Pskov, and from 1954 to 1957 as the superior of the Monastery of St Sergi at Zagorsk (with which he continues to have close ties). Pimen was consecrated bishop in 1957, and after having served as a suffragan first of Odessa and then of Moscow dioceses, he was made chancellor of the Moscow Patriarchate in 1960. Later that year he was elevated to archbishop and in 1961 he was made a permanent member of the Holy Synod and appointed Metropolian of Leningrad and Ladoga. In 1963, at the age of 53, he became Metropolitan of Krutitsy and Kolomna.[45] Patriarch Pimen seems to have had no formal theological training whatever. None of his official biographies mentions any theological study. Like other bishops we have mentioned, he is a product of Russia's long monastic tradition rather than of special 'job-oriented' episcopal training. He was however awarded an honorary doctorate by Moscow Theological Academy on 3 June 1971, the day of his enthronement as Patriarch.[46]

There is a long gap in Patriarch Pimen's official biography, from 1931 or 1932 until the end of the Second World War. In the shorter biographies these years are simply passed over without comment, but in the 20-page account of his life published on the occasion of his seventieth birthday,[47] such a gap would have been embarrassingly obvious. It is filled in by a statement that 'During the course of several years, Hieromonk Pimen fulfilled his monastic calling in the world' (p. 8), and that, at a time unstated, he was precentor of the Cathedral of the Epiphany (the Patriarchal cathedral) in Moscow (p. 9). There then follow a couple of paragraphs giving Pimen's views on religious music and the task of a precentor, followed by another describing how all the clergy and laity of the Russian Orthodox Church joined in the defence of their country during the 'heroic years of the Great Patriotic [i.e. Second World] War' (p. 10), but not mentioning Pimen specifically. Then the biography continues: 'The end of the Great Patriotic War found Hieromonk Pimen as priest in the Cathedral of the Epiphany in the ancient town of Murom in Vladimir diocese' (p. 10).

Such gaps in the biographies of a number of bishops and other church members are commonly to be found in the *Journal of the Moscow Patriarchate*, and it is generally assumed that the missing years were spent in labour camp. Many people in the church assume that this is true of Patriarch Pimen also, and revere him because of it. For example, one commentator wrote: 'he spent a long time in the concentration camps, where, according to rumours, he was beaten so badly that his kidneys were damaged'.[48] It is certainly highly likely that Pimen spent at least some of the missing years in labour camp, but this is not so clear-cut in his case as in the case of some other hierarchs who are known with some degree of certainty to have been imprisoned during these years: Metropolitan Iosif is a relevant example. There is evidence to suggest that Pimen was probably not imprisoned before 1936;[49] there are also persistent rumours that he spent several years in the army during this period of his life.

The only source which has given anything approaching authoritative information on the missing years in Pimen's life is the CRA Report (which did not reach the West until 1979), and even this contains information which is rather confusing. In a section headed 'Information (*spravka*) on Metropolitan Pimen of Leningrad and Ladoga (Izvekov S.M.)'[50] it gives what it states to be the true record as follows: 1926–32 precentor in Moscow, 1932–4 in the army, 1936–8 imprisoned, 1939 ran a health-education establishment in Andizhan in Uzbekistan, 1941–3 served at the front, 1944–5 imprisoned, 1946 onwards as in the biographies published by the *Journal of the Moscow Patriarchate*. The report states that Pimen has twice given false data about himself when supplying biographical information, disguising the years of imprisonment. In 1953 he reportedly wrote that he spent 1937–41 as a student in Fergana Pedagogical Institute while simultaneously teaching Russian in a school, and 1944–5 as a health instructor in Vorkuta in the far north of Russia. However, the CRA had evidently checked this information with its commissioner in Uzbekistan, who reported in 1963 that Pimen's presence in Fergana from 1937 to 1941 could not be corroborated. In 1959, according to the CRA, Pimen wrote that he spent 1936–8 as a health instructor on the Moscow–Volga Canal in Khimki, Moscow region, 1939–41 as a director of a health-education establishment in Andizhan, and in 1943–5 was demobilised from the army because of shell-shock and a wound and received treatment in hospitals in Frunze and Moscow. The CRA concludes that it is an 'incomprehensible and unexplained question' why Pimen gave this 'contradictory and false' information about himself.

However, the CRA's version of the missing years in Pimen's life is something of a puzzle. The report states that Pimen was sentenced in 1937 for deserting from the Soviet army, and that in 1943, as a major, he deserted again, lived for a while with false papers, was caught in 1944 and sentenced to ten years, but was amnestied because of the victory over Germany and released in 1945. This version is highly improbable: if Pimen really deserted once from the Soviet army it seems unlikely that he would have returned to it and reached the rank of major by 1943, and if he had deserted from the army a second time, and in wartime, it is most surprising that he was not shot.[51] The CRA officials who compiled the biography are of course well aware of this, and would have carefully checked all information in a report important enough to be sent to the Central Committee of the Communist Party, so we cannot assume that this passage is a result of the CRA being misinformed. It seems probable that Pimen really was imprisoned, but not for the reason given by the CRA; that he was one of the millions of victims of the 'cult of (Stalin's) personality', but that the CRA has chosen to avoid mentioning this in its report to the Central Committee. If this is so, it is still not clear, firstly why the CRA chose such an improbable cover story, and secondly why Pimen himself gave two contradictory versions of the way in which he spent the missing years. In fact, the CRA Report raises more questions than it answers. To sum up, we regard it as probable that the missing years were divided chiefly between the army and the labour camps, while noting that there are still many unanswered questions concerning this period of Pimen's life.

Since becoming Patriarch, Pimen has maintained a staunchly pro-government line in all his public utterances: we could quote many statements similar to those of other hierarchs quoted above. He has received a large number of foreign visitors to the USSR as the church's overseas contacts have continued to expand during the 1970s. However, he appears to be rather remote from all but the topmost hierarchs of the church, and to have little contact with church people at large. The Yakunin Report describes the Patriarch's isolation in some detail, attributing it largely to CRA policy but ending with the suggestion that Pimen could do more than he does to overcome it. Yakunin's account of the Patriarch's isolation is instructive:

> The Patriarch has no living contact with believers. The only form of communication with the people is divine services in the Yelokhovsky [so called from its situation on Moscow's Yelokhovsky Square, now renamed Bauman Square] Cathedral of the Epiphany and some Moscow churches. The Patriarch does not receive ordinary believers. The clergy are not received by him either. It is a rare event when the Patriarch receives priests from Moscow churches. When a priest is appointed incumbent of a Moscow church, he usually receives the patriarchal edict through a secretary. It is difficult for even a ruling bishop to be received by the Patriarch. The Patriarch is 'recommended' to travel abroad but he is 'not advised' to travel around the country and perform services in the dioceses (such services would promote the enlivening of religious life in the provinces — the authorities well know this, and so the Patriarch does not travel around the country). The Patriarch does not even officiate at services in the Moscow region, but only in the city of Moscow.
>
> In May this year [1979] Patriarch Pimen took a holiday, a cruise by steamer along the River Volga. Why could he not, on even one Sunday, have officiated at divine service in one of the many churches along his route, to the great joy of the believers? Patriarch Alexi did this in his time, and the local clergy and believing people met him with banners and icons and with bread and salt [traditional Russian sign of hospitality] to the sound of bells. But no, the authorities 'did not advise' it . . .
>
> In 1973 the 500-year jubilee of the Pskov Monastery of the Caves was celebrated; it was expected that Patriarch Pimen, a former superior of the monastery, would attend the festal ceremonies — but no, authorities 'did not recommend' it. The only exception to this rule was the Patriarch's trip to Leningrad to take part in the funeral of Metropolitan Nikodim. However, in his isolation the Patriarch is surrounded by the eyes and ears of the GB [i.e. KGB or secret police] and informers are included among those closest to him, among his personal attendants, subdeacons and personal secretary. Even his personal chauffeur is a KGB officer, a retired

major. He is just as closely enveloped in Peredelkino [a village near Moscow where the Patriarch has a country residence] and in the Monastery of the Dormition in Odessa, where the Patriarch takes his summer holiday. Sometimes the Patriarch takes holidays in special state sanatoria of the closed type. His food, medical service and personal doctor are from the 'Kremlyovka', the system providing services to the government.

In rare confidential conversations with people close to him, the Patriarch has said that he is in a 'golden cage'. Many hierarchs of the Russian Orthodox Church, quietening their consciences, like to repeat this phrase, which has become a byword, and apply it to themselves. But does this image correspond to reality? In part, yes. But is not the cage made of soft gold? Surely the pliant bars could be bent by strength of will?[52]

No doubt Yakunin is right to suggest that some people in the Patriarch's position could break out of the cage by sheer strength of will, and also that some bishops use it as a convenient excuse for inaction at times. But, bearing in mind the CRA's claim to vet all candidates for the episcopate and higher offices, it is probable that Pimen was advanced as a Patriarchal candidate precisely because he was thought to be by nature incapable of making any stand in the way that Yakunin was suggesting.

Pimen was elected Patriarch by the church's highest authority, composed of bishops, clergy and laity from every diocese (including those abroad) — the Local Council.

Excursus: The Local Council of 1971

A Local Council (*Pomestny Sobor*) is the supreme authority of a Local (or national) Orthodox Church, so called in contrast to the seven Ecumenical Councils, held between AD 325 and 787, which are the supreme authority of the whole church in all countries. The Russian Orthodox Church has held three Local Councils in the Soviet period: in 1917–18, when the Patriarchate was restored after an interval of over 200 years; in 1945, when Patriarch Alexi was elected; and in 1971, to elect his successor. (The election of Patriarch Sergi in 1943 took place at a Council of Bishops, not a Local Council with the participation of clergy and laity.) Patriarch Alexi died in April 1970, but the Local Council was not convened until the end of May 1971, after an interval of 13 months, although church regulations state that no more than six months should elapse between the death of a Patriarch and the election of his successor.[53] Apart from the Patriarchal election, the main item on the agenda of the 1971 Council was a discussion of the reform of parish life which had been introduced in 1961.

There are three main sources for our description of the 1971 Council. The first is the official report of the occasion in the *Journal of the Moscow Patriarchate*. The second is an account of the proceedings by one of the overseas participants, Nicolas Lossky. The third, and most revealing, is a report written some time after the Council by an anonymous witness of the proceedings who signed himself 'an observer'.[54]

The Council had 236 delegates, of whom 234 actually attended, including 74 from abroad. Each diocese sent its bishop, a priest and a layman to the Council.[55] There were also overseas guests.[56] The Local Council was preceded by a Council of Bishops held in the Novodevichi Monastery in Moscow on 25 May. The full Council met from 30 May to 2 June in the Holy Trinity Monastery of St Sergi in Zagorsk, 50 miles northeast of Moscow. The first day was devoted to a ceremonial liturgy and to a five-hour session of welcoming speeches. The second day was given over to reports: the first, from Metropolitan Pimen of Krutitsy, on the church's life from 1945 to 1971; the second, from Metropolitan Nikodim of Leningrad, on the Russian Orthodox Church's participation in the ecumenical movement; and the third, from Metropolitan Alexi of Tallinn, on the church's peacemaking activities. The anonymous observer reports that the overly pro-government tone of this third speech aroused the indignation of many delegates. The third day of the Council was devoted to discussion of these reports. The fourth day, 2 June, saw the election of the Patriarch and resolutions on the basis of the reports.

The Patriarchal Election

There was only one candidate for Patriarch, Metropolitan Pimen. No attempt was made to follow the electoral procedure formulated by the Council of 1917–18, which prescribed three candidates. Information circulated to delegates before the Council commenced, according to the observer, announced the single candidature and also stated that voting would be public, not by ballot. Both these facts were reportedly discussed at the Pre-Conciliar Council of Bishops, where opposition to them was expressed by some hierarchs, notably Archbishop Vasili of Brussels and his suffragan, Bishop Dionisi (Lukin) of Rotterdam. However, they were unable to accomplish any changes.

Two or three other possible candidates for the role of Patriarch of Moscow and All Russia have been mentioned. Perhaps the most obvious was Metropolitan Nikodim, who, as we have seen, was the object of discussions at the CRA. It is interesting to speculate what might have happened if he had become Patriarch. With his loyalty to the state established, he might have been free to turn his prodigious talents to the task of consolidating the church's position in the international arena, and of strengthening its position as an accepted part of Soviet life. This has in any case been achieved to some extent under Pimen's rule; maybe it would have been achieved to a greater extent, and certainly more dramatically, under Nikodim. However that may be, none of the bishops proposed his candidacy at the open voting session. Konstantinov thinks that the Soviet authorities were concerned about unfavourable reactions to Nikodim from Western circles in which his pro-government stance had aroused suspicions, and therefore did not let his candidacy go forward, which represents a retreat on their part.[57] Whatever view one takes of Nikodim's potential policies as Patriarch, it is clear that from the point of view of both church and state Pimen was the 'safer' candidate. That the choice between safety and a more adventurous course was not easy is indicated by the long interval before the Council was convened.

Another potential candidate was Metropolitan Iosif of Alma-Ata, whom we have already mentioned as enjoying great reverence because of his saintly bearing. Archbishop Vasili of Brussels describes the attempts to make him a candidate as follows:

when I was in Moscow in October 1970, I heard many stories about him as a possible candidate for the patriarchate. They said that the commissioner for religion in Alma-Ata had told him: 'Put in as a candidate for Patriarch — we'll support you!' Later I heard that a large group of clergy and believers, led by the former dean of the Patriarchal Cathedral in Moscow, Archpriest Ioann Potapov, wrote a letter to Metropolitan Iosif, signed by almost two thousand people, urging him for the good of the Church not to refuse election as Patriarch, and adding that if he did, he would have to answer for it before God at the Last Judgement. But Metropolitan Iosif still refused. However, the following opinion was more current among the Moscow clergy: 'Yes, of course Metropolitan Iosif is a good bishop, firm, energetic, holy living. But he would not be suitable as Patriarch. He's eighty years old (in fact he was 78), and besides that he was under German occupation and he's been in the camps: the authorities don't like that'.

During the Council, Archbishop Vasili had an opportunity of questioning Metropolitan Iosif about his possible candidature:

I'd never agree to that. In the first place I'm too old, also I've no theological education and not much secular either. I don't want to be upbraided for my ignorance in the Synod. They'd force me to agree with their opinions, because they're theologians. I'm an ignoramus and I'd have to do what they said.[58]

A third person mentioned as a possible candidate was Archbishop Yermogen of Kaluga. Since 1965 he had been known as a person who had led opposition to the 1961 reform, and it is said that reports filtered through from private sources to the effect that some of the overseas bishops tried to put him forward as a candidate, but were decisively stopped.[59] Yermogen had been demoted from his see and sent into forced retirement in the Zhirovitsy Monastery in Belorussia; he did not attend the Council. It appears that Metropolitan Filaret of Kiev was also mentioned as candidate, though his name seems not to have been vigorously canvassed. Another possibility which came to nothing was the idea of nominating an elderly and holy monk from Pochayev or Zagorsk.

Metropolitan Pimen was duly proposed unanimously and there was no vote. Two participants in the election, Archbishop Vasili and Nicolas Lossky, both reported that to hear delegate after delegate propose Metropolitan Pimen was impressive, rather than conveying a feeling of a rigged election:

> Everyone nominated Metropolitan Pimen. But it must be noted that, contrary to what one might think, this rather long and uniform procedure, far from becoming a predetermined masquerade, gave the impression more and more of a ceremony full of real dignity and an expression of real unanimity on the person of Metropolitan Pimen.[60]

Archbishop Vasili spoke of 'a great and profound spiritual unity among the Council members'.[61]

The enthronement of the new Patriarch followed immediately, on 3 June, in the Patriarchal cathedral in Moscow, and was performed by Patriarch Nicholas of Alexandria.

Although the Russian Orthodox Church is approaching its millennium, Patriarch Pimen is, surprisingly, only the fourteenth occupant of the Patriarchal throne. The Russian Metropolitanate was not elevated to Patriarchal status until 1589 and there were then ten Patriarchs in succession until 1700, when Peter the Great forbade the election of a new Patriarch. The church then had the status of a government department throughout the latter Tsarist period until the advent of the Soviet period. Since 1917 there have been four Patriarchs: Patriarch Tikhon (1917–25); Patriarch Sergi, who was Deputy-Locum Tenens and then Locum Tenens from 1927 to 1943 and Patriarch only until 1944; Patriarch Alexi (1945–70); and Patriarch Pimen. Patriarch Alexi's 25-year reign was by far the longest period of office of any Russian Patriarch. Patriarch Pimen therefore does not have as much of a Patriarchal tradition to draw upon as might be expected from the age of his church, and the influence of his two immediate predecessors is bound to be strong.

The 1961 Reform

The second major issue facing the Local Council of 1971 was whether or not to uphold the reform of parish life passed by the 1961 Council of Bishops.

As we saw in Chapter 2, the reform had undermined the authority of the parish priest and had led to a parlous situation developing in some parishes. By 1971, some bishops were of the opinion, firstly, that the reform was not compatible with the church's canons and therefore should not have been enacted, and, secondly, that it had caused many problems in practice in parish life and should therefore be repealed. The reform of 1961 was in accordance with the interests of the state, as we have seen, and was introduced with the implicit approval of the state, whose representatives were present at the Council of Bishops. The bishops who opposed the reform and wished to change it therefore had the powerful influence of state representatives to contend with.

The subject first arose at the Pre-Conciliar Council of Bishops on 28 May 1971. Lossky, in his article on the Local Council, said that this was the only occasion during the week when anything remotely resembling freedom of speech was possible.[62] The discussion was opened by the members of the Holy Synod, and according to the anonymous observer,

> Each of them began by declaring that the issue of the 'Synod of 1961' was 'not for discussion' . . . Archbishop Vasili of Brussels and Belgium asked for the floor and calmly, but obstinately and persistently, commenced a polemic against the 'Synod of 1961', asserting that it was uncanonical. A sharp clash with the Exarch of Ukraine, Metropolitan Filaret of Kiev and Galicia, took place. A sustained argument flared up. Then some other hierarchs spoke. Bishop Dionisi of Rotterdam gave a sharp, fiery speech against the 'preconciliar information', the open voting and the single candidature. This speech stunned the bishops. Silence fell: it was broken by Metropolitan Filaret of Kiev, who sharply opposed Bishop Dionisi. The older bishops kept silence. The younger careerists began to make objections to Bishop Dionisi. Archbishop Vasili stubbornly continued his polemic against the 'Synod of 1961'. The fruitless convention of bishops continued for five hours.

According to the observer, Archbishop Vasili asked Bishop Dionisi if he would repeat his speech before the full Council. However, older bishops who learned of the suggestion dissuaded him, saying that to do so would be to risk his life. (In the event, Dionisi did not attend the debate because of a heart ailment.) It was decided that the Belgian lay delegate would repeat the speech. The debates were scheduled for the third day of the Council. The observer continues:

> On the night before, a fierce argument flared up between Archbishop Vasili and Metropolitan Nikodim about the ill-starred 'Synod'. Metropolitan Nikodim told Archbishop Vasili that he was free to speak out, but that by doing so he would cause great harm to the Church, since the

Soviet government would not change the law.

Archbishop Vasili did not in fact speak out at the debate: when called to the rostrum, he announced publicly that he was not going to make use of his opportunity to speak — a brief but pregnant statement. The debate was carefully stage-managed:

> The speakers were called not in order of seniority, but in turn. During the debate the platform was cleared of guests (they were taken to see the sights of Moscow), the microphones did not work and the simultaneous interpreter was absent; the debate lasted eight hours. It was like trying to get blood out of a stone. Eulogies were sung to the Soviet government, and when, at last, the Belgian wished to speak and repeat the contents of Bishop Dionisi's speech, Metropolitan Nikodim adroitly closed the debate. The Belgians were beside themselves. Archbishop Vasili, gathering his delegation together, gave Metropolitan Nikodim a written protest in the name of the Archdiocese of Brussels and Belgium (and, consequently, in the name of the Dutch Vicariate), to the effect that the Archdiocese did not accept the resolutions of the 1961 Synod, as they were uncanonical.[63]

The Belgian protest carried no weight when the resolutions of the Council were adopted. A report based on Lossky's account of the proceedings describes how this was done:

> At 6 p.m. on 1 June, after an exhausting day of speeches from the floor, Metropolitan Filaret of Kiev hastily read three typed pages of resolutions which no one had the chance to see. They included putting the seal of approval on the 1961 regulations. Metropolitan Nikodim called for their adoption, but this was quickly contested by Lossky. Nikodim appeared to make a partial concession, saying that the text had been adopted 'by a majority'. Press releases nevertheless claimed unanimity and Lossky was refused permission to see the text itself. When it was finally made available to delegates on 6 June it had been further hardened, especially on point 4, regarding condemnation of the Russian Orthodox Church outside of Russia.[64]

The resolutions of the Local Council of 1971 were as follows: (1) to approve the actions of the Holy Synod since 1945, including the resolutions of the 1961 Council of Bishops; (2) to approve the granting of autocephaly to the Orthodox Churches in Poland, Czechoslovakia and America, and of autonomy to those in Japan and Finland; (3) to note the 'outstanding historical events' of the return to Orthodoxy in 1946 and 1949 of the Greek Catholics of Galicia and Trans-Carpathia; (4) to empower the Supreme

Church Authority to continue efforts towards reunion with the Russian Orthodox Church in Exile; (5) to approve the efforts made to promote relations with other Local Orthodox Churches; (6) to approve and ask for further development of ecumenical contacts with non-Orthodox churches; and (7) to recommend further development of the church's peacemaking activities. The Council also lifted the excommunication of the Old Believers laid in 1656 and 1667.[65] There is not space here to comment on these controversial and far-reaching issues, beyond noting that most of them represented important developments in the external relations of the church, which fall outside the scope of the present work.

The Failure of Reformist Bishops

It is clear from the accounts of the proceedings at the Council that only the overseas delegates dared speak out on controversial issues. This is evident from Metropolitan Iosif's words to Archbishop Vasili which we quoted above: 'We are cowed. We cannot speak.' However, some of the Soviet bishops had made their views known before the Council convened. They were Archbishop Yermogen (Golubyev) of Kaluga, Archbishop Pavel (Golyshev) of Novosibirsk, and Archbishop Veniamin (Novitsky) of Irkutsk.

Archbishop Yermogen had begun to campaign for greater freedom in the church in the mid-1960s. He enlisted other bishops to support him in a petition to the Patriarch to repeal the reform of 1961. He was also the confidant and supporter of Fathers Eshliman and Yakunin in their campaign for religious freedom (see Chapter 10). Father Yakunin in his 1979 Report has given some new information about these events:

> While having great love for *Vladyka* Yermogen, and profoundly revering his memory, nonetheless, in evaluating his role in church life in the sixties, we come to a sad conclusion. His objective role in the movement for the freedom of the Church is dramatic and highly ambiguous. Father Yermogen sincerely believed that in the period of 'restoration of socialist legality' which had commenced, it was possible to restore the rights of the Church simply by pointing out to the authorities instances of the violation of these rights and explaining to them what exactly were the legal rights of the Church and of believers.
>
> Believing, without sufficient grounds, that Patriarch Alexi was supporting him, he began to collect signatures of hierarchs under the renowned 'Appeal of the Ten', referring as he did so to the private blessing of the Patriarch. I remember that, meeting me within the walls of the Holy Trinity Monastery of St Sergi, Father Yermogen began to rejoice because the appeal had unexpectedly been signed by Archbishop

Grigori (Zaklyak) and he regarded this as a great success. The following dialogue ensued:

> Yakunin: *Vladyka*, did you tell him that the Patriarch had given you his blessing for this?
> Yermogen: Yes.
> Yakunin: But don't you think that he signed the appeal only through opportunist considerations, without investigating the situation, assuming that the Patriarch's blessing signified the authorities' blessing?

Vladyka Yermogen did not give a precise answer, and it turned out that I was right.

The rest is known: Patriarch Alexi refused to confirm that he had given his blessing for the collection of signatures, and *Vladyka* Yermogen was retired from the see of Kaluga by deceptive means. The hierarchs who had signed the appeal were summoned one by one to the Council [for Religious Affairs] and a written renunciation was demanded. Archbishop Grigori (Zaklyak) had already stated that he had been deceived into the escapade and into provocation. Some others renounced it in a milder form, but there were some who held out courageously, for example, Archbishops Pavel of Novosibirsk and Veniamin of Irkutsk.[66]

Archbishop Yermogen spent the rest of his life, until his death in 1978, in forced retirement in the Zhirovitsy Monastery in Belorussia, far from his home, where he was able to have little if any influence on church life. He wrote a number of letters and documents analysing the situation of the church,[67] but they seem to have fallen on deaf ears.

Archbishop Pavel was educated in Paris, but in 1947 he voluntarily offered his services to the Russian Orthodox Church and went to the USSR. He was made bishop in 1957 and served in several dioceses before his appointment to Novosibirsk. This is a large and important diocese, and Novosibirsk is near the new city of Akademgorodok, one of the most important scientific centres in the USSR. It can be assumed that the Holy Synod (and the CRA) regarded Pavel as a trustworthy person when they appointed him there.[68] In 1969 an interview with him was published in a Soviet newspaper for Russians overseas, and in it he made the same kind of pro-government statements as we have quoted above (see pp. 210–11). He was especially critical of the 'Karlovatsky' Church (the Russian Orthodox Church outside of Russia).[69] This does not, however, seem to have harmed his reputation as an independently minded person. The observer of the 1971 Council records that he was eagerly waited at the Council of Bishops which preceded it:

Everyone was waiting for the arrival of Archbishop Pavel of Novosibirsk,

who was known for his oppositionist views. To the great dismay of the
Council . . . news arrived that Father Pavel could not come, because he
had 'had an accident'.[70]

Lossky amplifies this by saying that Archbishop Pavel 'burned his hands at
the moment of leaving for Moscow'.[71] Not all the members of the Council
believed in this 'accident'. The observer quotes one (unnamed) hierarch as
saying:

> Father Pavel's guilt consists entirely of the fact that he attracts young
> people, and so they want to pin a charge of pederasty on him. They'll ruin
> Father Pavel, they'll ruin him. As soon as anyone takes a straight line,
> they ruin him.[72]

One source has reported that the 'accident' which prevented Archbishop
Pavel from attending the Local Council resulted from an unexpected
summons to visit the local CRA commissioner. When the archbishop sat
down in a chair, he felt a burning sensation in his back. Later it was discovered that the chair had been treated with a chemical: its effect was to
incapacitate him and prevent him travelling to Moscow.[73] Archbishop Pavel
alluded to this in a letter to the Patriarch:

> I have served almost fifteen years in the rank of bishop, and I have not
> once refused any appointment, nor have I ever thrust myself upon any
> see.
>   Almost eight years ago, Patriarch Alexi, who has reposed in God, sent
> me to Novosibirsk, saying: 'Bring order into the Novosibirsk Diocese.'
>   Since then I have laboured in this see, always remembering the words
> of His Holiness Patriarch Alexi. I have achieved something, although
> from the very beginning I felt opposition towards this aim from the com-
> missioner of the Council for Religious Affairs in Novosibirsk region,
> Alexander Sergeyevich Nikolayev, which led me to the necessity of
> making a complaint about him to the Chairman of the Council for
> Religious Affairs, Vladimir Alexandrovich Kuroyedov, in October 1971.
>   Despite the latter's promise to examine my complaint and give me a
> written answer to it, up to the present I have in fact received neither a
> written nor a verbal reply to my complaint. In spring last year, A. S.
> Nikolayev carried out a filthy provocation against me, which I disproved
> completely. But how it damaged my health!
>   Now you, Your Holiness, are translating me to another see to please
> A. S. Nikolayev, without there being any errors on my part to stimulate
> such a measure. I heard about this intention of yours last year. I have
> moved dioceses more than once. But now my age and my health are not
> such that I could easily bear these changes.

In Novosibirsk I have occupied a vast and difficult diocese, and I have been here significantly longer than my predecessors. Now I am being appointed to the quite insignificant diocese of Vologda, which has only seventeen parishes. I interpret this, Your Holiness, to mean that in your eyes I am capable of nothing better. By the same token, I do not exclude the possibility of further unmotivated transfers.

Perhaps, in general, my education and my pastoral and life's experience are insufficient for me to administer a diocese in the Soviet Union. In that case I am willing to go into retirement altogether, on condition that beforehand you offer assistance in acquiring a visa to France, where I could live in peace with my brother in Paris.[74]

This letter was written in February 1972; Archbishop Pavel's transfer to Vologda proceeded, and he remained there until October 1972, when the Holy Synod decided to retire him for 'violation of canonical standards, improper behaviour and incompetence in administering church affairs'.[75] It was not until October 1975 that he was allowed to emigrate to France.[76] Since then he has not to our knowledge made any public statement about the events we have described.

Archbishop Veniamin, as noted in Chapter 2, discovered that the reform of 1961 was causing problems in his diocese of Irkutsk, and wrote to the Commission preparing the Local Council to express his misgivings. Archbishop Vasili of Brussels learned of this, and was therefore expecting him to make a verbal contribution to the Council of Bishops preceding the Local Council. However, Veniamin remained silent. When Archbishop Vasili made his acquaintance later, he learned that Veniamin had been summoned to Moscow before the Council, and for a long time had been 'persuaded' not to speak out against the 1961 reform at the Council. Although Veniamin did not apparently suffer any physical violence, he may have been threatened with it, since the character of the 'persuasion', according to Archbishop Vasili, can be judged from a saying current in Moscow at the time and attributed to a deputy-chairman of the CRA, P. V. Makartsev: 'Anyone who opposes the resolution on parishes will break his leg.'

Archbishop Veniamin had been in German-occupied territory during the Second World War, and, like many Soviet citizens who suffered this fate, was despatched to the labour camps after the German withdrawal under suspicion of collaboration with the enemy. He spent twelve years in the camps of Kolyma in far eastern Siberia. It was said that beatings there had broken his spinal column, and Archbishop Vasili states that he remained hunchbacked all his life. When Archbishop Vasili asked him why he had not spoken out against the 1961 reform at the Council of Bishops, Veniamin replied that he had been deceived by being told that the subject would not come up for discussion. ' "But when you saw that there was a discussion, why did you not express your views too?" Archbishop Veniamin looked at me: "You know, I spent twelve years at hard labour in Kolyma. I haven't the strength to begin that again at my age. Forgive me!" '[77]

A fourth bishop whose protests have been summarily silenced at a later date is Bishop Feodosi of Poltava and Kremenchug, whose letter to President Brezhnev we have quoted in preceding chapters.[78] Although his complaints about the situation in his diocese, and the behaviour of the CRA commissioner, were forcefully worded, he did not say anything to suggest that the improvements he wanted were not well within the bounds of Soviet legislation on religion. Moreover, his letter could not have been regarded as an embarrassment to either church or state since it was not an open letter and was addressed only to Brezhnev, with copies to Patriarch Pimen and Metropolitan Filaret, the Exarch to Ukraine. The letter was written in 1977, but copies did not reach the West until 1980, long after it was clear that no reply was forthcoming. None the less, Feodosi was swiftly removed from Poltava, where he had served for twelve years, and sent, like Archbishop Pavel before him, to the 'insignificant' diocese of Vologda.[79] Shortly afterwards he was transferred again, to Astrakhan in the south of Russia, the reason given being that he needed to live in a warm climate for health reasons.[80] As a native Ukrainian, he would no doubt be more effectively employed in a Ukrainian diocese.

The cases of these four bishops exemplify the difficulties of developing an independent point of view within the episcopate of the Russian Church. A brave man might disregard the personal danger involved, but still be checked by the thought that he would lose any power to influence the state of the church, and might create an opening for a more compliant person to take his place. Furthermore, the fate of these four could well deter younger bishops from following their example. Were they then foolhardy to raise their voices in opposition? Father Yakunin thinks that, on the contrary, the error of Archbishop Yermogen was not to go far enough:

Having timidly begun a movement for the rights of the Church *Vladyka* Yermogen did not see before him the clear perspectives and the final aims of the path on which he had set out. Having begun and headed a movement for the freedom of the Church and the rights of believers, he renounced further struggle at the first trial (his retirement). Possessing great authority in the Church, *Vladyka* Yermogen by his own self-elimination and prolonged silence slowed down the movement which had begun. If *Vladyka* Yermogen had not spoken out at all, it is possible that another hierarch would have taken this mission upon himself (*Vladyka* Pavel/Golyshev/ said, for example, that he was ready to go to the end after *Vladyka* Yermogen; and other priests and laymen expressed the same readiness.) . . .

'No one who puts his hand to the plough and looks back is fit for the kingdom of God' [Luke 9, 72]. Archbishop Yermogen's unsuccessful démarche and the 'Letter of the Ten' were the episcopate's last humble attempt to protest officially against the relations which had been formed between Church and State. The silenced voice of Archbishop Yermogen is the silenced voice of the episcopate of the Russian Church.[81]

This is a harsh judgement, even though it is made by one who has shown himself ready to suffer imprisonment and hard labour for what he believes to be the truth. However, whether the Russian Orthodox bishops have been silenced by state pressure, by cowardice, by failure to recognise opportunities to defend their church, or by a mixture of all these things — and no one is in a position to make a final judgement — the fact remains that, for the present, they have been silenced.

Appendix 1: Dates of Birth and Consecration of Russian Orthodox Bishops in the USSR, Compiled 15 August 1982

(Note: Seniority in the Russian Orthodox Church is not by age but by rank and date of episcopal consecration. The hierarchs are listed in this order in the Church Calendar.)

		Birth	Consecration
Archbishop	Meliton (Solovyov) of Tikhvin	1897	1970
Metropolitan	Ioann (Razumov) of Pskov	1898	1953
Archbishop	Damian (Marchuk) of Volhynia	1899	1961
Archbishop	Kassian (Yaroslavsky) of Kostroma	1899	1961
Bishop	Viktorin (Belyayev) of Vilnius	1903	1973
Archbishop	Iosif (Savrash) of Ivano-Frankovsk	1909	1957
Metropolitan	Ioann (Wendland) of Yaroslavl	1909	1960
Archbishop	Nikon (Fomichev) of Perm	1910	1962
Patriarch	Pimen (Izvekov) of Moscow	1910	1957
Metropolitan	Nikolai (Yurik) of Lvov	1910	1965
Metropolitan	Alexi (Konoplev) of Kalinin	1910	1956
Archbishop	Mikhail (Chub) of Tambov	1912	1953
Archbishop	Mikhail (Mudyugin) of Vologda	1912	1966
Archbishop	Ionafan (Kopalovich) of Kishinyov	1912	1965
Bishop	Panteleimon (Mitryukovsky) of Kazan	1912	1975
Archbishop	Gleb (Smirnov) of Oryol	1913	1976
Metropolitan	Leonid (Polyakov) of Riga	1913	1959
Archbishop	Leonti (Bondar) of Orenburg	1913	1956
Bishop	Sevastian (Pilipchuk) of Kirovograd	1914	1977
Archbishop	Nikodim (Rusnak) of Kharkov	1921	1961
Archbishop	Pimen (Khmelevsky) of Saratov	1923	1965
Archbishop	Nikolai (Kutepov) of Gorky	1924	1961

		Birth	Consecration
Metropolitan	Sergi (Petrov) of Odessa	1924	1960
Metropolitan	Antoni (Melnikov) of Leningrad	1924	1964
Bishop	Savva (Babinets) of Mukhachevo	1926	1969
Archbishop	Antoni (Vakarik) of Chernigov	1926	1965
Archbishop	Feodosi (Dikun) of Astrakhan	1926	1967
Archbishop	Pitirim (Nechayev) of Volokolamsk	1926	1963
Archbishop	Feodosi (Protsyuk) of Smolensk	1927	1962
Archbishop	Melkhisedek (Lebedev) of Berlin	1927	1965
Bishop	Afanasi (Kudyuk) of Pinsk	1927	1980
Archbishop	Ioann (Snychev) of Kuibyshev	1927	1965
Archbishop	Varfolomei (Gandorovsky) of Tashkent	1927	1963
Archbishop	Simon (Novikov) of Ryazan	1928	1972
Bishop	Maxim (Krokha) of Omsk	1928	1972
Archbishop	Leonti (Gudimov) of Simferopol	1928	1961
Metropolitan	Filaret (Denisenko) of Kiev	1929	1962
Metropolitan	Alexi (Ridiger) of Tallinn	1929	1961
Bishop	Ioann (Bondarchuk) of Zhitomir	1929	1977
Archbishop	Yuvenali (Tarasov) of Irkutsk	1929	1975
Bishop	Varlaam (Ilyushchenko) of Chernovtsy	1929	1972
Archbishop	Gedeon (Dokunin) of Novosibirsk	1929	1967
Archbishop	Vladimir (Kotlyarov) of Krasnodar	1929	1962
Bishop	Amvrosi (Shchurov) of Ivanovo	1930	1977
Bishop	Anatoli (Kuznetsov) of Ufa	1930	1972
Bishop	Varnava (Kedrov) of Cheboksary	1931	1976
Archbishop	Serapion (Fadeyev) of Vladimir	1933	1972
Archbishop	Khrizostom (Martishkin) of Kursk	1934	1972
Bishop	Serafim (Tikhonov) of Penza	1935	1978
Metropolitan	Filaret (Vakhromeyev) of Minsk	1935	1965
Metropolitan	Yuvenali (Poyarkov) of Krutitsy	1935	1965
Metropolitan	Vladimir (Sabodan) of Rostov	1935	1966
Bishop	Damaskin (Bodry) of Poltava	1937	1972
Bishop	Khrisanf (Chepil) of Kirov	1937	1978
Bishop	German (Timofeyev) of Tula	1937	1968
Archbishop	Agafangel (Savvin) of Vinnitsa	1938	1975
Bishop	Antoni (Zavgorodny) of Stavropol	1938	1975
Archbishop	Makari (Svistun) of Uman	1938	1970
Bishop	Iov (Tyvonyuk) of Zaraisk	1938	1975
Bishop	Lazar (Shvets) of Argentina	1939	1980
Archbishop	Irinei (Seredny) of Alma-Ata	1939	1975
Bishop	Valentin (Mishchuk) of Zvenigorod	1940	1976
Archbishop	Platon (Udovenko) of Sverdlovsk	1940	1973
Bishop	Isidor (Kirichenko) of Arkhangelsk	1941	1977
Bishop	Ilian (Vostryakov) of Kaluga	1945	1979

		Birth	*Consecration*
Archbishop	Kirill (Gundyayev) of Vyborg	1946	1976
Bishop	Mefodi (Nemtsov) of Voronezh	1949	1980

Postscript to Appendix 1

At 31 December 1984 three of the bishops listed above had retired, and three new ones had been consecrated. The total of bishops of the Russian Orthodox Church in the USSR therefore remained 67.

On 12 October 1982, the Holy Synod approved the retirement of Archbishop Iosif of Ivano-Frankovsk and Kolomyya. Archbishop Makari of Uman was appointed to succeed him.

On 6 October 1983, the Holy Synod approved the retirement of Metropolitan Nikolai of Lvov and Ternopol. Archbishop Nikodim of Kharkov and Bogodukhov was appointed to succeed him, while retaining temporary administration of Kharkov diocese.

On 26 December 1984, the Holy Synod approved the retirement of Metropolitan Ioann of Yaroslavl and Rostov. Archbishop Platon of Sverdlovsk and Kurgan, temporarily administering Chelyabinsk diocese, was appointed to succeed him, while remaining a deputy-chairman of the DECR.

The following new bishops were consecrated:

Bishop	Sergi (Fomin) of Solnechnogorsk	1949	1982
Bishop	Alexander (Timofeyev) of Dmitrov	1941	1982
Bishop	Kliment (Kapalin) of Serpukhov	1949	1982

(Bishop Sergi was a deputy-chairman of the DECR: Bishop Alexander was Rector of the Moscow Theological Schools; Bishop Kliment was Administrator of the Patriarchal parishes in Canada and *ad interim* in the USA.)

On 26 December 1984, the following changes in diocesan appointments were made:

Archbishop Kirill of Vyborg, Rector of the Leningrad Theological Schools	to Smolensk
Archbishop Melkhisedek of Berlin and Central Europe (Exarch)	to Sverdlovsk
Archbishop Feodosi of Smolensk	to Berlin
Archbishop Platon of Sverdlovsk	to Yaroslavl ⎱ see
Metropolitan Ioann of Yaroslavl	retired ⎰ above
Archbishop Khrizostom of Kursk	to Irkutsk
Archbishop Yuvenali of Irkutsk	to Kursk

Appendix 2: Assignments of Bishops of the Moscow Patriarchate, Compiled 15 August 1982

As of 15 August 1982 the episcopate of the Russian Orthodox Church is composed of 76 bishops: Patriarch Pimen; 57 diocesan bishops serving in the USSR; 6 suffragan or titular bishops (see footnote on p. 206) serving in the USSR; 2 diocesan bishops temporarily assigned abroad; 2 suffragan or titular bishops temporarily assigned abroad; 8 bishops permanently based abroad.

Patriarch Pimen is also counted as a diocesan bishop. He has the Metropolitan of Krutitsy and Kolomna to assist him in administering Moscow diocese. This means that the Metropolitan is technically a suffragan, but in fact he has the status of a diocesan. In practice, the Patriarch assumes pastoral responsibility for churches in Moscow city, while the Metropolitan pays pastoral visits to churches in the surrounding Moscow region.

The diocesan bishops administer the dioceses listed in the Appendix to Chapter 1 (pp. 34–6). Some of them have additional responsibilities:

Metropolitan Filaret (Denisenko) of Kiev and Galicia, Patriarchal Exarch to Ukraine, permanent member of the Holy Synod, chairman of the Holy Synod's Commission on Questions of Christian Unity.

Metropolitan Antoni (Melnikov) of Leningrad and Novgorod, permanent member of the Holy Synod, chairman of the editorial board of *Bogoslovskye trudy* (*Theological Works*).

Metropolitan Yuvenali (Poyarkov) of Krutitsy and Kolomna, permanent member of the Holy Synod.

Metropolitan Alexi (Ridiger) of Tallinn and Estonia, permanent member of the Holy Synod, Chancellor (*upravlyayuschi delami*) of the Moscow Patriarchate, chairman of the Education Committee.

Metropolitan Filaret (Vakhromeyev) of Minsk and Belorussia, Patriarchal Exarch to Western Europe, permanent member of the Holy Synod, chairman of the Department of External Church Relations.

Archbishop Platon (Udovenko) of Sverdlovsk and Kurgan, a deputy-chairman of the Department of External Church Relations.

The suffragan or titular bishops serving in the USSR are:

Archbishop Pitirim (Nechayev) of Volokolamsk, chairman of the Publishing Department of the Moscow Patriarchate, suffragan of Moscow.

Archbishop Iov (Tyvonyuk) of Zaraisk, a deputy-chairman of the Department of External Church Relations, suffragan of Moscow.

Archbishop Kirill (Gundyayev) of Vyborg, rector of the Leningrad Theological Academy, suffragan of Leningrad.

Bishop Meliton (Solovyov) of Tikhvin, suffragan of Leningrad.

Archbishop Makari (Svistun) of Uman, suffragan of Kiev.

Bishop Afanasi (Kudyuk) of Pinsk, suffragan of Minsk.

The bishops serving temporarily abroad are:

Archbishop Melkhisedek (Lebedev) of Berlin and Central Europe, Patriarchal Exarch to Central Europe.

Bishop Lazar (Shvets) of Argentina and South America, Patriarchal Exarch to Central and South America.

Bishop Valentin (Mishchuk) of Zvenigorod, Patriarchal representative to the Patriarch of Antioch (Damascus), suffragan of Moscow.

Bishop Kliment (Seredny) of Serpukhov, assigned to Patriarchal parishes in Canada and temporarily the USA, suffragan of Moscow.

The bishops based permanently abroad are:

Metropolitan Antoni (Bloom) of Sourozh (London).

Archbishop Yakov (Akkersdijk) of The Hague and The Netherlands.

Archbishop Irinei (Zuzemil) of Vienna and Austria, and temporarily of Baden-Baden and Bavaria.

Bishop Longin (Talypin) of Düsseldorf.

Bishop Mark (Shavykin) of Ladoga, suffragan of Leningrad, resident in San Francisco.

Bishop Nikolai (Sayama) of Mozhaisk, suffragan of Moscow, incumbent of the Patriarchal daughter-church (*podvorye*) in Tokyo. (There are also two bishops of the Autonomous Japanese Orthodox Church whose photographs appear with those of the Russian Orthodox bishops in the Church Calendar.)

Bishop Serafim (Rodionov) of Zürich, suffragan of the Patriarchal Exarchate of Western Europe.

Archbishop Vasili (Krivoshein) of Brussels and Belgium.

For convenience, the *bishops with departmental responsibilities* may be regrouped as follows:

The Department of External Church Relations (DECR)
Chairman: Metropolitan Filaret of Minsk and Belorussia
Deputy-chairman: Archbishop Platon of Sverdlovsk and Kurgan; Archbishop Iov of Zaraisk

Holy Synod Commission on Questions of Christian Unity
Headed by: Metropolitan Filaret of Kiev

The Education Committee
Chairman: Metropolitan Alexi of Tallinn and Estonia
The chairman supervises theological education in: Moscow Theological Seminary and Academy — Rector, Archimandrite Alexander (Timofeyev)

(consecrated Bishop of Dmitrov on 12 October 1982); Leningrad Theological Seminary and Academy — Rector, Archbishop Kirill of Vyborg; Odessa Theological Seminary — Rector, Archpriest Alexander Kravchenko.

The Publishing Department
Chairman: Archbishop Pitirim of Volokolamsk

The Chancellery (administration) of the Moscow Patriarchate
Headed by: Metropolitan Alexi of Tallinn and Estonia

The Economic Management (*khozyaistvennoye upravleniye*)
Headed by: Archpriest Matvei Stadnyuk

The Pensions Committee
Headed by: Archpriest Dimitri Akinfiev

Patriarchal Exarchates
Exarch to Ukraine: Metropolitan Filaret of Kiev and Galicia
Exarch to Western Europe: Metropolitan Filaret of Minsk and Belorussia
Exarch to Central Europe: Archbishop Melkhisedek of Berlin and Central Europe
Exarch to Central and South America: Bishop Lazar of Argentina and South America

Ranks
There are 12 Metropolitans, 32 Archbishops and 22 Bishops based in the USSR. In the church as a whole, including the overseas hierarchs, there are 13 Metropolitans, 35 Archbishops and 26 Bishops.

The information in this appendix is taken from the Calendar of the Russian Orthodox Church, decisions of the Holy Synod recorded in issues of the *Journal of the Moscow Patriarchate*, *The Russian Orthodox Church: Organization, Situation, Activity*, and *The Moscow Patriarchate 1917–1977*, all published by the Moscow Patriarchate.

Postscript to Appendix 2
Since this Appendix was compiled, and up to the end of 1984, the following changes in episcopal appointments have been made.

Archimandrite Sergi (Fomin) (later consecrated Bishop of Solnechogorsk on 30 January 1983) has been a deputy-chairman of the DECR since his appointment on 16 July 1982.

In December 1983, Metropolitan Filaret of Minsk was elected to the new post of chairman of the Public Commission of the Soviet Peace Committee for Relations with Religious Peace Circles.

In June 1984, Metropolitan Vladimir of Rostov replaced Metropolitan Filaret of Minsk as Exarch to Western Europe.

On 26 December 1984, the Holy Synod made several changes in episcopal appointments. They included the following:

Archbishop Kirill of Vyborg was transferred from being Rector of the Leningrad Theological Schools to the Smolensk diocese. No replacement was announced at the time.

Archbishop Melkhisedek, Exarch to Berlin and Central Europe, was transferred to Sverdlovsk diocese. He was replaced by Archbishop Feodosi of Smolensk.

Bishop Sergi of Solnechnogorsk (see above) was appointed as the Church's representative at the World Council of Churches headquarters in Geneva. He replaced Protopresbyter Professor Vitali Borovoi, who was appointed a deputy-chairman of the DECR.

9 CHURCH−STATE RELATIONS

The continued existence of the Russian Orthodox Church and other religious bodies in the Soviet Union is something of an anomaly, given the attitude of the Communist Party to religion. The Communist Party of the Soviet Union (CPSU) makes no secret of its wish to eradicate all religious life. According to Marxism−Leninism, religion is part of the 'superstructure' arising from the economic base of society, and will wither away of its own accord once the economic base of bourgeois, capitalist society is replaced by a socialist, and, at some point yet to be reached in the future, a communist one. While it is generally believed, both inside and outside the Soviet Union, that few if any contemporary Soviet leaders retain the strength of ideological conviction necessary to effect this transformation, members of the CPSU continue to assert that religion will wither away. They further assert that vigorous propagandising of atheism is a necessary adjunct to this process. These assertions are backed up by periodic campaigns to revitalise and expand ideological education, which includes the propagation of what is officially termed 'scientific atheism'. Such calls for increased atheistic propaganda occur quite frequently in the Soviet press. Usually they have a routine air to them, repeat well-worn ideas, and rarely if ever have any fresh ideas or methods to suggest to the propagandists of atheism whom they are urging to increase their efforts. Moreover, the admission in some of these articles that religion continues to influence large numbers of Soviet citizens, and is attracting young people, is in itself an implicit admission that atheist propaganda is not succeeding. However, the fact that such articles continue to appear, in local and republican newspapers as well as in leading Soviet dailies, is clear evidence that the CPSU remains firmly committed to the eradication of religion, whatever the vicissitudes of this policy in the short term.

This was made clear at the Plenum of the Central Committee of the CPSU in June 1983, in a lengthy speech on ideological work by Konstantin Chernenko (then the Party's ideological chief, later that year to become leader of the Soviet Union after the death of President Andropov). He said:

> Work with such a specific group of the population as religious people must not be slackened either. Part of the people — and, frankly, not a very insignificant part — are still under the influence of religion. Numerous ideological centres of imperialism are trying to support and, moreover, foster religious sentiments and to impart to them an anti-Soviet and nationalist bias. A special stake is made on religious extremists.

At the same time allegations about 'violations of the freedom of conscience in the USSR' are spread. What can be said in this context? Everyone knows about our constitutional guarantees of the freedom of conscience. The communists are consistent atheists but they do not impose their world outlook on anyone. Our method is education, conviction and propaganda. But when we come across instances of violations of socialist laws and subversive political activity which is only camouflaged by religion, we act in accordance with the demands of our constitution.[1]

These remarks admittedly took up only two paragraphs in a three-page newspaper report, and they contain nothing new. (Attributing the survival of religion to hostile foreign influence is a routine assertion. Discussion of other points raised by Chernenko — for example, the constitutional guarantees for religious believers — follows.) None the less, we must not underestimate the significance of the fact that the issue was openly aired in this major public forum by the Soviet Union's chief of ideology.

The issue of religion has been raised in *Pravda*, the organ of the Central Committee of the CPSU, with somewhat increased frequency during the 1980s. This indicates continuing, even increased, Party commitment to the goal of eradicating religion (and was also doubtless prompted by the need to justify the increased repression of religious dissenters at this time — see Part 2). For example, a 1981 article, characterising religion as an 'alien ideology' which has no place in Soviet life, stated: 'there can be no thought of lessening ideological opposition to religion, nor of any re-examination of the Marxist view that religion is the "opium of the people" '.[2] A 1984 article by V. Klochov, a legal specialist in crime who often writes on religion in the Soviet press, elaborates the familiar theme that 'reactionary elements of contemporary religion' and 'imperialist forces' are abusing religion in a worldwide conspiracy against the state policies and socialist system of the USSR.[3] A subsequent editorial is devoted to youth, reflecting a growing concern in the Party over the attractiveness of religion to young people: it asserts that 'we should struggle against religion armed by our ideology . . . making use of our press and the power of the written word'.[4]

While the Party's commitment to eradicating religion is unwavering, its methods have changed. The emphasis on ideological work, on persuasion and changing believers' convictions, noted above, is marked. It has been recognised that the large-scale persecution of past decades failed to put an end to religion. After all, the Party unquestionably has the power to close down all religious institutions. Why has it not done so? At this point we need to recognise the distinction, blurred though it is, between the CPSU and the Soviet state. As the only political party in the country, the CPSU enjoys vast power, unquestionably more than the government possesses. This has been even more pronounced since the adoption in 1977 of the new Constitution, Article 6 of which made the leading role of the CPSU quite explicit:

The Communist Party of the Soviet Union (CPSU) is the leading and guiding force of Soviet society and the nucleus of its political system, of all state and public organisations. The CPSU exists for the people and serves the people.

Armed with the Marxist—Leninist teaching, the Communist Party shall determine the general perspective of society's development, and the guideline of the internal and external policy of the USSR, give guidance to the great creative endeavour of the Soviet people and place their struggle for the triumph of communism on a planned, scientific basis.

However, it is the Soviet government which runs the country and passes laws, and it is not always possible for the ideals propounded by the CPSU to be immediately translated into reality by the government. There are several reasons why the government has not taken measures to implement the eradication of religion desired by the Party.

Why Does the Russian Orthodox Church Still Exist?

In the first place, it would be impossible for the Soviet government to rid itself completely of the estimated 50 million members of the Russian Orthodox Church (plus possibly several millions more adherents) — not to mention an estimated 45—50 million Muslims and at least 12 million members of other religions and denominations.[5] Even if the Soviet government were to decide that it was prepared to antagonise such a large proportion of the Soviet population by closing down all institutional religious life, the task of doing so would be a massive one. The anti-religious campaign of 1959—64 took five years to close down more than half of the functioning Orthodox churches (as we saw in Chapter 1) as well as other institutions (see Chapters 4 and 5); presumably, therefore, it would take at least another five years to close down the remaining churches (and other institutions). The Soviet government would need to give the eradication of religion high and sustained priority over other goals. Even this, however, would not necessarily reduce the number of religious believers: the massive propagation of atheism during the anti-religious campaign of 1959—64 produced a number of highly publicised cases of renunciation of religion, including some renunciations by Orthodox priests, but it does not appear to have reduced the overall number of Orthodox believers at all (see Chapter 7). If the Soviet government did decide to close down all religious institutions (and accept the consequent redundancy of the Law on Religious Associations), it seems clear that many believers would carry on extra-legal activities in secret, and that the government would find it very difficult to supervise them. This would, after all be only a repetition of the situation (*mutatis mutandis*) before and during the Second World War (Great Patriotic War).

Now, as then, such lack of control over its citizens would be abhorrent to the Soviet state. It would clearly prefer to have religious activity out in the open, where it can see what is going on, and control and limit it.

Secondly, the Soviet government has already tried to eradicate the Russian Orthodox Church, and failed. Throughout the 1920s and 1930s, many thousands of Orthodox bishops and clergy, as well as lay people, were killed or died in labour camps, the clergy were virtually outlawed, monasteries and theological schools were all closed, few places of worship remained open, and the episcopate was reduced to only four ruling bishops still active on the eve of the Second World War. There seems little doubt that, if the war had not intervened, the church would have been extinguished altogether, or that at most a handful of bishops would have been permitted to survive to maintain a semblance of religious freedom. The concordat reached between church and state consequent upon the church's role in the war and the existence of flourishing religious institutions in the western territories incorporated into the USSR in 1940 and reoccupied at the war's conclusion (see Chapters 1 and 5) showed that there were still many millions of Orthodox believers, who flocked to the churches as soon as they were reopened. The rigours of the previous quarter century had done nothing to undermine their convictions. Their faith, having stood such a test, would certainly survive any less resolute attempts by the Soviet state to extinguish institutional religious life.

The third factor influencing the Soviet state to allow organised religious life to continue in the USSR is that it provides some backing for the state's assertions that it is truly democratic and permits true freedom of conscience, allowing its citizens freedom equally to believe or not to believe. This is important for Soviet policy in the international arena, where the USSR wishes to project itself as a country which allows more real freedom to the individual than do the capitalist countries. (It especially wishes to appear truly democratic in Third World countries which it is urging to adopt a communist system of government.) As we have seen in previous chapters, such freedom of religion as there is in the Soviet Union is very much more severely restricted than it is made out to be, but even this very limited religious activity is necessary to back up Soviet spokesmen's assertions that freedom of religions does exist. The usefulness to Soviet spokesmen of the limited remaining number of religious institutions has been exemplified on numerous occasions — for example, by members of the nationwide 'Knowledge' (*Znaniye*) society, who told a British journalist:

Sometimes, when we have met western atheists and humanists, they ask why we haven't closed all the churches and got rid of religion long ago. Bourgeois anti-clericalism makes the mistake of despising believers and expecting us to use administrative measures against them. We allow everyone freedom of conscience.[6]

As we have seen, the Soviet government does in fact use administrative measures, and very rigorous ones, against believers. Such measures consist of hampering them in the expression of their faith, and do not affect the basic issue of whether a Soviet citizen calls himself a believer or an unbeliever, which is why statements like the above can be made.

The Soviet Constitution and Believers

The basic issue is set forth in the Soviet Constitution, revised in 1977, Article 52 of which states:

> Freedom of conscience, that is, the right to profess any religion or not to profess any religion, to perform religious rites or to conduct atheist propaganda shall be guaranteed for all citizens of the USSR. Incitement of hostility and hatred on religious grounds shall be prohibited. The church in the USSR shall be separated from the state and the school from the church.

Even in this fundamental law of the land, we see an inequality between the believers, allowed only to perform religious rites, and atheists, who are allowed to conduct propaganda. This reflects an amendment made to the Constitution in 1936 under Stalin, at a time when massive persecution of religion was under way. The earlier, Leninist, Constitution of 1918 had stated that 'the right of religious and anti-religious propaganda is recognised for all citizens'. (This applied to the RSFSR only. The first Soviet Constitution was adopted in 1924.) The present situation means that atheists may propagate their beliefs freely by every means, with the extensive centralised resources of the Soviet state to back them up, while the opposing views of the believers may not be aired at all. Not only does this put believers at a disadvantage, but it means that they have to spend their lives in an insistently atheist, and very often openly anti-religious, atmosphere. Their children (as we noted in Chapter 7) are obliged to attend schools and higher educational institutions where, during the whole of their education, atheism is taught to them, and they are not only prevented from hearing the point of view of religious believers, but regularly hear it ridiculed.

The 1977 Constitution of the USSR was strongly criticised in draft form by the unofficial Christian Committee for the Defence of Believers' Rights in the USSR, in a letter to Mr Brezhnev.[7] Although comments and suggested amendments to the draft Constitution were then being published every day in the Soviet press, their letter was not published. The Christian Committee pointed out that, since the Constitution assigned a leading role to the Communist Party, whose rules bound its members to 'lead a resolute struggle against the survival of religion', believers were put in an impossible position. As citizens obliged to uphold the Constitution, they were, in theory, expected to participate in their own self-destruction. Moreover,

> a particular fear is aroused in believers by that clause of the Draft where for the first time in Soviet history 'the building of a communist (i.e. atheist, according to the authors of the Draft) society' is declared, *by legislation*, to be the supreme goal not only of the Party but of the whole State.[8]

By the adoption of the 1977 Constitution, in the Christian Committee's view: 'the borderlines between the Party and the State are obliterated once and for all, and the Soviet citizen's passport becomes a communist's Party card'.[9] Shortly afterwards, the Christian Committee appealed in another document to some of the foreign radio stations broadcasting to the USSR — the Voice of America, the BBC and Deutsche Welle — to broadcast special religious programmes for children, since the Constitution made it impossible for them to receive religious teaching legally within the USSR.[10]

This is the measure of religious freedom granted by the Soviet Constitution. All that is permitted is worship. Even this freedom is severely circumscribed — firstly by the Law on Religious Associations and, secondly, by the CRA, as we have shown in preceding chapters. The constitutional right to worship does not exist in practice for the many believers who do not live near open churches, and is undermined in many ways for those who do.

State Control of the Russian Orthodox Church

The ways in which the Soviet government controls and limits the different aspects of the life of the Russian Orthodox Church, principally through the CRA, have been thoroughly documented in the preceding chapters, and no further examples or illustrations are required here. We may summarise the government's policy towards the Russian Orthodox Church by saying that, while it permits the continuation of institutional church life, and even modest growth in some areas (for the reasons suggested above), the CRA exerts stringent control over every aspect of that life. Church officials are discouraged, and if necessary prevented, from taking any initiative to promote the growth of church life or to extend any Christian influence beyond the walls of the church. Clergy and bishops who none the less take such initiatives may expect sooner or later to be restrained (and perhaps demoted or even imprisoned) as we saw in Chapters 3 and 8. We have also described, in Chapter 7, the limitations suffered by lay people: the ways in which some lay people, notably the urban intelligentsia, have sought to overcome these limitations, are analysed in detail in Part 2. We shall also discuss in Part 2 the growing interest in Orthodoxy over the last two to three decades, and growth in church membership, particularly among young intellectuals, which is continuing in spite of, not because of, the Soviet government's policy towards the church. These factors — modest growth in institutional church life, plus growing interest in Orthodoxy, largely expressed unofficially through *samizdat* — have led some foreign observers to the misleading and fundamentally wrong conclusion that the 'influence' or the 'prestige' of the Russian Orthodox Church in Soviet society is increasing.[11] Such a conclusion may be reached only by ignoring the legal framework within which the church is obliged to operate, and in particular its close surveillance by the CRA. (The question of the church's external relations, and the light in which it is presented to foreigners, is discussed below.)

As far as legal provisions go, we should remind ourselves that only the parishes have any basis in law (see Chapter 2). The church's other institutions — the theological schools, monasteries, the Publishing Department of the Moscow Patriarchate and the Patriarchate itself — are nowhere mentioned in any published legislation, and their existence is entirely *de facto*, with, needless to say, the tacit approval of the Soviet government (see Chapters 1, 4, 5 and 6). At present, there is no sign that the government is thinking of abolishing or reducing any of these institutions; indeed, rather the reverse — its present interests seem to demand their promotion. The opening of the well-equipped new building for the Publishing Department (Chapter 6), the return of the Danilovsky Monastery in Moscow to the church (Chapter 5), and the recent opening of additional administrative premises for the Moscow Patriarchate[12] are all examples of this.

However, we should not forget that an observer in 1958, reviewing the post-war restoration of the Moscow Patriarchate, might well have made a very similar prognosis (allowing, of course, for the different circumstances then obtaining). Such an observer would have been quite wrong, as the virulent anti-religious campaign conducted by Khrushchev from 1959 to 1964 was to show. That campaign was, as we have noted, launched very much on the personal initiative of Khrushchev; there is at present no reason to think that any Soviet leader would wish to take a similar personal initiative against religion. The point is, however, that if a Soviet leader, or leaders, *did* choose to take such an initiative, there would be nothing in Soviet legislation to prevent them. The legal situation is almost exactly as it was in Khrushchev's day (the amendments to the Law on Religious Associations published in 1975 have not changed matters significantly). The power to make decisions in the area of religious policy rests entirely with the Soviet government: the church has no legal safeguards whatever. (The parishes, as noted, do have a legally prescribed existence, but they are registered only with the CRA's approval and may be deregistered at the CRA's discretion.) Church leaders may, indeed do, make representations to the government concerning their needs and wishes and their perceptions of their own situation, and these appear to be attentively listened to by the CRA; but the decision as to whether and how to act upon such representations is entirely in the hands of the CRA and the government. In such circumstances, while we may speak (as we shall do in Part 2) of the growing commitment of large numbers of Soviet citizens to Russian Orthodoxy, it is clearly meaningless to talk of the growing 'power' of the Russian Orthodox Church as an institution within Soviet society.

The duties and rights of the CRA are clearly set out in its Statute, but this is not generally available in the Soviet Union and believers are therefore unaware what legal powers belong to the supervisory government body which plays such a crucial role in their lives. A Statute for the CRA was approved on 10 May 1966 (after the CRA had been created on 8 December 1965 by the merger of the Council for Russian Orthodox Church Affairs and the Council for the Affairs of Religious Cults), but it was not published until 1971, and then only in a restricted-circulation handbook intended for workers professionally dealing 'with questions concerning religious cults'.[13] The Statute shows that one of the CRA's seven departments is involved exclusively with Orthodox Church affairs (this presumably includes the Georgian Orthodox Church as well as the Russian Orthodox). The powers of the CRA as defined in its Statute (which is given in full in the appendix at the end of this chapter, pp. 281–4) may be summarised as supervising legislation on religion, including making recommendations on proposed new legislation to appropriate government bodies, seeing that the existing laws are adhered to by religious associations, and observing and reporting on the lives of the associations. These tasks are carried out by the CRA in Moscow and by its representatives or commissioners (*upolnomochennye*) at republican and regional level throughout the Soviet Union. The references we have made to the activities of the commissioners in the preceding chapters show that many if not all of them keep a very close watch upon the lives of the religious associations, the clergy and the bishops.

We should, however, recognise that there is scope for variation in the way the commissioners carry out their duties. The zeal, or lack of zeal, with which a commissioner carries out his prescribed duties, dependent perhaps upon his age, health and personality, and also upon the relationship he has with local government bodies, doubtless means that believers in different regions of the country experience greater or lesser degrees of government control. (We should note that there are no known women commissioners, though there appears to be no explicit bar to a woman holding this post.) Those commissioners, a comparatively small number, about whom anything is known in the West appear to be those who are most ruthless towards believers, often exceeding their brief and interfering in the life of religious associations: evidently it is precisely this behaviour which has caused believers to send complaints about them abroad. Little or nothing is known of commissioners against whom believers have less obvious cause for complaint. It follows that, for example, the boorish behaviour of the commissioner for Poltava, Nechitailo, which caused Bishop Feodosi of Poltava to complain (unsuccessfully) to Brezhnev (see Chapter 8), cannot be taken to be typical. On the other hand, we should note that the CRA's Statute specifically mandates every commissioner to report to the CRA in Moscow about the situation of the religious associations in the area for which he is responsible, as well as to liaise with the appropriate local authorities, and presumably it would therefore be impossible for any commissioner to adopt an overtly tolerant attitude without both his superiors and his local colleagues being aware of it.

Soviet Spokesmen on Freedom of Religion

Official Soviet spokesmen commenting publicly on religion all consistently maintain that complete freedom of religion exists in the USSR. They do this by ignoring discussion of the legal situation of the churches and the role of the CRA and by emphasising the constitutional equality of believers and unbelievers. The chairman of the CRA, Vladimir Alexeyevich Kuroyedov, has pointed out in an article in the Soviet government newspaper *Izvestiya* that this is not the case elsewhere:

> The constitutions of bourgeois countries contain references to 'freedom of conscience', 'freedom of religion', etc., but not one of them acknowledges the right of the citizen to be an atheist. The interests of many millions of non-believing people are totally ignored and the proclaimed 'freedom of conscience' is reduced to the right to choose a religion.[14]

Kuroyedov fails to note that, while the right to be an atheist may not specifically be proclaimed in 'bourgeois countries', it is none the less enjoyed in practice. This legalistic distinction does nothing to prove that religious freedom is granted in practice in the USSR. The same viewpoint is found in another *Izvestiya* article by Kuroyedov which makes the following exaggerated claim:

> In general, in our country everything is done to guarantee freedom of conscience, and we have every right to affirm that our legislation on religious cults is the most humane and democratic in the world. It guarantees the interests of both believers and unbelievers to an identical degree.[15]

In the same article, however, Kuroyedov writes:

> The most important guarantee is the law on the separation of the Church

from the State. In accordance with this, the State does not interfere in the internal activities of religious associations, and the Church does not interfere in state affairs.[16]

In fact, this is only half true: it is ironic to say that the church 'does not interfere' in state affairs, when it is in fact rigorously excluded from them, but, as we have seen in previous chapters, the state does in fact interfere very considerably in the affairs of religious associations. Kuroyedov's assertions about freedom of conscience notwithstanding, the fact remains that administrative measures to curtail the freedom of the Russian Orthodox Church are widely used.

The issue of atheist education, which we referred to above, was discussed in a *Pravda* article by V. Klochkov, a doctor of juridical science whose commentaries on religion are published from time to time in leading Soviet newspapers. At the end of a fairly lengthy discussion of the Marxist–Leninist concept of law and freedom of conscience, Klochkov wrote:

And, of course, the unhindered conducting of scientific atheist propaganda, the spreading of a materialistic world-view, fully correspond to the democratic principles of the Soviet Constitution and to a scientific understanding of freedom of conscience. We do well to remember this, because there are people abroad who regard the noble work of enlightenment, of educating and bringing up Soviet citizens in the spirit of the humanistic ideals of communism, as allegedly 'spiritual violence' against believers, as 'violation of human rights'. It is difficult to imagine the true state of affairs in a more distorted way. Communists and all advanced Soviet citizens, acting in strict accordance with the democratic norms of socialist law, come forward as active champions of all-round social and cultural progress, as defenders of the most lofty moral ideals founded on scientific knowledge and responding to the deep-rooted interests of the working people, to the demands of the free and all-round development of members of society.[17]

This way of stating the issue would appear to do nothing to calm the anxieties of Soviet believers (it is not only 'people abroad' who raise the objections to which Klochkov refers). Even if the 'most lofty moral ideals really were being propounded by the Soviet education system, as Klochkov suggests, there would still be many who would not wish their children to be educated in a system which fosters 'scientific atheist propaganda', 'a materialistic world-view' and 'the spirit of the humanistic ideals of communism' to the exclusion of any other point of view. Klochkov is here simply asserting the right of the authorities to an ideogically unilateralist education system without considering the claims of other citizens, a stance which religious believers (and probably other groups also) must find very disturbing.

The Subservience of the Moscow Patriarchate

The Russian Orthodox Church has responded to the situation outlined above by adopting an attitude of total subservience to the Soviet state, dating (as we noted in the Introduction) from 1927. After ten years in power, during which time it employed considerable violence and coercion against the Russian Orthodox Church (markedly more than that used against some other religious groups and religions, which did not feel the full force of the government's anti-religious zeal until 1928 and afterwards), the new Bolshevik regime had forced the church into a position acceptable to it. That position has not altered very significantly from 1927 to the present, as far as the church's leadership is concerned. That is one reason why the Soviet government does not at present need to apply to the Orthodox church some of the especially harsh measures which it is using currently against smaller denominations — because it 'tamed' the Moscow Patriarchate long ago.

William Fletcher, in a perceptive article on the Russian Orthodox Church and modernisation,[18] has argued convincingly that the posture of total subservience is the only viable one for the church to assume. Having examined the theoretical alternative forms of church—state relations — theocracy, Caesaro-Papism, the church as the conscience of society, genuine as opposed to apparent separation of church and state — and shown that they are unworkable under present conditions, he concluded: 'Permanent, unrewarded subordination to the State is the Church's only recourse: no other approach is viable as a solution to church—state relations.'[19] This is almost certainly true so far as maintaining a visible institutional church presence in society is concerned. Those who argue against the policy of subordination initiated by Metropolitan Sergi — and they still exist among *samizdat* authors — must visualise some other form in which the church could have survived, an exercise by no means impossible, but so complicated by subsequent historical factors as to be speculative well beyond the limits of the present study.

The subservient position of the church, once adopted, increased as it was excluded from all influence in society. Fletcher has shown how the relations between church and state took on something of the nature of a bargaining relationship after the war: the church (as we have noted above) threw its weight behind the state during the war, and afterwards it assisted in 'the regime's drive for hegemony in Eastern Europe and in the subsequent peace campaigns'.[20] The anti-religious campaign of the early 1960s destroyed the reciprocal nature of the relationship: 'In effect, the State unilaterally withdrew its concessions while insisting on the continued — and in many respects increased — political service of the Church.'[21] The anti-religious campaign had not only reduced the institutions of the church considerably, it had also produced a shift within the framework of relations with the state:

> The Church's approach to its relations with the State remains that of complete subordination; but it receives very little in return. The Church continues to exist as an institution, but it is effectively cut off from any independent participation whatsoever in the corporate life of society.[22]

We have noted this enforced exclusion of the church from society many times in our analysis of its activities. The same impression was summed up succinctly by a journalist visiting the USSR:

> Go into any church in Russia and one will be astonished at the crowds. But come out again in the street, and go round the corner and there will be no resonance, no echo, no vibrations of any kind.[23]

Acceptance of this subservient role has unquestionably posed serious moral problems for the church's leaders. They have been obliged to renounce teaching and propagation of the faith to a considerable extent, and evangelism, charitable and missionary activity totally. It is not merely a question of trimming off peripheral accretions in order to maintain the central part of church life (even though the liturgy unquestionably is central to Orthodoxy, as we noted in Chapter 1); it is a conscious diminishing of the church's traditional activity in the world, based upon clear and unequivocal Gospel precepts. Not only this, but, as we shall see in Part 2, many members of the church continue to have to suffer very great hardship as a consequence of their faith, and the subservient church leadership not only fails to help them but denies publicly and repeatedly that they are suffering for their beliefs. The role adopted by the church unquestionably obliges its leaders to tell, and repeat, falsehoods. This has led to bitter criticism by laymen (such as Yuri Belov's letter to Archbishop Pitirim quoted in Chapter 8), who believe that their spiritual leaders are not only endangering their own souls through perjury, but are also guilty of betraying individual members of their flock whose consciences do not permit them to affirm these falsehoods by their silence. Why, then, do the church's hierarchs persist in silence and falsehoods? Why do they not speak out?

Why Are the Bishops Silent?

What would happen to any bishop who did speak out publicly and state that all was less than well with his church? Today they would certainly not meet such a grim fate as in the past: indeed, for the Soviet government to shoot or imprison a bishop who stepped out of line would be the clearest possible confirmation of all that its critics have been saying about the lack of religious liberty in the USSR. If Patriarch Pimen or a member of the Holy Synod were to deviate publicly from their unswerving loyalty to the state, they would no doubt be quickly retired due to 'ill-health' and then would disappear from public life entirely. (Possibly they might some time later be announced to have died of 'natural causes', as occurred in 1961 with Metropolitan Nikolai, who had displayed opposition to the emergent anti-religious campaign, and who was widely believed to have been murdered. In the present-day climate, however, enforced retirement and seclusion — the fate of Archbishop Yermogen after 1965 — is more likely.) No doubt there would also be a great deal of unpleasantness and victimisation — enough to make an honest man quail, but not to deter him utterly if he believed that the interests of the church would be served by his action.

However, one of the reasons why none of the present hierarchs is likely to take such a step is quite simply because the process of selection carried out by the CRA has been aimed at ensuring that precisely the kind of person who might do so has been excluded from any position of leadership. One example of the steps that have been taken towards this end is referred to in the CRA Report for 1970, which describes how the CRA bent Patriarch Alexi to its will. The report quotes some paragraphs from a stirring speech Alexi made at a Soviet disarmament conference in Moscow in 1960, when the anti-religious campaign was getting under way. It was an impassioned recital of the many services the Russian Orthodox Church had rendered to the nation in its long history, and its failure to mention the Soviet state's role was pointed. It referred to 'attacks and censure' against the church and concluded that Christ Himself had foreseen 'hostile thrusts' against the church and had said that the gates of hell would not prevail against it. Fletcher termed this speech 'an oration the like of which had not been heard in Russia for forty years', and indeed it was a resounding challenge to the state and its anti-religious policy.[24] The CRA Report notes that Patriarch Alexi's words had an effect which it regarded as harmful: 'The Patriarch's militant speech in defence of the Church was used not only by overseas propagandists, but also by the more active section of churchmen, by fanatics within the country.' Clearly the CRA had to take measures to deal with such a challenge, and it did so, apparently with success: 'It took much effort to bring pressure to bear upon the head of the Church, to influence him in the interests of the State. At the present time the relations of the head of the ROC to the State have become different.'[25]

By 1961, as we saw in Chapter 2, Patriarch Alexi was urging the church to adopt the state-inspired reform which subsequently undermined parish life. The price he paid for publicly defending the church in his speech was both increased CRA vigilance which made it impossible for him to do anything of the sort again, and also, almost certainly, great care on the part of the CRA to ensure that his successor would be unlikely to take any such initiative. The advantages and disadvantages here are finely balanced, but it would not be surprising if any leading hierarch tempted to emulate Patriarch Alexi's bold action in 1960 were to conclude that the price would be too high.

What of the less senior bishops — possibly under slightly less intense pressure from the CRA, less caught up in the daily business of running the Moscow Patriarchate, less exercised by the constant need to present a partial or distorted view to foreigners? They would no doubt have in mind the fates of bishops mentioned in Chapter 8: Archbishop Yermogen under a form of house arrest in a monastery far from his native city; Archbishop Pavel of Novosibirsk transferred to a small and insignificant diocese; or Bishop Feodosi of Poltava, transferred in a similar manner. A more recent, though less dramatic example is that of Archbishop Khrizostom of Kursk, whose conversations with the CRA we quoted in Chapter 8. As deputy-chairman of the Department of External Church Relations (DECR), he was known for occasionally unbending slightly and giving a frank personal viewpoint in his conversations with foreigners. The CRA Report for 1974 makes it clear that CRA officials were observing his activities closely, and in 1982 his retirement from the DECR was announced.[26] Though he continues as a diocesan bishop, his influence, and his opportunities for meeting foreigners, were clearly much less than formerly. In December 1984 he was transferred from Kursk to the very distant diocese of Irkutsk. Any bishop contemplating even a measure of independence in running diocesan affairs, not to speak of some public statement of his views on his church's freedom, or lack or it, would have to weigh his options very carefully. Would it be worth a few years of independent action in a diocese, or a few moments of publicly uttering independent personal views about the church, to spend the remainder of one's life ineffectually, moreover making way for some probably more complaisant hierarch to succeed one? In the present circumstances, even a bishop with serious personal misgivings about the line which he is expected to follow might well conclude that speaking out publicly, even while abroad, would not be the best course of action.

In any case, according to the Yakunin Report, the CRA has taken a further step to inhibit any such possible initiative:

> in order to hold the episcopate more firmly in submission, and so that no hierarch could 'mutiny' and repent publicly of having 'informed' . . . it became increasingly desirable for a candidate to possess some kind of moral defect, fixed by the authorities and making it possible to hold the hierarch in a mortal grip.[27]

As the moral defects of hierarchs do not usually become public knowledge, discussion of this assertion is somewhat difficult. However, attentive observation of members of the episcopate over a period of time tends to support this assertion in at least some cases.

Another reason why a bishop at odds with the situation of his church might be deterred from speaking his mind publicly is the likely effect that his initiative could be expected to produce. If he acted while still in the USSR, it might not be reported, or be misreported, or be just a nine days' wonder which would not significantly alter foreigners' perceptions of his church. If he acted while on a visit abroad, and then applied for political asylum, he would be widely assumed to have betrayed his church and his country. Would any hierarch have the courage to make some kind of public statement abroad and then return to the Soviet Union? And would he be admitted if he did?

The crucial issue is whether any such statement by a Soviet bishop — and he could make only one — would have any lasting effect abroad. Would it alter the relationship of Western churchmen to the Moscow Patriarchate and the Soviet government? Would it encourage them to support those working for greater freedom in the Russian Orthodox Church? Would he even be believed? Careful study of the response of Western churchmen to the calls for support from their Russian Orthodox counterparts over nearly two decades (about which we shall have more to say in Part 2) seem likely to lead any Russian hierarch to conclude that he would not find support sufficient to justify the likely consequences of any action he might take. Private conversations between Russian Orthodox hierarchs and a few trusted Western confidants over the years tend to reinforce this view. On occasion, Russian bishops have privately expressed amazement that their 'passport speeches' were received with credulity by Western listeners. Even though experienced Western churchmen have now become inured to such 'passport speeches' it still seems that the statements of Soviet (and other East European) church leaders are too often taken at face value by those who do not know enough about the context within which they should be interpreted. Recently a Russian Orthodox bishop told a Western confidant that he and his colleagues had tried to leave openings at international church assemblies such as the World Council of Churches for Western churchmen to press issues such as religious freedom in the USSR further, but had been disappointed by the lack of response. If this is their perception of the situation, then it is not surprising that the Russian Orthodox bishops remain silent as far as their personal opinions are concerned and publicly toe the Soviet line.

The importance of statements made in an international context should not be underestimated. The Russian Orthodox Church leadership, isolated from Soviet society, subservient to the regime, and having its major contacts with the Soviet authorities channelled through the vigilant and bureaucratic CRA, must perforce look to its foreign contacts to see what response might be expected of them. Its external relations are therefore of great significance.

External Relations

Since the end of the Second World War, the Russian Orthodox Church has, evidently at the behest of the Soviet government, been developing what is now a very sensitive web of relations with other Orthodox Churches, with other denominations in the Soviet Union and abroad, and with international Christian organisations. It would require a separate book to treat these fully, and we shall be able here only to refer briefly to some of the most significant of these relations. Our intention is to describe only how the Moscow Patriarchate organises its external relations, rather than to describe what those relations are.

This field is the responsibility of the Department of External Church Relations (DECR). Since it was founded in 1946, it has been identified in the minds of churchmen throughout the world with two successive chairmen, Metropolitan Nikolai of Krutitsy and Kolomna (1946–61) and Metropolitan Nikodim of Leningrad (1961–72), both of whom are tireless in travelling the world and in meeting seemingly endless delegations of foreign churchmen to Moscow. Metropolitan Nikodim was succeeded by his protégé and cousin, Metropolitan Yuvenali, but he retired in 1981 (because of ill-health). The present chairman is Metropolitan Filaret of Minsk (born 1935), who was created bishop at 30 and metropolitan at 40. He spent seven years as rector of the Moscow Theological Academy and five years in Berlin before being appointed to Minsk, and also to the Exarchate of Western Europe, a post which he held from 1978 to 1984.[28] He has been active in foreign relations for some years and has travelled extensively.

The two deputy-chairmen of the DECR are Archbishop Platon of Sverdlovsk and Kurgan (who previously spent some years representing his church in South America, and who replaced Archbishop Khrizostom in 1982), and Archbishop Iov of Zaraisk (who has served in the DECR since 1971 after graduating from the Moscow Theological Academy). The lay secretary of the DECR, Alexi Sergeyevich Buyevsky, has been at his post since 1946, a long time in one position even by Soviet standards. He meets all the most important delegations to Moscow and accompanies all the major church delegations abroad.

The DECR is situated in Chisty pereulok in central Moscow. In 1979 a branch was established in Leningrad under the chairmanship of Metropolitan Antoni. Its main responsibility appears to be looking after foreign church delegations to Leningrad.

The CRA Report for 1974 noted:

In connection with the growth of foreign tourism and of a certain interest among foreign citizens in the situation of religion and the church in the USSR, our demands on servants of the cult who are entrusted with contacts with foreigners are increasing.[29]

This comment suggests two things: first, that only priests considered reliable from the point of view of the CRA are permitted to meet foreigners, and, second, that they have 'demands' made upon them which presumably include some kind of preparatory briefing or training. The CRA Report continues: 'We should say that in the majority they justify this trust in them.' The CRA Report then gives what it regards as a satisfactory example of contact between foreigners and Russian Orthodox clergy:

In conversations with the clergy of foreign countries, Bishop Gedeon, the priests Kolodi, Burdin and others took up a patriotic position, revealed the libellous character of questions put by members of the American Council of Churches, especially Professors Price and Redigon . . . Taking as examples the activity of the churches in Novosibirsk region, Gedeon demonstrated that the constitutional position on freedom of conscience is strictly observed in the USSR. A member of the American delegation, the priest Berzensky, tried to give the priest Burdin a fur coat as a 'gift'. However, Burdin refused the gift, saying that 'he had a perfectly good Soviet fur coat'.[30]

It is not clear why the CRA should put the word 'gift' in inverted commas: the implication is that it regarded the fur coat as a bribe or inducement, but to what? This is not indicated in the report. The CRA clearly regards it as important that the Soviet clerics maintained a 'patriotic' position: this is a word which crops up again and again to describe a view which has less to do with love of country than with complete conformity to Soviet foreign policy. We could characterise this 'patriotism' as adhering to the line of 'my country right or wrong', were it not that the CRA's guidelines to clerics clearly preclude the possibility of their ever admitting to foreigners that their country *could* be wrong.

The CRA's demands upon 'servants of the cult' who meet foreigners also apply to those who travel abroad to represent their church. The KGB is also involved in vetting those who travel abroad, since, as the agency responsible for border controls in the USSR, it oversees applications for exit (and entry) visas. Moreover, it is generally recognised that in any group of Soviet citizens which travels abroad, one (at least) of them is detailed by the KGB to report on the activities of members of the group on their return. For example, the writer Anatoli Kuznetsov, who eventually managed to emigrate to the West, has recounted how two KGB officers made such a request to him before a trip abroad.[31] This has led to some rather loose accusations in religious circles in the West to the effect that most if not all churchmen from the USSR allowed to travel abroad are 'KGB agents'. The implication of this is that they are full-time employees of the KGB infiltrated into the churches. We cannot entirely rule out the possibility that there may be KGB professionals among the clergy and even the hierarchy of the Russian Orthodox Church, but generally speaking it is more probable that the KGB demands some control over the selection of the church's overseas delegations and requires that churchmen with whom the KGB has some influence, or over whom it has some control, accompany overseas delegations on important trips. Such 'agents' have a dual function. They both contribute to the KGB's intelligence files on foreign religious groups (and the KGB's propensity for collecting data from legitimate and open sources should not be underestimated) and also may inhibit unauthorised contacts or behaviour by other members of their delegation. (To our knowledge, no member of a Russian Orthodox delegation has ever defected while abroad.)

Sometimes, however, the activities of KGB recruits within the DECR, as in other parts of the church, do come to light. One such was Alexander Shushpanov, a translator for the DECR, who was revealed as a KGB agent by independent elements within the church in a letter sent to the West.[32] In a further letter to a priest in America, the Christian Committee for the Defence of Believers' Rights in the USSR disclosed that Shushpanov had contacted various independent or dissenting religious groups in the guise of a friend and helper from abroad: he told Catholics that he was Orthodox and Orthodox groups that he was a Catholic, even a Jesuit, and a 'specially trusted person of the Roman Curia'. He initiated an acquaintance between the Christian Committee and the then chaplain at the American Embassy, with the aim, as they discovered just in time, of concocting a case against them alleging contacts with the CIA. Shushpanov inveigled himself into a friendship with members of the Christian Seminar led by Alexander Ogorodnikov (see Chapter 12); he located copies of their *samizdat* journal and revealed them to the KGB, and he insistently offered to supply them with explosives and firearms, which they refused to accept.[33]

Once exposed as a KGB agent, Shushpanov could no longer continue working for the DECR. He was made churchwarden of the Church of St Nicholas in Kuznetsky, one of the best known in Moscow, whose priest (until his death in 1984) was the widely respected Father Vsevolod Shpiller (about whom more will be said in Part 2). In his role as churchwarden, Shushpanov meets many foreign visitors to the church, and plays the part of someone who has the interests of the Russian Orthodox Church at heart. He accepts printed materials from the West offered by foreigners, but in all probability he passes them on to the KGB, not to believers. Shushpanov's appointment is one more illustration of the ease with which non-believers can be infiltrated into parish executive committees (as we noted in Chapter 2). (A previous attempt to foist an unbelieving churchman on to Father

Vsevolod's church in 1966 has been described by Anatoli Levitin.)[34]

The Moscow Theological Academy's graduate course (*aspirantura*), which began in 1962, provides recruits for the DECR's work with foreigners. According to the CRA Report, the graduate course 'was created for preparing people for overseas work'.[35] The need for a special course was understandable in view of the church's isolation from foreign contacts before the war. There was no reservoir of people with overseas experience to support and gradually replace the leading figures in this field. Moreover, young men joining the church would almost certainly have no experience of foreign travel beforehand — a marked difference from the Western countries with which the church has ecclesiastical contacts. There was therefore a clear need for training the most capable young men quickly for the rapidly growing overseas work. However, this method does have the disadvantage that most if not all of the people responsible for the church's relations with foreigners are formed in the same mould and have little diversity of knowledge or experience to bring to their important task. (The contrast with their counterparts in Western churches is very marked indeed in this respect.) We should not overlook the fact that special training for expanding foreign relations commenced in 1962 (the year after the church's accession to the World Council of Churches) — a time which, as we have seen, was one of severe repression for the churches in the Soviet Union.

The CRA notes that in the 1973–4 academic year there were 13 students in the three-year graduate course; four graduated that year but four were expelled from the course 'for various reasons'. More up-to-date figures have not become available. The subjects the students studied were: Orthodox Local Churches and the overseas institutions of the Russian Orthodox Church; the Roman Catholic Church, Protestantism; the ecumenical movement; and either English or German language according to choice. There were also courses of lectures in philosophy, the history of philosophy, new philosophy, foreign literature, international organisations and diplomatic protocol.[36] This syllabus marks quite a departure from that of the seminaries and academies (described in Chapter 4), and is evidently intended to give students some idea of the thought-processes which have shaped the views of their foreign visitors.

As well as its full-time employees, who act as translators and guides for foreigners (*sotrudniki*), the DECR has young priests and monks attached to it in the capacity of 'assessor' (*referent*). They are not solely responsible to the DECR, but also work in parishes or study at the theological academy. According to the Yakunin Report the total number of DECR employees is more than all the other departments of the administration of the Moscow Patriarchate put together.[37] A more recent commentator has suggested that the DECR has a staff of about 100.[38] DECR employees are privileged in that they pay a much lower rate of tax than other members of the clergy: they are taxed under Article 5, along with the majority of members of the Soviet population, which means that they pay a maximum of 13 per cent income tax. The rationale behind this is evidently that their work, unlike that of a parish priest, is considered to be useful to the state; this is the principle upon which Soviet tax law is based (as we noted in our discussion of the taxation of clergy in Chapter 3). Some other members of the church also fall into the lower tax bracket: the Patriarch, the permanent members of the Holy Synod, executives in the Patriarchate, and some lecturers in the seminaries and academies.[39] Clearly, therefore, the state considers the work of the DECR, and of other sectors of the church leadership, to be of value to it, on a par with that of any Soviet worker. Indeed, this fact, taken in conjunction with the CRA's remarks quoted above, indicates that, from the state's point of view, the overseas relations of the Russian Orthodox Church are part and parcel of the state's foreign policy.

What have been the advantages to the Russian Orthodox Church of the work in which the DECR has been engaged since 1946? The most obvious is that a church which had been cut off from all contact with other churches for over 20 years,[40] and which was widely thought to have been virtually extinct, suddenly emerged on to the world scene and began to play a significant role in international ecumenical relations. The energetic work of the DECR, especially that of Metropolitans Nikolai and Nikodim, has put the Russian Orthodox Church firmly back on the map. This has been done in two ways: first, by participating in international organisations, and, second, by developing relations with individual churches around the world through talks and visits. By the 1980s, these relations have become very extensive and involve all major countries of the world.

This expansion of international contacts could have taken place only with the approval of the Soviet government, and has been achieved only by constant and total loyalty to the government and its foreign policy aims. The Russian Orthodox Church (like all other religious bodies in the Soviet Union which have foreign contacts) is in effect an extension of the state's foreign affairs apparatus. In its involvement in international Christian organisations, the chief of which are the World Council of Churches (WCC), the Prague-based Christian Peace Conference (CPC) and the Council of European Churches (CEC), the Russian Orthodox Church has at all times followed a line in total conformity with Soviet foreign policy. There is not space here to demonstrate the point in detail, but this has been done elsewhere by an acknowledged expert on the subject, William Fletcher.[41] Fletcher also shows how the Russian Orthodox Church, as the largest single member church of the WCC, has influenced that body to issue a number of statements on international affairs which, intentionally or not, support Soviet foreign policy objectives in the areas mentioned. The WCC did also condemn the Warsaw Pact invasion of Czechoslovakia in 1968, although Fletcher notes that it delayed for a week before doing so, in marked contrast to other Christian organisations which spoke out much more quickly.[42] We have already noted in Chapter 8 the single occasion when a Russian Orthodox delegate did express criticism of his government by supporting a motion which, *inter alia*, condemned the Soviet invasion of Afghanistan. These instances, however, are very much the exception rather than the rule. In external affairs, just as in domestic ones, its subservience deprives the church of any chance to think independently and creatively about the problems of the world and the possibility of a Christian solution to them.

This is not to say that the Russian Orthodox Church's foreign relations are not worth the candle. There is always some value in personal contacts, on both sides: some good personal relationships have been built up, many prejudices corrected, and many foreign churchmen have been amazed and moved by the splendour of Russian spiritual life and the deep fervour of the Russian Orthodox people. Some Russian churchmen have also been able to convey privately to the more perceptive and trustworthy of their contacts that their public statements are not always to be taken at face value. No doubt it is instructive for members of the Russian Orthodox Church to observe overseas churches which are able to engage freely in missionary work, evangelism and social action, and to make independent pronouncements on social and political issues (and even to criticise their own governments publicly), even though they cannot transplant any insights they may gain into their own church life.

On balance, it would seem that it can be in the Russian Orthodox Church's best interests for the stream of foreign visits to continue only if foreign church delegations are better informed as to the situation of the church with which they are dealing. Many churchmen faced with the multifarious and sometimes apparently insoluble problems of pluralistic societies are often first surprised and then refreshed to encounter the seemingly rock-like certainty about their church's role which Russian Orthodox representatives customarily display. Were they to realise that they are unable to choose any other role, and that, despite their millions of adherents, their role in society is remarkably circumscribed, it might be possible to proceed to a more mutually enriching dialogue.

The Peace Movement

The Russian Orthodox Church identifies itself wholeheartedly with the Soviet peace movement, and has done so ever since the movement got under way in the late 1940s. Indeed, the church predated the official peace movement by issuing a call for world peace at its Local Council in 1945, while the Second War was still in progress.[43] It was entirely natural for the church to identify itself with the wish for peace felt by the Soviet people as a whole.

Westerners who have not visited the USSR often fail to comprehend the enormity of the losses which the USSR sustained during the war and the lasting effect which they have had. The loss of more than 20 million lives cannot be soon forgotten and their memory is kept alive by the war memorials in every city, guarded by goose-stepping children in Pioneer uniforms, and by special lessons and clubs in schools where children are taught to revere the memory of the fallen. This loss is felt by the nation as a whole, and the church, identifying itself with the nation, shares in the sense of loss and joins with all the people in believing that nothing like it must be allowed to happen ever again.

The church was fully identified with the Soviet war effort from the very beginning of the war, from the moment of the news of the German invasion on 21 June 1941. As Struve has pointed out, the then head of the church, Metropolitan Sergi, as soon as he heard of the invasion, issued a pastoral letter condemning the aggressor, identifying the church with the destiny of the people, and giving its blessing to the struggle for victory; he did this without consulting the government, and ten days before Stalin issued his own appeal to the nation.[44] The future Patriarch, then Metropolitan Alexi, remained in Leningrad for the whole of the two-year blockade, sharing the privations of the people, and winning lasting respect and affection by his selfless concern for others. The Orthodox faithful raised many millions of roubles for the war effort: in the first year alone, the Moscow churches collected 3 million roubles, besides gifts of warm clothing for the armed forces. The church financed the building of a tank column named after Dimitri Donskoi, one of the greatest military leaders in Russian history.[45] It is largely due to this complete identification with the war effort that the church owes the post-war relaxation in church–state relations, and it was therefore quite natural for it to continue to identify with the nation in the heartfelt quest for peace.

We have already seen that the church contributes large amounts of money to the Soviet Peace Fund, from the income of its parishes (Chapter 2) and its clergy (Chapter 3). The remainder of its work for peace consists of numerous talks, meetings and conferences, both within the USSR and abroad. These activities are summarised in a 1978 publication of the church.[46] They consist of peacemaking activities in concert with other Orthodox Churches, with other denominations and religions, and in international secular organisations such as the World Peace Council, the Conference on Security and Cooperation in Europe, and various international movements for disarmament. In fact they closely parallel the ecumenical and foreign relations of the church as a whole. Within the USSR, the church is represented on various Soviet bodies working for peace: it has been represented on the Soviet Peace Committee since its formation in 1949; its representatives take part in the work of the Soviet Committee for Security and Cooperation in Europe; and Metropolitan

Alexi of Tallinn is a member of the board of the Soviet Peace Fund.

The activities of these bodies, and the church's peacemaking activity within international bodies, conform so entirely to Soviet foreign policy as to be little more than an extension of it. There is no point in making a virtue out of a church's opposition to its government, and it would certainly be a fortunate church that could freely agree with its government on every issue. However, there can be no doubt that in the case of the Russian Orthodox Church it is not a question of free agreement, but of state pressure. The reference in the CRA Reports to the church's foreign relations make that clear. Even without the evidence of the CRA Reports, a study of the church's public statements reveals that it has often supported its own government at the price of disagreement with other Christian bodies around the world. In the name of peace, the church has condemned the Hungarian uprising of 1956,[47] approved the Warsaw Pact invasion of Czechoslovakia in 1968,[48] and approved the Soviet invasion of Afghanistan in 1979,[49] thus taking a view diametrically opposed to that of the Christian world at large, particularly on Afghanistan. In the name of peace, the church's substantial contributions to the Soviet Peace Fund have been sent to, among others, 'fighting Vietnam' in the North and 'liberation movements' in Africa and Asia, but not to the casualties in any conflicts where the USSR does not have a political interest.[50] The church is involved, not in an even-handed effort to promote peace and help the victims of war, but in the furtherance of Soviet foreign policy objectives.

This means that the church's role is very far from that of attempting to forge and shape a programme for attaining objectives in which it believes and which are based upon Christian principles; it may only offer tacit support for policies already formulated, which take no account of any Christian worldview. The church is encouraged to supply Christian motivation for actions already decided upon, and to append biblical texts to its statements in support of peace, but this is a very far cry from being able to evolve a Christian response to the problems of the world. Moreover, the church is obliged to lend its support to actions, such as the invasion of Afghanistan, whose peacemaking nature is, to say the least, highly questionable. The natural yearning for peace, of the Soviet people at large as well as of the church, has been exploited and perverted into something which is very far from what it appears to be.

This is doubly unfortunate for the church because it affects the view of the church held by Soviet citizens. Its activity within the peace movement is the only area in which the Moscow Patriarchate is permitted to play any public part in the life of Soviet society as a whole. As previous chapters have shown, the church is rigorously excluded from the possibility of influencing society in any way, and unless a Soviet citizen who is not a believer happens to live near an open church, he would be unlikely to encounter any evidence of church activities in his normal daily life. However, church leaders sit alongside civilians from all walks of life at all manner of highly publicised gatherings in defence of peace. Functionaries of the Peace Fund attend diocesan and deanary meetings to congratulate the clergy on their work for peace and present them with diplomas and decorations. Church leaders are decorated for their services to peace: in July 1977 Patriarch Pimen was awarded the Order of the Red Banner of Labour by the Presidium of the Supreme Soviet of the USSR for his patriotic activity in the defence of peace,[51] a highly public act which was widely reported in the Soviet press. All this means that, when the Soviet populace sees any sign at all of public church life, they see it as passively echoing government sentiments, totally conformist to Soviet official policy, without, apparently, having any original or creative contributions of its own to make to the life of society.

The church's peacemaking activities show no sign of diminishing; if anything, they are increasing in scope. In 1977, on the initiative of Patriarch Pimen, a world conference entitled 'Religious Workers for Lasting Peace, Disarmament and Just Relations among Nations' took place at Zagorsk, attended by 633 delegates from 107 countries and including Buddhists, Hindus, Jews, Sikhs, Shintoists and Christians.[52] The effect of this has been to create an international forum which, in contrast to other bodies with which the Russian Orthodox Church is involved, is centred on Moscow and gives the Moscow Patriarchate a leading role in its activities. This was followed by a further conference in May 1982 entitled 'A World Conference of Religious Workers for Saving the Sacred Gift of Life from Nuclear Catastrophe', attended by nearly 600 participants — 401 Christians, 106 Muslims, 57 Buddhists, and also Jews, Hindus, Sikhs, a Shintoist and a Zoroastrian.[53] The *Journal of the Moscow Patriarchate* and other church publications continue to devote a substantial proportion of their space to the peacemaking and foreign relations activity of the church. In contrast to the shortage of information on some aspects of the church's internal life, the reader is overwhelmed by information on all aspects of its external life.

The casual observer, faced with such a wealth of information about the church's multifarious activities abroad, is likely to be so dazzled that he is blinded to the narrowness of the church's base in society at home.

Institutional Survival

The leaders of the Russian Orthodox Church evidently believe that, rather than making futile appeals for greater freedom, it is their duty to do all they can to keep the church alive as an institution, a visible presence, however limited, in Soviet society. They feel that they have a duty to minister to the people, who would have nowhere else to go if even the limited number of presently functioning churches were closed. This is the line the Moscow Patriarchate has taken since Metropolitan Sergi's Declaration of 1927, which immediately provoked a deep and bitter schism within the church which persists to this day.[54] In recent times the late Metropolitan Nikodim, an avowed supporter of Sergi's line, has been the most vigorous proponent of this view. As noted already, this policy necessarily involves repeated falsehood. Dimitri Pospielovsky, a Russian Orthodox historian living in Canada, has recounted a conversation with Nikodim on this question:

> To my remark that it is a bad temptation for a Christian to witness a bishop not telling the truth, he retorted: 'It is you people in the West that react this way. We're used to this sort of thing in the Soviet Union, and we don't react.'
> 'But it is terrible,' I said, 'that lies are accepted in such a way.'
> 'I didn't say this was good or bad. I'm just stating a fact,' said the Metropolitan with a sad smile. And then he went on to describe his own strategy as that of a man who in dense traffic prefers to select small side roads, and thus a longer distance, while still going towards his aim, rather than get stuck in a traffic jam or end up in an accident on the main road. He hoped that in this way he would achieve more for the Church in the long run.[55]

One can very readily sympathise with such an approach by a vigorous man with a mind of his own. In the situation within which the Russian Orthodox Church has to operate, it is refreshing to find such a realistic approach. (Just as it is revealing to learn that in the Soviet Union people are 'used to this sort of thing' when it comes to telling lies.) However, many people inside — and outside — the church would question the value of what is achieved by such methods. Can the end justify the means as easily as Metropolitan Nikodim supposed in the rather glib argument reported above? This is certainly true if one views the church as an institution and little else; if one believes that the church as a visible presence in society is its most valid expression. This is a tenable view, but, though it is the one adopted by the church's leadership, it is not the only possible view. The traditional Orthodox view of a true Christian is that, far from having a mind of his own, he strives to have a mind surrendered to God, which God can use as he chooses for purposes which he, not man, has ordained. Such a 'servant of God' (*rab Bozhi*), as pious Orthodox customarily refer to themselves, most certainly does not believe that the end justifies the means.

Hard times, however, breed hard decisions. Millions of Russian Orthodox held to the truth and went underground; the leadership compromised and remained in the open, able to take advantage of a change in government policy when it came. The fact that today the institutional church does exist, that churches, albeit few, are open, and that the faithful may receive the sacraments there, would seem to vindicate the church leadership's subservient approach to the state. However, Sergi's compromise with the state at first met with pronounced failure rather than success. Within two years of signing the Declaration of 1927, the Stalinist persecution of the church was under way, resulting, as we have noted in preceding chapters, in the almost total extinction of institutional church life by the end of the 1930s. Almost certainly the church would have been totally extinguished before very long, had it not been for the Second World War, and the survival of the faith revealed by it. Metropolitan Sergi's course was vindicated by an historical accident. It was the mass of the faithful, rather than the leadership, which kept the church alive.

The policy of Nikodim (and his fellow-bishops) may be too soon in time to be evaluated conclusively, but it seems that his known purpose that 'the State must never again feel that it can do without the Church, as it did during the anti-religious campaign' has not been fully realised. There has been a measure of success in that the state has been able to find a number of uses for a church which has proved difficult to get rid of, but this is not necessarily the same as feeling that it could not do without the church altogether — which would presumably be signalled by an end to anti-religious propaganda. In the present political situation, and given the present state of the Soviet people, the government appears to feel no pressing need to alter the status quo as regards the church, but if the political situation were to change (as it easily and suddenly might — for example, in the direction of a Russian nationalist-oriented regime), the regime's perceived need of the church might alter very rapidly. It could well be that the regime would feel that it needed the church more, not less, than at present; the point is that the initiative lies entirely with the state, and outside certain rather narrow limits there is very little the church can do about it.

This view is confirmed, as noted above, by the most recent historical precedent, the anti-religious campaign of 1959–64 waged under Khrushchev. Nothing has changed in the legislation on religion or in the church's position in Soviet society that would prevent a recurrence of persecution just as massive, if not more so, than that which closed over half the church's institutions 20 years ago. The policy advocated by Metropolitan Nikodim depends entirely upon the pragmatic instincts of the men in the Politburo. Similarly, any hopes which the church leadership may cherish of the future burgeoning of the regime under a government of Russian nationalist orientation[56] depend upon the power struggle within the higher echelons of the Soviet leadership. Metropolitan Nikodim's policy — the preservation of the institutional life of the church — contains no guarantee against the church's clock being set back 20 years, or more. The initiative, as we have said before, does not lie with the church, but with the state.

Traditionalism and Modernism

Metropolitan Nikodim's reformist efforts notwithstanding, the Russian Orthodox Church remains deeply conservative and almost totally unchanged in every aspect of its life — liturgy, festivals, vestments, customs, iconography, music. In this it does not differ greatly, on the surface, from any other Orthodox Local Church, since faithfulness to Tradition is an essential element of Orthodox belief. As Timothy Ware has pointed out, changelessness and a sense of living continuity with the church of the past are the Orthodox Church's distinctive characteristics.[57] 'The Orthodox Christian of today sees himself as heir and guardian to a great inheritance received from the past, and he believes that it is his duty to transmit this inheritance unimpaired to the future.'[58] Pre-eminent among the elements of Tradition are the Bible, the Creed and the doctrinal definitions of the Ecumenical Councils, but the writings of the Church Fathers, the examples of the saints and holy men, and the decrees and decisions of the church throughout the ages, are treated with great, if not equal, reverence. However, Ware adds the cautionary note that 'Tradition' is not the same as 'traditions', and that the result of uncritical acceptance of everything that comes from the past 'has frequently been stagnation'.[59]

The traditionalism of the Russian Orthodox Church has undoubtedly been one of the factors contributing to its survival. During the hardest years of persecution, the faithful were encouraged to persevere in their beliefs above all by a sense of continuity with the past, of being rooted in a great tradition, and by the timeless splendour and beauty of church services (when accessible) and of Orthodox customs. Tradition in the form of following daily and weekly routines — prayers, customs and rituals — can reinforce existing beliefs in circumstances so grim as to threaten to destroy faith completely. This has been one of the most obvious strengths of Russian Orthodoxy. By the same token, however, such circumstances make it virtually impossible for believers to engage in a constant creative re-examination and reaffirmation of the tenets of their faith. Persecution is not conducive to reform. Beliefs which are uncritically accepted and never thought through afresh certainly carry one through difficult periods in life, but over time they do tend to stagnate (as suggested by Timothy Ware). Things of greater and lesser significance come to be regarded as equally sacrosanct, equally unsusceptible to change. The important question today as far as the Russian Orthodox Church is concerned is whether, with all due allowances made for its characteristic traditionalism, it would be able to modernise in any way should it choose to do so.

There are several factors which encourage the present-day Russian Orthodox Church in its traditional attitudes. The Russian Church was cut off from Europe for many centuries and its people (as opposed, to some extent, to its intelligentsia) were untouched by the Renaissance, the Reformation and the Enlightenment. The church was the bulwark of the nation during the three centuries of the Mongol occupation of Russia, binding the people together by its rocklike refusal to budge or alter; its attempts to introduce reforms to the liturgy in the seventeenth century resulted in the bitter and painful Old Believer schism; and its ancient doctrine that 'Moscow is the Third Rome, and a fourth there will not be' (after the fall of Rome and Constaninople) makes it, in its own eyes at least, the last bastion of faithfulness to the Early Church. In the Soviet period, the experience of the government-backed Living Church in the 1920s, which quickly introduced many innovations, and initially looked as though it might supplant the Patriarchal Church, has left the church with an ingrained suspicion of reform.

However, there are those who, as in any church, believe that the church should adapt to modern conditions and make itself more relevant to modern life, with the aim of showing outsiders that the church, and Christianity, can fulfil their personal needs today as in the past. They include Metropolitan Nikodim and his supporters,[60] and also some of the independent thinkers within the church, as we shall see in Part 2. Such proponents of modernisation (it must be said, a very limited concept in comparison with some Western churches) are by no means oblivious to the riches of their church heritage and do not want to abandon them. On the contrary: it is their appreciation of the value of their tradition that makes them fear that they will stagnate, and become arid and immutable traditions, rather than living Tradition. One area of controversy is liturgical reform, advocated by some members of the church, but viewed with great suspicion by the majority. However, even such modest modernising ideas as are entertained by some members of the church are resolutely thwarted by the Soviet authorities.

It has been observed that the only areas in which the Russian Orthodox Church has modernised are political areas where the state forces it to modernise. These are all concerned with the church's external relations. It has swiftly adopted a most liberal and progressive position on such issues as pro-communist guerilla movements in the Third World, disarmament, and pro-Arab (and therefore to some extent pro-Muslim) policies; but has remained immovable on social issues such as abortion and family life in general, and implacable in its opposition to the ordination of women. It is liberal abroad and conservative at home, a dichotomy which has been brought about by the need to support Soviet foreign policy, and for no other reason. There is one exception to this rule, as Fletcher has pointed out: because of their involvement in international Christian bodies, especially the World Council of Churches, Russian Orthodox delegates have found themselves involved in discussion of a whole range of social problems — racism, capitalism, poverty, injustice and many more. But however progressive the positions they may express on such issues, they cannot put them into practice:

because the Church in Russia is rigidly excluded from the social dimension, the result has been the development of a small corps of internationalists whose concerns have no bearing whatsoever on the Church in Russia. Positions taken by Russian clergymen in international gatherings do not represent the domestic Church at all, and any new insights regarding the social role of Christianity which these internationalists may acquire are totally inapplicable at home.[61]

Innately conservative though the Russian Orthodox Church is, one reason why it is unable to make any moves at all towards modernisation is because the Soviet authorities seem to fear that a more up-to-date, more relevant church might have an increased influence in society.[62] It may seem contradictory to say that a conservative church is prevented from modernising, but it is important here not to confuse two distinct things. The church's conservatism is not in question: the point is that even if it were not conservative, the government's policy would probably remain the same — to consign the church to the past and prevent it updating its approach to a modern society. The state does not wish the church to appear more relevant to the daily life of Soviet citizens because it fears that the church, which it recognises can meet emotional and spiritual needs that the state cannot meet, would claim the primary allegiance of many more citizens, thus diluting their loyalty and commitment to the Soviet state. Whether or not the state is correct in this assumption is another matter. Modernisation is, in any event, an issue over which conservatives and liberals in almost any church would argue fiercely. The former point out that the church is already growing and attracting many new members; the latter argue that it could well attract a great many more.

Fletcher's conclusion seems sound: he believes that the Russian Orthodox Church has modernised by refusing to modernise. It has adapted to the society in which it finds itself in the only possible way — by withdrawing from it totally. It has been obliged to concentrate exclusively on the otherwordly and the transcendent, and (as we saw in Chapter 7), has suffered no diminution of commitment by the believing people. Indeed, this may well be a strength: as the church (along with other churches and religions) is the only place in Soviet society where the transcendent is publicly admitted to exist, it is likely to attract any enquiring individual who believes that there is more to life than the here and now. Fletcher states that the church has in fact selected the posture most likely to ensure its survival as a part, albeit an underprivileged part, of society. This is no doubt true, but it does not alter the essential falsity of the church's position. The Russian Orthodox Church has been obliged to abandon at least half its ministry — caring for the needy in the society around it — which the state has (theoretically) taken on. While there is nothing intrinsically wrong with its spiritual focus, one must conclude that it is fulfilling only a part of the role which a church is normally expected to perform.

The general thesis of the Yakunin Report is closely allied to this conclusion. Yakunin maintains that the Moscow Patriarchate, having abandoned all missionary, evangelistic and social activity, and having refused to protest when the few remaining institutions of the church are undermined and abused (in the ways we have described), is incapable of leading, or even responding to, any revival of religious life in the Soviet Union. He believes, along with many others, that a religious renaissance is taking place in Russia, especially among young people and the intelligentsia, but

> The Moscow Patriarchate in its present situation is incapable of reacting with animation to this process, of strengthening it and directing it into a churchly channel. This process of religious renaissance is taking place apart from the Moscow Patriarchate, and moreover the tragedy of the situation lies in the fact that the Moscow Patriarchate, against its will, has become an objective obstacle on its path, a brake.[63]

This is a fair summary, although more is done individually and secretly by some priests in the church (as noted in Chapter 3) than Yakunin allows for here. But he is right to conclude as follows:

> In the mission of salvation foreordained for the Church of Christ, the first and foremost aim is worldwide mission: 'Go therefore and make disciples of all nations, baptising them . . .' (Matt. 28, 19). This great command of the Saviour, given to the Church as it entered the world, becomes for the Russian Orthodox Church, in the conditions of total, singleminded atheism ruling in our country, a decisive task of exceptional importance, to which the Moscow Patriarchate in its present state is not remotely equal.[64]

If the Soviet government has been able to limit, undermine and neutralise the church's ministry to such a considerable extent, why is it that the church is not simply a whited sepulchre? Why is it that even casual visitors to the churches of the Moscow Patriarchate, or foreigners who do not understand the language or meaning of the service, find themselves enraptured, transported as though to another world? The answer is that the religious policy of the Soviet government is based on the belief that God does not exist. But millions of Soviet citizens believe, or are coming to believe, otherwise. They are finding that, however compromised the church as an institution may be, Christ's promise that 'Where two or three are gathered together in my name, there am I in the midst of them,' still holds true. Try as it may to crush church institutional life, the government cannot prevent its citizens from seeking, and finding, God.

The effect of the state's strict control over the institutional framework of church life has been to push the independently minded elements, and the vigorous renewal of the Christian faith which is taking place, outside this framework. In Part 2 we shall examine the development of dissent from the policies of the Moscow Patriarchate, and the differing alternatives put forward by the dissenters.

Appendix: Statute of the CRA*

STATUTE

of the Council for Religious Affairs (CRA) under the USSR Council of Ministers.

1. The CRA is a union organ, organised with the aim of consistent realisation of the policies of the Soviet state in relation to religion.

2. The chief tasks of the CRA are:

(a) To supervise the observance of the USSR Constitution and the Decree of 23 January 1918 'On the Separation of the Churches from the State and Schools from the Churches' which guarantee freedom of conscience, and the correct application and fulfilment within the entire territory of the USSR of the Laws of the USSR, Decrees of the Presidium of the Supreme Soviet of the USSR, Resolutions and Orders of the USSR Council of Ministers in questions concerning religion;

(b) To study and make public the practical application of the legislation on cults, working over the proposed laws of the USSR, Decrees of the Presidium of the USSR Supreme Soviet, Resolutions and Orders of the USSR Council of Ministers in questions concerning religion and submitting them to the USSR Council of Ministers;

(c) To inform the government of the USSR on the activities of religious organisations;

(d) To work with religious organisations in the realisation of international relations, participating in the struggle for peace, for strengthening friendship among nations.

3. The CRA with reference to the tasks placed upon it:

(a) Seeks to guarantee the rights of citizens of the USSR professing the religion of their choice or professing none at all, to fulfil their religious rituals or to carry out anti-religious propaganda;

(b) Supervises the observance of the legislation on cults by religious organisations or servants of the cult;

---

*English translation taken from *Religion in Communist Lands*, vol. 4, no. 4 (1976), pp. 32–4.

(c) Maintains communication between the government of the USSR and religious organisations when questions arise requiring the permission of the government of the USSR;

(d) Keeps a list of religious associations, prayer houses and buildings;

(e) Examines and decides, within the limits of its competence, questions connected with the activities of religious organisations in the USSR;

(f) Verifies the correct application of the legislation on cults by central and local organisations and also by responsible persons;

(g) Gives an authoritative opinion on projected legislative acts of union republics on questions concerning religion;

(h) Receives from ministries, departments and similar organisations, and also from local *soviet* organs information and materials in matters concerning religion.

4. The CRA has the right:

(a) To make decisions (upon recommendation of executive committees of *oblast*, regional Council of Workers' Deputies [i.e. *soviets*], Councils of Ministers of autonomous republics, and in union republics without *oblast* divisions — upon recommendation of the Councils of Ministers of union republics) on registration and removal from registration of religious associations, on opening and closing prayer buildings and houses;

(b) To verify the activity of religious organisations in their observance of the Soviet legislation on cults and to issue compulsory orders for eliminating violations of them;

(c) To draw persons guilty of violating the legislation on cults to the attention of disciplinary organs of civil or criminal jurisdiction;

(d) To give explanations to ministries, departments and other organisations and to local *soviet* organs on questions concerning the application of the legislation on cults;

(e) To introduce recommendations for changing commands, instructions, decisions, orders, resolutions and such-like acts which contradict the legislation on cults, to the organ submitting the act or to the next higher-ranking organ.

5. Councils of Ministers of union republics, ministries, departments and other central organisations, but also local *soviet* organs give consent to the measures taken by the CRA or its appointed plenipotentiaries in connection with the activities of religious organisations.

6. The CRA is composed of a chairman and his deputies appointed by the USSR Council of Ministers, and of council members who are appointed by the USSR Council of Ministers upon recommendation of the Chairman of the Council. The staff of the Council also includes the plenipotentiaries of the CRA assigned to union republics.

The structure and number of staff in the Council apparatus is approved by the USSR Council of Ministers.

7. The CRA at its meetings considers questions connected with the practical realisation of the policies of the Soviet State in relation to religion, the observance of the legislation on cults, takes decisions on registration and removal from registration of religious associations, on opening and closing prayer houses, provides explanations concerning the application of the legislation on cults, issues compulsory orders on eliminating violations of the legislation, introduces recommendations on changing acts contradicting the legislation on cults, hears reports from leading workers in the central apparatus and from the Council's plenipotentiaries, evaluates proposed laws of the USSR, Decrees of the Presidium of the Supreme Soviet of the USSR, Resolutions and Orders of the USSR Council of Ministers, and also other basic questions, which are within the competence of the Council.

8. The CRA has plenipotentiaries in union and autonomous republics, regions and *oblasts*, who, in their activity, are subordinate to the CRA.

Appointment to and release from duties of the plenipotentiary of the Council is done by the CRA upon recommendation of the corresponding republic Council of Ministers, regional or *oblast* executive committee of Councils of Workers' Deputies.

9. The plenipotentiary of the CRA:

(a) Supervises the correct application and observance of the legislation on cults by local religious organisations and servants of the cult, and also by local *soviet* organs, officials, and all citizens;

(b) Gives conclusions to the Council, and also to republic and local *soviet* organs and other republic, regional and *oblast* organisations on questions concerning religion;

(c) Informs the Council on the activities of religious organisations, on all violations of the legislation on cults in the territory of the republic, region, *oblast* and on measures taken concerning religion, conducted or noted by local *soviet* organs, and also on all decisions taken by them on these questions;

(d) Examines declarations and complaints and decides within the limits of his competency, those questions that are concerned with the activities of religious organisations;

(e) Gives assistance to the social commissions attached to the executive committees of city and regional Councils of Workers' Deputies in maintaining supervision of the observance of the legislation on cults.

10. The plenipotentiary of the CRA has the right:

(a) To verify the activities of local religious organisations in the area of the observance of the legislation on cults and to issue compulsory orders on the elimination of violations;

(b) To receive from local *soviet* organs scattered in the territory of the republics, regions, *oblasts* the necessary information, materials and forms on matters connected with religion;

(c) To provide explanations to republican and local soviet organs and other organisations of the republics, regions or *oblasts* on questions about the application of the legislation on cults;

(d) With the consent of the CRA to introduce recommendations for changes to commands, instructions, decisions, orders, resolutions and such-like acts that contradict the legislation on cults, to the organ issuing the act in question;

(e) To raise the questions before the responsible republic and local organs on calling in persons guilty of violating the legislation on cults to the disciplinary, administrative or criminal jurisdiction.

11. The plenipotentiary of the CRA carries out his duties in close co-operation with the responsible republic, regional or *oblast* organs.

12. The CRA and the plenipotentiary of the Council possess a seal with the coat of arms of the USSR and their respective designations on it.

(The structure of the CRA staff was approved on 17 March 1966 by a Resolution of the USSR Council of Ministers, No. 203.)

STRUCTURE

Central Apparatus of the Council for Religious Affairs under the USSR Council of Ministers

Department for Orthodox Church affairs
Department for the affairs of the Muslim and Buddhist religions
Department for the affairs of Catholic, Protestant and Armenian Churches, the Jewish religion and Sects
Department of International Relations
Juridical Department
Book-keeping
General Department

PART 2

PROLOGUE

The chapters which follow describe events involving dissenters in the Russian Orthodox Church in some detail, and analyse the ideas of nonconformist intellectuals within the church as expressed in *samizdat*. A few words of introduction are needed to set all this in context. As we noted in Chapter 7, there has been a noticeable increase of interest in religion, especially in Orthodoxy, among the Soviet intelligentsia in recent years. This phenomenon is commonly referred to now as the *Russkoye religioznoye vozrozhdeniye*, usually translated as 'the Russian religious renaissance', sometimes as 'the religious revival'. Neither term, especially the second, is entirely satisfactory: they convey the impression of an unimpeded, unopposed flowering and growth of faith, even of a mass movement, and they have a tinge of triumphalism about them. The reality is a slow, gradual, often painful process of people rediscovering their Christian roots; it has been gathering pace now for some 25 years or more. Once this qualification has been made, however, we should say at the outset that this religious renaissance (since no better term suggests itself) is of the greatest significance and should by no means be underestimated.

The return of large numbers of the intelligentsia to the Russian Orthodox Church is very remarkable. This is so not only because it is an outright rejection of decades of atheist propaganda and of the whole of the future towards which the Communist Party of the Soviet Union is striving. Long before the Revolution of 1917, from the mid-nineteenth century onwards, the intelligentsia had begun to reject the church. The present-day Russian intelligentsia has a profound awareness of its own history and roots, and cannot be ignorant of the irony that its members are finding a path to the future in a church which their forebears dismissed with contempt a century ago.

The beginning of the religious renaissance came at the end of the 1950s. (Ironically, it more or less coincided with the commencement of Khrushchev's anti-religious campaign). The process of de-Stalinisation, set off by Khrushchev's celebrated 'secret speech' to the Central Committee of the CPSU in 1956, played a key role. Soviet citizens now knew that they had been systematically lied to for nearly 30 years — and if one leader could lie to them, why not another? Thinking persons could no longer accept what they were told officially. To maintain their intellectual integrity, they had to think everything through for themselves, work out their own beliefs and their own approach to life. The area of enquiry thus opened up was very great, and included metaphysical and religious questions.

Another factor was that in the comparatively relaxed atmosphere following Stalin's death, Soviet citizens for the first time in 40 years had leisure to begin to talk guardedly to one another about their beliefs or their search for beliefs. The four decades after the Revolution were dominated by war, civil war, famine, political terror, and war again. People learned, especially during the terror of the 1930s, not to confide their deepest beliefs to anyone whom they did not know very well indeed. This is not to say that people did not think about religion — no doubt they did, as they reflected very urgently on the gravest issues of life and of death — merely that they would be reluctant to talk about it, and certainly would not write about it. Only in the post-Stalin period did it become possible for members of the intelligentsia (and others) to give wider currency to their views and speculations about religion, and to express the allegiance which many of them felt or began to feel towards the Russian Orthodox Church. The growth of *samizdat* over a comparable period adds force to this point.

In Chapter 12 we shall describe in some detail some of the better-known discussion groups or seminars for young people, which meet unofficially and have been subject to repression by the authorities. Such groups began to meet at the end of the 1950s, though, so far as we can judge, they were neither numerous or large. They have grown slowly but surely since then.

The impulses which lead Soviet citizens towards the Russian Orthodox Church are varied. For many, the search for meaning in life leads, often after much spiritual questing, to God, and in Russia and other parts of the Soviet Union this in turn leads naturally to the Orthodox Church. For some, the impulse may be aesthetic: the powerful assault upon the senses of Orthodox worship, and the beauty of the churches, both inside and out, offer an enticing alternative to the often drab round of daily life in the Soviet Union. Others are drawn to the church through their quest for historical roots, for a sense of individual and national identity pre-dating 1917. This inevitably involves a recognition of the central role which Orthodoxy has played in the lives of the Russian and other nations. This in turn involves another powerful impulse, the cultural one. As thinking people in the Soviet Union attempt to rediscover and resurrect the culture of their past (in its pure, as opposed to its ideologically distorted form), they encounter Orthodoxy at every turn — in art, architecture, music, literature, poetry. This may lead them to enquire as to the nature and beliefs of Orthodoxy. Another potent factor is the growth of nationalism in the various countries which form part of the Soviet Union. In Russia particularly, but also elsewhere, rediscovery of national self-identity inevitably involves Orthodoxy, so closely has the church identified itself with the nation in the past. The growth of Russian nationalism (which we shall refer to again in the following chapters) consequently involves a concomitant growth of interest in Orthodoxy.

With such different reasons for entering the Russian Orthodox Church, it could hardly be supposed that all its new members would be of like mind.

Nor could it be supposed that they would instantly find common ground with the traditionally minded members of the church, those who, usually through family ties, and often uneducated, formed and still form the bulk of the church's membership, and who kept the church alive (as noted in Part 1) through the decades of severe adversity. The confluence of newly converted intellectuals with the mass of the traditionally minded faithful, and still more the confluence of intellectuals of one viewpoint with those of another, has inevitably led to conflict, as we shall show.

The size and scope of the religious renaissance is a completely open question. No one, either inside or outside the Soviet Union, is in a position to know how many people, young or old, intellectuals or not, have become members of the Russian Orthodox Church (or, for that matter, of any other church), nor to state exactly what the nature of their beliefs may be — that is, the extent to which they may truly be considered Orthodox, to subscribe to all the doctrines and practices of the church. Even people who are themselves deeply involved in the religious renaissance offer different views as to its extent. There are those who suggest that it is very widespread and growing rapidly; but there are others who point out that it is limited in scope, being largely confined to young urban intellectuals, and therefore cannot be considered a mass movement. These views are of course impressionistic (though not to be dismissed on that account) rather than factual. In such a vast country as the Soviet Union, no one can have a comprehensive view. And Orthodox Christians living in Moscow and Leningrad sometimes appear, of necessity, to have a patchy understanding of what may be happening in the provinces.

We should also take note of the rather sceptical views of intellectuals not involved in the religious renaissance, who maintain that it is of limited scope, and that large numbers of people, including both intellectuals and non-intellectuals, remain untouched by it.

If we conclude that the religious renaissance is in fact limited in scope, this does not undermine its significance. Anyone who has newly discovered the spiritual riches of Christianity in its Orthodox form, and whose life has been changed as a result, and who has likeminded friends, cannot fail to perceive that a profound and meaningful change is taking place that must ineluctably have important consequences for the future of their country. On the other hand, anyone who has not had such an experience, or who has chosen to reject it, cannot but point to the relatively small proportion of the population thus far affected by it.

Having attempted to put the issue into some kind of perspective, it is only fair to point out that, after the most sustained and systematic attempt to eradicate religion yet seen in history, any kind of reawakening of impulse towards Orthodoxy (or other churches) in the Soviet Union, whatever its extent may be, must be considered one of the greatest miracles of Christianity in the twentieth century.

10 THE RISE OF ORTHODOX DISSENT: UP TO 1974

Members of the Russian Orthodox Church who dissented from the policies followed by the leaders of the Moscow Patriarchate did not make a public appearance until the end of the 1950s. Their existence was not noticed abroad until many years after that. Their alternative views were publicly expressed exclusively through *samizdat*, the manuscripts and typescripts which circulated clandestinely from hand to hand, and it was not for some years that reliable channels were discovered through which these could be secretly conveyed to the West. The early *samizdat* documents which did reach the West gave such a different picture of church life from that propagated by church leaders that, with a few exceptions, they aroused puzzlement and scepticism, and were ignored.

The Early Years

It was the onset of Khrushchev's anti-religious campaign which stimulated a few church members into a defence of religion in general and their church in particular. The post-war restoration of the Moscow Patriarchate, the reopening of churches, monasteries and theological schools, was such a piece of unlooked-for good fortune that at first no independent voice was raised against the restrictions on church activity which none the less existed, not even after the death of Stalin in 1953. However, the sharp increase in anti-religious literature from about 1958 onwards inspired a very few bold spirits to raise a voice in opposition. The church leaders, who no doubt disapproved as stongly as ordinary believers of the anti-religious onslaught, remained silent; Metropolitan Nikolai (Yarushevich), who did voice some opposition, was quickly retired and died soon afterwards.

The early phases of dissent in the Russian Orthodox Church, up to about 1967 or 1968, have been described more than once elsewhere;[1] and we shall therefore merely sketch in those years here (with the inclusion of some previously unavailable material) before moving on to a more detailed account of Orthodox dissent from the end of the 1960s onwards.

First in the field was Anatoli Levitin, who, writing under the pen-name A. Krasnov, produced a stream of *samizdat* articles from 1958 onwards. As we saw in Part 1, he defended specific people and institutions: the Pochayev monastery, the monks of the Pskov monastery, the Old Believer Yevgeni Bobkov. He also wrote detailed responses to articles critical of the church which appeared in the Soviet press, and sometimes submitted them to the publications in question. None of them was published, but his energetic activities did not pass unnoticed, and in 1965, after the anti-religious campaign abated, he was invited to a frank discussion with members of the anti-religious establishment.[2] Levitin's friend Vadim Shavrov, who had converted to Christianity while the two men were in labour camp together, offered vociferous opposition to the propagation of atheism: according to Levitin, he heckled a live broadcast of an anti-religious lecture so persistently that the programme had to be taken off the air.[3] Orthodox believers in Kirov diocese, led by the layman Boris Talantov, wrote several documents describing in great detail the closure of churches and other methods of repressing believers; Talantov, a retired schoolmaster, was arrested and died in labour camp.[4] A Moscow priest, the venerable Archpriest Vsevolod Shpiller, offered dignified resistance to attempts to undermine the life of his parish after the appointment of an unbelieving churchwarden.[5]

These protests were few and far between compared with the size of the anti-religious onslaught, but it must be remembered that most believers had no one to whom they could protest, and, at that time, no means of getting their protests out of the country. Parishioners who apparently remained silent when their churches were closed at the beginning of the 1960s were quick to protest when, at the end of the 1970s, the formation of the Christian Committee for the Defence of Believers' Rights in the USSR finally offered them an opportunity of doing so.

In 1964 an appeal was sent by an anonymous group of Orthodox believers to the Executive Committee of the World Council of Churches, which met in Odessa in February that year. The appeal asked the WCC to consider the situation of the Russian Orthodox Church, which for three or four years had been exposed to 'an unjust, persistent and cruel struggle', and described in detail some of the problems the believers were facing. It ended with a request that the appeal be circulated to the United Nations, the Eastern Patriarchs and the Pope, and that it be broadcast so that Christians all over the world could pray for the believers in the USSR. Explaining their anonymity, the authors said they were afraid of the KGB discovering their identity: 'if they seize us, they will crush us to dust'.[6] However, so far as is known, the WCC Executive Committee neither discussed nor publicised this appeal. The irony of the Russian Orthodox Church playing host to an international Christian conference while simultaneously being under severe attack by its own government has not been lost on several commentators who have pointed out that it was precisely during the anti-religious campaign that the church's international role developed most rapidly; whatever the other motivations for the church's increased activities overseas, one of them was clearly to distract international attention from the anti-religious campaign.

In Leningrad there existed between 1964 and 1967 a small group of would-be revolutionaries whose activities were to no little degree inspired and motivated by its leaders' commitment to Russian Orthodoxy. Usually known by its Russian acronym of VSKhSON, the All-Russian Social Christian Union for the Liberation of the People intended to extend its numbers gradually and secretly over a period of years until such time as it could organise a bloodless (it hoped) coup and institute a regime in which the Russian Orthodox Church would play a central role. However, its members were all arrested by the KGB, and have now all served their sentences of imprisonment, except for the leader, Igor Ogurtsov, who is still serving a total of 20 years in prison, labour camp and (from 1982) internal exile which has totally undermined his health. It was in Ogurtsov that the commitment to Russian Orthodoxy and the Russian nation was deepest and most inflexible. An exceptionally gifted man, he was years ahead of his contemporaries not only in his commitment to Russian national values, but in his ability to inspire and organise others to work in unity for his cause. The Russian nationalist motif will make its appearance many times in the following pages, but never in quite the same way that it did in the vision of this brilliant and singleminded man.[7] VSKhSON's ideas on the Russian Orthodox Church were not, like those of the other dissenters we are discussing, a reaction to the policies of the Moscow Patriarchate (to which the group paid little if any attention), but an expression of what it believed the church's ideal role to be. In this also Ogurtsov was ahead of his time.

An Appeal to the Patriarch: Eshliman and Yakunin

Of all the activities of dissenters in the church, the single most effective one — to date and for many years thereafter — was undoubtedly the two open letters written in 1965 by two Moscow priests, Father Nikolai Eshliman and Father Gleb Yakunin.[8] They at once attracted a good deal of publicity abroad, and among Russian Orthodox believers in the USSR they were subsequently seen as the starting-point for active and public opposition to the Moscow Patriarchate's policies. The first letter, dated 21 November 1965 (with an appendix dated 13 December) was addressed to Patriarch Alexi. It chronicled in great detail the repressive measures which were being used against the church by CROCA (Council for Russian Orthodox Church Affairs, a predecessor of the CRA) and the lack of resistance, even apparent acquiescence, of the church. The two priests urged the Patriarch to take action: 'The suffering church turns to you with hope. You have been invested with the staff of primatial authority. You have the power as Patriarch to put an end to this lawlessness with one word! Do this!'[9] The second open letter, dated 15 December 1965, was addressed to Mr Podgorny, then chairman of the Presidium of the Supreme Soviet of the USSR. It commenced with a protest against the 'illegal actions' of CROCA, which had 'flagrantly violated the principles of socialist law and the basic legislative requirements of the Soviet Government determining the relations of the Soviet State to the church'.[10] The two priests examined the 'illegal actions' in some detail, and concluded with a request that the policies of CROCA

> should be carefully and completely examined and legally condemned, so that all the activities of the council may be brought into complete compliance with the state's legislation on religion and the church . . . Moreover, all the churches, monasteries and theological schools illegally closed in the period 1961–64 should be rightfully returned to the Russian Orthodox Church.[11]

The Patriarch's response was to ban Eshliman and Yakunin from office; though they remain priests, neither has been able to exercise his priestly office from that day to this.

An interesting sidelight on this episode, revealing the influence of the CRA and the difficult position of the church's hierarchy, is disclosed in the section of the CRA Report which reports on interviews with leading hierarchs. The bishop responsible for dealing with Eshliman and Yakunin was the then Metropolitan Pimen of Krutitsy and Kolomna, now Patriarch, and the CRA believed that he was playing a 'double game':

> Pimen, at the Council, stated that, on the instructions of the Patriarch, he summoned Eshliman and Yakunin, condemned their action and acquainted them with the Patriarch's resolution warning the authors of the letter of the inadmissibility of similar actions in future. Pimen assured [us] that in doing so he gave Eshliman and Yakunin no documents.
>
> Pimen made an analogous statement on a second visit to the Council. However, as was subsequently made clear, Pimen had provided Eshliman and Yakunin with both the text of the instructions in the Patriarch's resolution, and of the written responses of several hierarchs to the letter of these priests.
>
> In connection with this fact, on 31 March 1966 Metropolitan Pimen was invited to the Council, where deputy chairman V. G. Furov told him of this. But Pimen denied everything, repeating that he had given no documents to Eshliman and Yakunin. However, at the end of the conversation he stated that there had been some talk about it in the patriarchate office, and that he would check and report on it. However, the promised report did not follow. But the next day, that is, the 1 April, the attached letter [not included in the copy of the report sent to the West] from workers in the office of the Moscow Patriarchate, Kolchitsky [text unclear] and Mityayeva, reached the Council, which confirmed the fact of Metropolitan Pimen's two-faced behaviour.[12]

The CRA evidently believed that Pimen, in this small way, was trying to give some slight support to the two priests. This is both a striking illustration of the cat-and-mouse game constantly being played between the CRA and the church hierarchs, and also an illustration of the fact that this game, however skilfully a hierarch may play it, often has only the most marginal effect on the believers in his care: Eshliman and Yakunin were no doubt more pleased than otherwise to receive the documents in question, but the difference it made to their situation was negligible.

(An independent source has confirmed that Eshliman and Yakunin did not in fact receive the documents directly from Pimen, while pointing out that they might well have reached them through intermediaries in the Patriarchate.)[13]

During a later conversation with the CRA, Metropolitan Pimen was asked what he thought had motivated Eshliman and Yakunin:

> Money, replied Pimen. I consider the removal of the church cash-box from the hands of the clergy, depriving them of the opportunity for unlimited gain, to be the chief motive. Shpiller is an example of the same thing . . . Patriarch Tikhon, remarked Pimen, said the money would spoil the Moscow clergy, and that if it were deprived of it, it would rebel.[14]

This is a curious assertion, in view of the fact that Eshliman and Yakunin stood to lose more than they gained by their action, and did in fact both lose their livelihoods. It is impossible to tell here whether Pimen is giving his true (and very cynical) opinion, thus demonstrating in private the support he has always given in public for the 1961 reforms, or whether he is giving the CRA the answer it wants most to hear, and, by allaying any suspicions of a principled opposition, discouraging any intention it may have had of taking further measures against the two priests.

Though the two priests' letters had little effect on their recipients, they did have a great effect on other members of the church. Inspired by their bold, unprecedented action, others began to formulate and publicise their own views about the Moscow Patriarchate's policies. Eshliman and Yakunin were the catalyst that inspired many to give expression to their long-pent-up feelings. Their influence extended even beyond the church, as Alexander Solzhenitsyn, recounting his long struggle with the Soviet literary establishment, has testified:

> in spring 1966, I had been delighted to read the protest written by two priests, Eshliman and Yakunin, a courageous, pure and honest voice in defence of a church which of old had lacked and lacks now both the skill and the will to defend itself. I read, and was envious. Why had I not done something like this myself, why was I so unenterprising? . . . I must do something similar![15]

(The Baptists in the Soviet Union pre-dated even Eshliman and Yakunin in their attempts to achieve freedom from state pressure. Their first *samizdat* appeals to Soviet leaders date from 1961, and by 1965 an independent group had already split off totally from the officially recognised Baptist Union and formed a separate structure with its own officials and organisation. Other Christian denominations, chiefly the Pentecostals, Seventh-Day Adventists and Catholics (in Lithuania), did not form organised movements for religious liberty until the 1970s.)

Two Schools of Thought: Democrats and Nationalists

By the end of the 1960s, the Russian Orthodox dissenters formed one of several groups of independently minded people seeking a greater measure of personal freedom in different spheres of Soviet life (see pp. 326–30). The largest and best-known of these was the loose association of reformist intellectuals which became known as the Democratic Movement. Its chief activity was to campaign for civil rights on the basis of appeals to Soviet laws, and to defend victims of injustice. On this level there was clearly scope for the democrats to work on behalf of Orthodox believers whose civil rights had been infringed, and they did so very readily. There was full and active co-operation between members of the Democratic Movement and the small but growing band of dissenters within the Russian Orthodox Church. The clearest instance of such co-operation came about because of the attempts of Orthodox believers in the small town of Naro-Fominsk, near Moscow, to register a church for worship. Meeting with no success, they then turned to members of the Democratic Movement in Moscow for support; Valeri Chalidze and Boris Zuckermann (the former not a declared believer, the latter a practising Jew) gave them legal advice, and Anatoli Levitin and others appeared on their behalf as witnesses in a court case. Chalidze described the whole attempt to register a church, including chicanery on the part of state agencies, in a long letter to members of the Presidium of the Supreme Soviet of the USSR.[16] The believers still did not succeed in registering a church, and have not up to the present, but this was no fault of the democrats, who gave them unstinting support. (The registration of a Baptist church in Naro-Fominsk in 1981 must have seemed very inconsistent to the Orthodox parishioners.)[17]

The other chief current of thought among the independently minded Soviet intelligentsia which had considerable influence upon members of the Russian Orthodox Church was Russian nationalism. Indeed, Orthodox thinkers were from the beginning among its chief proponents, believing as they did that their church was an integral part of their nation, and that Orthodoxy was an irreplaceable constituent element of the attempt to help Russians find their way back to their national roots and national consciousness. There was a good deal of fellow-feeling between the democrats and the nationalists, who recognised in one another small bands of dedicated idealists prepared to commit their entire lives to the seemingly impossible task of changing, or at least modifying, the monolithic Soviet political and ideological system. However, the two groups had completely different ideas about the direction of change and the future of the Russian nation and the Soviet Union as a whole, and this led to sharp exchanges of views in *samizdat* and elsewhere, conducted in the uncompromising and sometimes virulent tone customary in Russian polemics. These arguments were to play a significant role within Orthodox dissent, as well as among Soviet dissenters at large. The democrats, obviously, wanted to move towards democracy, and this inevitably meant studying and copying the democratic political systems of Western countries. To the Russian nationalists, the thought of aping the West in this way was anathema. This derived both from their view of the West — which they regarded as a Babylonian sink of vice and sexual permissiveness, unbridled consumerism and materialism, and rootless secularism — and from their conviction that Russia had a unique destiny which could be fulfilled only by adherence to the traditions of Russian history, culture and faith. The divergent positions adopted by the two groups had obvious associations with the nineteenth-century debate between the Slavophils and the Westernisers, who had faced the same problem of Russia's relationship with the West under different circumstances, but the democrats and nationalists of the late twentieth century were more preoccupied with their response to their immediate, and unique, situation than with their role in Russian intellectual history. None the less, large sections of the emergent Russian nationalist movement, which encompasses a range of different views, from pious patriots through principled nationalists to extreme Great Russian chauvinists, were dubbed 'Neo-Slavophil' by some Western commentators, and certainly much of their philosophical rationale derived from their nineteenth-century predecessors.[18] However, this term was rarely used in *samizdat* where the words 'Russophiles', 'patriots' or sometimes '*pochvenniki*' ('sons of the soil') were preferred. The nationalists believed that the moral and spiritual values which had upheld and inspired the Russian people throughout its history were essentially those of Russian Orthodoxy, and that these must be revived and reabsorbed into national life. They also believed that the Russian Orthodox Church would occupy a central role in national life in years to come, though various schools of thought which developed differed as to what precisely its role would be. Other important elements of nationalist thought included belief in the Russian people (as opposed to the intelligentsia) as the bearers of the spiritual power of Russian Orthodoxy, suspicion of Western democracy and a love of the Russian land and Russian culture, which was to some extent manifested in concern over the destruction of monuments of Russian culture, especially churches, and the poisoning of the environment by pollution.[19] Igor Ogurtsov and the VSKhSON group, mentioned above, were the first to develop these ideas and attempt to put them into practice.

Some of the more extreme Russian nationalists espoused the idea of Russian messianism, that is, the conviction that Russia not only had a unique destiny, but also a unique mission to reveal the truth which would save the world. This contrasted with the semi-isolationist views of the more moderate nationalists, whose chief concern was that Russia should retire to lick her wounds after the ordeals of the past decades and restore her national consciousness untroubled by thoughts of the world beyond.[20] One of the earliest *samizdat* articles on the theme of nationalism — 'Russian Messianism and the New National Consciousness', by V. Gorsky, published in 1970 — warned against the dangers of messianism and urged instead that the Russian nation should take the path of repentance for past wrongs.[21] This article provoked bitter criticism from nationalists of all shades of opinion, including Solzhenitsyn[22] and others,[23] not least because it was written pseudonymously, but also because it was felt that its criticism of 'messianism' was simply a cloak for an attack on the whole emergent nationalist movement. However, it did raise the concept of national repentance which was to reappear in subsequent nationalist writings.[24]

Russian nationalist ideas were not confined to *samizdat* and to dissenters. Love for the Russian countryside and the Russian past was evident not only in the works of Solzhenitsyn, including the short story 'Matryonin dvor' ('Matryona's Home') which was published officially in the Soviet Union,[25] but also in Vladimir Soloukhin's description of his experiences searching for icons in old Russian village churches 'Chernye doski' (*'Black Boards'*).[26] During the 1970s the trend was continued by several writers known as *'derevenshchiki'* ('village writers').[27] By the beginning of the 1980s, it had become clear that these pastoral tales often contained a clearly pro-religious element.[28] In art the Russian nationalist theme emerged principally in the paintings of Ilya Glazunov, who after initially incurring official odium was later able to hold official exhibitions which attracted vast crowds.[29] His work was praised by such Christian Russian patriots as Vladimir Osipov[30] and Father Dimitri Dudko.[31] The Russian nationalist tendency even flourished briefly in the pages of the Soviet newspaper *Molodaya gvardiya* (*Young Guard*), the organ of the Komsomol (Young Communist League) during the late 1960s and early 1970s, and though this line was quashed, and the editor of the newspaper sacked, the ensuing debate made it clear that there was support for it in influential party circles.[32] All this suggests that there were supporters of Russian nationalists in Soviet ruling circles whose influence might be expected to serve as a vehicle for the furtherance of ideals expressed in *samizdat* by nationalist dissenters. However, it is by no means clear whether they remain there in the early 1980s. In any case, how this might affect the Russian Orthodox Church is an open question. It seems improbable that such highly placed political figures would wish to usher in an era in which the church would be left free to forge its own role within the nation according to its own views of the spiritual needs of the people. More probably it would be assigned a more limited, figurehead role in the new scheme of things, its spiritual and moral authority over large sections of the population becoming a power base for the would-be new leadership. Though the church would find itself with more freedom than at present, and with opportunities to increase its influence and freedom of action by skilful manoeuvring, it could equally well become a political pawn in an attempt by a right-wing faction in the Soviet leadership to seize power in the post-*détente* era. The Russian nationalist option therefore constitutes a temptation and a possible danger for the church. If historical precedent is any guide, it is probably one that the hierarchy views with favour.[33]

Liberal Nationalism: Vladimir Osipov

The chief *samizdat* expression of Russian nationalist thought, in which Orthodoxy was accorded a prominent place, was the journal *Veche* (the name of the medieval Russian village popular assembly), ten issues of which appeared between 1971 and 1974. It was edited by Vladimir Osipov. Osipov, born in 1938, participated in informal cultural discussions held at the statue of Mayakovsky in Moscow from 1958, and was involved in *samizdat* from 1960, which led in 1961 to his being sentenced to a term of seven years in labour camp. An admirer of Yugoslav socialism at the time of his arrest, he was deeply impressed with the views of some members of the VSKhSON group whom he met in the labour camps, and emerged as an Orthodox Christian and a Russian patriot.[34] He maintained that *Veche* was an expression of 'loyal opposition', not opposed to Soviet power, and therefore not illegal, but critical. He criticised the VSKhSON group for its intention to use force against the Soviet regime[35] and believed that 'The only way is to convince the leaders, by energetic vocal effort, to be more tolerant and humanitarian, to respect the rights of man or, at the very least, their own Constitution of 1936. [In force when Osipov wrote these words in 1974; now superseded by the 1977 Constitution.]'[36] In this belief he was closer to many members of the Democratic Movement than to some of the more right-wing nationalists, and to some extent dissenters viewed him as positioned somewhere in between the two schools of thought. However, his deep, almost romantic patriotism was clearly expressed in his article 'Tri otnosheniya k Rodine' ('Three Attitudes Towards the Homeland'), which characterised the ideal attitude of a patriot as 'one of love' to the homeland, while bitterly castigating (in Aesopian language) the attitude of 'hatred' of the 'contemporary nihilist' (member of the Democratic Movement) and the attitude of 'opportunism' and 'speculation' (exemplified by official Soviet nationalism).[37]

Osipov's most pressing concern was the need to combat the immediate, practical problem of the decline of the Russian nation, as he made clear in his editorial in the first issue of *Veche*:

> Our moral state leaves very much to be desired. An epidemic of drunkenness. Disintegration of the family. A startling growth of boorishness (*khamstvo*) and vulgarity (*poshlost*). Loss of an elementary appreciation of beauty. An outburst of foul language — the symbol of brotherhood and equality in a pigsty. Envy and denunciations. A devil-may-care attitude to work. Thieving. A cult of bribery. Double-dealing as a method of social behaviour. Surely this cannot be us? Surely this is not the great nation which produced an immeasurable abundance of saints, zealots and heroes? Have we the right to call ourselves Russians? As though infected with fury, we have renounced our forefathers, our great culture, our heroic history and glorious name. We have renounced our nationality.[38]

Although this was clearly an appeal to nationalistic rather than to religious instincts, this catalogue of the nation's ills was not one to which an Orthodox (or any) Christian could be expected to remain indifferent.

An analysis of the contents of the first six issues of *Veche* according to subject-matter has shown that the second-largest category was that devoted to the Russian Orthodox Church and religious thought.[39] This included articles on church history, such as that on Patriarch Nikon and the seventeenth-century Old Believer schism,[40] coverage of Orthodox writers such as V. V. Rozanov,[41] Pavel Florensky,[42] Dostoyevsky[43] and others, reflections on religion by contemporary writers, such as the anonymous 'Notes of a Russian Christian'[44] and the review of a five-volume *samizdat* work entitled *Religiya i sovremennoye soznaniye (Religion and Contemporary Consciousness)*, [45] and coverage of the current situation of the Russian Orthodox Church, such as the Local Council of 1971[46] and the retirement of Archbishop Yermogen.[47] *Veche* also covered such issues as the contemporary attitude to Roman Catholicism, which many Neo-Slavophiles viewed with suspicion. Osipov himself stated unequivocally that he regarded Catholics as brothers in Christ,[48] but in this and other matters he did not impose his own moderate views on the contents of the journal as a whole, and published contributions from readers who believed that Catholicism constituted the greatest danger to the Russian Orthodox Church.[49] Osipov also published contributions from more extreme nationalists, leading to the appearance in the journal of chauvinistic and anti-semitic sentiments, which disturbed some commentators who criticised Osipov for failing to adopt a clear editorial line.[50]

Osipov ceased to publish *Veche* after the ninth issue, which appeared in December 1973. In March 1974 he issued a statement to the effect that the KGB was preparing a case against him on a charge of anti-Soviet agitation, and warning all *Veche* associates to be aware of KGB collaborators.[51] However, members of the editorial board produced a tenth issue, edited by I. V. Ovchinnikov. The history of the split in the editorial board remains somewhat obscure, but it was certainly inspired by the KGB. It has been suggested that the KGB feared a coalition of some members of the nationalist movement with the Democratic Movement due to Osipov's position as a potential mediator. However, the theory runs, they found it impossible to influence him against such a development because of his honesty and insistence on keeping *Veche* completely free from censorship, and so caused a split between him and his colleagues, possibly using Ovchinnikov as a provocateur.[52] In May 1974 Osipov wrote a *samizdat* article in which he continued his gradualist and realistic political approach by calling for a united front of patriotic and democratic forces in the nation, irrespective of their political and ideological beliefs, to struggle for a slow liberalisation and the strengthening of law and order.[53]

Veche's position in the spectrum of emergent Russian nationalist opinion was clarified in an article by Mikhail Agursky, a Jew converted to Orthodox Christianity, who made a significant contribution to the dissent movement in the USSR before emigrating to Israel in 1975. Though anti-semitic sentiments had, as noted, appeared in the pages of *Veche*, and were to recur in the works of other Orthodox *samizdat* authors, the real danger, in Agursky's view, lay in the overt and rampant anti-semitism to be found in both officially published and *samizdat* works by non-Christian extreme nationalists whom he saw as the forerunners of Soviet neo-Nazism. Agursky quoted a document from this school of thought which indicated that Christianity and the Orthodox Church were seen to be the chief obstacles to their racist ideas. He put forward the view (which other commentators have also advanced) that neo-Nazi elements within the Soviet leadership had attempted to take over *Veche* and make it an unofficial mouthpiece for their views, and that one of the chief reasons for their failure to do so was the position of Russian Christian nationalists such as Osipov, Leonid Borodin (a VSKhSON member) and Hierodeacon Varsonofi (Khaibulin). Agursky urged his fellow-Jews to realise that 'only Christian civilisation, only the Christian religion is a more powerful barrier in the path of the racism and Neo-Nazism that is again advancing upon the world'.[54]

As the debate between the democrats and the nationalists developed, it became clear that Orthodox Christian thought and the role of the church would have a significant part to play in the different schemes being proposed for the future of the country. Conversely, the debate within the church was deeply affected by the fact that the sympathies of different dissenters lay with the democrats or with varying shades of nationalist opinion. The democrats were no less patriotic than the nationalists, and just as concerned for the future of Russia and the Soviet Union, and they did not attempt to divorce the fate of their church from the fate of their country. Church dissent did not take place in a vacuum. Although much of the *samizdat* documentation on the church was concerned either with purely internal matters or, more often, with the relationship between the church and the state, concern for the Soviet people as a whole and the church's mission to them was never far from the author's minds.

Appeals to the 1971 Local Council

In the year that *Veche* commenced publication, 1971, some Orthodox dissenters attempted to open a discussion of purely theological issues within the church. They were spurred to do so by what they believed to be unacceptable theological innovations by Metropolitan Nikodim and others. Their objections took the form of an appeal to the Local Council, which took place in May to June that year, signed by four church members — a priest, Father Nikolai Gainov, and three laymen, Felix Karelin, Lev Regelson and Viktor Kapitanchuk. They were very critical of both the nature of the new ideas being expressed by Nikodim and others, and also of the fact that these ideas were being, as they put it, foisted upon the church without any previous general discussion. They therefore asked the Local Council to examine Nikodim's theological ideas, and circulated their appeal to all the bishops beforehand. According to the list of contents, the appeal contained 150 pages, divided into nine sections. Each of these contained lengthy quotations from speeches or articles by Metropolitan Nikodim and others (Metropolitan Ioann (Vendland), Metropolitan Nikolai (Yurik), Archpriest Liveri Voronov and Archpriest Vitali Borovoi), followed by questions posed by the authors concerning the theological implications of the remarks made.[55]

The four authors of the appeal considerd Nikodim's teachings to be 'not only new' but 'highly dubious' in areas concerning 'the apocalyptic aspects of the Divine Revelation', namely 'teaching on the thousand years' reign of Christ (Revelation 20, 1–11), teaching on the new creation (Revelation 21, 5), and teaching on the nations of the earth walking in the light of the New Jerusalem (Revelation 21, 24–22, 2)'.[56] The quotations which they give are mostly from speeches or articles given abroad at international Christian gatherings, chiefly the Christian Peace Conference, and are on the need to work for peace, to bring about the Kingdom of Heaven on earth. The modernistic ideas which are developed are exclusively in the overseas and peacemaking work of the church, not in its domestic life. There is not space here for an analysis of this detailed and complex material, but we will quote the chief objections of the authors of the appeal:

Three points in the activity of Metropolitan Nikodim and his fellow-thinkers arouse special alarm:

1. They do not attempt to found their new teaching on the religious experience of the Universal Church, but prefer to 'philosophise not according to the Fathers'.

2. They are imposing their teaching ambiguously — avoiding concrete designations — fragmentarily, scrappily, frequently interspersing short texts of significant religious and theological content into lengthy discussions on worldly themes, not so much appealing to the mind of the Church as gradually and imperceptibly changing the Church's spiritual atmosphere; and finally,

3. Metropolitan Nikodim and other persons who think as he does dare to foist their new teaching, which has not yet been examined by the collective mind of the Church nor approved by its collective authority, onto the Russian Church and even the whole of Christendom as a guide to action.[57]

The quotations and analysis which follow make it quite obvious that there was a case to be answered. Metropolitan Nikodim and the others clearly were introducing ideas which were new to traditional Orthodoxy and which had not been discussed by the church as a whole: for example, Metropolitan Nikodim implied that the end of the world was close at hand; he stated that knowledge was valuable and that technological progress was a great good; he asked for an agenda item at a pan-Orthodox conference concerning means of struggle against (*inter alia*) atheism to be removed; he and others implied that in accepting mankind in the Incarnation, Christ accepted the whole of the human race into his Body, that is, it became a 'potential church'.[58] These and the other matters mentioned are all far from simple, and admit of more than one opinion; the point at issue is that Nikodim and the others, representing the church abroad, were putting forward in the name of the church views which the church had not discussed. Whether the church would have agreed with the new ideas is another question: the authors of the appeal imply that it would not, and given the church's conservatism, they were probably right. Many of the views quoted are rather far removed from traditional Orthodox teaching. Nikodim might or might not have been able to convince other theologians of the truth of them, but the complaint of the four authors of the appeal is that he did not attempt to do so.

Though the authors of the appeal do not say so, it seems that this is an example of an issue we referred to in Chapter 9: the Moscow Patriarchate found itself obliged to adopt certain modernist views in order to 'keep up' in progressive Christian circles abroad, but was not permitted by the Soviet state to transfer modernistic ideas back home.

(*Veche*, in what was generally a favourable report on the Council[59] stated: 'They say (we cannot vouch for absolute authenticity) that Metropolitan

Nikodim, on learning of the appeal to the Council, broke down and wept, exclaiming "When did I ever say these things!"' However, all the remarks attributed to Metropolitan Nikodim (and to others) in the sections of the appeal which have reached the West are direct quotations from the *Journal of the Moscow Patriarchate*.)

The appeal was addressed to the 1971 Council because it was the most suitable forum for the issue to be raised. However, it was not mentioned. The official record contains reports on the church's ecumenical activity, by Metropolitan Nikodim, and on its peacemaking activity, by Metropolitan Ioann (Vendland),[60] which were approved by the Council without comment. In effect, then, the Council endorsed the new teachings which had crept into the church's overseas activity. The four authors made this point in a second document sent to the newly elected Patriarch Pimen after the Council.[61] They state that not only did the Council not discuss the issue they had raised, but no steps had been taken by the Patriarch after it was over; indeed, Nikodim had been given a decoration, signifying approval of his activity. Moreover, one of the compilers of the appeal, Father Nikolai Gainov, had been dismissed from his parish and was without means of live-lihood. It is clear from the circumstances that this was due to his participa-tion in the appeal. The four had had a conversation with Archbishop Pitirim, who had told them that no one would study their appeal, but they had been unable to see the Patriarch and letters to him had been unanswered.

Another document was addressed to the 1971 Council by three members of the church: Father Georgi Petukhov, Hierodeacon Varsonofi (Khaibulin) and layman Pyotr Fomin.[62] It begins with a rather strange, incoherent introduction, which attributes the growing immorality observ-able in the Russian nation to 'Zionism and satanism', but then rather suddenly changes tack and appeals to the Council to petition the state for various concession, such as opening of churches and monasteries, teaching of religion in schools, improved theological education, and so on. A priest from Irkutsk, Father Yevgeni Kasatkin, also wrote to the Council describ-ing the deleterious effects on parish life of the 1961 reforms in similar terms to the complaints which we discussed in Chapter 2.[63] Neither document was paid any attention during the Council proceedings. The *samizdat* author Anatoli Levitin, who had by then kept up a steady commentary on church affairs for more than ten years, was prevented from making any comment on the Council by his arrest on 8 May 1971.[64]

The failure of these appeals to the 1971 Council left no doubt that, if ordinary members of the church were to gain more freedom for it, they would have to think of other measures.

A Challenge to the Patriarch: The 'Lenten Letter' Debate

The next measure which was tried was a dramatic one which achieved worldwide publicity. The writer Alexander Solzhenitsyn, publicly identifying himself for the first time as a member of the Russian Orthodox Church, wrote an open letter to reproach to Patriarch Pimen. The 'Lenten Letter', as it was called, was as forthright and uncompromising as all Solzhenitsyn's writings. The writer bitterly criticised Patriarch Pimen for neglecting the religious education of childen, for acquiescing in the registration of baptisms, for allowing the church to be 'ruled dictatorially by atheists — a sight never before seen in two millennia!' Solzhenitsyn complained of the 'traditionally submissive' nature of pastoral letters, and of the fact that 'the Russian Church expresses its concern about any evil in distant Asia or Africa, while it never has anything at all to say about things which are wrong here at home'. These comments, and others — on the acute shortage of churches, on the forced retirement of Archbishop Yermogen — correctly point to the isolated, hemmed-in state of the church. In emphasising the church's failure to resist, Solzhenitsyn highlighted the central moral dilemma of the situation:

> By what reasoning is it possible to convince oneself that the planned *destruction* of the spirit and body of the church under the guidance of atheists is the best way of *preserving* it? Preserving it *for whom*? Certainly not for Christ. Preserving it *by what means*? *By falsehood*? But after the falsehood by whose hands are the holy sacraments to be celebrated?

Solzhenitsyn's own solution to the church's situation was sacrifice:

> Things were no easier at the birth of the Christian faith; nevertheless it held out and prospered. And showed us the way: *sacrifice*. Though deprived of all material strength, it is always victorious in *sacrifice*.[65]

Solzhenitsyn, and many who rejoiced to read his words, were clearly prepared to countenance the disappearance of officially permitted church life, a return to the pre-war situation, rather than compromise the truth. He regarded the church as a moral force, not an institution. A different view was put in a reply to the 'Lenten Letter' by a priest, Father Sergi Zheludkov. He took issue with Solzhenitsyn on two points, the first of which was that he thought it unfair publicly to criticise the Patriarch, who was quite unable to defend himself. Second, Zheludkov considered that Solzhenitsyn had not told the whole truth about the church; he himself believed that 'the legal Church organisation cannot be an *island of freedom* in our strictly unified society . . . There exists this strictly centralised system, and within it, surprisingly, is preserved an alien body — the Russian Orthodox Church.' Within this system the church 'is not permitted to do many things necessary for the existence of a real church life'. Thus far, there was no significant disagreement, but then Zheludkov continued:

What are we to do in such a situation? Should we say: all or nothing? Should we try to go underground, which in the present system is unthinkable? Or should we try somehow to accept the system and for the present use of those opportunities that are permitted? The Russian hierarchy took the latter decision.[66]

Here was the nub of the issue. Solzhenitsyn would surely have answered that the church should, if necessary, 'go underground' and would not consider it 'unthinkable' at all. These two short, stark letters of Solzhenitsyn and Zheludkov expressed the central conflict in the debate over the church: between those who believed that the church must be preserved as an institution and those who believed that the church was above all a metaphysical body.

Solzhenitsyn, in the 'Lenten Letter', viewed the church as moral force (or failed moral force), depending on the will of men. A more traditional, 'churchly' view, seeing the church as an instrument of divine grace, was put forcefully by the third person to join the fray, the layman Felix Karelin. He weighed in heavily on the side of Solzhenitsyn, in a letter deeply critical of Zheludkov's remarks. He first pointed out that it was highly presumptuous of Zheludlov to have answered as letter addressed to the Patriarch personally, and then defined the fundamental difference between his and Solzhenitsyn's letters:

the *writer* Alexander Solzhenitsyn asserts . . . that the human spirit, fortified by the grace of God, is stronger than all outward circumstances. The *priest* Sergi Zheludkov, on the other hand . . . insists that the social milieu is stronger than the human spirit and acts as a determining factor upon it.

Karelin took issue with Zheludkov over his concept of the church itself and his concept of the church in society. Regarding the former, he disagreed that the church 'cannot be an island of freedom': 'Spare us! This is precisely why Christ founded his Church, to be an island of freedom in a world enslaved by sin!' He also objected to the statement that the church was an 'alien body' within the state system:

It you mean a spiritual alienation . . . then . . . the Church is alien in the fullest sense of the word, it is another species, different from all the rest of mankind, 'a chosen race, a royal priesthood, a holy nation, God's own people' (1 Peter 2, 9–10). It is precisely this spiritual other-worldliness — more, its ontological otherness, which makes the Church an invincible kingdom.

This was not altogether fair to Zheludkov, who had said that it was the 'legal church organisation', not 'the Church', which could not be an island of freedom, and who in referring to the church as an 'alien body' evidently meant that it was such from the point of view of the state system, not from the church's own viewpoint. Karelin, however, like Solzhenitsyn, refused to limit the issue to what the state would or would not permit. This was clear in his second main objection to Zheludkov's letter, over the latter's concept of the church in society. Agreeing that the Russian Church 'exists in very strictly determined conditions', Karelin pointed out that these conditions were determined not by Soviet laws — which did not forbid church hierarchs to appeal for the opening of monasteries, churches and theological schools, nor ban priests from authority in church councils — but by 'foolish, irrational fear'. Here he allied himself with Solzhenitsyn's view. While agreeing with Zheludkov that 'there must be no incitement to sacrifice and martyrdom', Karelin pointed out that 'if a Christian voluntarily becomes a monk and also receives the elevated rank of bishop, he must be well aware of what he is doing . . . The work of a bishop is always sacrificial.' As regards the courage required to overcome fear on the part of church leaders, Karelin had this to say:

> the hero *acts bravely* and thus overcomes fear, not noticing that in doing so he is selling himself out to pride; the Christian *repents* of his fear, and overcomes it in God's strength. The hero shapes himself, the Christian moulds his soul.[67]

Solzhenitsyn and Karelin, though both rejecting the view of the church as primarily an institution, did so in different ways. Solzhenitsyn (as in the other areas of Soviet life to which he addressed himself) issued a robust challenge to the church to pluck up some courage and do what was right. Karelin — more in keeping with the kenotic element in Russian Orthodox tradition — suggested instead refraining from action, negating self in order to serve as the instrument of God. The two letters represented two distinct approaches to the nature of the church, which were to recur in the debate over its role. The former view, while willing to abandon institutional church life if necessary, none the less to some extent saw the church as having an institutional role in the sense that its role could be shaped by the will of man, subordinated to his policies, affected by his having or not having the courage to take certain actions. The latter view held that the role of the church was in the hands of God, who would unfold it to His servants if they were prepared to yield their wills and act in complete obedience to him.

The two views were not totally incompatible in that it required an act of will for a man to surrender himself to God, and courage to remain obedient to Him in hostile circumstances. However, the premises underlying the two approaches diverged in that the former called upon church members to take a moral initiative requiring boldness and resolution, while the latter urged them to subject their individual human qualities and capacities to the divine will and the collective mind of the church. Solzhenitsyn's clarion call was perforce too innovative for some church members steeped in the mainstream of traditional Orthodox thought.

The Legal Position: Igor Shafarevich

This intense religious controversy was followed by a document which cast a clear, logical eye on the church's position and starkly revealed the restraints upon it. 'Legislation on Religion in the USSR', by the mathematician Igor Shafarevich, took the form of a report to the three-man Committee for Human Rights headed by Academician Sakharov.[68] It was a further example of the support given by the human rights movement to the church. Though in theory concerned with all religions, the report in fact took most of its examples from the Russian Orthodox Church, to which Shafarevich belonged. The report was based largely on the 1929 Law on Religious Associations (before the 1975 revisions), and also on the Instructions issued to officials who had to implement the laws, and provided a systematic description of what the church could and could not do in different areas of its life. The importance of the report lay in the fact that the 1929 law was very difficult to obtain in the USSR, and therefore believers did not know what their rights were. There were frequent complaints in *samizdat* documents of that period that believers were expected to obey laws of whose content they were unaware. Shafarevich's report provided this information, albeit in a form which still made widespread circulation difficult. He was also able to obtain access to a secret, limited-circulation volume, *Legislation on Religious Cults*, which was intended for CRA commissioners, members of executive committees of *soviets* and others involved with religious associations.[69] Shafarevich was thus able to define far more clearly than had hitherto been possible the legal obligations of and restraints upon religious associations. As well as providing information of practical value to believers, his report pointed to shortcomings in the existing legislation, as stated in his conclusion:

(1) The laws existing at present on many most important issues do not provide sufficient guarantees for the normal development of religious life and the realisation of principle of freedom of conscience proclaimed in the Constitution [i.e. the Constitution of 1936 then in force].

(2) The Instructions which should clarify the application of the laws contain new regulations, which do not follow from the laws, and in some cases contradict them.

(3) There are weighty grounds for fearing that in practice both the instructions and the laws on religion are broken.[70]

As we saw in our analysis of legislation on religion in Part 1, Shafarevich's first and third conclusions are also applicable to the 1975 revision of the law.

Igor Shafarevich was one of many Soviet citizens who spoke out in defence of human rights and religious freedom at the expense of their careers. In the case of Shafarevich, this represented a loss to his country as well as to himself. He was one of the most gifted mathematicians in the Soviet Union, a child prodigy who became a corresponding member of the Academy of Sciences at the age of 35 (in 1958) and a Lenin Prize-winner. However, in 1975 his membership of Sakharov's Committee for Human Rights led to his dismissal from his lectureship at Moscow University, where he had taught for 30 years.[71] Like many whose religious or other beliefs were not fully in accord with the Communist Party's ideological line, Shafarevich was effectively reduced to the status of a second-class citizen, in the sense that his views and convictions were not allowed to contribute to the development of the society in which he lived, and led to personal disadvantagement.

Religious believers in the USSR are governed not only by the Law on Religious Associations analysed by Shafarevich, but also by other laws and instructions adopted from time to time. The adoption of a law in 1973 had serious consequences for believers: this was the Fundamentals of Legislation of the USSR and Union Republics on the Education of the People, passed by the Supreme Soviet of the USSR in July 1973 and effective from 1 January 1974. As is customary, the draft of this law had been published in *Izvestiya*, the government newspaper, on 4 April, to give Soviet citizens a chance to offer their views. Some Orthodox Christians did so: Viktor Kapitanchuk, Felix Karelin and Father Gleb Yakunin in a joint note; and Gennadi Shimanov in a separate letter dated 10 July.[72] Kapitanchuk, Karelin and Yakunin pointed out that, although the Soviet government in principle allowed parents to give their children a religious upbringing, as stated in the 1918 Decree on the Separation of Church and State, and elsewhere, this was implicitly denied in the new law, since it made no provision whatever for any kind of private religious education and upbringing. They also noted that the draft law stated that parents 'are obliged to bring up their children in a spirit of high communist morality'.[73] This, they stated, was illogical and inconsistent with other provisions of Soviet law: if the right to religious faith was recognised by law, parents who availed themselves of this right could not be expected to impart to their children an atheist worldview which they did not possess themselves. Shimanov came at greater length to similar conclusions. He also pointed out that the new law, which called for education in the spirit of communist morality, would be better served if the legislators showed true morality by treating religious believers as equal builders of the future of their country, instead of forcing them into the impossible position of teaching their children what they did not believe themselves.[74]

According to *Veche*'s editor, neither letter received a reply, and the law was promulgated with no alteration to the draft.[75] This legal anomaly continued to cause problems for believers of all denominations. Although they may appeal to other Soviet laws, or to the ratification by the Presidium of the Supreme Soviet of the USSR of the United Nations Convention on the Struggle against Discrimination in the Realm of Education,[76] they may still none the less be charged with failing to observe the Law on the Education of the People. This has led to some believers being deprived of parental rights (few Orthodox, but a number of Protestants). Furthermore, a strict interpretation of this law would render Christian parents culpable not only for giving their children religious education, but even for failing to give them an atheist education or upbringing. There has been no such charge, so far as is known, but the possibility exists in theory.

A Pastoral Initiative: Father Dimitri Dudko

As we saw in Chapter 3, church sermons are barred from making any contribution to the life of Soviet society, and tend on the whole to be far removed from the concerns of modern life. When, therefore, a Moscow priest began to speak openly and clearly on some of the problems of Soviet life, he at once found people from all walks of life flocking to his church. Father Dimitri Dudko was ordained priest in 1960 after a theological education which was interrupted by a spell of eight and a half years in labour camp.[77] Although the Soviet press has alleged that his sentence was for collaboration with the Germans during the War,[78] Dudko has maintained that this is untrue, that he was sentenced for the possession of manuscript religious verse, that his conviction was annulled, and his sentence shortened, by a special commission of the Presidium of the Supreme Soviet, and that he has a document to this effect.[79] This period of imprisonment, most of which he is said to have devoted to prayer,[80] seems to have been a kind of spiritual foundation for much of his subsequent ministry. From about 1962, Dudko served as priest in the Church of St Nicholas in the Transfiguration Cemetery (*na Preobrazhenke*) in Moscow. Natalya Solzhenitsyn, who knew Father Dimitri from about 1969, has described how Muscovites began coming to him for spiritual counsel:

That was the time of the beginning of religious searching for many people

. . . The return to the Church in those years was not yet a mass one, as it is now, but it was already having a noticeable influence on the general atmosphere of society. People were seeking living words about God, seeking spiritual preceptors. It was not easy to find them . . . There were not good pastors in every church. But all the same, people found Father Dimitri and came to him endlessly. With him you could meet young women with children, elderly men, youths, well-known writers, artists, and perfectly ordinary residents of the surrounding villages . . . Very Russian in spirit, [Father Dimitri] is also very Russian in appearance: thickset with a large head and bright blue eyes. He is affectionately attentive to everybody, he listens and does not say much about himself, but after every encounter with him you are left with the feeling: how deep and joyful is his faith! He is a man of surprising integrity and simplicity, and his preaching finds a direct and accurate path to a person's heart.[81]

By 1972, Father Dimitri's popularity had brought him to the attention of the Soviet authorities, and at the end of September 1972 he was informed that he was to be dismissed from his parish. Father Dimitri took the unusual step of informing his congregation of his impending dismissal in his sermon the next Sunday, and of appealing to them to support him. It was probably this bold step, and the resulting publicity of his plight, which saved him, for he was not in fact dismissed. The sermon was remarkable also for its mention of normally 'taboo' subjects — for example, the church's role in society:

The Church never stands aside . . . From this place, from which I have just greeted you on the day of Christ's Resurrection, people were exhorted to rally round and help those suffering at the front. There are other difficulties, perhaps as great as times of war — pervasive sin, when vice, like rust or vermin, is corrupting our families and morally crippling the rising generation, when moral standards are disintegrating, when drunkenness, hooliganism and murder are increasing . . .
. . . during the war many were calling for help, but today for some reason they are either unwilling or afraid. But the danger today is no less great.

Such a call to the church to be a moral force in society was, as we have seen in Chapter 3, far beyond the limits of what the CRA regards as desirable in sermons. And although the vices such as drunkenness and hooliganism to which Father Dimitri referred are no secret in Soviet society (they were and are the subject of frequent articles in the Soviet press), it was certainly something new for them to be described not as social problems, but as sin. Father Dimitri also stated in this sermon that 'There have been times of lawlessness in our country. Then I was subjected to slander and served a term of 8½ years.' Although the wording clearly places the time of his imprisonment in the Stalin era, the period of 'cult of personality' which had by then been denounced by Khrushchev, the public reference to labour camps was most unusual: in referring to what all his hearers knew of but none ever spoke of, Father Dimtri had broken another taboo. Another remarkable feature of this sermon was this remark:

> Among those who come into the church there are probably some who are sent here on purpose by someone else, people wishing to disturb our church order, who try to interfere in internal church affairs which they have no right to do under existing laws.[82]

Again, the presence of informers among church congregations was an open secret (as we saw from the description of the Minsk church in Chapter 2), but was somthing that was simply never mentioned. What was most striking about Dudko, and what drew people to his sermons, was his willingness to speak in a matter-of-fact way of what everybody knew to be true but none had the boldness to mention.

In December 1973, Father Dimitri began a series of conversations (*besedy*), or question-and-answer sessions, after the Saturday evening service in his church. Announcing his intention to do this, he referred to the need for sowing Christian knowledge among the faithful:

> A lot of people who come to church don't understand the service, the prayers, the Scripture . . . there are still superstitions among the faithful. Our purely Christian ideas are mixed with non-Christian ones . . . Books on religion are neither non-existent or hard to find.

Questions were to be written down and handed in in advance of the service; there was no need for questioners to give their name.[83]

Nothing like this had been known before in the Soviet Union. Never before had a priest stood up and given clear, simple, truthful answers to questions from his congregation about the Christian faith. The effect, on unbelievers as well as believers, was electrifying. People came from all over Moscow, and, in time, from much further afield, to hear him. Anatoli Levitin, who was present, described the congregation:

> The talks began at the end of December 1973 and by the beginning of January 1974 the whole of Moscow was already talking about them. Even people very far from the Church were speaking of them: professors and writers; believers in the transmigration of souls and those who believed in precisely nothing; those attracted by the philosophy of Yoga and those attracted by nothing at all. But above all, young people: dear Russian boys and wonderful Russian girls, ardent Jewish youths with fire in their

eyes and remarkable Jewish girls, impetuous and sharp, Baptists and Zen Buddhists, anthroposophists and Marxists — they all headed for this tiny cemetery church . . . Father Dimitri's listeners were won over by his sincerity, simplicity and enormous conviction; chiefly by his sincerity. Never, nowhere was there a single false note. All his answers to questions were direct, clear and precise, even when the question was put in a somewhat pointed manner.[84]

Father Dimitri's talks consisted mostly of the exposition of basic Christian doctrines. The questions make it obvious that many of his listeners had no clear idea of fundamental Christian beliefs, and that there was nowhere where they could find out what they were. Often Father Dimitri simply read passages out of books inaccessible to his audience. His preaching had a number of recurring themes, chief of which was the Resurrection. He spoke constantly of Christ's suffering and crucifixion, and of the Resurrection which followed, and drew a parallel with Russia, whose present suffering, he firmly believed, would be followed by rebirth and revival: 'A religious spring has begun here. It's still weak, but it will come.' 'If you want to believe in Russia, you've got to stand there next to Christ as He's nailed to the cross. In Russia today that's the only way you can believe.' He also had much to say about atheism and its destructive consequences: 'By undermining faith in God, atheism has also undermined all bases of social life . . . immorality, the collapse of the family, criminality and hooliganism — these are the fruits of atheism.' However, he did not fear the power of atheism: 'I don't think this will go on much longer . . . There are believers everywhere — among scholars, as well as the simple . . . I'm sure I've baptised at least 5,000 adults.'

Much of Father Dimitri's preaching had an utter simplicity which was easy to scorn until one actually tried to do as he said:

In order to follow Christ, one must first of all have a pure heart, without lusts and delusions. What lusts and delusions do we not have today? . . . We must seek the Kingdom of God and his righteousness . . . We should develop the spirit by fasting and prayer.[85]

A foreigner who attended some of Father Dimitri's talks summed up their content as follows:

What did it all mean? Well to me, then an atheist, just this. The immorality of Soviet society, its inhumanity and corruption, its lack of a moral code or credible ideals, means that Christ's teaching comes through to those whom it reaches as a shining contrast. It stresses the value of the individual, of humaneness, forgiveness, gentleness, love . . . As for me, the atheist, Father Dimitri that evening convinced me that the moral code of Christianity was not just something that could be cast aside as superseded; that, in fact, it had survived for two thousand years precisely because it did stress certain qualities essential in personal relations between men. The loss of these qualities is one of the most disturbing features of modern Soviet life.[86]

There was little political content in Father Dimitri's talks, and what there was consisted of reference to politically charged issues — such as the presence of informers in churches, or the existence of labour camps — when they arose naturally. He did not give his own political views, and he did not criticise the Soviet regime. Neither did he criticise the church leadership; indeed, he defended it:

Question: Father Dimitri, why do you set up the Church as an example? Open your eyes and look at today's clergy, even at the Patriarch himself — grovelling before the authorities, cowardly . . .
Answer: . . . You see the inadequacies of today's clergy and point to the Patriarch himself, but are you aware that you're looking at things too superficially? Who has fewer civil rights than the Patriarch? They say he's surrounded by thousands of informers. He so much as sighs and it's heard in every government department. Everything he does against his conscience he does under pressure and, of course, out of weakness, like any man. But you don't want to be compassionate. You sit in the judge's seat and pronounce sentence.[87]

However, everyone present at the talks knew that Father Dimitri could not continue to behave in this unprecedented manner without provoking some kind of response from the Soviet authorities. In fact it came through the Moscow Patriarchate. On Saturday 4 May Father Dimitri announced to his expectant congregation that there would be no talk that evening: 'The Patriarch has forbidden me to preach until I have had talks with him. Christ is Risen!'[88] Two weeks later, on 18 May, on what would have been the day of the tenth question-and-answer session, Father Dimitri took no part in the service, and afterwards gave a statement instead of a sermon. He said that though he had made repeated attempts to have an audience with the Patriarch, the latter had refused, and insisted, through his secretary, that Dudko write a note explaining why and in what way the Patriarch's name had been mentioned, the type of question discussed during the talks, and why Father Dimitri had not obeyed the area dean and the rector of the church when they had asked him to stop the discussions. Dudko gave full explanations of these matters in a note which he read out to the congregation. He said that he had not heeded the requests of the area dean and rector to stop the talks 'because I did not consider it a ban but advice, realising that no one can prohibit sermons'. He added that he had realised that so many people had begun to attend the talks that the church would not be able to hold them all and he alone would not be able to deal with all the questions, and therefore 'I was already thinking of coming to Your Holiness for your blessing on how I was to continue'. Father Dimitri concluded his explanatory note to the Patriarch by pointing out that people must have found some value in his talks for such interest to have been generated, and therefore 'I would ask you, Your Holiness, in the future to bless not only me, but also other priests in the search for living forms of communion between pastor and congregation.'[89]

Dudko informed his congregation that, after submitting this note to the Patriarch, he had been informed on 15 May that he had been placed at the disposal of Metropolitan Serafim of Krutitsy — in other words, that he would be removed from his church and transferred to a parish outside Moscow city.[90] He had then sent a petition to the Patriarch, which he also read out to his congregation of 18 May. The petition stated that he had again made several attempts to see the Patriarch, and had again been refused. He considered this 'a measure designed to paralyse my activity as a priest, since I have violated no canonical law'. In view of this, Dudko continued, 'I consider it necessary to retire from official church work.' He had come to this conclusion because there was 'a measure of reprisal' in the decision to transfer him; and it was 'an obvious intervention in internal church affairs on the part of certain persons who have no right to do so according to existing laws'.[91]

Members of the congregation stood outside the church after the service, waiting to see what would happen. Dudko came out escorted by two young men and was led to a waiting car. Many people assumed that he had been arrested, and a rumour to this effect spread quickly. However, it transpired that the young men were believers who were accompanying him for his own protection.[92]

Two days later, on 20 May, Dudko was banned from priestly office by Metropolitan Serafim for 'ignoring church discipline', until such time as he repented.[93] He wrote to the Metropolitan saying that, if he had violated church discipline, it had been involuntarily: he had thought that his petition to the Patriarch to be retired from priestly service had absolved him of any obligations to the Metropolitan. He continued:

Now, having thought everything over calmly, I see that I was wrong and that I involuntarily permitted a violation of discipline. Expressing my regret regarding this, I express my readiness to appear before Your Eminence at your first summons and I ask you to cover over all my mistakes with archpastoral love. At the same time I declare my readiness to serve Holy Church.[94]

Some time later, Dudko explained how he came to write this apology:

Metropolitan Serafim banned me from ministering in church because of 'violation of church discipline'. He banned me even when I had not served under him for a single day (is it possible?), and he himself, spreading his hands, recognised this — 'I don't have the right . . .'. The ban was in fact until such time as I should repent . . . 'Violation of church discipline', I thought. Although I haven't violated it, I repent. I thought a little more, and if you look into it further, then who of us is worthy to serve at the throne of God? I repented sincerely.[95]

After making his apology, Dudko was transferred to the Church of St Nikita the Martyr in the village of Kabanovo, some 50 miles from Moscow, where he served his first liturgy in September.[96] He and his family continued to live in their Moscow flat. A further two question-and-answer sessions, the tenth and eleventh in the series, were held in a private home at the request of parishioners.[97]

A careful study of the text of the question-and-answer sessions shows that Father Dimitri did not do the things he was glibly accused of: he did not criticise the church leadership (on the contrary, he defended it against other critics); he did not engage in political discussion; he did not attack the Soviet regime; he criticised atheism but expressed sorrow and sympathy for atheists; and he tried above all to preach simple, basic Christian truths. This did not prevent Soviet atheist publications from distorting his talks as follows:

the spiritual pastor used the church pulpit for sermons which were far from religious. The questions prepared beforehand by his stooges were formulated to give Dudko the opportunity, in his replies, of making attacks on the state authorities, of portraying our actual life in a distorted manner, of setting his flock against the 'godless'. He also made attacks on the Moscow Patriarchate.[98]

This is nothing but a gross distortion of the truth. However, despite the fact that he had violated neither state laws, nor in confining himself to basic Christian preaching, church regulations, everyone knew that Father Dimitri was stepping over a line which was invisible but known to all present. No one could have been more aware of this than Father Dimitri himself. One observer noted the strain that the talks imposed upon him:

Why does he do it? I can't understand how he continues. He is quite different from Solzhenitsyn. I have spoken to them both. Solzhenitsyn simply was afraid of nothing and nobody, but this man is afraid all the time. Yet he carries on.[99]

Response from the West: Yevgeni Barabanov

On the night of 24–25 August 1973 KGB officials conducted a seven-hour search of the Moscow flat of a young Orthodox art historian, Yevgeni Barabanov. A number of books, mostly on theology and religious philosophy, were confiscated, together with typewritten texts, personal notebooks and a portable typewriter.[100] On 27 August interrogations with a KGB investigator began. Barabanov was accused of having sent 'anti-Soviet materials' to the West and of having regularly supplied information to the editor of the Paris *Vestnik RSKhD* (*Herald of the Russian Student Christian Movement*). The search, confiscations and interrogations were by no means uncommon occurrences among nonconformist thinkers in the Soviet Union, but Barabanov's reaction was rather out of the ordinary. On 15 September he issued a defiant but carefully reasoned statement in which he admitted that he had sent materials abroad, and that he still considered that he had been right to do so. He pointed out that his action in sending materials abroad involved 'the most elementary, the most essential thing: the freedom to read and write, freedom of thought, the right of self-expression, without which a man loses himself and his own spiritual essence'. These rights were enshrined in the United Nations Declaration of Human Rights, signed along with other governments by the Soviet government. Moreover, Barabanov noted:

> Nor does Soviet legislation forbid those actions of which they are trying to accuse me . . . Appeal to the ideological struggle is nonsensical on a legal basis. It is only effective for those who wish to take part in that struggle. But I never gave any ideological oath and am under no obligation to adhere only to official opinions.

Here Barabanov succinctly illuminates an issue which we have already touched on in Chapter 9, and which has great significance for members of the Russian Orthodox Church, and equally for all whose opinions do not conform to those of the Communist Party of the Soviet Union. This is the conflict, indeed the overlap, between the Soviet state and the Communist Party. Soviet citizens can be, and are, prosecuted for actions which are not against the laws of the state, but which do conflict with the tenets of the minority Communist Party. Barabanov insisted that he was motivated by no ideological interests opposed to those of the CPSU:

> I have nothing to hide. I can speak openly about my actions before my nation and before the world. Let those people take cover who fear the light of publicity and who prosecute the free word. I did send manuscripts and documents to the West, and I did it completely disinterestedly. I repeat: I have nothing to do with some mythical ideological enemies into

whose hands I am supposed to be playing. Up to now the West has offered the only possibility of preserving these documents, saving them from physical destruction or oblivion.

His motivation was entirely different:

I was guided not only by my rights of free spiritual orientation, but also by the demands of Christian duty and conscience, for I am convinced that genuine spiritual values cannot be created in a closed atmosphere where there is disinformation.

Then Barabanov lists some of the materials which he transmitted to the West. They include the human rights journal *A Chronicle of Current Events*; works, unpublished in the USSR, of the great Russian poets Anna Akhmatova, Marina Tsvetayeva, Osip Mandelshtam and Boris Pasternak; materials on 'the history of Russian culture, of the Church, religious philosophy and unofficial theology'; works by the religious philosopher Nikolai Berdyayev and the martyrs Father Pavel Florensky and Lev Karsavin; poems 'commemorating the tragic image of the prisons and camps of our time'; the prison diaries of Eduard Kuznetsov, 'who sacrificed himself for the right of the Jews to emigrate to Israel'; and finally photographs of 'contemporary social activists and writers suffering persecution, people of good will'. This is a most impressive list, including as it does some of the greatest writers of the Soviet period, and fully justifies Barabanov's claim that 'I considered, and still consider, the materials that I sent out as a serious contribution to Russian culture, Russian thought and self-awareness.'

There was no need for Barabanov to have admitted publicly to sending out so much material. To have kept quiet, or to have admitted responsibility for only some of these works, might have seemed a more prudent course to most people. But he was motivated by larger concerns than his own immediate fate:

If I am arrested I shall consider it an act of gross arbitrariness. But the question does not simply concern me, but Russian culture: should it exist regardless of whether or not it is permitted by the official ideology and censorship? Should manuscripts perish if the authorities will not publish them here? . . . To allow this would be to allow an injury not only to Russian, but to world culture. The world would not know the whole truth about our country, all the complexity of her life, her spiritual problems, the tragic nature of her historical experience. Our century would be deprived of some of its meaning and depth if it did not draw this experience into itself.[101]

Barabanov had some well-known supporters for his statement: Alexander

Solzhenitsyn, in whose flat the above statement to the press was made,[102] and the scientist Mikhail Agursky, who quickly issued an appeal to Christian and Jewish organisations abroad to support Barabanov.[103] It instantly achieved a great deal of publicity in the West and resulted in many statements of support for Barabanov and many messages sent directly to him in Moscow. Solzhenitsyn recorded:

> The Western reaction to Barabanov's declaration was one of the many things in those months that exceeded our expectations . . . After the West had remained apathetically silent about the annihilation of whole peoples in our country, about events involving millions, its current reaction to such an insignificant event in the East as the public vilification of a little group of dissidents amazed us . . . the West was in a state of high excitement, had been stirred more deeply than ever before.[104]

Why was there a wave of sympathy and action in the West on Barabanov's behalf when many others in a similar plight had been virtually ignored? Partly it was that, after several years of campaigning by democrats, nationalists, Christians, Jews and others in the USSR, people in the West were finally beginning to realise that his was no flash in the pan but a serious commitment to human rights by some of the best-educated and most gifted minds in the country. The best known of these, Solzhenitsyn and Sakharov, were constantly in the international news during the summer of 1973. However, Barabanov was not simply lucky in his timing: both his boldness in making his statement and the eminent reasonableness of its wording struck a responsive chord not only among Christians, but also among those who cherished Russian culture and who valued freedom of thought. Just over a week after making his statement, Barabanov was able to write a letter of thanks to those in the West who had supported him, including the Mayor of New York, Mr Lindsay; two French academicians, Gabriel Marcel and Pierre Emmanuel; and four universities, those of Paris, Louvain, Geneva and Columbia (New York), which had invited him to give lectures.[105]

A Challenge to the Soviet Leaders: Alexander Solzhenitsyn

For the next few months events involving independently minded members of the Russian Orthodox Church, among others, followed fast upon one another, and Solzhenitsyn was at the centre of them. His *Letter to Soviet Leaders*, dated 5 September 1973, but not published until the following year, set forth a number of proposals for the development of the Russian nation and Soviet society which generated a good deal of controversy in Soviet nonconformist circles. As regards the role the Russian Orthodox

Church was to play, Solzhenitsyn did not make this entirely clear, though he evidently valued its moral authority. In his view, some kind of authoritarian system was desirable for his country, and he approved of the authoritarian order of the first seven centuries of Russian Orthodoxy — before it was 'battered by Patriarch Nikon and bureaucratised by Peter the Great' — because it 'possessed a strong moral foundation, embryonic and rudimentary though it was — not the ideology of universal violence, but Christian Orthodoxy'.[106] Some of Solzhenitsyn's critics concluded from this remark that he wanted to replace Marxist ideology with an authoritarian Orthodox ideology; Sakharov and the writer Lev Kopelev both voiced this apprehension.[107] In fact, however, Solzhenitsyn did not express such a wish, and a few pages later he implicitly contradicts it:

> [the Soviet leaders should] allow competition on an equal and honourable basis between all ideological and moral currents, in particular between *all religions* . . . (I myself see Christianity today as the only living spiritual force capable of undertaking the spiritual healing of Russia. But I request and propose no special privilege for it, simply that it should be treated fairly and not suppressed.)[108]

This was a far cry from the leading role which, as we shall see, some of the more right-wing Russian nationalists were to envisage for the Russian Orthodox Church. The *Letter to Soviet Leaders*, while it certainly embodied many of the patriotic ideals and proposals advocated by the nationalists was, in the context of Russian nationalist opinion in the Soviet Union, closest to the liberal nationalism and gradualist approach typified by Osipov. Mikhail Agursky pointed this out succinctly:

> It appears quite obvious that the sole realistic alternative for those who would truly desire to revive Russian life in its fundamental form would be the acceptance (in its basic form, to be sure) of the humanistic programme proposed by Solzhenitsyn in his *Letter to Soviet Leaders*. Unfortunately, Western public opinion views this programme as something of an extreme form of Russian nationalism. It does not understand that this is the only humanistic alternative in Russia to racism and neo-Nazism.[109]

For democrats such as Sakharov, however, the acceptance of some kind of authoritarian system of government was the chief stumbling-block. Solzhenitsyn believed that an authoritarian form of government, stripped of its ideological monopoly, was necessary at least as a transitional stage, since to advance more quickly would be more abrupt a change than the system could safely sustain. The issue of authoritarianism, and of Russia's ability or inability to embrace democracy, continued to be the chief bone of contention between the democrats and even the moderate nationalists.

At the beginning of 1974, after the publication of *The Gulag Archipelago*, Solzhenitsyn was subjected to an intense campaign of vilification in the Soviet press, and Soviet citizens were urged in every way to denounce him. But he was not entirely without support: 'three fearless young men — Boris Mikhailov, Vadim Borisov, Yevgeni Barabanov (each of whom has small children) — have come to my defence in public, armed only with the knowledge that they are right'.[110] These three, who are all Orthodox Christians, issued statements in support of Solzhenitsyn. Barabanov's statement said that he saw no reason to condemn a man for revealing an important historical truth:

> Solzhenitsyn is not calling for revenge. His book, the book of a Christian, leads us to a true understanding and to final forgiveness. Upon our shoulders lies the burden of historical responsibility. We can no longer avoid it and wait: history may not grant us another similar occasion.[111]

Solzhenitsyn: Criticism and Admiration within the Church

On 12 February 1974, Solzhenitsyn was forcibly exiled from his native land. Criticism and vilification of him in the Soviet press continued unabated, and one of the contributors to it was Metropolitan Serafim of Krutitsy and Kolomna. *Sovetskaya Rossiya* quoted him as saying that he regarded the decision to expel Solzhenitsyn as the 'only correct measure' for dealing with him, and he added: 'Solzhenitsyn is sadly well known for his actions in support of circles hostile to our homeland and our people.'[112] In a long letter to *The Times* of London, Metropolitan Serafim repeated the accusation that Solzhenitsyn had acted against the interests of his country and his people, and concluded: 'In the eyes of believers of the Russian Orthodox Church he has long forfeited the right to call himself a Christian.'[113] This provoked leading churchmen into writing responses which vigorously defended Solzhenitsyn and rejected all Metropolitan Serafim's assertions.[114] Most significant was a letter from Metropolitan Antoni of Sourozh (London), then Patriarchal Exarch in Western Europe. He stated unequivocally that in his own name and that of his clergy and believers he wished 'to disown the statements about Solzhenitsyn in the letter of Metropolitan Serafim of Krutitsy and Kolomna'. He went on:

> Far from being a traitor to his country, Solzhenitsyn shows a deep and committed love 'unto death' for Russia in his fearless struggle for human dignity, truth and freedom . . . he believes that a nation which cannot openly face its recent past, cannot solve its problems in the present and the future.[115]

Archbishop Vasili of Brussels also spoke out publicly in Solzhenitsyn's defence, and declared that he was in complete disagreement with Metropolitan Serafim's remarks.[116] He sent a telegram to Patriarch Pimen, dated 17 February 1974, which moved the Patriarch to respond as follows on 11 March:

> In his statement on the actions of Alexander Solzhenitsyn, His Eminence Metropolitan Serafim correctly expressed the opinion of his fellow citizens, which every person has the right to do. His Grace Archbishop Vasili, who has spent the greater part of his life in emigration, cannot on this issue be entirely impartial towards what is happening in his Soviet homeland.[117]

This carefully worded resolution avoids committing the Holy Synod or the church as a whole to support of Metropolitan Serafim's statements. It follows the main theme of the obviously centrally organised campaign against Solzhenitsyn by concentrating on his alleged betrayal of his united countrymen.

The Metropolitan's statement drew strong criticism from members of his church within the Soviet Union. Father Gleb Yakunin addressed him a brief open letter, asking: 'Are you not afraid, Your Eminence, dreadfully afraid? And don't you feel a twinge of conscience? Our martyrs have perished in the Gulag camps. Don't you know about this?'[118] This was a reference to the fact that, in uncovering the history of the Soviet labour camps and their inmates, Solzhenitsyn had also uncovered an important part of the history of the Russian Orthodox Church during the Soviet period. The concern for the memory of Orthodox martyrs was to be an important preoccupation of some independently minded Orthodox in following years. Another strong reproach was addressed to the Metropolitan by the literary critic Yevgeni Ternovsky and the artist Eduard Shteinberg: they told him that Orthodox Christians had read his words 'not only with bewilderment, but also with great sorrow', and asked: 'will not any Christian, reading your hard-hearted words, feel that Christ has abandoned you, since you have abandoned him?'[119] These are harsh words; but this was indeed an occasion when a church hierarch seems to have been over-eager to do the bidding of the Soviet authorities. There was no need for the church to say anything at all about Solzhenitsyn's expulsion, and it is probable that a simple refusal to make a statement, or even skilful delaying tactics to lessen its impact, would not have had unbearable consequences for the Metropolitan. Possibly his nerve had already been weakened by his responsibility as diocesan bishop for Father Dimitri Dudko, whose question-and-answer sessions were still in progress. It is conceivable that the authorities approached him, rather than another hierarch, to make a statement for this very reason, since he had no more connection with Solzhenitsyn than any other bishop.

An uncompromising and strongly worded statement on the expulsion of Solzhenitsyn was issued by a young Orthodox layman, Lev Regelson, to the Soviet government. He accused the present leadership of being as guilty as their predecessors of the death of millions in the Gulag Archipelago, of the fratricide of millions of their countrymen, and of a whole catalogue of crimes in every field of Soviet life. This sweeping condemnation ended with an appeal:

> Know that your souls, whatever grave sins they may be burdened with, are precious to God, more precious than all the treasures in the world . . . Take Russia away from Cain and give her to God, for Abel's blood cries out of the earth.

The most surprising statement on Solzhenitsyn, and one which shocked many members of the Russian Orthodox Church, was that given by the greatly respected Moscow priest, Archpriest Vsevolod Shpiller, in an interview with a correspondent of the Novosti Press Agency only a few days after Solzhenitsyn's expulsion. The form of his statement was perhaps more surprising than its content. Shpiller's basic contention was that Solzhenitsyn was not a 'Christian writer', as had been said in the West. He did *not* say that Solzhenitsyn was not a Christian, but he did say: 'I hold to be deeply mistaken that view of him which considers him a "religious writer", and moreover one who expresses the view, the thoughts and feelings, of us Orthodox people here.' Shpiller characterised Solzhenitsyn as a writer who 'seeks truth everywhere . . . is engrossed by striving towards it', but who has not understood that 'For us Christians, truth and good, like falsehood and evil, are greater and deeper than simply ethical or moral ideas and concepts'. In the Christian understanding, these qualities were found 'in the spiritual (*dukhovny*) depths of the human soul', and 'it was not given to Solzhenitsyn to plumb these depths'. This is a surprising statement to make of the author of *Cancer Ward* and *The First Circle*. So is Shpiller's further assertion that Solzhenitsyn's works 'strike [one] by the absence of love', and that in its place there is 'malice and irritation'. That is almost the opposite of Barabanov's view of *The Gulag Archipelago*, quoted above.

Shpiller, however, was speaking not of Solzhenitsyn's portrayal of the human soul, but of his understanding of the church, and the way in which the church had shaped his views. He introduced the concept of 'churchliness' (*tserkovnost*) into his statement. In his view, Solzhenitsyn's 'churchliness' was deficient:

> It was not given to Solzhenitsyn, whose one-sided glance slipped over the surface of church life, to see in it that which perhaps really makes or could make our Russian Orthodox Church the salt without which contemporary Christianity will become savourless.

Christian churches all over the world, according to Shpiller, were in a state of crisis, but this was not a 'crisis of faith' but a 'crisis of understanding of the Church', the chief aspect of which was: 'how should one understand that "the Church is *not* of this world but is *in* this world"?' He pointed out that in his 'Lenten Letter' to the Patriarch two years previously, Solzhenitsyn had ignored the otherworldly nature of the church and presented its 'essentially sacramental nature' as something of second- or third-rate importance, while 'It is supposed that first-rate importance belongs to activism, barely distinguished from the activism of ordinary organisations which belong entirely to this world.' Shpiller continued: 'One's position on *this* issue is correctly considered to be one of the criteria, a standard, of churchliness and non-churchliness.' Shpiller rejected as 'cruel and unjust' the suggestion that the Russian Orthodox Church had retreated from activism into sacramental life for the sake of self-preservation, and said that, on the contrary, it had been seeking over the decades for that feature which would distinguish 'the true and just safe-guarding of the Church from its corrupting self-preservation'. This seeking formed part of 'the spiritual experience of our Church', but 'Solzhenitsyn did not approach it even from afar. He did not know how to and he did not want to.' Solzhenitsyn, 'together with many who have merely drawn near to the Church', had 'remained alien to it', making demands upon it rather than entering into it.[121]

The importance of the concept of 'churchliness' is great, not only in this controversy, but in the whole area of the return of many Russian intellectuals to the church. Critical, independent thinkers often clashed with traditional views. To a pious, traditional Orthodox believer, 'churchliness' means being completely imbued with the teachings, worship, practice and traditions of the church, so that all one's thoughts and actions result from them rather than from one's own reflection or rationalisation. It is not enough simply to take some Christian concepts, or some Orthodox traditions, and weave them into one's own thinking: to be truly 'churchly', a member of the church in the fullest sense, one has to give oneself over entirely to the church's collective wisdom. The concept of *sobornost*, or 'conciliarity', is relevant here: an Orthodox Christian does not think, speak or act as an individual, but as a member of the church, a church which includes the Holy Fathers, the saints, and the great teachers and leaders of the past as well as the present, all of whose views, arrived at through prayer and fasting by the grace of the Holy Spirit, form his views. Traditional Orthodoxy does not demand that the gifts and talents of the individual be suppressed, but that they may be exercised only after he has undergone the kenotic experience of denying self and surrendering himself to the collective mind of the church. Among those baptised into the Russian Orthodox Church in recent years are some who do not understand, or have not yet understood, or have rejected this concept of 'churchliness', and this inevitably leads to tension. There are many who have adopted some of the values, even forms, of Orthodoxy and transposed them into their own scheme of things. To a traditional Orthodox believer, this is like skimming off the cream to decorate one's own confections, and ignoring the wholesome, health-giving milk.

This, then, was what Shpiller meant by saying that Solzhenitsyn was not a Christian writer, and his viewpoint seems understandable if we recall that, in the 'Lenten Letter' to the Patriarch and the *Letter to Soviet Leaders*, Solzhenitsyn had viewed the church primarily as a moral force, one of the potential forces for good which would (or would not) shape the future of Russia. However, the manner in which Shpiller expressed his viewpoint, and its timing, aroused serious misgivings as to his motivation. He could have voiced his views on the 'churchliness' of Solzhenitsyn (and other new members of the church) at any time, and through a more 'churchly' medium than the Soviet press agency. Moreover his remarks were misdirected: Solzhenitsyn had never claimed to be a religious or a Christian writer, and those in the West who had made the claim on his behalf could hardly be expected to understand Shpiller's correct but rather esoteric exposition of the nature of Orthodox churchliness. Shpiller must have realised that, in giving this interview only days after Solzhenitsyn's deportation, he would be seen as allying himself with those uttering all manner of vilification against the writer: and so he was. His interview was published in a grossly distorted form in an English-language book aimed at destroying Solzhenitsyn's credibility,[122] and other members of the Russian Orthodox Church criticised him bitterly.

The criticisms did not appear for some time because Shpiller's interview was not published within the USSR until April, and then only in the small-circulation duplicated *Information Bulletin* of the DECR. On 6 May eleven believers, including Mikhail Agursky and Vladimir Osipov, wrote a bitter statement, accusing Shpiller of secret machinations against Solzhenitsyn since 1972, of 'elaborate lies and crude hypocrisy', and of much besides.[123] On 7 May Agursky alone wrote Shpiller an open letter which also contained bitter epithets, but in which he promised to offer his hand and 'promote the restoration of your good name', if Shpiller would repent publicly.[124] In August came an open letter from a member of the Georgian Orthodox Church, Merab Kostava, staunchly defending Solzhenitsyn and insultingly addressing 'Citizen' (not 'Father') Shpiller.[125] Mikhail Agursky, meanwhile, had had second thoughts, and in August wrote a letter in which he admitted that he had been over-hasty in applying terms to Shpiller which should not be used between believers, and apologised unreservedly for them, although he remained convinced that the basic criticisms were correct, and that Shpiller's interview had been a 'tragic mistake'. However, he had realised upon reflection that another reason for Father V. Shpiller's mistake is the conflict between two types of faith which have co-existed in Orthodoxy for a long time. Solzhenitsyn is a bearer of one type of faith, the sacrificial type, actively involving itself in life, but Father V. Shpiller is a bearer of the other type of faith, purely sacramental, summoning to a retreat from surrounding life. Therefore his speech against Solzhenitsyn in ordinary circumstances, when it could not have been used for political ends, could have been justified (although I personally consider myself as belonging to the same type of faith as Solzhenitsyn).[126]

Here Agursky (a recent convert to Orthodoxy) throws light on the views of those who were then coming to the church, and who were to be more in evidence in years to come. What the traditionally minded Orthodox saw as 'churchliness', they were inclined to view as 'purely sacramental' and 'a retreat from life'. (Whereas the 'churchly' Orthodox would argue that, like the great Russian monks of the past, one needs to retreat from life in order to equip oneself to face it later.) But Agursky, like many newcomers to the church, clearly regarded involvement in life as 'sacrificial', and as a different, but equally valid, form of Orthodoxy.

Without wishing to impose artificial divisions upon the natural flow of events, it is possible to regard 1974, and above all the expulsion of Solzhenitsyn, as an important watershed for independently minded Soviet citizens, including members of the Russian Orthodox Church. By 1974, those who had by now been working for many years for freedom of thought and freedom of expression in the USSR had realised that the collective leadership under Brezhnev was not going to accede to their demands for reform. They had realised that support from the West was not going to be as swift or as strong as they had hoped at first. And the banishment of Solzhenitsyn had shown that, however much fame an individual might have in the West, even to the extent of being awarded a Nobel Prize, he would none the less not be allowed to remain in peace to put his ideas into practice in his native land. As regards the Russian Orthodox Church, there was a growing awareness among the independent thinkers that they need not expect much help from the West and would have to look more to their own resources. This did not happen overnight, nor did it happen to the same extent among the various groupings in the church, but there was a small but perceptible shift in that direction. The courses adopted by the different groupings became slightly more divergent: there was more specialisation in different approaches to the church's problems. Special study groups for young people grew in size and numbers. The chief events before 1974 — the appeal of Eshliman and Yakunin, the articles of Levitin, the letters to the 1971 Local Council, Solzhenitsyn's 'Lenten Letter' and the ensuing debate, Shafarevich's report — had all centred on the role of the Moscow

Patriarchate and the possibilities for changing it. But it became clear that, for the foreseeable future, the Moscow Patriarchate was not going to change, and exhortations addressed to it dwindled with the passing years. Some of the later events during this period — the founding of *Veche* in 1971, Father Dimitri Dudko's question-and-answer sessions in 1973–4, Barabanov's transmission of materials abroad up to 1973 — heralded the kind of activity which was to develop in the late 1970s, activity which was not greatly concerned with the Moscow Patriarchate because the latter was thought to be largely irrelevant to the task of forging a viable role for Orthodox Christianity in Soviet society.

Excursus: Orthodox Involvement in Non-church Dissent

Beyond the attempts to bring about a greater measure of freedom for Orthodox Christians, the dissent movement in the USSR in the 1960s and 1970s was widespread and varied. There were Solzhenitsyn and others within the literary establishment; many artists kicking against the restraints of socialist realism; some neo-Marxists; the Jewish emigration movement; the Democratic Movement, with the renowned Academician Andrei Sakharov at its head; and potentially most explosive of all, the nationalist movements in Ukraine, the Baltic countries and elsewhere, and not least in Russia itself. A number of Orthodox who played little or no part in purely church-oriented dissent were at the forefront of those defending the civil rights of their fellow-citizens. Generally speaking, these were often people converted to Orthodoxy in the course of their work for human rights. However, there were also some existing members of the church who threw themselves into the dissent movement working for greater individual liberty in Soviet society as a whole. Without casting doubt on their commitment to individual liberty and human rights, it is likely that they were also influenced by the consideration that the church (and other religious groups) would enjoy a greater measure of freedom in a freer society. It was, partly, a new approach to an old problem, a recognition that freedom is indivisible.

It was on the practical rather than the philosophical level that human rights activists and church dissenters, both Orthodox and non-Orthodox, became embroiled in one another's concerns. People who could argue for hours without agreement over the future of Soviet society would happily co-operate in circulating one another's *samizdat* articles, hiding them from house-searches by the KGB and the militia, arranging meetings with overseas journalists and other foreign visitors, and supporting the families of those who were arrested. A continuing feature of the dissent movement has been the issuing of *samizdat* statements of support for dissenters arrested, harassed, seriously ill in prison or otherwise afflicted, and Orthodox dissenters were as prominent as any other group in the long lists of signatures, whether or not the signers agreed with the views of the person concerned. There has been, and still is, a strong sense of fraternity between human rights activists and some church members, a sense that they are battling selflessly for justice in various spheres, and an awareness that the same forbidding penalties of prison, labour camps and forcible confinement to psychiatric hospitals looms over them all.

Anatoli Levitin was the first Orthodox Christian to identify himself wholeheartedly with the Democratic Movement, and in 1969 was one of the founders of the Action Group (*Initsiativnaya gruppa*) for the Defence of Human Rights. His pioneering role was recognised by 32 leading dissenters who signed a statement of protest when he was arrested in 1969:

> In the post-Stalin years he was the first person active in the religious sphere in our country to . . . raise his voice in defence of civil rights and of those people who have become victims in the struggle for these rights.[127]

Something of the atmosphere of those years at the end of the 1960s and beginning of the 1970s is conveyed in a description of the gatherings which took place in Anatoli Levitin's home:

> an oil stove . . . fills the seven-metre square room with a stifling and all-pervasive smell . . . What strikes you most of all in his home is the number of young people . . . the potatoes . . . were put on the stove and boiled with an onion for a long time. This was the usual food in Anatoli Emmanuilovich's house . . . lengthy arguments had begun long before the tea was brought. Anatoli Emmanuilovich's was the only place in Moscow where theoretical conversations about every subject under the sun were held: about the situation of the Church, about the history and the fate of Russia, about the Democratic Movement. You could talk and argue about whatever you liked, thanks to the religious and political tolerance of the host, and thanks to his colossal erudition. 'A corner of old Russia' — he liked to say of his flat . . . Often atheists came to him, and a long argument would begin as to whether God exists or not.

After his release from prison in 1970 Levitin held a celebration:

> The whole of Moscow came . . . There was a very warm, free and easy atmosphere. Father Gleb Yakunin said a prayer, at which everyone present stood in silence, even the non-believers. We sang *Mnogaya leta* [*Many Years*]. Tony Astrakhan [*Washington Post* correspondent] gave a short toast to Anatoli Emmanuilovich and the Democratic Movement. We dispersed to our homes late in the evening, greeting the KGB agents standing at the doorway with friendly laughter.[128]

In 1968 a priest from Pskov, Father Sergi Zheludkov, wrote to a leading human rights activist, Pavel Litvinov, to offer him unstinting support.[129] He also wrote to ecclesiastical leaders abroad, including Professor Hromadka in Prague, the president of the Christian Peace Conference, to ask them to concern themselves on behalf of the imprisoned Anatoli Marchenko and other dissenters in difficulties.[130] In 1973 Zheludkov was one of eleven Soviet intellectuals who announced their wish to form a group affiliated to Amnesty International, knowing that the organisation's members work only on behalf of prisoners in countries other than their own.[131] This identification with non-religious activists was at least partly a consequence of Zheludkov's theological views, which included the concept of a church composed of 'people of good will' who identified themselves with the church by their behaviour without necessarily having any kind of religious experience. In his letter to Litvinov, Zheludkov expressed his idea thus: 'Today in Russia many call themselves atheists only because of a short-coming in their education.'[132] This radical view caused controversy in Orthodox circles, as we shall see in the following chapter.

Other believers who spoke out on human rights issues included Lev Regelson, later well known for his involvement in church affairs, whose first public protests were in defence of the parapsychologist Eduard Naumov, who was imprisoned and otherwise repressed.[133] In 1977 he wrote a protest against the practice of dismissing dissenters from their jobs and making it impossible for them to obtain further employment.[134] The same year, he and Zheludkov joined other Soviet dissenters in signing a statement supporting the Charter 77 movement in Czechoslovakia.[135] A Ukrainian priest, Father Vasyl Romanyuk, was sentenced to a long term of imprison-ment for signing a statement in support of a leading nationalist activist, Valentyn Moroz.[136] Ironically, Moroz was one of five Soviet political and religious prisoners sent to the USA in 1979 in exchange for two Soviet spies; he was at liberty while Father Romanyuk continued to serve out his sentence. In labour camp Romanyuk met the leading Jewish dissenter, Eduard Kuznetsov, and supported him in difficulty by writing a glowing testimonial to his character.[137]

It is not always clear whether involvement in human rights activity by a particular individual precedes or follows conversion to Christianity. Some people who have worked for human rights for many years have later acknowledged themselves to be Orthodox Christians — for example, Tatyana Khodorovich, a linguist and longstanding dissenter. Among many other activities, she campaigned insistently for the release of a psychiatric hospital detainee, Leonid Plyushch, who was an avowed neo-Marxist.[138] The historian Mikhail Bernshtam, interned in a psychiatric hospital for a year after he had written a book on Soviet history and allegedly formed an anti-Soviet group among his students, became active in the human rights movement after his release.[139] Sergei Soldatov, a Russian living in Estonia, became secretary and ideologue of the Democratic Movement of Estonia.[140] The mathematician Tatyana Velikanova, a tireless helper of the afflicted, was a member of the Moscow group set up to monitor the implementation of the Helsinki Agreements, and was involved in the production of the chief human rights *samizdat* publication, the *Chronicle of Current Events*, until her arrest in 1979.

Other longstanding dissenters apparently embraced Orthodoxy after committing themselves to fight for human rights. While faith· was a motivating force for Christians such as Anatoli Levitin and Zheludkov, it seems that for these people faith was the result of their general quest for individual freedom. Alexander Ginzburg, one of the most respected people in the human rights movement, was active from the end of the 1950s, and was imprisoned three times. Whilst in labour camp he became an Orthodox Christian, though he has not been greatly involved in church matters. The same could be said of a number of other converts to the Orthodox faith, who, generally speaking, regard the church leadership as an ally of the Soviet government in repressing dissent. Ginzburg was a member of the Moscow Helsinki Monitoring Group, where he specialised in helping oppressed Baptists, Pentecostals and Adventists, whose courage and depth of faith deeply impressed him. At one of Ginzburg's trials, the so-called 'Trial of the Four' in 1968, two of his three co-defendants, Yuri Galanskov and Vera Lashkova, either were or later became Orthodox believers. Lashkova was one of many young people who were greatly influenced by Anatoli Levitin, who was responsible for bringing many young people to the Christian faith and helping them to grow in it.

Two members of Academician Sakharov's Committee for Human Rights, Andrei Tverdokhlebov and Igor Shafarevich, also became Orthodox Christians at some point during the course of their human rights activity. Tverdokhlebov was also the secretary of the Moscow group of Amnesty International. Lev Lukyanenko, a Ukrainian lawyer sentenced to 15 years' imprisonment (commuted from the death sentence) for participating in a neo-Marxist discussion group, became a Christian while in labour camp. On his release, he soon became active in the Ukrainian Helsinki Monitoring Group, and also complained to the Soviet authorities that the town where he was sent to live, Chernigov, had only one Orthodox church, insufficient for the number of people who wished to worship.[141] He was arrested again in 1978 and sentenced to a further 15 years, imprisonment.

Some Orthodox Christians chose to express independent views through art rather than through overt dissent or church-related activity. Pyotr Starchik composed songs and sang them to friends who visited his flat. He was forcibly committed to psychiatric hospital because some of them were judged to be 'anti-Soviet' in character.[142] The painter Yuri Titov produced a number of striking paintings on Christian themes, obviously influenced by traditional iconography, in the 1960s and early 1970s. In 1972 he and his wife were permitted to emigrate to France, but only after both had been forcibly confined to a psychiatric hospital for two or three weeks.[143] Another artist, Yuri Ivanov, spent 16 years in prison (1955–71), where he drew sketches of his fellow-prisoners, some of which have reached the West. After his release he continued to be under surveillance, and on one occasion was detained while visiting the Zagorsk monastery. He was forcibly committed to a Leningrad psychiatric hospital for 16 months during 1973 and 1974.[144] The biologist Abramkin was arrested in 1979 for his participation in the nonconformist *samizdat* journal *Poiski (Quests)*.[145]

The Orthodox Church throughout its history, in Russia and elsewhere, has not been noted for involvement in social or political reform, and those of its members identified with dissent in the Soviet Union are very much pioneers. There is little or no sign of their example spreading to the Orthodox Church at large, just as there is no sign of the general dissent movement spreading to the mass of the Soviet population. Throughout the whole 20 years or so of Soviet dissent, most of the activity has been carried on by a quite small number of people, most of them intellectuals. However, as their number has been regularly diminished by arrests and emigration, so it has continued to be replenished by new, hitherto silent, dissenters. This is true of the Orthodox dissenters as well as of the rest. Lack of overt support for the dissenters does not necessarily imply disapproval of their activities. On the other hand, it is known that some Orthodox do not believe open dissent to be the correct path for the church to follow. Some, including the church leadership, are afraid of antagonising the state to such an extent that they lose even such limited freedom as they presently have. Others, motivated more by spiritual than pragmatic considerations, believe that it is wrong for the church to agitate about rights; they think that the church should be prepared to adopt a servant role, accepting whatever humiliations come to it, and trust God for the grace to function in whatever historical circumstances it may find itself. Both support and criticism of dissenters continue to be expressed in intellectual circles within the church. However, it is difficult to say precisely how church members at large regard them. It is probable that many admire their bravery and commitment, but lack the conviction, or the courage, to follow their example.

The encounter between the Orthodox dissenters and other human rights activists has been a fruitful one. It has demonstrated both to Soviet nonconformists, and to the world at large, that, however conservative and restricted their church may be, some of its boldest spirits are not content to see the status quo in either church or society remain unchallenged. They have shown that their faith is not bounded by the four walls of a church building, but overflows into their whole lives and motivates their concern for their fellow-men.

11 THE GROWTH OF ORTHODOX DISSENT: 1974−6

Shortly after Solzhenitsyn's expulsion from the Soviet Union came the publication of an important book edited by him and containing articles by himself and six other Russian Orthodox writers: Mikhail Agursky, Yevgeni Barabanov, Vadim Borisov, Igor Shafarevich, the pseudonymóus F. Korsakov and the anonymous A.B. *Iz-pod glyb* (From Under the Rubble)[1] assessed the future of the countries which form the Soviet Union with an eye unclouded by Marxist−Leninist dogma — no small achievement for writers who had lived all their adult lives under the Soviet regime and educational system — and which looked to the Russian Orthodox tradition and Russian patriotic values of the past to provide a guide to the future. As Max Hayward pointed out in his introduction to the English translation of the book, the seven authors were consciously associating themselves with the authors of *Vekhi* (*Landmarks*) published in 1909, and its sequel *Iz glubiny* (*De Profundis*) published in 1918; many of the authors of these works had had Marxist backgrounds, but had rejected them in favour of a return to the traditional spiritual values, and in most cases had embraced the Russian Orthodox Church. The authors of *Iz-pod glyb* had also subjected Marxism to a searching scrutiny, found it wanting, and had instead found values which they believed to be satisfying, both for themselves and for the future of their country, elsewhere, and chiefly in Orthodoxy. They had done this after a void of 60 years during which no such intellectual or spiritual enquiry had been possible.

The seven authors had come by different paths to the belief that Christianity held the clue to the future of Russia. The second main theme which united them was a deep patriotism which avoided narrow nationalism. These seven authors, different though they were in their personalities and backgrounds, could perhaps best be described as belonging to the moderate wing of the nationalists with which Solzhenitsyn had already been identified. Although some of them (Shafarevich and Agursky, and to a lesser extent Barabanov and Borisov) had given support to the Democratic Movement at different times, they had mostly shifted away from any belief they may once have had that democracy, at any rate in its Western, parliamentary form, held the clue to the future. On the other hand, they did not place a supreme and exclusive value on nationalist qualities. Though convinced that the future of their country must be developed through capacities and values which Russians could find and nurture within their own history and culture, they did not reject intercourse with and learning from the West, as did more extreme nationalists. National repentance for past wrongs formed an important part of their thinking, especially Solzhenitsyn's, and this was an important element of Slavophil thought. (However, Solzhenitsyn bitterly castigated what he believed to be the false repentance of V. Gorsky and others, whose rejection of messianism he regarded simply as hatred of Russia, based upon a distorted version of Russian history.) However, although the authors of *Iz-pod glyb* regarded traditional Russian values as important, even crucial, the book as a whole looked firmly towards the future, not the past. The seven writers were rooted to the Russian past, specifically its Christian past, but were not shackled by it. Their orientation was not 'anti-Soviet' in that they did not attack the Soviet regime: they were far more inclined to be self-critical and to accuse themselves and their compatriots of the moral guilt of failing to stand up to the excesses of the regime. Indeed, in their discussion of the future of their country, they paid little or no attention to the Soviet state. Ironically, by following a line of thought totally divorced from Marxist doctrine, they had come to the implicit assumption that the state would wither away.

Internal Critics of the Church

One of the eleven essays in *Iz-pod glyb* was devoted exclusively to a discussion of the Russian Orthodox Church; this was 'The Schism Between the Church and the World' by Yevgeni Barabanov. The main thesis of this essay was that the church had too readily accepted its subordinate relationship to the state, and had forgotten, or chosen to forget, its more fundamental relationship to the world. The hierarchy had accepted the limited degree of freedom offered to it, and had abandoned its responsibility for the Christianisation of Russia. The church made no response to the 'remarkable, deeply moral and indispensable summons' issued by Eshliman and Yakunin, Archbishop Yermogen, Anatoli Levitin, Boris Talantov and Solzhenitsyn in his 'Lenten Letter' — and, Barabanov wrote, everyone knew that the hierarchy had no intention of doing anything of the kind. In part, this situation resulted from the close union of church and state in the past, the 'symphony' existing between church and state since the time of the Emperor Constantine, which meant that the church was identified with the empire, and this left it unprepared to form a relationship with a new, hostile, atheistic state. This, however, was only an explanation for the position in which the church found itself, not a justification for it. There was nothing surprising in the fact that the state tried to limit the life of the church, since, according to its governing ideology, religion and the church were doomed to extinction. 'What is surprising,' wrote Barabanov,

> . . . is that this particular ideological position should begin to sap our own
> ecclesiastical consciousness. It goes without saying that we do not

profess the necessity for us ourselves to die off, but more often than not we do regard the present state of affairs as something natural and normal.[2]

For example, it was said that the restrictions on church life 'correspond to the secret desires of many ecclesiastics' who believed that the liturgy was not only central to Christianity but 'in itself *is* Christianity, and that the Christian needs nothing besides'. State pressure to prevent the church involving itself in social activity combined with this mentality to produce 'a certain weird and wonderful ecclesiology', which led to church leaders saying: ' "You are right to prohibit these things . . . We have not yet learned how to pray — how could we get involved in kindergartens. The Church is for prayer, and not for worldly cares.' " Barabanov noted that 'In an ecclesiology such as this there is of course no room for the problems of the Christianisation of Russia.'[3]

Barabanov's analysis of the condition of his church was important because he was a person who, from inside the church, was prepared to look dispassionately at some of the reasons frequently advanced to explain its problems, and to find them wanting. He understood the church's historical position, and he understood the centrality of the liturgy in Orthodox life, but he did not think that they were a sufficient explanation for the problems of the Russian Orthodox Church. Looking deeper, he suggested that

> The Russian Orthodox Church is displaying with peculiar vividness just a few of the symptoms of that universal malady which has today affected Christianity, with varying degrees of severity, all over the world. There-fore many of our problems need to be examined in a wider perspective, namely, that of the general crisis of the consciousness of the Church in the secular world. There exists not only an opposition between the Church and the State, the Church and a totalitarian system, but also a more fundamental opposition, that between the Church and the world.[4]

The church had failed to recognise and cope with this more fundamental opposition: instead of acknowledging its responsibility to transform the world and to assist the creation of the Kingdom of God within the world, it had retreated, and delimited its God-given task to being no more than that of ensuring individual salvation. After His Transfiguration, which is such a central part of Orthodox liturgy and worship, Christ came down into the world again, to heal the sick, to suffer and to die. The church had forsaken this responsibility for the world, and consequently, 'The world, of course, has abandoned the Church, since the traditional groove reserved for creativity turned out to be too restricted for man.' It was now the world, not the church, which was creating a new civilisation, and the church was left 'dragging along behind'.[5] The church had lost the initiative.

It is evident that a better future for Russia is inseparable from Christianity. And if Russia is to have a renaissance, it can only be accomplished on a religious foundation. But will the Church have enough strength to start this renaissance?

The answer to this question was self-evident. Barabanov refused to accept the view that it was a question of 'only a crisis of church government': in fact, 'we are experiencing something much bigger — a crisis in church consciousness itself'.[6] Somehow the church must find the means to 'counter the godless humanism which is destroying mankind'. 'We are too passive in our attitude to the world.' A radical solution was needed, leading 'not to a reformation but to a transformation of Christian consciousness and life'.[7]

What was refreshing about this was the refusal to narrow the focus of the church's vision, to blame all its ills upon the suppression by the Soviet state. Solzhenitsyn admitted that the Russian nation had made mistakes and needed to repent, and Barabanov similarly admitted that the Russian Orthodox Church needed to repent of past errors and failures and find a new way in the future. It was not sufficient for the church simply to *be*, waiting for the world to come to it: it had a duty to go to the world, bringing it the Gospel, transforming it.

Barabanov's essay bore some echoes from an earlier *samizdat* article by Mikhail Meerson-Aksyonov, 'The People of God and the Pastors'.[8] Meerson-Aksyonov was also a church member, an 'insider' who was not prepared to lay all the blame for the church's predicament on its enthralment by the state. He demonstrated a knowledge of the historical and other circumstances which had led to the present state of affairs, but did not regard them as absolving the church from the need to deal with its problems. Meerson-Aksyonov pointed out that recent debate on the church, especially Solzhenitsyn's 'Lenten Letter' and the responses to it, had centred on the hierarchy, and on accusations and defences concerning its role. However, there was no good reason for identifying the whole church with its hierarchy. Meerson-Aksyonov wished to broaden the debate. He discussed the history of the church at some length, pointing out that the division into clergy and laity had not existed in the early church, and had come about only as a result of historical circumstances. The clergy became a band of professional religious activists removed from the world, and the church's involvement in society at large dwindled. Whereas 'the early Christian Church was a place of true creative freedom', the formation, over centuries, of the priesthood and the consequent development of church services which became their 'professional affair' meant that 'the living organism of religion is transformed into a ritual'. There was no place here for human creativity, as formerly, and so 'It should come as no surprise that . . . the intelligentsia, the most creative part of human society, left the Church.'[9] Like Barabanov, Meerson-Aksyonov was concerned that the church had acquiesced too readily in the withdrawal of its Christianising influence from the world at large.

Furthermore, he pointed to another consequence of the division between clergy and laity, the fact that the hierarchical structure which had resulted has become an instrument for the church's captivity by the state. Once Metropolitan Sergi had decided in 1927 to give in to the state's demands, the hierarchs subordinate to him had either to comply or to leave: 'the circle was closed, and the Church became a prisoner of its own hierarchical structure'.[10] Picking up a point from the 'Lenten Letter' debate, Meerson-Aksyonov asserted that Christ did indeed intend the church to be an 'island of freedom', but: 'does it follow that everywhere and at all times every local church can truly be an island of freedom?' No: the state will always attempt to subjugate it, with greater or lesser success depending upon prevailing circumstances. 'Only the Ecumenical Church can be free . . . Even if at a specific moment a society will appear victorious over a part of such a Church, no "gates of hell" will ever be capable of prevailing against it.'[11]

How was the Russian Orthodox Church, meaning all its members, to cope with the lack of creative reaching-out to the world around it and with its hierarchy's subordination to the state? Like Barabanov, Meerson-Aksyonov believed that all church members must seek actively to meet the spiritual needs of the society in which they lived:

> The Church does not have the right today to be closed up within itself, to be an archaism, to be a museum of restored antiques into which the restlessly creative human spirit dares not enter . . . The Christian today is called above all to be a conscious witness of his faith, and departure from the world is far from the best means to testify to it.

Different means of seeking God had been appropriate at different times in history, but 'the constant groans of the world around us today remind us that salvation does not come individually'. And for the church to meet this need in its present condition, 'Laymen must cease being members of a flock at a time when there are not enough shepherds.'[12]

Meerson-Aksyonov pointed out that criticism of the church hierarchy had been voiced largely by 'the non-churchgoing intelligentsia', while the believing people held a quite different view:

> It is enough to take just one look at how people crowd in at a liturgy when the bishop is serving and how long they will wait for his blessing in order to see that for them the hierarchs remain the sovereign successors of the Apostles.

How can Christians who 'are afraid openly to practise our faith but instead come in the night like Nicodemus . . . accuse the bishops, who at least profess their Christianity openly?' The critics were not fulfilling a crucial aspect of their faith, to be witnesses to it. They were holding aloof.

> It would be desirable for convinced Christians to stop looking at the Church with the eyes of accidental guests, occasional users who do not even have the right of 'voicing an opinion'. The theoretical preparation and the search for practical paths for the *new* missionary orientation of Christianity in a secular society belong to the Church intelligentsia, free from hierarchical responsibility and conservative consciousness.[13]

A sympathetic response to Meerson-Aksyonov's article came in the form of a thoughtful essay, 'Gift and Responsibility' by A. Kolesov,[14] who developed several points raised by Meerson-Aksyonov, and with great subtlety and insight described the states of mind of members of the intelligentsia who had joined the church and revealed why they were failing to fulfil their Christian responsibility to the world around them. The basic thesis of the article was that the gift of faith carried with it a concomitant responsibility to the church and to the world. The gift of faith was given when a person responded to God's call, but that call involved becoming a member of a particular church at a particular moment in history, and the new member had a responsibility to act within the given situation, and to accept the church's misfortunes as his own.[15]

> It is so easy to forget the agonising situation of the Church, to shield ourselves from the 'torment' of the Church and remain inside our own splendid experiences of churchliness. This religious 'hedonism', in essence, represents a flight from the Church, a rejection of its present, real fate.[16]

These thoughtful and penetrating articles demonstrated that a new element was entering into the debate about the church, a readiness to be self-critical and to assume responsibility for the role of the church. The discussion was lifted above the level of church–state relations. Some of the church's new members believed that it was not enough simply to continue endlessly blaming the state for all the ills of the church. They believed that Orthodoxy was inherently strong enough and vital enough to carve out its own role, and need not be at the mercy of outside forces.

The Decline of Liberal Nationalism

According to one of the contributors to *Veche*, Gennadi Shimanov, three currents of thought emerged among nationalists after its demise: a liberal–democratic group, a centrist group and a rightist group.[17] Shimanov himself claimed to belong to the centrist group; we shall examine his views later in this chapter (pp. 339–45). Shimanov suggested that Solzhenitsyn was a representative of the liberal–democratic group, and that Osipov was, like himself, a centrist. However, it seems to us that Osipov had more in common with Solzhenitsyn than with Shimanov as time went on, and that, in view of the conciliatory, mediating role which Osipov attempted to play between the nationalists and the democrats, it is more logical to regard him too as belonging to the liberal–democratic group. Osipov and an associate, Vyacheslav Rodionov, commenced publication of a new *samizdat* journal, *Zemlya* (*Land* or *Earth*), two issues of which appeared during 1974.[18] *Zemlya* continued the Christian patriotic line begun by *Veche*, and especially emphasised, in the tradition of the nineteenth-century *pochvenniki*, the need to keep in touch with primeval roots, with Mother Earth (*Mat Zemlya*). The editorial to the first issue stated forcefully:

> Nationalism alienated from Christianity is unthinkable. Any form of pagan or atheistic nationalism is devil worship (*besovshchina*). For Russians, such a 'nationalism' means a new abyss and final ruin. People without mercy, generosity and love to God and man are not Russians.

It added that the journal's guiding principles would, as before, be the line of the Slavophils and Dostoyevsky.[19] The criticism of 'pagan or atheistic nationalism' was a reference to the right-wing group of the three designated by Shimanov — this was evidently the same as the anti-Christian, anti-semitic racist tendency against which Agursky had also warned (see pp. 300–19).

The first issue of *Zemlya* did not feature the lengthy theoretical articles on these themes which had characterised *Veche*, but concentrated on current events. The controversy over Father Dimitri's Dudko's 'conversations', which had recently been stopped, was represented by letters in support of Dudko written by Igor Shafarevich to Archbishop Pitirim of Volokolamsk and Archbishop Vasili of Brussels, the article 'Father Dimitri Dudko' written by A. Krasnov (the pen-name of Anatoli Levitin), and the transcript of the first five 'conversations'. There was also an account of the threatened attempt to close the Cathedral of the Dormition in Vladimir (see Chapter 1, p. 20) and a list of the numbers of open churches in the diocesan centres. This concern for the current practical problems of the Russian Orthodox Church suggests why Shimanov viewed the journal as being aligned with the democrats. The patriotic tendency was represented in this issue chiefly by Osipov's article 'Posledny den Moskvy' ('Moscow's Last Day'), which was a lament for the destruction of old Moscow due to the city architect's policy of pulling down many beautiful and historic buildings and monuments.

The second issue, however, showed that more substantial original material was being assembled. It included an article by Valentina Mashkova (Osipov's wife), entitled 'Kto dolzhen pokayatsya?' ('Who Must Repent?'), which took up the theme already raised in *samizdat* of the need for national repentance, and warned, as Solzhenitsyn had done in *Iz-pod glyb*, against a false repentance which would consist simply of denigrating Russia and ignoring all the good, even holy qualities which the nation embodied. In what was clearly a criticism of V. Gorsky's article (see p. 297), Mashkova censured 'religious' intellectuals who remained outside the church but advocated a semi-repentance which was more an apology for their situation than an act of personal contrition. She concluded:

> Only inwardly belonging to the Church, to its living organism, sanctifies a man and makes him an irreplaceable member of it . . . You who hate Russia, who do not understand her, who do not enter [the church] yourselves and do not let others enter — you should repent![20]

Among articles on history, economics, art, Christian doctrine and other subjects which appeared in this issue was a brief interview with Anatoli Levitin-Krasnov, the social-democrat and human rights activist, who was about to emigrate. He expressed an understanding attitude towards the national–religious line of *Zemlya*, and a willingness to contribute to it from abroad, provided that no 'chauvinist and anti-semitic tendencies' appeared in it. This provoked an indignant editorial comment to the effect that the Russian nationalist, who was 'above all an Orthodox Christian', could not possibly harbour such sentiments.[21] However, it was clear that Osipov's sincere attempt to unite Christian and patriotic virtues and form a middle way between the democrats and the nationalists was compromised by the appearance of these unhealthy tendencies among some of the more extreme nationalists whose general views about the Russian nation he shared.

Osipov's attempt to create, through *Veche* and then *Zemlya*, a forum for a loyal opposition which remained faithful to Soviet power, was unsuccessful. The Soviet authorities were unimpressed by his open, legal behaviour, and the latter issues of *Veche* routinely contained reports of interrogations, detentions and searches of its editor by the militia. On 28 November 1974, three days after the publication of the second issue of *Zemlya*, Osipov was arrested, and charged with 'anti-Soviet agitation and propaganda' (Article 70 of the Criminal Code). His wife, Valentina Mashkova, invited Western readers to compare any issue of *Veche* with Article 70 of the Criminal Code to see if there were any substance in the charge. Osipov was held in pre-trial detention in various prisons for longer than the nine months maximum permitted under Soviet law, and was eventually brought to trial from 24 to 26 September. Western journalists who tried to attend were prevented from entering the courtroom. Osipov was sentenced to eight years in strict regime labour camp, which he served in the Mordovian camp complex.[22] His editorial assistant on *Zemlya*, Vyacheslav Rodionov, announced his intention of continuing publication and issued a statement giving the address to which contributions should be sent.[23] However, no further issues of the journal appeared.

The *samizdat* journal *Moskovsky sbornik* (*Moscow Miscellany*) was intended, according to its editorial, to become a periodical published at irregular intervals, but in fact only one issue, dated September 1974, ever appeared.[24] It has been described by commentators as the mouthpiece of the 'centrist' group among the nationalists, no doubt because three of its most substantial contributions were a lengthy historical essay, 'Mif o Rasputine' ('The Myth of Rasputin') by Anatoli Skuratov, a nationalist who had written long theoretical articles on the Slavophiles in *Veche*; the article 'Moskva — Treti Rim' ('Moscow — The Third Rome') by Shimanov (see pp. 344–5); and 'Opyt teleologicheskogo opravdaniya natsii' ('An Attempt at a Teleological Justification of the Nation') by A. Borisov.[25] However, it also included an article by Mikhail Agursky, the Jewish convert to Christianity, who was, as we have seen, hostile to the more right-wing manifestations of Russian nationalism, on the purely religious topic of the forms of worship and communal life to be adopted by Christianised Jews in the USSR, and the inappropriateness of expecting them to adopt Russian cultural forms to express their faith.[26] Other, more heterogeneous, material included (like *Zemlya*) an article on the fate of Father Dimitri Dudko, a translation from Louis Fischer's biography of Lenin, a critical response by Leonid Borodin to Anatoli Levitin's article 'Zemlya dybom', and extracts from *Otchizna neizvestnaya*, the moving and beautifully told story of a priest exiled to Siberia, which was later to be hailed as a minor spiritual classic.[27] Although contributors such as Shimanov, Borodin and Agursky were prominent in Orthodox intellectual circles, *Moskovsky sbornik* did not adopt such a clearly and exclusively Christian line as *Zemlya* had done.

Orthodox Messianism: Gennadi Shimanov

Gennadi Shimanov was a prolific *samizdat* writer on nationalist and other themes. Although, as we have noted, he claimed to belong to the centrist group among the nationalists, the rightist group was non-Christian, even (as Agursky has suggested) anti-Christian and neo-pagan. This means that within Christian intellectual circles Shimanov was viewed as something of an extremist, and Jewish intellectuals also regarded him in this light.

Shimanov grew up as a communist, the son of a militantly atheist mother, but became a Christian after a period of intense and unhappy thought and searching during which he came close to suicide. He read Dostoyevsky, but became a more convinced communist, believing in the need for authoritarian power; he read Berdyayev, and was presented with the choice between God and nothing; but he did not find the truth he had been seeking all his life until he chanced to read the words 'Christ is Risen!' in, ironically perhaps, a Baptist journal.[28] Still close to despair, he decided to seek out a quiet place where he could reflect upon his new-found faith, and took the original step of having himself committed to a mental hospital for a few weeks. He complained to a psychiatrist in the local clinic of insomnia and a fear of hallucinations, and added that he heard 'voices' intermittently. In the psychiatric hospital he had food and shelter, was safe from arrest for 'parasitism', and had peace to think undisturbed.[29] Apparently, he was discharged without difficulty. However, as a result of his stay, he was placed, like all psychiatric patients, on the so-called psychiatric register, which meant that he was liable to further enquiries and possibly check-ups by psychiatrists. Shimanov emerged from the psychiatric hospital in 1962, at the age of 25, with his faith intact and even deepened, and with a desire to share it with others. In time a group of believers gathered around him. In May 1969, after a series of thwarted attempts, the psychiatric hospital authorities succeeded in having him recommitted, and it was made clear to him that his faith was the reason for this. His psychiatrist engaged him in conversations about his Christian beliefs, and Shimanov's explanation and defence of them make for instructive reading. His replies to the psychiatrist revealed a deep and mature Christian faith expounded in a clear and logical manner.[30] Unlike many other dissenters, including Christians, who have been compulsorily interned in psychiatric hospitals, Shimanov was released quite quickly, due probably to his calm but determined attitude and the resolve he showed in staging a hunger-strike when other methods failed. However, since his discharge, Shimanov has frequently been contacted by staff from the local psychiatric clinic.[31]

By about 1975, Shimanov had come to believe that a return to the Christian faith would not in itself be sufficient to meet the needs of the Russian people. He became convinced, first, that Orthodoxy was the only true form of Christianity, and, second, that Orthodoxy must be closely bound up with Russian national values. Shimanov's vision for the future demanded an indissoluble unity of the church and the nation:

> the revival of religious consciousness in our country will inevitably entail, although not at once, the revival of our *Russian national consciousness*. Yes, we must remember that we are Russians, and remember it not in order to forget it again a moment later, but in order to unite our hearts forever with the hearts of the people, to unite our fates with the fate of our Fatherland, to unite our hopes with the hopes of the best Russian people for a *religious–national revival of Russia*. For a *solely* religious revival is not enough, it is religiously incomplete, religiously powerless, it bears the imprint of the waning of the Protestant–Catholic world.[32]

Shimanov's rejection of Protestantism and Catholicism was bound up with his sweeping rejection of the West in its entirety. He made it clear that the Russian national revival must be based on Orthodoxy and only Orthodoxy:

> The numerous as yet unresolved problems connected with the nationalist theme and the future of Russia now pose the question of the necessity of working out a *Russian national ideology* which would have *Orthodoxy* as its spiritual foundation and its spiritual banner and which would resolve these problems in a *Russian-Orthodox* spirit.[33]

Since the Bolshevik Revolution and the existence of Soviet power were historical facts, they should not be ignored or resisted, in Shimanov's view: they must be woven into the plan for the vision of the religious–national renaissance:

> The cherished dream of the anti-Soviets is to unite everyone on an anti-Soviet platform. 'Soviet power is the greatest of evils', is their favourite slogan. But we must look at things with sober eyes, with Orthodox eyes. The greatest of evils is not to seek God's truth and not to build one's life according to that truth. You will seek and you will build, and no power will be able to stop you doing so. Soviet power is not only godlessness and the greatest threat in the world, it is also a kind of mystery and an instrument of Divine Providence. *To oppose this power of ours is to go against God.*[34]

Not surprisingly, this view attracted strong criticism from other dissenters. We should note that Shimanov did not think the Soviet authorities were above all criticism: we have seen that he objected to the new Education Law (pp. 308–9) and he was later to write a complaint to Patriarch Pimen (see Chapter 12, pp. 372–3). However, even his fellow-nationalist, Osipov, thought Shimanov was going too far, and wrote him an open letter in which he said: 'A direct and honest attitude towards Soviet laws is not that worshipping obeisance before the regime which you propose'.[35] This drew an indignant response from Shimanov in the form of an article entitled 'Kak otnositsya k sovetskoi vlasti' ('How to Relate to Soviet Power'). He accused Osipov of an excessive desire to appease liberal opinion and over-eagerness to fall in with the ideas of non-believing liberals, such as Sakharov, Amalrik and Grigorenko: 'Is not comparing oneself with people who are indifferent to the Orthodox faith or who have only just joined it and are therefore imbued with alien elements to behave in an un-Russian way?'[36] Shimanov agreed with Osipov and the liberals that Soviet power was undesirable and must be superseded, but disagreed with them over the means by which this was to be accomplished. He wrote to Osipov: 'Is it not time to realise that communism in our country will be overcome only in an Orthodox and spiritual way, and certainly not in a liberal way?'[37] The role of the Russian nation in the gradual overcoming of communism was to be crucial:

> Essentially the only support for the Soviet state is Russia, the Russian people. For what have, say, the Baltic people in common with the Caucasians? The Tuvins with the Moldavians? The Tadzhiks with the Finns? It is only the Russian people which unites them in one great association. And now this support, this link is literally melting away, the Russian people is ever more quickly disappearing both physically and morally.[38]

This was a reference to the decline of the Russian people, both physically and morally, which was a central concern of all patriotic Russians, not only those who held nationalist views. Shimanov believed that the revival of Russian national values on the basis of Orthodoxy would both halt the decline of the Russian people and lead to the disappearance of the communist system:

> The process of the return of the Russian spirit, the process of the return of the *Russian consciousness* has already begun, and nothing can stop it. Now it is extremely important for us to restore a healthy and truly Orthodox attitude to our State. In my opinion it is unnecessary to be troubled because it is officially atheistic at present (it is well known that Paul, until his conversion, was Saul), but it is necessary to believe in and work for the good of the Church, for the good of Russian society and the Soviet State. There can be no doubt that Orthodox Christians ought to be the *best* citizens of our Motherland, i.e. deeply moral, hardworking, sober people . . . Moreover, they must be ardent patriots, ready always, both by word and deed, i.e. with weapons in their hands, to defend their Fatherland from all its enemies. In the present atmosphere of inner *emptiness* and inward *running wild* they must be the true *strength*, the true *health* and the true *support* of our Russian people and our State — and so it will undoubtedly be to the glory of God and the triumph of our Orthodox Church![39]

The triumphalist note evident here was also to be found in Shimanov's reply to Osipov. Osipov, he believed, was wrong to pose the question of the relationship to Soviet power in a purely juridical manner, as though it were a political system like any other: it was a special power which had arisen in a special country, one which had been 'the spiritual centre of history for the last thousand years'. Soviet power could be understood only through Christian truth, which 'has been gently and tactfully rejected by the Western world'.[40] This messianism was more clearly spelled out elsewhere, when Shimanov was considering whether there were any force in the world sufficient to combat the recent course of Western history and return to religious and national cultural values:

> Only one country is in a condition to do this — Russia! Only Russia! Because there is no other people in the world which has exhibited, not as a day-dream but as a fact, such an improbable range of contradictions in its spiritual and social life, always going to the brink, to the very last point, as our Russian people has done . . . [This] will doubtless lead it finally onto the path of salvation, and with it many, many other peoples.[41]

Shimanov appeared to view the Bolshevik Revolution and its painful aftermath almost as a guarantee of the special role Russia was destined to play. How could there have been so much human suffering, so much blood spilled, resulting in the rule of a godless power in the midst of a Christian nation, if it were not to lead to the revelation of some great new truth? Such a cataclysmic upheaval could not be an accident; there must be an explanation for it; and this would yield the clue to Russia's divinely ordained future. In his reply to Osipov, Shimanov compared the October Revolution to a black cloud, a threat, but suggested that it would be wiser to work with it rather than against it. It was like a painful operation on the body of Russia, necessary to save it from a fatal disease: like death, the death a seed suffers before it can bear fruit; like the Cross of the Crucifixion, a symbol of tragedy whose real meaning is victory. Here and elsewhere Shimanov suggested that in the dialectic of history, the October Revolution was the antithesis which must inevitably lead to a synthesis with its predecessor, the Orthodox life of the Russian people.[42] This gradual historical process, Shimanov believed, was the only way to true freedom. Democrats and liberals agitated about freedom without understanding what it really was: 'The entire West is currently in the embrace of this "freedom".' Russia must seek a different freedom:

> *Only freedom received from Christ truly liberates.* It creates instead of destroying, it does not humiliate or wear down the one who has been liberated, but lays upon him the lightest and brightest of yokes and gives him the spiritual strength to bear that yoke. Only in this, in this yoke, and in everything organically connected with it, lies the salvation of Russia and the salvation of the whole world.[43]

The theme of the significance of the October Revolution appeared again in Shimanov's article 'Kak ponimat nashu istoriyu' ('How to Understand Our History'), which was a critical commentary on Solzhenitsyn's *Letter to the Soviet Leaders.* Shimanov asserted that Solzhenitsyn had failed to elaborate the significance of Russian history, particularly the Revolution, in the *Letter.* (Interestingly, Levitin-Krasnov, at the opposite end of the political spectrum from Shimanov, also charged Solzhenitsyn with failing to analyse the Revolution in his *Letter*. His social-democratic corrective view was, however, very far removed from Shimanov's theocratic one.[44] In any case, this hardly seems a fair charge to bring against the author of the *Gulag Archipelago*, given that the *Letter to Soviet Leaders* was more in the nature of a political and social programme than a historical analysis.) Where Solzhenitsyn had urged the Soviet leaders to renounce a moribund Marxism-Leninism as a prelude to finding a way forward to national regeneration, Shimanov went much further: 'only authentic, reborn Christianity' could lead Russia and mankind out of their 'unbearable dead-end', and this meant the creation of a 'new theocracy'. What force would be capable of accomplishing this? Only that force which had turned against God and tried to turn the whole world around to suit it — Soviet power. Its authoritarian nature and maximalist vision could be transformed, under the influence of truth, 'from a minus to a plus'.[45] Since, Shimanov continued, it was unrealistic for the Soviet system either to pursue communism (here he agreed with Solzhenitsyn), or to give up its grandiose schemes, it could justify itself by adopting Orthodoxy and thus acknowledging itself to be God's instrument in the creation of a new Christian world. But how could Soviet power make such a vast change and follow a course contradictory to that which it had been proclaiming? Simply by referring to the dialectical nature of Marxism–Leninism and authorising the influential cadre of ideologues to represent the change in this light, using the state's 'fantastic means for propaganda'. Shimanov depicted the scene, not without humour:

> Let us suppose that tomorrow they write in the newspapers (first of all in very small print, but after a month or two in large print) that they say, comrades, there has been a mistake, and God, it turns out, despite the errors of the last few decades, exists (and they would quote the opinions of two or three scholars, and they would explain judiciously and in detail why such a mistake had occurred) — and half the reading population would at once, their eyes never leaving the page, believe, and the rest would be disturbed and begin to think seriously for the first time in their lives.[46]

Shimanov developed his views on the coming transformation of Soviet power in his article 'Moskva — Treti Rim' ('Moscow — The Third Rome'). He argued that Moscow did not cease to be the Third Rome* because of the October Revolution, but, on the contrary, was preserved as the Third Rome precisely because of this 'most powerful spiritual movement', which neither

---

*After the fall of Rome and the capitulation of the Second Rome, Constantinople, to the Muslim Turks, the Russian Orthodox saw themselves as the last remaining Christian state, and formulated the doctrine: 'Moscow is the Third Rome, and a fourth there shall not be.'

her friends nor her enemies had recognised as such. Moscow's role as the Third Rome had a worldwide significance: the Revolution had not occurred merely to bring about the 'Orthodoxification' (*pravoslavizatsiya*) and russification of Russia, but of the whole world.[47]

It was only to be expected that such sweeping views as this would draw criticism from other dissenters, particularly non-Russians. Shimanov's thoroughgoing commitment to his country and his faith may have been impressive, but it led him to ignore the claims of major sections of the population, those of other nations and other faiths. His assertion that the 'ideal state' would be achieved with the transformation of the Communist Party into the Orthodox Party of the Soviet Union[48] could hardly be viewed with approval by Protestants and Catholics, not to mention the democrats and liberals whom Shimanov so despised. And his insistence on the need for Russian national values to be predominant in the building of the new, transformed state led him into sharp conflict with the aspirations of the national minorities — Ukrainians and many others — who already resented what they saw as Russian domination. Though we cannot devote more space here to the considerable ramifications of the purely national, as opposed to religious, consequences of Shimanov's views, we should note that there was a particularly sharp reaction from Jews, who accused him of anti-semitism.[49] The question of the relationship between Orthodox Christians and Jews was also the cause of conflict between Shimanov and other rightist Orthodox, Felix Karelin and L. Ibragimov, on the one hand, and more liberal Orthodox such as Yevgeni Barabanov and Father Alexander Men, on the other hand.[50]

The Controversy between the Nationalists and the Liberals in the Church

Shimanov's belief, shared by other nationalists, that the Orthodox Church was the only true church and the only possible saviour for Russia was very far removed from the self-critical attitude advocated by people like Barabanov and Meerson-Aksyonov, and naturally led to controversy. Shimanov was, for example, very critical of some radical suggestions put forward by Father Sergi Zheludkov, who formulated the phrase *'Khristianstvo dlya vsekh'* ('Christianity for all'). He used this concept to suggest what the church's attitude should be to those who lived a life worthy of a Christian and were a force for good in society, but did not have the gift of faith: he called them 'people of good will' (*lyudi dobroi voli*). Evidently he had been impressed by the selfless attitude and positive moral approach of those, principally members of the contemporary intelligentsia, with whom he had begun to work in the human rights movement. He suggested that Karl Rahner's term 'anonymous Christians' might apply to them: they lived, unconsciously perhaps, a Christian life without ever having thought about the Christian faith, and without having accepted all the beliefs and dogma of the church. Zheludkov pointed to the contrast between the good done by some anonymous Christians and the passive or even negative contribution of some merely nominal Christians, who subscribed to church dogma but lacked real faith. However, even the anonymous Christians were not totally divorced from the church:

> We must not forget that the greatest representatives of anonymous-Christian humanism were brought up in the Christian Church, nurtured in a Christian culture. The future will show in practice what influence the Christian Churches of faith have had on the pan-human Church of people of good will. It is a fact that it exists today — and this is Christianity for all.[52]

Zheludkov was not proposing a programmatic reform; his suggestions were tentative, advanced in the form of a correspondence with rather sceptical friends. However, they met with an unsympathetic and dismissive response from other members of the church. Zheludkov was not without some theological support for his views: it has always been a feature of Orthodoxy to regard all men and women as potential sons and daughters of the church, which is an abiding presence in society, waiting to receive them until such time as their life's experience shall make them aware of their need of it. (This is why the Orthodox Church does not normally engage in active proselytisation, and tends to view with suspicion the emphasis on instant conversion experiences characteristic of many Protestant Churches.) One might have expected more support for his views from the nationalists, who believed that all Russians were really Orthodox in their heart of hearts. Once more we see that many church members still shied away from accepting the contribution of those whose *tserkovnost* (churchliness) was deficient: offered the concept of a broad church, most traditionally minded Orthodox clung to the concept of a narrow one.

This issue was taken up by Yevgeni Barabanov in his essay 'Pravda gumanizma' ('The Truth of Humanism'),[53] in which he argued that, despite the traditional dangers of humanism for Christians, they could not afford to ignore the new affirmation of human values, long suppressed by totalitarianism, which people were developing outside the church. 'Christianity for all', whatever its theological shortcomings, had been an attempt to respond to this significant phenomenon, which could not be ignored, and the failure to give it serious consideration bespoke a narrow, defensive frame of mind within the church. This could be dangerous for the church's future:

> What if we live in the Church as merely passive consumers? What if our Christianity is nominal? What if we have no other concerns apart from

our misgivings about 'how not to fall into heresy' and to maintain the purity of our vestments, free from 'worldly dirt'? Will not the Lord then find himself sons and workers outside the walls of the Church? And has perhaps already found them?[54]

Barabanov accepted that 'The fullness of good is God, and beyond Him there is not and cannot be any authentic good', he knew that this fullness was in the church, 'everything is in her and she is everything',[55] and he acknowledged that 'the truth of the new humanism is only a partial and incomplete truth'.[56] None the less, he believed the church must ask itself:

Why are we so deaf to this great 'common cause' of bringing the world into the Church (*votserkovleniye mira*)? Why are we so silent and indifferent before the onslaught of falsehood and inhumanity? Surely our churchliness (*tserkovnost*) is not merely a feeling of powerlessness and thirst for spiritual consolation? Surely the words about Christian responsibility for the fate of the world are not meaningless and empty chatter?[57]

Christianity, Barabanov and Zheludkov believed, was a matter of will as well of belief, of works as well as faith. In a land where the mere survival of the churches in the face of the massive physical and ideological pressures of atheism is often regarded as miraculous, their maximalism showed that Christianity had not simply been preserved as a relic of the past, as a kind of cultural artefact, but had a vital, creative role to play in the present. Here there was perhaps a point of contact with the nationalists, who believed that only Orthodox Christianity had sufficient vitality to regenerate and transform the Russian nation, and, some of them believed, the whole world. However, where the nationalists believed that the non-Christian world must accept traditional Orthodoxy and enter into the church, these more radical thinkers believed that the church had the responsibility to forsake its narrow, comfortable patterns of thought and reach out to the world. It is interesting that their thinking derived in part from Vladimir Solovyov, who was one of the leading developers of Slavophil thought in the late nineteenth century, and therefore a source of inspiration for the nationalists also. He too had aroused controversy by his suggestion that Christianity was not simply a matter of individual salvation and nothing besides, but a task involving responsibility to the world.[58]

Where Zheludkov and Yevgeni Barabanov had voiced opinions which were theologically opposed to the views of the Russian nationalists, Meerson-Aksyonov added political ones. He declared roundly: 'I am convinced that the path to the rebirth of the conciliar structure of Orthodoxy in Russia today must pass through the democratisation of Soviet society, and be a part of the national movement for civil rights.'[59] He also made a contribution to the discussion about the role of the intelligentsia in the struggle for human rights and its relationship to the church. He suggested (to summarise a detailed and closely argued article) that representatives of the nineteenth-century intelligentsia had left the church because they found it narrow and stultifying, incapable of meeting the needs of a rapidly changing society, and had embraced liberal beliefs; and this liberal tendency was now emerging in the new, contemporary intelligentsia which had taken up the task of defending human rights, a task the church was incapable of undertaking. The liberal intelligentsia, then, was a kind of supplement to the church, formed out of historical necessity because of the church's failure to fulfil its divinely ordained mission to the world.[60] There was an echo here of Shimanov's commentary on the nineteenth-century intelligentsia in his article 'Moskva — Treti Rim', where he contrasted the faithful Orthodox people with the parasitic upper classes, and suggested that the Revolution could have been avoided if the latter had lived truly Christian lives instead of forsaking the church. However, he was inclined to excuse their falling away on the grounds that they lived 'in an atmosphere, in a spiritual current, which came to us from the West'.[61] Here there was a clear difference of interpretation. Meerson-Aksyonov suggested that the intelligentsia had left the church because the church was not creative enough and outward-looking enough to hold them; Shimanov suggested that they were the unfortunate victims of the alien, decadent influence of the West. This divergence of opinion illustrated the grounds upon which the nationalist and liberal schools of thought have developed among the Orthodox intelligentsia: the key issues were the attitudes to the West and to Russian Orthodox tradition. The more liberal thinkers were prepared to look at the West, and at the Catholic and Protestant Churches, with eyes which were critical but basically sympathetic; they wanted to learn what they could and to adopt any ideas which might help in their own situation. This did not mean that they wished to abandon their own traditions and their own roots; simply that they recognised that Christianity was universal, not the especial property of the Russian nation. For the nationalists, on the other hand, especially the more extreme ones such as Shimanov, Russia and Orthodoxy were the repository of all truth, and anything coming from the West was an 'infection' to be rigorously shunned. (Shimanov's criticisms of the West, which he had never visited, were rather vague and unsubstantiated — if he had read Western authors, he rarely quoted or referred to them — and this constituted a flaw in his arguments. His anti-Western motif was remarkably similar to that found in the official Soviet press, which, as we shall see in the following chapters, was to rely ever more heavily upon alleged Western subversion as an explanation for the growing dissent within the church and in Soviet society generally.) As for Russian Orthodox tradition, the nationalists seem to have regarded it as sacrosanct. Their close identification of Orthodoxy with the

Russian nation and their belief in the union of the two as the only realistic path into the future meant that every custom, every aspect of specifically Russian Orthodoxy was an anchorage, a solid base to which they could return as a refuge from the disastrous turmoils and upheavals of recent decades. The more liberal thinkers, on the other hand, were prepared to recognise that Russian Orthodoxy could in the course of the centuries have become encrusted with purely cultural, purely national practices and beliefs which might constitute an obstacle to the rediscovery of the true Orthodox tradition. It was, perhaps, a question of distinguishing between Tradition and traditions, as a perceptive English Orthodox writer has noted:

> There is a difference between 'Tradition' and 'traditions': many traditions which the past has handed down are human and accidental — pious opinions (or worse) but not a true part of the one Tradition, the essential Christian message.[62]

For the nationalists, the often evocative and beautiful accretions of Russian Orthodoxy were an essential part of the task of regenerating the Russian nation, while for the no less patriotic liberals they were a potential stumbling-block which might prevent the Russian Church playing its full part in the Church Universal.

It would be a mistake to think of the dissenting Orthodox intelligentsia as drawn up into two separate and irreconcilable camps. The two sharply opposed schools of thought we have described certainly exist, but there are many shades and gradations of opinion within them and between them. Moreover, there is a strong unifying factor, namely that adherents of both viewpoints are concerned above all to work out the future of the church according to independently formulated ideas based on purely Christian principles, irrespective of the political pressures from the state which influence the hierarchy. In this situation, such sharp diversity of opinion is undoubtedly healthy, indicating as it does that freshness and variety of thought have been able to spring up despite all attempts to stifle and crush it. A monolithic Orthodox dissent would be an easy victim for the far greater monolith of the Soviet state, whereas diverse and constantly ramifying Orthodox thought may in time surround and even overgrow it.

It is clear that the nonconformist members of the Russian Orthodox Church are far more sharply divided over their attitude to the Russian nation than over their attitude to the Soviet state. Broadly speaking, they all oppose the state's interference with the life of the church — and turn aside from such necessary but mundane opposition to discuss ever more eagerly and intensely the role of the church within Russia, and, as a corollary, within Europe and within the world. The Soviet state cannot be ignored, but its annoyances fade into insignificance when visionary eyes are focused upon the future. It follows from this that, if the Soviet system were to collapse overnight, the fundamental debate over the future of the Russian Orthodox Church would continue no less intensely than at present.

Another unifying factor for all the protagonists in this debate was that they all constantly had hanging over them the same threat, that of the loss of liberty and perhaps health due to repression by the state. Shimanov had been incarcerated in a psychiatric hospital, and Yevgeni Barabanov was threatened with the same fate in September 1975. In a forceful and moving appeal to world public opinion, he wrote:

> It turns out that disagreement with bureaucratic ideology and religious conviction are entirely sufficient grounds for being called not simply a criminal, but an even more terrible word — madman. I say 'terrible' not only because our psychiatric hospitals are immeasurably more terrible than prisons and concentration camps, but because this cure for dissent is a monstrous moral distortion, a crime against the very nature of man, against the right to think, speak, believe and be free; it is a spiritual murder.[63]

Westerners who had responded to Barabanov's appeal the previous year responded again; there was a great deal of publicity about the threat against him, and it was successful: he was not in fact committed to a psychiatric hospital.

An Appeal to the CPSU

An issue upon which all shades of opinion among Orthodox dissenters, and indeed dissenters in general, could have agreed was the necessity to combat the falsehood which had insidiously seeped into every part of Soviet life to an almost Orwellian extent. Solzhenitsyn, with his famous challenge to 'live not by lies' (*zhit ne po lzhi*), made this question a central one for all nonconformist intellectuals. The theme was taken up in an appeal to the Twenty-fifth Congress of the CPSU in 1976 by two members of the Russian Orthodox Church, Hierodeacon Varsonofi (Khaibulin) and layman Gleb Mileshkin. They pointed out that the Communist Party's attempts to deny religion and root it out had met with no success whatever, and that although it had reduced the episcopate to a state where it spoke only part of the truth, this had only increased the desire of the people to tell the whole truth:

> This desire becomes overwhelmingly strong when a catastrophically huge accumulation of falsehood threatens to corrupt and break up everything: the personality, the family, the nation, humanity, our very Earth.

This rather rambling document embodied the idea that, as the Communist

Party had evidently failed to halt the decline of morality in the land, it would be better advised to enlist the church as its ally rather than to deprive it of rights:

> If there were firm juridical guarantees that the State would not interfere in the internal life of the Church, Christians would be joyful comrades-in-arms of Communists in achieving their social and economic ideals, which would in no way contradict Christianity, so long as the CPSU, in its strategy and tactics, would strictly observe the principle of non-interference in the free development of a God-like human personality.

Perhaps not all Christians would acquiesce with such a ready commitment to the achieving of social and economic ideals, but the basic point of the appeal, that the state was depriving itself by alienating Christians, was well founded. The appeal concluded with a number of requests which were more reasonable than the very lengthy preamble might have led the reader to expect: that believers should be granted true equality by the state renouncing atheism as it had renounced religion; that the CPSU should adopt a neutral, not hostile, attitude towards religion; that religious propaganda should be allowed alongside anti-religious propganda; that the school should be separated not only from the church, but also from atheism.[64]

The preamble to the appeal attributed great significance to alleged appearances of the Virgin Mary at Zeitun, near Cairo, for a whole year from 1968 to 1969. Though the references to the appearances in the appeal did little to help the writers' case, and can hardly have been expected to have made much impression upon the addressees at the CPSU Congress, they evidently aroused considerable interest among some Orthodox activists, who believed that, like the Fatima appearances in Portugal, they were relevant to Russian Christians. (The appearances of the Virgin Mary to three children at Fatima in Portugal in 1917 are widely believed to have foretold the Bolshevik Revolution.) Hierodeacon Varsonofi was particularly seized by the significance of the Zeitun appearances, and spent much time and effort writing about them in *samizdat* and distributing his works. He was a theological student at Zagorsk when he began to do this, and he has recounted in detail how his distribution of religious *samizdat*, including literature about the Zeitun appearances, led to his being transferred from the residential to the correspondence course, and eventually to his expulsion. He obtained work as a parish priest in Vladimir region and continued his activities, and especially his efforts to attract young people into the church, ignoring warnings from both church and state officials to desist. Finally, and obviously under KGB pressure, the Archbishop of Vladimir and Suzdal dismissed him from his parish.[65]

Appeals for Freedom for the Church: Yakunin and Regelson

Between 1974 and 1976, a number of important documents on the state of the Russian Orthodox Church were issued by the banned priest Father Gleb Yakunin, and the layman Lev Regelson.[66] Since being banned from the priesthood in 1966, Yakunin had remained silent until the end of 1973, when, as noted in Chapter 10, he was among those who criticised the new law on education. Regelson had not been an especially vocal advocate of reform in the church since co-signing the appeal to the 1971 Local Council, though he had protested on other issues, as noted above (p. 328). From 1974, however, they evidently came to an agreement that a series of public documentary appeals, most of them jointly signed, would be a good and useful means of drawing attention to some of the ills of their church. Most of their documents were directly concerned with church matters. However, they did address other issues. Both of them criticised the expulsion of Solzhenitsyn, as we noted in Chapter 10, and they jointly published an impassioned denunciation of the murder, apparently with official sanction, of the dissenter and translator Konstantin Bogatyrev.[67]

Another of Yakunin's and Regelson's joint statements had no direct bearing on internal church affairs, but drew upon the church's experience under Soviet rule to issue a warning to Christians in Portugal, at a time when dictatorship in that country had been overthrown and the political future was uncertain. The 'Appeal to the Christians of Portugal' commenced with a reminder of the appearances of the Mother of God in Fatima, Portugal, in which she was said to have foretold the revolution of October 1917 in Russia, and urged Portuguese Christian to heed the prophecy of Fatima and the experience of Christians in the Soviet Union:

> Now, at the crossroads of history, your country may become the key to the spread of totalitarianism in Europe. Or it could be a bulwark against it, if, by a decision coming from the depth of your hearts, you should reject temptation, and stop the evil of which the Most Holy Mother of God spoke in Fatima.[68]

It is not known what effect this unexpected letter from Moscow may or may not have had on the situation in Portugal, but its effect within the USSR is a little easier to gauge: the social activism and participation in political life advocated by Yakunin and Regelson did not escape the attention of the Soviet authorities, and they were to refer to this 'Appeal to the Christians of Portugal' in interrogations, investigations and trials of believers far more frequently than to the other appeals by Yakunin and Regelson.

The remaining documents jointly signed by Yakunin and Regelson, which are all concerned with internal church matters, may be divided into those which address specific grievances and those which are concerned with larger issues. Three documents belong to the first group. The first was a letter to Archbishop Pitirim from Yakunin, strongly criticising the former's interview stating that there was no need for the church to teach religion to children or to engage in charitable activity. (We noted in Chapter 8 that Archbishop Vasili of Brussels also criticised Pitirim's interview — see pp. 213–14).[69] The second was a letter to an English pastor, Rev. David Hathaway, who had just founded an organisation named Christian Prisoners' Release International (CPRI). Yakunin and Regelson wrote to offer support and encouragement in this venture, and to suggest specific courses of action Hathaway should adopt in working for Christian prisoners in the USSR. Unfortunately, CPRI proved to be a short-lived organisation.[70] The third document was a letter written by Yakunin to the CRA chairman, V. A. Kuroyedov, protesting about the difficulties he had encountered in his employment since beginning to make public statements. Since being forbidden to exercise his priestly ministry, he had worked in churches in various capacities, such as watchman, but had more than once been deprived of employment under various subterfuges. The timing of these dismissals, according to Yakunin, made it clear that they 'exposed an aspiration to suppress free discussions within the Church'.[71]

In 1975, Orthodox Easter coincided with Lenin's birthday. In the Soviet Union, this day has become known as a *subbotnik* or 'Red Saturday' (originally they were usually held on Saturday — *subbota*), when the populace, emulating Lenin's example, 'voluntarily' puts in an extra day's work for the state. Easter Day 1975 was therefore declared to be a working day,[72] and this naturally aroused indignation among the believers, who would have to do a full day's work after standing through the all-night Easter service, and would not be able to enjoy the usual festivities afterwards. Yakunin addressed an indignant rebuke to the Politburo:

> Your ideologists affirm that one should not insult the religious feelings of believers. But here, as elsewhere, your theory disagrees with your practice. By ordering people to work on the Easter holiday, you insulted the religious feelings of millions of believers. If you order a working day on 1 May or 7 November, the number of those insulted would be much less.[73]

However, the Soviet authorities appeared not to heed this appeal, since in 1982 Easter was again declared a working day.[74]

In May 1975, Yakunin and Regelson, joined this time by layman Viktor Kapitanchuk, wrote to Patriarch Pimen and to the heads of three jurisdictions of the Russian Orthodox Church overseas to urge them to begin preparations for the commemoration and glorification of the martyrs of the church in the USSR during the early decades of the Soviet regime. That year, 1975, was the fiftieth anniversary of the greatly loved Patriarch

Tikhon, who, the authors asserted, had been the leader of those bishops who had offered spiritual opposition to the anti-religious excesses of the Soviet regime. The compromises of his successor — Metropolitan, later Patriarch, Sergi — were based on 'purely human calculations', and in their view, the position he adopted was 'one of the main reasons for the shattered position of the Russian Church at the present time and the loss of her inner freedom'. This is a view with which very many, though by no means all, members of the church would agree: the rightness or otherwise of Sergi's position has been debated, and no doubt will continue to be debated, endlessly. The authors of this appeal suggest that the church's main attention should be directed not to this debate, but to 'the glorious reality of the holiness of the Russian Church and to its many confessors and martyrs, which was the Church's answer to the unprecedented magnitude of the persecution'. The Moscow Patriarchate, however, has repudiated the martyrs by ignoring them. The three authors suggest that the period of the rehabilitation of victims of the 'cult of personality' (i.e. after Khrushchev's 'secret speech' denouncing Stalin in 1956) offered an opportunity for the Moscow Patriarchate to revive the memory of the Orthodox martyrs, but it was ignored. They point out that the act of glorification is not necessary so much for the martyrs themselves — who have now been 'rewarded by the blissful glory of God' — as for the church on earth. They believe that 'By refusing to glorify the multitude of martyrs, we impoverish ourselves to the utmost, we disarm ourselves; their great beneficial power remains unrealised, hidden from us.' The Orthodox concept of *sobornost* ('unity' or 'conciliarity') is invoked here. The concept of *sobornost* unites all members of the church, living or dead, in everlasting fellowship. The deceased martyrs and saints are just as much members of the church as those who are visible here on earth. To fail to recognise them, to ignore them, is a violation of *sobornost*, a disruption of its unity. While such disruption of unity can hardly be supposed to affect those who have departed this life and are seated with God, it does have the effect of spiritually diminishing the church on earth.

Yakunin, Regelson and Kapitanchuk pointed out that preparation for the glorification of martyrs was difficult on the most practical level, since documents, letters, photographs and other material mementoes were swept away during the years of persecution. They therefore appealed to the leaders of the divided Orthodox jurisdictions to begin by collecting and studying the necessary materials: the great aim of canonisation of the martyrs should be sufficient to overcome 'interjurisdictional rivalry, distrust and even hostility'.[75]

Yakunin and Regelson evidently attached great importance to their jointly signed documents, and it was therefore a little surprising that they did not seek the support of like-minded members of the church (with the one exception of Kapitanchuk's signature on one appeal) to give greater weight to their views. The absence of other signatures suggested that others may not have supported their initiative. Perhaps some were afraid of the consequences, but we have already seen that there were a number of Orthodox believers who were prepared to sign public appeals and endure whatever harassment might result. This suggests that other Orthodox dissenters may not have agreed either with Yakunin's and Regelson's views, or with the means they chose to express them, or both. However, it is also likely that Yakunin and Regelson did not in fact approach anyone to co-sign their appeals for purely pragmatic reasons first, the practical difficulties of agreeing texts and circulating documents for signature without discovery; and second, the fact that a document able to be signed by many people with strong individual views would inevitably have to be watered down somewhat to obtain general agreement, and might therefore lose something of its cutting edge.

The Nairobi Appeal

Of all the documents under the joint authorship of Yakunin and Regelson, there was one above all others which attracted worldwide publicity, was debated in church circles throughout the world, and resulted in a small but appreciable alteration in the attitude of overseas churches and ecclesiastical organisations towards the Moscow Patriarchate. It was probably the most effective religious *samizdat* document to come out of the Soviet Union. This was the appeal to delegates to the Fifth Assembly of the World Council of Churches in Nairobi in November 1975.[76] The appeal commenced with the assertion that

> only at the foot of the Cross of Golgotha can be born a love passionate enough truly to overcome the strife which alienates denominations from one another, and prepare Christian hearts for genuine unity . . . we presume that doubts about the spiritual quality of the ecumenical movement may be banished only if the confession of the Cross in its original Gospel sense — as signifying the endurance of trials and tribulations for the sake of Christ's Name — is made the basis for Christian unity.

Few Christians would dissent from such a view. Yakunin and Regelson went on to link it specifically with the Russian Orthodox Church: they pointed out that the 'new efforts of Christian love' which arose in it in response to suffering 'give hope that a complete victory over Christian divisiveness may be possible'.

Yakunin and Regelson listed responses to their church's plight under the Soviet regime from various Christian denominations and from Jews and Muslims. These had come in response to the Local Council of 1918, the famine of 1921, and the mass arrests and executions of 1922 and after. These protests achieved the release of Patriarch Tikhon from prison. Worldwide prayer for the Russian Orthodox Church in 1930, in which Pope Pius XI played a leading role, was 'a great step towards genuine ecumenism'. However, the Moscow Patriarchate at that time denied that persecution was taking place, which caused Christians overseas to wonder if they were doing the right thing. Yakunin and Regelson then considered the entry of the Russian Orthodox Church into the World Council of Churches in 1961, which they noted was accompanied by 'an increasing wave of anti-religious terror' and the declaration of the CPSU that 'this generation of Soviet people will live under communism'. They gave an interesting account of the reaction of ordinary church people to the entry into the WCC: they stated that they 'never had any particular illusions' about it, and realised that it 'obviously followed the government's own strategic aims, which had nothing to do with the task of consolidating Christian positions in the modern world'. Despite this sceptical view, Orthodox believers 'still hoped that Christian solidarity and determination to achieve genuine unity would prove stronger than the influence of anti-Christian forces', and that the WCC would initiate prayer and support for persecuted members of the church.

Yakunin and Regelson then briefly considered the main concerns of the WCC to date: the struggle for peace and attempts to prevent nuclear war; study of political and military conflicts in Vietnam, the Middle East, Nigeria and Cyprus; study of explosive areas such as Cuba and Northern Ireland; racial, ethnic and national discrimination; social injustice, population control and the fight against hunger. They pointed out that, among all these serious problems, 'the matter of religious persecution failed to occupy the place it deserves'. There was no protest from the WCC concerning the anti-religious campaign in the USSR, nor when Christianity was made illegal in China, nor when religion was crushed in Albania. This analysis of the WCC's preoccupations would seem, broadly speaking, to be a fair one. However, Yakunin and Regelson were optimistic: they could not believe that 'a feeling of genuine Christian solidarity will not after all eventually emerge', and they hoped that the WCC's support for a dissenting Soviet Baptist, Georgi Vins, earlier that year would be an initiative which would be followed up.

The appeal then proceeded to practicalities. Yakunin and Regelson wrote that 'We are aware that many Christians are deeply concerned about the suffering of their brethren and wish with all their hearts to help them, but often do not know how to proceed.' They therefore followed up this perfectly correct assumption with eight eminently practical forms of suggested action. These were: that information about suffering Christians should be provided by every means of mass communication; that prayer, sermons, discussion and meditation based upon such information should be regularly organised; that personal contacts through letters and visits would be greatly valued; that appropriate protests directed towards the persecutors would certainly be effective; that confessors of other religions and fighters for freedom and human dignity also deserved support by the international Christian community; that the 'barbaric methods' of psychiatric abuse must be countered with an 'implacable struggle'; that Christians who wished to emigrate from the USSR, 'exhausted after many years of oppression and humiliation', should be supported, both to leave their country and to return to it; and finally that ways should be found to provide the copies of the Holy Scripture which Christians in the USSR urgently needed.

These requests appear to have been very carefully thought out. Most of them could readily be undertaken by any separate church, or even by small groups within churches, so that, if the appeal did not reach the WCC, or arrived too late, or was ignored by it, or if its recommendations were not followed up (as Yakunin and Regelson must no doubt have feared), their suggestions could none the less have been taken up by other Christian bodies without difficulty. Furthermore, Yakunin and Regelson appear to have given some consideration to the probability that their suggestions would be opposed, or even suppressed, by the Russian Orthodox Church's delegation to the Assembly — again, a perfectly correct assumption, as it turned out. This is suggested by the fact that it would not have been possible for the delegation to prevent the adoption of any of their suggestions. How could any one delegation have prevented the Assembly from voting to circulate information about persecuted Christians, praying for them, writing them letters, and so forth? True, the proposal could be watered down by applying it to all countries without mentioning names — but who would forget where the proposal had originated? In view of some of the views Yakunin and Regelson had expressed elsewhere, the Nairobi Appeal is remarkable for its restraint: there was no challenge to expel the Russian Orthodox Church from the WCC, to denounce the Moscow Patriarchate, to criticise the Soviet government for its persecution of religion. A great deal of the subsequent effectiveness of the appeal was due to its skilful wording and the extremely practical nature of its requests.

The appeal from Yakunin and Regelson was not on the agenda of the Assembly, and no one knew in advance that it would arrive, so that it was no easy matter to slot it into the proceedings. However, an English translation of it was printed in a local Christian newspaper, *Target*, which was published daily while the Assembly was in progress and was distributed to all the delegates along with official conference papers. The appeal aroused great interest among delegates and was widely discussed on an informal basis. It appeared in *Target* on 25 November 1975, two days after the beginning of the conference; it was not until three days later that a response from the Russian Orthodox delegation was published. (A response from the Soviet Baptist delegation was also published, but it did not refer specifically to the appeal and did not respond to the particular points raised by Yakunin and Regelson.) One observer noted in confidence that the Russian text of the Russian Orthodox delegation's response was typed on a Cyrillic electric typewriter which must have been provided by the Soviet Embassy, since there was no one at the conference who could have had access to such a facility. The reply, which was signed by Metropolitan Yuvenali, chairman of the DECR and head of the delegation, began with an attempt to undermine the credibility of the authors of the appeal: Yakunin had been 'in conflict with his own church authorities for some time' and Regelson, on the basis of the appeal to the 1971 Local Council which he had co-signed, was dubbed a person 'known for his anti-ecumenism'. Yuvenali then noted that Patriarch Tikhon had 'gained the opportunity to conduct the activities of the Moscow Patriarchate in a normal fashion', and that this line had been followed by Patriarchs Sergi and Alexi and 'the vast majority of the Church's faithful'. Yakunin and Regelson, by implication, were trouble-makers of dubious standing.

Metropolitan Yuvenali then stated that 'we do not disguise the fact that there have arisen and that there do arise problems in the life of the Church', but he ascribed these exclusively to violations of the laws on religion, 'both by local representatives of the state authorities and by members of church communities'. The uninformed reader of *Target* might have thought that Yuvenali's admission that state officials sometimes broke laws showed that he was not under pressure to whitewash the state completely. However, it is routine in the USSR to attribute any friction in church–state relations to 'mistakes' by local officials: this avoids the necessity of probing trouble-spots more deeply. So it was on this occasion: Metropolitan Yuvenali refrained from discussing the church's position in any detail and passed on to a tribute to the 'highly beneficial activity' of the CRA in dealing with infringements of the law. Yuvenali then stated:

> Not infrequently rumours of these infringements are brought to the attention of western Christians in an exaggerated — sometimes, distorted — form, which provokes an inadequate response from these Christians, thus complicating the resolution of our internal church problems.

Here he touched upon a genuine problem. The censorship which exists in the USSR, and the restrictions upon the means of communication available to believers, do mean that information often reaches Western Christians in a partial, delayed, and, possibly, distorted form, so that the reader is often left wanting to know more about a given situation. If news of such violations of laws could be made available in a fuller, official form, it would no doubt help Western Christians not to act in a way which complicated the resolution of internal church problems. However, Metropolitan Yuvenali's argument here was weakened by his use of the word 'rumours': as he had admitted that violations of laws did occur, why refer to reports of them as 'rumours'?

There is a further curious statement in the following paragraph, in which Yuvenali stated that every country has its laws, and that his church could not condone anyone who broke them. He continues:

At the same time we cannot but note the fact that our society is evolving in the direction of ever-increasing development of democratic principles. The Church has found its level in this process.[77]

The remarkable implication of these words was that Soviet society had not yet achieved full development of democratic principles, which is very far from customary Soviet assertions about the benefits of fully fledged socialist democracy. This letter showed every sign of having been put together hastily and under pressure, and — aid from the Soviet Embassy notwithstanding — it did not really provide an adequate response to the carefully thought-out appeal from Moscow. Its rather stereotyped assertions were exactly what readers would have been expecting, and therefore they made little or no impression on the Assembly delegates.

The story of subsequent events at the Assembly has been recounted in detail elsewhere,[78] and we will not repeat it here. Suffice it to say that an unsuccessful attempt was made to raise the issue of 'restrictions on religious liberty particularly in the USSR' during a debate on disarmament and the Helsinki Agreements (see p. 418), which because of confusion over procedural issues was referred back to committee; that as a result an open hearing on religious liberty in the USSR was held at an evening session after the closure of official proceedings; that the hearing was prolonged and lively and that the Russian Orthodox delegates played a conspicuous role in it; that afterwards a committee sat until the early hours of the morning drafting a substitute amendment; and that this amendment was presented to the Assembly next morning, 9 December. It read:

The Assembly requests the General Secretary to see to it that questions of religious liberty be the subject of intense consultations with the member Churches of the signatory States of the Helsinki Agreement and the first report be presented at the next Central Committee meeting of August 1976.

It was eventually accepted together with the following addition, which strengthened the expression of the Assembly's concern about violations of religious liberty:

This Assembly recognises that all the signatory nations appended below have equal responsibility to observe and carry out all the principles of this solemn agreement.

There are several conclusions to be drawn from the appeal, the debate and the resolution adopted by the Assembly. The first is that the course of action adopted was a considerable transmutation of that suggested by Yakunin and Regelson. Instead of peaceful protests, days of prayer and letters to suffering believers, there was to be a report to the WCC Central Committee. However, given the nature of the WCC it would not have been realistic to expect anything else, and the fact that the appeal was widely published gave sanction to the more direct initiatives of many organisations and churches around the world. The fact that the report was to be on religious liberty in all countries which had signed the Helsinki Agreement, as opposed to the USSR specifically, undoubtedly diminished the force of the resolution. It was clearly framed in this manner in order to avoid embarrassing the Russian Orthodox delegation, and perhaps even provoking their withdrawal from the WCC. Metropolitan Yuvenali had been understood to say at one point in the debate that his church might have to consider withdrawal if the USSR were named in a damaging manner in any resolution. The delegates in general seem to have displayed great understanding and sympathy for the Russian Orthodox delegation, and to have tried to help them in their awkward predicament. The Assembly clearly wished to play a mediating role between the two schools of thought in the Russian Orthodox Church, rather than to grasp the nettle of uncompromising condemnation of religious persecution. To the most active campaigners for religious liberty in the USSR, this no doubt looked like pusillanimity.

However, veterans of WCC meetings and other international ecumenical gatherings felt that much progress had been made. The fact that the general secretary had been mandated to prepare a report as early as August the following year was seen to express a general wish for urgent action. And the fact that Russian Orthodox and other delegates had publicly debated the issue of religious liberty in the USSR for the first time ever was seen as a major step forward.

The fact that the issue was eventually dealt with in the context of the Helsinki Agreements was significant. This meant that henceforward only WCC member churches from the European and North American countries which had signed the Agreements would be involved in the discussion of religious liberty. This fact reflected the attitude of the predominantly Third World membership of the WCC, which, generally speaking, viewed the whole issue as a purely European affair which was less important than the social, economic and other problems they faced in their own countries. Although the debate on religious liberty has been carried on within the WCC since the Nairobi Assembly, it is only part of it, not the whole, that has been involved.

The Russian Orthodox delegation did not have to return empty-handed to report to the CRA, since Metropolitan Nikodim was elected at the Assembly to be one of the WCC's several presidents. These are honorary rather than executive posts, but influential none the less. It had been noted for some time before the Assembly that Russian Orthodox representatives had been dropping obvious hints in WCC circles to the effect that they expected Nikodim to be elected, and had even hinted that they might withdraw if he was not. Many delegates reportedly had grave reservations about electing a man who constantly asserted that there was no persecution of religion in his country, but these yielded to a combination of procedural obstacles and a desire to compensate the Russian Orthodox delegation for their embarrassment over the Yakunin–Regelson appeal.

Responses to the Nairobi Appeal

Patriarch Pimen and the Holy Synod evaluated the Nairobi Assembly at length in a letter to the WCC's chairman and general secretary, dated 3 March 1976, which they published in the *Journal of the Moscow Patriarchate*.[79] They made a number of critical comments, chief of which were that the Orthodox voice was submerged by that of the Protestant majority, that the experience of the socialist countries in matters of social and economic justice was virtually ignored, and that on many issues related to the church's mission in the world there was too much emphasis on humanistic ideas and concepts of social justice and too little on the scriptural and spiritual foundations for this. These criticisms by the Russian Orthodox Church have all become familiar ones in recent years. Concerning the debate on religious freedom in the USSR, the Holy Synod broached it by stating that the discussion on the Helsinki Agreements had been in principle a good thing, but that it had been used to 'compromise the Soviet Union', and that 'objective illumination' of it had been hampered because no one from the Soviet Union or any other socialist country had been invited to take part in the preparations or the debate. People from the Soviet Union who had wished to speak during the discussions 'seldom received the opportunity to do so'. Objections to the procedure adopted for handing the Yakunin– Regelson appeal followed.[80] There was only one direct reference to the appeal:

> an attempt was made — not without the encouragement of certain WCC officials — to substitute the voice of Russian Orthodox Church delegates by that of ecclesiastical dissidents whose relations with the ecclesiastical authorities are strained and who do not share the mood of the great majority of Church members.

Such directness is unusual for the *Journal of the Moscow Patriarchate:*

this was probably the first, possibly the only, time that the word 'dissident' has appeared in its pages. The Holy Synod continued by deploring tendencies to direct contacts with such people by the WCC, which implied distrust in the leadership of the church, and warned that such contacts 'may lead to a weakening of our ties with the World Council of Churches'.[81] These were strong words, and they were repeated by the Russian Orthodox leadership during 1976. Metropolitan Nikodim stated in an interview:

> Certain circles, indirectly connected with the WCC staff, tried to create an anti-Soviet atmosphere at and around the assembly . . . it was an attempt made by reactionary forces in the West . . . the anti-Soviet clamour had been programmed, so to speak, and prepared beforehand.[82]

This allegation is a surprising one in view of the well-known fact that no one had been aware of Yakunin and Regelson's appeal until it arrived, and that it was not even on the agenda. However, Archbishop Pitirim made a similar statement later that year, blaming foreign organisations for fomenting trouble at Nairobi.[83] The three main elements in the Moscow Patriarchate's response were, to sum up: an attempt to discredit Yakunin and Regelson as being unrepresentative of the church; a deliberate accusation that some (unnamed) members of the WCC staff had tried to stir up 'anti-Soviet' sentiments; and the laying of the blame for the events at Nairobi on 'reactionary' and 'anti-Soviet' organisations in the West — the latter being a very common allegation by Soviet religious leaders at difficult moments. Their response was evasive, and, not unexpectedly, completely ignored the issues raised by the appeal.

An entirely different view of the proceedings at Nairobi was taken by Archbishop Vasili of Brussels, who wrote to Dr Potter, the WCC's general secretary, thanking him warmly for the 'courageous intervention of our Christian brothers in the West' in defence of Christians in the Soviet Union. The archbishop continued:

> This kind of intervention and protest, if it is continued in the future, could have a great influence on the situation of Christians in the USSR and will actively serve the improvement of their lot and help them in the struggle for religious freedom, as experience has already shown in many similar cases.[84]

The responses to Yakunin's and Regelson's appeal, which had received great publicity in the West, clearly disturbed the Soviet authorities. From January 1976, a number of major articles in the Soviet press reasserted the official Soviet view that freedom of religion existed in the USSR. (The fact that over a month elapsed before these began to be published suggests that the CRA had been completely taken by surprise by the events in Nairobi.)

An interview with the Deputy Minister of Justice of the USSR was published in *New Times*,[85] and shortly afterwards followed an interview with the CRA chairman, Vladimir Kuroyedov, in *Izvestiya*.[86] The first part of this long interview was devoted to a recital of the freedoms believers enjoyed under Soviet law and the benefits they had received from the Soviet state — church buildings, educational establishments, freedom to publish, and so forth. Kuroyedov stated:

> we have every right to affirm that our legislation on religious cults is the most humane and democratic in the world. It guarantees the interests of both believers and unbelievers to an identical degree.

Such a statement could be made only by ignoring the detailed analysis of Soviet laws on religion made by Igor Shafarevich in his report to the Human Rights Committee. In the second part of his article, Kuroyedov turned to the question of dissenters:

> Quite often reports appear in the West about people who have been sentenced here and are serving sentences allegedly for religious convictions. Such reports are gross falsehoods.

Kuroyedov maintained that people were sentenced for breaking the law, not for their religious convictions. Such people were 'usually pursuing careerist, mercenary goals and at the same time using religion as a cover'. He mentioned specifically Father Dimitri Dudko, Father Gleb Yakunin and Lev Regelson, and also the Baptist Georgi Vins. Father Dimitri's parishioners, according to Kuroyedov, had 'rejected the services of the priest Dudko, expelling him from his church for preaching with an anti-social content'. Yakunin had been under ban since 1966 for 'improper activity and violation of church discipline'. And Regelson was merely 'a person without a defined occupation' — an ironic comment, in view of Regelson's unsuccessful efforts to be reinstated as a physicist. Kuroyedov expressed surprise that Dr Potter of the WCC should have taken upon himself a 'far from honourable mission, that of popularising the slanderous letter about the situation of believers in the USSR', which had been 'cooked up by' Yakunin and Regelson. The whole thrust of Kuroyedov's article was against 'bourgeois propaganda' in the West which, he claimed, distorted the situation of religious believers in the Soviet Union because of hostility to socialism.

This attempt to throw all the blame for dissent on to the West was to become more and more frequent in the years to come. The Soviet press has never advanced any suggestions as to the causes of dissent other than that dissenters are motivated by an egoistical desire for fame and self-advancement, and that they are dupes of Western subversion. Since most of the dissenters thus described have received lengthy terms of imprisonment, and since they mostly commenced their public activities long before becoming known in the West, these claims are unconvincing. There was an ideological dilemma for the Soviet press, since to suggest that there were serious, rational grounds for dissent would have been tantamount to admitting that the Marxist–Leninist ideological system was not capable of solving all social and political problems. (The Soviet press not infrequently carries articles and debates on social and economic problems, but never suggests that a solution to them cannot be found within the Marxist–Leninist framework.) So Kuroyedov in his *Izvestiya* interview and other commentators on the subject were obliged to shift the whole question on to a rather crude ideological level, refusing to admit that, in what was supposedly a debate about religion, there could be any other standpoints than those of democratic socialism and the reactionary bourgeois camp.

Kuroyedov's interview in the government paper *Izvestiya* was followed by an editorial in the Communist paper, *Pravda*, which repeated the main points he had made. Both papers included a quote from Patriarch Pimen to the effect that no one in the USSR was sentenced for his religious beliefs. *Pravda* stated that believers were sentenced only for activities which harmed citizens' health or led to their non-fulfilment of their duties as citizens.[87] This article was reproduced in several Soviet newspapers.

These articles were followed in September 1976 by a book containing strong criticisms of religious believers. *Diversiya bez dinamita* (*Diversion Without Dynamite*), co-authored by a writer, A. Belov, and a KGB major, A. D. Shilkin, was published in a second edition revised to include pejorative statements about several named Orthodox Christians.[88] Eshliman and Yakunin, Anatoli Levitin, Zheludkov, Felix Karelin and Boris Talantov, who had all figured in the first edition in 1972, were now joined by Father Dimitri Dudko, Lev Regelson and Yevgeni Barabanov. The main thrust of the book was against research centres and radio stations in the West which were allegedly carrying out 'diversion' in the USSR, not with 'dynamite' but with books, radio broadcasts and 'disinformation' of all kinds suggesting that religious liberty did not exist in the USSR. The Orthodox and other believers who were named were said to be totally unrepresentative of Christians in general, but were none the less eagerly seized upon by the 'bourgeois clericalist' Western organisations for their 'anti-Soviet propaganda'. The aim of the book was thus to isolate the nonconformists from other believers, declare them law-breakers, and thus render them ripe for arrest and imprisonment.

The line adopted in this book and the press articles was the same as before, and the points they made had all been made before, but now they were being given much more prominent coverage. The revised second edition of *Diversiya bez dinamita* and the press campaign made it clear that the Soviet government regarded the activities of the dissenters, and especially the Nairobi Appeal, as a serious threat.

Yakunin and Regelson Respond to the Press Campaign

Yakunin and Regelson referred to the press articles in a further letter, dated 6 March 1976, addressed to Dr Potter.[89] They began by thanking him personally, and participants in the Assembly 'who showed a sincere and effective concern for the fate of the confessors and martyrs who are victims of such inhumanity'. They contrasted this attitude with a strongly worded criticism of

> those who take the initiative in seeking a spiritual union with the implacable enemies of the Church, who place their hopes not in Christ, but in the mighty ones of this world, who themselves become channels for anti-Christian influences

— a clear reference to the leaders of the Moscow Patriarchate. In the preamble to this letter, Yakunin and Regelson clearly aligned themselves with those who viewed the church as the metaphysical Body of Christ, rather than as an institution which must be preserved at all costs. Yakunin and Regelson then summarised the main points of the Soviet press articles in some detail for Dr Potter's benefit. They pointed out that the articles were 'aimed at preventing a broad international movement in defence of human rights' and 'intended to hamper the activity of the sub-committee of the WCC, organised at the behest of the Nairobi Assembly to investigate the situation of religion and believers'. They also pointed out that the willingness of Soviet officials to admit some isolated instances of violation of believers' rights 'may cause confusion to world public opinion and the members of the WCC sub-committee, pre-empting any formal possibility of accusing the Soviet State of anti-religious policy on the basis of individual, although flagrant, cases'. Yakunin and Regelson therefore suggested that the WCC sub-committee should base its deliberations upon an analysis of Soviet legislation on religion. They then discussed in detail four basic principles of the legislation on religion, which in their opinion 'determine its discriminatory character':

1. The unjust registration of religious societies as a sanctioning act.
2. Religious societies are deprived of property rights to the prayer buildings and basic items of the cult.
3. Religious societies are forbidden to carry on missionary and cultural-social activities.
4. The educational system is discriminatory in character; organised forms of private religious education are forbidden.

They proceeded to elaborate on these points (the points raised in their analysis have been covered in Part 1 of the present work).

Yakunin and Regelson then warned Dr Potter that since the Nairobi Assembly the CRA had directed its local officials to organise a campaign to collect signatures from clergy and believers assuring the WCC that all was well in the Russian Orthodox Church. Yakunin and Regelson pointed out that no amount of signatures could prove that there was religious liberty: 'Freedom is its own witness.' The only proof of absence of religious discrimination would be 'tens of thousands of new religious societies, churches, prayer houses, circles for religious instruction, associations for charitable and religious–cultural purposes, which would quickly spring up of themselves as soon as genuine religious freedom was established in the USSR'.

An example of the attempt to collect signatures to neutralise their appeal to the Nairobi Assembly had been given by Yakunin and Regelson in a letter to Patriarch Pimen only two days before their letter to Dr Potter.[90] It described an occurrence in the Church of St Nikolai in the village of Pushkino, Moscow region, where the priest was Archpriest Dimitri Sagan. According to Yakunin and Regelson, on 18 February 1976 he preached a 'most unusual sermon', in which he 'went on to distort completely the content and sense of our communication' by asserting, *inter alia*, that Yakunin and Regelson had written that 'believers are not allowed into the church to pray'. He appealed to his congregation, which consisted 'on a weekday of elderly women who had not only never heard of the Nairobi appeal, but knew nothing of the existence of the WCC itself', and they naturally agreed that they were allowed to pray in church, and began to move forward to receive the text of the statement they were being asked to sign. However, Sagan's dreams of being the first in Moscow diocese to achieve the desired signatures, and thus curry favour with his superiors and perhaps being reinstated in the DECR (which is the motivation Yakunin and Regelson impute to his action), were shattered by a bizarre occurrence: 'one little old lady whispered very audibly: "Orthodox believers! They want us to join with the Catholics!" Thereupon, to Father Dimitri's chagrin, most of the congregation rushed from the church.' Yakunin and Regelson pointed out in their letter to the Patriarch that it would not be at all difficult to organise the collection of signatures against the Nairobi Appeal, since many clergy and church workers would be afraid to refuse to sign for fear of losing their jobs. Even so, they concluded,

However wide an audience this campaign reaches, we are confident that the more letters of protest, the more signatures they show, then the more it will be an obvious, vivid and convincing dramatisation of our appeal to the WCC, and the more it will be an indication of the slavery of the Church in Russia.

Yakunin's and Regelson's version of events in Pushkino was corroborated in a further letter to Dr Potter from Father Sergi Zheludkov.[91] He summarised the restrictions on believers in the USSR with regard to the small number of churches, baptism, religious education, higher education and other matters, and ended with this statement:

> This whole issue of the legal and (in practice) illegal *lack of full rights* for believing citizens has been sufficiently illuminated in the well-known report of Academician Igor Shafarevich [see pp. 307–8] and in other truthful and responsible documents. Like so many, I have remained silent, consoling myself with the knowledge that the truth was known. But I felt myself obliged to speak out before you when I heard of this unscrupulous attempt, by means of this so-called 'parishioners' letter', to slander our brothers and deceive the World Council of Churches in your person.

As well as the evidence provided in these letters from Yakunin and Regelson and Zheludkov, Dr Potter and his WCC colleagues also had made available to them a report entitled *Religious Liberty in the Soviet Union* compiled, at the request of a member church of the WCC, by three Western European research centres.[92] Its five sections included a note on the six member churches of the WCC in the USSR; an account of relations between the WCC and these churches; a chapter on legislative discrimination against believers in the USSR; the 6 March letter from Yakunin and Regelson to Dr Potter; and a selection of *samizdat* documents from all the main denominations in the USSR. When the WCC Central Committee met in Geneva from 10 to 18 August 1976 it also had presented to it a report from a special informal consultation which had been held in Montreux, Switzerland, on 19 March between about 30 representatives of churches in countries which had signed the Helsinki Declaration.[93]

According to a journalist who was present at the Geneva meeting, the first days were very tense because of unease over the question of religious liberty in the Soviet Union. Both journalists and Central Committee members kept referring to the subject, and Archbishop Scott, the chairman of the Central Committee, admitted at a press conference that there could be serious differences of opinion in the debate for human rights, scheduled for 12 August. Metropolitan Yuvenali made a statement seriously criticising the WCC for failing to respond to the Holy Synod's letter of 3 March. On 12 August, Dr Potter gave his eagerly awaited report. The gist of it was that the issue of the freedom of believers was too large a one to be decided at the current meeting, and that he therefore proposed the creation of two special commissions. One would be part of the WCC Commission on International Affairs, and would be responsible for gathering, sifting and preparing information for discussion; the other would be composed of representatives of European and North American churches, and would take appropriate decisions.[94]

It is not within the scope of the present work to discuss the subsequent activity in defence of religious liberty in the Soviet Union within the WCC. The WCC's policy of consulting member churches before issuing a statement on any event in a given country has meant that its support for those working for religious freedom (including Yakunin and Regelson themselves in following years) has sometimes been muted, or even entirely private. But the fact that the WCC was finally obliged to incorporate into its structure machinery for dealing with the issue of religious liberty in the USSR (and elsewhere) is of no little historical significance, and credit for this belongs to the authors of the appeal to the Nairobi Assembly, Father Gleb Yakunin and Lev Regelson.

Although attempts to persuade the leaders of the Russian Orthodox Church to change their stance had diminished from about 1974, the preoccupations of Orthodox dissenters were still concentrated upon the state of the Russian Orthodox Church and the possibilities for improving it. Barabanov and Meerson-Aksyonov voiced the views of those who believed that the church must find strength within itself to overcome its disabilities, while the letters and appeals of Yakunin and Regelson were aimed at reducing state pressure on the church. While these two tendencies are not necessarily mutually exclusive, they did in fact become more sharply opposed in following years. Both, however, saw the central problem as being that of forging a viable role for the Orthodox Church in Soviet society. This concern did not decrease in succeeding years, but at the same time Orthodox dissenters began to exhibit more awareness of the fact that other religious believers were in a situation similar to their own. Ecumenical contacts began to develop on a limited scale.

12 THE FLOWERING OF ORTHODOX DISSENT: 1976–9

The Ecumenical Appeal

The first open expression of ecumenical co-operation was the appearance in June 1976 of a *samizdat* appeal to the Presidium of the Supreme Soviet of the USSR and to the World Council of Churches from 27 Christians belonging to six denominations.[1] As noted in its opening words, it was the first time in the history of the Soviet Union (indeed, of Russia) that members of different denominations had united in this way. Nearly half the signatories — twelve out of the 27 — were members of the Russian Orthodox Church. The other denominations represented were the Community of Evangelical Christians-Pentecostals, the Evangelical Christian-Baptist Church, the All-Union Church of True and Free Adventists, the Church of Christ[2] and the Catholic Church of Lithuania.

The ecumenical appeal was a carefully reasoned, lengthy account of the relations between religious communities and the Soviet state, consisting of ten sections. The first six sections gave a concise and well-argued exposition of by now familiar complaints: that Soviet legislation discriminated against believers, that they did not have equal rights with atheists, and that, beyond this, the state continually interfered both in the lives of religious communities and in the lives of individuals, by the obligatory teaching of atheism. The appeal's arguments were specifically addressed against the view of religious life in the USSR given by CRA chairman, Vladimir Kuroyedov, in his article in *Izvestiya* the previous January (see Chapter 11, p. 363).[3] Kuroyedov had repeated at length the customary assertions that Soviet laws granted true freedom for believers, and that individuals who were regarded in the West as persecuted for their faith were in fact law-breakers. The whole thrust of Kuroyedov's article was against 'reactionary circles in the West' which had 'put into circulation the filthy invention that there is no freedom of conscience in the USSR'. It concluded: 'In the cohesive Soviet society there is no division of people into believers and unbelievers. Both labour hand in hand for the good of their Motherland.'[4] This assertion was taken up in section seven of the ecumenical appeal:

> How can this be reconciled with the existence of a large number of believers sentenced for 'violation of the legislation on religious cults'? If the reason is not found in a hostile posture of believers towards the State, as V. A. Kuroyedov admits, this means that it lies in defects of the legislation itself or in its incorrect application.

The authors of the appeal then continued by making what were probably some of the most penetrating observations on the legislation on religion to date. They pointed out that

> Christianity arose far earlier than Soviet legislation on religion and therefore it is logically impossible to expect that it could have taken account in advance of the demands of this legislation. In precisely the same way it is unrealistic that Christianity, in the twentieth century of its existence, should revise its basic tenets.

At a superficial reading it might appear that the appeal was advancing an argument for disobeying the law, but in fact the point being made was that what Soviet law permitted was not full-blooded Christianity. When Kuroyedov spoke of freedom of religion for Christians, he was speaking of religion as defined by Marxist–Leninist theory, not the Christian religion as it has developed over 20 centuries. The ecumenical appeal was making the eminently logical point that Christians should be able to define their own beliefs and practices, not to have them defined by atheists, if they were to be considered truly free. Kuroyedov was able to pontificate about the existence of religious freedom in the USSR only because he and his political masters had defined what religious freedom consisted of. The appeal continued:

> If the right of religion to exist is honestly acknowledged, then it is impossible to deny the right to discuss the laws which regulate the situation of believers. These laws change: they have changed in recent years, consequently, discussion and criticism of them is natural.[5]

This section of the appeal was a thrust aimed at the heart of the Soviet government's policy on religion, which was simultaneously to repress it and to claim that it was free. Its arguments gnawed away at this dichotomy not so much by presenting evidence of repression (which was barely mentioned), but by revealing the logical inconsistency of the arguments used to demonstrate the supposed 'freedom of religion'.

The following section of the appeal pointed out that the worst effect of the existing situation of religion was on the country itself, not on the believers. The state needed to unite all citizens and eliminate internal contradictions, but

> at the same time tens of millions of believers are artificially brought into a state of *conflict* with the State in which they live. An ambiguity is created in their relationship with the State: they are loyal citizens, but they do not feel the corresponding attitude to themselves on the part of the State.

For a Christian, his faith was the most fundamental thing in life, and so an attempt to limit religion to worship was tantamount to an attempt to destroy religion altogether.

> It is easy to indicate who *suffers* from such a situation — the believers, the people as a whole, the international prestige of the State . . . But to whom it is *useful*? This is far harder to say. Most probably, it is useful to *no one*.

In other words the 'obsolete concepts of militant atheism' were being given precedence over what would be in the interests of all concerned: 'it would be so simple to alter this situation — *there is nothing whatever to prevent it*!'[6]

The remaining sections of the ecumenical appeal were devoted to listing the practical and legal changes which would be required to bring out true freedom for religious believers — all points which had been mentioned in many previous *samizdat* documents. It concluded by summing up its chief theme: that the abnormal position into which religion was forced was 'a terrible injury to our people' and 'an ailment of our society'.[7] Its authors ended by noting that they were not the first to make such requests, and that they were not so naive as to expect an immediate response, but 'a sense of responsibility to our country and to history impels us to express our views in the hope that our words will be heard — if not now, then at least before it is too late'.[8]

The ecumenical appeal was impressive both because of the force of its realistic and logically reasoned arguments, and because of its interdenominational support. The chief feature of this support was the number and stature of the Orthodox signatories as compared with those of other denominations. Not only were nearly half the signatories Orthodox, but they included nearly all those who had been most active among the independently minded Orthodox: Father Dimitri Dudko, Father Sergi Zheludkov, Father Gleb Yakunin, Hierodeacon Varsonofi (Khaibulin), Yevgeni Barabanov, Vadim Borisov, Boris Mikhailov, Lev Regelson, Felix Svetov, Tatyana Khodorovich, Igor Khokhlushkin and Igor Shafarevich. While the large number of Orthodox signatories may be explained by the fact that numbers of signatures were in very rough proportion to the size of each denomination represented (excepting the Church of Christ), it remained true that the stature of the Orthodox signatories was greater than that of the other denominations, some (though not all) of which were not represented by their best-known or most responsible members. Furthermore, the tone of the whole document suggested that it was probably originally drafted by an Orthodox believer or believers. The examples used to illustrate points and the wording of the documents strongly indicate this. This ecumenical venture, therefore, was most probably a venture by independently minded Orthodox who reached out to members of other denominations, rather than one which originated with another denomination or denominations and attracted the support of Orthodox believers. Although a few individual Orthodox Christians had done much to help members of other denominations (as mentioned earlier), this ecumenical spirit was on the whole a new development in the Russian Orthodox milieu.

An Open Letter to Patriarch Pimen

Another public document about the state of the Russian Orthodox Church, in the form of an open letter to Patriarch Pimen, was issued by Gennadi Shimanov in July 1976, shortly after the ecumenical appeal had been made public.[9] Shimanov asked why the Moscow Patriarchate did not protest about the lack of religious literature, the shortage of workshops for producing icons, the small numbers of churches, and so on. He pointed out that violation of the laws would be wrong, but requesting that they be altered was not. If, for whatever reason, the church was unable to print enough religious literature to satisfy the needs of its members, what was to prevent it asking the Soviet government for permission to receive literature from Christians abroad? There was no law against this. Why did the Moscow Patriarchate not protest against compulsory atheist education, why did it not request the opening of church schools and church libraries, such as existed in communist Hungary and communist Poland? Thus far, Shimanov's requests were not so very different from those of the ecumenical appeal, and the reader may wonder why he did not sign it after publication (a possibility which its authors specifically mentioned). It would probably have been more effective to give added weight to that already impressive appeal instead of issuing another one with only one signature. The answer was contained in the last few paragraphs of Shimanov's open letter. He wrote:

> the elimination from Soviet legislation and Soviet practice of destructive points will lead to the moral health of Soviet society, because it will unite it with the thousand-year-old moral roots of Russia, and will strengthen Soviet power itself, because it will liquidate the soil in which anti-Soviet attitudes sprout and will attract millions of Soviet patriots to the side of a harmonised Soviet State.

This was not so very far removed from the ecumenical appeal's argument that the normalisation of the position of religion in the Soviet Union would bring as many benefits to the people and society as a whole as to believers themselves. The difference was that Shimanov here linked the potential benefits to Soviet society with the 1,000 years of Russian Orthodoxy and with Russian patriotism rather than with Christianity in general. Shimanov continued:

> There are serious grounds for hoping that in the not too distant future

the Soviet leaders will realise this and will go to meet their own best interests, and also world public opinion and the petitions of our Church.

Shimanov did not say what these 'serious grounds' were, but he was clearly urging Patriarch Pimen not only to defend the interests of the church, but also to be in a position to benefit from the expected change in the Soviet leaders' attitude. Shimanov believed that, 'Correctly understood, the interests of the Church and the Soviet State are the same.' They were the same not only in the creation of a truly human society on earth, but also because of the characteristics of Russian history.

> The Soviet State as a matter of fact deeply *needs* the Orthodox Church, and the forthcoming transfiguration of our country into an Orthodox theocratic spirit is *necessary* to it, because only such a transfiguration will justify and save Soviet power from the merciless judgement of history.

This was a logical consequence of Shimanov's views as given in other *samizdat* documents, which we discussed in Chapter 11 (see pp. 339–45). It was clear that Shimanov could not have signed the ecumenical appeal because he did not believe in the ability of any Christian denomination except Russian Orthodoxy to challenge, subdue and transfigure the Soviet state. The peculiarly Russian nature of Orthodoxy was as important to him as its Christian content. Moreover, he believed that Russian Orthodoxy needed the Soviet state: 'Orthodoxy, currently in a state of paralysis, *needs* the religio-historical phenomenon of the Soviet State for its triumph in history.'

Once more we see the divergence between the liberals and the nationalists among the Orthodox intellectuals. All wanted to see the Russian Orthodox Church freed from state restraints and able to carry on normal church activities freely, and all believed that Soviet society as a whole would be better-off if this were so. But the authors of the ecumenical appeal wanted the laws to be changed in order to leave all Christian denominations free to define their own sphere of action and to live in accordance with beliefs worked out since the foundation of Christianity — broadly speaking, a reform in the direction of democracy, giving the churches some of the basic democratic freedoms. Shimanov, on the other hand, did not appear to be at all concerned with the non-Orthodox churches, and, far from wanting the church to be separate from the state, envisaged some kind of union or transformation of the state in an encounter with specifically Russian Orthodoxy. Russian nationalism played as great a role in his scheme of things as did Orthodoxy.

The Christian Committee for the Defence of Believers' Rights in the USSR

An important event which took place in December 1976 allied some members of the Russian Orthodox Church closely with the Democratic Movement. This was the founding of the Christian Committee for the Defence of Believers' Rights in the USSR.[10] The declared aim of the Christian Committee was 'to help believers to exercise their right of living in accordance with their convictions'.[11] In performing this task, it was complementing and aiding the work of two other kinds of official groups of Soviet citizens. It was continuing in greater depth one aspect of the work of human rights groups which included a concern for religious believers in their work for human rights in general; and at the same time it was able to co-operate with committees and groups of various denominations of believers working to defend the rights of their own members. The Christian Committee was set up in close consultation with the Moscow Helsinki Monitoring Group, which felt the need for another more specialised group to deal with all the material on religious groups which it was receiving. (The Helsinki Monitoring Group similarly spawned another specialist body, the Working Commission for the Investigation of the Use of Psychiatry for Political Purposes.)

Although the Christian Committee claimed strong support and co-operation from members of other denominations, its initial membership was exclusively Orthodox. The three founding-members were Father Gleb Yakunin, Hierodeacon Varsonofi (Khaibulin) and, as secretary, Viktor Kapitanchuk. The Committee's founding Declaration explained that since the Russian Orthodox Church had been the dominant religion in Russia for centuries, and had sometimes been guilty of persecuting non-Orthodox believers, the Committee's founding-members felt a particular obligation to atone for the wrongs of their church's past by doing what they could to help members of other denominations. There was also a practical reason for the Committee's unidenominational membership. In March 1978, in a conversation with a foreign visitor,[12] its members explained that they would have liked the Committee to be interdenominational, but that after a good deal of thought they had decided against this, chiefly because it would be difficult to keep up communications with various groups of believers over long distances. However, it is known that some Orthodox refrained from giving overt support to the Committee's work because they believed the principle of interdenominational responsibility to be an important one.[13]

Although its concern was interdenominational, the Christian Committee did in fact play a special role in the defence of Orthodox Christians, since it was the only body in the Soviet Union actively working on their behalf. Other sizeable denominations suffering persecution — the Reform Baptists, Pentecostals, True and Free Seventh-Day Adventists and Lithuanian Catholics — had already formed their own unofficial bodies to try to protect their members' interests. The Russian Orthodox Church, though far larger than any of them, had not previously adopted any comparable means of trying to defend its members' interests. As we have seen, such a reaction as there was to the pressures on Orthodox believers had come from a relatively small number of individuals, often with differing viewpoints. There were two probable reasons for their failure to take swifter and more united action. First, although, as we have seen, the Orthodox Church had been under very considerable state pressure, it had not been subjected to the more dramatic forms of open persecution which other denominations have suffered in recent years. Second, there was no tradition in the Orthodox Church of fighting for the civil rights of its members.

The Christian Committee was founded on 27 December 1976. It announced its existence at a press conference in Moscow, produced its Declaration stating why it had been formed and what it intended to do, and immediately distributed three documents describing particular injustices suffered by different groups of religious believers, thus setting the pattern for its future work. Its founding Declaration is an admirably clear and concise statement of purpose. It pointed out that, though the Constitution of the USSR proclaimed freedom of conscience, there was inevitably conflict between believers and a government whose declared aim was to construct a non-religious society, leading sometimes to 'violations by the state administrative authorities of even those rights which believers legally possess'. It might be objected that such matters were properly the concern of the church's leaders, not of unofficial groups of believers acting on their own initiative. The Declaration had a reply to this:

> At present, the bishops of the Russian Orthodox Church and the leaders of other religious organisations do not concern themselves with the defence of believers' rights, for a variety of reasons. In such circumstances, the Christian community has to make the legal defence of believers its own concern.

The phrase 'for a variety of reasons' covered the whole bitter and controversial debate about the continued silence of church leaders on the problems faced by their members as a result of state policies.

The Christian Committee listed five ways in which it intended to help believers attain their rights 'to live in accordance with their convictions':

1. To collect, study and distribute information on the situation of religious believers in the USSR.
2. To give legal advice to believers when their civil rights were infringed.
3. To appeal to state institutions concerning the defence of believers' rights.
4. To conduct research, as far as this was possible, to clarify the legal and factual position of religion in the USSR.
5. To assist in putting the Soviet legislation on religion into practice.

The Committee has fulfilled its first and fourth aims by compiling and sending to the West a large number of documents. It also fulfilled its third aim to some extent, since among these documents are some addressed to Soviet state institutions on particular problems. We have no way of knowing whether the Christian Committee found it possible to realise its second and fifth aims.

The Christian Committee was fortunate in finding friends in the West who were willing to publish and circulate its documents promptly: the Washington Research Center in San Francisco. The Center produced 11 volumes of Russian texts and one volume (vol. 3) of selected English translations, under the title *Documents of the Christian Committee for the Defense of Believers' Rights in the USSR (DCCDBR)*.[14] These volumes contained 396 documents totalling 1,189 pages of Russian text. Another 21 documents, intended for an as yet unpublished vol. 13, brought the total to 417 documents and 1,302 pages. A further six documents reached the West separately, making a total of 423, by March 1980. (After this date the nature of the Committee's activities changed radically, as we shall see.)

The majority of the documents were signed by the denominational representatives who submitted them to the Christian Committee. However, the Christian Committee itself signed 64 documents. Forty-six of them were concerned with denominational issues, eight were concerned with problems involved in the Committee's work, and ten discussed more general but substantial issues.

These ten general documents reported in depth on problems affecting the situation of the churches as a whole, particularly the Russian Orthodox Church, as opposed to individual groups or believers. The first was the founding Declaration mentioned above, and the second was a detailed commentary on the draft of the new Soviet Constitution, which we discussed in Chapter 9.[15] A third general document, which we quoted in Chapter 3, concerned economic discrimination against church employees.[16] Also in 1977, the Christian Committee issued a commentary on foreign religious broadcasts, which form an extremely important source of both news and devotional material for Soviet believers.[17]

On 11 April 1978 the Christian Committee wrote a letter to the Ecumenical Patriarch Demetrios,[18] appealing to him to come to the aid of the Russian Orthodox Church, since the Russian bishops had abandoned their responsibility to defend oppressed Christians and the flouted rights of the church: 'If the forces of ecumenical Orthodoxy, and its free voice, do not come to the aid of the captive Russian Church, then only divine intervention will be able to save us.'

The next three general documents were addressed to the Pope. The first, 'to the successor of Pope John Paul I', with a covering letter to three cardinals, expressed the hope that the next Pope would wish to establish good relations with the Russian Orthodox Church, and that these relations would be based on a true understanding of the position of the Russian

Orthodox Church and its relationship with the Soviet state.[19] It must have been a great joy to the Christian Committee when the recipient of their letter, the Polish Pope John Paul II, was revealed to be a man with a lifetime's experience of relations between the church and a communist state. The second letter, dated 22 November 1978, was addressed to Pope John Paul II and other Christian leaders, including the heads of Orthodox autocephalous churches, the Archbishop of Canterbury, the World Council of Churches and President Carter of the USA. It urged the adoption of an international 'pact on religious rights' or 'Convention on the struggle against religious discrimination', analogous to international agreements on human rights. An international agreement of this kind should protect the internal life of religious communities against state interference, and should also decide upon a definition of the term 'confession of a religion' which would make it impossible for a state to limit believers merely to the 'performance of a cult'.[20] The third of these letters, addressed to Pope John Paul II and dated 2 April 1979, gave evidence of the close relations between the Moscow Patriarchate's Department of External Church Relations and the Council for Religious Affairs. It warned against the danger of thinking that official bodies of the Russian Orthodox Church were free and representative entities.[21]

Probably the most significant of all the Christian Committee's documents was the 'Report of Father Gleb Yakunin to the Christian Committee for the Defence of Believer's Rights in the USSR on the Current Situation of the Orthodox Church and the Prospects for a Religious Renaissance in Russia', which we quoted extensively in Part 1 and to which we shall refer again at the end of this chapter.

The tenth of the general documents, an undated 'Appeal to Christians of the Whole World',[22] was signed jointly by the Christian Committee and the Christian Seminar on Problems of the Religious Renaissance (see below, pp. 381–90). It spoke of the urgent need for Christian literature in the USSR and appealed to Christians to do all they could to provide the means to send Christian books there. Tourists were urged to help: 'Let everyone who travels to Russia take with them at least one Bible and one prayer book, which are pemitted to be taken through Soviet customs.'

The overwhelming majority of the documents issued by the Christian Committee were concerned with specific cases of violations of believers' rights. They were characterised by an evident desire to achieve accuracy, provide as many factual details as possible, and avoid any histrionics and sensationalism, even when recounting incidents causing great distress to the victims. Believers who were themselves involved in these incidents, or denominational bodies representing them, have written 359 of these documents, and a further 46 were signed by the Christian Committee, often in support of denominational reports describing particular incidents.[23]

Of those documents which deal with incidents concerning Orthodox believers, very few reached the West independently of the Christian Committee. They furnished a very valuable source of previously unobtainable information about problems of Orthodox parish life. Many of the cases which we quoted in Part 1 of believers unable to reopen closed churches, of CRA interference in parish life, and of the disruptive activities of immoral parish priests, were based on documents made available by the Christian Committee. In many cases the grievances of parishioners dated back for many years, and it is clear that they had no means of making them known to the general public until the new channel provided by the Christian Committee became available.

The Christian Committee documents also added a great deal to knowledge in the West of the affairs of the Christian Seminar (see below) and of the arrests, trials and imprisonment of individual Orthodox believers.

To what extent did the Christian Committee make available information which would not otherwise have reached the West on non-Orthodox denominations? In the case of the Protestant denominations (Reform Baptist, Pentecostal, and Seventh-Day Adventist), about half the 177 documents sent out by the Christian Committee had already reached the West by other routes. Of the rest, some reached the West by other routes than the copies sent by the Christian Committee, but many did not, and are available only because the Christian Committee sent them out. Of the 49 Catholic documents forwarded by the Christian Committee, almost all reached the West through other channels as well, chiefly through the *samizdat Chronicle of the Lithuanian Catholic Church*. However, in many cases copies sent by the Christian Committee reached the West first, and in some cases the Christian Committee has provided the West with its only Russian (as opposed to Lithuanian) text. It seems, then, that the Christian Committee's chief contribution to the already established denominational groups was to provide additional, faster channels for getting information to the West, due to the fact that it was based in Moscow, where contact with foreigners, especially Western correspondents, is easier than anywhere else in the country.

Although the Christian Committee claimed to defend all religious believers in the USSR, only two of its documents related to non-Christian believers. Both concerned Iosif Begun, a Jewish believer who was sentenced to a term of internal exile for giving private lessons in Hebrew.[24] The Christian Committee could not fairly be accused of pro-Christian bias, however, since there was no non-Christian religious cause which it could sensibly have included in its programme. Certainly Soviet Jews were, and are, enduring all kinds of hardships, but these are overwhelmingly concerned with their ethnic, not their religious, status. The current major preoccupation of Soviet Jewry is the right to emigrate, and this is not a purely religious concern. Iosif Begun's case was connected with his religious beliefs, and the Christian Committee was quick to take it up. Soviet Islam is under close state control, like all religions in the USSR, but there is little evidence of violation of specific legal rights of Muslim believers. A Christian Committee report on Soviet Buddhists would certainly have been welcome, but apparently the Committee was unable to find a satisfactory means of obtaining information from the Buryat ASSR in the Soviet Far East where most Buddhists live. We should also note that little or no information on the violation of rights of Jewish, Muslim or Buddhist believers reached the West from any other sources during the period in which the Christian Committee was active.

The Christian Committee evidently managed to win the support and respect of Roman Catholic, Reform Baptist, Pentecostal and Adventist activists, and must be credited with being at the forefront 'of a highly practical ecumenical venture which was something quite new for the Soviet Union. The ecumenical appeal had shown that there was willingness for some interdenominational co-operation, and the Christian Committee developed this initial venture. However, the interdenominational co-operation appears to have been on a purely practical, rather than a theological, basis, and took place between the Christian Committee and the denominational groups concerned, rather than among the denominational groups themselves. It was all focused on Moscow, with the obvious practical aim of getting documentation sent to the West.

The Christian Committee's example inspired others to follow suit. In November 1978 the Catholic Committee for the Defence of Believers' Rights was formed in Lithuania. When it made public its formation, it stated its intention of working in close co-operation with the Christian Committee, which in fact organised the press conference in Moscow at which the Catholic Committee made its announcement. Many of the Catholic documents subsequently sent to the West by the Christian Committee were compiled and signed by the Catholic Committee. In 1978 a similar committee was formed in Romania: the Christian Committee for the Defence of Religious Freedom and Freedom of Conscience (ALRC). The founders of ALRC apparently heard of the existence of the Moscow Christian Committee on foreign radio broadcasts, and it was one source of inspiration for their own initiative.[25]

For the first three years of its existence, there were only six members of the Christian Committee altogether, and no more than four at any one time. The three founder-members were joined on 29 December 1977 by a second layman, Vadim Shcheglov. It was announced that if any of the three founder-members were arrested, there were other people ready to take their places, and Shcheglov's function would be to reveal their names.[26] Shortly after this, Khaibulin left the Committee. He was attached to a parish in Vladimir region, and communication between him and the other members in Moscow was known to be difficult. In May 1979 Father Vasili Fonchenkov joined the Committee. On 1 November 1979 Yakunin was arrested, and shortly afterwards it was announced that his place would be taken by Father Nikolai Gainov. On 12 March 1980 Viktor Kapitanchuk was also arrested. From March 1980, therefore, the Christian Committee has consisted of Father Nikolai Gainov, Father Vasili Fonchenkov and Vadim Shcheglov. Another ten people had reportedly joined the Committee after the arrests, but were not prepared to reveal their names because of inevitable KGB pressure if they did so.[27] Stanislav Zherdev, a Pentecostal who emigrated to the West on 5 August 1980, subsequently announced that he was one of the 'secret' members. Evidently the Christian Committee had decided that the time for interdenominational membership had come.

The six known members of the Christian Committee had very different backgrounds and were differently treated by the Soviet authorities. Yakunin, Khaibulin and Kapitanchuk had all been active in the defence of freedom of religion and had signed, separately, many appeals and protests, as a result of which Yakunin and Khaibulin had lost their posts in parishes. Kapitanchuk, however, unusually for one active in any sphere of dissent in the USSR, retained his job as a chemist up to the time of his arrest. Vadim Shcheglov had not been involved in any independent public activities up to the time he joined the Christian Committee. He had been a Christian for only six years (having been converted after reading a book by Metropolitan Anthony (Bloom) of Sourozh). He was not dismissed from his work as a mathematician in the Ministry of Health after his membership of the Christian Committee was announced.

The most unexpected members of the Christian Committee were Fonchenkov, who had no previous public involvement in the defence of believers' rights, and Gainov, who had very little. Both held official positions within the Russian Orthodox Church, and they must have realised that these would be put in jeopardy by their membership of the Christian Committee. Father Vasili Fonchenkov, born in 1932, was baptised at the age of 18, studied history, and worked in museums. (His autobiography includes a fascinating snippet of information. During Khrushchev's anti-religious campaign, the museum where Fonchenkov worked was turned into a centre for atheist work. Despite this, some of the workers were converted to Christianity, and one of them, besides Fonchenkov himself, became a priest.) He graduated from the Theological Academy at Zagorsk in 1972, and was appointed a lecturer there, as well as occupying a post in the Department of External Church Relations. From 1976 to 1977 he was incumbent of the Church of St Sergi in East Berlin, and edited the journal of the Central European Exarchate of the Moscow Patriarchate, *Stimme der Orthodoxie* (*The Voice of Orthodoxy*).[28] He was clearly a person trusted by the church and the CRA, and with the prospect of a good career before him.

On joining the Christian Committee, Fonchenkov issued a statement[29] in which he pointed out that the Moscow Patriarchate had never condemned the activities of the Christian Committee, and hoped that his own membership of the Committee would not attract condemnation either. Neither he nor other Committee members were openly censured by church leaders, but, though Father Vasili continued lecturing at the Moscow Theological Schools for some time after joining the Christian Committee, he was eventually dismissed from his lectureship. He retained his parish in Moscow.

As noted in Chapter 10, Gainov was dismissed from his parish after co-signing an appeal to the 1971 Local Council. However, at the time when he joined the Christian Committee in November 1979, he was priest in the parish of Tsarevo, Moscow region. He was not dismissed from his parish on joining the Christian Committee.

The arrest of Viktor Kapitanchuk on 12 March 1980 marked the end of the first and most productive phase of the work of the Christian Committee. With the disappearance of the three founder-members, the authors and compilers of the prodigious amount of material forwarded by the Committee, this aspect of its work came virtually to a standstill. It is true that Gainov and Shcheglov issued a statement on the same day announcing that the Christian Committee intended to continue its work 'in accordance with the founding Declaration adopted in 1976'. It also stated that the ten new unidentified members had been selected from about 250 applicants. But in practice, only a handful of documents have reached the West, and these have all been brief reports of particular acts of repression. There has been none of the careful documentations of particular grievances, or long general analytical documents, as formerly. This may be because the present members, forewarned by the fate of their predecessors, have decided to conduct the Committee's work on a more low-key level. As we shall see in the following chapter, dissenters have had to operate in a more repressive atmosphere since 1980, and it is difficult for the Christian Committee to ascertain facts about incidents of repression, or to forward their documents to the West. However, in April 1981 it was reported that the Committee's activity was continuing despite the difficulties, and that the enlarged secret membership included Baptists, Adventists and Pentecostals.[30]

The Christian Seminar

By 1976, the unofficial attempts at reform within the church had been in progress for more than a decade without making any difference at all to the structure or the policies of the Moscow Patriarchate. Two consequences of this fact which had been developing for some time now began to make themselves obvious. The first was that independently minded Orthodox were beginning to devote more of their energies to independent, unofficial church life than to attempts to reform the Moscow Patriarchate; and the second was that the Soviet authorities were beginning to criticise and suppress such activists more vigorously. Their repressive activities will be discussed in the following chapter. Both these processes were exemplified in the Christian Seminar. This was an informal study group for young intellectuals who had recently become members of the Russian Orthodox Church, and who wished to learn more about their new-found faith. It had been founded by Alexander Ogorodnikov in September or October 1974,[31] at a time when, as we noted at the end of Chapter 10, the formation of special-interest groups among Orthodox dissenters was beginning to increase.[32]

The Christian Seminar was by no means unique. For many years there have been reports, almost always undocumented, of groups of young Orthodox meeting together to discuss and study their faith. Often this seems to have been a fairly deep and systematic study of Scripture, the Church Fathers and the great Russian philosophers and theologians, though with the ever-present limitation that students were restricted to study of such religious books as they could manage with great difficulty to obtain. Often these little groups appear to have been gathered around priests, who, as we saw in Chapter 3, are able to conduct such a ministry among young people if they act with a carefully judged combination of determination and caution. Many young people also went for advice and lively discussion sessions to the layman Anatoli Levitin, who helped and influenced a great many people along their path to the Christian faith. Such little groups have been gathering since at least the mid-1960s.[33] Since they depend for their continued existence on secrecy, very little is known of the activity of these groups, and it is impossible to say how many people are involved, even in Moscow and Leningrad, where foreigners are sometimes able to make contact with them. As for the provinces, all we can say is that study groups are definitely known to exist there, though precisely where, and on what scale, we cannot guess. Occasionally members of these groups appear in Moscow and Leningrad to make contact with Christians there, mainly for the purpose of obtaining religious literature brought in from the West. Then they disappear again, and even Christians in the capital cities are unable to maintain contact with them and their groups' activities. The activities of the Christian Seminar were as unpublicised as those of any other group during the first two years of its existence, although it did not shun contacts with foreigners: at least one Western Christian is known to have been warmly welcomed to to its meetings in 1974. However, from the summer of 1976 onwards the Christian Seminar was for some reason singled out for brutal and continued persecution. From that time a stream of information about its activities and the fates of its members has reached the West. For this reason, we are able to discuss this particular study group in some detail.

The reasons for forming the Christian Seminar were set out in two letters written to the general secretary of the WCC, Dr Philip Potter, during summer 1976 (see note 31). They reflect the experience of many young

Soviet urban intellectuals. Ogorodnikov wrote that he and his friends

> grew up in atheist families. Each of us has undergone a complex, some-times agonising, path of spiritual questing. From Marxist convictions, via nihilism and the complete rejection of any ideology, via attraction to the 'hippy' lifestyle, we have come to the Church.[34]

The joint letter from Ogorodnikov and Razveyev spelled out this painful process. They became part of an 'intellectual ferment' in Soviet society, which 'was at first just a cry of pain, a desperate attempt to escape from the spellbound spiritual captivity of ideology'. They began to 'suspect all ideologies in principle' and 'found ourselves in a new blind alley' because they had 'eliminated the human element'. 'Modern non-religious humanism, in declaring man to be the highest and only standard of value, ends up by justifying all his actions, even the evil he has done in history'. It was of course precisely the evil done by man in history, especially during the Stalinist period, from which this generation of Soviet intellectuals was seeking to find a way back. At this point, they write, 'a revision of our moral values became necessary'. Expelled from academic institutes, they were obliged to take menial jobs as, for example, night-watchmen, and

> aspiring Russian thought matured in agonising disputes (sometimes lasting for weeks), which opened up to us the truth of Russian religious philosophy. Khomyakov, Dostoyevsky, V. Solovyov, Fr S. Bulgakov and G. Florovsky brought us up to the threshold of the Church and set us before its doors.

As with so many others, it was the great Russian thinkers of the nineteenth and early twentieth centuries whose influence proved decisive. The final stage was effortless: 'our ailing souls heard at last the quiet call of God. The world was transformed, it acquired wholeness and integrity.'[35]

However, acceptance of Orthodoxy and membership of the church did not mean the end of their difficulties.

> New problems awaited us within the sacred portals of the Church. On the one hand, our involvement in the Church was hindered by a pagan element of intellectual pride, on the other, by the lack of a flourishing religious community life within the Russian Orthodox Church, which deprived us of the opportunity to serve the Church actively.[36]

> We were soon convinced that our problems were not being raised in church sermons, which are the only means for the religious education of believers, nor in the pages of the church journal, the *Journal of the Moscow Patriarchate*, which, moreover, is inaccessible to the ordinary Christian.[37]

The letter concludes: 'All this forced us to try and solve our problems ourselves.' Their reasons for beginning the Christian Seminar were:

— the thirst for a living Christian fellowship of love;
— the clearly-recognised need for theological education, which we could not obtain by any other means;
— a duty to carry out missionary work.[38]

It is not entirely clear whether this rejection of the institutional church constituted a complete break or not. It seems probable that individual Seminar members may have continued to visit churches and to take communion, though this is not explicit. Anatoli Levitin, writing generally about young converts to the church, has said:

As a rule, they rarely went to church: Church Slavonic was alien to them and their atheist education; and religious rituals confused them. They would start by reading religious literature, and would often meet other religious people to argue and talk about religion. Gradually, however, they would be overwhelmed by a desire to pray, and would begin turning to prayer more and more as life threw up difficulties in their path. Gradually they would get used to the atmosphere in church; and communion would become a spiritual necessity to them.[39]

We should also recall that, as noted in Chapter 7, attendance at church by a young person, if noticed by the authorities, could lead to problems, even expulsion, from their place of study or employment.

This at least partial rejection of the institutional church did not pass unnoticed by its leadership. Metropolitan Filaret of Minsk, asked in an interview in Paris in January 1980 why the church hierarchy had done nothing to help Christian Seminar members who were being persecuted, replied that, as they had gone off on their own, he was unable to help them.[40]

Christian Seminar members did, however, have guidance from older and more experienced church members. Alexander Ogorodnikov and others regarded Father Dimitri Dudko as their spiritual father, a relationship in which the spiritual son or daughter voluntarily submits themselves to obedience. Anatoli Levitin was close to Ogorodnikov, and after his emigration in 1974 was referred to as the overseas representative of the Christian Seminar. Another older Christian, Mikhail Agursky, told the present author after his emigration that he had visited the Christian Seminar to give a lecture to them.

Dissatisfaction with church services was a reason for joining the Christian Seminar mentioned by several members. Yelena K. 'used to go to church, but the services struck her as tired and dead. Now she has found the

Seminar, where she gets support, has learned bravery, and has found peace.' Vladimir Blagovestov 'went to church but wasn't satisfied. Then he came to the Seminar and found God.' The most frequently mentioned reason for joining the Seminar was the opportunity to meet other young people in the community and discuss freely. A. Yevgeni stated: 'The greatest thing about the Seminar is the opportunity to meet and discuss with other young people. This is something that can't be done in church.' Sergei Yermolayev found that 'One of the greatest things about the Seminar is free fraternal intercourse with young people.' 'Andrei' (no surname given) believed that 'Meetings with other Christians are the important thing — just like the early Christians, who met together and confirmed each other's faith.' And Alexander Shchipkov pointed out the value of 'Life in a community (Christians are among Christians — not one atheist).' The absence of atheists must have been particularly refreshing for people accustomed to live their whole lives in an atmosphere saturated with atheist teachings, faced with the task of justifying their beliefs to those around them. That they did not shrink from this difficult task is evidenced by the emphasis on missionary activities in writings by Seminar members, and by the fact that new members kept appearing. As Seminar member Vladimir Blagovestov wrote: 'To argue successfully against atheism, you need more than just the Holy Scriptures. You need knowledge of science, philosophy, mathematics etc. Here the Seminar is a great help.'[41]

It has sometimes been assumed that the Christian Seminar's independent existence, without official sanction from either church or state, meant that its activities were illegal. However, a careful study of the relevant legislation casts doubt on this. We saw in Chapter 2 that the Law on Religious Associations, adopted in 1929 and revised in 1975, stated (Article 2): 'Religious associations of believers of all denominations shall be registered as religious societies or groups of believers.' However, the Law on Religious Associations does not specifically state that the forming of religious associations is to be the *only* means whereby people may fulfil their religious needs. We have seen that other aspects of religious life for which there is no legal basis continue to exist with the tacit complicity of the state. For example, the monasteries and convents, to which foreign visitors are taken, have no basis in law. Neither does the *Journal of the Moscow Patriarchate*, though it continues to be published without hindrance.

The Christian Seminar did not attempt to register as a state-recognised religious association. Indeed, it did not attempt to form itself into what the Soviet government (or Western secular or ecclesiastical authorities) would necessarily recognise as a 'religious association'. It had no chairman or secretary, no treasurer or auditing commission, no funds at all, as far as we know; there was no formally prescribed membership, no election of officers, no structure of any kind. In what sense, then, could it be called a religious association which should seek registration under Soviet law? In practice, the Christian Seminar was a small group of people, probably not even with a constant membership, which met informally in the homes of its members. There did not appear to be any legal basis for the Soviet government to take action against them. Furthermore, an Instruction on the implementation of the Law on Religious Associations makes it clear that activity by believers outside registered associations is countenanced under the law. Article 22 (Part 3) of this Instruction reads: 'Believers who have not formed a society or group must notify the authorities regarding each prayer meeting separately.'[42]

This view of the legality of the Christian Seminar's activity is strengthened by the fact that the nine members of the Seminar known to have been arrested have not been charged with participating in meetings of the Christian Seminar. A variety of other charges (described in Chapter 13) have been preferred.

A good deal of information is available about the members of the Christian Seminar who have been arrested, but little or nothing is known about those who continued to participate in the Seminar's activities without attracting the attention of the KGB. To what extent the arrested members of the Seminar were typical of the membership of the whole Seminar is therefore difficult to judge. Evidently they were its leading spirits, possibly more dedicated, or more intellectually or spiritually gifted than the others.

Alexander Ogorodnikov, the Seminar's founder, was born in 1950. He is married to Yelena Levasheva and they have a young son. He is reported to have been an excellent student in the three educational institutes which he attended: Moscow State University, the Urals University (in their respective philosophy departments), and the All-Union State Cinematography Institute in Moscow. His interest in Christianity began when he saw Pasolini's film *The Gospel According to Saint Matthew* at the Cinematographic Institute. Although he received a higher grant in recognition of his ability, he was expelled after the institute's authorities discovered that he was a Christian.[43]

Another early member of the Christian Seminar was Vladimir Poresh, sometimes described as its co-founder along with Ogorodnikov. His path to the church, described by his school-teacher, Tatyana Shchipkova, also involved a long process of agonised intellectual and spiritual questing, which at one time brought him close to suicide. He too read Berdyayev, Khomyakov, Solovyov and Dostoyevsky, and gradually: 'I came to the conclusion that God exists. He cannot not exist, otherwise there would be no sense in anything.'[44] In 1975 he met Ogorodnikov. By this time he had left school in Smolensk and was studying in Leningrad State University. He specialised in Romance philology, and after graduation worked in the Academy of Sciences Library in Leningrad. He has published academic works in his subject. Poresh became the Seminar's Leningrad representative. He is married to Tatyana Kupatadze and they have two daughters.

Tatyana Shchipkova also joined the Christian Seminar. Born in 1930, she is its only longstanding member known to be older than her twenties or early thirties. She lectured at the Smolensk Pedagogical Institute for 17 years, and was a specialist in Romance languages — Latin, Old French and Old Romanian. She wrote of the Seminar:

These meetings of young Orthodox believers, their discussions, lectures and arguments, gave me what I had been unable to find either at academic conferences or in the company of my respectable friends — warm Christian fellowship, completely untrammelled thinking, and total immersion in the spiritual realm.[45]

It is unusual for a practising Christian to be a teacher in the Soviet Union (except in Lithuania),[46] since teachers are thought to be in a position to influence ideologically the minds of their students. Shchipkova, however, not only maintained her post for a considerable time, but also managed to give her students some unbiased knowledge of the Christian faith:

I had a set class on the Latin language during the first year during which I have been accustomed for the last 13 or 14 years to familiarise the students not only with the grammar but also with the culture and history of ancient Rome . . . I told the first-year students about the rise of Christianity, the person of Christ, His commandments, and the significance of Christianity for the subsequent fate of Rome, Europe and humanity.[47]

Shchipkova held the degree of candidate of philological sciences (equivalent to a PhD).

Lev Regelson assumed leadership of the Christian Seminar after Ogorodnikov's arrest in November 1978. As a slightly older (born 1940) and more experienced Christian, it was thought that he should be able to give them the teaching they needed. We have already seen that Regelson had been very active in the defence of religious freedom. Before this, he had graduated as a physicist from Moscow University, and had worked for a time in the Moscow Planetarium. He lost his job after he refused to make a secret of his new-found Christian faith.[48]

These brief biographies indicate that the Christian Seminar was able to attract highly intelligent and gifted people who gained entry to some of the highest educational institutes in the Soviet Union, and at least some of whom held responsible positions in the Soviet academic world. Many, possibly the majority of Seminar members were students, including Sergei Yermolayev, Boris Razveyev, Sergei Shuvalov, Valentin Serov, Alexander Shchipkov (son of Tatyana Schchipkova) and Yelena Kashtanova. Several of these were expelled when their connection with the Seminar was discovered. Only one Seminar member has been described as a worker, Viktor Popkov, who worked in the Smolensk Exhibition Hall. The names of other members of the Christian Seminar have been included in or appended to documents sent to the West: Alexander Argentov, Georgi Fedotov, Alexander Kuzkin, Gennadi Kurganov, Marina Timonina, Yelena Levasheva, Oleg Tripolsky, Vladimir Burtsev and others. Some names appear in early documents and then disappear, indicating that the Seminar probably had a fluctuating membership.

Most of the Christian Seminar members lived in or near Moscow. Vladimir Poresh and Tatyana Shchipkova are described as the Seminar's representatives in Leningrad and Smolensk respectively, and other members living in these two cities are named, but it appears that Seminar meetings did not take place there, but in Moscow. Shchipkova specifically mentioned travelling from Smolensk to Moscow for meetings.[49] Seminar meetings have been reported in Chistopol (Tatar ASSR) and in Redkino (near Kalinin), but this was clearly because Ogorodnikov was living there for a time.

The Ideas of the Christian Seminar

The ideas of the Christian Seminar were expressed through its *samizdat* journal, *Obshchina* (Community) and other writings. Unfortunately, only one issue of *Obshchina*, no. 2, has reached the West. The first issue, and possibly subsequent ones, were confiscated by the KGB before they were ready for circulation. The second issue of *Obshchina* consists of 284 type-written pages, and the contents fall into four main categories, as Philip Walters has noted.[50] The first category, totalling about 75 pages, might be called 'contemporary theory': it included summaries of Seminar source material, declarations of principle, descriptions of topics to be discussed, testimonies by various members about the Seminar, letters to and from young Christians abroad, and an item on the sixtieth anniversary of the appearance of the Virgin at Fatima. This section also included three articles. 'Dai krovi-priimi dukh' ('Give Blood and Receive the Spirit') by Vladimir Poresh, a theological response to contemporary reality; Ogorodnikov's 'Kultura katakomb' ('Culture of the Catacombs'), a survey of Soviet youth and its movement towards Christianity; and a scholarly article by Viktor Kapitanchuk on the concept of Sophia, the Wisdom of God, 'Ontologiches-kaya problema v russkoi sofiologii' ('The Ontological Problem in Russian Sophiology'). The second section, again comprising about 75 pages, contained documentation of contemporary events, including events at the Monastery of the Caves in Kiev, a letter from the imprisoned Christian Igor Ogurtsov (the former leader of VSKhSON — see p. 292), descriptions of events at Easter 1977 in Kiev, and a letter about KGB disruption of a meeting of Baptists in Rostov, as well as accounts of the troubles of

Seminar members. The third section, of about 70 pages, included reprinted documents of historical and literary interest with commentaries by Poresh: these comprised works by Bulgakov, Andrei Bely and the philosopher Lev Shestov; there were also extracts from the memoirs of a member of the Red Guard about the murder of the Imperial family. The fourth category consisted of about 40 pages of poems by the Leningrad poet Oleg Okhapkin, with an introduction by his friend Poresh. Walters records that Ogorodnikov was mainly responsible for gathering material on the activities of the Seminar members and the violation of their rights by the authorities, while Poresh, helped by Okhapkin (who otherwise was not much involved with the Seminar), compiled the sections of *Obshchina* which were of a theological, philosophical, historiosophical or artistic nature.

The main character of the lists of subjects studied in the Seminar[51] was their eclecticism. This was no doubt due to the difficulties of obtaining books, the result being that the Seminar studied any it managed to lay hands on. The main generalisation to be made is that Russian thinkers mentioned above as having formed the major influence in leading Seminar members to the church featured largely. Existentialists were also prominent.[52] More infrequent topics included: the church and the modern industrial world; the sermons of Billy Graham; and the fate of modern humanism. The Seminar began its study with the Bible and the Church Fathers before moving on to the nineteenth-century Russian writers,[53] in which they seem to have followed the same pattern as other study groups of which anything is known.

Slavophil thinkers were prominent in the list of Russian authors, and the Christian Seminar shared their ideas to some extent, in that they found much inspiration in their Russian past, and that their writings attacked Western enlightenment as a source of godlessness. However, they lacked any 'bellicose anti-westernism', and did not share the traditional Slavophil antipathy to Western democracy. Moreover, they did not share the Slavophil view that Russia was destined to play a leading role in world history; on the contrary, they emphasised that Christians throughout the world must co-operate together.[54]

The evident desire that Seminar members had for contact with young Christians from other countries seems to have grown, or perhaps simply to have been more openly expressed, with the passage of time. Several letters signed by Seminar members have been addressed to Christians in different countries, and one or two refer to meetings which have taken place. One of the most expressive is a letter to American young people which states:

> The time has come for us, living as we do on different continents and raised in different historical traditions, to open our hearts to each other and unite our efforts in creative searching. We feel your influence around us at every step . . . We are grateful to you for the spirit of liberation,

which has filtered through the customs barriers and the infernal wailings of the radio-jammers . . . we turn to other people with our souls laid open. Open your hearts to us, as we are opening our own to you.[55]

Poresh expressed this desire for international contact in a letter to Alexander Solzhenitsyn: 'Dear Alexander Isayevich, if possible, please put us in contact with religious communities and groups of young people of our type in the USA and other countries. We are tolerant towards any confession and have a wide understanding of this.' This letter was one of the pieces of evidence brought up at Poresh's trial, alleged to be of anti-Soviet content.[56]

At least one Seminar member was a Protestant, Pyotr (no surname given). He wrote:

As a Protestant I have noted with humble satisfaction the interested attention of those present, which provoked a discussion of the role of laymen, i.e. simple believers, in the life of the Church, and of the community as the most fruitful form of Christian unity. It is to my own brethren in faith that God has granted to work on these problems over the centuries. And we are ready to put forward the fruit of our labours for the examination of our Orthodox friends, feeling it our duty to pray that our mistakes should not be repeated by others.[57]

The Seminar's most fruitful contacts with foreigners seem to have been with Italian Catholics, especially the youth organisation Communione e Liberazione. Whether or not this contact arose by chance, it reflects a view of the Seminar members that it is in co-operation with the Roman Catholic Church in particular that interconfessional contacts can be most effective. In this they were following one of the thinkers who has had most influence on the Seminar (and on many other independently minded Orthodox), Vladimir Solovyov.[58] We may recall that the VSKhSON movement had also shown interest in 'the social doctrine of the Catholic Church' and in Solovyov's ideas.[59]

The most central idea of the Christian Seminar, as noted above, was the idea of community, a Christian community based on love and freedom, in which the concept of *sobornost* was central. Though separate from the world, it did not ignore the world, indeed the Christianisation of the world, of culture, was to be its object. As Walters has commented: 'The gulf between the secular world and the Church is to be bridged: the world is to become the Church.'[60] He quoted Poresh's visionary words at his trial:

Poresh: . . . we need the whole world.
Judge: What? What do you need?
Poresh: The whole world.[61]

The '37' Seminar

One other study group about which a good deal is known is the religio-philosophical seminar in Leningrad, sometimes referred to as the '37' group (the name derives from the number of the flat in which the first meetings were held). The '37' seminar did not attempt to hide its existence, and it published a *samizdat* journal, also called *37*, of which some issues have reached the West. Moreover, one of the founders, Tatyana Goricheva, was deported from the USSR in 1980 (because of her involvement in the nascent Soviet feminist movement — see below, pp. 397–8) and has provided further information about the seminar's activities since her arrival in the West. The seminars began in October 1975.[62] A large proportion, possibly even a majority, of the members were Orthodox, but it was from the beginning more ecumenically oriented than the Christian Seminar in Moscow.[63] Its members included a fair number of unbelievers: agnostics, atheists, and devotees of non-Christian beliefs such as yoga and paganism. Some Baptists also attended (which is rather unusual for Soviet Baptists).[64] There were also Jews and Catholics.[65] Goricheva has noted that, whereas the Christian Seminar in Moscow, with its predominantly Orthodox membership, debated such topics as 'Orthodoxy and Russia' and 'Orthodoxy and History', the Leningrad seminar held discussions entitled 'Christianity and Culture', 'Christianity and Patriotism' and 'Christianity and Us'.[66] However, the nucleus which began the seminars — Goricheva, the poet Victor Krivulin, and others — were all Orthodox Christians.

Goricheva stated that about 40–50 people attended the fortnightly seminars when they began,[67] and a foreign visitor to Leningrad in 1980 was told that about 50 people were still gathering regularly. The seminars could hardly have been any larger, since they were held in cramped private dwellings.

Most of the members of the '37' seminar, whether Christians, Jews or unbelievers, belonged to the nonconformist creative intelligentisa. Many were poets, writers, philosophers and artists who were unable to publish or exhibit their creations officially, and therefore resorted to *samizdat* and unofficial exhibitions. The seminar was strongly oriented towards culture and to attempts to find a new direction for Russian culture. Its founders wanted to build a bridge between Christian and contemporary unofficial culture which would enable them to find a creative way forward from what they saw as the stagnant, hopeless impasse of post-Stalinist society. The seminars were a means of demonstrating to the creative intelligentsia of Leningrad that Christianity was a foundation upon which such efforts might be based. This message evidently fell upon fertile ground, and it seems that least some of the unbelievers in the seminar became Christians, as Goricheva notes: 'in 1975, when we began to publish *37*, only Viktor Krivulin and I were baptised. Now all the members of the editorial board are baptised.'[68] The '37' seminar was not drawn exclusively from the ranks of the nonconformists, however: its members also included people officially employed as engineers, physicists, mathematicians and sociologists.[69]

As with members of the Christian Seminar and other converts to Orthodoxy, the '37' seminar was considerably influenced by the great Russian writers and philosophers of the past, particularly those of the late nineteenth and early twentieth centuries. Their attempts to forge a new culture were to be a continuation with Russian thought of the past. Goricheva, after emigrating, evaluated the seminar's involvement with contemporary culture as follows:

> In the sixties, when the breakdown of the myth of Stalin and of the ideals of communism began, we saw that culture was a new point of departure . . . Cultural values helped us to come out of the underground towards the light . . . Our culture recognises itself to be a creation of God. Here the human impulse and courage which create culture are indissolubly united with humility. In this way an ecclesiastical culture is created; and a new Orthodox poetry, a new Orthodox philosophy, are born. The great Russian culture has, in its leading exponents, Gogol, Dostoyevsky, and, in philosophy, Berdyayev, Bulgakov, Florensky, always been closely tied to the Church.
>
> In the sixties we had nothing, and now we have created a bridge to this tradition, to the philosophers of the beginning of the century. But in comparison with them we have something extra, which is a great experience of suffering. This has introduced an important element into Russian culture, a greater rigour and attention in tracing back every reality to its spiritual foundation. We shall not fall again into what was tried by the authors of the beginning of the century, aestheticism, humanism or liberalism. What attracts people is the fundamental thing, the spiritual struggle.[70]

The first year of the '37' seminar was devoted to a careful study of the Church Fathers. Members prepared and read papers on Philo of Alexandria, the Gnostics, Tertullian, Athanasius the Great, Clement of Alexandria, Origen and others.[71] As Goricheva commented: 'We are all young in the faith and we had to begin by getting to know the treasures of Christian knowledge.'[72] The second year saw a marked change in the subject-matter of the seminars. Its members now found they needed to make a response to the growing interest in religion among the nonconformist intelligentsia, and the discussions became creative rather than educative in character. They began to hold seminars with such titles as 'Religion and Ethics', 'Religion and Culture', and 'Contemporary Neo-Christians'.[73] The sixth issue of *37* contains a summary of a seminar on 'Christianity and Ethics', which commenced with a paper by Goricheva, who is a graduate in philosophy of Leningrad University. She suggested that the opposition between religion and ethics noted by some philosophers was a by-product of secularisation, and needed to be broken down. Religion should 'liberate itself from its haughty, malevolent attitude to culture and morals, while the anti-church, tamely humanistic orientation of modern man needs to accept the absolute values which it can find only by turning to Christ'. Goricheva continued by examining the relations between religion and ethics, referring to Kant, with whom, on the whole, she disagreed, and to the Scriptures. Her conclusion was that love was the key, and that an 'intentional ethic of love' was a possible way of reunifying religion and ethics. Discussion followed, and was greatly enlivened by a participant named Levin, who in contrast to the general mood was not at all impressed by the 'ethic of love', or indeed by the 'dream' as he called it, of the Christian renaissance, and preferred his own idea of 'rational egoism'.[74] This summary is of interest because it demonstrates two of the main concerns of the '37' seminar: its wish to bridge the gulf between the Christian church and the world, and its view that the best means of doing this is through love — that is, through obedience to Christ's command to love. It also shows that the seminar was a forum for genuine exchanges of opposing views.

As well as the broader philosophical topics mentioned above, more specialised ones were tackled. In May 1976 there were four weekly seminars, two on poetry and two on theology: 'The Poem as a Genre in the Poetry of the Beginning of the 20th Century. Andrei Bely, "Christ is Risen"' (7 May); 'The Works of Gregory the Theologian' (14 May); 'The Religion of the Old Testament' (21 May); and 'The Poem in Contemporary Leningrad Poetry' (28 May).[75] As time went on, the topics became more comprehensive and required fuller preparation, so the seminars met only monthly. In 1980, according to a foreigner who visited one of the seminar members, there was a seminar on Rozanov in May and one on Solovyov in September. The seminars began and ended with prayer: sometimes members prayed in the Orthodox way at the beginning and in the Baptist manner at the conclusion.[76] In 1979, a circle devoted to the study of Catholic theology was formed, and its members sometimes met for prayer with young Catholics.[77]

The '37' group regarded itself as part of the church, not as a separate or alternative body. Its Orthodox members attended church and went to confession and communion. They saw themselves as a part of the church which was able to reach out to the world around, not as a splinter group in conflict with the institutional church. Although the founding-members of the group were lay people, not priests, it does not seem that the Leningrad priests or hierarchy had misgivings about their activities. One seminar member told a foreign visitor that the late Metropolitan Nikodim of Leningrad had helped them privately — for example, by giving them books. Goricheva stated that some Orthodox priests attended the seminar, 'but we asked them, for their own sakes, to come in mufti'.[78] Like other independently minded Orthodox, the seminar members were grieved by their church's subservience to the state and by what they saw as the overly compliant attitude of some hierarchs, but they accepted that they were part of the mystical organism of the church and bore responsibility for it. As Goricheva said: 'Not through our devotion to the Church do we want to begin to reform it but rather through repentance and the renouncing of our old, sinful life.'[79]

The '37' members also rejected any suggestion that they were in opposition to Soviet society. The fifth issue of *37* contains the editors' reply to an article about the seminar which appeared in the US newspaper *Herald News*. They rejected the article's statement that they were in any way an 'underground' group. They also objected to the way the article politicised their activities and cast them in the light of opponents of the Soviet system. They explained that their objective of helping to create a new culture was far more profound and comprehensive than any mere opposition to the existing order would have been: 'to think of [unofficial culture] as the antithesis of state politics and even art would be to insult it'.[80]

The journal *37* commenced publication in 1975, and by 1981 20 issues had been produced. This is a creditable achievement for a *samizdat* journal. (Although *samizdat* journals which record events, usually acts of repression — for example, the *Chronicle of Current Events*, *Jews in the USSR*, and the *Chronicle of the Lithuanian Catholic Church* — have managed to keep going despite immense difficulties for many years, journals of ideas have tended to be rather short-lived, as were *Veche*, *Zemlya*, *Poiski*, and others.) The main sections of the journal were devoted to philosophy and to literature, especially poetry, reflecting the preoccupations of Goricheva and Viktor Krivulin respectively. After a number of issues had been produced they thought of producing two separate journals instead, but this did not in fact happen. There were also sections reprinting writings of Russian authors from the past, and giving translations of foreign authors. The final section, entitled 'Chronicle', reported the activities of the seminar and of the world of unofficial culture generally: for example, it gave information about forthcoming showings of unofficial art in private dwellings. The 'Chronicle' section in issue no. 17 is particularly interesting, since it gives evidence of the seminar's relations with outsiders. It contained an appreciation of the journal *Obshchina* produced by the Christian Seminar in Moscow; an account of a conversation between Vladimir Poresh and members of the '37' group; an interview with an overseas visitor belonging to the Anglican Church; and replies to a questionnaire sent to readers of *37*.

The response aroused by the readers' questionnaire indicated that *37* was being read by a variety of people interested in different aspects of the seminar's activities. The replies printed were from a poet aged 32, a writer aged 34, a sociologist aged 48, an art historian aged 66, and an engineer aged 23.[81] They all wrote that they had read the journal with great interest, and in some cases had passed it around among family and friends, but none the less they all saw weaknesses of which they were very critical. All the readers picked different things to criticise, but there were some common denominators in what they said. No one appears to have been very impressed with the poetry, although some poems had given pleasure, but the general feeling was that there was nothing new in it. Reactions to the articles on philosophy were more mixed: some critics offered commendation while others complained of the poor quality of some articles. An exception was the philosophical articles by Goricheva, which earned general praise. A general criticism was that the philosophy section was 'elitist', that it mirrored the preoccupations of the authors and was of limited interest to a wider audience. One or two readers felt that the literary and philosophical sections were not sufficiently integrated, and that the journal as a whole lacked cohesion and had no unifying editorial standpoint. However, every reader found some items of value and interest in the journal, and most of them spoke approvingly of the 'Chronicle' section. The criticisms should not be taken to mean that *37* was thought to be failing in its task, but rather that it had succeeded in finding a readership anxious to help it define and fulfil its task more fully. Stringent, often harsh, criticism is the normal reaction to anything new in Russian intellectual circles, but it does not necessarily represent hostility towards the enterprise concerned. As one of the critics wrote: 'If I have subjected some sections to criticism, it does not mean that they are bad, but that they could be better.'[82]

The reaction of the editors of *37* to *Obshchina* is interesting in the light of these comments.[83] Generally speaking, it was one of approval, and several articles are singled out for commendation. But the strongest impression upon the *37* editors was of the unified editorial viewpoint clearly expressed in all the items, despite the diversity of subject-matter. As indicated above, this was in sharp contrast with the diverse character of *37*, and its editors clearly took exception to it. Though impressed with the dynamism and depth of faith evident in the pages of *Obshchina*, they objected to its declamatory character. Some of its conclusions, in their opinion, were insufficiently substantiated, leading sometimes to 'a blunting of the sense of reality, a distortion of historical perspectives'. As an example they quote the following statement by Ogorodnikov, and in doing so throw an interesting light on the difference between the two groups:

> Our task stands thus: either we can, albeit at the price of our life, transform the world (our inner world, and that means the face of the world also), or else our weakness will be destruction — a fitting reward for nonentities.[84]

At first sight it is hard to see what the '37' group were objecting to, since they themselves also believed that the church had a responsibility to the world, and that it was its duty to transform and Christianise the world.

In fact, they wrote, they appreciated this aspect of Ogorodnikov's statement; it was the 'superfluous self-confidence' that offended them. They took Ogorodnikov to mean that the fate of humanity depended upon a small group of people in Moscow, and that was certainly implicit in his words. It was the all-or-nothing tone of *Obshchina* which made them wary of it. The '37' group, as we have seen, were open to a wide variety of people and views, and though they did not compromise their Christian convictions, they wanted to share them rather than impose them. It would be a mistake to take the comparison between the two seminars any further than this, since the only evidence available to us is the subjective opinions of the people involved. Probably the lines they adopted were influenced by personalities as much as by convictions, and also to some degree by the atmosphere of their respective cities. It is no surprise to find that the Christian Seminar in the capital, Moscow, the centre of government and ideology, had a comparatively more hard-headed and doctrinaire attitude, while in Leningrad, the 'city of poets', the '37' group was rather more relaxed and open in its approach.

A meeting which took place between the '37' group and Vladimir Poresh, the Leningrad representative of the Christian Seminar, made it clear that their differences were those of form rather than substance, and that there was more to unite than to divide them. It transpired that though the '37' group had been formed as a response to the needs of the nonconformist creative intelligentsia, while the Christian Seminar was the result of the reaction of some young Orthodox intellectuals to the needs of Soviet youth in general, their common ground was a belief in the need for the Christian transformation of culture and society, and particularly of their own generation. They agreed that they were moving towards each other: *37* was the fruit of people in the world of culture turning to religion, while *Obshchina* was moving from religion towards culture.[85]

One member of the '37' seminar, summarising its guiding principles, wrote that among its Orthodox members: 'There are "rebels", but there are also conservatives, although numerically most support those who are seeking a "third way".'[86] The means of finding this third way was through following Christ's commandment to love, not opposing or criticising what they saw as wrong in church or society but rising above it to find a better way forward. Goricheva wrote that they were faced by a religiosity which did not take serious account of the world and a mankind which put the joys of the present above shadowy promises about the afterlife.

And so, on the one hand there is the egoism of holiness, on the other hand, the egoism of the flesh. As we see, the extremes coincide. The true way is narrow, it lies somewhere in the middle, although it is by no means a tepid or indifferent middle . . . We religious people must take care that we do not have to choose between religion and Christ or between faith in

God and love to our neighbour.[87]

The writings of the '37' group were permeated with the idea that the third way, if it was to be found, must commence with themselves and their own personal lives. They recognised that they could not bring about change in society or in the church unless they themselves were changed. This attitude revealed a Christian maturity and sense of responsibility remarkable in people so recently converted to Christianity. It was perhaps most clearly seen in the following comment in one of the papers read at the seminar:

> For a Christian, it is important not only to build a religious life, but also to make one's whole life religious . . . We should bear in mind that the authorities subject us above all not to persecution but to *temptation*: the temptation of throwing ourselves backwards or forwards. And our only aid against this is abiding within oneself — prayer . . . Berdyayev challenged people to live not by taking offence, but by accepting blame (*ne obidoi a vinoi*). Many are indignant at this: why should there be further blame when there seems to be no end to oppression and accusation? To live not by taking offence but by accepting blame means to be spiritually reborn. We must concentrate our attention not on the fact that we are insulted, persecuted and oppressed, but on the fact that we rarely, infinitely rarely, act through love, that we make little effort to draw closer to God.[88]

Orthodox Women and Feminism

A feminist movement began in Leningrad in September 1979[89] and spread rapidly. At the end of the year it produced a *samizdat* almanac entitled *Zhenshchina i Rossiya* (*Woman and Russia*) which attracted much interest in the West among members of the women's liberation movement and many others. The almanac was quickly published in the West in Russian and English.[90] In contrast to most Western feminism, the Soviet women's movement from its inception included a number of Orthodox believers who made an important Christian contribution to its ideas. They included Tatyana Goricheva, Natalya Malakhovskaya, the secretary of the editorial board of *37*, and the poetess Yuliya Voznesenskaya, all of whom contributed to *Zhenshchina i Rossiya*. Goricheva's article was the only one of the twelve items in the almanac which had a positive tone. All the others were overwhelmingly negative, consisting as they did of an account of the always grim and sometimes nightmarish conditions in which Soviet women have to live, work, give birth and bring up their children. Goricheva, by contrast, wrote of the significance of Mary, the Mother of God, for womankind. She herself found release from the image of womanhood fostered by Soviet society through contemplation of the virtues exemplified by the Mother of God: purity, chastity, self-givingness, fullness of humanity: She wrote: 'Prayer to the Most Holy Queen helped me to discover and resurrect my female self in all its purity and absoluteness.'[91] This was a far cry from Western feminism. Not only did it reflect the very different experiences of women in Soviet and Western societies, it was also an illustration of the involvement of the church with the world which the '37' group and others advocated. The participation of the Orthodox women meant that from the beginning this important new social development, which was concerned above all with social justice, contained a significant Christian element. However, in the *37* journal Goricheva wrote an article critical of the more strident, negative elements to be found in *Zhenshchina i Rossiya*, and also of the attitudes of Western feminists. She wrote:

> Emancipation of women has produced paradoxical results: in our times the most emancipated women in Russia are to be found in the Church . . . Those who acknowledged neither gods nor men have submitted to the Christian God, because in Him they have found Life and Truth and the Way, and they have submitted to Him with a readiness to give up everything, to sacrifice everything.

She added her hope that the journal would not make women 'blinded by their grief and pain' but would help them to 'overcome sufferings by love, for without Love, we are nothing'.[92]

The Christian feminists emphasised their dedication to the Virgin Mary by forming the Mariya Club and by producing a second feminist almanac also entitled *Mariya*. The first issue appeared in March 1980, and five issues had been produced by summer 1981.[93] A feminist émigré, Sofiya Sokolova, said early in 1981 that the Club had expanded considerably and that its structure resembled that of a Christian community. Most of its members were young mothers, who helped one another in material ways and in looking after their children, and shared housekeeping expenses.[94] The Mariya Club was not the only direction in which the women's movement developed — another club which formed was more interested in the socio-political aspects of feminism — but it was none the less an important Christian response to an urgent and large-scale social need. This response extended beyond even the massive needs of Soviet women to those of women in Afghanistan: in June 1980 the Mariya Club sent a letter to Afghan women who had demonstrated against the Soviet invasion.[95]

The Search for Historical Roots

Most of the thought and activity of Russian Orthodox dissenters during the 1970s was devoted, quite understandably, to grappling with the immediate problems which confronted them. Many of them found that in order to do this, they needed to look back to the past, to study their own history, so that they could see how their present position had developed. They quickly realised that they could not grasp the main features of their present situation, and devise means for changing it, without a thorough understanding of its historical antecedents. This meant that they had to study, first of all, the history of the Russian Orthodox Church during the Soviet period. They could not afford to neglect the pre-revolutionary period either, but knowledge was weakest, and information most unobtainable, for the immediate past. The search to uncover this past coincided with a growing historical awareness among the Soviet intelligentsia in general. As the Stalinist years faded into the past, thinking citizens began to realise that they had been fed only with the CPSU's version of Soviet history, and that books or other materials to support alternative views were unobtainable. Since alternative views clearly must exist, not a few questing spirits wished to track them down. The single most powerful impulse in this direction was Khrushchev's 'secret speech' unmasking Stalinism and the 'cult of personality' which he gave in 1956. People who were then students, in their late teens or early twenties, were stunned to realise that everything they had been told until then was now admitted to be untrue. Everything they had been taught about Stalin and the attitude they should have to him was demolished overnight. There were many who realised that, if they had been deceived once, they could be deceived again. A government or Party leader might speak authoritatively to them today — but what might his successor say tomorrow? Once a chink had been made in the monolith, it broadened rapidly into a gaping fissure through which passed many members of the intelligentsia who would never again believe what they were told, and would have to work everything out for themselves from first principles. But where were they to obtain the materials for independent study and deliberation? These were locked away in specialised rooms of libraries and archives, available to only the most trusted and politically reliable researchers. Very few people could obtain access to the raw materials upon which an independent view of Soviet history could be built up.

This is why Solzhenitsyn's *Gulag Archipelago* was regarded as such an amazing achievement by his countrymen. Not only did it tell a harrowing story which no one before had had the means to tell, but it represented an unshakable determination to track down the truth about the immediate past from its few survivors with practically none of the usual tools of historical research at the author's disposal. The publication of *The Gulag Archipelago* showed that the task was possible, and probably encouraged young Orthodox believers faced with the almost insurmountably difficult task of writing their own recent history. The archives of the Moscow Patriarchate were closed to them, historical archives in Soviet libraries and museums are normally available only to accredited researchers working on officially approved subjects, and such works as existed in the West, in Russian, English and German, were extremely difficult for them to obtain. They had to piece their evidence and their sources together painstakingly from the words of survivors and such written materials as had been preserved and were beginning to be released by those who had guarded them jealously during the years of hardship. Using such sources, some young Orthodox writers attempted to assess their church's response to the Soviet regime, to document and analyse it, searching for clues that would enable them to formulate their own response. Some writers elected to devote the major part of their efforts to historical studies rather than to public activity, believing that this was the surest way forward in the long term. Given the difficulties they faced, it is too soon for much of substance to have been produced yet. The fact that we cannot examine the results of these prodigious efforts constitutes an unavoidable imbalance in the present study.

One work which has emerged, and which formed a first step on the long historical path which had to be trodden, was Lev Regelson's *The Tragedy of the Russian Church 1917–1945*. The first part of the book is a narrative of the years in question, and the second is a valuable collection of documentary material, much of it previously unknown, at any rate in the West.[96] The difficulties of collecting and preserving so much material can scarcely be imagined by anyone unfamiliar with Soviet conditions. Indeed, Regelson himself noted that in 1968 his work was brought to a standstill when a valuable archive of material was confiscated by the authorities, and could be resumed only when a fuller archive was made available to him 'by the grace of God'.[97] This illustrates two things: first, that the contemporary historian of the Russian Orthodox Church in the Soviet Union must be patient and painstaking in his search for materials; and, second, that he is entirely dependent on those who, often at great personal danger, have carefully collected and stored documentary materials from the past. Regelson's work centred on the most controversial issue of the recent past, Metropolitan (later Patriarch) Sergi's decision in 1927 to declare unequivocal support for the Soviet state in order to keep the institutional church alive. As we have seen, this decision would be no less fiercely debated had it to be made afresh today. Regelson was unreservedly opposed to Metropolitan Sergi's standpoint. He used every conceivable chance to criticise him and could find no extenuating circumstances whatever for his actions. This impaired his book as a historical work, but showed vividly the crucial importance of the issues of the past in the process of working out the attitude of the contemporary church to the Soviet state and to the world. As Regelson said:

We should like to hope that events separated from us by decades will attract the attention not only of church historians, but of all those who hold dear the imminent fate of the Church, of those who clearly understand that our future is rooted in our past.[98]

Two other important historical works which appeared in *samizdat* were the massive collection of essays on the Living Church by Anatoli Levitin and Vadim Shavrov and the three-volume history of the church by Vladimir Rusak; both were major feats of gathering scattered material.[99]

The Canonisation of Martyrs

The call by some Orthodox believers for the canonisation of martyrs of the Soviet period, which we mentioned above, has been a practical consequence of this growing awareness of recent history. Regelson's book provided material towards this end by including extensive (though still incomplete) biographical information about many of those who perished. Father Dimitri Dudko also spoke up in support of the canonisation of the martyred, including Tsar Nicholas II. This occasioned some dismay among those who otherwise supported him, both in the USSR and abroad, but Dudko, while noting this, persisted.[100] Even late in 1979 he was still urging the glorification of Nicholas II among others who suffered, on the basis that objections on political grounds were irrelevant when it was a question of a man laying down his life for the church. Nicholas should be canonised not for his political successes or failures, but solely for his readiness to sacrifice himself.[101] This view was supported by the authors of the 1975 appeal for canonisation of the martyrs, Father Gleb Yakunin, Lev Regelson and Viktor Kapitanchuk, joined now by Father Vasili Fonchenkov, in an open letter to all Russian Orthodox Christians. While admitting that Nicholas II may have been 'a bad sovereign and a sinful Christian', some of whose actions were harmful to the church, they pointed out that a martyr was created on the basis of his death for the Christian faith, not on the quality of his life. Nicholas II and his family qualified for the status of martyr on this ground, the more so because the Tsar was held to have a special position in the church, to be anointed as an Orthodox ruler. However, there was not much public support for these arguments. The four authors addressed another issue in their letter, the fact that the Russian Orthodox Church in Exile had taken a decision to canonise martyrs of the twentieth century. The authors urged restraint: they pointed out that such a serious step should be performed by the Russian Orthodox Church as a whole, not by one jurisdiction in isolation.[102] This was not a contradiction of their May 1975 letter, which had been addressed to leaders of all the jurisdictions (see pp. 353–4); rather, it was an affirmation of a central point of that letter, the need for true unity in the church as a whole. Clearly, the cause of unity would not be served if, in order to honour the martyrs who form part of the unity (*sobornost*) of the church, one jurisdiction were to increase the disunity existing between it and other earthly members of the church. Despite this appeal, the Russian Orthodox Church in Exile canonised the martyrs of the twentieth century, including the Imperial family, on 1 November 1981, which occasioned some controversy in the Orthodox world.

Attitudes to Russian Orthodox Jurisdictions Overseas

Towards the end of the 1970s there were some scattered signs that some members of the church in the USSR were looking to the overseas jurisdictions to provide the leadership which their own episcopate could not or would not give. An anonymous letter from 'an ordinary Orthodox Christian from the USSR' stated that 'some laymen and priests of the Moscow Patriarchate' looked with 'love and gratitude' to the episcopate of the Russian Orthodox Church in Exile, and wished to know more about them than the hostile remarks which were frequently addressed at them in the Soviet press.[103] Father Dimitri Dudko engaged in correspondence with leaders of overseas jurisdictions, asking that there should be more understanding and closer contact between them, and even suggesting that bishops might come from abroad to ordain worthy candidates for the priesthood secretly.[104] However, the clearest expectation of leadership from the overseas jurisdictions was expressed in the Yakunin Report. We quoted in Part 1 many passages from the analytical introductory section of this report, which examined the various aspects of the Moscow Patriarchate's work and found them sadly lacking. This was less a thoroughgoing analysis of the Moscow Patriarchate — Yakunin admitted that it was too short to be that — but more a series of studies of 'its most scandalous fragments', selected with the aim of proving that the Moscow Patriarchate was incapable of coping with the revival of religious feelings which was taking place, especially among young people, in the Soviet Union. Moreover, it had even abandoned many of its longstanding members in areas, especially Siberia, where there were very few churches. Yakunin quoted a visitor from Kamchatka as saying to him:

> For us in Kamchatka, the question of jurisdictions is purely theoretical. What do we gain from the mere consciousness of unity with the Moscow Patriarchate, if Christians are dying without communion and confession, and children are without baptism? We need unity with a real Church, communion with Christ in the sacraments of the Church. We are ready to accept any other hierarchy if the Moscow Patriarchate does not come to us. Let it be the Greeks, the Americans, the Paris jurisdiction or the 'Karlovtsy' jurisdiction [i.e. the Russian Orthodox Church in Exile, so-called because it was formed in Sremci-Karlovci in Yugoslavia] ...

Let it be anyone at all, if only they bring us God's grace and the light of Orthodox truth.[105]

Yakunin offered a pragmatic solution to this dilemma, the creation of unregistered Orthodox communities similar to the unregistered Baptist, Pentecostal and Adventist communities which exist in the USSR. He pointed out that these communities, unhampered by state control of their leadership, carried on an active ministry of preaching and evangelisation which led to an influx of new converts to replace their arrested leaders. He carefully pointed out that unregistered communities were not the same as catacomb or underground communities, since 'they do not hide themselves from the State, but refuse registration and other forms of state control'.[106] He gave a simple but very clear analogy of what he was proposing:

the ideal form of existence for the Church in contemporary conditions should be a structure built on the principle of a school experiment in physics: two communicating vessels filled with liquid. The point of this visual aid is to demonstrate the change in the level of the liquid in one vessel subject to a change in the level of the other. In a church structure built in an analogous manner, the two communicating vessels are two church organisations: an official one, registered by the State, and an unofficial unregistered one.

Such a dynamic structure would permit the Church to endure the harshest persecution on the part of the State, since pressure on the official part of the Church would only strengthen and fortify the unregistered Church, and would raise the level of religious life in it.[107]

Such a structure would require the ordination of priests in secrecy, such as was practised by both Patriarch Tikhon in the early 1920s and later by Metropolitan Manuil (Lemeshevsky), but Yakunin believed that there was no hope of such independent action from the present episcopate. He therefore advocated that the many keen young candidates for the priesthood who existed in the USSR should be able to receive ordination from any sister Orthodox Church. Yakunin admitted that this suggestion ran against the canonical principle of the territorial integrity of each Local Orthodox Church, but did not regard this as an insuperable obstacle. On the grounds that 'The Sabbath was made for man, not man for the Sabbath', he argued that historical changes rendered alterations in the application of the canons legitimate. He also pointed out that, as the Moscow Patriarchate had violated the territorial principle by having some parishes on the territory of the Orthodox Church of America, some reciprocal activity by the latter would restore the balance.

This was an eminently practical approach to a difficult problem, and, on the technical level, would seem to have had the makings of a workable solution. However, perhaps the most outstanding fact related to the Yakunin Report was the total lack of response to it in *samizdat*. Since the report was written in August 1979, no *samizdat* document reaching the West has commented upon it. This is very surprising, since an original idea normally sparks off a lively debate between its supporters, detractors and modifiers. It is probable that silence should be taken to denote dissent from Yakunin's views rather than agreement with them. Yakunin was arrested shortly after completing his report, in November 1979, and this fact must have weighed with those who might have taken issue with him. Opposition to his ideas would have enabled the KGB investigators to make capital out of the fact that not even members of his own church agreed with his views. Conversely, the fact that in all the protests against his arrest, no one specifically supported his proposals, cannot be overlooked. It seems that the majority of members of the Russian Orthodox Church were not prepared to regard the creation of unregistered communities and the acknowledgement of an overseas episcopate as a valid solution to their problems.

Yakunin's proposal was a neat practical solution, but too radical for the Russian Orthodox Church. Rightly or wrongly, its members felt that they had not built up 1,000 years' worth of experience, in suffering and in triumph, simply to cast it aside to follow the example of some youthful Protestant communities. They were searching, ever more eagerly, for a solution, a way forward, which would be in the tradition of the past, its logical historical and spiritual development.

13 THE REPRESSION OF ORTHODOX DISSENT: 1976–80

By the mid-1970s, most of the Orthodox dissenters mentioned in the preceding chapters had suffered discrimination of various kinds as a result of their activities. They shared this fate with numerous other Soviet dissenters. The majority of the Orthodox activists — and they included a number of highly educated specialists — lost their jobs and were unable to pursue their chosen careers. Shafarevich was dismissed from his lectureship at Moscow University, Barabanov lost his job in the publishing house Iskusstvo (Art), the physicist Regelson lost his post at the Moscow Planetarium, the poet Viktor Krivulin was not officially published in the Soviet Union, and Tatyana Goricheva, an exceptionally able philosopher who had corresponded with Heidegger during the course of her studies, was unable to find work in her field. All these were graduates of Moscow and Leningrad Universities, and as such were clearly of above-average ability. In denying them the right to work, the Soviet authorities were injuring their own interests almost as much as those of the people concerned, since they were depriving their country of the talents and abilities of some of its most gifted and highly educated people. Others encountered difficulties in education: Alexander Ogorodnikov and others were expelled from higher educational institutes (as we noted in Chapter 7), and the historian Vadim Borisov, at Moscow Univeristy, was refused permission to present his thesis on the Orthodox Church in the fourteenth and fifteenth centuries. In order to avoid being imprisoned on a charge of parasitism, all these people had to find jobs: some scraped a living by doing translations while others found all doors closed to them but those leading to the most menial and unsatisfying work. Many found it difficult to provide food, clothing and accommodation for themselves and their families, and relied upon parents who often did not share their convictions, their already hard-pressed friends, and gifts from abroad. They also had to face difficulties of a bureaucratic nature with various local Soviet bodies concerning work, children's education, health, accommodation, and so forth — an endless round of petty annoyances which consumed time and sapped vitality. Others had suffered the far more serious hardships of prison and labour camp, such as Anatoli Levitin, Igor Ogurtsov, Vladimir Osipov, Father Vasyl Romanyuk, Sergei Soldatov and others. Some, though they bore no trace of insanity, suffered the horrifying experience of forcible confinement to psychiatric hospitals: they included Gennadi Shimanov, Pyotr Starchik and Yuri Ivanov. Others again decided to emigrate because they could see no future for themselves in their native land, or else the authorities pressured them into leaving as a means of silencing their protests. Mikhail Agursky, Mikhail Meerson-Aksyonov, Anatoli Levitin, Tatyana Khodorovich, Mikhail Bernshtam and Yevgeni Vagin were among the Orthodox Christians who made the difficult decision to leave.

Everyone who became involved in the human rights movement and in dissent within the Russian Orthodox Church knew full well the kind of penalties that lay ahead. The fact that they persisted in their activities is a measure of their commitment to their aims. It is important to remember this in assessing the conflict between the church hierarchy and the dissenters over the role of the church: it is not simply a question of a continuing debate within the church, the clash of two conflicting viewpoints, but a grim struggle in which one side has the spectre of labour camps and psychiatric hospitals constantly at its shoulder. This is one reason for the often strident polemical tone found in *samizdat* writings, which sometimes seem harsh to Western readers: their writers know that they are not merely engaging in an academic or ecclesiastical discussion, but writing words for which they may have to pay with their careers, their health and their liberty.

The Press Campaign Grows Harsher

From the mid-1970s onwards, the Soviet government began to take an even harsher line against church dissenters (and dissenters in general). This line was clearly aimed only against active dissenters. The Soviet attitude to the church as a whole did not alter significantly, and if anything appeared to soften slightly, thus heightening the contrast between dissenters and other church members. Anti-religious propaganda continued unabated, and efforts were made to intensify it. But actions specifically directed at dissenters increased markedly, beginning early in 1976. This began with the press campaign which we outlined in Chapter 11 (see pp. 362–4). However, as noted, neither the press nor the revised edition of *Diversiya bez dinamita* said anything startlingly new about religious believers; indeed, their comments could be termed routine for Soviet anti-religious literature. A few months later, however, there followed a bitter personal attack on four Orthodox Christians which pulled no punches whatever. The article 'Svoboda religii i klevetniki' (Freedom of Religion and the Slanderers) appeared in two parts in the leading Soviet weekly, *Literaturnaya gazeta* (*Literary Gazette*), on 13 and 20 April 1977. It was entirely devoted to vilifying Father Dimitri Dudko, Father Gleb Yakunin, Lev Regelson and Alexander Ogorodnikov.[1] On 27 April the four men responded by holding a press conference in Dudko's Moscow apartment where they produced statements signed by themselves and their friends denying *Literaturnaya gazeta*'s accusations and presenting what they said was the true version of events referred to.[2] As is customary in such cases, these documents have not been published in the USSR, and therefore readers of *Literaturnaya gazeta* have been left with a one-sided story. Anatoli Levitin in Switzerland issued a statement denying the accusations against the four on the basis of his personal knowledge of them, and urging Christians in the West to support them.[3]

Like *Diversiya bez dinamita*, Roshchin's article complained that Western radio stations and newspapers were constantly harping on the alleged 'persecution' of certain religious believers. The purpose of his article was to show that they were not the 'fighters for religious freedom' that they were given out to be, but people who flouted Soviet laws from unworthy motives. Yakunin was said to be acting from anti-Soviet rather than religious motives and to want fame above all; Father Dimitri Dudko and Alexander Ogorodnikov were accused of preying upon young people in order to influence them; Dudko was also accused of having collaborated with the Nazis; and Lev Regelson was said to have been acting from mercenary motives, with the aim of receiving money and parcels from abroad. These were only the main charges: there were numerous other innuendoes and jibes, too numerous to relate here. The entire tone of the article was slanted in such a way as to belittle its subjects. Here, for example, is Roshchin's account of how Yakunin became a priest:

> In contrast to Ogorodnikov, Yakunin was at least able to graduate from an agricultural institute, and even worked for about a year as a hunts-man. But after a few months he grew bored with catching wild animals: he thought it more advantageous to catch men's souls. Yakunin threw up his work and got himself fixed up in the Moscow Seminary. However, he was not able to study there for long — he was soon dismissed for indecent behaviour. Yakunin did not lose heart, and mobilising his acquaintances, got himself work in one of the Moscow churches. After a time he was even able to gain the rank of priest.[4]

Roshchin was here describing events which are by no means uncommon: a young man feels a vocation to the priesthood after training in some other field and enters (as opposed to 'getting himself fixed up in') an officially recognised establishment; having been expelled, he follows the perfectly proper course of finding work in churches until such time as he can find a bishop who will accept him for ordination. There was nothing at all suspicious in any of this; but Roshchin's account was so loaded with innuendo that the discerning reader was less inclined to accept his other statements at face value. The most potentially damaging statement here was that Yakunin was dismissed for 'indecent behaviour', but the total absence of any kind of supporting evidence made it impossible to take this charge seriously.

Roshchin quoted a letter sent by Lev Regelson to an American businessman, Henry Dakin, as evidence that Regelson was trying to get money from abroad by dubious means: this letter allegedly dropped from Ogorodnikov's pockets when he was pulling out his documents to show to militia officers who had asked to see them.[5] However, Regelson stated that the letter was found when Ogorodnikov was searched illegally, without the sanction of the Procurator, and that Roshchin had distorted the text of his letter to Dakin. Study of another copy of his letter which Dakin received showed that this was true. Dakin issued a statement complaining that Regelson's private letter to him had been published in a newspaper without authorisation, and also in a distorted form.[6]

Father Dimitri was accused, *inter alia*, of having private talks with young men and girls who 'glanced into' his church, and of then inviting them to his flat. These talks were by no means an 'explanation of the essence of religion', since Father Dimitri broke off the conversation 'if a person of ecclesiastical rank entered the room'. Roshchin gave the example of Olga F., whose mother 'was naturally disturbed' when she learned of this, 'demanded an explanation' from Father Dimitri and finally 'put a stop to her daughter's "spiritual refinement" '.[7] However, the girl in question, Olga Fyodorova, wrote to the editor of *Literaturnaya gazeta* to say that Roshchin's version of events was completely misleading, that Father Dimitri had given her advice during a period of family tension, and that he himself had invited her mother to his home in order to help them overcome their frictions. Fyodorova was far from being the bewildered, duped victim whom Roshchin depicted: she ended her letter: 'Now that I am independent and adult I find it impossible to write about Dimitri Sergeyevich [Dudko] without acknowledging my debt of gratitude to him.'[8]

These are only a few of many examples which could be given of Roshchin's distortions. Since they were so easily shown to have been distortions and untruths (not only by those concerned, but also by outsiders such as Fyodorova and Dakin), the reader may wonder what the point of Roshchin's article was. Its obvious purpose was to isolate the four men from the mass of law-abiding Orthodox Christians by declaring them to have broken the law and therefore to be candidates for arrest. Roshchin made this quite specific. He stated that Dudko 'does not so much preach the Ten Commandments as transgress them, and at the same time the laws of his country'. Ogorodnikov 'has no relation whatever to the existing Russian Orthodox Church'. As for Yakunin and Regelson: 'In every article, in every letter of Yakunin, Regelson and company there are knowingly false fabrications defaming the Soviet system, the Soviet State and the Soviet people.'[9] These words correspond very closely to the words of article 190/1 of the Criminal Code of the RSFSR, which provides for up to three years' imprisonment for offenders. The clear threat of arrest contained in the article was referred to by Yakunin at the press conference of 27 April. He pointed out that several people engaged in defence of human rights (Anatoli Shcharansky, Yuri Orlov, Alexander Ginzburg, Vladimir Bukovsky, Zviad

Gamsakhurdia) had been arrested after the publication of similar articles in the Soviet press. He also pointed to the current wave of arrests of human rights activists involved in the Helsinki Monitoring Groups,* which were decimated during the summer of 1977. Yakunin stated that the fact that they had not been arrested after publication of the article did not mean they would not be arrested in the near future, and that in publishing the article the Soviet authorities wanted to test what the reaction of world public opinion and world Christianity might be to the repression of Russian Christians.[10]

We do not know whether the Soviet authorities considered Western reaction to Roshchin's article and the replies to it to be a deterrent or not, but the fact is that they did stay their hand for a time. The most likely explanation for this is that they were so involved with the arrests and investigations of Helsinki Monitors, and with preparation for the series of trials which took place in 1978, that they preferred to leave the purely religious cases until they had leisure to deal with them.

Mounting Pressure against Father Dimitri Dudko

Father Dimitri Dudko was the victim of increasingly harsh pressure by the KGB from the time when he was appointed to a parish in the village of Kabanovo, Moscow region, after being dismissed from his Moscow city parish (see Chapter 10, p. 315). This had begun as early as March 1975, before the press campaign and other measures got under way. In this month Father Dimitri was severely injured in a car 'accident' in which he broke both legs. He and his friends believed that the incident had been engineered by the KGB, because of the suspicious way in which it occurred. A lorry reversed into the car in which he was a passenger and the driver drove off immediately without waiting to see what had happened. Militia men refused requests to go to the scene of the accident, and no legal action was taken.[11]

At the end of 1975, Father Dimitri was dismissed without warning from his parish in Kabanovo, against the will of his parishioners. When they learned of his dismissal, more than 300 of them signed a petition in his support.[12] A second petition, signed by 100 or so parishioners, was addressed to Patriarch Pimen. It stated that the churchwarden, Ye. I. Kharitonova, had cancelled the agreement with Dudko without the agreement of the parish council, and added that she had been ordered to do this by the local district executive committee. These parishioners, whom Father Dimitri had served for less than a year and a half, testified to his ministry as follows:

---

*Groups of Soviet citizens formed in Moscow, Ukraine, Lithuania, Georgia and Armenia to monitor Soviet compliance or non-compliance with the Final Act of the Conference on Security and Cooperation in Europe, signed 1 August 1975, in the field of human rights.

we have recognised him as a conscientious pastor and have grown very fond of him. His sermons, in which Father Dimitri calls people to faith in God and to a moral life, have been especially conducive to the creation of a healthy spiritual atmosphere in our church.[13]

Other protests about Dudko's dismissal included one by several leading Orthodox intellectuals, among them Igor Shafarevich, Vadim Borisov, Felix Svetov and Igor Khokhlushkin. Their statement revealed that the district executive committee had attempted to justify its interference by telling parishioners that it had had instructions from an unnamed organisation in Moscow (clearly the CRA). The statement denounced this as violating the separation of church and state 'in the crudest manner'.[14]

This new trouble of Dudko's caused concern abroad, and the World Council of Churches enquired about him. Metropolitan Serafim of Krutitsy, as Dudko's diocesan bishop, responded in a statement dated 13 January 1976. He said that the church executive committee had broken off its contract with Dudko because 'he had systematically included in his sermons and talks political material of an anti-social character, containing tendentious criticism of the life of our State'. This was in marked contrast to the assessment of his parishioners quoted above. Father Dimitri was also said to have used the small parish house next to the church for 'special meetings' for people who came out from Moscow to hear his talks and sermons. It is not easy to see what was reprehensible about this, since anyone making the journey of two hours or more from Moscow to hear a sermon would certainly be in need of rest and refreshment before returning, especially in winter. Metropolitan Serafim's statement added that Dudko was still a member of the Moscow clergy, currently awaiting reassignment, and that he was therefore in no danger of arrest for 'parasitism', as had been alleged in the West.[15] It had in fact been no secret that many people, especially young people, who had attended Father Dimitri's church in Moscow had been travelling out to Kabanovo, and it seems clear that the authorities had decided to put a stop to this in the hope of curtailing his growing influence. Before long he was transferred to another village church, in Grebnevo, some two hours' journey to the southeast of Moscow.

However, it was not long before moves began to be made against Dudko at Grebnevo also. The measures taken by the authorities affected both him personally and also his many 'spiritual children', as he called the young people who surrounded him, and whom he taught and guided. In December 1977 it was reported that the CRA commissioner for Moscow region, A. Trushin, had called together the parish council and asked them to end their agreement with Dudko. They refused.[16] On 16 May 1978 Father Dimitri wrote to the local district executive committee, of Shchelkovo district, Moscow region, protesting against attempts by state officials to put pressure on his congregation, especially the parish council. He listed his grievances: official complaints had been made to the churchwarden about the young people who came to visit him; the gate to his house was locked; letters to him were confiscated; and parishioners were sometimes afraid to speak to him.[17] Evidently there was no improvement, judging by a further letter which Father Dimitri wrote to CRA chairman, Vladimir Kuroyedov, on 7 August. He alleged that the local authorities were harassing his spiritual children, trying to find out the identity of people attending his church with the aim of having them dismissed from their jobs.[18] In December 1977 it was reported that Dudko's 17-year-old son Mikhail had been subjected to a forcible psychiatric examination (often a prelude to compulsory psychiatric detention), after he had been found to wear a baptismal cross, and this was widely interpreted as a move by the authorities to intimidate his father.[19]

Far from being intimidated, Father Dimitri began a venture unprecedented for a church in the Soviet Union: in September 1978 he started a parish magazine. *In the Light of the Transfiguration* was a brief newsletter, which contained devotional material and spiritual advice, answers to parishioners' questions, and also regular reports of the harassment of church members, which became more frequent and more vicious as time went on.[20] The parish newsletter had no pretensions to profundity of thought, but it was remarkable as an attempt to provide a common forum for members of a particular parish and to compensate, in however modest a way, for the lack of spiritual literature.

On 11 November 1978 occurred what can only be described as a raid on Father Dimitri's accommodation next to the church, where he sometimes stayed overnight. A group of men dressed in militia uniforms arrived at night, broke down the door and forced their way inside, brandishing pistols and threatening to shoot everyone. They dragged Vladimir Sedov, one of Father Dimitri's spiritual children, out into the snow in his underwear and beat him with their pistols. Then they took him to the local militia station, where he was detained and denied medical attention for his injuries.[21] Dudko wrote letters of complaint to the militia department, the district executive committee, the Politburo and Patriarch Pimen,[22] and the Christian Committee addressed a similar complaint to Kuroyedov,[23] but without result.

Despite such brutality, the young people who travelled to Grebnevo were not deterred. In October 1979 it was reported that Dudko had been summoned to Metropolitan Yuvenali (who had replaced Serafim as Metropolitan of Krutitsy) and given a serious warning about his sermons, which had been attracting large crowds.[24] This move through church channels was followed by a new measure by the state authorities. On Saturday 20 October two militia officers and 20 men in civilian clothes entered the church, where Father Dimitri was taking evening service, and demanded to see the documents of all present. They threatened to detain members of the congregation, including Dudko, if they refused to comply. This was a gross violation by the state of the constitutional freedom of worship. A report of the incident said that Father Dimitri was exhausted by the wave of hostile actions.[25]

In the midst of all this pressure from outside, Dudko also had to deal with a certain amount of criticism from within the Russian Orthodox Church, and with some trouble among his spiritual children. We do not know the precise nature of the criticisms of Father Dimitri (which were probably verbal, not written), but they can be inferred from a letter he wrote on the subject in January 1977. He wrote that he had been grieved because some people had said he was turning away from Orthodoxy. His own view was that he was not disobeying the episcopate, but that he had to judge whether or not an instruction was from God; similarly, he felt that the church canons should not be a brake on any new kind of activity, but a guide for Christian initiatives. Dudko pointed out that his spiritual children were all very different from one another, and if some of them were inclined towards Protestantism, then there was all the more reason for him to love them and care for them.[26] This suggests that the charge of 'sectarianism' was among the criticisms made. Such a charge is likely to be levelled at any Orthodox pastor who seeks to draw people to the faith and teach them without support from fellow-clergy and hierarchs: because he is acting without the overt blessing of the church, he is likely to diverge, or be thought to diverge, farther and farther from it, in the sense that he is acting on his own initiative and not within the *sobornost* of the whole church. If this is taken to its logical conclusion, the pastor and his flock eventually cease to become Orthodox, and become 'sectarians'. Father Dimitri's undoubted loyalty to Orthodox tradition and love for his church do not seem to have been sufficient to protect him entirely from such suspicions, which came from other independently minded Orthodox as well as from official circles. However, Dudko evidently believed that, under conditions when the church is prevented by external forces from giving its blessing to its pastors to draw in new members to the church and nurture them in the faith, then the true priest and pastor will do so of his own accord.

By 1980, problems had begun to occur among Father Dimitri's spiritual children. The pressures they had been subjected to, particularly after some of them had been summoned as witnesses in the criminal investigations against Father Gleb Yakunin and Alexander Ogorodnikov after their arrests, were bound to have their effect, especially as many were still young in the Christian faith. Dudko appealed for unity among them. Disagreements and mutual suspicions were growing.[27] By this time there must have been strong suspicions that the KGB would have infiltrated among their number, and this no doubt helped to cause strained relations. A little later, Father Dimitri noted sadly that some of his spiritual children had left him, without explanation, apparently because they could not bear the pressures.

He expressed another misgiving: not all his spiritual children were willing to accept authority, and sometimes wanted to start teaching before they had learned.[28] This is another example of the problem we noted in Chapter 10: enthusiastic new members of the church wanting to make their own contribution and express their own ideas before attaining what traditional Orthodox believers would regard as a sufficient measure of 'churchliness'.

Father Dimitri's time in Grebnevo was marked by increasing hostility and brutality from agents of the state, attempts by church hierarchs to curb his activities, and a somewhat mixed reception from ordinary members of the Russian Orthodox Church. It would seem that, despite the reservations and misgivings about his activities in the minds of some Orthodox, Father Dimitri in general enjoyed the respect and supportive concern of many believers. Those who did have reservations mostly refrained from expressing them, not wishing to give the KGB further ammunition to use against Dudko. And the many people who made the long journey from Moscow to hear his sermons, and who surrounded him and his family with love and care, evidently found in him a real source of spiritual strength and guidance. No one, however, whatever their attitude to Father Dimitri's ministry, could fail to be aware that trouble was in store. The increasingly violent nature of the KGB's reprisals, and their obvious concern at the growth of Father Dimitri's fame, in the West as well as in the Soviet Union, inevitably bred fears that worse was to come. His spiritual children, fearing another 'accident' which might cost him his life, were constantly at his side, ensuring that he was never left alone. Thus for three years or more Dudko was at the centre of a web of tensions, suspicions and anxieties, spiritually supported by his faith and his spiritual children, but physically and mentally under constant threat from the almost unbearable tensions mounting up around him.

The Suppression of the Christian Seminar

The KGB used similarly harsh measures against members of the Christian Seminar during this time. The first documents from them to arrive in the West, in summer 1976, were appeals to help two Seminar members, Alexander Argentov and Georgi Fedotov, who had been forcibly incarcerated in psychiatric hospitals, though neither had any history of psychiatric illness and both were thought by their friends and families to be quite well.[29] The fact that it was their religious beliefs which led to their confinement was made quite clear in a long conversation between Fedotov's doctor and Alexander Ogorodnikov, who attempted to visit Fedotov in hospital. During the course of it, the psychiatrist stated:

Religion for him [Fedotov] is an obsessional *idée fixe*. There are believers who pray, take communion, and then go back to normal life. They don't stick their noses into things that don't concern them. They just get on with their jobs . . . I'm not against belief, though I'm an atheist through and through. You won't succeed in converting me. Your Eduard [Fedotov's name from birth; Georgi is his baptismal name] is living in a world of illusions, and I want to bring him back to real life . . . Belief is connected with his illness. He doesn't just simply believe — he's a fanatic. He's isolated from life. But he's a fine lad, capable. There are often spiritually sensitive people among believers. We want the best for him.[30]

Ogorodnikov was unable to convince him that Christianity was not merely worship and prayer isolated from 'normal life', but something which colours and fashions the whole life of the committed believer. Though this psychiatrist seems to have been more humane than many in his profession, he could not be shifted from the official Soviet view of religion as a matter confined to church buildings and separated from real life. Argentov's doctor, by contrast, was much more forthright: 'We'll beat your religion out of you!' he is reported to have said.[31]

There was a great deal of publicity in the West about the cases of Fedotov and Argentov, and both were released after a few weeks. This did not prevent other Seminar members from being interned in psychiatric hospitals later: Sergei Yermolayev and Alexander Kuzkin were both interned for a time during 1978 and 1979, and Fedotov was recommitted in January 1980.[32] Moreover, Fedotov suffered lasting effects from drug treatment:

In the course of three months, apart from neuroleptic drugs, Fedotov was given three injections of Moditen Depo without his consent, as a result of which his organism was severely intoxicated and he underwent a severe form of depression . . . The destructive actions of the neuroleptic drugs have produced an irreversible effect on Georgi: he has a serious form of vegetative dystonia [loss of muscle-tone] and asthenia [debility].[33]

This was undoubtedly the worst measure employed against Christian Seminar members, but the documents record a host of other more or less serious reprisals. Between September 1976 and April 1977, 31 Seminar members were interrogated, searched and pressurised, and Ogorodnikov had his residence permit withdrawn and lost his job.[34] In the year to August 1979, no less than 32 instances of harassment of Seminar members occurred.[35] Valentin Serov was attacked at night in a Moscow street by unknown assailants who used professional methods. They broke his arm, then kicked him brutally as he was lying on the ground.[36] A 21-year-old girl connected with the Seminar was harassed in the street by two men who shoved her, trod on her feet, hit her, and then followed her home and tried to force their way after her into her flat.[37] Yevgeni Nesterov was summoned for interrogation by the KGB: when he returned home he found that a KGB agent, S. Pavlenko, had forced his way in and was carrying out an illegal search of his flat. The next day Pavlenko returned and harassed Nesterov's bedridden mother, as a result of which she suffered severe heart trouble and had to go into hospital.[38]

There were many searches of the homes of members of the Christian Seminar, during which books, typewriters and other personal property were routinely confiscated. Some idea of the invasion of privacy and general disruption caused by such a search was given in a lengthy account by Tatyana Shchipkova of a search of her apartment on 21 May 1978:

They behaved themselves unexpectedly politely, tried not to break or smash anything. There was no scattered powder, fragments scrunching underfoot, piles of linen dumped out onto the floor . . . But all the same, it was loathsome. Something sticky and paralysing. You feel soiled by strangers' dirty hands, by strangers' searching looks. Dirty shoes trample not the carpet, but your soul, loathsome hands sort through letters from beloved people who died thirty years ago. But this did not turn out to be the most terrible thing for me. It is horrible, opposed to nature, that people who have burst into your house with an axe in their hands find this [behaviour] so natural themselves that they feel no irritation or antipathy towards the mistress of the house. When they asked me at the end of the search, which lasted six hours, whether I had any complaints, I thought and said 'No', because, really, what complaints could there be? People were just fulfilling their difficult overtime work in the designated area. This area turned out to be my home, and the material, my dear and indispensable books and extracts.[39]

A total of 78 items, mostly *samizdat* manuscripts and typescripts, including materials for the forthcoming issue of *Obshchina*, were confiscated.[40]

The KGB's zeal in this case extended to a Seminar member who had left Smolensk that same night: Sergei Yermolayev was ordered off the Smolensk Moscow train at 2 a.m. and subjected to a two-hour search, conducted without a search-warrant, at the end of which two typewriters were confiscated from him.[41] Yermolayev and a friend were later involved in a curious incident which led to them both being arrested and sent to labour camps. In order to 'test freedom of speech in practice' they shouted slogans such as 'Down with the Communist Party of the Soviet Union!' while travelling on the Moscow Metro. However, though both had committed the same rash act, Yermolayev received a stiffer sentence — four years compared with his friend's three and a half years.[42] Furthermore, Yermolayev was sent to serve his sentence in the Buryat Autonomous Republic in the Soviet Far East, while his friend was sent no further than Gorky, about 260 miles from

Moscow. It seems likely that Yermolayev's membership of the Christian Seminar persuaded the Soviet authorities to give him the harsher sentence.

After the search of her flat, Tatyana Shchipkova encountered further difficulties, which she described in a document entitled 'Has a Soviet Teacher the Right to Freedom of Conscience?'[43] The KGB gave her to understand that she might forfeit her career as a teacher if she persisted in her allegedly 'anti-Soviet' activities, and she decided to forestall a possible public smear campaign by telling her students the truth herself. After telling them about the part played by Christianity in ancient Rome, as was her custom, she added that she herself was a Christian, like many educated people in the Soviet Union, and explained what it meant to be a Christian. She told the students that 'although I had done nothing illegal or immoral, I was not sure whether I would be allowed to continue working with them'. The effect on the students was considerable:

> We are not in the habit of telling the truth about ourselves, and so the students were unaccustomed to hearing it. They were stunned by what I said, listened in total silence and did not ask a single question. No one, it seems, ran off to report on me.[44]

This bold step did not help her case. She was summoned to a departmental meeting where she was charged with conducting religious propaganda among the students, and despite her explanation of what had actually occurred, all her colleagues voted for her dismissal. There followed council meetings of both the faculty and the institute, at which more of her colleagues rose to denounce her. Shchipkova writes that she knew she had sympathisers present, but 'no one dared speak out in my defence, for this would have been tantamount to surrendering their jobs'.[45] The decision was taken to dismiss her 'for teaching of an anti-scientific nature'. However, Shchipkova records that in her work-book — the record of employment and of conduct at places of employment, which Soviet citizens must keep throughout their working lives and present at each new job they take up — she found a different formulation:

> 'dismissed due to the unsuitability of the post held as a result of the person in question being underqualified'. This note was entered immediately before three comments expressing gratitude for my excellent educational work with the students.[46]

Shchipkova had been working at the institute, without criticism, for 16 years.[47] In November that year, at a meeting at the Linguistic Institute of the USSR Academy of Sciences in Leningrad, Shchipkova was stripped of her degree of candidate of philological sciences. Vladimir Poresh was present, but was not allowed to speak.[48]

Alexander Ogorodnikov had continued to encounter many problems in obtaining a residence permit and in finding employment. He had moved out of Moscow to Redkino, in Kalinin region, some two hours' journey by train from Moscow, where Seminar meetings took place. On 20 November 1978, Ogorodnikov was arrested at Redkino railway station, and was charged with failure to find gainful employment, or 'parasitism'. According to his friends, however, who at once wrote an explanation of the circumstances of his arrest, Ogorodnikov was in the act of travelling to complete the formalities for a job for which he had already been accepted.[49] His trial took place in Konakovo, Kalinin region, on 10 January 1979. As is usual in the trials of dissenters in the USSR, the courtroom was packed out before-hand with 'members of the public' admitted well before the start of the proceedings by the KGB, so that Ogorodnikov's friends were unable to enter due to lack of space. Even his wife and his parents were able to enter the courtroom for only part of the trial, and after lengthy arguments and protests. Defence witnesses requested by Ogorodnikov were not allowed to be called — another common feature of trials of dissenters. (A detailed transcript of the trial was later pieced together by one of Ogorodnikov's friends, who heightened these and other features of the trial by scripting it as though it were a play or farce, where all the leading participants knew their lines beforehand and the outcome was known to them all in advance.)[50] An additional feature of this trial was that relevant medical evidence was passed over by the judge. Ogorodnikov's defence lawyer stated during the trial that Ogorodnikov suffered from a serious disease of the blood, as a result of which his spleen had been removed, and asked that a medical commission be consulted to determine the degree of his unfitness for work. Despite its obvious relevance to Ogorodnikov's difficulties in finding permanent employment, this petition was denied. Ogorodnikov was sentenced to one year in labour camp, and was sent to eastern Siberia to serve his term. As we shall see, this sentence passed on the Christian Seminar's founder was by no means the end of its troubles, and several members were to follow Ogorodnikov into labour camps.

The Orthodox in the Context of Soviet Repression of Dissent

During 1978 and 1979 the arrests and trials of Helsinki Monitors were pro-ceeding apace. Nearly all the leading figures and earliest members of the five groups were arrested sooner or later. In Moscow and Lithuania, new members came forward, enabling both groups to maintain a precarious existence on into the 1980s, but the Georgian and Armenian groups were forced to abandon their activities, and the Ukrainian group was crippled. Orthodox Christians active in the Helsinki groups suffered along with the rest: Alexander Ginzburg was arrested in February 1978 and sentenced to eight years' special regime labour camp and Lev Lukyanenko was arrested in December 1977 (after only 18 months at liberty since the end of a previous 15-year sentence) and sentenced to ten years in labour camp and five years' internal exile. (Ginzburg was one of five Soviet prisoners released on 27 April 1979, stripped of Soviet citizenship, and deported to the USA in exchange for two Soviet spies.) The activities of the Helsinki Monitors had generated much publicity and a great deal of public support for them in the West, and this had clearly disturbed the Soviet government. The authorities evidently made it a priority to silence these political activitists, as they thought of them, even at a cost of a temporary slowing down of their repression of the religious activists against whom they had already begun to move so determinedly.

The arrests of the Helsinki Monitors and the lengthy terms of imprisonment to which they were sentenced marked the commencement of a new period of repression by the Soviet government which has shown no sign of abating, and in which religious believers have suffered alongside others of all stripes viewed as political deviants. This repression was chiefly the consequence of the failure of the policy of *détente* with the West which flowered briefly during the mid-1970s, and of which the signing of the Final Act of the Helsinki Agreements in August 1975 was the most obvious sign. This represented a substantial political advantage to the Soviet Union, recognising as it did (*de facto* if not *de jure*, since the Final Act did not have treaty status) the post-war political boundaries of Europe, with the implicit recognition of Eastern Europe as a Soviet sphere of influence. However, a consequence of the signing of those sections of the Final Act which made provisions concerning various areas of human rights and freer exchange of information between signatory states was that Western countries now began to pay closer attention to what advocates of human rights in the Soviet Union had been saying for some years past. Protests by Jewish and other would-be emigrants, by Academician Sakharov, who was awarded the Nobel Peace Prize in 1975, by some nationalist movements, and by religious believers of various denominations, were the subject of great debate and of some action by Western bodies in the light of the undertakings made at Helsinki. The open declaration by the new President of the USA, Jimmy Carter (elected in 1976), that human rights and the observation, or lack of observation, of them would form a major part of his foreign policy played a significant part in focusing international attention on the Soviet Union's failure to live up to the obligations it had undertaken at Helsinki. The activities of the Helsinki Monitors added fuel to the fire, and they were therefore the first to be dealt with once the Soviet government had taken the decision which confronted it. That decision was a simple alternative: either the authorities must take the demands of the dissenters and human rights activists seriously and make some attempt to accommodate them within the Soviet system, or they must remove them from the scene. The decision to do the latter was evidently taken as early as late 1976 or early 1977, after which the arrests of Helsinki Monitors proceeded despite international protests. After this time, protest abroad was no longer sufficient to guarantee any Soviet dissenter immunity from arrest. The Soviet government had clearly decided to face out protest from abroad and relinquish the possible advantages of *détente* in order to preserve its monolithic system intact. It shrank from the alternative, which was to allow at least some measure of political reform in the hope of pacifying the dissidents. No doubt it thought that, once started, even minimal reforms might open the floodgates leading to all kinds of demands for further social and political change, and preferred the familiar routine of repression to the more demanding social and ideological exercise of developing totalitarian Marxism–Leninism in the direction of social democracy.

By the summer of 1979, the trials of the Helsinki Monitors were over, and the KGB once again turned its attention to religious dissenters. The timing of the wave of arrests which followed makes it clear that religious activists were regarded as one section of an undesirable political and social phenomenon — dissent in all its forms — rather than as a peculiarly religious or Christian threat to the Soviet system. At this stage — late 1979 and early 1980 — Christians were simply one of many groups whose activities were arousing too much support within the Soviet Union and too much interest abroad, and who must be silenced along with nationalists, Jews, various emigration movements, campaigners against the abuse of psychiatry for political motives, *samizdat* authors, remaining advocates of the free trade union movement, and even incapacitated people who had formed a movement to press for the rights of the disabled. During the 1970s, the total number of known Christian prisoners had averaged about 100, but after the arrests of late 1979 and early 1980 the number quickly regained the total of 300 or more which had been the average during the anti-religious campaign of the early 1960s. The number of unregistered Baptist prisoners grew from 39 in 1979 to 104 in 1981, and the number of Orthodox prisoners from 27 to 36 in the same period. By August 1982 there were 162 Baptist and 41 Orthodox prisoners, and the overall number of known Christian prisoners was 393.[51]

A Wave of Arrests

Vladimir Poresh was arrested in August 1979 and charged under Article 70, 'anti-Soviet agitation and propaganda', and specifically with preparing and circulating *Obshchina*. Alexander Ogorodnikov, due for release upon completion of his one-year sentence in November 1979, was instead transferred to prison in Leningrad and interrogated in connection with the same case. Other Orthodox Christians arrested at this time were Valeri Abramkin, a member of the editorial board of the new *samizdat* journal *Poiski* (*Quests*), who was later sentenced to three years in labour camp, and Tatyana Velikanova, one of the compilers of the *Chronicle of Current Events*. She was later sentenced to four years in labour camp to be followed by five years' internal exile. Velikanova's selfless efforts to give advice and help to many different people whose human rights had been infringed had earned her enormous respect and affection in nonconformist circles in Moscow. She was arrested on the same day as Father Gleb Yakunin, 1 November, and many people were quick to appeal publicly for support for them both.

It was clear from the many *samizdat* protests against Yakunin's arrest that the detention of such a prominent figure in the struggle for the rights of religious believers was taken to be a direct challenge by the state to the movement as a whole. An appeal by two Orthodox lay people, Alexi and Irina Zalessky, urged their fellow-Christians to stand firm:

> The authorities think that if they can remove the 'ringleaders' then the rest — small fry, in their opinion — will scatter like beetles and hide in crannies . . . Our reply to the authorities when they arrest priests or laymen who are struggling for human rights must be firm and unambiguous: do not imagine that arrests and repressive measures will have the effect you are hoping for. Your aim is to extinguish the religious movement and the human rights movement: on the contrary, you will reinforce them. When any religious activist or human rights defender is arrested or dismissed from his job, dozens more will stand up to take his place . . . In the past you meant to destroy religion by pulling down churches and arresting priests; but religion rose again like Christ crucified. History repeats itself.[52]

The protests on Yakunin's behalf also made it clear that his work with the Christian Committee had won him friends and supporters in other denominations who were prepared to speak out publicly on his behalf. This was, and remains, the exception rather than the rule among religious dissenters. For example, an appeal signed by 300 Pentecostals declared:

> Whenever you meet Gleb Yakunin you feel joy and admiration for this selfless man . . . [his] contribution to the struggle for believers' rights in the USSR is immense. We call on the governments and parliaments of all countries, on Christians throughout the world, and on all men of good will to join in the struggle for the release of Gleb Yakunin with all the strength God gives you![53]

An appeal demanding the immediate release of Father Yakunin, signed by Igor Shafarevich and over 70 others, adopted a more general, but forthright and uncompromising, tone:

For tens of thousands of years, as far as the gaze of historians penetrates back into the past, religion has formed an inalienable part of life of human society. It would be naive to suppose that this side of our existence could be eliminated at some moment in time . . . We view the arrest of Father Gleb as an obstacle to the normalisation of religious life on the part of the authorities.[54]

Father Nikolai Gainov, who had not engaged in any public protests since the unsuccessful letter to the Local Council in 1971, now wrote openly to Patriarch Pimen asking him 'to do everything possible for the release' of Yakunin.[55] It was then announced that Gainov had taken over Yakunin's place on the Christian Committee.[56] Shortly after this the Christian Committee, consisting now of Father Nikolai Gainov, Father Vasili Fonchenkov, Viktor Kapitanchuk and Vadim Shcheglov, put out brief informational statements about persecution of Christians of various denominations,[57] evidently hoping to continue the Committee's activities as in the past.

A feature of Yakunin's arrest was the harsh, even malicious, attitude which the KGB adopted towards him and his family. This was also demonstrated during a house-search which preceded his arrest, on 28 September, and two further searches afterwards, on 1 and 13 November. When Father Gleb was taken from his home at 8 a.m. on 1 November by senior KGB lieutenant Novikov, he tried to say goodbye to his children, but Novikov told him that this was not necessary, as he would be returning home after questioning. In fact he did not return, and his wife, Iraida Georgievna, had to make several telephone calls before finally being told that he had been arrested and taken to Lefortovo investigation prison. Even then, and for some time afterwards, she was not told on what charge he had been arrested.[58] During the three house-searches, many personal possessions of the family were confiscated, including the icons which they used for family prayers.[59] Mrs Yakunin and her daughter were subjected to a body search by an unauthorised woman, the only purpose of which seemed to be to humiliate them.[60] Also confiscated was money given by a Christian in Krasnoyarsk to further the work of the Christian Committee, in the form of four savings books totalling 1,589 roubles.[61] More seriously, items of value were taken: the icons mentioned above, a crucifix, spoons and a cigarette case made 'of white metal'.[62] The confiscation of the valuables gave rise to fears among Father Gleb's family and friends that the KGB intended to concoct a case against him on a charge of 'speculation' — unauthorised dealings in valuable objects — a serious crime in the Soviet Union, but in the event this came to nothing. The confiscation of money and valuables by the KGB remains an unexplained and unauthorised action.

The arrests of Orthodox and other dissenters were stepped up at the turn of the year and during the first weeks of 1980. At this time, other events began to dominate the scene. During the final days of 1979, the Soviet Union invaded Afghanistan, and worldwide condemnation of this action followed swiftly. This increased the fervour behind the already existing movement in many countries to boycott the Olympic Games scheduled to be held in Moscow in summer 1980. The Soviet government appears to have concluded that with international odium against it already so great, the arrest of more dissidents could hardly make matters worse, and that this might indeed be an excellent opportunity to remove them from public life before the Olympic Games commenced. There could have been no clearer indication of this new hardline approach than the forcible exile of Academician Sakharov to Gorky in January 1982, despite strong and continuing worldwide protests.

Lev Regelson (who had assumed leadership of the Christian Seminar after the arrest of Ogorodnikov) was arrested in Tallinn on 24 December. He had gone there in a vain attempt to avoid arrest.[63] Another Christian Seminar member, Tatyana Shchipkova, was brought to trial in Moscow on 8 January 1980 and sentenced to three years in labour camp on a charge of 'malicious hooliganism' (article 206 of the Criminal Code). This related to an incident which had occurred during 1979, when Shchipkova was present during the search of a friend's flat. One of the officials conducting the search had attempted to wrest a book from her hand, and when she refused to relinquish it he had twisted her arm. She had slapped his face in retaliation, and this constituted her 'crime'.[64] Two other Christian Seminar members were arrested early in 1980: Viktor Popkov, a worker from Smolensk, on 8 January, and Vladimir Burtsev, a technician from Moscow, on 8 February. A court in Smolensk sentenced them both to 18 months in labour camp on charges of 'forgery' under Article 196 of the Criminal Code, at a joint trial on 8–9 April. Though Popkov had previously been told, during a KGB investigation in June 1978, that his participation in the Christian Seminar, and the Seminar's activities, constituted 'anti-Soviet activity', this played no part in the charge against them and the court proceedings. (The charge in fact related to inaccurate work-sheets that they had been obliged to file by a foreman on a summer work project; this was to cover up the fact that they had been coerced into working illegally long hours.)[65] The charges against Shchipkova, Popkov and Burtsev served to underline once more the KGB's failure to find any illegality in the existence and activities of the Christian Seminar. (Burtsev and Popkov were subsequently released conditionally before completion of their sentences, with compulsory allocation to hard labour.)[66]

The Arrest of Father Dimitri Dudko

Amid this long procession of arrests and trials, the greatest shock and international protest was undoubtedly occasioned by the arrest of Father Dimitri Dudko on 15 January 1980. Unlike the other Orthodox who were arrested, he had not been directly involved in work for believers' rights, and he was still working as an officially recognised parish priest in Grebnevo. He had, however, continued to make outspoken comments on current events, particularly the arrest of Yakunin, in his parish newsletter *In the Light of the Transfiguration*, and the Soviet authorities had no doubt been particularly angered by his repeated calls for the canonisation of twentieth-century Russian martyrs, including Tsar Nicholas II and his family. The pressure on Dudko and his spiritual children had increased greatly towards the end of 1979; incursions into the church by militia officers who behaved boorishly and threateningly had become more frequent. Father Dimitri knew that he was in danger, as is clear from a letter he wrote to a friend abroad at the end of December, in which he wrote: 'If anything happens to me, let this be my word from captivity. I ask you to pray.'[67]

Father Dimitri was arrested at his church in Grebnevo at 8 a.m. by twelve KGB officers and driven to Lefortovo prison. His Moscow flat was searched from 8 a.m. to 8. p.m., and the homes of three of his spiritual children and of Viktor Kapitanchuk were also searched. All religious literature was confiscated from Dudko's home: Bibles, prayer books, religious books and manuscripts, all Father Dimitri's sermons, a complete set of a children's religious magazine, *Trezvon* (*Peal of Bells*), published in the USA, as well as a typewriter, a tape-recorder and all the family's money. Dudko's son had been sent home from the institute where he studied to witness the proceedings, but had refused to sign the protocol of the search since there was no ground for the confiscation of the money and of purely religious literature. There was also a search of the parish house in Grebnevo, which lasted until 2.30 a.m. the following morning, where money and a typewriter were among the items confiscated.[68] It was reported the Dudko would be charged under Article 70 of the Criminal Code ('anti-Soviet agitation and propaganda').[69]

Protests against Dudko's arrest appeared with remarkable speed: no fewer than 95 signatures to an appeal were gathered on the very day of the arrest. The appeal addressed 'To Christians of the whole world' said that Father Dimitri's appearance in their country had been a miracle, and the extent of his influence inconceivable.[70] Another of the numerous appeals issued at this time, originating in Leningrad, stated that the recent arrests demonstrated:

that religious teaching, contact among believers and people who are interested in questions of morality and conscience which cannot be solved by an atheistic State, or discussion of contemporary spiritual problems are seen by the [Soviet] authorities as *de facto* anti-State activities.[71]

This point was taken up in an appeal issued by the Leningrad religious seminar, which commented that the authorities were evidently determined to stamp out all kinds of independent thought, no matter how little they were opposed to the official ideology.[72] An open letter to Patriarch Pimen from 55 parishioners and spiritual children urged him to pray for Father Dimitri and to take up his case with the authorities.[73] The Christian Committee, in a statement mourning the arrest of this 'true pastor of Christ', saw the recent arrests as 'the beginning of a new, unsurpassed persecution of Christianity in Russia', but warned that 'however cruel the authorities are, they will not succeed in stifling the spiritual renaissance which has begun, in killing the living Christian spirit in Russia'.[74] The theme running through these and other protests was that, as Father Dimitri had been a priest working legally and openly in a parish, with a ministry confined to preaching and pastoral work, his arrest was to be taken as a move by the authorities against active Christianity as such, not merely against those who made a point of working publicly for believers' rights and true freedom of religion.

A new note was introduced in a statement by four Orthodox intellectuals, Igor Shafarevich, Vadim Borisov, Igor Khokhlushkin and Leonid Borodin, who suggested that the KGB might have been encouraged to arrest Dudko because a number of Russian-language publications in the West had recently published critical comments about him. (These had centred on Dudko's repeated support for the canonisation of Nicholas II.) The four authors of the statement said that these comments, which had gone so far as to suggest that it was no accident that Dudko still remained at liberty despite his outspoken sermons and articles, might well have been taken by the Soviet authorities to mean that his arrest would not provoke very vigorous protests in the West.[75] It is impossible to know whether this supposition by these four very experienced observers of the Soviet scene was in fact correct. As noted above, from the invasion of Afghanistan at the end of 1979 and thereafter, no dissenter was sufficiently illustrious to be saved from arrest, with the exception of Academician Sakharov, whose worldwide renown as a Nobel Laureate meant that he was subjected to administrative exile rather than to arrest and legal processes. It is conceivable, however, that Dudko, by now possibly the best-known person in the West after Sakharov, might have been removed from the scene by some means other than arrest — transfer to a remote parish, for example — had there not been controversy in the West (and among nonconformist Orthodox in the USSR) over his views on canonisation of martyrs. This possibility reveals another aspect of the difficulty Soviet dissenters have in holding free and open debates on controversial matters. A dissenter may be inhibited from expressing disagreement with the opinion of another dissenter for fear that the KGB may manipulate his words to discredit and isolate him, in order to diminish protest when he is arrested. This undoubtedly impairs the climate of freedom of thought and expression even among those dissenters who have had the moral courage to renounce career, a peaceful life and even physical freedom in order to seek and proclaim the truth.

Dudko's arrest also provoked an unprecedented spate of activity abroad. Church members of all denominations engaged in special prayers and appeals, many public statements were made by church leaders, and both Christian and secular press gave coverage to the arrest and to Father Dimitri's career. Some statements were linked to other arrests, to criticism of the Soviet invasion of Afghanistan and to the proposed boycott of the Moscow Olympic Games: for example, the newly elected Archbishop of Canterbury, Dr Robert Runcie, publicly criticised the pre-Olympic wave of arrests[76] and this led to the Russian Orthodox representation at his subsequent enthronement being substantially and pointedly reduced.[77] Orthodox bishops overseas spoke up on Father Dimitri's behalf. Archbishop Vasili of Brussels appealed directly to Mr Brezhnev to release Dudko,[78] and received a warm letter of thanks from some of Father Dimitri's parishioners.[79] In London, Metropolitan Antoni of Sourozh attended a special church service to support Dudko and other Orthodox prisoners, at which he served a *moleben*, or service of intercession, for them.[80] The Primate of the Orthodox Church in America, Metropolitan Theodosius (who had met Father Dimitri at his own request during a visit to Moscow in 1978) issued a statement expressing his concern over the arrest[81] and later made a second statement addressed to President Carter.[82] Never before had Orthodox churchmen in the West in communion with the Moscow Patriarchate made their disapproval known so strongly.

Perhaps the most unexpected appeal for Dudko came from an Anglican priest in Capetown, South Africa, Rev. David Russell, who was under a banning order after having outspokenly criticised injustice in South Africa. He was due to appear in court on 25 January for having violated his house arrest in order to attend the Synod of his church, and was also charged with possessing a banned book (a biography of the black activist Steve Biko). Despite his own predicament, on 18 January he sent a cable to President Brezhnev urging him to 'apply wisdom and compassion' and release Dudko.[83]

Bishops of the Moscow Patriarchate who travelled abroad from the Soviet Union at this time faced insistent questioning from the press about the arrests of Dudko and Yakunin. Archbishop Pitirim of Volokolamsk said in Stockholm that Father Dimitri, with whom he had studied in the seminary in 1945, was a 'nervous and unbalanced person' who might be supposed liable to break the law.[84] This comment could as well be taken as an attempt to exculpate Father Dimitri because of his temperament as to cast a slur on his character. The Archbishop added: 'We pray for him.' In West Germany shortly afterwards, Archbishop Pitirim said that there was 'no wave of arrests' and that reports of stepped-up arrests and persecution of priests in the Soviet Union were 'absolutely false'. He added that the situation of the Orthodox Church and the clergy in the Soviet Union had 'stabilised' over the last 15 years.[85] He went on to state that the cases of Dudko and Yakunin were exceptional, and said that the Patriarchate would be advised of the charges against the two priests once the investigation of their cases had been completed.[86] These remarks met with widespread indignation and disbelief from the press and other commentators. There was a clear clash of perspective. The Archbishop, from his own view of the church's situation, was confining himself to as few comments as possible on what he believed to be the literal truth. The arrests of a number of leading Orthodox dissenters did not constitute a 'wave' considered against the numbers of the church as a whole; it was indeed not true that persecution of priests in general in the Soviet Union had increased; the cases of Dudko and Yakunin certainly were exceptional; and the church's situation undoubtedly had stabilised since the end of the anti-religious campaign in 1964. However, whether the Archbishop was giving his true personal opinion or merely carrying out the behests of the CRA, his taking refuge in these comments avoided the point of the issue, which was the genuine concern felt in the West for Dudko and Yakunin. His replies were taken to mean that he was washing his hands of the two brave priests and their undeserved sufferings and was suggesting that there was no cause for concern, and this made him appear personally uncharitable and even treacherous towards his fellow-priests. By contrast, Metropolitan Alexi of Tallinn was altogether more distant and official in his replies to similar questions during a visit to Austria. He stated that the Moscow Patriarchate had made enquiries of the CRA about Dudko and been told that he had not been charged; he added that the Patriarchate knew nothing of the reasons for the arrest and could not base its stance on Western speculations. He further remarked, apparently gratuitously: 'In the Soviet Union, citizens are never arrested for their religious or ideological convictions.'[87] This 'stonewalling' approach contrasted with Archbishop Pitirim's (admittedly unsuccessful) efforts to advance some kind of explanation of the current situation; it showed that there could be some variations in the stances adopted by church leaders, even within the very strict restraints upon bishops imposed by the CRA, which we examined in Part 1.

In practical terms, however, these subtleties were of little moment to the arrested priests, as their defenders were quick to point out. One of Father Dimitri's spiritual children, Pavel Protsenko, wrote an open letter to Archbishop Pitirim complaining about the 'concealed slander' in his words about Father Dimitri;[88] and a human rights activist who had emigrated, Yuri Belov, accused him of remaining silent while the persecution of believers in the USSR continued.[89] As we have already commented (p. 221), the esoteric fencing game continually carried on between the bishops and the CRA, with all its implications for the moral stance of the bishops concerned, has little or no immediate practical consequence for the church at large.

Further Arrests

Whatever the effectiveness or otherwise of support from the West for Soviet dissenters and prisoners, it gave them 'an enormous moral boost', according to Viktor Kapitanchuk, the secretary of the Christian Committee. He added that this was particularly true for those who lived in the provinces and were more isolated and vulnerable to persecution than those in large cities.[90] This suggests that Western protests were having a certain, unquantifiable, effect even if they were apparently unable to affect matters materially.[91] Kapitanchuk was at this time encountering increased pressure from the KGB. On 31 January he was summoned for questioning in connection with the case of his imprisoned fellow-Christian Committee member, Father Gleb Yakunin, but refused to give evidence on religious and ethical grounds. He was warned that if he did not cease his human rights activities immediately, he would be arrested, but despite this threat he refused to give any assurances.[92] Kapitanchuk was in fact arrested on 12 March. His wife Tatyana received a telephone call informing her that her husband was being charged under Article 190/1 of the Criminal Code ('anti-Soviet slander'), which carries a maximum penalty of three years' deprivation of freedom.[93] Like the other arrested Orthodox Christians, Kapitanchuk was taken to Lefortovo investigation prison.[94]

As we noted in Chapter 12, Father Nikolai Gainov and Vadim Shcheglov issued a statement on the day of Kapitanchuk's arrest to the effect that the Christian Committee would carry on its work, and that ten new, anonymous, members had been selected from over 250 applicants (see p. 380). They did in fact manage to send a few reports abroad shortly afterwards,[95] but after this no more documents reached the West, and this aspect of the Christian Committee's activity ceased.

The scaling-down of the Christian Committee's activities was no doubt the reason why its three remaining members escaped arrest, although they continued to be the objects of official attention, particularly the secretary, Vadim Shcheglov. Shortly after Kapitanchuk's arrest, he was warned that he too would be arrested if he did not immediately stop his activities on behalf of believers.[96] On 19 May he was summoned for an interview with his director at work (in the Ministry of Health, where Shcheglov worked as a mathematician), who told him that a practising believer should not be employed in a responsible position, and chided him for keeping 'undesirable company' (a reference to Academician Sakharov, whom Shcheglov had visited in exile in Gorky). The same day, Shcheglov was summoned for a similar conversation by the secretary of the Party committee in the

Ministry of Health. This interview ended when the secretary learned that the Shcheglov family intended to leave Moscow for the duration of the forth-coming Olympic Games.[97] Father Vasili Fonchenkov issued a statement at this time saying that he too was under threat of arrest. He had been summoned for an interrogation by the KGB on 16 May, during the course of which he had learned that his joining the Christian Committee a year previously was regarded by the KGB as having 'inflicted damage upon the interests of the Soviet State'. His statement concluded:

> In the event that any kind of materials or reports harmful to the Christian Committee for the Defence of Believers' Rights or its members should be circulated in my name, I ask that they should be regarded as invalid, as not conforming to my conviction on the usefulness of the Committee's activity in defence of rights.[98]

Pressure on Orthodox and other Christians continued during the spring and summer as they were summoned for questioning about the cases of those already arrested, or threatened with arrest themselves. Various Christians were summoned for interrogation in connection with Father Gleb Yakunin and Viktor Kapitanchuk,[99] but it was notable that there were no summonses in connection with Father Dimitri Dudko's case.[100] One believer, Tatyana Lebedeva, summoned for questioning on 27 March in the case against Lev Regelson, 'refused to assist in the fabrication of a case against him on religious and moral grounds'. After this, the officials questioning her threatened and abused her, and discussed in front of her what the fate of her 9-year-old daughter would be were she to be arrested.[101] Two Christian Seminar members who had already been forcibly interned in psychiatric hospitals were recommitted early in 1980. Georgi Fedotov was arrested on 18 January after reporting the arrest of Dudko to foreign corre-spondents. He was committed to Moscow Psychiatric Hospital Number 14, and was initially treated with haloperidol, triftazin and aminazin.[102] He was released a few months later.[103] Alexander Kuzkin was taken from work on 7 March by officials who lectured him on the unacceptability of preaching Christianity among his colleagues at work, and suggested that he should be admitted to a psychiatric ward for examination. Kuzkin said that he did not need an examination as he had already been examined by an independent Soviet psychiatrist and a foreign psychiatrist.[104] At this, one official left the room to consult his superiors by telephone, and on his return told Kuzkin he could go free until 10 March. However, Kuzkin was subsequently arrested and taken to Butyrki prison, where he was given a psychiatric examination and charged under Article 190/1 of the Criminal Code ('anti-Soviet slander').[105] On 23 May, 35-year-old Ignati Lapkin, a follower of Dudko, was arrested in Barnaul, Siberia. He had been criticised in the Soviet press for his activities and contacts with other Orthodox believers.[106]

In Leningrad, the feminists also experienced growing repression. Tatyana Goricheva had refused to give evidence in the case of Vladimir Poresh the previous November, when KGB officers had called at her home. She had declined to accompany them to their headquarters for further questioning, but was taken there none the less after they had summoned a detachment of militia to back them up.[107] On 29 February, Goricheva was involved in the search of the home of poetess Yuliya Voznesenskaya, another Christian feminist, whom she had chanced to visit. Twenty-five books were confiscated from Goricheva, while Voznesenskaya lost about 300 books and two suitcases full of papers — her entire archive. On the same date, feminist Sofiya Sokolova was searched and then questioned for a whole day, and had 23 books confiscated, including a copy of *The Gulag Archipelago*.[108] In July three feminists were forcibly deported from the Soviet Union: they were Tatyana Mamonova, and the two Orthodox Christians Tatyana Goricheva and Natalya Malakhovskaya.[109] Other dissenters had been deported during the pre-Olympic period, but the exiling of three leading feminists (they were flown to Vienna on a special aeroplane) suggested that the Soviet authorities feared the consequences of the rapid growth of the feminist movement.

The Trial of Vladimir Poresh

Poresh's trial took place in central Leningrad from 23 to 25 April, accompanied by all the usual difficulties over the admission of his family and friends to the courtroom. A lengthy *Samizdat* account of the trial which reached the West[110] formed a moving testimony both to the depth of the Christian qualities which characterised Poresh himself — principally his humility and selflessness — and to the profoundly spiritual attitude which he and his friends had towards his trial and imprisonment. After sentence was pronounced, and the court attendants had unceremoniously pushed Poresh's family and friends out of the courtroom and into a hallway, they all spontaneously broke into an Easter chant from the Orthodox liturgy, and continued singing until they were hoarse. In Soviet courts, the accused is allowed to make a final speech at the conclusion of the proceedings, before sentence is pronounced, and in his final word Poresh said that the Procurator had asked for a 'short' sentence for him, and added: 'I would have asked for a longer one, but I know that this would be too great an honour for me. There are people who have done much more for the Church than I have.' He spoke of the 'constant sense of joy' experienced during the trial by himself, his family and friends (whom he had not seen for nine months), and said of their relationship: 'This is a new religious community . . . This new spiritual reality, this communal Christian view of the world, is being created everywhere, even here in this courtroom.' Poresh was sentenced to five years' strict regime labour camp to be followed by three years' internal exile.[111]

Father Dimitri Dudko's 'Recantation'

The grim round of arrests and trials was suddenly broken on 20 June by a fresh move in the KGB's campaign against religious dissenters. To the profound shock and distress of his friends and spiritual children, Father Dimitri Dudko appeared on Soviet television to make a public 'confession' or 'recantation' of his former views and activities.[112] It was given extensive publicity in the Soviet press. A TASS press release the same day reported on the broadcast, the Novosti Press Agency released the text of Dudko's statement to foreign correspondents, and Radio Moscow gave it full coverage in its foreign service. The next day the text of Dudko's statement was published in *Izvestiya*.[113] It was dated 5 June, that is, over two weeks before the date of publication. (No reason for the delay has been given, but the obvious explanation is that this time was needed to co-ordinate the release of the statement by the media after Dudko had signed it.) The statement was subsequently reprinted in a number of other leading Soviet newspapers.[114] On Saturday, 21 June Dudko was allowed to return home.[115] Some three weeks later, a penitent letter from Dudko to Patriarch Pimen, also dated 5 June, was published, first in the Moscow Patriarchate's *News Bulletin* on 9 July, and later in the *Journal of the Moscow Patriarchate*.[116]

Dudko's statement commenced with an admission of criminal guilt. He said that after his arrest he had initially maintained that he was struggling against atheism, not against the Soviet state, but after reflection he realised that: 'I was arrested not for believing in God but for crime.' (The words 'God' and 'Church' are capitalised through the *Izvestiya* statement, a departure from standard Soviet practice.) He went on to describe the stages by which he had reached this conviction: he had tried to teach the bishops that they were adopting the wrong course, which concealed a desire to bring the church into conflict with the state; he had not been sufficiently grateful when he had been humanely released from his previous term of imprisonment; he had published statements and books containing 'anti-Soviet slander' in the West; he had tried to do everything on his own instead of in concert with the people of the fatherland he claimed to love. Above all, he had been the source of information discrediting his country which had been picked up in the sensation-hungry West and had come to realise that 'The West . . . is amusing itself with you.' Moreover, he had not wanted to keep in step with the church of which he was a member — 'forgetting that our Church does precisely what it is necessary for her to do'. All these considerations led to the categoric statement. 'I renounce what I have done, and I regard my so-called struggle with godlessness as a struggle with Soviet power.' The second part of Dudko's statement was concerned with his meetings with foreigners, several of whom he named, and to whom he admitted giving 'slanderous materials which were used in hostile propaganda against our State'.[117] He concluded by saying that he had written to the Patriarch asking him to forgive him, and to accept him 'as a newborn child' into his flock; and also appealed to his 'former likeminded colleagues' (*byvshye yedinomyshlenniki*) to work together with their government and people, who were 'given to us by God'.

There were two recurring threads running throughout this statement: first, Dudko's involvement with the West and the way he was 'used' by it; and, second, his public recognition and acceptance of the Moscow Patriarchate's established relationship to the state. The nub of the whole issue was Dudko's implicit 'betrayal' of the Soviet fatherland, and this was described in terms of his willingness to supply harmful information about it to the West, and of his disregard of the wise policies of his own ecclesiastical superiors in their attitude to the state. The statement was not about the Christian faith — it was explicitly stated that Dudko was not asked to deny his faith — but solely about church–state relations and the way in which they were perceived in the West.

The concern with Western reactions to Dudko's activities amounted almost to an obsession in the statement, as demonstrated above all by the editorial choice of title for it in the *Izvestiya* reportage. Where the reader might have expected (if one can speak of expectations in such an unprecedented affair) something like 'Priest Acknowledges Guilt' or 'Church "Dissident" Confesses', he read instead 'The West is Seeking Sensations'. The burden of guilt was shifted from Dudko himself to the West and he was made to seem the naive dupe of political machinations. This impression was reinforced when, at the end of a passage in which Father Dimitri reflected upon love to his fatherland and his neighbour, and upon the words of St Serafim of Sarov and St John the Evangelist, the reader suddenly found him condemning 'the sabre-rattling of the Carter administration [which is] threatening fratricidal war and arousing the indignation and protest of all peoples by its aggressive intentions'.

Father Dimitri's return to an acceptance of the established pattern of church–state relations was given almost equal prominence in the statement. He specifically renounced actions taken on his own initiative, and appealed to others not to do so, but to act in concord with the people (*narod*) and the church, thus implicitly identifying the church with the Soviet people and with Soviet policies. Dudko's willingness to accept the church's relationship to the state was even more pronounced in his letter to Patriarch Pimen. He spoke of having had to humble his pride, and of being 'reduced to dust' before realising that

I tried to instruct you, to tell you that you were following the wrong path.

But you were following the right path, because your predecessors also followed it. By travelling that road the Church has stood fast and is carrying on its work, while another road would have ended in mere sensation-seeking or political intrigue, in which I found myself involved and of which I now sincerely repent.

God's work is done meekly and quietly, patiently and humbly, not in the way I imagined.[118]

There could be no more complete acceptance of the church's position as defined by the Soviet state. These words were precisely what the Soviet authorities required to reassert their view of the church's proper place, and to invalidate the former words and actions not only of Dudko, but of other nonconformist activists also.

This raised the question as to whether Dudko's confession was genuine or whether it was fabricated by the KGB. In a sense, the question was almost redundant in the light of the circumstances in which it was made. Dudko had displayed no doubts about the course of his ministry before his arrest, and so it was quite obvious that a statement produced after five months' isolation in prison and constant interrogation by the KGB could not be called an act of free will. It was also clear, however, that the KGB could not simply have broken him by means of drugs, torture, threats or any other methods and then immediately released him unless they were sure that he would not retract his statement and reveal the pressures under which it had been made. Clearly, they had reached some kind of agreement with him which went farther than inducing him to sign a document in a moment of weakness. It was to be some time before fragmentary indications of the nature of this agreement emerged.

Western commentators quickly asserted that Dudko could not have composed the text of the statement himself. It was too much in the style of usual Soviet press items, and far too well tailored to Soviet policy objectives, for anyone to think that it represented the spontaneous reflections of a deeply religious, deeply patriotic penitent. They concluded that Father Dimitri was compelled by unimaginable pressures into signing a prepared text.[119]

This view was also predominant in Soviet dissident circles in the wake of the televised confession. The overwhelming majority of public comments were written in sorrow rather than in anger, and among those who knew the resources available to the KGB and the lengths to which they were prepared to go to attain their objectives, there was no one willing publicly to sit in judgement over Father Dimitri. Those church members who felt they could not excuse his action (they were mostly those who had harboured reservations about his activities for some time before his arrest) kept silent. The word 'betrayal' was on everyone's lips, and even those who wrote in support of Dudko realised that the independent movement within the

Russian Orthodox Church had been dealt a probably irreparable blow, but they adopted the charitable attitude of hating the sin while loving the sinner. One Moscow believer said:

> We know all too well what measures can be employed in such cases. This could have happened to any one of us . . . we can never forget that Father Dimitri has brought the light of God to thousands of people. Now the authorities want to make him pay by discrediting him . . . by sowing the seeds of doubt among the faithful about his spiritual integrity. However, all that Father Dimitri has accomplished over the past twenty years cannot be wiped out.[120]

This thought was taken up by a believer named M. Probatov, who wrote: 'The truth preached by Father Dimitri remains. This truth of the Holy Bible he once gave me, and no one will ever be able to rob me of it.' Probatov also pointed out that 'Father Dimitri battled incessantly and alone. He was surrounded by people who needed his support, but who were unable to support him in his most difficult hour.' This sense of aloneness was, as we shall see, to be a continuing affliction for Father Dimitri. Probatov, however, restored some sense of perspective to the disaster which had occurred by recalling that 'we shall have all eternity before us': 'I believe that in eternity you will stand beside me again — strong, brave and radiating pure light, as I shall remember you to my dying day.'[121] More ominously, a lengthy, reflective statement by Irina Zalesskaya ended with a postscript which many others were to repeat in the months to come: 'If I should make a similar "confession" or renounce my views, I ask that this be considered the result of physical or psychological torture.'[122]

Immediately after his release, Father Dimitri was reported to be resting near Moscow,[123] and later he visited his brothers and sisters in his native region of Bryansk, during the Olympic Games period, when the authorities obviously wanted him well away from Moscow and possible contacts with foreigners.[124] Later he was said to be visiting Tula region.[125] He officiated at a liturgy for the first time since his release, according to Anatoli Levitin, on 21 September (1980), the feast of the Nativity of Our Lady, when he concelebrated with Metropolitan Yuvenali.[126] Shortly after this, he was appointed to a large, rich parish[127] in Vinogradovo, Moscow region, some 40 kilometres from Moscow.[128] However, the case against him had not been formally dropped. The fact that it was continuing was confirmed when one Igor Chapkovsky was told that a search of his Moscow home on 15 August was connected with 'the Dudko case'.[129]

Father Dimitri's friends and spiritual children were naturally concerned to discover his state of mind after his release and to establish exactly what had happened to him. However, it proved difficult to do so. After his release he was, not surprisingly, in a very confused state of mind, and this seems to have persisted for many months. Quite soon he began to express his thoughts and feelings on paper, and so it was eventually possible to form some idea of how his 'recantation' had come about. However, these writings reached the West in some cases after lengthy delays, and were not all published. Nevertheless, Dudko's statement entitled 'To all my Spiritual Children', dated 27 July, was published fairly quickly. In it he expressed the deep remorse and anguish which was to permeate all his written reflections. He wrote:

> I cannot forgive myself for my weakness, and my heart is torn asunder seeing your confusion and hearing garbled interpretations. I shudder at the thought of how I must appear to everyone, into what temptation I have led people, how I have disheartened those whom I had previously heartened. I prostrate myself before you and beg for your forgiveness.

He went on to ask his spiritual children to remain united, because it was not just he but the whole of the Russian Orthodox Church that was on trial. It was a time for mercy, not judgement. He concluded with a reminder that they were not fighting the Soviet authorities: 'It is godlessness we seek to combat, we are fighting for souls, striving to bring them to God, so that there might be one flock with one shepherd, the Lord our God.'[130] At about the same time, Dudko also wrote to Archbishop Vasili of Brussels, whom he had mentioned in his 'recantation', asking his forgiveness for tarnishing his name.[131] These partial retractions naturally drew a response from the KGB, and it was soon reported that two officials had visited Dudko at his home and asked him to sign a document entitled 'Gratitude to the Soviet Government'. Dudko refused to comply, and was then summoned to Moscow for further questioning.[132]

Dudko gave further details of his imprisonment and his interrogations, which continued after his release, in a series of his parish newsletter *In the Light of the Transfiguration* which reached the West much later.[133] The newsletters consisted solely of his reflections upon his experiences after his arrest. They were rambling and repetitious, bearing no evidence of editing or revision. Father Dimitri added to the newsletter the subtitle *Newspaper– Sermon* (*Gazeta–propoved*), and made it clear that his chief concern, for the future as in the past, was his work as a preacher and the overriding need to preach Christianity to the godless. However, this was not a confident, optimistic assertion, but a recognition that, crushed and abject as he felt himself to be, he had nothing left to hold on to but the fact that he was still a priest with a duty to preach. The other main theme running through the newsletters was Father Dimitri's overwhelming sense of loneliness and abandonment by his friends. He seems to have been genuinely surprised that some of his spiritual children had left him, that people did not gather round him as formerly, or telephone to ask how he was.

This sense of aloneness was expressed clearly in a document accompanying the newsletters, dated 31 July, which was a sentence-by-sentence analysis of his *Izvestiya* statement.[134] He seemed unable to understand how people could have taken it seriously, or believed that he had written it of his own free will: 'We have all learned now to read between the lines. For the time being my statement in the press is being read as though it were a piece of normal writing, and that is why many are reacting strongly against it. I wish to be the first to read my statement between the lines.' The analysis which follows certainly illuminated the real meaning and intentions behind the printed words. Some phrases were simply 'theirs' (the KGB's) which Dudko was obliged to include — for example, the 'sabre-rattling of the Carter administration'.[135] Others were written by Dudko, but carefully worded so that, he hoped, a discerning reader would not be deceived. For example, in his statement he renounced 'illegal contacts with abroad' — but what in fact constituted an illegal contact? There was after all no law against meeting foreigners. By renouncing specifically 'illegal' contacts, Dudko felt he was leaving the way open for those which could not be proved to be illegal. Dudko commented: 'Here I learned something from the Chekists [i.e. KGB officials; derived from the name of the first Soviet secret police body, the *Cheka*] — I didn't spend five months in prison for nothing.'[136] However, these and other subtleties were lost upon his readers. In his detailed commentary upon his statement, Dudko suffered a loss of perspective: he seems to have been quite unable to take a broader view, and to realise the sheer impact made by the fact of his statement, however worded, and particularly by his unexpected appearance upon television to read it.

In this analysis of his press statement, Dudko explained how it came to be written. He wrote several variants of what he wanted to say, and his KGB interrogators took them off for correction. Then they presented him with a typed final version and asked him to write it out himself. The KGB had reworked his versions and thrown in some phrases of their own. Dudko wrote: 'Of course, my words were there, and even my trend of thought (*napravleniye*), but as a whole it had been composed by them.'[137]

Dudko also gave an explanation, in the series of newsletters, of why he had consented to write any statement at all. It hinged upon his relationship with his KGB interrogator, Vladimir Sergeyevich Sorokin. Father Dimitri wrote several times that he wanted to find a way to reach the atheists, to speak to them in their language. He commented that it was a mistake to think that people who worked for the KGB were not human beings.[138] Once this step had been taken, he quickly came to view his interrogator as a fellow-human being, even a brother: he referred to Vladimir Sergeyevich at one point as 'my own (*rodnoi*) brother', and even 'my own interrogator'.[139] It seems that the interrogator was quick to take advantage of what he doubtless saw as a weakness, and to establish friendly and confidential relations with Father Dimitri. In a conversation with Vladimir Sergeyevich, Dudko told him that he did not hate him, because he made a distinction between him and the system which he served.[140] As a priest, he felt obliged to establish cordial relations, and attempt to preach the Gospel, to any individual he might meet, no matter if he were acting in a professional capacity and representing the interests of an opposing ideology. It seems that this was Father Dimitri's undoing. Many prisoners who have survived Soviet secret police interrogations, from Stalinist times to the present day, have testified that their only hope of maintaining their personal integrity was to remain obdurate to all suggestions, refusing to concede even the slightest degree to their interrogators. Once Dudko had made a small concession, the skilled KGB interrogator knew how to exploit it.

Perhaps the most dominant theme in the newsletters was the need for humility (*smireniye*). Father Dimitri believed that his humbling of himself, his willingness to admit he could have been wrong, was a more truly Christian way, and one which made it easier for him to talk openly to his interrogators. Vladimir Sergeyevich reproached him: 'You should have been strong! A priest must be strong!' but Father Dimitri responded: 'you forget that we have other ways: humility and repentance'.[141] Father Dimitri wondered why even believers did not understand this simple fact: 'we understand a heroic feat (*podvig*) . . . but we don't understand humility and love to our enemies'.[142] It appeared from the newsletters that Dudko deliberately chose to embrace shame and humiliation, with a purpose: 'I voluntarily took the path of shame, in order to do something further.'[143] And elsewhere:

Heroism for the sake of one's own good name can become a grief for others.

Should one renounce heroism for the sake of others? [Should one] humble oneself, single oneself out, even soil oneself a little? But we must act, for everything is perishing. It is not fame which acts, but shame. So one chooses shame.

I chose shame.[144]

This suggested that it was not weakness or fear which caused Dudko's repentance, but a decision to regain his freedom, even at the cost of his own personal reputation, in order to act as a priest and to preach to those 'perishing' around him.

Dudko's misfortune was that he reached this decision after weeks of feverish, introspective thought, under great pressure, and in isolation. When he emerged, there were few, if any, of his friends who thought that he had made the right decision. His explanations and reflections after his release do not appear to have made any difference to this general view. There were those who thought it unwise for him to analyse his action in a way which at times amounted almost to self-justification. In the news-letters, Dudko said at one point that in prison he undertook no action without praying, so that God must for some reason have allowed his confession to come about.[145] Later he wrote categorically: 'This would not have happened if God had not tolerated it', and concluded that the purpose was to humble him.[146] No one appeared to support this view. Indeed, Nikita Struve was moved to write a strong criticism of Dudko's apparent attempts at self-justification in the Paris journal *Vestnik RKhD*.[147] This reportedly upset Father Dimitri considerably, and he wrote a reply in which he asked for prayer. The reply also said: 'I have tried to find a common language with those who have left me in my grief, and unfortunately I have not achieved this goal.'[148] This was a succinct statement by Dudko of what he had tried to do, and his own admission, at length, that it had failed.

Dudko's account of his experiences in the newsletters, longwinded and disordered though it was, made it possible to put into perspective some of the suppositions which had been made regarding his televised statement. Some of those who saw his television broadcast thought that he might have been under the influence of drugs, because of his cheerful, even euphoric, air and the fact that he appeared to have put on weight.[149] However, Dudko's own account suggested that drugs would have been superfluous. Some Western commentators picked up from sources in Moscow the story that Dudko had been threatened with homosexual assault while in prison[150] and there was some support for this in Dudko's comment that his voluntary confession might have thrown the KGB off course: 'They could have pre-sented me in a different light. After all, there had already been talk of sodomy and drunken orgies.'[151] Another question was whether representa-tives of the Moscow Patriarchate were involved in Father Dimitri's change of heart during his five months in Lefortovo prison. There were some grounds for believing that Dudko was visited by Metropolitan Yuvenali, possibly more than once, and that he was even taken for a meeting with Patriarch Pimen.[152] This cannot be verified, but it was not implausible. Knowing Dudko's willingness to humble himself before his hierarchical superior during critical confrontations, as evidenced by his submission to Metropolitan Serafim in 1974 (see p. 314), it was more than likely that the KGB would have enlisted the help of the church, and there was no reason to suppose that either Metropolitan Yuvenali or the Patriarch would have been unwilling to persuade him to conform to the status quo of church–state relations.[153] There was, however, no direct mention of episcopal intervention in Father Dimitri's reflections in the newsletters, apart from a brief state-ment that in future issues of his newsletter he might speak of his 'conversa-tions with the ruling bishop',[154] but this was not followed up. There was also an unexplained reference to a conversation with 'a highly placed person', which could have meant either Metropolitan Yuvenali or the Patriarch.[155] However, Father Dimitri's loyalty to his hierarchy was as explicit in the newsletters as it had previously been elsewhere, and the absence of any clear mention of intervention by the Moscow Patriarchate cannot therefore be taken to mean that such did not take place.

The investigation of Dudko's case continued for some time after his release. Within three days he was summoned to the Lubyanka, where a senior KGB official made it clear that he could be rearrested. Investigator Sorokin continued to visit him, and after Dudko had written some of the above-mentioned statements partially retracting his confession, began to demand that he should make a new statement, and even hold a press conference for foreign correspondents. Father Dimitri categorically refused.[156] At length, on 18 November, Sorokin told him that he need not sign any further statement, and that the KGB hoped to avoid a trial.[157] However, they continued to summon people as witnesses in his case, which they had not done when he was in prison.[158]

A foreigner who visited Dudko about a month after the end of the series of *In the Light of the Transfiguration* quoted above — that is, in March 1981 — in the company of one of his spiritual children, found that he was still somewhat confused and uncertain as to what had actually happened to him, although he continued to dwell on the main themes of the newsletter as outlined above. He repeatedly asked for prayer, and he maintained that his proper activity was that of an Orthodox priest, to preach and teach, and that he was continuing to do this. As regards other occurrences, he and the spiritual daughter present did not entirely agree. Dudko said that he had been offered the choice of death, possibly by firing squad on a charge of treason (Article 64 of the Criminal Code), or continuing his work: he chose the latter because he was anxious about his family and spiritual children; the choice of death would have been 'for himself'. However, he firmly denied that he had felt a 'fear unto death' while in prison, an explanation of his behaviour apparently current among his spiritual children. He denied that he had been administered any drugs, while admitting that they could have been put into his food without his knowledge; and he denied that any hierarch from the Patriarchate had been to visit him in prison, while admitting that someone from the Patriarchate had arranged to have the eucharist brought to him so that he could take communion at Easter. He denied that he had been taken out of Lefortovo during his imprisonment, but yielded to the spiritual daughter's firm assurance that some of his flock knew for a fact that he had been in a psychiatric hospital for a time. (It is fairly common for religious and political prisoners in the Soviet Union to be taken to psychiatric hospitals for examination during pre-trial detention.) Clearly, then, he was still in a state of confusion and uncertainty even nine months after his release, and this suggests that the full story of his five months in Lefortovo may never be known for certain.[159]

Shortly afterwards, on 7 March 1981, nine months after his release, the case against Dudko was finally dropped. According to TASS, the decision was taken on the grounds of his age (59) and his 'repentance'.[160]

The Trial of Father Gleb Yakunin

The trial of Father Gleb Yakunin took place in Moscow from 25 to 28 August 1980. About a week before this, his wife Iraida had been officially informed that the trial would 'definitely' not take place in August and 'maybe not even in September', evidently a move by the Soviet authorities to minimise advance publicity and prevent protests in the Soviet Union and abroad.[161] As usual, Yakunin's family and friends and Western correspondents were unable to enter the courtroom, which had been packed out in advance by 'burly young men in ill-fitting suits' in the words of one correspondent.[162] Yakunin's wife was the only person admitted to the trial. Evidently she must have been the source for a partial description of the proceedings which later reached the West by different channels.[163]

The basis of the charge of 'anti-Soviet agitation and propaganda' (Article 70 of the Criminal Code) against Yakunin was the extensive documentation issued by the Christian Committee, but the judge, Lubentsova, dismissed as 'irrelevant' Yakunin's attempt to explain the activities of the Committee. Although many church members testified at the trial, those favourable to Yakunin were excluded. The judge remarked that some witnesses 'had not bothered to turn up, for example the Poluektovs and Fonchenkov'. In fact, Father Vasili Fonchenkov, Larisa Poluektova, an Orthodox laywoman, and her daughter Valera had waited outside the court every day, but had been refused admittance, even when Father Vasili produced his summons.[164]

Unusually for the trial of a church dissenter, two people with official posts in the church testified against Yakunin. They were A. I. Osipov, Professor of Theology at the Moscow Theological Academy, and the monk Iosif Pustoutov, who is attached to the Department of External Church Relations. They frequently represent the church abroad, and they both testified that the work of the Christian Committee had had a harmful effect on the church's international contacts. Other church witnesses included a Moscow priest named Anatoli Kuznetsov; Alexander Shushpanov, a churchwarden earlier exposed by Yakunin as a KGB collaborator (see Chapter 9, p. 268); and the *samizdat* author Felix Karelin.[165] They all spoke of their differences of opinion with Yakunin and stated that the work of the Christian Committee was harmful to the Russian Orthodox Church. Evidence of a less substantial nature was given by a priest from Lvov, Krivoi, who had served a sentence for trafficking in icons on the black market, and who reportedly descended to personal abuse of Yakunin, concluding with the assertion: 'I once saw him drink two bottles of vodka.'[166] In contrast to these witnesses, surprising evidence was given by A. Zagryazkina, whom Yakunin had described in Christian Committee documents as a disruptive influence and an instrument of the KGB in Moscow parishes where she had been employed (see Chapter 2, p. 72). Although she had spoken negatively about Father Gleb during the pre-trial investigation, Zagryazkina changed her mind, for unknown reasons, in court, and stated that, although she had had personal differences with Father Gleb, she considered him to be a man who lived a truly Christian life, had pure principles, and was an example to everyone.[167]

Two further witnesses were Lev Regelson and Viktor Kapitanchuk, who were brought from Lefortovo prison to the court. Conflicting statements were issued regarding their evidence. A TASS report stated that they had both regretted their participation in the sending of documents abroad, and blamed Yakunin as bearing the greatest responsibility for the transmission of such information. Sources in Moscow initially dismissed this as a false statement, designed to undermine sympathy for Regelson and Kapitanchuk at their own forthcoming trials. However, both men later recanted from their former activities at their trials, and it has since become known that they gave extensive evidence against Yakunin at the pre-trial investigation. It had been thought that Dudko might be summoned as a witness, but he was not. He subsequently disclosed that he had been questioned and had hoped to be called as a witness, but the KGB had clearly been afraid that he might use the occasion as an opportunity to retract his own earlier 'confession'.[168]

Yakunin was sentenced to five years' imprisonment followed by five years' internal exile, the sentence called for by the prosecution. (It is unclear why the court refrained from imposing the maximum sentence under Article 70 — seven years' imprisonment followed by five years' exile. It is possible that Western protests before and during* the trial helped to reduce the sentence.) Father Gleb's final word was brief: 'I thank God for this test that He has sent me. I consider it a great honour, and, as a Christian, accept it gladly.'[169]

The fear that Yakunin might be charged with speculation or currency offences, arising from the confiscation of valuables from his home and the evidence given at his trial by Krivoi, was borne out by the court's recommendation after his sentence had been read out that he should be remanded for further trial on these charges, under Articles 154 and 88 of the Criminal Code. The latter charge carried a possible death penalty.[170] However, a few weeks later it was reported that the charges had been dropped, and the icons and other valuable objects had been returned to Mrs Yakunin.[171] It was not clear why the KGB should have abandoned this case after taking pains to set it up over a period of many months. Perhaps it was impossible to find enough witnesses to testify convincingly against Yakunin on such a serious

---

*For example, during the course of the trial, three telegrams from Britain, signed by 23 churchmen, including 17 bishops, a cardinal and a former Archbishop of Canterbury, were sent to the judge, Lubentsova, to the Procurator-General of the USSR, and to Mrs Yakunin.

charge, or possibly Western protests against his first sentence were sufficiently great to discourage a second trial and sentence. Another puzzle was
the delay of over six months before Yakunin's appeal against his sentence
was heard, and rejected, on 12 March 1981.[172] Normally appeals in political
cases are heard, and invariably turned down, within a week or two of the
trial.

A report of Father Gleb's trial in the trade union newspaper *Trud*
(*Labour*), a report of which was broadcast by TASS, gave prominence to
the evidence of Shushpanov, Regelson and Kapitanchuk, and also to the
statements made by Zagryazkina at the pre-trial investigation rather than at
the trial itself. Once more, there was an evident attempt to blame Western
agencies for Yakunin's behaviour, and much was made of his contacts with
'anti-Soviet organisations' in the West and his meetings with their 'emissaries'. As with Dudko, the blame was shifted to external forces; as it was
ideologically impossible to admit that discontent with the existing situation
could have arisen spontaneously within Soviet society, it could only have
been inspired from elsewhere. The article concluded with the assertion that
Yakunin would not have been worth anyone's attention were it not that he
was part of a 'shrill campaign, which in the West has been given the name of
"the defence of human rights in the Soviet Union" '.[173]

A protest against the sentencing of Yakunin and of Tatyana Velikanova,
who had been sentenced on 29 August to four years' imprisonment plus five
years' internal exile,[174] was quickly issued with 57 signatures, headed by that
of Andrei Sakharov.[175] In the West, a telegram was sent by the British
Council of Churches to President Brezhnev, with a copy to Patriarch
Pimen, urging the court to reconsider its decision.[176] However, a request to
the World Council of Churches to support Yakunin met with no response at
this time.[177]

Further Trials

The trial of Alexander Ogorodnikov, which lasted from 3 to 7 September,
was held in the provincial town of Kalinin, and thus attracted far less
publicity than previous trials. His mother was admitted briefly to the courtroom, but his father and wife were excluded on the pretext that they would
be called as witnesses, which they were not. Other Christian Seminar
members were brought from their places of imprisonment to testify,
including Vladimir Poresh, who reportedly tried to take all the 'blame'
upon himself. Ogorodnikov was sentenced to six years' strict regime labour
camp followed by five years' internal exile.[178]

The Moscow Helsinki Monitoring Group issued a statement which drew
attention to the severity of the sentence, and noted that it was 'a clear
indication of the intention of the authorities to stamp out the movement

for freedom of conscience'. The statement also pointed out that, though the charges against Ogorodnikov were not clear, it was known that they included publication of *Obshchina*: however, since the journal had been published before his arrest for 'parasitism' in 1979, and he had not been charged with involvement in it at that time, the bringing of charges in 1980 constituted 'an illegal method of extending his period of punishment'.[179]

After the trial, Ogorodnikov's brother, Rafail, a monk in the Pskov monastery, asked permission to visit him in gaol to give him Holy Communion, but met with a refusal. Shortly afterwards, he was ordered out of Pskov diocese by the bishop, Metropolitan Ioann.[180] In Ogorodnikov's case, as in Yakunin's, the trial in court was followed by a trial in the press. The popular weekly *Ogonyok* carried two articles denouncing the Christian Seminar and its leader in what amounted to a vicious personal attack upon his character and morals. It is of interest that, among several inconsistencies and unsubstantiated assertions in the article, there were statements which are at variance with those made in the 1976 press attack on Ogorodnikov in *Literaturnaya gazeta*.[181] The article included the by now familiar attempt to shift responsibility for dissident behaviour on to Western 'subversion', in the form of a vague allegation that Ogorodnikov and Poresh were acting as the paid agents of some person or organisation abroad.[182]

Lev Regelson's trial took place in Moscow from 22 to 24 September. He too was charged with 'anti-Soviet agitation and propaganda' and witnesses testified that he had 'prepared, duplicated and sent abroad a number of slanderous materials jointly with Gleb Yakunin' — that is, the documents discussed in Chapter 11 of this book (pp. 352–7). According to a TASS report on the trial, Regelson was also accused of 'maintaining criminal ties' with named foreign correspondents of the Western media and with 'representatives of foreign organisations'.[183] Regelson pleaded guilty. He said that he regretted the harm he had brought to his country, and that in future he would not mix his religious activity with politics. Viktor Kapitanchuk, giving testimony as a witness, gave detailed information about his own work for the Christian Committee. Yakunin was not called as a witness, but the judge read out a statement by him taking full responsibility for the documents written by him and Regelson. In view of his 'sincere repentance', Regelson was given a five-year suspended sentence, and was released at once at the end of his trial. He spoke to Western journalists immediately after his release and confirmed his statements at the trial. He said he was 'prepared to go to prison for the faith, but not for human rights'.[184]

Viktor Kapitanchuk also pleaded guilty to a charge under Article 70 at his trial on 8–9 October, and was also released with a suspended five-year sentence. TASS took the opportunity to defend Soviet policy towards dissenters by issuing a commentary on the trial. This asserted that documents Kapitanchuk had issued through the Christian Committee alleging that people had been persecuted for their religious beliefs were slanderous because the people in question had been imprisoned for criminal offences or hospitalised because they were genuinely insane.[185] According to TASS, Kapitanchuk said that he had 'inflicted damage on the Soviet State for which I am very sorry'.[186] Kapitanchuk also gave the names of a number of Western correspondents to whom he had given information, some of whom were still working in Moscow and therefore subject to reprisals.[187] This suggested that he had decided to go beyond merely 'repenting' to avoid a term in labour camp and was willing to give further information useful to the Soviet authorities.

Although it is still not clear precisely what induced Regelson and Kapitanchuk publicly to recant, it is known that they were treated quite differently from Father Dimitri. Whereas he had suffered physically and mentally in Lefortovo prison, they were apparently put in comfortable cells, with access to radio, television and foreign religious literature to help them to 'think through' their positions. It is not known why the KGB decided to give them this most unusual treatment, but the success of their policy suggests that they have considerable psychological insight and manipulative skill. One report suggested that Regelson and his investigator had attempted to deceive one another; the investigator had pretended to be a secret believer within the KGB who wanted to help Regelson, and Regelson had pretended to believe him, but he had become too deeply implicated and could not extricate himself.[188]

After Regelson's release, it was reported that he intended to reassume leadership of a group to be called the Christian Seminar, but that it would now be run on a semi-official basis. Regelson had to inform the authorities in advance of the time and place of each meeting.[189] However, little further was heard of these meetings, and it appears that they had little or no support from other Seminar members, and may not have continued for any length of time. Members of the original Seminar continued to meet separately on an informal basis. Moreover, Regelson visited other Christian activists in an attempt to persuade them to change their point of view and renounce their former activities as he had done. He is known to have visited Tatyana Poresh in Leningrad and Viktor Popkov, though reports that he was to be taken to visit Vladimir Poresh and Alexander Ogorodnikov in labour camp have not been substantiated.

The reactions of Moscow believers to the two recantations are perhaps best summed up by a brief statement issued by Vadim Shcheglov, the secretary of the Christian Committee:

I, Vadim Ivanovich Shcheglov, member of the Christian Committee for the Defence of Believers' Rights in the USSR, do hereby declare that all my activities within the Committee were conducted in strict accordance with the aims set out in the Committee's founding statement and with full observance of the laws of our country. Recently I have become a target for illegal persecution by the authorities — my telephone has been arbitrarily disconnected and I am to be demoted at work. In the expectation of being arrested I declare that I do not reject my views, nor any of my activities, as they were consonant with the aims of the Committee and Soviet law. Should I be arrested and give testimony which contradicts the above statement, such testimony would have been extracted from me against my will and conscience by the application of illegal methods.[190]

The Response of the World Council of Churches

The World Council of Churches responded to the trials in October (despite its earlier refusal to take action — see p. 441) in the form of a letter to Metropolitan Yuvenali, which expressed concern over 'a number of serious problems' in connection with the trials which were troubling the WCC. The Council was concerned that the allegedly 'non-religious' basis on which the trials were said to be conducted might not be understood by the Soviet population, and that this might 'influence Soviet public opinion against the life of the churches'; it believed that the sentences passed were 'disproportionate with the seriousness of the crimes which have allegedly been committed'; and it feared that the timing of the trials, a few weeks before the opening of the Madrid Conference to review implementation of the Helsinki Agreements signed in 1975, would do nothing to establish 'an atmosphere conducive to *détente*'.[191] Metropolitan Yuvenali's reply, written after consultation with the Council for Religious Affairs, as the letter makes clear, was courteous but yielded nothing to the point of view expressed by the WCC. The Metropolitan assured the WCC that the Soviet media had informed the population adequately about the trials; that severe verdicts had been incurred only by defendants who had refused to admit their guilt; and that an 'objective approach to this question' would 'not create any difficulties' regarding implementation of the Helsinki Agreement. This was a bland reiteration of the existing Soviet viewpoint, and in no sense an attempt to give a meaningful response to the points raised in the letter.[192] The WCC's intervention may have marked a shift in relations with the Russian Orthodox Church, but it was too late to have any effect on the situation.

Repression Continues After 1980

The campaign against Orthodox (and other) dissenters continued throughout 1980 into 1981 and afterwards, though on a reduced scale now that fewer of them remained at liberty. Orthodox who belonged to the women's movement were an especial target for the KGB. The homes of Galina

Grigoreva and Natalya Lazareva were searched on 11 September 1980 and copies of their articles on the condition of Soviet women and children were confiscated. Lazareva was arrested on 24 or 25 September, and at her trial on 11 January 1981 she was charged on the basis of these materials with 'anti-Soviet slander' under Article 190/1 of the Criminal Code and sentenced to ten months' imprisonment. This relatively short sentence was probably due to her admission that the views expressed in her articles were one-sided although the facts she had cited were correct.[193] House-searches took place on 24 September in the homes of the Dmitrievs, Natalya Volokhonskaya and Sofiya Sokolova, who was later forced to emigrate. On 14 December Natalya Maltseva was arrested after a house-search, and the homes of Tatyana Belyayeva (who later emigrated) and Galina Zlatkina were also searched. Further searches followed on 29 December in the homes of Galina Grigoreva once more, Yelena Borisova (from whom part of the archive of the journal *Mariya* was confiscated) and the poetess Kari.[194] Natalya Savelyeva, aged 23, was interned in a psychiatric hospital near Leningrad,[195] but was released after a short time because the medical commission could find no grounds for detaining her.[196] In summer 1981 the KGB complained to the West German consulate about a German woman language student who had formed an 'undesirable friendship' with some of the feminists. Four 'Mariya' Club members — Yelena Shanygina, Irina Zhosan, Natalya Savelyeva and Klavdiya Rotmanova — protested without success on her behalf. Shanygina came under pressure from the KGB, who hinted that her two children, aged 2 and 4, could easily be run over in the street; she applied to emigrate but was prevented from doing so.[197] Lazareva, having completed her ten-month sentence, was arrested again on 13 March 1982 and on 1 July 1982 she was sentenced to four years' strict regime labour camp plus two years' internal exile.[198]

In March 1981 the *samizdat* journal *37* ceased publication after 20 issues. Its editor, Viktor Krivulin, a paraplegic with a wife and child, was warned by the KGB that he would be arrested and sent to labour camp or expelled from the USSR if he continued publication, and he reluctantly signed an undertaking to cease publishing the journal. He did, however, continue to edit another *samizdat* journal, *Severnaya pochta* (*Northern Post*), which was devoted to poetry, the ninth issue of which appeared early in 1981.[199]

During spring 1981 it became clear that repression had not ceased as the number of arrests and trials subsided. A foreign visitor reported that the authorities were attempting to tighten the reins on unofficial or semi-official culture, especially if a religious element was involved. There were attempts to stop meetings in private flats and to reduce the number of *samizdat* journals with a philosophical, religious or political content. One consequence was a growing dearth of religious literature due to confiscations during house-searches. In Leningrad alone some 20 flats had been searched shortly before the Twenty-sixth Congress of the CPSU which

began on 23 February and religious and other literature had been confiscated.[200] Further arrests continued sporadically in 1982.

The Effect of KGB Repression

The KGB's campaign against public dissent within the Russian Orthodox
Church, which began in 1976, reached its zenith in 1979 and 1980, and continued relentlessly through 1981 and 1982, was successful. The series of
trials of Orthodox believers during 1980 removed the best-known and most
active leaders from the scene. With Father Gleb Yakunin, Alexander
Ogorodnikov, Vladimir Poresh and others despatched to labour camps and
exile for ten years or more, and Father Dimitri Dudko, Lev Regelson and
Viktor Kapitanchuk discredited, the KGB had effectively crushed open
protest and dissent within the Orthodox Church. After this, Orthodox
believers were far less willing to protest openly about the injustices they
perceived. No doubt the prospect of a term in labour camp was a deterrent
to even the most courageous, but an even more powerful disincentive to
open protest must have been the consideration that more than a decade of
public dissent had resulted in no change whatever in the situation of the
church. Appeals to Soviet legality had not improved the lives of believers;
reasoned arguments addressed to the Soviet government had brought about
no change in policy; and support and publicity in the West, though it had
increased markedly by 1980, had still not reached a sufficient level to
convince the Soviet government that it would lose anything by continuing to
repress dissent of all kinds. Not only was there no change in the church's
situation, there was no indication that either the Soviet state or the church
hierarchy had shifted their position in the slightest, or even given serious
consideration to any of the proposals put forward by the would-be
reformers. If anything, attitudes hardened. Improvements in official church
life at the beginning of the 1980s, such as the reduction in the taxation of
clergy (see Chapter 3, p. 87) and the opening of extensive new offices for
the Publishing Department of the Moscow Patriarchate (see Chapter 6,
p. 167) were an indication that the state was ready to make concessions in
return for obedient compliance with its policies; the contrast between this
and the harsh treatment meted out to dissenters served only to increase the
gulf which separated them from the silent majority within the church. A
'divide and rule' policy was clearly in operation.

However, what the KGB's campaign failed to do was to remove the
misgivings and dissatisfaction believers felt concerning the position of their
church. They had been intimidated, not reassured. None the less, any
Orthodox Christian wishing to change the church's situation could hardly
fail to conclude at this time that public protests were unlikely to be effective
and more than likely to result in his being imprisoned and unable to do

anything further in the service of the church for many years to come. The problems of the church were no less grave than they had ever been, but the concerned believer must clearly find new ways of attempting to solve them.

Though open protests dwindled almost to nothing, the Orthodox renaissance was by no means a thing of the past. Faith was strong, Christians' vitality was undiminished though its expression was subdued, and the church continued to attract converts. Despite the hardships, Christians continued to derive joy and comfort from the practice of their faith, as one believer wrote:

> What a joy it is that we have a Saviour and such good friends who, with their prayers, warm words of encouragement and occasional postcards, help us to live through these difficult times . . . Today I went to confession and Holy Communion, and came away in joy and peace. All that had been unclean, frightening and sad in my heart was washed away; life no longer seems unbearable.[201]

With the traumatic events of 1980 behind them, Orthodox Christians remained true to their beliefs and continued to find comfort in their faith as they considered the problems their church still faced and attempted to devise a path forward for the future.

CONCLUDING SUMMARY: UP TO 1985

Active dissent may have declined in the Russian Orthodox Church since 1979, but faith has not. Believers may have become more wary about the way in which, and the extent to which, they express their views as to their legal rights. But they do not believe any less strongly than formerly, they have not ceased to meet informally to discuss their beliefs, and they have not ceased to regard Orthodox Christianity as having an important, even crucial, role to play in the future of their country. Nor have their disagreements on the latter point abated.

Spiritual life has if anything deepened following the traumatic events which we narrated in the last chapter. Believers are even more aware than formerly of the suffering and humiliation which open spokesmen may incur, and have taken counsel accordingly. Anyone today concerned to act as best he or she may for the future of their church may well conclude that, for the present at any rate, informal and unpublicised attempts to strengthen spiritual life are preferable to public action. Accordingly, prayer groups, discussion groups and seminars have increased considerably in numbers. No precise information is available, which is not surprising, given the fate of well-known seminars which we discussed in Chapter 13. The groups appear to be informal in their structure, to have loose but unsystematic contacts with one another, and not to be centrally organised. The KGB, however, incorrectly believes them to be part of a centralised conspiracy, and is determined to discover and liquidate them all.

The repression against active members of the Russian Orthodox Church, which began to intensify in 1979, has continued. People who can by no means be called dissenters, who have not offered public opposition to the Communist Party's policy on religion, but have attempted to express their beliefs, and help others to do so, in private ways, have been arrested and sentenced. We have already mentioned, in Chapter 6, the arrest of Zoya Krakhmalnikova, who was the editor of the purely religious *samizdat* journal *Nadezhda*. She was sentenced to one year in labour camp plus five years' internal exile, which she is serving in Krasnoyarsk. On 23 January 1985, her 57-year-old husband, Felix Svetov, was arrested after a search of his home during which religious literature was discovered, and is awaiting trial. Both of them might possibly have escaped arrest during the 1970s (though they might well have been subjected to forms of intimidation), and this is an indication that the attitude of the authorities towards independently minded religious believers has hardened.

Another case which reinforces this point is that of Sergei Markus. He was arrested in January 1984 and sentenced in July to three years in labour camp. Before that, he had been a leading member of a group known as the Ecumenists, an ecumenical discussion group which had sought both to advance understanding between Christians of different denominations, and to reach out to non-Christians. Markus did not write about or publicise his views, and the only threat which he and his colleagues represented to Soviet authority was that they would talk to acquaintances about their Christian view of life. His case demonstrates the likelihood that there are many such groups of whom nothing can be known until one of their number comes to attention by some form of official reprisal.

Father Alexander Men, a widely respected priest with a parish at Pushkino, near Moscow, an energetic and scholarly man who has for many years had a flourishing pastoral ministry, was detained on 26 January 1984 and his home searched. Subsequently there were rumours that he might be moved further from Moscow.

During the 1980s, the scope of the subject-matter of Orthodox *samizdat* reaching the West has diminished. Protests, appeals and complaints on behalf of particular individuals and communities continue to reach the West, as does a certain amount of information about trials and about the situation of prisoners. But there has been very little *samizdat* of ideas. The works of spirituality, theology, philosophy, literature, etc., are now sparse (though it is true that *Nadezhda* continues to appear). *Samizdat* journals have ceased publication. This is due to the fact that many of the leading *samizdat* authors have either been imprisoned or have emigrated. Those who remain at 'liberty', which involves continued discrimination, repeated interrogations and sometimes surveillance, have been pressurised by the KGB into refraining from publishing further *samizdat* works under threat of arrest. No doubt unknown *samizdat* authors are still writing 'for the drawer', as the phrase goes, or perhaps for a very limited circle of acquaintances, but they probably feel that it is not worth the risk of trying to send their works abroad. It is also some time since there has been any kind of collective appeal discussing the larger issues — legal, ideological, etc. — underlying the continuing violations of believers' rights. In this case, however, Soviet believers may well consider that enough of this kind of documentation has already been sent to the West; quite sufficient to enable Western Churches to take action on their behalf should they choose to do so. If the response from Western churches and other bodies has not been all that the dissenters hoped for, all the more reason not to court repression by sending further futile appeals.

One exception to this general picture was the appearance of two issues of a new journal entitled *Mnogaya leta* (*Many Years*) in 1980 and 1981. Its editor was Gennadi Shimanov, and its chief contributors were Shimanov himself, Felix Karelin and L. Ibragimov (the pen-name of Vladimir Prilutsky). These three were the best known of the right-wing Russian nationalists within the church, and the tone of the journal was therefore

predictable. Other Orthodox criticised it in very strong terms. One anonymous *samizdat* reviewer dubbed it 'a coagulation of hatred', and said that
several articles were virulently anti-semitic. The *Mnogaya leta* authors
strongly criticised the West, especially America, which they regarded as
being in the thrall of a Jewish—Masonic—plutocratic conspiracy, and they
also strongly criticised Jews, including those within the Russian Orthodox
Church. They regarded these various groups and forces as threatening to
the Russian nation and its church. Their solution was that there should be a
concordat between the Orthodox Church and the Soviet state (as we have
seen, Shimanov had advanced this argument in earlier writings). Perhaps
this was why the KGB allowed the journal to appear at a time when it was
suppressing other journals. The appearance of *Mnogaya leta* at first led
commentators to believe that the Soviet authorities were favouring the more
extreme nationalists in the church over against other dissenters (who, as we
saw in the previous chapter, were experiencing severe repression at that
time). It seemed that this strengthened the argument for the existence of
supporters of Russian nationalism in very senior positions which we discussed earlier. There is probably more than a grain of truth in this.
Certainly leading nationalist figures were not arrested at a time when other
leading dissenters were. However, there have in fact been no further issues
of *Mnogaya leta* since 1981. Whether this is due to KGB suppression or to
other reasons is not known. Moreover, the arrests of Leonid Borodin (a
former VSKhSON member and contributor to *Moskovsky sbornik*) on 12
May 1982 and of another nationalist writer, Anatoli Senin, on 15 February
1983 suggest that nationalists can no longer expect immunity. As far as is
known, no measures have been taken against Shimanov and Karelin (the
letter had no doubt earned official favour by testifying against Father Gleb
Yakunin at his trial).

Three important documents concerning increasing repression of believers
did, however, reach the West in the summer of 1983. The first, written in
June, was stated to be by authors from several different denominations.
However, unlike previous such collective appeals, they remained anonymous, which in itself was an indication of worsening conditions. They
stated unequivocally: 'there has been a hardening of government policy
towards religion following the changes which have taken place in the Soviet
leadership'. (This was during Yuri Andropov's brief tenure of power.) The
appeal continued by chronicling various acts of repression which had taken
place recently against believers of different denominations: they included
house-searches, confiscations of religious literature, breaking up of prayer
meetings, and arrests. It concluded with an appeal to Christians in the West
to pray for Soviet believers, 'whose situation could, in the near future,
become much worse'.

The second document came from Deacon Vladimir Rusak, whose lengthy
history of the Russian Church we quoted from in Chapter 6 and referred to

in Chapter 12. It was addressed to the World Council of Churches Assembly in Vancouver, and reached the West just after the Assembly had commenced. The matter was not included in the official proceedings, but was raised by the Archbishop of Canterbury (to whom a copy of the appeal was addressed), both directly with the Russian Orthodox delegation and in a radio interview with the BBC. The Archbishop also raised the case of Father Gleb Yakunin publicly. Other British delegates supported this stance in plenary sessions. Rusak raised both his own case — he had been dismissed from his Moscow parish and from his job in the Publishing Department of the Moscow Patriarchate after it became known that he had written a history of the church — and also the situation of his church generally. It was felt to be difficult for the World Council of Churches to intervene in a case involving an individual's relationship with his own church hierarchy; and the more general issues he raised were to be dealt with as appropriate through the WCC's normal procedures.

A third document, also addressed to the Vancouver Assembly, came from the Christian Committee for the Defence of Believers' Rights in the USSR. They referred to the appeal addressed to the previous WCC Assembly in Nairobi by Yakunin and Regelson, and said that the situation of believers had deteriorated even further since then. They singled out five examples of ways in which this deterioration had occurred: (1) increased numbers of Christian prisoners (currently 300); (2) 20,000 Pentecostals wished to emigrate because of religious persecution but were not allowed to do so; (3) compulsory anti-religious indoctrination in schools and elsewhere; (4) attacks on believers in the media; (5) discrimination against believers in the areas of equal pay, education, medical assistance, recreation and housing — a 'policy of genocide'. The appeal also referred to the fate of Christian Committee members: Father Gleb Yakunin imprisoned, Vadim Shcheglov pressurised into emigrating (he had arrived in the West earlier in 1983, and later went to live in the USA), and Fathers Nikolai Gainov and Vasili Fonchenkov under pressure from the church authorities. This appeal, however, was not publicly referred to during the Assembly.

Orthodox Christians continued to be involved in the support of those, believers and non-believers, whose civil rights were violated, and to accept the consequences. A succession of Orthodox Christians were administrators of the Russian Social Fund, established after his deportation by Alexander Solzhenitsyn and using his royalties from *The Gulag Archipelago*. The administrator was responsible for ensuring that funds were disbursed to the families of political and religious prisoners. The first administrator was Alexander Ginzburg, who, as we have noted, was deported to the USA in May 1979. Subsequent administrators were Valeri Repin, Sergei Khodorovich, Andrei Kistyakovsky and Boris Mikhailov. Repin was arrested, but after 15 months' imprisonment recanted his activities publicly on television in March 1983. Khodorovich was arrested and sentenced in

January 1984 to three years' strict regime camp. He was brutally beaten up during his pre-trial detention. Andrei Kistyakovsky was the Russian Social Fund's administrator for a short time during 1983, but resigned in October due to ill-health. Boris Mikhailov subsequently announced that he had assumed the administrator's responsibilities, but shortly afterwards retracted this due to the pressure he was under, and by February 1984 the fund had no publicly declared administrator.

Valeri Fefelov, himself disabled, was one of the founders of an unofficial Group for the Defence of the Rights of the Disabled. He was forced to emigrate in 1982.

Yelena Sannikova was involved in helping the oppressed in a number of ways, including through the Russian Social Fund. She was arrested in January 1984 at the age of 24. After her arrest, Fefelov wrote of her: 'In a word, her life means "service", given with the love of a deeply believing Christian, who has been led by her beliefs never to align herself with Soviet tyranny but rather to seek to preserve the dignity of man.' She was sentenced the following October to one year of strict regime camp followed by five years of internal exile.

Valeri Senderov, a talented mathematician, was co-author (with Boris Kanevsky) in 1980 of a *samizdat* work entitled 'Intellectual Genocide' which documented discrimination against Jews in university entrance examinations. Senderov was one of several people whose flats were searched on 6 April 1982 in connection with the unofficial production of large quantities of Orthodox literature (see Chapter 6, p. 166). Senderov was arrested the following June (so was Kanevsky). He was charged with publishing and sending abroad the information bulletin of the unofficial trade union group, SMOT. He was tried in February 1983 and sentenced to seven years' strict regime camp plus five years' internal exile.

Another Orthodox Christian who spoke out in defence of Jews was Dr Ivan Martynov, a historian from Leningrad. In December 1983 he wrote an open letter to the Academy of Sciences of the USSR protesting against growing anti-semitism in the Soviet Union. He spoke with admiration of a number of his Jewish colleagues. To add force to his letter, he resigned his Doctorate of Pedagogical Sciences, conferred on him by the Academy in 1970. In January 1985 Martynov was sentenced to 18 months' forced labour with compulsory 20 per cent deduction of pay. On 10 April 1985 he wrote a letter to Western Christians appealing for support, since he and his wife were expected to exist on only 20 roubles a month (the average monthly wage at that time was 180 roubles).

On a completely different level, we should note here that two priests who have figured significantly in previous chapters, Fathers Sergi Zheludkov and Vsevolod Shpiller, both died at an advanced age during January 1984; and Father Nikolai Eshliman died on 3 June 1985.

During 1984 several items of new legislation were enacted which indicated an increasingly repressive attitude to dissenters generally, including Christians. In January 1984, Article 70 of the Criminal Code ('anti-Soviet agitation and propaganda') was amended to include a new clause. This stated that it was now an offence 'to use [for anti-Soviet purposes] money or material goods received from Western organisations or persons acting in their interests'. The previous maximum term under this article, seven years' deprivation of liberty plus five years' internal exile, was now increased to ten years' deprivation of liberty plus five years' exile. This was clearly intended to stop prisoners' families and others in need receiving material aid from the West, and was probably especially aimed at Solzhenitsyn's Russian Social Fund.

In March, it was reported that as from 1 August following, it would no longer be possible to send parcels with pre-paid duty to the USSR. (Previously, agencies in various Western countries had been licensed by the Soviet authorities to collect import duties from the senders of parcels.) This meant that, in future, the recipients would have to pay duty upon receipt of a parcel. As these duties are extremely high, however, this was prohibitive for the already impoverished recipients. This was a significant step, since the foreign currency revenues from these parcels were reportedly very high. The Soviet Union normally tries to attract foreign currency (which it needs to buy goods from the West) by every conceivable method. This means that increasing pressure on dissenters was regarded as having priority over maximising foreign currency earnings, and the decision therefore must have been taken at a very high level.

In July 1984, an administrative (not criminal) regulation came into force which made it an offence punishable by fine for a Soviet citizen to allow a foreigner to stay overnight in his home, or to give him a lift in his car. It was also no longer possible for Soviet citizens to invite foreigners to stay with them (including relatives).

There has been speculation as to whether changes in leadership in recent years herald any change for the churches in the USSR. Before discussing top leadership, we should note that in December 1984, the elderly chairman of the CRA, Vladimir Kuroyedov, was replaced by Konstantin Kharchov, an engineer from Siberia and a former ambassador to Guyana. Little more is known of Kharchov, who has no known previous direct connection with religious (or atheist) affairs, although he was in leadership work in the Far Eastern Maritime Province and was Communist Party secretary in Vladivostok, and can hardly have been unaware of the persecution of religious believers, especially Pentecostals, in that area. Kuroyedov's retirement is thought to be due to age, and there is no reason as yet to expect that Kharchov's appointment heralds any change on religious policy.

The changes in the Soviet leadership since the death of President Brezhnev in 1983 have been the subject of worldwide comment, and all that need be said here is that they did not appear to affect policy on religion.

The increased repression of religious and political dissent began under Brezhnev (though it is true that Andropov, his successor, as the former head of the KGB, would have been very influential in this matter). Clearly, there has been change with the advent to power of the comparatively youthful and vigorous Mikhail Gorbachov. However, any speculation that there will be liberalisation in the area of religion (or any other) would be premature at the time of writing. Changes may perhaps be in the offing in the economic field, but in political areas, including the political control of religion, there is as yet no sign of any change of policy.

Whatever the political situation, and whatever the vicissitudes it has to face, it is clear that the spiritual vitality of the Russian Orthodox Church is undimmed. However politically captive its leadership may be, the body of the faithful simply continue to persist in their beliefs, and to add new members to their ranks. On the evidence of the preceding pages, we must expect that the largest national church in the world will continue to be a shining example of the power of the Christian faith to inspire people to overcome unprecedented persecution and suffering.

NOTES

1. Some frequently-cited *samizdat* sources have been referred to in abbreviated form in the end-notes to the chapters which follow. They are: the CRA Report, The Yakunin Report and the DCCDBR (Documents of the Christian Committee for the Defence of Believers' Rights in the USSR). Bibliographical details are given in the end-notes to the Introduction immediately following (pp. 455–6). Bibliographical references follow in the '*Samizdat*' section of the bibliography (pp. 518–19).

2. Frequently-cited sources have been designated in the notes and bibliography by abbreviations. A list follows:

AS	*Arkhiv samizdata*
CCE	*Chronicle of Current Events*
DCCDBR	*Documents of the Christian Committee for the Defense of Believers' Rights in the USSR*
JMP	*Journal of the Moscow Patriarchate*
KC archive	Keston College archive
KNS	*Keston News Service*
LFM	*Letters from Moscow*
RCDA	*Religion in Communist-Dominated Areas*
RCL	*Religion in Communist Lands*
RL in SU	*Religious Liberty in the Soviet Union*
SOP	*Service Orthodox de Presse*
Vestnik R(S)Khd	*Vestnik Russkogo (Studencheskogo) Khristianskogo Dvizheniya* (*Herald of the Russian (Student) Christian Movement*)

3. Variations in Russian personal names may be observed between the text and notes on one hand, and the bibliography on the other. This is because different transliteration systems have been used by the author and by the named person in question. For example, the surname Meerson-Aksyonov is spelled consistently by the author in the text and notes, but the alternative spelling Meerson-Aksenov appears in the bibliography. This writer, now resident in the USA, has, quite properly, chosen to transliterate his name in the latter way on his published materials.

A somewhat different issue concerns *samizdat* writers in the USSR who have been obliged to use pseudonyms. An example is Anatoli Levitin, who, while resident in the Soviet Union, used the pseudonym A. Krasnov on his *samizdat* writings. Since emigrating to Switzerland in 1974, he has used the name Anatoli (or A.) Levitin-Krasnov, or, sometimes, Krasnov-Levitin. Variations on these names are therefore evident in the text, notes and bibliography, according to the time of writing of the works cited and the designation upon the original text.

Other examples of variations in personal names will also be evident.

Introduction

1. In the *samizdat* form in which the CRA Report has reached the West, it is prefaced by the title 'Extracts from Informational Reports of the Council for Religious Affairs under the Council of Ministers of the USSR to the Central Committee of the CPSU'. There are extracts from three reports, dated 1968, 1970 and 1974. They are signed by V. Furov, a deputy chairman of the CRA and head of the department which deals with the Russian Orthodox Church. There is also a section of brief reports on discussions held between CRA officials and two leading hierarchs of the Russian Orthodox Church, some of which are dated 1966, 1967 and 1968 (some are undated). The two hierarchs are the then Metropolitan of Krutitsy and

Kolomna, now Patriarch Pimen; and Metropolitan Alexi of Tallinn and Estonia, then and now chancellor (*upravlyayushchi delami*) of the Moscow Patriarchate. Some of these reports are unsigned and some are signed by A. Plekhanov.

A photocopy of the CRA Report is in the archives of Keston College, Heathfield Road, Keston, Kent, BR2 6BA, England, henceforward referred to as KC archive. Parts of it have been published in Russian in *Vestnik RKhD*, Paris: the extracts from the 1974 report in no. 130 (1979), pp. 275–344; from the 1970 report in no. 131 (1980), pp. 362–72; and from the 1968 report (biography of the then Metropolitan Pimen and his conversations with CRA officials) in no 132 (1980), pp. 197–205.

An English translation of the CRA Report has been published in *Religion in Communist-dominated Areas*, New York, vol. XIX, nos 9–11 (1980), and subsequent issues, and is to be reprinted in a forthcoming book. (English translations of extracts in this book are the author's own.)

The extracts from the 1974 report have been published in French as a book, *Report secret au comité centrale sur l'état de l'église en URSS*, introduction by Nikita Struve (Seuil, Paris, 1980). This book dates the report as 1975 not 1974; this is owing to a misprint in the *Vestnik RKhD* editions of the report (no. 130, 1979, p. 287) where a date in September 1974 is wrongly printed as September 1975, leading to the false conclusion that the report was written later than indicated. Dimitri Pospielovsky (cited above) also dates the report later than its authors indicate. He writes: 'We date the report as probably 1978 because, although the information given covers roughly the period from 1967 to September 1975, it mentions both Mstislav and Bogolep as ruling bishops of Kirov. Mstislav died in 1978 and the next incumbent was Bogolep.' In fact, however, Bogolep was not bishop of the Russian diocese of Kirov and Slobodskoi, but of the Ukrainian diocese of Kirovograd and Nikolayev. The CRA's listing of Bogolep as Bishop of Kirov (*Vestnik RKhD*, no. 130, 1979, p. 279) is erroneous. There seems no reason to doubt the 1974 date of the report.

2. *The Documents of the Christian Committee for the Defense of Believers' Rights in the USSR* (*DCCDBR*) have been published by Washington Research Center, 3101 Washington Street, San Francisco, California 94115, USA. They are in the form of photographic reproductions of the original Russian texts. There are twelve volumes, of which vol. 3 consists of selected English translations of documents from vols 1, 2 and 4. From vol. 13, the task of publishing was assumed by CCDBR Publications, Glendale, California, while responsibility for editing and translating was taken over by the Society for the Study of Religion under Communism, Box 2310, Orange, California 92669. (See Chapter 12, note 14.)

3. 'Report of Father Gleb Yakunin to the Christian Committee for the Defence of Believers' Rights in the USSR on the Current Situation of the Russian Orthodox Church and the Prospects for a Religious Renaissance in Russia', 15 August 1979, published in *DCCDBR*, vol. 11, pp. 1128–68. A partial but extensive translation into English is given in the same volume, pp. xvi–xxx. See also *Arkhiv samizdata (AS)*, Radio Liberty, Munich, no. 3751.

1. Churches and Dioceses

1. Georges Florovsky, 'The Elements of Liturgy in the Orthodox Catholic Church', *One Church*, vol. XIII, nos 1–2 (1959), p. 24 (New York); quoted in Timothy Ware, *The Orthodox Church* (Penguin Books, Harmondsworth, 1963; revised 1964), p. 271.

2. Michael Bourdeaux, *Opium of the People* (reprinted Mowbrays, London and Oxford, 1977), p. 87.

3. Jonathan Steele, 'Churches Are Seen But Not Heard', *Guardian*, 20 November 1979, p. 21.

4. I. N. Yudin, *Pravda o peterburgskikh svyatinyakh* (*The Truth about the Petersburg Shrines*) (Lenizdat, Leningrad, 1962), p. 8.

5. J. A. Hebly, *The Russians and the World Council of Churches* (Christian Journals Ltd, Belfast, Dublin and Ottawa, 1978), p. 114.

6. *Nauka i religiya* (*Science and Religion*), no. 11 (1962), p. 60; V. K. Tancher, *Osnovy ateizma* (*The Foundations of Atheism*) (Izdatelstvo Kievskogo universiteta, Kiev, 1961), p. 181.

7. Yudin, *Pravda o peterburgskikh*; Fathers N. Eshliman and G. Yakunin, 'Declaration to the Chairman of the Presidium of the Supreme Soviet of the USSR', 21 November 1965, translation in Michael Bourdeaux, *Patriarch and Prophets* (reprinted Mowbrays, London and Oxford, 1975), p. 191.

8. William C. Fletcher in his article in the symposium *Religion and Modernization in the Soviet Union*, ed. Dennis J. Dunn (Westview Press, Boulder, Colorado, 1977), p. 235, note 21, helpfully lists estimates of the number of open churches in 1939. The figure of 4,225 churches was given by the press department of the Soviet Embassy in London, while another Soviet source stated that there were 'nearly 4,000' open churches. In the West, Konstantinov estimated 3,200 open churches and Kurt Hutten, 1,500. Bourdeaux gave a figure of only 100 open churches. This figure of 100 is also given by another source not cited by Fletcher: Nikita Struve, *Christians in Contemporary Russia* (Harvill Press, London, 1967), p. 57. It is possible that the lower figures reflect the position before September 1939, while the higher ones indicate the number of churches after the annexation of eastern Poland and western Ukraine by the USSR which took place in that month. This is described by Wassilij Alexeev and Theofanis G. Stavrou in *The Great Revival: The Russian Church Under German Occupation* (Burgess Publishing Company, Minneapolis, Minnesota, 1976), pp. 44ff.; they say that there were 1,299 parishes in the annexed territories.

9. See Alexeev and Stavrou, *The Great Revival*, for an account of the reopening of churches in German-occupied areas.

10. The Statute of the CRA was published in V. A. Kuroyedov and A. S. Pankratov (eds), *Zakonodatelstvo o religioznykh kultakh* (*Legislation on Religious Cults*) (Yuridicheskaya Literatura, Moscow, 1971); however, it was for restricted circulation and has reached the West only in photocopied form (copy in KC archive). An English translation of the Statute is given in *RCL*, vol. 4, no. 4 (1976), pp. 32–4, reproduced in the appendix at the end of Chapter 9 of the book (pp. 281–4). The clause cited, 3d, is on p. 282.

11. Paul Masson, *La Libre Belgique*, 10 October 1979.

12. Steele, 'Churches Are Seen'.

13. *Spravochnik propagandista i agitatora* (*The Propagandist's and Agitator's Handbook*) (Izdatelstvo politicheskoi literatury, Moscow, 1966), p. 149.

14. Ye. I. Lisavtsev, *Kritika burzhuaznoi falsifikatsii polozheniya religii v SSSR* (*A Critique of Bourgeois Falsification of the Situation of Religion in the USSR*) (Mysl, Moscow, 1971), p. 9.

15. *Vestnik RKhD*, no. 130 (1979), p. 298.

16. *Russkaya mysl*, 13 March 1975, p. 8.

17. *Russkaya mysl*, 22 May 1975, p. 12.

18. F. Luzhin, 'Gosudarstvobesiye' ('State Demonism') (Moscow, 1976), in *Vestnik RKhD*, no. 118 (1976), p. 265.

19. 'Irina Zholkovskaya-Ginzburg's Testimony on the Russian Orthodox Church before the Commission on Security and Cooperation in Europe' (in Washington DC), 21 May 1980; KC archive.

20. Lecture to staff members working on the *Great Soviet Encyclopaedia*, May 1976, by V. Furov, reported in the *Chronicle of Current Events*, no. 14 (Khronika Press, New York, 1976), pp. 609 (which wrongly gives the lecturer's name as Furin); English translation in *RCL*, vol. 6, no. 1 (1979), p. 33.

21. Vladimir Kuroyedov, *Religiya i tserkov v sovetskom obshchestve* (Politicheskaya Literatura, Moscow, 1984).

22. Dimitry Konstantinov has suggested that there were 4,000 churches in 1975 and 'not more than 3,000' in 1982 (*Stations of the Cross*, Zarya, London, Ontario, 1984, p. 15). Konstantinov specifies that he is counting only churches which appear to be open all the time for worship, and notes that there are others which are apparently open only occasionally. Given the caveat we have made above, that many of our estimated 6,000–6,500 churches are not open permanently, this makes the discrepancy between our estimate and Konstantinov's much smaller. Another western author, Dimitri Pospielovsky, cites a source claiming that 'inside figures of the Patriarchate' for 1972 showed 6,850 registered churches. He assumes a 'further slight decline' in the number of churches during the 1970s. This coincides quite well with our estimate based on other sources within the Soviet Union (Pospielovsky, *The Russian Orthodox Church under the Soviet Regime 1917–1982*, St Vladimir's Seminary Press,

Crestwood, New York, 1984, p. 401).

23. Trevor Beeson, *Discretion and Valour* (Fontana, Glasgow, 1974), pp. 287–8. A publication of one of the overseas churches under the jurisdiction of the Moscow Patriarchate subsequently broke this figure down to 3,200 parish churches and 500 chapels (*One Church*, vol. 28, no. 6 (1974), pp. 275–6).

24. Beeson, *Discretion and Valour*, p. 302. A Romanian publication subsequently gave a higher figure of 10,000 parishes, though without indicating whether or not the number of churches had increased correspondingly (*Romanian Orthodox Church News*, vol. V, no. 4 (1975), p. 62).

25. Beeson, *Discretion and Valour*, p. 302.

26. Father Miguel Arranz SJ, interview 'Inside the Russian Church — by a Jesuit at Work in Leningrad', with Desmond O'Grady, *Catholic Herald*, 28 March 1980, p. 10. Archbishop Khrizostom, deputy chairman of the Department of External Church Relations, has also told foreign visitors that there are 43 churches in Moscow.

27. *Baptist World Alliance News Service*, 11 April 1980.

28. Michael Binyon, 'Latvian Diary', *The Times*, 28 March 1980, p. 16.

29. Vladimir Smirnov, interview with (then) Bishop Serapion of Irkutsk, 29 April 1978, Novosti Press Agency; copy in KC archive. Bishop Serapion repeated the same figure a year later to a Western visitor, Michael Bourdeaux ('Pilgrimage to Siberia', *Christianity Today*, 7 September 1979, p. 24).

30. Archbishop Pavel (Golyshev) in a letter to Patriarch Pimen dated February 1972 (*Vestnik RKhD*, no. 103 (1972), pp. 173–4).

31. This pattern is apparent from the admittedly incomplete data provided by the 'From the Dioceses' section of *JMP* since 1965, and is borne out by such other figures as are available. Struve (*Christians in Contemporary Russia*, p. 180ff.) noted this pattern, relying for the most part on information pre-dating the end of the anti-religious campaign in 1964; and Christel Lane, relying principally upon data provided by Soviet sociologists, came to the same general conclusion in 1970s (*Christian Religion in the Soviet Union*, Allen & Unwin, London, 1978, p. 46).

32. This pattern is noted and developed at some length by Gleb Rahr, 'Skolko v Rossii pravoslavnykh khramov?' ('How Many Orthodox Churches Are There in Russia?'), *Posev*, January 1974, pp. 39–44.

33. Rahr (ibid., p. 39) quotes a figure of 950 churches; Philippe Sabant ('Religion in Russia Today', *The Tablet*, 19 January 1980, p. 55) gives a figure of 947 parishes. However, Father Sergei Hackel (in a letter to the present author), gives a figure of 989 churches, quoted to him in summer 1979 by both the Metropolitan of Lvov and the diocesan secretary.

34. *Vestnik RKhD*, no. 130 (1979), p. 299.

35. Ibid., p. 300. The figures given add up to 364, not 363: the figures are the same in the photocopy of the typewritten report; there is no misprint in *Vestnik*. Errors in simple addition are a recurring feature of the CRA Report.

36. Bohdan R. Bociurkiw, 'The Orthodox Church and the Soviet Regime in the Ukraine, 1953–1971', *Canadian Slavonic Papers*, vol. XIV, no. 2 (summer 1972), pp. 193–4, 196.

37. Frank E. Sysyn, 'The Ukrainian Orthodox Church in the USSR', *RCL*, vol. 11, no. 3 (1983), p. 252. (Ukrainian Catholics have been outlawed in the USSR since being forcibly incorporated into the Russian Orthodox Church in 1946.)

38. This figure was given by Metropolitan Filaret of Minsk and Belorussia during a talk in London in 1980 (*KNS*, no. 112 (29 November 1980), p. 18).

39. Rahr ('Skolko v Rossii'), gives a figure of 76 churches; the churches mentioned in *JMP* since 1965 total 69.

40. Rahr ('Skolko v Rossii'), states 100 churches; Masson (*La Libre Belgique*) says there are 101 parishes.

41. Arranz, 'Inside the Russian Church'; these figures have also been given to foreign visitors by Archbishop Khrizostom.

42. Ukraine is the only region of the Soviet Union to be recognised as an Exarchate of the Moscow Patriarchate, due to its size and its history. However, Ukrainian Orthodox resent their lack of an autocephalous church, particularly when they contrast their status with that of the Georgian Orthodox Church, which has its own Patriarch and is an autocephalous church recognised by Moscow Patriarch (Sysyn, 'The Ukrainian Orthodox Question', pp. 254–6).

Most of the population of Georgia are nominally Orthodox, but they number 5 million compared to Ukraine's 50 million.

43. Apparently these dioceses have lapsed or fallen vacant on the death of the bishop, but issues of *JMP* for the relevant years do not indicate why no new bishop was appointed.

44. *Christian Science Monitor*, 2 July 1973, p. 6.

45. Lev Lukyanenko, 'Christmas Appeal to Atheists', *ABN Correspondence*, vol. XXVIII, no. 5/6 (September–December 1977), p. 7.

46. *JMP*, no. 2 (1979), p. 24; no. 5 (1979), p. 36.

47. Professor Harry Rigby, Australian National University, in a conversation with the present author.

48. Igor Ratmirov, 'Restavratsiya ili diskriminatsiya?' ('Restoration or Discrimination?') *samizdat*; summarised in *Religiya i ateizm v SSSR*, no. 5 (92) (May 1975), pp. 9–10.

49. Ibid., p. 10.

50. *JMP*, no. 3 (1980), p. 18.

51. Vladimir Kuroyedov, 'Ravny pered zakonom?' ('Equal Before the Law?'), *Literaturnaya gazeta*, 7 July 1982.

52. *Glaube in der 2. Welt* (G2W), 2 December 1977.

53. Smirnov, 'Interview'.

54. Bourdeaux ('Pilgrimage to Siberia') says that Bishop Serapion had consecrated four churches the previous year (1978), in which case the diocese may have a total of 30 churches, not 29.

55. *Daily Telegraph*, 29 October 1978, p. 6.

56. *JMP*, no. 8 (1978), p. 11.

57. *The Yakunin Report*, p. 25 (footnote).

58. Ibid. This comment by Father Yakunin belies a comment in the *International Herald Tribune* ('Russian Believers Plead', 4 September 1977), which states: 'According to Rev. Gleb Yakunin . . . not a single church has been opened in Russia since World War II.'

59. *JMP*, no. 5 (1980), p. 21 (Prokopevsk); no. 6, p. 17 (Pavlysh), p. 18 (Salkovo), pp. 18–19 (Drakino); no. 10, p. 20 (Obilnoye, Izobilny, Alexandriya); no. 11, pp. 12–15 (Sofrino).

60. Open letter from Siberia to all Orthodox Christians, from parishioners of the Church of the Protecting Veil, Asino, Tomsk *oblast*, in *SMOT* (Free Interprofessional Association of Workers) *Information Bulletin* (*samizdat*), no. 15 (April–May 1981).

61. We have used the translation 'commissioner' for the Russian word *upolnomochenny*, which can be perhaps more precisely, but more cumbersomely, translated 'plenipotentiary'. We believe that 'commissioner' conveys the same sense of a person commissioned and empowered by a particular body for a particular task. It is preferable to the words 'official' and 'representative', which are sometimes used, because they are applied to a number of different kinds of officials of various Soviet bodies, while *upolnomochenny* (at least in the contexts referred to in this book) invariably refers to a member of the CRA.

62. *Vestnik RKhD*, no. 117 (1976), p. 214.

63. See, for example, photographs in the book *Razrushennye i oskvernennye khramy* (*Destroyed and Profaned Churches*) (Posev, Frankfurt/Main, 1980), and in the booklet *The Land of Closed Churches* (Hans Neerskov, Danish European Mission, Søborg, no date).

64. 'Plea to Patriarch Pimen from Father Gleb Yakunin', 17 April 1976, *AS*, no. 2563, p. 4.

65. Law on Religious Associations, Articles 5 and 10, in *Review of Socialist Law*, vol. 1 (September 1975), pp. 223–4.

66. Ibid.

67. See their letter to Dr Eugene Carson Blake, general secretary of the World Council of Churches, signed by 36 citizens of Gorky, November 1968; translation in M. Bourdeaux, H. Hebly and E. Voss (eds), *Religious Liberty in the Soviet Union* (Keston College, Keston, 1976), pp. 56–7.

68. Report of the Christian Committee for the Defence of Believers' Rights in the USSR, 22 August 1977; *DCCDBR*, vol. 4, p. 433.

69. Letter to L. I. Brezhnev, general secretary of the Central Committee of the CPSU and chairman of the Presidium of the Supreme Soviet of the USSR, and A. N. Kosygin, chairman of the Council of Ministers of the USSR, from Veniamin F. Kozulin, 14 September 1977;

DCCDBR, vol. 4, p. 470.

70. Letter to Brezhnev and Kosygin from Orthodox citizens of Gorky, 1,600 signatures (not appended to copy received), undated; *DCCDBR*, vol. 4, p. 471.

71. The conference reviewed the application of the so-called 'Helsinki Agreements', the Final Act of the Conference on Security and Cooperation in Europe, signed on 1 August 1975 by 35 countries, including the USSR; among its wide-ranging undertakings was the statement: 'The participating States will respect human rights and fundamental freedoms, including the freedom of thought, conscience, religion or belief . . . [they] will recognise and respect the freedom of the individual to profess and practice, alone or in community with others, religion or belief acting in accordance with the dictates of his own conscience' (Section (a), Para. VII).

72. Appeal (*obrashcheniye*) of Orthodox Christians in Gorky (USSR) to the Belgrade Conference to review the application of the Helsinki Agreements, January 1978; *DCCDBR*, vol. 4, pp. 473–4.

73. 'Russian Believers Plead', *International Herald Tribune*, 4 September 1977.

74. Open letter from citizens of Gorky to the editorial board of the newspaper *Gorkovskaya pravda* (*Gorky Truth*), undated but after 14 October 1978, 27 signatures, of which three appear on copy received, *DCCDBR*, vol. 7, pp. 858–63.

75. Ibid., pp. 864–5.

76. *DCCDBR*, vol. 4, pp. 475–81 (Sitskoye); vol. 7, pp. 848–50 (Bolshoi Khomutets); vol. 9, pp. 985–8; vol. 11, pp. 1186–95; vol. 12, pp. 1248–50 (Kotovo); vol. 11, pp. 1182–5 (Lozovaya); vol. 11, pp. 1171–3 (Balashovka); vol. 1, pp. 101–7 (Velikiye Zagaitsy); vol. 4, pp. 468–9 (Budki); and vol. 2, pp. 228–31 (Khotovitsa).

77. *DCCDBR*, vol. 11, pp. 1171–3.

78. Ibid., pp. 1191–3.

79. *DCCDBR*, vol. 1, pp. 101–2.

80. The alteration was due to the revision of the Law on Religious Associations in 1975. For a discussion of this, see Walter Sawatsky, 'The New Soviet Law on Religion', *RCL*, vol. 4, no. 2 (1976), pp. 4–10, esp. p. 7.

81. *Religiya i ateizm v SSSR*, nos 7–8 (94–5) (July–August 1975), p. 6, quoting *Ukrainsky visnik*, nos 7–8, compiled in Ukraine in spring 1974 and published in Paris in 1975.

82. See documents in *DCCDBR*, no. 1; official documents pp. 72–4; letters from parishioners to Kuroyedov, 24 January 1975 and undated, pp. 75–6.

83. Untitled document signed by 'Believers of the Rechitsa Prayer-house of the Holy Dormition', and headed 'BSSR, Gomel obl., g. Rechitsa, Prayer house dedicated to the Dormition of the Mother of God', undated, but 1979, after 1 September and before 12 November, when it was received in the West (KC archive).

84. To the Secretary-General of the United Nations, Mr Kurt Waldheim, from parishioners of the Church of the Epiphany in Zhitomir, 16 August 1975, translation in Bourdeaux, Hebly and Voss (eds), *Religious Liberty in the Soviet Union*, pp. 62–3.

85. A. Krasnov, 'Zemlya dybom' ('The Earth Turned Upside Down') (*samizdat*, Moscow, 1974), *AS*, no. 1876, p. 72.

86. To His Holiness Patriarch Pimen of Moscow and All Russia, from 'the servant of God, Yuri', signed Yu. Belov, 12 December 1978, Moscow; *DCCDBR*, vol. 7, p. 857.

87. See, for example, Ye. Ukhov, 'Klyuchi Svuyazhka' ('The Keys of Sviyazhsk'), *Trud*, 18 August 1981, p. 4; English translation in *KNS*, no. 132 (10 September 1981), pp. 13–15.

88. The journalist Vasili Yelesin in *Nash sovremennik*, no. 10 (1978), p. 172, attributed the moral degradation of the peasants to the absence of churches in rural areas, according to Mikhail Agursky, 'The Attitude to Religion in the New Russian Literature', *RCL*, vol. 10, no. 2 (1982), p. 147.

89. John Dunlop, *The Faces of Contemporary Russian Nationalism* (Princeton University Press, Princeton, NJ, 1983), pp. 74–5. The foregoing account of VOOPIK is derived from pp. 66ff.

90. A. Viktorov, 'Spasat etot unikany pamyatnik' ('Save this Unique Monument'), in *Dekorativnoye iskusstvo v SSSR* (*Decorative Art in the USSR*), no. 7 (1982); *KNS*, no. 183 (22 September 1983), pp. 5–6. The same issue of *KNS* (pp. 5 and 7) gives two other examples of endangered churches: the church in Rovenki, Belgorod *oblast*, which is falling down for lack of funds to restore it even though it has been designated a historical monument; and the seventeenth-century church in Borovsk, Kaluga *oblast*, reportedly scheduled for demolition.

See also *AS*, nos 4995, 4996.

91. *Agitator*, no. 8 (1972), p. 34.

92. Article 52 of 1977 Soviet Constitution.

93. *Chronicle of the Lithuanian Catholic Church*, no. 24, 1 October 1976, English version, p. 32.

94. Ibid., p. 33.

95. *Cahiers du Samizdat*, May 1977, p. 3, quoting *Vstrechi*, published in Frankfurt/Main by the NTS (Natsionalny Trudovoi Soyuz: National Labour Union), no. 178 (February 1977).

96. *AS*, no. 3751, p. 38. *JMP*, no. 3 (1979), pp. 70–5; no. 4, pp. 73–7; no. 5 (1979), pp. 73–7.

97. *The Russian Orthodox Church: Organisation, Situation, Activity*, English edition (Moscow Patriarchate, Moscow, 1958), pp. 38–9.

98. Quoted in *Aktualnosti Krščanska sadašnjosti* (*AKSA: Actualités of Contemporary Christianity*), 21 November 1980.

99. *The Moscow Patriarchate 1917–1977* (Moscow Patriarchate, Moscow, 1978), p. 28.

100. *Pravoslavny tserkovny kalendar* (*Orthodox Church Calendar*), 1980, p. 137.

101. Arranz, 'Interview', quotes Archbishop Khrizostom in *Le Figaro* 'recently'.

102. *Vestnik RKhD*, no. 130 (1979), p. 277.

2. Parish Life

1. Hieromonk Nikon (Yakimov), 'Vpechatleniya ochevidtsa' ('Impressions of an Eyewitness'), *Vestnik RKhD*, no. 132 (1980), pp. 206–8.

2. A. Udodov, '*Skolko pravoslavnykh v Rossii?*' ('How many Orthodox Are There in Russia?'), *Posev*, February 1976, p. 41.

3. Yakunin Report, p. 24.

4. Letter to Dr Philip Potter, secretary-general of the World Council of Churches, from Alexander Ogorodnikov, 27 July 1976; English translation in *RCL*, vol. 4, no. 4 (1976), p. 46.

5. Zakon o religioznykh obyedinyeniyakh (Law on Religious Associations), Article 60. The 1929 law was amended by Decree of the Presidium of the Supreme Soviet of the RSFSR on 23 June 1975, and the amendments were published in *Vedomosti Verkhovnogo Soveta* (*Annals of the Supreme Soviet*), no. 27 (873) (3 July 1975). The complete text of the revised law was published in Russian by Khronika Press, New York, 1975, and in English translation in *The Review of Socialist Law*, vol. 1 (September 1975), pp. 223–34.

6. Law on Religious Associations, Article 17.

7. *Polozheniye ob upravlenii Russkoi Pravoslavnoi Tserkvi* (published in the church's Calendar for 1946), pp. 58–60; this was not available to the present author, who has used the English translation in William B. Stroyen, *Communist Russia and the Russian Orthodox Church 1943–62* (Catholic University of America Press Inc., Washington DC, 1967), Appendix E, pp. 136–40. A commentary giving the main points of the Statute is to be found in *The Russian Orthodox Church: Organization, Situation, Activity*, Russian and English editions (Moscow Patriarchate, Moscow, 1958), pp. 29–38.

8. The revised version is given in *JMP*, no. 8 (1961), pp. 15–17; English translation in Stroyen, *Communist Russia*, Appendix F, pp. 141–3 (which, however, contains inaccuracies); *Vestnik RKhD*, no. 133 (1981), pp. 214–20.

9. Law on Religious Associations (henceforward LRA), Article 3.

10. This is made clear in *The Russian Orthodox Church: Organization, Situation, Actvity*, p. 36: 'Each parish consists of a group of faithful.'

11. LRA, Article 12.

12. LRA, Article 13.

13. LRA, Article 14.

14. LRA, Article 54.

15. LRA, Article 56; 1961 amendments to 1945 Statute, *JMP*, no. 8 (1961), p. 16, section 2g.

16. LRA, Article 15.

17. *JMP*, no. 8 (1961), p. 16, section 2b.

18. LRA, Article 16.

19. 'Explanatory Instruction of the Oblast Representative (Regional Commissioner) of the Council on Religious Affairs. Concluding a Contract with the "Group of Twenty", the Legal Organ of a Parish', English translation in R. Marshall, T. Bird and A. Blane (eds), *Aspects of Religion in the Soviet Union 1917–1967* (The University of Chicago Press, Chicago and London, 1971), p. 461.

20. *JMP*, no. 8 (1961), p. 16, section 2e.

21. Ibid.

22. See, for example, 'Excerpts from Listeners' Letters Programme, with Metropolitan Alexius of Tallinn and Estonia', Radio Moscow in English for north America, 00.30 GMT, 26 February 1977, *Summary of World Broadcasts*, SU/5459/B/1, 10 March 1977.

23. LRA, Article 54.

24. *JMP*, no. 8 (1961), p. 16, section 2f. Prosphora are small loaves of bread sold before the beginning of the liturgy and passed to the priest at the altar, accompanied by a request for prayer for a named person, either for the health of a living person or for the soul of someone departed. The priest cuts a fragment from the loaf at a credence table in the sanctuary as he prays. The remainder of the loaves are distributed to the congregation at the end of the service. The bread is not formally blessed in Russian practice, but is treated with reverence, because it has played its part in the eucharistic process.

25. See note 22.

26. LRA, Article 55.

27. LRA, Article 40.

28. *JMP*, no. 8 (1961), p. 16, section 2e; LRA, Article 54.

29. Paul Masson, *La Libre Belgique*, 13–14 October 1979; Michael Bourdeaux, *Land of Crosses* (Augustine Publishing Company, Chulmleigh, Devon, 1979), p. 173.

30. LRA, Article 29.

31. Letter to the general secretary of the Central Committee of the CPSU and chairman of the Presidium of the Supreme Soviet of the USSR, Leonid Ilich Brezhnev, with copies to Patriarch Pimen and Metropolitan Filaret of Kiev and Galicia, Patriarchal Exarch for Ukraine, from Bishop Feodosi of Poltava and Kremenchug, Poltava, 26 October 1977, *AS*, no. 4456; Ukrainian translation published in *Suchasnist*, nos 7–8 (1981), pp. 159–85.

32. *AS*, no. 4456, pp. 4–5.

33. Ibid., pp. 5–12, 24.

34. Ibid., pp. 24–5.

35. Alain Woodrow (*Le Monde*, 7 September 1978, p. 6) gave the income as 1 million roubles in 1977; Masson (*La Libre Belgique*, 10 October 1979) as 1.2 million; and a foreign visitor in 1981 as 1.3 million (confidential report in KC archive).

36. Confidential report, 1981 (KC archive).

37. Ibid.

38. Woodrow, *Le Monde*.

39. Confidential report, 1981 (KC archive).

40. Masson, *La Libre Belgique*.

41. Michael Binyon, *Life in Russia* (Hamish Hamilton, London, 1983), p. 232.

42. *DCCDBR*, vol. 1, pp. 61, 67. (The figure of 106,000 roubles a year given on p. 50 must be a misprint.)

43. *DCCDBR*, vol. 5, part 1, p. 689.

44. *DCCDBR*, vol. 1, p. 50.

45. Letter to Mr Brezhnev from Bishop Feodosi, 26 October 1977, p. 18.

46. Ibid.

47. Ibid., p. 17.

48. See note 22.

49. 'Osnovnye voprosy deyatelnosti komissii sodeistviya pri ispolkomakh i raionnykh sovetov deputatov trudyashchikhsya po kontrolyu za soblyudeniyem zakonodatelstva o kultakh', *Vestnik RKhD*, no. 83 (1967), pp. 3–6.

50. Alexander A. Bogolepov, 'The Legal Position of the Russian Orthodox Church', in Marshall, Bird and Blane (eds), *Aspects of Religion*, p. 217.

51. Yakunin Report, p. 20.

52. *JMP*, no. 8 (1961), pp. 3−29.

53. 'Arkhiyereisky sobor 1961' ('The Council of Bishops 1961') unsigned and undated, 35pp., *AS*, no. 701, received in the West by the middle of the 1960s; photocopy of original typescript in KC archive. Partial English translation in *RCL*, vol. 9, no. 1 (1981), pp. 24−7.

54. 'The Council of Bishops', p. 12.

55. Ibid., p. 18.

56. *JMP*, no. 8 (1961), p. 6.

57. 'The Council of Bishops', p. 1.

58. 'The Fiftieth Anniversary of the Restoration of the Patriarchate: A Historical, Canonical and Legal Inquiry', Archbishop Yermogen, Zhirovitsy Monastery, 25 December 1967; English translation in M. Bourdeaux, *Patriarch and Prophets* (reprinted Mowbrays, London and Oxford, 1975), p. 245.

59. 'The Council of Bishops', p. 2.

60. Ibid., p. 16; *JMP*, no. 8 (1961), p. 5.

61. *JMP*, no. 8 (1961), p. 6.

62. Bogolepov, 'The Legal Position', p. 215.

63. A western writer on the 1959−64 anti-religious campaign takes the view that the 1961 Council of Bishops was an important part of it: Michael Bourdeaux, 'The Black Quinquennium', *RCL*, vol. 9, nos 1−2 (1981), p. 20.

64. 'The Council of Bishops', p. 16; *RCL*, vol. 9, no. 1 (1981), p. 25.

65. 'The Council of Bishops', p. 8.

66. Bogolepov, 'The Legal Position', p. 198.

67. 'The Council of Bishops', p. 8.

68. Ibid., pp. 8−9.

69. *JMP*, no. 8 (1961), pp. 5−6.

70. Ibid., pp. 10−11.

71. CRA Report: Transcript of a Conversation with Metropolitan Pimen in the CRA Office on 21 February 1967, signed A. Plekhanov; p. 2 of the copy in KC archive.

72. 'The Council of Bishops', p. 27; *RCL*, vol. 9, no. 1 (1981), p. 26.

73. *RCL*, vol. 9, no. 1 (1981), p. 26.

74. Ibid.

75. Ibid.

76. 'The Council of Bishops', p. 11.

77. Ibid., p. 12.

78. Canons cited in A. Levitin-Krasnov, *'Bolnaya tserkov'* (*The Ailing Church*), *samizdat*, 27 August 1965; *AS* no. 886, p. 7.

79. 1945 Statute, paragraph 41; 1961 amendments, paragraph 5; English translation taken (with slight amendments) from Stroyen, *Communist Russia*, pp. 139, 142.

80. *JMP*, no. 8 (1961), p. 5.

81. 'The Council of Bishops', p. 26; *RCL*, vol. 9, no. 1 (1981), p. 25.

82. 'The Council of Bishops', p. 30.

83. *JMP*, no. 8 (1961), p. 6.

84. 'The Council of Bishops', p. 20.

85. Ibid.

86. It has been impossible to ascertain whether this photo was ever published.

87. 'The Council of Bishops', p. 2.

88. Ibid., p. 3.

89. Ibid.

90. Ibid.

91. Ibid., p. 29; *RCL*, vol. 9, no. 1 (1981), p. 27.

92. 'The Council of Bishops', p. 26; *RCL*, vol. 9, no. 1 (1981), p. 26.

93. 'The Council of Bishops', p. 33.

94. Ibid., p. 34.

95. Ibid., p. 32; *RCL*, vol. 9, no.1 (1981), p. 27.

96. Timothy Ware, *The Orthodox Church* (Penguin Books, Harmondsworth, 1963; revised 1964), pp. 213−14, 302.

97. Part I, paragraph 7; Stroyen, *Communist Russia*, p. 137. See also the commentary on the Statute in *The Russian Orthodox Church: Organization, Situation, Activity*, p. 33.

98. *JMP*, no. 8 (1961), p. 15.

99. Bourdeaux, *Patriarch and Prophets*, quotes Yermogen, and Eshliman and Yakunin, extensively.

100. Zapiska Presedatelyu Komissii po podgotovke Pomestnogo Sobora (Note to the Chairman of the Commission for preparing the Local Council), 24 December 1970, and Proyekt redaktsii IV razdela 'Polozheniya ob Upravlenii Russkoi Pravoslavnoi Tserkovyu' (Draft Revision of section IV of the 'Statute on the Administration of the Russian Orthodox Church'), 22 April 1971, *Vestnik RKhD*, no. 120 (1977), pp. 294–305.

101. See note 99.

102. *Vestnik RKhD*, no. 120 (1977), p. 296.

103. Ibid.

104. Ibid.

105. Ibid., pp. 297–300.

106. *Vestnik RKhD*, no. 100 (1971), pp. 206–12.

107. *The Chronicle of Current Events*, no. 34 (31 December 1974; Khronika Press edition), pp. 52–3.

108. Complaint to the regional procurator from the church council of St Barbara's Church, signed by the deputy-churchwarden, Ye. I. Shumyakova, and four others, undated but apparently written after the middle of 1975 and before the end of 1977; *DCCDBR*, vol. 1, pp. 77–8.

109. 'News from the USSR', reported by Anatoli Levitin-Krasnov, *Russkaya mysl*, 27 October 1977, p. 3.

110. *The Chronicle of Current Events*, no. 42 (8 October 1976), p. 83.

111. Declaration to the Chairman of the Council of Religious Affairs under the Council of Ministers of the USSR, V. A. Kuroyedov, from Father Gleb Yakunin, 21 March 1977, *AS*, no. 2970; also *DCCDBR*, vol. 2, pp. 164–5.

112. The documents are all published in *DCCDBR*, as follows: vol. 1, pp. 50–71; vol. 2, p. 232; vol. 4, pp. 434–7 and 452–67; vol. 5, Part 1, pp. 689–96; vol. 6, pp. 731–2; vol. 7, pp. 833–4 and 866–76; vol. 11, pp. 1196–7.

113. Letter to L. A. Levanova from V. Shendrik, 17 October 1977; *DCCDBR*, vol. 2, p. 232.

114. Letter to CRA Chairman Kuroyedov and CRA Chairman for Ukraine, K. Z. Litvin, from 27 parishioners, 28 August 1977; *DCCDBR*, vol. 1, p. 68.

115. Ye. Yachnik, 'Vot tebe i "Bozhii slugi"' ('So Much for the "Servants of God"'), *Sovetskaya Kirgiziya* (*Soviet Kirgizia*), 5 February 1976, p. 4.

116. Daily talk by Vladimir Pozner, Radio Moscow in English for North America, 23.00 GMT 24 April 1976, *Summary of World Broadcasts*, SU/5193/A1/5, 27 April 1976.

117. *Molodyozh Moldavii*, 29 April 1982; English translation taken from *KNS*, no. 149 (20 May 1982), p. 1.

118. *Posev*, June 1973, p. 12.

119. *The Times*, 27 April 1981, p. 6.

120. The foreign visitor wishes to remain anonymous; the confidential report is in KC archive.

3. The Clergy

1. Statute of the Church, as reformed in 1961, *JMP*, no. 8 (1961), p. 16.

2. Statute, section 10, in ibid; *The Moscow Patriarchate 1917–177* (Moscow Patriarchate, Moscow, 1978), p. 29.

3. Statute, section 11, *JMP*, no. 8 (1961), p. 17.

4. Law on Religious Associations (LRA), Article 3.

5. Ibid., Article 19.

6. Ibid., Article 58.

7. Ibid., Article 59.

8. Letter from Bishop Feodosi of Poltava and Kremenchug to L. I. Brezhnev, 26 October

1977, *AS*, no. 4456, pp. 25–6.

9. Ibid., pp. 16, 26.

10. M. Meerson-Aksyonov, 'L'Église en URSS', *Études*, June 1973, p. 928. Mikhail Meerson-Aksyonov was an Orthodox layman when he emigrated from the USSR in 1972, and has since been ordained priest.

11. Metropolitan Filaret was speaking at a gathering in the Russian Orthodox Church in London on 4 November 1980; see *KNS*, no. 112 (29 November 1980), p. 19.

12. A. F. Okulov and D. M. Ugrinovich, 'Problemy filosofii religii na XIV Mezhdunarodnom filosofskom kongresse v Vene' ('Problems of the Philosophy of Religion at the XIVth International Philosophical Congress in Vienna'), in *Voprosy nauchnogo ateizma (Questions of Scientific Atheism)*, no. 7 (Mysl, Moscow, 1969), p. 406.

13. 'Extracts from Informational Reports of the Council for Religious Affairs under the Council of Ministers of the USSR to the Central Committee of the CPSU', signed Furov; 'From the Report for 1970' (typescript, KC archive), p. 13.

14. Ibid.

15. '"*Bezobidny*" *Kompromiss*?' ('A "Harmless" Compromise?'), *Komsomolskaya pravda*, 10 September 1980; see commentary in *KNS*, no. 109 (16 October 1980), pp. 7–8.

16. Yakunin Report, p. 14.

17. Ibid.

18. Ibid.

19. J. A. Hebly, *The Russians and the World Council of Churches* (Christian Journals Ltd, Belfast, Dublin and Ottawa, 1978), p. 114.

20. Alain Woodrow, 'La Vie religieuse en URSS', *Le Monde*, 7 September 1978, p. 6.

21. 'Unseparate Church and State', *Time*, 23 June 1980, p. 54.

22. Father Miguel Arranz SJ, 'Inside the Russian Church — by a Jesuit at Work in Leningrad', interview with Desmond O'Grady, *Catholic Herald*, 28 March 1980, p. 10.

23. Alan Nichols, 'Documentary Record on the Australian Anglican Delegation's Visit to the Soviet Union, Poland and Yugoslavia', 14 June–4 July 1976 (18-page duplicated typescript, KC archive), p. 8.

24. 'The Other Side of the Penny: Impressions of Six Weeks with the Russian Church', April–June 1973, Rev. O. and Mrs X. Fielding-Clarke, 42 St John Street, Wirksworth, Derby, DE4 4DS (12-page duplicated typescript), p. 6.

25. *Vestnik RKhD*, no. 130 (1979), p. 297.

26. *RCL*, vol. 6, no. 1 (1978), p. 32.

27. *Vestnik RKhD*, no. 130 (1979), p. 297.

28. Ibid., p. 298.

29. Ibid., p. 299.

30. Ibid., p. 300.

31. 'Archbishop of Canterbury Talks with Soviet Correspondents', Reuters, 29 September 1977; summarised in 'Current Abstracts and Annotations', *Radio Liberty*, no. 10 (28 October 1977), p. 7.

32. *Russkaya mysl*, 31 October 1974, p. 5.

33. *Vestnik RKhD*, no. 130 (1979), p. 298.

34. Ibid., p. 299.

35. Ibid., p. 298.

36. Ibid., p. 299.

37. Letter from Bishop Feodosi to Brezhnev, 26 October 1977, *AS*, no. 4456, pp. 22–3.

38. Paul Masson, *La Libre Belgique*, 13–14 October 1979, p. 6; Woodrow, 'La Vie religieuse', p. 6.

39. Alan Nichols, 'Documentary Record', p. 3.

40. Jonathan Steele, 'A Useful Opium for the State?', *Guardian*, 21 November 1979, p. 15.

41. Mervyn Matthews, *Privilege in the Soviet Union* (Allen & Unwin, London, 1978), p. 33, footnote.

42. Ibid., p. 92. The 1985 figure was given by a recent *émigré*, Valeri Fefelov, in *Le Monde*, 2–3 March 1985.

43. Letter from Bishop Feodosi to Brezhnev, p. 18.

44. V. A. Mezentsev (ed.), *Otvety veruyushchim (Answers to Believers)* (Politicheskaya Literatura, Moscow, third edition 1971), pp. 246–7.

45. The basic tax law is the Edict of the Presidium of the Supreme Soviet of the USSR, 30 April 1943, '*O podokhodnom naloge s naseleniya*' ('The Income Tax on the Population'). The decision to tax 'servants of the cult' under Article 19 is contained in a resolution of the Council of Ministers of the USSR, 3 December 1946, no. 2584. See *Sbornik zakonov SSSR 1938–1975* (*Collection of Soviet Laws*) (Izdaniye 'Izvestiya Sovetov Deputatov Trudyashchikhsya SSSR', Moscow, 1975), vol. 1, pp. 544–56.

46. 'O diskriminatsionnom kharaktere gosudarstvennykh nalogov v SSSR na dukhovenstvo i rabotnikov religioznykh organizatsii' (The Discriminatory Character of State Taxes in the USSR on the Clergy and Workers of Religious Organisations'). Report to the Christian Committee compiled by Father Gleb Yakunin, 1 July 1977; *DCCDBR*, vol. 1, pp. 31–5.

47. Ibid., p. 35.

48. *Vedomosti verkhovnogo soveta SSSR*, no. 48 (26 December 1980), p. 1027; Michael Binyon, 'Tax Cuts and Social Benefits for Soviet Clergy', *The Times*, 4 November 1980, p. 7; the edict was approved by the Supreme Soviet on 24 November 1980, according to *Izvestiya*, (25 November 1981, p. 2), and came into effect from January 1981.

49. Oxana Antic, 'Taxation of Clergy in the USSR', *Radio Liberty Research*, RL 254/81, 24 June 1981.

50. Appeal (*obrashcheniye*) to the chairman of the Constitutional Commission, L. I. Brezhnev, from members of the Christian Committee for the Defence of Believers' Rights in the USSR, 22 July 1977, Moscow; *DCCDBR*, vol. 1, p. 30.

51. Jonathan Steele, 'A Useful Opium'.

52. *Sovetskaya Rossiya*, 18 August 1973; reported in *RCL*, vol. 2, no. 2 (1974), p. 32.

53. V. Vladimirov, 'Dokhodnoye mesto' ('A Lucrative Place'), *Kommunist Tadzhikistana*, 3 April 1977, p. 2.

54. CRA Reports, 'From the Report for 1968' (typescript, KC archive), pp. 4, 9.

55. Ibid., p. 4.

56. Ibid., p. 5.

57. Ibid.

58. Ibid., pp. 7–8.

59. Ibid., p. 8.

60. 'Executive Bodies, Safes, Violation of Legislation and Interference by Priests in the Economic and Financial Activity of Religious Communities', *Vestnik RKhD*, no. 130 (1979), pp. 337–44.

61. CRA 1968 Report, p. 7.

62. Metropolitan Serafim of Krutitsy, circular 900, 13 December 1974, *Vestnik RKhD*, no. 118 (1976), pp. 287–91.

63. Father Gleb Yakunin, Commentary on the Edict of Metropolitan Serafim of Krutitsy and Kolomna, 2 December 1975, *Vestnik RKhD*, no. 118 (1976), pp. 291–7.

64. *Vestnik RKhD*, no. 130 (1979), p. 310.

65. *Russkaya mysl*, 8 November 1979, p. 6.

66. *JMP*, no. 8 (1978), p. 7.

67. Originally published in *Vedomosti verkhovnogo soveta RSFSR*, no. 11 (19 May 1961), Edict 273, and amended in ibid., no. 38 (23 September 1965), Edict 932.

68. *Posev*, February 1976, p. 39.

69. 'Svidetelstvo svyashch. Yevgeniya Solodkogo' ('Testimony of the Priest Yevgeni Solodki'), 28 March 1980, *Vestnik RKhD*, no. 131 (1980), pp. 380–2.

70. *The Russian Orthodox Church: Organization, Situation, Activity* (Moscow Patriarchate, Moscow 1958), p. 72.

71. Yakunin Report, pp. 18–19.

72. *JMP*, no. 6 (1979), pp. 19–20, 44.

73. *JMP*, no. 1 (1980), pp. 23–4, 27.

74. *JMP*, no. 3 (1980), pp. 18–19.

75. *JMP*, no. 4 (1980), pp. 10–11, 14–15, 16–17.

76. *JMP*, no. 5 (1980), p. 20.

77. *JMP*, no. 1 (1980), p. 30 (English edition).

78. *JMP*, no. 4 (1980), p. 21 (English edition).

79. Letter to Patriarch Pimen from 12 parishioners (names and addresses appended, undated but from internal evidence written in 1978); *DCCDBR*, vol. 7, pp. 837–43. A

covering letter to the Patriarch from the Christian Committee is dated 6 December 1978, in ibid., pp. 831–2.

80. V. Moskvitin, 'Pastyr vo khmelyu' ('The Tipsy Pastor'), from unnamed, undated local Soviet newspaper, recounting incident on 21 February 1974 (photocopy of article in *DCCDBR*, vol. 7, p. 844).

81. Ibid., p. 839.

82. His behaviour and its consequences for the parish are described in several documents written by parishioners (*DCCDBR*, vol. 1, pp. 78–98; vol. 2, pp. 223–5).

83. *DCCDBR*, vol. 1, p. 84.

84. Ibid., pp. 84, 87.

85. Ibid., p. 87.

86. *DCCDBR*, vol. 2, p. 225.

87. *DCCDBR*, vol. 1, p. 88; *JMP*, no. 12 (1977), p. 6, which states that Bogolep was retired on 6 October 1977 at his own request because of a 'prolonged and serious illness'.

88. Biographical information, anonymous, undated, in *DCCDBR*, vol. 1, p. 118; and private letter from two Orthodox believers in Leningrad to a friend in the West, undated but before 14 October 1977 (copy in KC archive).

89. *USSR News Brief*, supplement no. 2 (30 June 1981).

90. 'Reports from Russia', no author but probably the Christian Committee for the Defence of Believers' Rights in the USSR, undated but after 13 June and before 19 November 1980 (typescript; copy in KC archive), p. 2.

91. 'Goneniya na svyashchennika' ('Persecution of a Priest'), anonymous, probably Kiev, soon after 15 January 1982, *AS*, no. 4603; *Vestnik RKhD*, no. 136 (1982), pp. 267–9.

92. *KNS*, no. 125 (4 June 1981), pp. 5–6.

93. *SMOT Information Bulletin*, no. 19 (August–September 1981), p. 32.

94. *Vestnik RKhD*, no. 136 (1982), pp. 270–1.

95. *KNS*, nos 184 (6 October 1983) and 188 (1 December 1983); *RFE/RL Research Paper*, RS 246/84, 16 November 1984.

96. English translation in *KNS*, no. 182 (8 September 1983).

97. Copy of Russian appeal and English translation in KC archive. See also *KNS*, nos 180 (11 August 1983) and 188 (1 December 1983).

4. Theological Education

1. The closure of the theological schools and the work involved in reopening them is described in Nikita Struve, *Christians in Contemporary Russia* (The Harvill Press, London, 1967), pp. 120–37.

2. Walter Kolarz, *Religion in the Soviet Union* (Macmillan, London, 1961), p. 90; he states that the figure of 1,500 students 'may be on the optimistic side'.

3. Compare the list of ten theological schools given in *The Russian Orthodox Church: Organization, Situation, Activity* (Moscow Patriarchate, Moscow), pp. 103–4, published in 1958; and of five theological schools given in *The Moscow Patriarchate 1917–1977* (Moscow Patriarchate, Moscow), p. 35, published in 1978.

4. *Russkaya mysl*, 31 October 1974, p. 5.

5. This report was published in Russian in *Religiya i ateizm v SSSR*, no. 131 (June 1978), pp. 2–17. However, we have chosen to quote from the author's later, slightly expanded, English version delivered as an address to a conference of the Fellowship of St Alban and St Sergius in Hoddesdon, England, in August 1978. A copy of this untitled, undated address is in KC archive, together with two letters to the present author, dated November 1981, in which Mr van der Voort has kindly clarified certain points. We have taken the liberty of correcting some phrases in the English text of his address.

6. *The Russian Orthodox Church: Organization, Situation, Activity*, p. 116.

7. *The Moscow Patriarchate 1917–1977*, p. 35.

8. Archbishop Pitirim (ed.), *The Orthodox Church in Russia* (Thames & Hudson, London, 1982), p. 243.

9. Jonathan Steele ('Churches Are Seen But Not Heard', *Guardian*, 20 November 1979) said there were 22 girls on the course, but a photograph in *JMP* (no. 5, 1980, p. 15) shows a photograph with a *total* of 22 students, of whom 4 are boys. In the same *JMP* report the rector said there were 'slightly over twenty' boys and girls (p. 16).

10. *JMP*, no. 9 (1980), p. 37.

11. *JMP*, nos 8 (1980), p. 17. and 9 (1981), pp. 27–8.

12. *Ecumenical Press Service*, 83, van. 33.

13. Theo van der Voort, untitled, undated report in KC archive, p. 10.

14. Raymond Oppenheim, 'Russian Orthodox Theological Education in the Soviet Union', *RCL*, vol. 2, no. 3 (1974), pp. 4–8, p. 7.

15. Ibid., p. 5.

16. Philippe Sabant, 'Religion in Russia Today', *The Tablet*, 19 January 1980, p. 55; confidential report from a visitor to the Soviet Union, 19 November 1979 (filed in KC archive).

17. *JMP*, no. 9 (1980), p. 37.

18. Archbishop Pitirim (ed.), *The Orthodox Church in Russia*, pp. 244, 248.

19. Ibid., p. 243.

20. Dimitri Pospielovsky, *The Russian Church under the Soviet Regime* (St Vladimir's Seminary Press, Crestwood, New York, 1984), p. 452. He attributes the success achieved by the church in sending theology students abroad to the late Metropolitan Nikodim (d. 1978), and the subsequent decline in this programme to the lack of dynamism of his successor, Metropolitan Yuvenali.

21. *The Moscow Patriarchate 1917–1977*, p. 36. Hierarchs' visits to the theological schools are frequently reported in *JMP*.

22. Van der Voort, untitled, undated report in KC archive, p. 7.

23. Oppenheim, 'Russian Orthodox Theological Education', pp. 5, 7, 8.

24. Confidential report in KC archive, 19 November 1979.

25. *Ostkirchliche Information*, 81-X/7.

26. Archbishop Kirill in the film *Candle in the Wind*.

27. Professor T. H. Rigby, Australian National University, Camberra, letter to the present author, 14 May 1984 (in KC archive).

28. Archbishop Pitirim (ed.), *The Orthodox Church in Russia*, p. 244.

29. Ibid., p. 242. Cf. the earlier church publication, *The Russian Orthodox Church*, compiled in 1980 (Progress, Moscow), which stated that there were 'many' candidates of theology, 48 masters and 15 doctors (p. 97). The awarding of 12 master's degrees over two years suggests the continuing expansion of higher theological education, while the fact that no doctorates were awarded over the same period perhaps reflects the high level of sustained academic achievement required for this degree.

30. Oppenheim, 'Russian Orthodox Theological Education', p. 5.

31. *The Russian Orthodox Church: Organization, Situation, Activity*, p. 115.

32. CRA Report for 1974, *Vestnik RKhD*, no. 130 (1979), p. 324.

33. *Russkaya mysl*, 31 October 1974, p. 5.

34. Oppenheim, 'Russian Orthodox Theological Education', p. 5.

35. Archbishop Pitirim (ed.), *The Orthodox Church in Russia*, p. 244.

36. William B. Stroyen, *Communist Russia and the Russian Orthodox Church 1943–1962* (The Catholic University of America Press Ltd, Washington DC, 1967), p. 72, citing *JMP*, no. 7 (1947), p. 26.

37. Ibid.

38. *The Russian Orthodox Church: Organization, Situation, Activity*, p. 117.

39. Van der Voort, untitled, undated report in KC archive, p. 10.

40. Struve, *Christians in Contemporary Russia*, pp. 124–5; Oppenheim, 'Russian Orthodox Theological Education', p. 4.

41. Oppenheim, 'Russian Orthodox Theological Education', p. 8.

42. Van der Voort, untitled, undated report in KC archive, p. 4; *JMP*, no. 3 (1978), pp. 15–17.

43. *The Catholic Herald*, 19 November 1980, reporting on a speech by Pitirim at a press conference in Rome. The increase of 100 students is more or less consistent with the figures quoted in the appendix to this chapter (pp. 120–1).

44. Oppenheim, 'Russian Orthodox Theological Education', p. 7; van der Voort, untitled,

undated report in KC archive, p. 5.

45. *JMP*, no. 1 (1979), p. 16.

46. Oppenheim, 'Russian Orthodox Theological Education', p. 7; van der Voort, untitled, undated report in KC archive, p. 5.

47. *Vestnik RKhD*, no. 130 (1979), pp. 322–3.

48. Oppenheim, 'Russian Orthodox Theological Education', pp. 5, 7, 8; Alan Nichols, 'Documentary Record on Australian Anglican Visit' (18-page duplicated typescript, KC archive).

49. Van der Voort, untitled, undated report in KC archive, p. 8.

50. Archbishop Pitirim (ed.), *The Orthodox Church in Russia*, p. 243.

51. Van der Voort, untitled, undated report in KC archive, pp. 8–9.

52. Oppenheim, 'Russian Orthodox Theological Education', p. 8.

53. *The Russian Orthodox Church: Organization, Situation, Activity*, pp. 117–8; Oppenheim, 'Russian Orthodox Theological Education', p. 8; van der Voort, untitled, undated report in KC archive, p. 6.

54. Van der Voort, ibid., p. 7.

55. Ibid., p. 6.

56. Ibid., pp. 6–7.

57. *The Russian Orthodox Church: Oganization, Situation, Activity*, p. 118.

58. Van der Voort, untitled, undated report in KC archive, p. 9.

59. *JMP*, no. 4 (1980), pp. 78–80.

60. *International Herald Tribune*, 19 June 1974.

61. Confidential report dated July 1976 (KC archive).

62. *Vestnik RKhD*, no. 130 (1979), p. 317.

63. Ibid., p. 318.

64. Ibid.

65. Van der Voort, untitled, undated report in KC archive, p. 10.

66. Ibid.

67. A. Levitin-Krasnov, 'Le KGB et les jeunes seminaristes russes', *Catacombes*, October 1975, p. 8. (Text of a speech given in Lucerne on 24 October 1974, shortly after Levitin's emigration from the USSR.)

68. Ibid.

69. Van der Voort, untitled, undated report in KC archive, p. 10.

70. A. Krasnov (pseudonym), 'V chas rassveta' ('At the Hour of the Dawn'), *Posev*, May 1968, p. 54.

71. Levitin-Krasnov, 'Le KGB'.

72. Van der Voort, untitled, undated report in KC archive, p. 11.

73. Open letter to Archbishop Vladimir of Vladimir and Suzdal, from Hierodeacon Varsonofi (Khaibulin), 23 November 1975 (typescript, KC archive), pp. 14–15.

74. Levitin-Krasnov, 'Le KGB'.

75. Father Lev Konin, 'Prekratit psikhiatricheskiye repressii v SSSR! Otkrytoye pismo pravoslavnogo svyashchennika iz psikhiatricheskogo zastenka' ('Stop Psychiatric Repression in the USSR! An Open Letter from an Orthodox Priest in a Psychiatric Torture-Chamber'), 6 May 1977, *DCCDBR*, vol. 1, pp. 112–16 (this quotation, pp. 114–15).

76. Levitin-Krasnov, 'Le KGB'.

77. Jonathan Steele, 'A Useful Opium for the State?', *Guardian*, 21 November 1979, p. 15. A similar story is recounted by one Father George, studying at the Moscow seminary, interviewed in a television programme broadcast in the USA. He grew up in a non-Christian family, but at the age of 15 entered a church in Moscow. He was intrigued, wanted to know more, and began to read all the theological books he could lay hands on. The result, he told his interviewer, Rev. Bruce Rigdon, was that 'gradually . . . my world views became religious ones' ('The Church of the Russians', part 2, an NBC Religious Program, in association with the National Council of Churches of Christ, original broadcast 17 July 1983).

78. Steele, 'A Useful Opium'.

79. *Russkaya mysl*, 31 October 1974, p. 5.

80. *The Russian Orthodox Church: Situation, Organization, Activity*, pp. 104, 115.

81. Van der Voort, untitled, undated report in KC archive, p. 7.

82. Oppenheim, 'Russian Orthodox Theological Education', p.8; Stroyen, *Communist*

Russia, pp. 79–80; Yakunin Report, p. 29.

83. Oppenheim, ibid.

84. Van der Voort, untitled, undated report in KC archive, pp. 7–8.

85. Paul Masson, *La Libre Belgique*, 12 October 1979 (Masson quoted Archbishop Kirill as saying that a quarter of the students were foreigners, but subsequent checking has shown that this in incorrect).

86. *Information Bulletin* of the Department of External Church Relations of the Moscow Patriarchate, no. 1 (1985), p. 16; this reported on decisions taken by the Holy Synod on 26 December 1984. See also *KNS*, no. 218 (7 February 1985), p. 13.

87. Oppenheim, 'Russian Orthodox Theological Education', p. 6.

88. A. Krasnov-Levitin, 'Bolnaya tserkov' ('The Ailing Church'), 27 August 1965, *AS*, no. 886, pp. 24–8.

89. The Yakunin Report, p. 29.

90. Van der Voort, untitled, undated report in KC archive, p. 11.

91. *Vestnik RKhD*, no. 130 (1979), p. 321.

92. Ibid., p. 319.

93. Ibid., p. 320.

94. Ibid., p. 323.

95. Van der Voort, untitled, undated report in KC archive, p. 12.

5. Monasticism

1. 'The Conversation of St Serafim with N. A. Motovilov', quoted from the English translation in G. P. Fedotov (ed.), *A Treasury of Russian Spirituality* (Sheed & Ward, London, 1977), p. 266.

2. These monasteries and convents are listed in the CRA Report for 1970, p. 26. All of them continue to be mentioned quite frequently in the 'From the Dioceses' section of the *JMP*.

3. L. I. Denisov, *Pravoslavnye monastyri Rossiiskoi imperii* (*Orthodox Monasteries of the Russian Empire*) (Izdaniye A. D. Stupina, Moscow, 1908).

4. CRA Report for 1970, p. 20, KC archive; Nikita Struve, *Christians in Contemporary Russia* (The Harvill Press, London, 1967), p. 90.

5. See, for example, W. Alexeev and T. Stavrou, *The Great Revival* (Burgess Publishing Company, Minneapolis, Minnesota, 1976), pp. 180–1.

6. CRA Report for 1970, pp. 22–3.

7. Alexander Bogolepov ('The Legal Position of the Russian Orthodox Church', in R. Marshall, T. Bird and A. Blane (eds), *Aspects of Religion in the USSR* (University of Chicago Press, London and Chicago, 1971), p. 206, gives a total of 89 monasteries at the beginning of the 1950s; the encyclopaedia *Der Grosse Herder* (vol. 7, p. 1441, quoted in *RL Research Paper*, no. 267/76 (20 May 1976)) gives a figure of 90 in 1958.

8. *The Russian Orthodox Church: Organization, Situation, Activity* (Moscow Patriarchate, Moscow, 1958), p. 78.

9. See Marite Sapiets, 'Monasticism in the Soviet Union', *RCL*, vol. 4, no. 1 (1976), p. 29; Struve, *Christians in Contemporary Russia*, pp. 303–10.

10. This figure was given on joining the World Council of Churches; J. A. Hebly, *The Russians and the World Council of Churches* (Christian Journals Ltd, Belfast, Dublin and Ottawa, 1978), p. 114.

11. *The Moscow Patriarchate 1917–1977* (Moscow Patriarchate, Moscow, 1978), p. 34.

12. CRA Report for 1970, p. 25.

13. Philippe Sabant, 'Religion in Russia Today', *The Tablet*, 19 January 1980, p. 55; Sapiets ('Monasticism', p. 30) states that there were about 90 monks in 1976, half of whom were ordained priests.

14. *JMP*, no. 7 (1983), p. 8.

15. Anon., *An Early Soviet Saint: The Life of Father Zachariah*, translated by Jane Ellis (Mowbrays, London and Oxford, 1976), pp. 52–3.

16. Sapiets, ('Monasticism', p. 30) states that there were about 60 monks in 1976; James

Moss ('The Remnants of Orthodox Monasticism', *The Chelsea Journal*, September–October 1976, p. 258), said that there were 80 monks in 1976; Sabant ('Religion in Russia Today', p. 55) gave a figure of 'about sixty monks and a score of novices' in 1980; and Paul Masson (*La Libre Belgique*, 15 October 1979) said that there were 100 monks, including 15 novices.

17. Sapiets, 'Monasticism', p. 31, quoting Anatoli Levitin.

18. Masson, *La Libre Belgique*.

19. Walter Kolarz, *Religion in the Soviet Union* (Macmillan, London, 1961), p. 74, footnote; he points out that the word is derived from the Greek *'lavros'*, 'meaning street or passageway and also a whole row of monastic cells'.

20. Moss, 'The Remnants', p. 257.

21. Alan Nichols, 'Documentary Record of Australian Anglican Visit' (18-page duplicate typescript in KC archive), p. 10; Moss ('The Remnants', p. 257) also states that there are 40 monks.

22. Sapiets, 'Monasticism', p. 31.

23. *The Orthodox Church*, March 1981, p. 7.

24. Sapiets, 'Monasticism'.

25. Reported by a French visitor in that year, according to Moss, 'The Remnants', p. 258.

26. The superior of the convent, Mother Margarita, said in an interview in February 1982 that the number of nuns 'had remained steady at about 100 for many years'. At that time there were 95 nuns; Nigel Wade, *Daily Telegraph*, 26 February 1982, p. 6. A slightly higher figure was given at the same time by Archbishop Makari of Uman, a suffragan of Kiev diocese, who said in an interview that there were 'up to 120 nuns' (film *Candle in the Wind*, Pacem Productions, California). This indicates that even people in a position to know the true figures often give approximations. Foreign visitors may or may not have a correct impression: Masson (*La Libre Belgique*) in 1979 said there were 105 nuns and Sabant in 1980 said there were 'over a hundred' ('Religion in Russia Today', p. 256); but Nichols, who visited the convent in 1976, reported 'fifty or so' nuns ('Documentary Record', p. 8).

27. *Daily Telegraph*, 26 February 1982, p. 6.

28. Moss, 'The Remnants', p. 258.

29. *Daily Telegraph*, 26 February 1982, p. 6.

30. Ibid.

31. Nichols, 'Documentary Record', p. 8.

32. Film *Candle in the Wind*.

33. Nichols, 'Documentary Record', p. 8; Moss, 'The Remnants', p. 258.

34. Masson, *La Libre Belgique*.

35. Moss, ('The Remnants', p. 258) says there were 150 nuns in 1976; Masson (*La Libre Belgique*) reported 96 nuns in 1979; and Sabant ('Religion in Russia Today', p. 56) said there were 'about 80' in 1980.

36. Script of 'The Church of the Russians', NBC television documentary, Part 2, p. 11.

37. Moss, 'The Remnants', p. 259; Sapiets, 'Monasticism', p, 32; *JMP*, no. 4 (1975), p. 12.

38. Sabant, 'Religion in Russia Today', p. 256; Sapiets ('Monasticism', p. 32) had stated there were 120 in 1976.

39. Sabant, 'Religion in Russia Today', p. 256.

40. Zagorsk, 53; Pskov, 66; Pochayev, 45; Odessa, 39; Vilnius, 26; Zhirovitsy, 61; Protecting Veil, Kiev, 168; St Florus, Kiev, 144; Korets, 144; Alexandrovka, 50; Krasnogorsk, 85; Mukachevo, 123; Chumalevo, 41; Zhabka, 70; Pühtitsa, 105; Riga, 55. Total, 1,275.

41. Sapiets, 'Monasticism', p. 33.

42. Ibid., p. 31; Moss, 'The Remnants', p. 258.

43. Sapiets, ('Monasticism', p. 31) and Moss ('The Remnants', p. 258) both say there were 150 nuns in 1976; Sabant ('Religion in Russia Today', p. 256) says that there were over 100 in 1980.

44. Michael Binyon, *The Times*, 28 March 1980, p. 16.

45. *RL Research Paper*, no. 267/76, p. 4; nine of the closed monasteries are listed.

46. *The Times*, 13 June 1983.

47. *JMP*, nos 9 (1983), pp. 7ff., 11, 12, and 1 (1984), pp. 9, 18, 19; *KNS*, no. 176 (16 June 1983), p. 4.

48. See his biography in *JMP*, no. 8 (1983), p. 26.

49. *JMP*, no. 1 (1984), p. 19.

50. *JMP*, no. 10 (1983), p. 2 (English and Russian versions).

51. CRA Report for 1970, p. 26.

52. Ibid., p. 22. An English translation of the section of the CRA Report on monasteries is found in *The Orthodox Monitor*, nos 11–12 (January–June 1981), pp. 87–97. (Translations in this chapter are the author's own.)

53. CRA Report for 1970, p. 24 and passim.

54. Yakunin Report, p. 25.

55. CRA Report for 1970, p. 21.

56. Ibid.

57. Ibid.

58. Ibid., p. 22.

59. Ibid., p. 24.

60. Ibid., p. 23.

61. Ibid.

62. Ibid.

63. Ibid., p. 24.

64. Ibid., p. 22.

65. Ibid., pp. 27–8.

66. Yakunin Report, pp. 26–7.

67. CRA Report for 1970, p. 28.

68. Nikolai Shemetov, 'Russkaya Pravoslavnaya Tserkov v nashi dni' ('The Russian Orthodox Church in Our Times'), Dialogue No. 4, *Religiya i ateizm v SSSR*, no. 171 (November 1981), p. 6.

69. The Yakunin Report, p. 28.

70. Masson, *La Libre Belgique*.

71. Film *Candle in the Wind*.

72. *Daily Telegraph*, 26 February 1982, p. 6.

73. Shemetov, 'The Russian Orthodox Church in Our Times', p. 5.

74. Tatyana Goricheva, 'Letters to a Spiritual Brother', January–June 1979, *Russia Cristiana*, no. 6 (1982), pp. 43–4. German translation in Tatiana Goritschewa, *Die Rettung der Verlorenen* (Brockhaus Verlag, Wuppertal, 1982), p. 43.

75. *KNS*, no. 184 (6 October 1983), p. 3.

76. Hegumen Savva, 'Reply to a Friend's Letter', the introduction to the *samizdat* book *Kratkoye opisaniye Pskovo-Pecherskogo Monastyrya* (*A Short Description of the Pskov Monastery of the Caves*), undated, KC archive; this translation is taken from *RCL*, vol. 4, no. 1 (1976), pp. 45–8.

77. See M. Bourdeaux, *Patriarch and Prophets* (reprinted Mowbrays, London and Oxford, 1975), for a letter describing the persecution, which was written by the Spiritual Council of the Pochayev Monastery, pp. 97–116; for accounts of the persecution of two of the monks, pp. 74–84; and for Grigorigan's statement, p. 267; also Anatoli Levitin, 'Golosuyet serdtse' ('The Heart Votes'), 12 March 1963 (typescript in KC archive).

78. Letter to Comrade V. V. Kuroyedov, chairman of the Council for Religious Affairs, from Archimandrite Samuil, superior of the Pochayev Lavra, and Hegumen Vsevolod, secretary of the Spiritual Council, 29 September 1973; *DCCDBR*, vol. 1, p. 43.

79. 'Reuter Concoction Refuted by Church Leader', interview by Archimandrite Samuil and Metropolitan Filaret of Kiev with a Novosti Press Agency correspondent, *Soviet News*, 12 March 1974, p. 91.

80. Letter to the chairman of the Ternopol regional executive committee from Archimandrite Yakov, 11 November 1976; *DCCDBR*, vol. 1, p. 44.

81. Letter to the Christian Committee for the Defence of Believers' Rights, to Father Gleb Yakunin, from Filipp Afanasevich Baidyug, undated but after August 1976 and before the end of 1977; *DCCDBR*, vol. 1, p. 45.

82. Reported by Anatoli Levitin, *Russkaya mysl*, 8 December 1977, p. 4.

83. *Russkaya mysl*, 29 June 1978, p. 5.

84. *KNS*, no. 112 (29 November 1980), pp. 15–16. See also *KNS*, no. 116 (29 January 1981), pp. 2–3.

85. For example, the festival on 4–5 August 1980 celebrated by Metropolitan Filaret of Kiev and five other bishops; *JMP*, no. 4 (1981), p. 15.

86. *JMP*, no. 12 (1975), pp. 8–11.

87. Anonymous *samizdat* report, 1981, 2pp. (photocopy of typed original in KC archive; English translation in *KNS*, no. 124 (21 May 1981), p. 13). See also report in *Vestnik RKhD*, no. 136 (1982), pp. 260–1, and summary in *KNS*, no. 141 (28 January 1982), p. 7.

88. Letters to Patriarch Pimen from Hegumen Apelli and Brother Nestor, both 12 August 1981, *Russkaya mysl*, 4 March 1982; English translation in *KNS*, no. 150 (4 June 1982), p. 10.

89. Appeal by Hegumen Apelli (Stankevich), undated but after August 1981 and before November 1982; English translation in *KNS*, no. 162 (18 November 1982), p. 12.

90. Struve, *Christians in Contemporary Russia*, p. 310; M. Bourdeaux, *Patriarch and Prophets*, (Mowbrays, London and Oxford, 1975), pp. 77ff.

91. *Russkaya mysl*, 18 October 1984, p. 7; English translation in *KNS*, no. 212 (8 November 1984), p. 23.

92. *Uspenskaya Pochayevskaya lavra* (izd. Moskovskoi Patriarkhii, Moscow, 1983), 16pp. with illustrations; see *JMP*, no. 7 (1983), p. 80.

93. Obituary in *JMP*, no. 6 (1975), pp. 19–20.

94. G. Gerodnik, *Pravda o Pskov-Pecherskom Monastyre* (*The Truth about the Pskov Caves Monastery*) (Izd. Politicheskoi Literatury, Moscow, 1963); A. Krasnov, 'Otvet G. Gerodniku' ('Reply to G. Gerodnik'), 1963 (English translation in Bourdeaux, *Patriarch and Prophets*, pp. 93–7).

95. CRA Report for 1970, p. 24.

96. Ibid.

97. Ibid., p. 25.

98. *JMP*, no. 7 (1975), p. 19.

99. Plea (*prosheniye*) to His Holiness Patriarch Pimen of Moscow and all Russia from Anastasiya Kleimenova, 27 October 1978; *DCCDBR*, vol. 7, pp. 835–6.

100. Letter to Patriarch Pimen of Moscow and All Russia from the Christian Committee for the Defence of Believers' Rights in the USSR, 16 December 1978; *DCCDBR*, vol. 7, pp. 831–2.

101. Untitled *samizdat* document, signed by 'Orthodox Christians', dated April 1983; English translation in *KNS*, no. 180 (11 August 1983), pp. 12–13.

102. The Yakunin Report, p. 6. See also Dimitri Pospielovsky, (*The Russian Orthodox Church under the Soviet Regime 1917–82* (St Vladimir's Seminary Press, Crestwood, New York, 1984), p. 429) who additionally cites 'oral testimony of Russian clerics'.

103. *KNS*, no. 180 (11 August 1983), p. 7.

104. Yakunin Report, pp. 27–8.

105. *Russkaya mysl*, 29 June 1978, p. 5.

106. Ibid.

107. Oxana Antic, 'The Condition of the Kiev Monastery of the Caves', *Radio Liberty Research*, RL 42/79, 7 February 1979.

108. *Pravda*, 11 November 1978, p. 3.

109. Declaration (*zayavleniye*) to the chairman of the Presidium of the Supreme Soviet of the USSR, Leonid Ilich Brezhnev, from Brothers of the Kiev Caves Lavra, 12 signatures, 18 September 1977; *DCCDBR*, vol. 2, p. 233 (English translation in *RCL*, vol. 7, no. 4 (1979), pp. 257–8).

110. Appeal (*obrashcheniye*) to L. I. Brezhnev from Alexander Ogorodnikov, Vladimir Poresh and Nikolai Khovansky, 10 November 1977; *DCCDBR*, vol. 1, p. 46.

111. Antic, 'Condition of the Kiev Monastery', p. 2; *Russkaya mysl*, 24 November 1977, p. 13.

112. 'To Orthodox Christians in the Soviet Union', from the Christian Committee for the Defence of Believers' Rights in the USSR, 11 November 1977, Moscow; *DCCDBR*, vol. 1, p. 36.

113. *Trud*, 5 June 1984; see commentary in *KNS*, no. 202 (21 June 1984), pp. 4–5.

114. Antic, 'Condition of the Kiev Monastery', p. 2.

115. 'K arestu pravoslavnoi monakhini Valerii Makeyevoi' ('On the Arrest of the Orthodox Nun Valeriya Makeyeva'), a report by her friends, unsigned, summer 1978; *DCCDBR*, vol. 7, p. 845 (English translation in *The Samizdat Bulletin*, no. 74 (June 1979)).

116. Appeal (*obrashcheniye*) by the Christian Committee for the Defence of Believers' Rights in the USSR, 24 April 1979; *DCCDBR*, vol. 10, pp. 1080–83.

117. *Vozzvaniye* (appeal) to Member of Parliament Mrs Margaret Thatcher from Abbess Magdalina of the community of nuns in Zhitomir (secular name Lyubov Nikanorovna Dubinovich), also signed by four other nuns (signatures illegible), undated but September–October 1979 (KC archive).

118. Circular from the Working Group on the Internment of Dissenters in Mental Hospitals, 3 September 1979, London.

119. *Vesti iz SSSR* (*News from the USSR*), no. 7 (1981), p. 8.

120. Appeal from Abbess Magdalina — see note 117.

121. Conversation between Anatoli Levitin and Jane Ellis, 12 March 1975 (tape-recording and transcribed summary in KC archive).

122. 'L'Eremo dello 'starets' Tavrion' ('The Hermitage of *Starets* Tavrion'), *Russia Cristiana*, no. 168 (1979), pp. 22–30 (English translation in *RCL*, vol. 10, no. 1 (1982), pp. 96–100; a different English translation was published in *The Orthodox Monitor*, nos 11–12 (January–June 1981), pp. 120–5.)

6. Publications

1. Paul Masson, *La Libre Belgique*, 11 October 1979.

2. Ibid.

3. John Paxton (ed.), *The Stateman's Year Book 1980–81* (Macmillan, London, 1980), pp. 1224, 1226.

4. '*The Moscow Patriarchate 1917–1977* (Moscow Patriarchate, Moscow, 1978), p. 26.

5. Walter Sawatsky, 'Bibles in Eastern Europe Since 1945', *RCL*, vol. 3, no. 6 (1975), p. 9.

6. Vladimir Rusak, 'Tipograficheskaya problema' ('The Problem of Printing'), p. 20 in *Svidetelstvo obvineniya. Tserkov i gosudarstvo v Sovetskom soyuze* (Testimony of the Prosecution, Church and State in the Soviet Union), *samizdat*, Moscow, 1980.

7. Sawatsky, 'Bibles', p. 13, note 8, which provides further details.

8. Rusak, 'Tipograficheskaya problema', p. 20.

9. Philippe Sabant, 'Religion in Russia Today', *The Tablet*, 19 January 1980, p. 56.

10. Rusak, 'Tipograficheskaya problema', p. 21.

11. Ibid.

12. *KNS*, no. 186 (3 November 1983).

13. Vladimir Pozner, '"Unexpected" Reason for Ban on Bible Imports', Radio Moscow in English for North America, 23.30 GMT, 21 January 1978, *Summary of World Broadcasts*, 26 January 1978, SU/5723/A1/6.

14. *Ecumenical Press Service*, no. 16 (8 June 1978), p. 7.

15. *One World*, no. 38 (July–August 1978), p. 6; *JMP*, no. 6 (1978), p. 3.

16. Pozner, '"Unexpected" Reason'.

17. *One Church*, no. 3 (1979), pp. 111–12; *UBS World Report*, no. 141 (January 1982).

18. *The Moscow Patriarchate 1917–1977*, pp. 26–7, and issues of *JMP* list the publications but not the numbers printed: these are given in the 1974 CRA Report (*Vestnik RKhD*, no. 130 (1979), p. 328), and *Episkepsis*, no. 252 (20 May 1981), p. 6.

19. Rusak, 'Tipograficheskaya problema', p. 22.

20. *Vestnik RKhD*, no. 130 (1979), p. 328.

21. Masson, *La Libre Belgique*.

22. Rusak, 'Tipograficheskaya problema', pp. 22, 23.

23. *The Russian Orthodox Church* (Progress, Moscow, 1982), p. 42.

24. *JMP*, no. 6 (1983), p. 80.

25. *The Moscow Patriarchate 1917–1977*, p. 27; *Vestnik RKhD*, no. 130 (1979), p. 326.

26. *Vestnik RKhD*, no. 130 (1979), p. 326.

27. CRA Report for 1970, (KC archive), p. 18; this gives the dates for publication of *JMP* in the 1930s, but states erroneously that it recommenced in 1941. The fortieth anniversary of the journal was celebrated by its staff on 22 September 1983 (*JMP*, no. 10 (1983), p. 5).

28. *Vestnik RKhD*, no. 130, (1979), p. 327.

29. Ibid., p. 328; CRA Report for 1970, p. 18.

30. The Yakunin Report, p. 34.

31. Masson, *La Libre Belgique*.

32. Rusak, 'Tipograficheskaya problema', p. 21, 22.

33. *Vestnik RKhD*, no. 130 (1979), p. 329.

34. Rusak, 'Tipograficheskaya problema', pp. 21, 22.

35. *Vestnik RKhD*, no. 130 (1979), p. 328.

36. The Yakunin Report, p. 34.

37. Ibid., p. 35.

38. CRA Report for 1970, p. 18.

39. Luzhin, '*Gosudarstvobesiye*', *Vestnik RKhD*, no. 118 (1976), p. 264.

40. A. Levitin-Krasnov, 'Censorship and Freedom of Speech', *Radio Liberty Research*, RS 85/79, 25 May 1979; reprinted in *The Orthodox Monitor*, nos 9–10 (July–December 1980), pp. 31–3.

41. Rusak, 'Tipograficheskaya problema', pp. 6–12.

42. *Vestnik RKhD*, no. 130 (1979), p. 329.

43. Ibid., p. 330.

44. Ibid.

45. Ibid., p. 331.

46. Ibid., pp. 329–30.

47. Ibid., p. 332.

48. Ibid.

49. Ibid., p. 333.

50. Ibid., p. 337.

51. Rusak, 'Tipograficheskaya problema', pp. 24–8.

52. 'Soviet Archbishop at Media Festival', *The Orthodox Church*, September 1979, p. 7.

53. Letter to the publisher Zhizn s Bogom (La Vie avec Dieu), from 'a priest', Moscow, October 1979; *Religiya i ateizm v SSSR*, April 1980, p. 13.

54. *Sovetskaya Rossiya*, 8 and 9 July 1982. Reports of the searches and arrests are given in *Vestnik RKhD*, no. 136 (1982), pp. 277–8; *USSR News Brief*, no. 10 (1982); *KNS*, no. 151 (17 June 1982), p. 6; analysis in *KNS*, no. 180 (11 August 1983), p. 10.

55. *KNS*, nos 155 (12 August 1982), p. 2, and 158 (23 September 1982), pp. 12–13; also *samizdat* appeals and reports by Krakhmalnikova's husband, Felix Svetov, and others in KC archive.

56. Rusak, 'Tipograficheskaya problema', p. 18.

57. Michael Binyon, 'Moscow Opens Lavish Bible Centre', *The Times*, 23 September 1981, p. 6; correction 6 October 1981, p. 8; *JMP*, no. 1 (1982), p. 22.

58. Rusak, 'Tipograficheskaya problema', p. 19.

7. The Laity

1. Pierre Pascal, *The Religion of the Russian People* (Mowbrays, London and Oxford, 1976), pp. 51–3.

2. Alexei Puzin, *Religion in the USSR* (Novosti Press Agency Publishing House, Moscow, 1967), p. 32.

3. Yu. T. Mashkov, 'Golos s rodiny' ('A Voice from the Homeland'), *Russkoye vozrozhdeniye*, no. 4 (1978), p. 12.

4. For example, an article reporting on an Australian Anglican visit to the Russian Orthodox Church gave an estimate of 'between 40 and 50 million members' (*Southern Cross*, August 1976, p. 4), while an American journal asserts that 'according to USSR government estimates' there are '30 million members who regularly attend services', adding that 'some Orthodox priests put baptised membership at 60 million' (*Time*, 23 June 1980, p. 54).

5. For example, Archbishop Pitirim was quoted in a *samizdat* source as having given a figure of 30–50 million believers (F. Luzhin, 'Gosudarstvobesiye' ('State Demonism'), *Vestnik RKhD*, no. 118 (1976), p. 264.

6. Robert Conquest (ed.), *Religion in the USSR* (The Bodley Head, London, 1968), p. 64,

citing *World Christian Handbook*, p. 221.

7. Jonathan Steele, *Guardian*, 20 November 1979. (The context makes it appear that Khrizostom was referring to religious believers in general, but from our knowledge of the approximate size of other religious bodies, it is clear that his 36—40 million applied to the Orthodox Church.)

8. 'The Church in the Soviet Union', interview with Anatoli Levitin-Krasnov, *Russkaya mysl*, 5 December 1974, p. 5.

9. According to the 1979 census, the populations of these republics were: RSFSR 136.5 million; Ukraine 50 million; Belorussia 10 million; Moldavia 4 million; a total of 200.5 million.

10. It is of interest that Western estimates of the number of Russian Orthodox believers have risen considerably over the last 10 or 15 years, as the facts of the church's life have become more widely known. This is shown most strikingly in the report on religious conditions in the USSR and Eastern Europe prepared by a working party of the East—West Relations Advisory Committee of the British Council of Churches (Trevor Beeson, *Discretion and Valour* (London, Collins/Fontana, 1974; Collins/Fount, 1982)). The first, 1974 edition stated that 'informed observers usually estimate figures ranging between 25 and 30 million' (p. 77). The revised edition of 1982, having reviewed pertinent evidence, concluded: 'Taking the evidence as a whole, it seems reasonable to suppose that the number of Orthodox believers in the Soviet Union is not much less than fifty million' (p. 58).

11. Christel Lane, *Christian Religion in the Soviet Union. A Sociological Study* (Allen & Unwin, London, 1978), p. 46.

12. Ibid.

13. William C. Fletcher, 'Backwards From Reactionism: The De-modernization of the Russian Orthodox Church', in Dennis J. Dunn (ed.), *Religion and Modernization in the Soviet Union* (Westview Press, Boulder, Colorado, 1977), p. 228.

14. William C. Fletcher, *Soviet Believers. The Religious Sector of the Population* (The Regents Press of Kansas, Lawrence, 1981), pp. 208—9, 211.

15. Ibid., in the chapter 'The Number of Believers', pp. 57—74.

16. Ibid., pp. 209—11.

17. There are other religious groups not yet mentioned which should also be included here, but their numbers, so far as is known, are not significant. Orthodox sects as the Molokans, Dukhobors, and others still exist, but are probably numbered only in thousands, and the same is true of Protestant sects such as the Jehovah's Witnesses. However, there are almost certainly more than a million Old Believers (Lane, *Christian Religion in the Soviet Union*, p. 114), though information about them is scarce. Another sizable group about whom very little is known is the True Orthodox (who went underground in the 1920s and 1930s in opposition to the Russian Orthodox leadership's policy of accommodation with the Soviet state). They are still believed to be widely spread (Lane, ibid., pp. 89—90; Fletcher, *The Russian Orthodox Church Underground 1917—1970* (Oxford University Press, London, 1971) Chapter 8, *passim*), but there is no indication of this group's current size, though Lane concludes that it is 'not insignificant in numerical terms'. It is quite possible that some of those identified by Soviet sociologists as Orthodox are in fact True Orthodox, though it is equally possible that the strong emphasis on secrecy fostered by the True Orthodox would lead them to avoid sociological questionnaires or supply misleading replies. We should therefore allow a minimum figure of 2 million for the Old Believers, True Orthodox and smaller sects, while noting that the number of True Orthodox might have to be revised upwards.

18. Nikita Struve, *Christians in Contemporary Russia* (The Harvill Press, London, 1967), p. 176.

19. Lane, *Christian Religion in the Soviet Union*, p. 60.

20. Fletcher, *Soviet Believers*, pp. 186—94.

21. Christopher A. P. Binns, 'Soviet Secular Ritual: Atheist Propaganda or Spiritual Consumerism?', *RCL*, vol. 10, no. 3 (1982), pp. 304—5.

22. Alan Nichols, 'Documentary Record of Australian Anglican Visit' (18-page duplicate typescript in KC archive), p. 4.

23. Father Dimitri Dudko, 'Kreshcheniye na Rusi' ('Baptism in Russia'), *Vestnik RKhD*, no. 117 (1976), pp. 188—208.

24. Steele, *Guardian*, 21 November 1979, p. 15.

25. Ye. Duluman, 'Narusheniye pravoporyadka i koshchunstvo' ('Violation of Law and

Order and Blasphemy'), *Pravda Ukrainy*, 11 March 1973, p. 3.

26. Film *Candle in the Wind* (Pacem Productions, California, 1982), p. 9 of script.

27. *Komsomolskaya pravda*, 18 January 1985; report in *KNS*, no. 217 (24 January 1985).

28. Letter to the Committee for Human Rights at the United Nations (*sic*) from residents of Vladimirets raion, Rovno oblast, Ukrainian SSR, 21 signatures, dated 15 February 1978 (?); *DCCDBR*, vol. 2, p. 227. See below for fuller comment.

29. Yu. Safronov, 'Avtoritet ateista' ('The Authority of the Atheist'), *Izvestiya*, 12 November 1971, p. 3.

30. Binns, 'Soviet Secular Ritual', p. 303.

31. Fletcher, *Soviet Believers*, p. 185.

32. Ibid., pp. 194–6.

33. Lane, *Christian Religion in the Soviet Union*, p. 60.

34. Ibid., p. 61; Binns, 'Soviet Secular Ritual', p. 304.

35. Binns, 'Soviet Secular Ritual', p. 305.

36. Lane, *Christian Religion in the Soviet Union*, p. 60.

37. Ibid., p. 41.

38. Lane, *Christian Religion in the Soviet Union*, p. 60.

39. Fletcher, *Soviet Believers*, p. 197.

40. Ibid., p. 185.

41. Ibid., p. 195.

42. Gleb Rahr, 'Combien d'Orthodoxes y a-t-il en Russie?', *Catacombes*, February 1973, pp. 6 and 12. Rahr's figure of 115 million Orthodox believers represented 60 per cent of the traditionally Orthodox population of the USSR. Some Soviet *émigrés* might dispute such a figure, but one, A. Udodov, who had spent some time in labour camps and had later lived in Minsk, stated that he thought that Rahr's figure of sixty per cent of Orthodox believers was about right (Skol'ko pravoslavnykh v Rossii?' ('How many Orthodox Are There in Russia?'), *Posev*, February 1976, pp. 38–41).

43. *Vestnik RKhD*, no. 130 (1979), p. 328.

44. Lane, *Christian Religion in the Soviet Union*, p. 47.

45. Ibid., pp. 47–8.

46. Fletcher, *Soviet Believers*, pp. 76–82.

47. Ibid., pp. 82–5.

48. Lane, *Christian Religion in the Soviet Union*, p. 47.

49. Fletcher, *Soviet Believers*, pp. 85–9. Fletcher cites figures which show that in the late 1960s the Soviet population was made up to 54.9 per cent women (114,776,000) and 45.04 per cent men (94,050,000), while the population over the age of 50 consisted of 65.11 per cent women. In the RSFSR (a traditionally Orthodox region) the disparity was more pronounced: 55.6 per cent women to 44.4 per cent men in 1969, though this was an improvement on the 1959 figures of 59 per cent women and 41 per cent men (p. 88).

50. Ibid., p. 92.

51. Ibid., pp. 94–9 (quote p. 99).

52. Lane, *Christian Religion in the Soviet Union*, p. 48.

53. Fletcher, *Soviet Believers*, p. 95.

54. M. K. Teplyakov, 'Sostoyaniye religioznosti naseleniya i otkhod veruyushchikh ot religii v Voronezhskoi oblast (1961–1964 gg)' ('The Situation of the Religiousness of the Population and the Departure of Believers from Religion in the Voronezh Region (1961–1964)'), in N. P. Krasnikov (ed.), *Voprosy preodoleniya religioznykh perezhitkov v SSSR* (*Problems of Overcoming Religious Survivals in the USSR*) (Nauka, Moscow, 1966), pp. 31–52, cited by Fletcher, *Soviet Believers*, p. 101.

55. Fletcher, *Soviet Believers*, pp. 99–105.

56. D. M. Ugrinovich, *Vvedeniye v teoreticheskoye religiovedeniye* (*Introduction to Theoretical Religious Studies*), Moscow, 'Mysl' (Mysl, Moscow, 1973), p. 137; cited by Fletcher, *Soviet Believers*, p. 103. Fletcher notes that Ugrinovich did not indicate what became of the remaining 7.8 per cent.

57. Fletcher, *Soviet Believers*, p. 111.

58. Lane, *Christian Religion in the Soviet Union*, p. 48.

59. Ibid., p. 49.

60. Anatoli Levitin-Krasnov, 'Religion and Soviet Youth', *RCL*, vol. 7, no. 4 (1979),

pp. 234–5.

61. Ibid., p. 236.

62. Letter to the Committee for Human Rights at the United Nations (*sic*) from residents of Vladimirets raion, Rovno oblast, Ukrainian SSR, 21 signatures, dated 15 February 1978 (?); *DCCDBR*, vol. 2, p. 227.

63. '"Bezobidny" Kompromiss?' ('A "Harmless" Compromise?'), *Komsomolskaya pravda*, 29 September 1980; quoted in *KNS*, no. 109 (16 October 1980), pp. 7–8.

64. 'Shkola molodogo ateista' ('School of the Yound Atheist'), *Molodyozh Moldavii*, (28 March 1981); cited in *KNS*, no. 122 (24 April 1981), p. 7.

65. *Nauka i religiya*, no. 4 (1982); cited in *KNS*, no. 149 (20 May 1982), pp. 2–3.

66. Letter to 'The deeply-respected head of our Russian Orthodox Church, Father Pimen', from Zinaida Romanovna Girinkova, undated but after 31 August 1977 and before spring 1978; *DCCDBR*, vol. 1, pp. 108–10.

67. *Human Rights in the USSR*, no. 6 (1973), p. 13.

68. *Nauka i religiya*, no. 12 (1970), p. 14.

69. *Russkaya mysl*, 13 May 1982, p. 7.

70. *Sovetskaya Rossiya* (18 May 1984); see *KNS*, no. 201 (1984), p. 3.

71. 'Elgin Greets Soviet Union Churchmen', *Daily Courier News* (Elgin, Illinois), 6 March 1975, p. 10.

72. *Episkepsis*, 1 June 1977, p. 6.

73. 'Garantirovano vsem' ('Guaranteed to Everyone'), *Golos rodiny*, no. 1 (1980), p. 7.

74. Kornel and Nekrasov, 'Khameleon' ('The Chameleon'), *Moskovsky komsomolets*, 11 April 1959. 'More on the Chameleon', ibid., 13 October 1959.

75. A. Krasnov, 'O dvukh yumoristicheskikh statyakh i odnom seryoznom dele' ('On Two Humorous Articles and One Very Serious Matter'), *Dialog s tserkovnoi Rossiei* (Ichthus, Paris, 1967), pp. 21–9.

76. Information (*spravka*) signed by the deputy-head of administration of Moscow State University hostels, signature illegible, undated; *DCCDBR*, vol. 4, p. 512.

77. Statement (*zayavleniye*) to the rector of Moscow State University, Academician Logunov, from Sergei Borisovich Bogdanovsky, undated; *DCCDBR*, vol. 4, pp. 509–10 (this quotation p. 510).

78. Statement to the Moscow State University Committee of the Young Communist League, from Sergei Borisovich Bogdanovsky, 15 May 1978; *DCCDBR*, vol. 4, p. 511.

79. Information, reporting on Young Communist League meeting of 15 May 1978; *DCCDBR*, vol. 4, p. 511.

80. Extract from Order No. 232 UbB, 15 May 1978, signed B. M. Logvinenko, official stamp (illegible on copy received); *DCCDBR*, vol. 4, p. 513.

81. Open letter to the editor of *Literaturnaya gazeta* (*Literary Gazette*) from Alexander Ogorodnikov, 27 April 1977; English translation in Father Gleb Yakunin and Lev Regelson, *Letters from Moscow*, ed. Jane Ellis (co-published by Keston College and H. S. Dakin Company, San Francisco, 1978), pp. 110–2 (this quotation p. 110).

82. Boris Roshchin, 'Svoboda religii i klevetniki' ('Freedom of Religion and the Slanders'), *Literaturnaya gazeta*, 13 April 1977; English translation in Yakunin and Regelson, *Letters from Moscow*, p. 75.

83. *KNS*, no. 112 (29 November 1980), p. 19.

84. The Yakunin Report, p. 24.

85. B. Shirskov, 'Ubezhdat faktami' ('Convince by Facts'), *Meditsinskaya Gazeta* (Medical Gazette), 24 March 1970.

86. I. I. Ogryzko, *Deti i religiya* (*Children and Religion*) (Lenizdat, Leningrad, 1970), pp. 57–8.

87. Michael Bourdeaux, *Patriarch and Prophets* (reprinted Mowbrays, London and Oxford, 1975), p. 171.

88. Ibid., pp. 196–8, 202, 220.

89. Ibid., pp. 306, 309–10.

90. Yakunin and Regelson, *Letters from Moscow*, pp. 89, 92.

91. Letter from Father Sergi Zheludkov to Dr Philip Potter, General Secretary of the WCC, 10 April 1976, p. 3; in *Religiya i ateizm v SSSR*, May 1976, pp. 11–13.

92. Anatoli Levitin-Krasnov, 'Zemlya dybom' ('The Earth Turned Upside Down'),

Moscow, March 1974, *AS*, no. 1876, pp. 79–80.

93. V svete preobrazheniya (*In the Light of the Transfiguration*), no. 44 (62) (December 1979); in *Russkaya mysl*, 14 February 1980, p. 5.

94. Letter from Bishop Feodosi of Poltava and Kremenchug to L. I. Brezhnev, Poltava, 26 October 1977, *AS*, no. 4456, pp. 19ff., 27–8.

95. Ibid., p. 21.

96. Donald A. Lowrie and William C. Fletcher, 'Khrushchev's Religious Policy', in R. Marshall, T. Bird and A. Blane (eds), *Aspects of Religion in the Soviet Union* (University of Chicago Press, Chicago and London, 1971), p. 139, citing Yu. Rozenbaum, 'Takoi zakon yest' ('There Is Such a Law'), in *Nauka i religiya*, no. 4 (1964), pp. 83–5, and no. 8 (1964), p. 89.

97. 'Circular of the Council for Russian Orthodox Church Affairs', Marshall, Bird and Blane (eds), *Aspects of Religion in the Soviet Union*, pp. 459–60.

98. Circular no. 1917, 22 December 1964, signed on behalf of Patriarch Alexi by Archpriest Victor Ippolitov, secretary of the Metropolitan of Krutitsy and Kolomna; text given in Anatoli Levitin, 'Bolnaya Tserkov' ('The Ailing Church'), *samizdat* typescript, Moscow, 1965, p. 11; also referred to in the open letter to Patriarch Alexi from Fathers Nikolai Eshliman and Gleb Yakunin, 21 November 1965 (English translation in Bourdeaux, *Patriarch and Prophets*, p. 197).

99. *Veche*, no. 4 (31 January 1972), *AS*, no. 1140, pp. 170–1.

100. *Vestnik RKhD*, no. 118 (1976), p. 290.

101. Duluman, 'Narusheniye'.

102. 'Soobshcheniya iz Rossii' ('Report from Russia'), anon., undated but between 13 June and 19 November 1980 (typescript in KC archive).

103. Letter to the 'Minister of Internal Affairs, Shchelokhov, from the Christian Committee for the Defence of Believers' Rights, undated but after 9 August 1977, and before spring 1978; *DCCDBR*, vol. 1, p. 3.

104. Letter to citizen V. A. Kapitanchuk from R. Gadeliya, major of the Ministry of Internal Affairs in the Abkhazian Autonomous SSR (Georgia), dated (illegible) 1977; *DCCDBR*, vol. 2, p. 226.

105. *Frankfurter Allgemeine Zeitung*, cited in *KNS*, no. 130 (13 August 1981), pp. 6–7.

106. *The Ukrainian Review*, no. 4 (1976), p. 88.

107. V. Shevelev, '*Neprostaya arifmetika*' ('Not Simple Arithmetic'), *Nauka i religiya*, no. 2 (1973), pp. 46–8.

108. *KNS*, no. 125 (4 June 1981), pp. 5–6.

109. Anatoli Kuznetsov, *Religiya i ateizm v SSSR* no. 5 (104) (April 1976), p. 3.

110. Father Gleb Yakunin, open letter to the Politburo of the CPSU, 19 April 1975; English translation in Yakunin and Regelson, *Letters from Moscow*, p. 32.

8. The Episcopate

1. *JMP*, no. 1 (1954); the words are those of Patriarch Alexi.

2. *JMP*, no. 11 (1980); the words are those of Metropolitan Alexi of Tallinn, quoting the words used by the future Patriarch Sergi at his episcopal consecration.

3. *Prosheniye* (plea) to Patriarch Pimen from Father Gleb Yakunin, 17 April 1976, *AS*, no. 2563, p. 4.

4. In fact, for unknown reasons, Bishop Ilian did not go to Czechoslovakia, and has remained in the USSR. It has been suggested that the local population in Czechoslovakia might have objected to receiving a Soviet bishop. However, another bishop consecrated, like Ilian, in 1979 for service in Czechoslovakia, has settled there: Bishop Nikanor of Podolsk, a suffragan of Moscow diocese. Ilian was assigned to Perm diocese because of the illness, then death (on 3 June 1981) of Archbishop Nikolai (Bychkovsky), *JMP*, no. 9 (1981), pp. 25–6).

5. These six are: Bishop Anatoli of Ufa and Sterlitamak, who has served in Damascus; Archbishop Leonti of Simferopol and Crimea, who has served in Damascus and Central Europe; Bishop Maxim of Omsk and Tyumen and Archbishop Nikodim of Kharkov and Bogodukhov, who have both served in Argentina; Bishop Varfolomei of Tashkent and Central

Asia, who has served in Vienna; and Archbishop Vladimir of Krasnodar and Kuban, who has served in Geneva, Damascus and Berlin.

6. See Nikita Struve, *Christians in Contemporary Russia* (The Harvill Press, London, 1967), pp. 162–4; and Nadezhda Teodorovich in her essay, 'The Rejuvenation of the Russian Clergy', in William C. Fletcher and Anthony J. Strover (eds), *Religion and the Search of New Ideals in the USSR* (Praeger, New York, Washington and London, 1967), pp. 36 and 38.

7. *The Moscow Patriarchate 1917–1977* (Moscow Patriarchate, Moscow, 1978), p. 28.

8. This is pointed out by Struve, *Christians in Contemporary Russia*, p. 142.

9. The chief instances of this practice are: Archbishop Damian (Marchuk), assigned to the diocese of Volhynia, where he was born, since 1964; Archbishop Gedeon (Dokunin), born in Siberia, who has governed Novosibirsk diocese since 1972; Archbishop Ioann (Snychev) of Kuibyshev, who spent his childhood in the neighbouring region of Orenburg; Metropolitan Ioann (Wendland), who has served in Yaroslavl diocese since 1967, though he was born and grew up in Leningrad; Archbishop Iosif (Savrash) who, as bishop of his native Ivano-Frankovsk since 1957, has the longest period of unbroken service in a single diocese; Archbishop Kassian (Yaroslavsky), Bishop of Kostroma since 1964, who was born in nearby Yaroslavl; Archbishop Leonti (Bondar), who has been in the diocese of Orenburg since 1963, though most of his life previously had been spent in Belorussia and Lithuania; Archbishop Nikodim (Rusnak), bishop of Kharkov since 1970, who was born in Ukraine; Metropolitan Nikolai (Yurik), bishop of his native Lvov since 1965; Archbishop Pimen (Khmelevsky), born in Smolensk but bishop of Saratov since 1965. This makes a total of ten bishops who have served in the same diocese for at least ten years. There are several other bishops who have remained continuously in one diocese for a number of years, an indication that the policy may be continuing.

10. 'Church-State Relations in the USSR', Radio Moscow in English for North America, 00.30 GMT, 26 February 1977; *Summary of World Broadcasts*, SU/5459/B/1, 10 March 1977.

11. 'Interview Given by Metropolitan Filaret of Kiev and Galich to a Novosti Press Agency Correspondent', *JMP*, no. 5 (1976), p. 5 (English edition).

12. BBC External Services, Current Affairs Research and Information Section, Report no. 1/75, 5 February 1975, 'Statement by Metropolitan Yuvenali, Head of the Foreign Relations Department of the Moscow Patriarchate, Recorded for the BBC on 26 January 1975'. The statement has been published in *RCL*, vol. 3, nos 1–3 (January–June 1975), pp. 24–5.

13. Interview with the magazine *Gésu* (*Jesus*) published in Milan; quotations here taken from extracts in Russian translation in *Posev*, no. 2 (1980), pp. 41–2.

14. Bishop Serapion of Irkutsk, quoted in an interview by Vladimir Smirnov of Novosti Press Agency, 25 April 1978 (KC archive).

15. Archbishop Mstislav of Kirov, interviewed by *Golos rodiny*, no. 11 (1969), p. 4.

16. Archbishop Nikodim of Kharkov, interviewed by *Golos rodiny*, no. 18 (1980), p. 12.

17. Reported in *CSCE Weekly Review*, 29 February–6 March 1980, p. 5; and idea nos 11–12, 1980 (17 March 1980), p. 3.

18. *Religiya i ateizm v SSSR*, April 1980, pp. 6–7.

19. A report of the meeting was issued under the title 'Threats to Peace' by the World Council of Churches Executive Committee, Liebfrauenberg, Woerth, France, 11–15 February 1980, Document No. 19 (revised), Final Version (copy in KC archive); some background to the meeting and the vote is given in a *Radio Liberty Research Paper*, 21 February 1980, RL 76/80.

20. *Vestnik RKhD*, no. 114 (1974), pp. 268–70.

21. *Service Orthodox de presse et d'information* (*SOP*), no. 15 (February 1977), p. 5.

22. The quotations below from the section of the 1974 CRA Report on the episcopate have all been taken from *Vestnik RKhD*, no. 130 (1979), pp. 276–80, 284 and 286–7.

23. The list must be dated after 3 September 1974 because it reflects the appointment on that date of Bishop German to the diocese of Vilnius. It is also dated after 23 October, the date of the death of Archbishop Mefodi of Omsk, who does not appear on the list. (Mefodi was 'widely believed to have been murdered as recently as 1974', according to Trevor Beeson, *Discretion and Valour* (second revised edition, Collins, London, 1982), p. 78.) It must be dated before 26 December because it does not reflect the translation of Bishop Maxim from Argentina to Minsk, which the Holy Synod decided on that day. (See the decisions of the Holy Synod in *JMP*, nos 11 (1974), p. 3, and 2 (1975), p. 2; and the report of Archbishop Mefodi's

death in no. 12 (1974), p. 15.)

24. The 14 missing bishops are: the five permanently based in Western Europe — Vasili in Brussels, Iakov in the Hague, Serafim in Zurich, Pyotr (L'Huillier) in France (who transferred to the Autocephalous Orthodox Church of America in 1979) and Antoni in London; Nikolai in Tokyo; Irinei and Alexi in West Germany; Filaret in Berlin and Maxim in Argentina; Mark in San Francisco and Makari in New York (until 26 December, when he was sent to Geneva); Viktorin for a brief spell in Vienna (3 September–13 March); and Serapion in Damascus, until he was recalled to Irkutsk on 17 April 1975.

25. Of the remaining seven hierarchs in this category, Archbishop Grigori of Mukhachevo retired, and Metropolitans Palladi of Orel, Serafim of Krutitsy and Kolomna and Iosif of Alma-Ata, Archbishop Alipi of Vinnitsa and Bishops Iona of Stavropol, Platon of Voronezh and Nikolai of Perm have all died. Metropolitan Serafim had been assigned to the first category only 'recently'.

26. Four members of the second category had died; Metropolitan Nikodim of Leningrad and Archbishops Mikhail of Kazan, Mstislav of Kirov and Yermogen of Krasnodar (then Bishop of Kalinin); and Archbishop (then Bishop) Kliment of Sverdlovsk has retired.

27. Six of the seven remaining hierarchs in this category have died: Archbishops Veniamin of Cheboksary, Palladi of Zhitomir, Flavian of Gorky, Feodosi of Ufa, and Ioasaf of Rostov; and Bishop Bogolep of Kirov; and Archbishop Donat of Kaluga has retired.

28. Anatoli Levitin has pointed out that this is sufficient grounds for regarding the entire episcopate of the church as uncanonical. 'A bishop is considered canonical when he has been elected by his flock and then confirmed and consecrated by a council of bishops. Any kind of participation at all in the election of a bishop by a civil authority, according to the canons, renders the consecration invalid and the consecrated person is unfrocked' (See 'My Reply to Hieromonk Chrysostomus' (*Russkaya mysl*, 13 March 1975, p. 8), for Levitin's debate with Chrysostomus on this subject.

29. Yakunin Report, p. 11.

30. Ibid.

31. *JMP*, no. 12 (1975), p. 10.

32. Ibid., pp. 13–14.

33. *Vestnik RKhD*, no. 116 (1975), pp. 225–9; this translation taken from Translation Service no. 9 (1976), 'The Voice of Soviet Christians', 25 March 1976, Keston College.

34. These conversations are recorded in an untitled section of the CRA Report. They are dated between 31 March 1966 and 26 February 1968; some are signed by A. Plekhanov and some are unsigned. The conversations on this date with Metropolitans Pimen and Alexi are published in *Vestnik RKhD*, no. 132 (1980), pp. 203–5; the remainder are in KC archive.

35. See, *inter alia*: the official obituary of Metropolitan Nikodim in *JMP*, no. 4 (1979), pp. 25–29; the obituary by D. Pospielovsky, 'Metropolitan Nikodim and His Times', *Posev*, no. 2 (1979), pp. 21–6; comments by D. Pospielovsky, John Lawrence and Paul Oestreicher, *RCL*, vol. 6, no. 4 (1978), pp. 227–34; and comments by Anatoli Levitin-Krasnov in his *samizdat* article 'The Ailing Church', 27 August 1965, *AS*, no. 886. Beeson (*Discretion and Valour*, pp. 78–80) gives a good summary, but cf. Raymond Oppenheim's review in *RCL*, vol. 11, no. 1 1983, pp. 109–12.

36. *RCL*, vol. 6, no. 4 (1978), p. 232.

37. *JMP*, no. 4 (1979), pp. 24–7.

38. In 1969 the Russian Orthodox Church issued an encyclical allowing Roman Catholics to receive confession and communion from Orthodox priests, and the Roman Catholic reciprocated. This was done on Nikodim's initiative, and his official explanation was that it applied to cases where Roman Catholics lacked their own clergy and in cases of emergency. This explanation would appear not to cover tourists to Leningrad, where there is an open Catholic church. Also, Nikodim gave communion to Roman Catholic clergy and laity at an Orthodox liturgy which he celebrated during a visit to the Vatican. See Dimitri Pospielovsky, *RCL*, vol. 6, no. 4 (1978), p. 228.

39. *JMP*, no. 19 (1975), p. 50 (English edition).

40. 'A Changing World (Information and Analysis of Theological and Pastoral Trends in the Church Following the Meeting in Zagorsk in 1973)', delivered in the Roman Catholic Church in Trento, 24 June 1975; *JMP*, no. 10 (1975), pp. 47–53.

41. *JMP*, no. 10 (1975), p. 51.

42. For example, a letter of the Christian Committee for the Defence of Believers' Rights in the USSR to the successor of Pope John-Paul I, dated 1 October 1978, states that 'it is widely known among the clergy and people of the Russian Church that Metropolitan Nikodim was an active collaborator of the organs of the KGB' (*DCCDBR*, vol. 5, part 2, p. 706).

43. *RCL*, vol. 6, no. 4 (1978), p. 230.

44. *Posev*, no. 2 (1979), p. 23.

45. This biographical information is taken from the official biographies pubished in *JMP*, no. 6 (1971), p. 23, and (on the occasion of the Patriarch's seventieth birthday) in *JMP*, no. 7 (1980), p. 3. There is a discrepancy between them: the former states that Pimen was made hierodeacon on July 1930 and hieromonk on 12 January 1931; the latter gives the same days and months but the years as 1931 and 1932 respectively.

46. The late Dr Nadezhda Teodorovich, an authority on the Russian Orthodox episcopate, has pointed out that even the citation for his honorary doctorate makes no mention of any theological (or other) education: 'for his nourishing of the theological schools during his tenure of the Locum Tenency of the Patriarchal See, to mark his election as Patriarch and to acknowledge his many years of ecclesiastical and social activity, and as testimony to the fact that the recipient of the award has become a teacher, preceptor and the chief prelate of the Russian Orthodox Church' (*Religiya i ateizm v SSSR*, no. 9–10 (59–60), (September–October 1972), p. 8, footnote 1; condensed from *JMP*, no. 7 (1971), p. 76). Pimen's own awareness of his deficiency in this respect is demonstrated in his humble speech to members of his diocese on becoming Metropolitan of Leningrad: 'I have brought no brilliant gifts of intellect, nor splendour of thought, nor oratory, nor beautiful preaching, I have brought you only one thing . . . God's peace' (Beeson, *Discretion and Valour*, p. 18).

47. *JMP*, no. 7 (1980), pp. 4–24.

48. *Russkaya mysl*, 2 October 1975, p. 14.

49. This evidence comes in a *JMP* article on St Pimen's Church in Moscow, where the then monk Pimen was choirmaster between 1927 and 1931. This includes two photographs of Pimen with the choir, one dated 1928 and the other dated 1936. The dating of the second photograph is a surprise since the article makes it clear that his formal connection with the church ended in 1931. However, careful comparison of the two photographs suggests that the time-lapse indicated between them is probably correct, and there is no strong reason to doubt the 1936 dating. The monk Pimen has shoulder-length hair in both photographs, suggesting that he was not imprisoned between 1932 and 1936 (in which event his head would have been shaved). This assumption is given some support by the CRA Report (discussed immediately below), which does not suggest that Pimen was imprisoned before 1936. However, the *JMP* article gives no indication what happened to Pimen between 1932 and 1936. See *JMP*, no. 11 (1981), pp. 23–5, and *RCL*, vol. 10, no. 2 (1982), p. 193.

50. *Vestnik RKhD*, no. 132 (1981), pp. 197–8.

51. According to the Criminal Code of the RSFSR promulgated in 1926 and revised in 1953, the relevant section (unrevised) states: 'Absence without leave for more than twenty-four hours is desertion and entails — deprivation of freedom for a term of five to ten years, and in wartime, capital punishment — execution by shooting with confiscation of property. (Edict (*Ukaz*) of the Presidium of the Supreme Soviet of the USSR 6 July 1940)' (*Ugolovny kodeks RSFSR* (Gosyurizdat, Moscow, 1953), p. 57). This would have been applicable to Pimen's alleged second, wartime desertion in 1943. The same penalty would have covered the first peacetime desertion, under the 1927 USSR Statute on Military Crimes, according to Harold J. Berman, *Soviet Criminal Law and Procedure* (Harvard University Press, Cambridge, Mass., second edition 1972), p. 41.

52. Yakunin Report, pp. 3–8. Patriarch Pimen has been identified as a member of the *nomenklatura*, that is, belonging to one of those key positions, appointments to which are made by the higher authorities in the Communist Party: Michael Voslensky, *Nomenklatura. The Soviet Ruling Class: An Insider's Report* (Doubleday, New York, 1984), p. 75.

53. See the 1945 Statute of the Russian Orthodox Church, Part 1, para. 14 (for reference, see Chapter 2, note 7).

54. The official report of the Council is in *JMP*, nos 6, 7 and 8 (1971), and of the enthronement of Patriarch Pimen in no. 9 (1971). (The minutes were later published as a volume by the Moscow Patriarchate.) Several photographs of the occasion appear in *The Moscow Patriarchate 1917–1977*, though the Council is mentioned only briefly, on p. 22. The report of

Nicolas Lossky, the lay delegate of the French diocese at the Council, is in *Contacts*, no. 4 (1971), pp. 359−85. The report of the anonymous observer (*nablyudatel*) is in *Russkaya mysl*, 20 October 1975, p. 14. Secondary reports are given in: Michael Bourdeaux and Kathleen Matchett, 'The Russian Orthodox Church in Council 1945−1971', in B. Bociurkiw and J. Strong (eds), *Religion and Atheism in the USSR and Eastern Europe* (Macmillan, London, 1975), pp. 37−55, which quotes Lossky extensively; and Archpriest D. Konstantinov, *Zarnitsy dukhovnogo vozrozhdeniya* (*Summer Lightning of the Spiritual Renaissance*) (Zarya, London, Ontario, 1973), pp. 107−19.

55. A list of the delegates in typewritten form was issued by the Moscow Patriarchate (copy in KC archive). The two missing delegates were Archbishop Antoni of Vilnius, who died on 28 May, and Archbishop Pavel of Novosibirsk, of whom more will be said later. Bourdeaux and Matchett ('The Church in Council', p. 50), state that only 233 delegates were present, citing Lossky; the identity of the third absent person is unknown. Information on the numbers and composition of the Council is given in *JMP*, no. 6 (1971), p. 20.

56. A list of overseas visitors is given in *JMP*, no. 6 (1971), pp. 18−19.

57. Konstantinov, *Zarnitsy*, p. 112.

58. *Vestnik RKhD*, no. 116 (see note 33).

59. Konstantinov, *Zarnitsy*, p. 115.

60. Bourdeaux and Matchett, 'The Church in Council', p. 51, quoting Lossky.

61. *Episkepsis*, 20 July 1971, p. 13; this quotation from Bourdeaux and Matchett, 'The Church in Council'.

62. Bourdeaux and Matchett, 'The Church in Council', p. 50.

63. *Russkaya mysl*, 2 October 1975, p. 4.

64. Bourdeaux and Matchett, 'The Church in Council, p. 54.

65. *JMP*, no. 6 (1971), pp. 3−7.

66. Yakunin Report, pp. 9−10.

67. These are published in Michael Bourdeaux, *Patriarch and Prophets* (reprinted Mowbrays, London and Oxford, 1975), pp. 238−54.

68. This is pointed out by Bourdeaux and Matchett, 'The Church in Council', p. 49.

69. *Golos rodiny*, no. 22 (1969), p. 4.

70. *Russkaya mysl*, 2 October 1975, p. 14.

71. Quoted in Michael Bourdeaux, 'How Soviet State Kept Control of Church Council', *Church Times*, 17 March 1972, p. 11.

72. *Russkaya mysl*, 2 October 1975.

73. This information comes from a confidential but reliable source.

74. *Vestnik RKhD*, no. 103 (1972), pp. 173−4.

75. *JMP*, no. 11 (1972), p. 2.

76. *SOP*, no. 7 (April 1976), p. 3.

77. Archbishop Vasili (Krivoshein), 'Archbishop Veniamin (Novitsky)', *Vestnik RKhD*, no. 120 (1977), pp. 289−94.

78. *AS*, no. 4456, dated 26 October 1977.

79. *JMP*, no. 11 (1979), p. 4.

80. *JMP*, no. 2 (1980), p. 2.

81. Yakunin Report, pp. 10−11.

9. Church−State Relations

1. *Sovetskaya Rossiya*, 15 June 1983, p. 3; English translation taken from *Soviet News* (London), 16 June 1983, p. 204.

2. V. Ostrozhinsky, 'Vrazhdebnaya ideologiya' ('The Alien Ideology'), *Pravda*, 21 October 1981; commentary in *KNS*, no. 136 (5 November 1981).

3. V. Klochkov, 'Teoreticheskiye voprosy' ('Questions of Theory'), *Pravda*, 25 May 1984; commentary in *KNS*, no. 202 (21 June 1984).

4. 'Atheist Convictions for the Youth' (editorial), *Pravda*, 18 October 1984; commentary in *KNS*, no. 212 (8 November 1984).

5. The number of Muslims is given by specialists on Islam in the USSR, Alexandre Bennigsen and Marie Broxup, in *The Islamic Threat to the Soviet State* (Croom Helm, London, 1983), p. 1. Very approximate estimates of the other religious groups are as follows: 5.5 million Roman Catholics, possibly 1.5 million or more Eastern-rite Catholics, over 3 million Baptists, 2.5–3 million Jews (not all of whom are religious), up to 0.5 million Pentecostals, 0.5 million Buddhists, and unknown numbers of much smaller groups: Seventh-Day Adventists, Methodists, Mennonites, Lutherans, Jehovah's Witnesses, True Orthodox, Old Believers and other sects of Orthodox origin. The number of Old Believers, about whom little is known, could well be a million or more, which would mean that our estimate is on the low side. There are large but unknown numbers of members of the Georgian Orthodox Church (population of Georgia 5 million) and of the Armenian Apostolic Church (population of Armenia 3 million).

6. Jonathan Steele, *Guardian*, 22 November 1979, p. 10.

7. Appeal to L. I. Brezhnev, 22 November 1979, chairman of the Constitutional Commission, from the Christian Committee for the Defence of Believers' Rights in the USSR, 8 June 1977; English translation in *RCL*, vol. 6, no. 1 (1978), pp. 34–6.

8. Ibid., p. 35.

9. Ibid., p. 36.

10. Open letter dated 11 November; *DCCDBR*, vol. 1, pp. 37–8.

11. See, for example, Michael Binyon, 'Salving the Soul of Russia', *Sunday Times* colour supplement, 8 January 1983. This article was republished in a revised form in the same author's *Life in Russia* (Hamish Hamilton, London, 1983), pp. 232–6. Another example was the two-part NBC film documentary 'The Church of the Russians', narrated by Rev. Bruce Rigdon and screened in the USA on 24 June and 1 July 1983. For further comments, see *KNS*, nos 204 (19 July 1984) and 205 (2 August 1984).

12. The new administrative building was blessed by Metropolitan Alexi on 23 June 1983. It houses the chancery of the Moscow Patriarchate, the Education Committee and the Pensions Committee. It is located at No. 56 Chisty pereulok (*JMP*, no. 9 (1983), pp. 17–18). The DECR is situated in the same street.

13. V. A. Kuroyedov and A. S. Pankratov (eds), *Legislation on Religious Cults* (*Collection of Materials and Documents*) (Yuridicheskaya Literatura, Moscow, 1971). The book is marked 'For Official Use Only' (*Dlya sluzhebnogo polzovaniya*) on the title-page, and each of its 21,000 copies was numbered to restrict its circulation. (The number in the photocopied copy which reached the West had been erased.) See article by Walter Sawatsky, 'Secret Soviet Lawbook on Religion', *RCL*, vol. 4, no. 4 (1976), pp. 24–31. An English translation of the CRA Statute is appended to the article, pp. 31–4.

14. Vladimir Kuroyedov, 'On Freedom of Conscience, both Real and Imaginary', *Izvestiya*, 28 January 1978; English translation (abridged) in *RCL*, vol. 4, no. 4 (1978), p. 261.

15. Izvestiya, 31 January 1976; English translation in *RCL*, vol. 4, no. 2 (1976), p. 43.

16. Ibid., p. 42.

17. V. Klochkov, 'Law and Freedom of Conscience', *Pravda*, 10 September 1982, pp. 2–3.

18. William C. Fletcher, 'Backwards from Reactionism: The Demodernization of the Russian Orthodox Church', in Dennis J. Dunn (ed.), *Religion and Modernization in the Soviet Union* (Westview Press, Boulder, Colorado, 1977), pp. 205–38.

19. Ibid., pp. 219–20.

20. Ibid., p. 218.

21. Ibid., p. 215.

22. Ibid.

23. Jonathan Steele, *Guardian*, 20 November 1979, p. 21.

24. CRA Report for 1970, pp. 15–16; Fletcher, *Nikolai* (Macmillan, New York, 1968), p. 188.

25. CRA Report, 1970, p. 16.

26. *JMP*, no. 10 (1981), p. 4. The official reason given for Khrizostom's resignation was 'ill-health', which is customary on such occasions.

27. Yakunin Report, p. 9.

28. *JMP*, no. 1 (1979), p. 12.

29. *Vestnik RKhD*, no. 130 (1979), p. 304.

30. Ibid., pp. 304–5.

31. John Barron, *KGB: The Secret Work of Soviet Secret Agents* (Corgi books, London, 1975), p. 138.

32. Declaration to Patriarch Pimen from the Christian Committee for the Defence of Believers' Rights in the USSR, *Russkaya mysl*, 9 March 1978, p. 5.

33. Open letter to Professor Archpriest John Meyendorff from the Christian Committee, 16 October 1978; *DCCDBR*, vol. 5, part I, pp. 687−8.

34. A. Krasnov, 'Kaplya pod mikroskopom' ('A Drop under the Microscope'), December 1966, *Vestnik RKhD*, no. 83 (1967), pp. 7−28; English (abridged) in M. Bourdeaux, *Patriarch and Prophets* (reprinted Mowbrays, London and Oxford, 1975), pp. 307−24.

35. *Vestnik RKhD*, no. 130 (1979), p. 324.

36. Ibid.

37. Yakunin Report, p. 35.

38. Rev. Richard Harries, 'Assessing Soviet Peace Rhetoric', September 1984; unpublished typescript on file at Keston College. (The article is a reflection of Rev. Harries's views after a visit to the USSR as part of a British interdenominational delegation in the same month.)

39. Father Gleb Yakunin, 'The Discriminatory Character of State Taxes in the USSR on the Clergy and Workers in Religious Organisations', 1 July 1977; *DCCDBR*, vol. 1, p. 32, footnote 3.

40. The Russian Orthodox Church was completely cut off from the West from 1917 to 1943, when the Archbishop of Canterbury visited Metropolitan Sergi in Moscow. Thereafter talks began with members of what was to become the World Council of Churches. See J. Hebly, *The Russians and the World Council of Churches* (Christian Journals Ltd, Belfast, 1978).

41. William C. Fletcher, 'Religion and Soviet Foreign Policy: A Functional Survey', in B. Bociurkiw and J. Strong (eds), *Religion and Atheism in the USSR and Eastern Europe* (Macmillan, London, 1975), pp. 171−89.

42. Ibid., pp. 184−5.

43. *The Moscow Patriarchate 1917−1977* (Moscow Patriarchate, Moscow, 1978), p. 56.

44. Nikita Struve, *Christians in Contemporary Russia* (The Harvill Press, London, 1967), pp. 59−61.

45. *The Russian Orthodox Church: Organization, Situation, Activity* (Moscow Patriarchate, Moscow, 1956), Chapter 7, 'Patriotic Activity of the Russian Orthodox Church during the Great Patriotic War', pp. 199−208.

46. *The Moscow Patriarchate 1917−1977*, Deacon Vladimir Rusak, 'Peacemaking of the Russian Orthodox Church', pp. 60−9. (For information on Rusak's other activities, particularly after being dismissed from the Publishing Department of the Moscow Patriarchate, see Chapter 13.)

47. *JMP*, no. 1 (1957), p. 37.

48. *JMP*, no. 10 (1968), pp. 2−3.

49. *JMP*, no. 5 (1980), pp. 3−6.

50. A. Vsevolodov, 'The Soviet Peace Fund', *Sovetskaya yustitsiya*, no. 9 (1970).

51. Novosti Press Agency, 7 July 1977.

52. *The Moscow Patriarchate 1917−1977*, pp. 64−5.

53. Richard Chartres, 'The Moscow Peace Conference, May 1982', *RCL*, vol. 10, no. 3 (1982), pp. 337−9; *KNS Special Supplement*, no. 150 (4 June 1982).

54. The True Orthodox Church or True Orthodox Christians, who went into schism during the 1920s, are reputedly still numerous and spread throughout the Soviet Union, though information is hard to come by because their corporate life is carried on entirely underground. They are believed to have some priests and perhaps two or three bishops. Members live their daily lives in a normal way but meet together for worship and fellowship in great secrecy, in a 'cell' system. Great emphasis is placed upon never revealing one's membership of the church or the names of fellow-members. True Orthodox who have been arrested and imprisoned have made a great impression upon their fellow-prisoners because of their piety and strict dedication to their beliefs. They are noted for refusing to co-operate in any way at all with the Soviet system. The most comprehensive treatment of the True Orthodox to date is William C. Fletcher, *The Russian Orthodox Church Underground 1917−1970* (Oxford University Press, London, 1971).

55. Dimitri Pospielovsky, 'Metropolitan Nikodim Remembered', *RCL*, vol. 6, no. 4 (1978), p. 230.

56. The issue of Russian nationalism is too large a one to discuss in detail here. We shall refer to it in more depth in Part 2, where we examine the *samizdat* writings of some nationalist authors. Suffice it to say that there are some persuasive arguments to foster the growth of Russian nationalist ideas in Soviet ruling circles, chief of which are the mobilisation and demographic ones. (The need for a powerful appeal to mobilise the population for a possible future conflict, perhaps with China — as in the Great Patriotic War; and the need to restore the declining Russian birthrate and deal with family and social problems.) Articles of a Russian nationalist nature have been published by a number of members of the Soviet literary and journalistic establishment and (although their views have sometimes been contested by more orthodox Marxist–Leninists writing in rival newspapers and journals) they clearly would not have survived as long as they have (allowing for some vicissitudes) if they had not had protectors in high places. But the accession to power of a Russian nationalist regime is at present speculative and the subject of much controversy. (The most thorough examination of the issue to date is John Dunlop's *The Faces of Contemporary Russian Nationalism* (Princeton University Press, Princeton, New Jersey, 1983).) However, the church's position if a putative regime of Russian nationalist orientation were to come to power is not altogether clear. Almost certainly such a regime would see the church as an ally, to a greater or lesser degree, and would accord it more freedom than it has at present. Unquestionably too the church would find the ideals and policies of such a regime more acceptable than those of the present regime. But would the church in fact be given any measure of real independence? Would its own voice be heard freely, or would it merely be a prop to further the aims of the new regime? That can only be speculative at present (and much would depend on the precise nature within the spectrum of Russian nationalist views of the beliefs of those who might come to power). The church could well find itself no freer than it was during the last two centuries of Tsarist rule.

As for the church's own attitude to such a regime, it seems more than likely that the church hierarchy, and very likely the broad masses of the faithful, would embrace it warmly. (Intellectuals would probably continue to be as divided as they are at present, as we shall see in Part 2.) This would be because such a regime would undoubtedly appear to be an improvement on the present one. Moreover, it would involve no change in policy for the church, which can be said to have maintained a policy of staunch patriotism, if not always of outright nationalism, quite consistently since 1917 — indeed, as we have noted, it was very largely this stance which led to its post-war restoration. We should note, however, that this stance on the part of the church leadership has been perceived as unbalanced by some church members. For example, Father Gleb Yakunin has described in some detail the excessive glorification of Stalin by the church leadership. Yakunin suggested that, after Stalin's policies took a pro-Russian nationalist turn from 1935 onwards, the church hierarchy was hoping that he would be a 'new Constantine', declare the country a pan-Slav Orthodox empire, and make Orthodoxy the state religion. He points out that the church leadership has never repented of its adulation of Stalin — even though Khrushchev would have welcomed the slightest sign of such repentance. ('The Moscow Patriarchate and the Cult of Stalin', *Russkoye vozrozhdeniye*, no. 1 (1978), pp. 103–37). With such precedents in mind, we should assume that the church leadership would be unlikely to be as critical about the nature of any emergent nationalist regime as many of its members would be.

Finally, speculation about the emergence of a Russian nationalist regime and the church's relationship to it must take into account the question of the situation of members of the church in non-Russian republics. Russian nationalist writers, both official and unofficial, vary quite widely in their recommendations as to Russia's future relationship to the minority nationalities in the USSR. As far as the church is concerned, the problem would be particularly acute in Ukraine, where, as we have seen, a large proportion of the church's institutions and of its faithful are to be found (and where Ukrainian nationalism is strong, particularly in western Ukraine).

57. Timothy Ware, *The Orthodox Church* (Penguin Books, Harmondsworth, 1972), pp. 203–7.

58. Ibid., p. 204.

59. Ibid., p. 205.

60. See, for example, the article 'Izmenyayushchi mir' ('The Changing World') by Metropolitan Nikodim, *JMP*, no. 10 (1975), pp. 56–60. He discusses the adaptation of the church to the modern world — for example, the use of Russian in services: this has been welcomed by

some laity, but congregations tend to be suspicious of change. In an interview with a foreign journalist, Archbishop Kirill of Vyborg and Bishop Makari of Uman also expressed a desire to encourage thinking young people by a revitalisation of theological thought, but without abandoning Orthodox dogma and liturgy (Paul Masson, *La Libre Belgique*, 11 October 1979). Some translations of the psalms into modern Russian have been unofficially produced (*Vestnik RKhD*, no. 136 (1982), pp. 5–10).

61. Fletcher, 'Backwards from Reactionism', pp. 226–7.

62. See, for example, the article by Ye. D. Kondryatev, 'Criticism of Orthodox Theological Concepts of the "Reconciliation" of Science and Religion', *Voprosy nauchnogo ateizma*, no. 19 (1976), pp. 229–43. Kondryatev expresses the fear that modernisation in the church after the pattern of the Catholic Church in the West might increase its influence among thinking people in the Soviet Union. An earlier book contends that, despite the efforts of some Orthodox thinkers to bring religion up to date, they have failed to do so because religion is quite simply incompatible with science and with the modern world in general (M. P. Novikov, *Pravoslaviye i sovremennost (Orthodoxy and the Modern World)* (Izd. Moskovskogo Universiteta, Moscow, 1965). Similar views are expressed in articles by N. Krasikov ('Posle pomestnogo sobora' ('After the Local Council'), *Nauka i religiya*, no. 12 (1975), pp. 38–40) and I. Yershov ('The Social Activity of the Individual and Modernist Religious Conceptions', *Lyudina i svit*, no. 4 (1977), pp. 34–8).

63. Yakunin Report, p. 1.

64. Ibid., p. 37.

10. The Rise of Orthodox Dissent: up to 1974

1. The most important *samizdat* documents from this period are translated in Michael Bourdeaux, *Patriarch and Prophets: Persecution of the Russian Orthodox Church* (reprinted Mowbrays, London and Oxford, 1975). Analytical accounts are given in: Michael Bourdeaux, 'The Black Quinquennium: The Russian Orthodox Church 1959–1964', *RCL*, vol. 9, no. 1 (1981), pp. 18–23; Bohdan R. Bociurkiw, 'Religious Dissent and the Soviet State', in B. Bociurkiw and J. Strong (eds), *Religion and Atheism in the USSR and Eastern Europe* (Macmillan, London, 1975); Gerhard Simon, *Church State and Opposition in the USSR*, translated by Kathleen Matchett (C. Hurst & Company, London, 1974), pp. 125–30.

2. An account of this meeting, and other articles by Levitin, appear in Bourdeaux, *Patriarch and Prophets*. A collection of Anatoli Levitin's writings is expected to appear in English shortly: Anatoli Levitin-Krasnov, *One Man's Witness*, ed. Jane Ellis (St Vladimir's Seminary Press, Crestwood, New York, and Darton, Longman & Todd, London, forthcoming).

3. Interview between Anatoli Levitin and Jane Ellis, 6 March 1975; cassette recording in KC archive.

4. Bourdeaux, *Patriarch and Prophets*, pp. 125–54.

5. Ibid., pp. 305–29. See Chapter 9, pp. 268–9.

6. Appeal to the World Council of Churches, Odessa, from Orthodox Christians in Russia, Ukraine and Belorussia, 2 February 1964; English translation in M. Bourdeaux, H. Hebly and E. Voss (eds), *Religious Liberty in the Soviet Union* (Keston College, Kent, England, 1976), pp. 54–6.

7. The extensive documentation on VSKhSON has been collected in *Vserossiisky sotsial-Khristiansky soyuz osvobozhdeniya naroda — programma, sud, v tyurmakh i lageryakh*, compiled by John Dunlop (YMCA Press, Paris, 1975), and analysed in John Dunlop, *The New Russian Revolutionaries* (Nordland Publishing Company, Belmont, Mass., 1976).

8. Abridged translation in Bourdeaux, *Patriarch and Prophets*, pp. 189–223.

9. Ibid., p. 218.

10. Ibid., p. 189.

11. Ibid., pp. 193–4.

12. 'Report (*spravka*) on a Conversation with Metropolitan Pimen of Krutitsy and Kolomna (Izvekov S.M.)', signed Plekhanov (?), photocopy of typescript in KC archive.

13. Private letter to the present author.

14. 'Notes of a Conversation Which Took Place in the Council on 21 February 1967 with Metropolitan Pimen (Izvekov S.M.)', signed A. Plekhanov, p. 2; photocopy of typescript in KC archive.

15. Alexander Solzhenitsyn, *The Oak and the Calf*, translated by Harry Willetts (Harper & Row, New York, 1979), pp. 150–1.

16. The letter, and several of the documents relating to the case, are in Valeri Chalidze, *Prava cheloveka i sovetsky soyuz* (Kronika Press, New York, 1974), pp. 213–47; translated as *To Defend These Rights: Human Rights and the Soviet Union* (Collins & Harvill, London, 1975), pp. 199–208.

17. *Bratsky vestnik (Fraternal Herald)*, no. 5 (1981), p. 71; *RCL*, vol. 10, no. 2 (1982), p. 194.

18. The main nineteenth-century Slavophils were I. V. Kireyevsky (1806–56), A. S. Khomyakov (1804–60), Yu. F. Samarin (1819–76), and the brothers K. S. Aksakov (1817–60) and I. S. Aksakov (1823–86). Their ideas were taken up and developed by F. M. Dostoyevsky (1821–81), N. Ya. Danilevsky (1822–85), K. N. Leontyev (1831–81) and V. S. Solovyov (1853–1900).

19. For fuller treatment of the ideas of the neo-Slavophils, including their political thought, see John Dunlop, 'The Eleventh Hour', *Frontier*, vol. 18, no. 2 (1975), pp. 71–81; Philip Walters, 'A New Creed for Russians?', *RCL*, vol. 4, no. 3 (1976), pp. 20–6.

20. Among nationalist writers on themes concerning the Russian Orthodox Church, messianism was reflected chiefly in the writings of Gennadi Shimanov, while the more liberal trend was exemplified by Solzhenitsyn and Vladimir Osipov: the works of these three writers will be discussed in this and the following chapter.

21. This article and two others — O. Altayev, 'The Dual Consciousness of the Intelligentsia and Pseudo-Culture'; and M. Chelnov, 'How to Be?' — appeared as a collection under the title *Metanoia (Conversion)* and were published in *Vestnik RKhD*, no. 97 (1970), pp. 4–96.

22. In A. Solzhenitsyn (ed.), *From Under the Rubble* (Collins/Harvill, London, 1975), see pp. 121–7.

23. Letters by V. Prokhorov, L. Ibragimov and K. Radugin protesting against the publication of the three articles were published in *Vestnik RKhD*, no. 106 (1972); a critical article by Leonid Borodin, '*Vestnik RKhD* and the Russian Intelligentsia', appeared in *Veche*, no. 8 (19 July 1973), pp. 171–211 (photograph of typed original in KC archive).

24. Chiefly by Solzhenitsyn, also in *From Under the Rubble*; see pp. 331–2.

25. *Novy mir (New World)*, January 1963.

26. 'Chernye doski' ('Black Boards'), appeared with a collection of short stories in *A Winter's Day* (Moscow, 1969); translated as *Searching for Icons in Russia* (Harvill Press, London, 1971).

27. Emerging in the 1950s, the *derevenshchiki* ('village writers') reacted against the stereotyped, production-orientated rural writing of the post-war decade. Their portrayal of the Soviet village was realistic, stressing the harshness of rural life, and frequently depicting the peasant as the victim of city-dwelling bureaucrats. Thus V. Ovechkin's 'Raionnye budni' ('District Weekdays') clearly blamed the government apparatus for conditions in the countryside — a courageous step bearing in mind that it was written in 1952. Another theme of these writers was emphasis on the moral importance of peasant links with the soil. This is the theme of V. Belov's 'Privychnoe delo' ('That's How It Is') (1966), a tragic love story in which the hero comes to terms with life as he begins to appreciate the endless renewal of life that comes through the soil. In the last decade the most prominent 'village writer' has been Valentin Rasputin, whose stories have been much praised for their incisive characterisation of peasant psychology. See Deming Brown, *Soviet Russian Literature since Stalin* (Cambridge University Press, 1978), pp. 218–52.

28. See analysis by Mikhail Agursky in 'The Attitude to Religion in the New Russian Literature', *RCL*, vol. 10, no. 2 (1982), pp. 145–55.

29. Glazunov held exhibitions in Moscow in 1978 and in Leningrad in 1979; *Komsomolskaya pravda*, 3 June 1978, and *The Times*, 16 June 1978.

30. 'Russky khudozhnik Ilya Glazunov' ('The Russian Artist Ilya Glazunov'), *Veche*, no. 8 (19 September 1973), pp. 212–32.

31. *Russia Cristiana*, no. 165 (1979), pp. 55–64.

32. For a summary of this, see Michael Meerson-Aksyonov, 'The Debate Over the National

Renaissance in Russia', in M. Meerson-Aksyonov and Boris Schragin (eds), *The Political, Social and Religious Thought of Russian Samizdat — An Anthology* (Nordland Publishing Company, Belmont, Mass., 1977), pp. 345–7. A more detailed, and vivid, account appears in Solzhenitsyn, *The Oak and the Calf*, pp. 244–56. A more thorough analysis is given in Alexander Yanov, *The Russian New Right* (Institute of International Studies, University of California, Berkeley, 1978), pp. 39–61; however, the book as a whole is a tendentious and unconvincing polemic against all shades of Russian nationalist opinion, which is sometimes represented in a manner amounting to caricature.

33. We have in mind not only the 'symphony' between the church and Tsarism still viewed by many as an ideal form for church–state relations, and the intensely patriotic stance taken by the church during the Second World War, but also the hierarchy's attitude to Stalin during and after the war and after his death, as analysed by Father Gleb Yakunin in his article 'Moskovskaya Patriarkhiya i "kult lichnosti" Stalina', ('The Moscow Patriarchate and the "Cult of Personality" of Stalin'), *Russkoye Vozrozhdeniye*, no. 1 (1978), pp. 103–37, and no. 2 (1978), pp. 110–50. Father Gleb points out that the excessive praise heaped upon Stalin by the church during his life and at his funeral was never subsequently retracted or modified, even though the period of destalinisation inaugurated by Khrushchev in 1956 offered ample opportunity for this, and suggests that the church leadership was remaining faithful to the hope of a Russian national renaissance favourably disposed to the church of the kind initiated by Stalin at the height of the war effort.

34. See Dunlop, 'The Eleventh Hour', p. 74; and Philip Walters, 'Vladimir Osipov: Loyal Opposition?' *RCL*, vol. 5, no. 4 (1977), pp. 229–33.

35. Vladimir Osipov, 'Berdyaevsky kruzhok v Leningrade' ('The Berdyaev Circle in Leningrad' — Osipov's appellation for VSKhSON), January 1972, *AS*, no. 1163, pp. 164–5; *Vestnik RKhD*, nos 104–5 (1972); cited in Walters, 'Vladimir Osipov', p. 230.

36. Vladimir Osipov, 'Otkrytoye pismo Gennadiyu Shimanovu' ('Open Letter to Gennadi Shimanov'), 29 April 1973, *AS*, no. 1732, and 'Pyat vozrazhenii Sakharovu' ('Five Objections to Sakharov'), April 1974, *AS*, no. 1696; both cited in Walters, 'Vladimir Osipov'.

37. Vladimir Osipov, 'Tri otnosheniya k Rodine', 25 March–2 April 1970, *AS*, no. 1147; *Vestnik RKhD*, no. 103 (1972), pp. 216–22; later published as a book by Posev, Frankfurt, 1978; English translation in Meerson-Aksyonov and Schragin (eds), *Political, Social and Religious Thought*, pp. 394–403.

38. *Veche*, no. 1 (January 1971), *AS*, no. 1013, p. 2.

39. The analysis by John Dunlop, 'The Eleventh Hour', p. 74, shows that the 893 pages in the Radio Liberty *Arkhiv Samizdata* edition of *Veche* nos 1–6 are divided as follows between what he calls 'somewhat arbitrary categories with obvious overlap': (1) nineteenth-century Slavophiles and nationalists, 213pp.; (2) the Russian Orthodox Church and religious thought, 156pp.; (3) problems of neo-Slavophilism in the 1960s and 1970s, 80pp.; (4) Solzhenitsyn, 78pp.; (5) the thought of anti- and non-Slavophiles, 66pp.; (6) ecology, 60pp.; (7) Russian architecture, 57pp.; (8) neo-Slavophil poetry, 41pp.; (9) discussion of music, 41pp.; (10) fiction and memoirs, 31pp.; (11) literary criticism, 29pp.

40. *Veche*, no. 8 (19 September 1973), pp. 87–110; photograph of typed original in KC archive.

41. Ibid., pp. 31–86.

42. *Veche*, no. 6 (19 October 1972), *AS*, no. 1599, pp. 25–33.

43. *Veche*, no. 4 (31 January 1972), *AS*, no. 1140, pp. 6–14.

44. *Veche*, no. 1 (January 1971), *AS*, no. 1013, pp. 48–51; English extracts in *RCL*, vol. 1, no. 1 (1973), pp. 21–3.

45. *Veche*, no. 1 (January 1971), pp. 121–31.

46. *Veche*, no. 2 (19 May 1971), pp. 33–47, and no. 5 (25 May 1972), *AS*, no. 1230, pp. 45–53; see also pp. 301–3 of the present chapter.

47. *Veche*, no. 6 (19 October 1972), pp. 34–42; see also Chapter 8, pp. 239–40.

48. Ibid., p. 18; this statement was made in an interview with two Western newspaper correspondents.

49. Letters from V. N., 'Otryvki iz dnevnika' ('Extracts from a Diary'), *Veche*, no. 4 (31 January 1972), pp. 40–4; and N. V., 'K pismu V. N. o katolitsizme' ('On V. N.'s Letter about Catholicism'), *Veche*, no. 6 (19 October 1972), pp. 129–30.

50. Walters, 'Vladimir Osipov', p. 233.

51. 'Ekstrennoye zayavleniye dlya pechati' ('Emergency Statement to the Press'), 7 March 1974, *AS*, no. 1705; English translation in Meerson-Aksyonov and Schragin (eds), *Political, Social and Religious Thought*, pp. 605–6.

52. Meerson-Aksyonov and Schragin, ibid., pp. 349–50 and 605–6.

53. Vladimir Osipov, 'K voprosu o tseli i metodakh legalnoi oppositsii' ('On the Question of the Goals and Methods of Legal Opposition'), May 1974, *AS*, no. 1760.

54. Mikhail Agursky, 'The Intensification of Neo-Nazi Dangers in the Soviet Union', plus appendices, in Meerson-Aksyonov and Schragin (eds), *Political, Social and Religious Thought*, pp. 414–48.

55. Appeal (*obrashcheniye*) to the Local Council of the Russian Orthodox Church, compiled by Father Nikolai Gainov and laymen Felix Karelin, Lev Regelson and Viktor Kapitanchuk, 26 April 1971 (copy of typewritten text in KC archive). Only the first 41 pages, up to partway through section 3, are included. The entire text is summarised in *Veche*, no. 2 (19 May 1971), *AS*, no. 680, pp. 33–47.

56. Gainov *et al.*, 'Appeal', pp. 2–3.

57. Ibid., pp. 3–4.

58. *AS*, no. 680, pp. 37–8, 39–40, 45.

59. *Veche*, no. 3 (19 September 1972), *AS*, no. 1108, p. 55.

60. *JMP*, no. 6 (1971), pp. 4–5.

61. Plea (*prosheniye*) to His Holiness, the Most Holy Patriarch Pimen of Moscow and All Russia, from Gainov, Karelin, Regelson and Kapitanchuk, 22 September 1971, *RRS*, no. 1021.

62. Plea to the Local Council of the Russian Orthodox Church 1971, date unclear on copy received, *RRS*, no. 1108, pp. 62–7.

63. Appeal to the Council, from the area dean of the second Irkutsk area, Father Yevgeni Kasatkin, undated, *AS*, no. 1108, pp. 56–61.

64. In fact he had been arrested in autumn 1969, investigated and then released pending trial in August 1970, then tried and sentenced in May 1971; *Chronicle of Current Events*, no. 29 (Amnesty International, London), p. 76 (Henceforward cited as *CCE*).

65. Letter dated Lent 1972, Week of the Adoration of the Cross (sent on 17 March, according to Solzhenitsyn in *The Oak and the Calf*, p. 329); English translation in Gerhard Simon, *Church, State and Opposition*, translated from German by Kathleen Matchett (C. Hurst & Company, London, 1974), pp. 202–5.

66. Letter dated Easter 1972; English translation in Simon, *Church, State and Opposition*, pp. 206–8.

67. Letter dated Easter 1972, Week of the Paralytic; English translation (abridged) in *Eastern Churches Review*, vol. 5, no. 1 (Spring 1973), pp. 44–52. The same issue contains translations of Solzhenitsyn's letter (pp. 37–41), and Zheludkov's letter (pp. 41–4), as well as a brief reply from Solzhenitsyn to Zheludkov, 28 May 1972, (p. 44).

68. I. R. Shafarevich, *Zakonodatelstvo o religii v SSSR* (YMCA Press, Paris, 1973); unpublished English translation available in typescript from Keston College.

69. A copy of this book was subsequently leaked to the West. For a description of its contents, see Walter Sawatsky, 'Secret Soviet Lawbook on Religion', *RCL*, vol. 4, no. 4 (1976), pp. 24–31. See also p. 258.

70. Shafarevich, *Zakonodatelstvo*, p. 66.

71. See statement by Alexander Solzhenitsyn, 14 October 1975, *Vestnik RKhD*, no. 116 (1975), p. 258.

72. *Veche*, no. 8 (19 September 1973), pp. 113–19 and 120–36 respectively; photograph in KC archive.

73. Ibid., p. 116.

74. Ibid., p. 133.

75. Ibid., p. 112. The text of the law is published in *Sbornik zakonov SSSR 1938–1975* (Izdaniye Izvestiya Sovetov Deputatov Trudyashchikhsya SSSR, Moscow, 1975), pp. 143–8.

76. Ratified 2 July 1962; *Sbornik zakonov*, vol. 2, p. 251.

77. Anatoli Levitin-Krasnov, 'Father Dimitri Dudko', Moscow, May 1974, *AS*, no. 1975, pp. 3–4.

78. Belov and Shilkin, *Diversiya bez dinamita* (*Diversion without Dynamite*) (Politicheskaya Literatura, Moscow, 1976), p. 100; Boris Roshchin, 'Freedom of Religion and the Slanderers', *Literaturnaya gazeta*, 20 April 1977. (English translation in Father Gleb Yakunin

and Lev Regelson, *Letters from Moscow*, ed. Jane Ellis (co-published by Keston College, Keston, England, and H. S. Dakin Company, San Francisco, California, 1978), p. 82; henceforward cited as *LFM*.)

79. Statement by Father Dudko at a press conference *apropos* of Roshchin's article, 27 April 1977; English translation in *LFM*, p. 90.

80. Anatoli Levitin-Krasnov, 'Father Dimitri Dudko', p. 4.

81. Radio broadcast by Natalya Solzhenitsyn, 2 August 1979, quoted in Father V. Potapov, 'Pravoslavnoye inakomysliye v SSSR' ('Orthodox Nonconformism in the USSR'), *Russkoye vozrozhdeniye (Russian Renaissance)*, nos 7–8 (1979), p. 84.

82. Sermon by Father Dimitri Dudko, 1 October 1972, English translation in *RCL*, vol. 1, nos 4–5 (1973), pp. 54–5.

83. Father Dimitri Dudko, *Our Hope* (the text of all the question-and-answer sessions) (St Vladimir's Seminary Press, Crestwood, New York, 1977), p. 13.

84. Anatoli Levitin-Krasnov, 'Father Dimitri Dudko', pp. 10–11.

85. Quotations from *Our Hope, passim*; summary based on Jane Ellis, 'Father Dudko: The Flower of Russia's "Religious Spring"', *The Times*, 29 January 1980, p. 12.

86. Anon., 'Fr Dimitri Dudko: An Eye-witness Account', *RCL*, vol. 4, no. 2 (1979), p. 23.

87. Dudko, *Our Hope*, pp. 183–4.

88. Ibid., p. 225; 'Eye-witness Account', p. 24.

89. Dudko, *Our Hope*, pp. 225–7; the English translation quoted here is taken from M. Bourdeaux and M. Rowe (eds), *May One Believe — In Russia?* (Darton, Longman & Todd, London, 1980), pp. 25–6.

90. Letter from Matfei Stadnyuk, the Patriarch's secretary, to Father Dimitri Dudko, 15 May 1974, *Vestnik RKhD*, nos 112–13 (1974), p. 267.

91. Bourdeaux and Rowe (eds), *May One Believe*, p. 27.

92. 'Eye-witness Account', pp. 26–7; Dudko, *Our Hope*, p. 229.

93. *Vestnik RKhD*, nos 112–13 (1974), letter, undated but between 15 and 20 May 1974.

94. *Vestnik RKhD*, nos 112–13 (1974), p. 268; letter, but probably 23 and 24 May 1974.

95. 'Press Conference at the Apartment of Father Dimitri Dudko', 27 April 1977. *LFM*, p. 91.

96. Dudko, *Our Hope*, p. 10; 'Special Broadcast by Levitin-Krasnov on Father Dimitri Dudko', 18 June 1975, RL Research Dept, RS 295/75, p. 4.

97. The text of these, together with the nine talks given in church, is given in *Our Hope*.

98. Belov and Shilkin, *Diversiya*, p. 99.

99. Observer quoted in 'Eye-witness Account', p. 26.

100. 'Protocol of a Search', Moscow 24 August 1973, *AS*, no. 1493.

101. Yevgeni Barabanov, press statement, 15 September 1973; English translation in *RCL*, vol. 2, no. 1 (1974), pp. 29–31.

102. Solzhenitsyn, *The Oak and the Calf*, p. 356.

103. Appeal dated 21 September 1973; English translation in *RCL*, vol. 2, no. 3 (1974), p. 24.

104. Solzhenitsyn, *The Oak and the Calf*, pp. 356–7.

105. Letter dated 23 September 1973, *AS*, no. 1489.

106. Alexander Solzhenitsyn, *Letter to Soviet Leaders* (Index on Censorship and Fontana Books, London, 1974), p. 52.

107. Meerson-Aksyonov and Schragin (eds), *Political, Social and Religious Thought*; Sakharov's view is given in his article on p. 300, Kopelev's in his article on pp. 334–5.

108. Solzhenitsyn, *Letter to Soviet Leaders*, p. 56.

109. Meerson-Aksyonov and Schragin (eds), *Political, Social and Religious Thought*, p. 418. Orthodox thinkers made substantial contributions to the extensive debate over the *Letter to Soviet Leaders* conducted among Soviet intellectuals. Agursky gave it a detailed and appreciative analysis in 'Mezhdunarodnoye znacheniye "Pisma k vozhdyam" A. Solzhenitsyn' ('The International Significance of A. Solzhenitsyn's "Letter to Soviet Leaders"'), 9 June 1974, *AS*, no. 1965. Anatoli Levitin-Krasnov was however very critical of it, particularly of its advocacy of some authoritarian form of government; A. Krasnov, 'Zemlya dybom' ('The Earth Turned Upside Down'), Moscow, 1974, *AS*, no. 1876, pp. 7ff. Vladimir Osipov was sympathetic to Solzhenitsyn's views and critical of Levitin-Krasnov's (also of the responses of democrats such as Sakharov and Roy Medvedev) in his article 'On the Questions of the Goals

and Methods of Legal Opposition' (see note 53). Leonid Borodin was scornfully critical of the views of Levitin-Krasnov, whom he called a dilettante, in his article 'Mersi — ili volosy dybom' ('Merci! Or Hair on End') in *Moskovsky sbornik, samizdat*, Moscow, September 1974.

110. Solzhenitsyn, *The Oak and the Calf*, p. 537.

111. Yevgeni Barabanov, 'Put sovesti' ('The Way of Conscience'), 28 January 1974, *AS*, no. 1603, p. 3.

112. *Sovetskaya Rossiya*, 16 February 1974, p. 3.

113. *The Times*, 1 March 1974, p. 15.

114. The Bishop of Manchester and Professor Dimitri Obolensky, *The Times*, 6 March 1974, p. 13.

115. *The Times*, 7 March 1974, p. 11.

116. *Le Soir* (Brussels), 17–18 March 1974.

117. Contained in a letter to Archbishop Vasili from Metropolitan Yuvenali, chairman of the DECR, 11 March 1974, *AS*, no. 483; photocopy in KC archive.

118. Open letter to Metropolitan Serafim of Krutitsy and Kolomna from Father Gleb Yakunin, 18 February 1974; English translation in *LFM*, p. 21.

119. Open letter to Metropolitan Serafim of Krutitsy and Kolomna from Yevgeni Ternovsky and Eduard Shteinberg, Moscow, 17 February 1974, *AS*, no. 1606.

120. Lev Regelson, letter to the Soviet government on the expulsion of Solzhenitsyn, Moscow, 17 February 1974; English translation in *LFM*, pp. 12–20; this quotation, p. 20. (A greatly abridged English translation is given in *The Oak and the Calf*, p. 538.)

121. Archbishop Vsevolod Shpiller, 'Report to the Council for Religious Affairs under the Council of Ministers of the USSR Concerning an Interview with a Correspondent of APN on A. Solzhenitsyn as a Religious Writer', Moscow, 18 February 1974, *AS*, no. 1738.

122. V. Shpiller, 'The Vicious Has No Future' (*sic*), in *The Last Circle* (a collection of articles) (Novosti Press Agency Publishing House, Moscow, 1974), pp. 144–7.

123. 'Concerning the Statement of Archpriest V. Shpiller against Solzhenitsyn. An Open Letter', signed Mikhail Agursky, Vladimir Osipov, Leonid Borodin, Yevgeni Ternovsky, Vladislav Ilyakov, Nikolai Ivanov, Valentina Mashkova, Vyacheslav Rodionov, Stanislav Sery, Georgi Dudnikov, Eduard Shteinberg, 6 May 1974, *Russkaya mysl*, 20 June 1974.

124. Open letter from Mikhail Agursky, 7 May 1974, ibid.

125. Open letter to Archpriest Vsevolod Shpiller from Merab Kostava, 28 August 1974, *AS*, no. 2106.

126. Mikhail Agursky, letter to the editors of the newspaper *Russkaya mysl* and the journal *Vestnik RKhD*, 8 October 1974, *AS*, no. 1971.

127. To the Public of the Soviet Union and of foreign countries, 26 September 1969, Zampira Asanova and 31 others; English translation in *Religion in Communist-Dominated Areas* (*RCDA*), vol. 8, nos 23–4 (December 1969), pp. 218–19.

128. 'Documents: Anatoli Levitin', (an account of receptions in Levitin's home by a friend who had emigrated, Andrei Dubrov), *RCL*, vol. 2, no. 2 (1974), pp. 21–3.

129. Bourdeaux, *Patriarch and Prophets*, pp. 339–41; letter dated 30 March 1968.

130. *Posev*, no. 11 (1968), pp. 10–11.

131. *RCL*, vol. 2, no. 1 (1974), p.35.

132. Bourdeaux, *Patriarch and Prophets*, p. 340.

133. *LFM*, pp. 22–7, 136–8.

134. Lev Regelson, 'Obrashcheniye k uchastnikam Belgradskoi konferentsii o prinuditelnom trude v SSSR' ('Appeal to Delegates to the Belgrade Conference on Forced Labour in the USSR'), 16 September 1977, *AS*, nos 404–6.

135. N. Meiman and 61 other signatories, 'Zayavlenie v poderzhku Kharti 77' ('Statement in Support of Charter 77'), 12 February 1977, *AS*, no. 2966; *RCL*, vol. 6, no. 1 (1978), p.46.

136. *Ukrainsky visnik* (*Ukrainian Herald*), no. 4 (January 1971), pp. 52–4; English in Alan Scarfe (ed.), *A Voice in the Wildnerness* (Society for the Study of Religion and Communism, Wheaton, Illinois, 1980), pp. 17–18.

137. 'Obrashcheniye k yevreyam i vsem lyudyam dobroi voli s prizyvom vystupit za osvobozhdeniye Eduarda Kuznetsova i yego sotovarishchei' ('Appeal to Jews and All People of Good Will to Appeal for the Release of Eduard Kuznetsov and His Comrades'), *AS* no. 3064.

138. *AS*, no. 1550, June 1973; *AS*, no. 2006, 20 December 1974 (with Yuri Orlov).

139. Sydney Bloch and Peter Reddaway, *Russia's Political Hospitals — The Abuse of Psychiatry in the Soviet Union* (Gollancz, London, 1977), p. 353.

140. S. Soldatov, 'Aktsiya 10 v podderzhku DDE', February 1978, *AS*, no. 3241.

141. 'Zvernennya do ateistiv', *Visnik*, 1 May 1978; Translated into English as 'Christmas Appeal to Atheists', *ABN Correspondence*, September–December 1977, pp. 4–7.

142. Document no. 8 the Group to Promote the Implementation of the Helsinki Agreements in the USSR, 'O zloupotrebleniyakh psikhiatrici' ('On Abuses of Psychiatry'), 12 October 1976, *AS*, no. 2818.

143. Bloch and Reddaway, *Russia's Political Hospitals*, p. 392.

144. Ibid., p. 364; *RCL*, vol. 2, nos 4–5 (1974), pp. 57–8.

145. *CCE*, no. 55, 31 December 1979 (Khronika Press, 1980), p. 14.

11. The Growth of Orthodox Dissent: 1974–6

1. A. Solzhenitsyn (ed.), *Iz-pod glyb* (YMCA Press, Paris, 1974); translated as *From Under the Rubble* (Collins & Harvill Press, London, 1975).

2. Yevgeni Barabanov, 'The Schism Between the Church and the World', in Solzhenitsyn (ed.), *From Under the Rubble*, p. 179.

3. Ibid., p. 180.

4. Ibid., p. 181.

5. Ibid., p. 186.

6. Ibid., p. 191.

7. Ibid., pp. 192–3.

8. English translation in Michael Meerson-Aksenov and Boris Shragin (eds), *The Political, Social and Religious Thought of Russian Samizdat — An Anthology* (Nordland Publishing Company, Belmont, Mass., 1977), pp. 511–41.

9. Ibid., pp. 532–3.

10. Ibid., p. 530.

11. Ibid., pp. 524–5.

12. Ibid., pp. 534–5.

13. Ibid., pp. 538–40.

14. English translation in Meerson-Aksenov and Shragin, ibid., pp. 542–56.

15. Ibid., p. 547.

16. Ibid., p. 551.

17. John Dunlop, 'The Eleventh Hour', *Frontier*, vol. 18, no. 2 (1975), p. 75.

18. *Zemlya*, no. 1 (1 August 1974), *AS*, no. 1909, 32pp.; no. 2 (25 December 1975), *AS*, no. 2060, 67pp.

19. *Zemlya*, no. 1 (1 August 1974), p. 2.

20. *Zemlya*, no. 2 (25 December 1974), pp. 9–10.

21. Ibid., pp. 20–1.

22. Reports of Osipov's arrest and trial are given in *CCE*, no. 37 (30 October 1975), pp. 7–9.

23. Statement for the press by the assistant editor of the journal *Zemlya*, Vyacheslav Rodionov, 15 December 1974, *AS*, no. 2061, 2pp.

24. Copy in KC archive; 197pp.

25. This could be a misprint for V. (Vadim) Borisov, who wrote the article 'Personality and National Awareness' in *Iz-pod glyb*, but if so the misprint occurs twice, on the contents page and the first page of the article.

26. 'O perspektivakh khristianstva sredi yevreyev' ('On the Perspectives for Christianity Among the Jews'), 13 June 1974, *Moskovsky sbornik*, pp. 80–7; KC archive. English extracts in *RCL*, vol. 3, nos 4–5 (1975), pp. 31–2.

27. Translated into English by Marite Sapiets as *The Unknown Homeland* (Mowbrays, Oxford, 1978).

28. Shimanov has given a lengthy autobiographical account of his religious quest in *Pered smertyu* (*Before Death*), Moscow, 1962–66; the first *samizdat* edition, dated 1969, was lost, so

the author rewrote it for a second *samizdat* edition dated 1974; copy in KC archive, 62pp. The above summary is from the sections 'Yunost' ('Youth'), pp. 5–11, and 'Khristos Voskres!' ('Christ is Risen!'), pp. 28–9.

29. Ibid., section entitled 'V sumashedshom dome razmyshlyayu o razume' ('In the Mental Hospital I Meditate on Reason'), pp. 31–5.

30. Shimanov described his hospitalisation very fully in *Zapiski iz krasnogo doma*, the fourth section of *Pered smertyu*, which was not included in the copy received in KC archive. An English translation entitled *Notes from the Red House* was published by Diane Books, Glendale, California, 1972 (second edition). This has been adapted as a play, *Catwalk*, by the English Christian playwright Murray Watts, in a version very faithful to the original text. For an account of Shimanov's hospitalisation in the context of Soviet psychiatric abuse, see S. Bloch and P. Reddaway, *Russia's Political Hospitals* (Gollancz, London, 1977), pp. 158–70.

31. According to Bloch and Reddaway (*Russia's Political Hospitals*, p. 168), Shimanov had been contacted regularly up to their interview with him in June 1976 'at any time, and invariably before major public holidays'. No doubt this was designed to prevent any initiatives he might have been planning for these non-working days when it might have been possible to attract the attention of a large segment of the Soviet population: such 'prophylactic' measures by the Soviet authorities have been observed in the cases of a number of known dissenters, and have included such occasions as visits by foreign heads of state, when dissenters have sometimes been temporarily imprisoned.

32. Gennadi Shimanov, *Protiv techeniya* (*Against the Current*), a collection of articles, Moscow, 1975, 119pp.; copy in KC archive. This quote from 'Vera v chudo' ('Belief in a Miracle'), p. 56.

33. Ibid., p. 60.

34. Ibid., p. 23; from 'Otryvki iz dnevnika' ('Notes from a Diary').

35. Vladimir Osipov, 'Otkrytoye pismo Gennadiyu Shimanovu' ('Open Letter to Gennadi Shimanov'), *AS*, no. 1732; in *Volnoye slovo* (*The Free Word*), *Iz zhurnala Veche*, 1975, p. 14.

36. Shimanov, 'Kak otnositsya k sovetskoi vlasti' ('How to Relate to Soviet Power'), reply to V. N. Osipov, Moscow, 2 June 1974, *Protiv techeniya*, pp. 95–105; KC archive; this quote, p. 100.

37. Ibid., p. 101.

38. Shimanov, 'Put zhizni' ('The Path of Life'), *Protiv techeniya*, p. 62.

39. Shimanov, 'Razumnaya uzost' ('Prudent Narrowness'), *Protiv techeniya*, p. 66.

40. Ibid., p. 101.

41. Shimanov, 'O Tserkvi v sovremennoi Rossii' ('The Church in Contemporary Russia'), *Protiv techeniya*, pp. 73–4.

42. Ibid., pp. 103–4.

43. Ibid., p. 104.

44. A. Krasnov, 'Zemlya dybom' ('The Earth Turned Upside Down'), Moscow, 1974, *AS*, no. 1876, 104pp., p. 7ff.

45. Shimanov, *Protiv techeniya*, pp. 89–90.

46. Ibid., p. 91.

47. Ibid., p. 110, 'Moskva–Treti Rim' ('Moscow–The Third Rome'); this was republished in *Moskovsky sbornik*.

48. Shimanov, *Idealnoye gosudarstvo* (*The Ideal State*), Moscow, 29 May 1975; copies of first and second version in KC archive; p. 8 of second version.

49. In an interview given to the Jewish *samizdat* journal *Yevrei v SSSR* (*Jews in the USSR*), Shimanov did not seek to avoid the charge of anti-semitism, though he substituted the term anti-Judaism; he spelled out his views on the question in detail, maintaining that he wanted for his fellow-Russians and the Russian nation only what Jews wanted and worked for for the Jewish people: G. M. Shimanov, 'Otvety voprosam korrespondentaz hurnala *Yevrei v SSSR*' ('Answers to Questions of a Correspondent of *Jews in the USSR*', Moscow, 13 May 1976; copy in KC archive, 13pp.

50. *Priglasheniye k dialogu* (*Invitation to Dialogue*) comprises six articles by Shimanov, Karelin and Ibragimov which form detailed and harsh criticisms of the positive attitude to Judaism expressed by Barabanov and Father Men (a Jewish convert to Christianity) in interviews which they gave to *Yevrei v SSSR*: Moscow, 1978; copy in KC archive, 40pp.

51. 'Problemy sovremennogo Khristianstva (Iz lichnoi perepiski)' ('Problems of

Contemporary Christianity (From Personal Correspondence)'), *Vestnik RKhD*, nos 115 (1975), pp. 5–16, and 118 (1976), pp. 32–45.

52. *Vestnik RKhD*, no. 115 (1975), pp. 14–15.

53. Yevgeni Barabanov, 'Pravda gumanizma', Moscow, 1975, pp. 11–26 of the collection of articles *Samosoznaniye* (*Insights*), compiled by P. Litvinov, M. Meerson-Aksyonov, B. Shragin (Khronika Press, New York, 1976). The compilers wrote that the unifying theme of the articles was a liberal–democratic view: though the history of Russian liberalism, which had arisen at the end of the nineteenth century, was not long or successful, it was still alive in *samizdat*. It is interesting that Barabanov was invited to contribute to both this liberal–democratic symposium and to the more conservative, patriotic *Iz-pod glyb*. In fact, neither of his articles supported one view or the other; his concern was for the church and society, or the world, at large, irrespective of the political or social system in which it found itself.

54. 'Pravda gumanizma', pp. 20–1.

55. Ibid., p. 19.

56. Ibid., p. 26.

57. Ibid.

58. Barabanov wrote an article giving a detailed commentary on Solovyov's 1891 lecture on this theme, 'O prichinakh upadka srednevekovogo mirosozertsaniya' ('The Reasons for the Decline of the Medieval World-View'): the article was entitled 'Zabyty spor' ('A Forgotten Argument'), *Vestnik RKhD*, no. 118 (1976), pp. 117–65.

59. Mikhail Meerson-Aksyonov, 'La Chiesa ortodossa nello Stato ateo', *Russian Cristiana*, no. 168 (November–December 1979), pp. 9–21; this quote, p. 19.

60. Mikhail Meerson-Aksyonov, 'Rozhdeniye novoi intelligentsii' ('The Birth of a New Intelligentsia'), in Litvinov *et al., Samosoznaniye*, pp. 89–116.

61. Shimanov, *Protiv techeniya*, p. 108.

62. Timothy Ware, *The Orthodox Church* (Penguin Books, Harmondsworth, 1963), p. 205.

63. Statement by Yevgeni Barabanov, 8 September 1975, 25 September 1975, p. 3; English translation in Bordeaux *et al.*, *Religious Liberty in the Soviet Union* (henceforward *RLinSU*), p. 63.

64. 'Appeal to the XXVth Congress of the CPSU by a group (*sic*) of Christians of the Russian Orthodox Church', Hierodeacon Varsonofi (Boris Khaibulin), Murom, Vladimir region and Gleb Mileshkin, Balta, Odessa region, undated but evidently written before the CPSU Congress on 24 February 1976, *AS*, no. 2567.

65. 'Open Letter to His Grace Archbishop Vladimir of Vladimir and Suzdal, member of the delegation of the Russian Orthodox Church to the Assembly of the World Council of Churches in Nairobi, and to the entire respected Assembly, from a cleric of the Vladimir Diocese of the Moscow Patriarchate, Hierodeacon Varsonofi (Khaibulin)', 23 November 1975, Murom, Vladimir region; copy in KC archive.

66. Translations of these documents, with explanatory background material, are given in Gleb Yakunin and Lev Regelson, *Letters from Moscow*. ed. Jane Ellis (Keston College and H. S. Dakin Company, San Francisco, 1978); henceforward *LFM*.

67. Father Gleb Yakunin and Lev Regelson, 'Na smert Bogatyreva' ('On the Death of Bogatyrev'), 27 June 1976, *Russkaya mysl*, 23 September 1976, p. 5; *LFM*, p. 70 (Russian text, p. 72).

68. 'Obrashcheniye k Khristianam Portugalii' ('An Appeal to Christians of Portugal'), Father Gleb Yakunin and Lev Regelson, Moscow 3 April 1975, *Vestnik*, no. 116 (1975), pp. 253–6; *LFM*, pp. 29–31.

69. Father Gleb Yakunin, 'Pismo arkhiepiskomu Pitirimu' ('Letter to Archbishop Pitirim'), editor of the *Journal of the Moscow Patriarchate*, 26 November 1974), *Vestnik*, no. 114 (1974), pp. 265–7; *LFM*, pp. 27–8.

70. Father Gleb Yakunin and Lev Regelson, 'Letter to the Reverend David Hathaway', Moscow, 4 April 1976; Russian text in KC archive; *LFM*, pp. 67–9.

71. Father Gleb Yakunin, 'Letter to V. A. Kuroyedov, chairman of the Council for Religious Affairs', 14 January 1976, *Vestnik*, no. 117 (1976), pp. 263–4; *LFM*, pp. 47–8.

72. *KNS*, no. 9 (25 April 1975).

73. Father Gleb Yakunin, 'Politbyuro Ts.K.KPSS — Otkrytoye pismo' ('Open Letter to the Politburo of the Central Committee of the CPSU'), Moscow, 19 April 1975, *Vestnik*, no. 115 (1975), pp. 219–20; *LFM*, pp. 32–3.

74. *Izvestiya*, 8 April 1982, p. 1; *KNS*, no. 147 (22 April 1982).

75. Father Gleb Yakunin, Viktor Kapitanchuk, Lev Regelson, 'Appeal for the Glorification of Russian Martyrs in the USSR', Moscow, 25 May 1975; *Russkaya zhizn*, 4 December 1975; *LFM*, pp. 34–40.

76. Father Gleb Yakunin and Lev Regelson, 'Obrashcheniye k delegatam V assembleya Vsemirnogo Soveta Tserkvei' ('Appeal to the delegates of the Fifth Assembly of the World Council of Churches'), Moscow, 16 October 1975, *AS*, no. 2380; *LFM*, pp. 41–6, reprinted from *RCL*, vol. 4, no. 1 (1976), pp. 9–14.

77. *RCL*, vol. 4, no. 1 (1976), pp. 15–16.

78. Accounts of events in the Assembly are given in David Kelly, 'Nairobi: A Door Opened', *RCL*, vol. 4, no. 1 (1976), pp. 4–8; and Elena Pozdeeva, 'The Report Card of the Moscow Patriarchate's Delegation in Nairobi', *Radio Liberty Research*, 23 February 1976, RL 104/76.

79. *JMP*, no. 4 (1976), pp. 7–13.

80. Ibid., p. 11.

81. Ibid., pp. 12–13; translation taken from the English edition of *JMP*, p. 16.

82. *Moscow News*, 7–14 February 1976; extracts in *LFM*, pp. 134–5; summary on radio by TASS in English, 12.51 GMT, 29 January 1976, *Summary of World Broadcasts*, 31 January 1976, SU/5122/A1/5–6.

83. *Golos rodiny*, no. 41 (October 1976), pp. 12–13.

84. Letter to Dr Potter from Archbishop Vasili of Brussels and Belgium (Moscow Patriarchate), undated, *Vestnik RKhD*, no. 120 (1977), p. 313.

85. Interview with the Deputy Minister of Justice of the USSR, A. Sukharev, *New Times*, 4 January 1976.

86. Vladimir Kuroyedov, 'Sovetsky zakon i svoboda sovesti' ('Soviet Law and Freedom of Conscience'), *Izvestiya*, 31 January 1976, p. 5; English translation in *RCL*, vol. 4, no. 2 (1976), pp. 41–6.

87. *Pravda*, 20 February 1976.

88. A. Belov and A. D. Shilkin, *Diversiya bez dinamita* (Izd Politicheskoi lituratury, Moscow, 1976).

89. 'Generalnomu Sekretaryu Vsemirnogo Soveta Tserkvei Filippu Potteru' ('Letter to the General Secretary of the World Council of Churches, Philip Potter'), from Father Gleb Yakunin and Lev Regelson, members of the Russian Orthodox Church, Moscow, 6 March 1976 (in KC archive); English translation in *RLinSU*, pp. 40–53; *LFM*, pp. 53–66.

90. 'Yego Svyateishestvu, Svyateishemu Pimenu, Patriarkhu Moskovskomu i Vseya Rusi' ('To His Holiness, the Most Holy Pimen, Patriarch of Moscow and all Russia'), from Father Gleb Yakunin and Lev Regelson, 4 March 1876, *Religiya i ateizm v SSSR*, May 1976, pp. 13–15; *LFM*, pp. 49–52.

91. 'Letter to Dr Philip Potter, General Secretary of the World Council of Churches', from Father Sergi Zheludkov, Pskov, 10 April 1976 (copy in KC archive).

92. Michael Bourdeaux, Hans Hebly and Eugen Voss (eds), *Religious Liberty in the Soviet Union, WCC and USSR, A Post-Nairobi Documentation* (Keston College, 1976).

93. Helene Posdeeff, 'Geneva: The Defence of Believers' Rights', *RCL*, vol. 4, no. (1976), p. 6.

94. Ibid., pp. 6–8.

12. The Flowering of Orthodox Dissent: 1976–9

1. Appeal of members of the Christian Churches of the USSR to the Presidium of the Supreme Soviet of the USSR and the World Council of Churches (27 signatures), 20 June 1976, *Vestnik RKhD*, no. 118 (1976), pp. 301–13.

2. The inclusion of the Church of Christ alongside the other much larger and older communities is somewhat anomalous. At the time of the ecumenical appeal it was believed to have no more than a handful of members, who had formerly been reform Baptists, and it has not been very active, at least in *samizdat*, since then. Although its members initially had some contact with the Church of Christ in the USA, it is not affiliated to it.

3. *Izvestiya*, 31 January 1976.

4. Ibid., p. 4.

5. *Vestnik RKhD*, no. 118 (1976), pp. 308–9.

6. Ibid., pp. 309–10.

7. Ibid., p. 312.

8. Ibid., p. 313.

9. Gennadi Shimanov, 'Open Letter to His Holiness Patriarch Pimen of Moscow and All Russia', Moscow, 15 July 1976; abridged English translation published as a pamphlet by Monastery Press, 8011 Champagneur Ave., Montreal, Quebec, Canada H3N 2K4, of the Free Russian Orthodox Church Outside of Russia.

10. The following pages are largely based on the present author's article 'The Christian Committee for the Defence of Believers' Rights in the USSR', *RCL*, vol. 8, no. 4 (1980), pp. 279–91.

11. See the founding 'Declaration' of the Christian Committee dated 27 December 1976; English translation in *RCL*, vol. 6, no. 1 (1978), pp. 33–4.

12. A copy of the visitor's report is filed in KC archive.

13. Ibid.

14. From vol. 13 the task of publishing was assumed by CCDBR Publications, Glendale, California, while responsibility for editing and translation was assumed by the Society for the Study of Religion under Communism, also in California. The Russian texts intended for vol. 13 were not published as such, and instead selected English translations from vols 4–12 were published as vol. 13 under the title *The CCDBR Documents: Christian Committee for the Defense of Believers' Rights in the USSR*, translated by Maria Belaeffa, edited by Alan Scarfe (Door of Hope Press and Society for the Study of Religion under Communism, Glendale/Orange, California, 1982). Earlier volumes of *DCCDBR* may be ordered from Washington Research Center, 3101 Washington Street, San Francisco, California 94115.

15. *DCCDBR*, vol. 1, p. 22, and pp. 23–6 (illegible), dated 23 June 1977; *AS*, no. 3143; English translation in *RCL*, vol. 6, no. 1 (1978), pp. 34–6.

16. *DCCDBR*, vol. 1, pp. 30–5; English translation in KC archive.

17. *DCCDBR*, vol. 1, pp. 37–8.

18. *DCCDBR*, vol. 2, pp. 159–63; English translation in *DCCDBR*, vol. 3, pp. 290–7, and in *RCL*, vol. 7, no. 3 (1979), pp. 191–4 (abridged).

19. *DCCDBR*, vol. 5, part 2. An English translation was prepared for vol. 5, part 3, but not published; copy in KC archive.

20. *DCCDBR*, vol. 7, pp. 922–6.

21. *DCCDBR*, vol. 10, pp. 1007–10.

22. *Russkaya mysl*, 27 September 1979, p. 4.

23. The breakdown of these documents is as follows: Orthodox — 154, including 20 signed by the Christian Committee; Reform Baptist — 100, including 5 signed by the Christian Committee; Pentecostal — 25, including 5 signed by the Christian Committee; documents issued jointly by Reform Baptists and Pentecostals (mostly on the emigration issue) — 17, including 5 signed by the Christian Committee; True and Free Seventh-Day Adventists — 37, including 3 signed by the Christian Committee; Roman Catholic — 49 (nearly all from Lithuania but with some from Moldavia), including 1 signed by the Christian Committee; Georgian Orthodox — 5, including 3 signed by the Christian Committee; Jewish — 2, both signed by the Christian Committee; other — 16, including 2 signed by the Christian Committee. This last category comprises documents covering more than one denomination, and those concerning non-religious matters (mostly appeals on behalf of arrested members of Helsinki Monitoring Groups who had helped religious believers).

24. *DCCDBR*, vol. 1, p. 20, and vol. 2, p. 170; English translation in KC archive.

25. Alan Scarfe, 'Dismantling a Human Rights Movement: A Romanian Solution', *RCL*, vol. 7, no. 3 (1979), pp. 166–70, describes the formation of ALRC, though without mentioning the small contributory inspiration provided by the Christian Committee.

26. *DCCDBR*, vol. 1, pp. 41–2.

27. Statement by Father Nikolai Gainov and Vadim Shcheglov, 12 March 1980; English translation in *RCL*, vol. 8, no. 4 (1980), p. 298.

28. *DCCDBR*, vol. 10, p. 1077; English translation in *RCL*, vol. 8, no. 4 (1980), pp. 297–8.

29. Ibid., pp. 1078–9.

30. KNS, no. 121, (9 April 1981), p. 3.

31. October 1974 according to a letter from Alexander Ogorodnikov to Dr Philip Potter, General Secretary of the WCC, 27 July 1976 (English translation in *RCL*, vol. 4, no. 4 (1976), pp. 45–7); September 1974 according to a letter to Dr Potter from Ogorodnikov and Boris Razveyev, 5 August 1976 (English translation in *RCL*, vol. 7, no. 1 (1979), pp. 49–50).

32. The discussion of the Christian Seminar which follows is largely based on the present author's article 'USSR: The Christian Seminar', *RCL*, vol. 8, no. 2 (1980), pp. 92–101.

33. Michael Aksenov-Meerson, 'The Russian Orthodox Church 1965–1980', *RCL*, vol. 9, nos 3–4 (1981), p. 106.

34. *RCL*, vol. 4, no. 4 (1976), p. 46.

35. *RCL*, vol. 7, no. 1 (1979), p. 49.

36. Ibid.

37. *RCL*, vol. 4 no. 4 (1976), p. 46.

38. *RCL*, vol. 7, no. 1 (1979), pp. 40–50.

39. Anatoli Levitin, 'Religion and Soviet Youth', *RCL*, vol. 7, no. 4 (1979), p. 236.

40. *Idea* (Informationsdienst der Evangelischen Allianz), no. 3 (1980), 28 January 1980.

41. *Obshchina*, no. 2 (1978), pp. 35–48; photograph of typed original in KC archive.

42. Instructions of the People's Commissariat of the Interior, 1 October 1929; amended 28 January 1932, Article 22, Part 3.

43. Anatoli Levitin has said that Ogorodnikov's marks at the Institute are known to have been excellent, all 4s and 5s (out of 5 — the universal Soviet marking system). Ogorodnikov's claim that he was expelled because he was a Christian has been discussed in Chapter 7, and is also referred to in the following chapter.

44. Tatyana Shchipkova, 'Spiritual Pilgrimage of Vladimir Poresh', 28 February 1979; English translation in *RCL*, vol. 8, no. 2 (1980), pp. 101–3.

45. Tatyana Shchipkova, 'Has a Soviet Teacher the Right to Freedom of Conscience?', undated but July–September 1978; *DCCDBR*, vol. 4, pp. 497–506; English translation (abridged) in *RCL*, vol. 8, no. 2 (1980), pp. 106–9. A brief biography of Scchipkova is given in *KNS*, no. 122 (24 April 1981), pp. 16–17.

46. For a selection of documents on Christian teachers in Lithuania, see Michael Bourdeaux, *Land of Crosses* (Augustine Publishing Company, Devon, 1979), pp. 219–22.

47. *RCL*, vol. 8, no. 2 (1980), p. 106.

48. An account of this is given by Anatoli Levitin-Krasnov in Chapter 1 of Father Gleb Yakunin and Lev Regelson, *Letters from Moscow*, ed. Jane Ellis (Keston College and H. S. Dakin Company, San Francisco, 1978); henceforward *LFM*.

49. *RCL*, vol. 8, no. 2 (1980), p. 106.

50. This analysis, and other insights which follow, owe much to the article by Philip Walters, 'The Ideas of the Christian Seminar', *RCL*, vol. 9, nos 3–4 (1981), pp. 111–22.

51. Letters to Dr Potter, *RCL*, vol. 4, no. 4 (1976), p. 46; vol. 7, no. 1 (1979), p. 50.

52. Walters, 'The Ideas', p. 113.

53. Ibid.

54. Ibid., p. 120, note 21.

55. 'Young Russia to Young America', members of the Christian Seminar on Problems of the Religious Renaissance, August (?) 1979; copy in KC archive.

56. 'Zapis protsessa Vladimira Poresha v Lengorsude' ('Note on the Trial of Vladimir Poresh in Leningrad City Court'), soon after 25 April 1980, *AS*, no. 4022, p. 59.

57. *Obshchina*, *AS*, no. 3452, p. 41. Walters ('The Ideas', p. 120, note 32) notes that 'an early example of the interest of Ogorodnikov in the witness of members of other faiths was the film *Dzhizes pipl* (*Jesus People*) which he was planning to make and which may have been one of the factors leading to his expulsion from the Moscow Cinematography Institute'.

58. Walters, 'The Ideas', p. 116.

59. Yevgeni Vagin, former VSKhSON member now in Rome, in *Russkoye vozrozhdeniye*, no. 1 (1978), p. 57; Walters, 'The Ideas', p. 121, note 39.

60. Walters, 'The Ideas', p. 118.

61. *AS*, no. 4022, p. 59.

62. Ye. Giryayev, 'Religiozno-filosofsky seminar v Leningrade', *Vestnik RKhD*, no. 123 (1977), p. 170.

63. Giryayev (ibid., p. 169) says that a majority of the members were Orthodox, but then

contradicts this by stating (p. 170) that 'a no less numerous group' were agnostics and atheists.

64. Ibid.
65. Tatyana Goricheva, 'Religious Revival', *Light in the East*, vol. 4, no. 1 (January 1981), p. 7.
66. Ibid.
67. Ibid.
68. *Catacombes*, February 1981, p. 11.
69. Giryayev, 'Religiozno-filosofsky', p. 170.
70. Interview with Tatyana Goricheva, 'Gli Occhi di Fede di una Donna Russa' ('A Russian Woman's Eyes of Faith'), *Litterae Communionis*, no. 6 (June 1981), pp. 18–19.
71. Giryayev, 'Religiozno-filosofsky', p. 170.
72. Goricheva, 'Religious Revival', p. 7.
73. Giryayev, 'Religiozno-filosofsky', pp. 170–1.
74. *37*, no. 6 (June–August 1976), pp. 212–5; copy in KC archive.
75. *37*, no. 5 (May 1976), p. 181; copy in KC archive.
76. Goricheva, 'Religious Revival', p. 7.
77. Letter from Goricheva to Theo van der Voort, undated but shortly before 12 November 1979; copy in KC archive.
78. Goricheva, 'Religious Revival', p. 7.
79. Ibid.
80. *37*, no. 5 (May 1976), pp. 181–4.
81. *37*, no. 17 (1979), pp. 210–16; copy in KC archive.
82. Ibid., critic no. 6, p. 215.
83. Ibid., pp. 196–202.
84. Ibid., p. 200.
85. Ibid., pp. 202–5.
86. Giryayev, 'Religiozno-filosofsky', p. 170.
87. Ibid., pp. 173–4.
88. Ibid., pp. 172–3.
89. *Mariya, spetsialny vypusk* (special issue), no. 1, published by the Mariya Club in Frankfurt, September 1981. This was an *émigré* publication, not identical to the Russian *samizdat* journal *Mariya*, and was produced by Yuliya Voznesenskaya after her emigration.
90. *Zhenshchina i Rossiya*, 10 December 1979, Leningrad, published by Des Femmes, Paris, 1980; English translation, *Woman and Russia*, published by Sheba Feminist Publishers, London, 1980.
91. Ibid., p. 31. See also Goricheva's speech at a meeting in Rimini, Italy; text in *Russia Cristiana*, no. 180 (1981), pp. 40–5.
92. T. Goricheva, 'Paradoksy zhenskoi emansipatsii' ('Paradoxes of Female Emancipation'), *37*, no. 19 (September–December 1979), no page numbers; copy in KC archive.
93. *Mariya*, special issue, no. 1, Frankfurt, p. 1.
94. *Russkaya mysl*, 26 February 1981, p. 6; see also *Mariya*, ibid.
95. *Russkaya mysl*, 19 June 1980, p. 3; English translation in *Guardian*, 31 July 1980, p. 8.
96. Lev Regelson, *Tragediya russkoi tserkvi 1917–1945* (YMCA Press, Paris, 1977); English translation (of Part 1 only), by Jane Ellis, is in KC archive.
97. Ibid., p. 14.
98. Ibid., p. 59.
99. Anatoli Levitin-Krasnov and Vadim Shavrov, *Ocherki po istorii russkoi tserkovnoi smuty* (*Essays on the History of the Russian Church Troubles*) (Institut Glaube in der 2. Welt, Küsnacht, Switzerland, 1978). Vladimir Stepanov (Rusak's pseudonym), *Svidetelstvo obvineniya. Tserkov i gosudarstvo v Sovetskom Soyuze* (*Testimony of the Prosecution. Church and State in the Soviet Union*), Moscow 1980, 3 vols; typescript reprinted by Institut Glaube in der 2. Welt, Küsnacht, Switzerland. We cited one section of this extensively in Chapter 6 (see pp. 150–68 *passim*).
100. Father Dimitri Dudko, 'O chem propovedovat?' ('What Should We Preach About?'), *Russkoye vozrozhedeniye*, no. 2 (1978), pp. 10–26.
101. Father Dimitri Dudko, 'Chto znachit proslavleniye russkikh muchenikov' ('The Meaning of the Glorification of the Russian Martyrs'), 10 May 1979, *Russkaya mysl*,

13 December 1979, p. 9; *Russkoye vozrozhdeniye*, nos 7–8 (1979), pp. 31–2.

102. 'K russkim pravoslavnym khristianam v otechestve i v rasseyanii sushchim' ('To Russian Orthodox Christians in the Homeland and in Diaspora'), Moscow, 12 September 1979, *Russkaya mysl*, 6 October 1979, p. 5.

103. 'Letter from Russia', signed R. Kh., *Russkaya mysl*, 17 March 1977, p. 10.

104. *Newsletter of the Saint George Orthodox Information Service*, no. 5 (April 1980).

105. Yakunin Report, p. 38.

106. Ibid., p. 39.

107. Ibid., p. 40.

13. The Repression of Dissent: 1976–80

1. Boris Roshchin, 'Svoboda religii i klevetniki' ('Freedom of Religion and the Slanderers'), *Literaturnaya gazeta*, 13 and 20 April 1977, Moscow; English translation in Gleb Yakunin and Lev Regelson, *Letters from Moscow*, ed. Jane Ellis (Keston College and H. S. Dakin Company, San Francisco, 1978), pp. 74–83 (henceforward *LFM*).

2. The press conference consisted of introductory remarks by Father Gleb Yakunin, a statement by Father Dimitri Dudko, and a statement by Konstantin (no surname) identified as a spiritual son of Father Dimitri. Eleven documents signed by the four men mentioned in the article and their supporters were distributed to Western correspondents. The statements and documents have been translated into English in *LFM*, pp. 84–115.

3. Anatoli Levitin-Krasnov, 'Save these Honest People!', published in *Novoye russkoye slovo*, 7 May 1977; English translation in *LFM*, pp. 116–17.

4. *LFM*, p. 77.

5. Ibid., pp. 79–80.

6. Ibid., pp. 102, 118.

7. Ibid., p. 81.

8. Ibid., p. 100.

9. Ibid., pp. 83, 79.

10. Ibid., pp. 85–7.

11. L. Ivanov, 'Outspoken Priest Nearly Killed in Road "Accident"' (based on telephone conversation with Anatoli Levitin), *The Guardian of Liberty*, May–June 1975, p. 8.

12. *The Chronicle of Current Events*, no. 38 (31 December 1975), p. 68 (henceforward *CCE*).

13. Petition to Patriarch Pimen of Moscow and All Russia from parishioners of the Church of St Nikita the Martyr in the village of Kabanovo, Orekhovo-Zuyevsky district, Moscow region, undated but January 1976, about 100 signatures; English translation in *RLinSU*, p. 66.

14. Declaration to Representatives of the Christian Churches, seven signatures, 15 January 1976; English translation in *RLinSU*, p. 66. Copies of related documents in KC archives.

15. Statement (*zayavleniye*) of Metropolitan Serafim of Krutitsy and Kolomna to the Department of Communication of the WCC, 13 January 1976; copy in KC archive.

16. *Russkaya mysl*, 8 December 1977, p. 4.

17. Ibid., 7 December 1978, p. 4.

18. Ibid., 26 October 1978, p. 5.

19. *Informationsdienst G2W*, nr. 17 (2 December 1977), p. 6; *Catacombes*, 15 December 1977, p. 6.

20. Nos 1, 12 and 13 (September–26 November 1978), in *Vestnik RKhD*, no. 127 (1978), pp. 237–47. Subsequent issues in *Vestnik RKhD* and KC archive. English translation of no. 1 in *The Samizdat Bulletin*, no. 71 (March 1979).

21. *DCCDBR*, vol. 7, p. 823.

22. Ibid., pp. 824–8.

23. Ibid., pp. 829–30.

24. *Information Bulletin* of the Department of External Church Relations of the Moscow Patriarchate, nos 18–19, 15 October 1979.

25. *USSR News Brief*, nos 24–6 (1979); anonymous letter from Grebnevo dated 21 October

1979, *Russkaya mysl*, 15 November 1979, p. 15.

26. *Vestnik RKhD*, no. 120 (1977), p. 314.

27. 'In the Light of the Transfiguration', no. 45 (63) (9 December 1979) in *Russkaya mysl*, 21 February 1980, p. 4.

28. Issues of 'In the Light of the Transfiguration' dated 6 December 1979, in *Russkaya mysl*, 29 February 1980, p. 5.

29. *CCE*, no. 41 (3 August 1976), pp. 12–14 (Argentov); *AS*, no. 2818 (12 October 1976) (Fedotov).

30. 'A. Ogorodnikov's Conversation with a Soviet Psychiatrist', *Obshchina*, no. 2 (Moscow-Leningrad, 1978), pp. 159–63; English translation in *RCL*, vol. 8, no. 2 (1980), pp. 109–12 (quotation from p. 111).

31. Letter to Dr Potter of the WCC from Alexander Ogorodnikov, 27 July 1976; English translation in *RCL*, vol. 4, no. 4 (1976), p. 47.

32. *Information Bulletin of the Working Commission to Investigate the Use of Psychiatry for Political Purposes*, no. 21 (18 February 1980).

33. Letter to Dr Philip Potter, secretary-general of the WCC, from ten friends of Ogorodnikov and members of the Christian Seminar, 18 April 1977; English translation in *LFM*, pp. 104–8.

34. Ibid.

35. 'A Short History of Repressions Against the Seminar on Problems of the Religious Renaissance During the Last Year', 15 August 1979, *AS*, no. 3748.

36. Letter to Dr Potter from Alexander Ogorodnikov; letter to the Procurator-General of the USSR from the Christian Committee, undated but probably 1976, after 13 July; *DCCDBR*, vol. 1, p. 6.

37. Ibid.

38. Ibid.

39. *DCCDBR*, vol. 4, pp. 486–92; English translation in vol. 3, pp. 303–9; this quotation, p. 309.

40. 'Protocol of a Search', 21 May 1978, signed by Senior Investigator Kleshcheva; *DCCDBR*, vol. 4, pp. 493–5. Several of the confiscated items listed here subsequently appeared in *Obshchina*, no. 2 (1978), so evidently they were not the only copies. Perhaps the members of the Christian Seminar had profited by the experience of losing all extant copies of materials for *Obshchina*, no. 1, in a similar search.

41. Letter to the Procuracy of the USSR from Sergei Yermolayev, 27 May 1978; *DCCDBR*, vol. 6, pp. 734–5.

42. *CCE*, no. 52, 1 March 1979, p. 29.

43. Undated, but written between July and September 1978; *DCCDBR*, vol. 4, pp. 497–506; English translation of pp. 497–502 in *RCL*, vol. 8, no. 2 (1980), pp. 106–9.

44. Ibid., p. 107.

45. Ibid.

46. Ibid., p. 108.

47. Ibid.

48. Untitled, undated description of the meeting, signed by T. Shchipkova; *DCCDBR*, vol. 11, pp. 1178–80.

49. Telegram to the Procurator of the USSR from seven members of the Christian Seminar and Kapitanchuk for the CCDBR, 26 November 1978; *DCCDBR*, vol. 7, p. 855.

50. Vladimir Belozerov, 'Sud-spektakl nad Aleksandrom Ogorodnikovym' ('The Theatrical Performance of Alexander Orgorodnikov's Trial'), 10 December 1978; *DCCDBR*, vol. 9, pp. 976–82. (This date must be a misprint: all other sources give the trial date as 10 January 1979).

51. See *Christian Prisoners in the USSR 1979*, published by Keston College (Keston, England), and *Soviet Christian Prisoner List 1981*, published in 1981 by the Society for the Study of Religion under Communism (Orange, California); also updates in *KNS*.

52. 'Appeal to the Christians of our Country', undated, *Russkaya mysl*, 17 January 1980; English translation in *RCL*, vol. 8, no. 4 (1980), pp. 292–3.

53. Declaration by Stanislav Zherdev, Anatoli Vlasov, Nikolai Romanyuk and others, Moscow, November 1979; English translation in *RCL*, vol. 8, no. 4 (1980), p. 293.

54. 'K arestu o. Gleba Yakunina' ('On the Arrest of Fr Gleb Yakunin'), Igor Shafarevich

and 22 others, 4 November 1979, *AS*, no. 3853; the same text was reissued on 14 November 1979 with a total of 73 signatures, ending with the statement that the collection of signatures was continuing on 19 November; *Russkaya mysl*, 17 January 1980, p. 4.

55. Appeal (*obrashcheniye*) to His Holiness Patriarch Pimen from Fr Nikolai Gainov, 4 November 1979, *Russkaya mysl*, 17 January 1980, p. 4.

56. *Le Monde*, 7 November 1979, p. 8; Gainov's signature appears under a CCDBR document dated 10 November 1979, *Russkaya mysl*, 10 January 1980, p. 4.

57. Reports (*soobshcheniya*) of the Christian Committee for the Defence of Believers' Rights in the USSR, 19 November 1979, Moscow, *Russkaya mysl*, 10 January 1980, p. 4. (The date '1976' in this source must be a misprint.) The reports concerned the interrogation of Tatyana Goricheva and others in Leningrad; the difficulties of a Leningrad Baptist family who wished to emigrate; the breaking-up of a Pentecostal prayer meeting and the arrest of the Pentecostal Fyodor Sidenko in Starotitarovskaya, Kuban.

58. Open letter to the Procurator-General of the USSR from Iraida Georgievna Yakunin, 17 November 1979, *Russkaya mysl*, 10 January 1980; English summary in *KNS*, no. 90 (25 January 1980), pp. 2–3. For a summary of the illegalities committed during the searches and arrest, see also appendix (*prilozheniye*) to the open letter of Iraida Yakunin by lawyer (pensioner) S. V. Kallistratova, issued on the same date and printed/summarised in the same nos of *Russkaya mysl* and *KNS*.

59. Ibid.

60. Ibid.

61. 'Declaration (*zayavleniye*) by a member of the Christian Committee for the Defence of Believers' Rights in the USSR, Priest Gleb Yakunin', 10 October 1979; *DCCDBR*, vol. 12, pp. 1242–3.

62. Ibid.

63. *KNS*, no. 89 (10 January 1980), p. 1.

64. Declaration (*zayavleniye*) to the Moscow CRA commissioner, A. S. Plekhanov, from V. Poresh, V. Popkov and V. Burtsev, 26 February 1979, *AS*, no. 3545.

65. *KNS*, nos. 92 (18 February 1980), p. 3; 94 (20 March 1980), p. 7; 96 (17 April 1980), p. 3.

66. *KNS*, no. 96 (17 April 1980), p. 3.

67. Letter to Father Viktor Potapov in Washington, 20 December 1979, *Russkaya mysl*, 31 January 1980, p. 6; English translation in *KNS*, no. 90 (25 January 1980), p. 13.

68. Details were given by Mrs Dudko in a telephone call to the West on 16 January, reported in *Russkaya mysl*, 31 January 1980, p. 6; these and subsequent details were reported in *KNS*, nos 90 (25 January 1980), p. 2, and 91 (7 February 1980), p. 2.

69. Viktor Kapitanchuk was reported in *Russkaya mysl* (14 February 1980, p. 5) as saying that Father Dudko might be charged under Article 70; *USSR News Brief* (no. 2, 31 January 1980) reported that he had been so charged.

70. *Russkaya mysl*, 29 February 1980, p. 4.

71. *KNS*, no. 94 (20 March 1980), p. 3.

72. 'Appeal from Leningrad', by members of the Leningrad religious seminar and others, *Russkaya mysl*, 29 February 1980, p. 3.

73. Open letter to His Holiness Patriarch Pimen from seven named and 48 unnamed spiritual children of Father Dimitri Dudko, 17 February 1980, *Russkaya mysl*, 20 March 1980, p. 4.

74. 'Appeal to the Christian Public' ('Obrashcheniye k Khristianskoi obshchestvennosti'), by Christian Committee members Father Nikolai Gainov, Viktor Kapitanchuk and Vadim Shcheglov, Moscow, January 1980; photocopy of handwritten and typed version in KC archive.

75. 'On the Arrest of Fr Dimitri Dudko', V. Borisov, I. Shafarevich, I. Khokhlushkin and L. Borodin, 16 January 1980, *Russkaya mysl*, 27 March 1980, p. 4. The same four authors later issued an appeal to the Catholic hierarchy in Western countries to support Father Dimitri: Appeal to the editorial boards of leading Catholic newspapers in Argentina, Brazil, Italy, Spain, Mexico and France, Easter 1980, *Russkaya mysl*, 24 April 1980, p. 4; English extracts in *KNS*, no. 98 (15 May 1980), p. 3.

76. *The Times*, 12 March 1980, p. 4.

77. Only Archbishop Pitirim of Volokolamsk attended, whereas the delegation was

originally to have consisted of Metropolitan Yuvenali, Metropolitan Filaret of Minsk, and Archbishop Pitirim; see *JMP*, no. 5 (1980), p. 7.

78. *Russkaya mysl*, 31 January 1980, p. 3.

79. Letter to His Grace Vasili, Archbishop of Brussels and Belgium, from Nikolai Popovich, Nikolai Chestnikh, Vladimir Sedov and others, Moscow, 17 February 1980, *Russkaya mysl*, 20 March 1980, p. 4.

80. The service was held in St Martin-in-the-Fields Church, London, on 9 March 1980, and was organised by Clergy to Defend Russian Christians, an association of British clergy formed as a response to the arrests in the Soviet Union. See press reports in, e.g. the *Church Times*, 14 March 1980, p. 1.

81. English version of the statement in *The Orthodox Church*, vol. 16, no. 3 (March 1980), pp. 1–2; Russian in *Russkaya mysl*, 29 February 1980, p. 1.

82. English version in *The Orthodox Church*, ibid., p. 1.

83. Appeal to Soviet President, the *Baptist Times*, 31 January 1980, p. 3.

84. *Russkaya mysl*, 14 February 1980, p. 1.

85. *Frankfurter Allgemeine Zeitung*, 4 March 1980, p. 6.

86. *KNS*, no. 94 (20 March 1980), p. 2.

87. Ibid., p. 3.

88. Letter to Archbishop Pitirim of Volokolamsk from Pavel Protsenko 10–17 February 1980, *Russkaya mysl*, 24 April 1980, p. 4; English translation in *KNS*, no. 100 (12 June 1980), p. 11.

89. *KNS*, Ibid., p. 2.

90. *KNS*, no. 92 (18 February 1980), p. 3.

91. Among other statements of support by Western church leaders were those by Metropolitan Antoni of Sourozh; Archbishop Methodius Fouyas of the Greek Orthodox Archdiocese of Thyateira and Great Britain; the Most Rev. Derek Worlock (Roman Catholic), Archbishop of Liverpool; Bishop Basil of Washington (Orthodox Church in America) (see *KNS*, no. 92 (18 February 1980), pp. 12–13); Archbishop Anthony of Geneva and Western Europe (Russian Orthodox Church in Exile); Rt Rev. David Sheppard (Anglican), Bishop of Liverpool; and Most Rev. Michael Bowen (Roman Catholic), Archbishop of Southwark (see *KNS*, no. 94 (20 March 1980), pp. 16–17).

92. *KNS*, no. 92 (18 February 1980), p. 3.

93. *KNS*, no. 94 (20 March 1980), p. 2.

94. Report (*soobshcheniye*) on the arrest of Viktor Kapitanchuk, anon., undated, but thought to be Moscow, 12 March 1980, *AS*, no. 3957.

95. These were biographies of Yakunin, Regelson and Kapitanchuk; an 'appeal' (*obrashcheniye*) to Kurt Waldheim from V. B. and A. A. Konopatsky, 1979; and an 'appeal' to the government of Canada from Pyotr Ivanovich Dubinetsky (? the spelling of this name is unclear), Khartsyzsk, Donetsk region. They were published as 'unedited documents for inclusion in Volume 13' of *DCCDBR* by Washington Research Center in San Francisco. There was also an Easter greeting to prisoners from the Christian Committee: 'Dlya slova bozhiya net uz!' ('There Are No Bounds for the Word of God!'), Easter 1980; copy in KC archive.

96. *KNS*, no. 98 (15 May 1980), p. 3.

97. *KNS*, no. 99 (29 May 1980), p. 3.

98. Declaration (*zayavleniye*) by Fr Vasili Fonchenkov, member of the Christian Committee, to the Christian Committee for the Defence of Believers' Rights in the USSR, 17 May 1980, *AS*, no. 4157.

99. They included Fonchenkov and the Pentecostal Stanislav Zherdev (*KNS*, no. 99 (29 May 1980), p. 3), and another Pentecostal, Boris Perchatkin (*KNS*, no. 100 (12 June 1980), p. 3).

100. *KNS*, no. 96 (17 April 1980), p. 3.

101. *KNS*, no. 99 (29 May 1980), p. 2.

102. *KNS*, no. 97 (1 May 1980), p. 3.

103. *KNS*, no. 104 (7 August 1980), p. 8.

104. These are the Soviet psychiatrist Alexander Voloshanovich, who subsequently emigrated, and Dr Gerard Low-Beer of the Royal College of Psychiatry in London, who visited the USSR in April 1978. These two psychiatrists, working in association with the unofficial Working Commission for the Investigation of the Use of Psychiatry for Political

Purposes, professionally examined a number of political and religious dissenters who had been forcibly committed to psychiatric hospitals. This incident with Kuzkin is one of several which indicates that their efforts were taken seriously by the Soviet authorities.

105. *KNS*, no. 99 (29 May 1980), p. 2.

106. *KNS*, no. 101 (26 June 1980), p. 5.

107. Report from the Christian Committee, 19 November 1979, *Russkaya mysl*, 10 January 1980, p. 4.

108. Vadim Nechayev, 'Golosa russkikh zhenshchin' ('The Voice of Russian Women'), *Russkaya mysl*, 3 April 1980, p. 10.

109. *KNS*, no. 103 (23 July 1980), p. 6; *Le Monde*, 22 July 1980. See interview with Goricheva and Malakhovskaya in *Guardian*, 31 July 1980, p. 8.

110. 'Zapis protsessa Vladimira Poresha v Lengorsude 23–25.4.80' ('Transcript of the Trial of Vladimir Poresh in Leningrad City Court 23–25 April 1980'), anon., Leningrad, shortly after 25 April 1980, *AS*, no. 4022; English extracts (evidence of witness Oleg Okhapkin and final word by Poresh) in *RCL*, vol. 10, no. 3 (1980), pp. 344–50; other extracts in *The Orthodox Monitor*, nos. 9–10 (July–December 1980), pp. 48–51.

111. Ibid., *AS*, no. 4022, p. 61.

112. He was interviewed on the popular Soviet current affairs programme 'Vremya' ('Time') by one 'Sergi Dmitrievich' (no surname given) who was identified simply as 'a journalist' (*KNS*, no. 101 (26 June 1980), p. 1).

113. 'Zapad ishchet sensatsii . . . : Zayavleniye svyashchennika D. Dudko' ('The West Is Seeking Sensations . . . : Statement of Priest D. Dudko'), *Izvestiya*, 21 June 1980, p. 6; English translation in *The Orthodox Monitor*, nos 9–10 (July–December 1980), pp. 23–6.

114. *Pravda Ukrainy*, 22 June 1980, p. 4; *Sovetskaya Belorussiya*, 22 June 1980, p. 3; *Pravda vostoka*, 24 June 1980, p. 3; *Zarya vostoka*, 22 June 1980, p. 3; *Sovetskaya Moldaviya*, 22 June 1980, p. 3; *Sovetskaya Rossiya*, 22 June 1980, p. 5; *Bakinsky rabochy*, 26 June 1980, p. 4.

115. *KNS*, no. 101 (26 June 1980), p. 1.

116. *JMP*, no. 7 (1980), p. 40.

117. One of the people named as having received documents was Archbishop Vasili of Brussels. According to two French Orthodox writers, he corresponded with Father Dudko, but did not receive documents. (Olivier Clement and Nicolas Lossky, '''L'Aveu'' et le martyre: A propos du P. Doudko', *La Croix*, 20–21 July 1980, p. 2.) Since the Archbishop was able to refute the *Izvestiya* statement, one may wonder why he was named there: Clement and Lossky suggest, very plausibly, that because of his open support for Father Dudko and other noncomformists, he was, in the eyes of the Soviet government 'un homme à abattre'. Another curious statement was that, having seen the 'subversive character' of some of his foreign contacts, Father Dudko subsequently refused to meet 'a member of the English Parliament, D. Atkinson' (David Atkinson, Conservative member for Bournemouth 1977–). Mr Atkinson, however, has said that he did meet Father Dimitri Dudko while he was in Moscow in 1980 (*Daily Telegraph*, 21 June 1980, p. 1). It is not at all clear why *Izvestiya* should have missed the chance to attack a member of the political party led by Mrs Margaret Thatcher, who at that time was implacably opposing the sending of British athletes to the Moscow Olympics Games.

118. *JMP*, no. 7 (1980), p. 4.

119. For example, *KNS*, no. 101 (26 June 1980), pp. 1–2; Clement and Lossky, '''L'Aveu'''; and the recently emigrated Yuri Belov, as quoted in Pietro Modesto, 'The ''Confession of Guilt'' of the Orthodox Priest Father Dudko', *Informationsdienst*, published by Kirche in Not/Ostpriesterhilfe, Königstein, no. 79, 28 November 1980. The two latter suggest that, as a priest, Father Dudko could not have been responsible for the text of the statement because it attributed to Christ words in fact written by St Paul ('For there is no authority except from God, and those that exist have been instituted by God. Therefore he who resists the authorities resists what God has appointed . . .' Romans 13, 1–2). In fact, the statement attributed these words to Christ only by implication, by stating that they were 'in the Gospel' (when in fact they occur in the Epistles). However, Russians often use the word 'Gospel' (*Yevangeliye*) rather loosely to mean the whole New Testament, not just the four Gospels, and it seems likely that this was the case here. This does not suggest that the KGB was not involved in writing the statement, merely that its officers were not as careless as has been supposed.

120. *KNS*, no. 101 (26 June 1980), pp. 1–2.

121. M. Probatov, Moscow, 27 June 1980, in *Russkaya mysl*, 17 July 1980, p. 4; English translation in *KNS*, no. 104 (7 August 1980), p. 12.

122. Statement by Irina Zalesskaya, Moscow, 22 June 1980, in *Russkaya mysl*, 31 July 1980, p. 4.

123. *KNS*, no. 102 (10 July 1980), p. 2.

124. *Religiya i ateizm v SSSR*, no. 11/59 (November 1980), p. 5.

125. *KNS*, no. 106 (4 September 1980), p. 4.

126. *Religiya i ateizm v SSSR*, no. 11/59 (November 1980).

127. Ibid.

128. *KNS*, no. 111 (13 November 1980), p. 2.

129. *KNS*, no. 106 (4 September 1980), p. 4.

130. 'Vsem moim dukhovnym detyam' ('To all my Spiritual Children'), Father Dimitri Dudko, 27 July 1980 (in KC archive); English translation in *KNS*, no. 111 (13 November 1980), pp. 1–2.

131. Letter to Archbishop Vasili of Brussels from Father Dimitri Dudko, undated but probably July 1980 (in KC archive); English translation in *KNS*, no. 111 (13 November 1980), p. 2.

132. *KNS*, nos 106 (4 September 1980), p. 4, and 111 (13 November 1980), p. 2.

133. *In the Light of the Transfiguration*, nos 69–83, dated 9 November 1980 to 22 February 1981, 133 consecutively numbered A5 pages (copy in KC archive). Nos 69 and 70 are not the same as issues bearing the same numbers put out by Father Dudko's parishioners after his arrest (no. 69 (no. 1, 1980), copy in KC archive; no. 70 (no. 2, 1980), 3 February 1980, *Russkaya mysl*, 20 March 1980, p. 5). He said here (p. 5) that he was dissatisfied with those issues and decided to recommence the series where he had been obliged to stop it. The documents containing these issues of the parish newsletter also contain other statements by Father Dudko: 'Moye pokayaniye' ('My Repentance'), undated, pp. 61–71; 'To All My Spiritual Children' (see note 130), pp. 77–9; 'Moi vopl' ('My Cry'), undated, p. 102; 'Rasprostranyayutsya slukhi' ('Rumours Are Spreading'), undated, pp. 103–9; 'Obrashcheniye k bezbozhnikam' ('Appeal to the Godless'), 26 December 1980, p. 133. The whole collection is entitled *Pritcha o nepravednom domopravitele: tragediya-Monolog* (*The Parable of the Unjust Steward: A Tragic Monologue*). These documents by Father Dudko did not reach Keston College until April 1982, though it seems that at least one copy had reached the West earlier but was not circulated.

134. Father Dimitri Dudko, 'Khozhdeniye po krugam . . .' ('A Passage through the Circles [of Hell]'), 31 July 1980 (date 31 June at end of document is a misprint), 22 pages (copy in KC archive).

135. Ibid., p. 12.

136. Ibid., p. 15.

137. Ibid., p. 1.

138. *In the Light of the Transfiguration*, p. 31.

139. Ibid., pp. 28–9.

140. Ibid., p. 30.

141. Ibid., p. 22.

142. Ibid., p. 23.

143. Ibid., p. 9.

144. Ibid., p. 112.

145. Ibid., p. 64.

146. Ibid., p. 127.

147. *Vestnik RKhD*, no. 132 (1980), pp. 230–2.

148. *Vestnik RKhD*, no. 133 (1981), p. 293; English translation in *KNS*, no. 128 (16 July 1981), p. 6.

149. *KNS*, nos 101 (26 June 1980), p. 2, and 102 (10 July 1980), p. 2. After his release Father Dudko appeared to have lost about 40 pounds in weight. It is known that rapid weight loss and gain is a side-effect of some mind-altering drugs.

150. 'Warum Dudko Widerrief' ('Why Dudko Recanted'), *Menschenrechte*, September–October 1980; *Russland und Wir*, September 1980, p. 12.

151. *In the Light of the Transfiguration*, p. 122.

152. Interview with Anatoli Levitin-Krasnov in *Religiya i ateizm v SSSR*, no. 11/159 (November 1980), p. 4; *USSR News Brief*, no. 8 (1980), pp. 13–14.

153. It is a matter for conjecture as to why, if Metropolitan Yuvenali had indeed performed the useful service of persuading Father Dudko to recant, he was subsequently removed from the post of chairman of the Department of External Church Relations in April 1981. It may be that his performance in this post was assessed quite separately from his performance as Metropolitan of Krutitsy and Kolomna, in which capacity he acted as Father Dudko's diocesan bishop. Alternatively, he may have been demoted from one of his posts as a punishment for allowing Father Dudko's activities to reach a pitch at which his arrest was, in the view of the KGB, necessary.

154. *In the Light of the Transfiguration*, p. 80.

155. Ibid., p. 17. This term is unlikely to mean a senior KGB official, since Father Dudko several times refers to such a person using the quite different terms the 'big chief' or the 'highest chief' (*bolshoye* and *vyssheye nachalstvo*).

156. *In the Light of the Transfiguration*, pp. 17, 56, 67–8, 98–9; 16 July 1981, p. 6.

157. Ibid., pp. 73, 75.

158. Ibid., p. 75.

159. Report of a foreign visitor to the USSR, spring 1981; copy in KC archive.

160. TASS report cited in *KNS*, nos 125 (4 June 1981), p. 7, and 128 (16 July 1981), p. 6.

161. *KNS*, no. 106 (4 September 1980), p. 3.

162. Nigel Wade, *The Daily Telegraph*, 26 August 1980, p. 22.

163. Reports of the trial appeared in *Russkaya mysl*, 4 September 1980, p. 3, and *KNS*, no. 106 (4 September 1980), pp. 2–4. According to the latter, a *samizdat* transcript of the trial was being prepared, but this has not been received in the West. Some details about the trial later appeared in a *samizdat* document entitled 'Rasprava' ('Reprisal'), by Monk Inokenti, Moscow, September 1980 (copy in KC archive). This was an indignant diatribe against the authorities for their arrest of Father Gleb and their conduct of the trial, and an appraisal of Yakunin's significance as a standard-bearer of Christianity in a hostile world.

164. *KNS*, no. 106 (4 September 1980), p. 4.

165. Karelin's willingness to testify against Father Yakunin represents a complete *volte-face* from his views a decade earlier, when, as we noted in Chapter 10 (p. 301), he was one of the signatories to the appeal to the 1971 Local Council. Moreover, Karelin had played a key role in providing important documentation used by Fathers Eshliman and Yakunin in their open letter to Patriarch Alexi in 1965. It seems that in the intervening years, Karelin had come to share the views of Gennadi Shimanov, and to believe that the way forward for the Russian Orthodox Church lay in some kind of union with the Soviet state, not in opposition to it.

166. *KNS*, no. 106 (4 September 1980), p. 3.

167. Ibid.

168. *In the Light of the Transfiguration*, pp. 84–5.

169. *KNS*, no. 106 (4 September 1980), p. 3.

170. *KNS*, no. 107 (18 September 1980), p. 1.

171. *KNS*, no. 113 (11 December 1980), p. 2.

172. *KNS*, no. 120 (26 March 1981), p. 3.

173. L. Kolosov, 'Komu sluzhil "otets" Gleb?' ('Whom Did "Father" Gleb Serve?'), *Trud*, 2 September 1980; broadcast by TASS, 2 September 1980, in Russian and English and summarised in *Summary of World Broadcasts*, SU/6514/C1/1, 4 September 1980.

174. *KNS*, no. 106 (4 September 1980), p. 5.

175. A. Sakharov *et al.*, 'Kto osuzhdyon?' ('Who is Condemned?'), Moscow, 29 August 1980, *AS*, no. 4076.

176. *KNS*, no. 106 (4 September 1980).

177. Ibid.

178. Ibid., p. 6; *KNS*, no. 107 (18 September 1980), p. 2; *CCE*, no. 58 (1980), p. 33.

179. Document no. 141 of the Moscow Helsinki Monitoring Group, 23 September 1980, signed by Yelena Bonner, Sofiya Kallistratova, Ivan Kovalyov, Naum Meiman and Felix Serebrov; English translation in *KNS*, no. 112 (29 November 1980), p. 7.

180. *KNS*, no. 113 (11 December 1980), p. 6.

181. For a detailed analysis of the article, see Paul Lucey, '"Aliens": A Study in Character Assassination', *KNS*, no. 145 (25 March 1982), pp. 9–15; also a commentary by Anatoli

Levitin, dated 12 October 1982, in *Russkaya mysl*, 12 November 1981, p. 7.

182. Viktor Pronin, 'Chuzhaki' ('Aliens'), *Ogonyok*, 23 and 30 August 1981.

183. 'Lev Regelson Goes on Trial', *Radio Liberty Research, RL 337/80*, 23 September 1980, p. 1; *CCE*, no. 58 (1980), p. 33.

184. *Russkaya mysl*, 2 October 1980, p. 4; *KNS*, no. 108 (2 October 1980), p. 2.

185. *Guardian*, 10 October 1980, p. 6.

186. *Daily Telegraph*, 9 October 1980, p. 6.

187. *Le Monde*, 11 October 1980, p. 3; *KNS*, no. 109 (16 October 1980), p. 2.

188. Confidential report by a Western visitor to the USSR, spring 1981; copy in KC archive.

189. Ibid.

190. Vadim Shcheglov, open letter, 8 October 1980 (handwritten original in KC archive); English translation in *KNS*, no. 112 (29 November 1980), p. 4.

191. Letter to Metropolitan Yuvenali from Dr Konrad Raiser, acting general secretary of the WCC, dated 1 October 1980, published 30 October 1980, after an 'appropriate delay' to enable the Metropolitan to consider it (copy in KC archive); summary in *KNS*, no. 111 (13 November 1980), p. 4.

192. Letter to Dr Konrad Raiser from Metropolitan Yuvenali, Moscow, 29 October 1980; English text in *KNS*, no. 112 (29 November 1980), pp. 20–1; commentary ibid, pp. 22–3.

193. *Russkaya mysl*, 26 February 1981, p. 6; *KNS*, no. 116 (29 January 1981), p. 5.

194. *Russkaya mysl*, 26 February 1981, p. 6.

195. *KNS*, no. 118 (26 February 1981), p. 6.

196. *KNS*, no. 121 (9 April 1981), p. 8.

197. *KNS*, no. 130 (13 August 1981), p. 7.

198. *KNS*, nos 145 (25 March 1982), p. 1, and 153 (15 July 1982), p. 1.

199. *KNS*, no. 120 (26 March 1981), p. 6.

200. Ibid., p. 18.

201. *KNS*, no. 114 (22 December 1980), p. 1.

BIBLIOGRAPHY

This bibliography is comprehensive for books, articles and periodicals, but selective for *samizdat*. The inclusion of every *samizdat* document cited would make the bibliography excessively lengthy, and in any case, all the documents are collected in either or both of two archives (see below under 'Archives').

We have therefore selected *samizdat* items which are in the form of articles, book or journals, rather than appeals, complaints or statements protesting about persecution and discrimination against believers. The selection is therefore representative of ideas and opinions rather than facts. We have, however, included some of the most significant 'protest' items, concentrating on those which cover a range of issues and are analytical rather than those which give details of a specific case or limited number of cases. These are listed below under '*Samizdat*'. The other *samizdat* items — articles, books and journals — are listed under the appropriate heading along with non-*samizdat* sources, but are distinguished by (S).

Books

Alexeev, Wassilij, and Theofanis G. Stavrou *The Great Revival. The Russian Church under German Occupation* (Burgess Publishing Company, Minneapolis, Minnesota, 1976)

Anon. Untitled Russian typescript (S), translated into English by Jane Ellis as *An Early Soviet Saint: The Life of Father Zachariah* (Mowbrays, London and Oxford, 1976)

Anon. *Otchizna neizvestnaya* (S), translated into English by Marite Sapiets as *The Unknown Homeland* (Mowbrays, Oxford, 1978)

Barron, John *KGB: The Secret Work of Soviet Secret Agents* (Corgi Books, London, 1975)

Beeson, Trevor *Discretion and Valour* (Collins/Fontana, London, 1974; revised edition Collins/Fount, London, 1982)

Belov, Anatoli, and Andrei Shilkin *Diversiya bez dinamita* (*Diversion Without Dynamite*) (Politicheskaya Literatura, Moscow, 1976)

Bennigsen, Alexandre, and Marie Broxup *The Islamic Threat to the Soviet State* (Croom Helm, London, 1983)

Berman, Harold J. *Introduction and Analysis to Soviet Criminal Law and Procedure* (Harvard University Press, Cambridge, Mass., second edition 1972)

Binyon, Michael *Life in Russia* (Hamish Hamilton, London, 1983)

Bloch, Sydney, and Peter Reddaway *Russia's Political Hospitals — The Abuse of Psychiatry in the Soviet Union* (Gollancz, London, 1977)

Bociurkiw, Bohdan R., and John Strong (eds) *Religion and Atheism in the USSR and Eastern Europe* (Macmillan, London, 1975)

Bourdeaux, Michael *Patriarch and Prophets: Persecution of the Russian Orthodox Church* (reprinted Mowbrays, London and Oxford, 1975)

—— *Opium of the People* (reprinted Mowbrays, London and Oxford, 1977)

—— *Land of Crosses: The Struggle for Religious Freedom in Lithuania, 1930–1978* (Augustine Publishing Company, Chulmleigh, Devon, 1979)

Bourdeaux, Michael, Hans Hebly and Eugen Voss (eds) *Religious Liberty in the Soviet Union: A Post-Nairobi Documentation* (Keston College, England, 1976)

Bourdeaux, Michael, and Michael Rowe *May One Believe — in Russia?* (Darton Longman & Todd, London, 1980)

Brown, Deming *Soviet Russian Literature Since Stalin* (Cambridge University Press, 1978)

Chalidze, Valeri *Prava cheloveka i Sovetsky Soyuz* (Khronika Press, New York, 1974), translated into English by Guy Daniels as *To Defend These Rights: Human Rights and the Soviet Union* (Collins & Harvill, London, 1975)

Christian Prisoners in the USSR 1979 (Keston College, Keston, England, 1979)

Conquest, Robert (ed.) *Religion in the USSR* (The Bodley Head, London, 1968)

Denisov, L. I. *Pravoslavnye monastyri Rossiiskoi imperii* (*Orthodox Monasteries of the Russian Empire*) (Moscow, 1908)

Dialog s tserkovnoi Rossiei (*Dialogue with Ecclesiastical Russia*) (Ichthus, Paris, 1967)

Dudko, Father Dimitri *O nashem upovanii* (YMCA Press, Paris, 1975), translated into English by Paul D. Garrett as *Our Hope* (St Vladimir's Seminary Press, Crestwood, New York, 1977)

Dunlop, John *Vserossiisky sotsial-khristiansky soyuz osvobozhdeniya naroda — programma, sud, v tyurmakh i lageryakh* (*The All-Russian Social-Christian Union for the Liberation of the People - Progamme, Trial, In Prisons and Camps*) (YMCA Press, Paris, 1975)

—————— *The New Russian Revolutionaries* (Nordland Publishing Company, Belmont, Mass., 1976)

—————— *The Faces of Contemporary Russian Nationalism* (Princeton University Press, Princeton, N.J., 1983)

Dunn, Dennis J. (ed.) *Religion and Modernization in the Soviet Union* (Westview Press, Boulder, Colorado, 1977)

Fedotov, G. P. (ed.) *A Treasury of Russian Spirituality* (Sheed & Ward, London, 1977)

Fletcher, William C., and Anthony J. Strover (eds) *Religion and The Search for New Ideals in the USSR* (Praeger, New York, Washington and London, 1967)

—————— *Nikolai* (Macmillan, New York, 1968)

—————— *Soviet Believers. The Religious Sector of the Population* (The Regents Press of Kansas, Lawrence, 1981)

Gerodnik, G. *Pravda o pskov-pecherskom monastyre* (*The Truth about the Pskov Caves Monastery*) (Politicheskaya literatura, Moscow, 1963)

Goricheva, Tatyana *Die Rettung der Verlorenen* (Brockhaus Verlag, Wuppertal, 1982)

Hebly, J. A. *The Russians and the World Council of Churches* (Christian Journals Ltd, Belfast, Dublin and Ottawa, 1978)

Kolarz, Walter *Religion in the Soviet Union* (Macmillan, London, 1961)

Konstantinov, Archpriest D. *Zarnitsy dukhovnogo vozrozhdeniya* (*Summer Lightning of the Spiritual Renaissance*) (Zarya, London, Ontario, 1973)

Konstantinow, The Very Rev. D. *Crown of Thorns* (Zarya, London, Ontario, 1979)

—————— *Stations of the Cross* (Zarya, London, Ontario, 1984)

Krasnikov, N. P. *Voprosy preodoleniya religioznykh perezhitkov v SSSR* (*Problems of Overcoming Religious Survivals in the USSR*) (Nauka, Moscow, 1966)

Kuroyedov, V. A., and A. S. Pankratov (eds) *Zakonodatelstvo o religioznykh kultakh* (*Legislation on Religious Cults*) (Yuridicheskaya literatura, Moscow, 1971)

Kuroyedov, Vladimir *Religiya i tserkov v sovetskom obshchestve* (*Religion and the Church in Soviet Society*) (Politicheskaya literatura, Moscow, 1984)

Lane, Christel *Christian Religion in the Soviet Union* (Allen & Unwin, London, 1978)

The Last Circle (Novosti Press Agency Publishing House, Moscow, 1974)

Levitin-Krasnov, Anatoli, and Vadim Shavrov *Ocherki po istorii russkoi tserkovnoi smuty* (*Essays on the History of the Russian Church Troubles*) (Institut Glaube in der 2. Welt, Küsnacht, Switzerland, 1978)

Lisavtsev, Ye. I. *Kritika burzhuaznoi falsifikatsii polozheniya religii v SSSR* (*A Critique of Bourgeois Falsification of the Situation of Religion in the USSR*) (Mysl, Moscow, 1971)

Litvinov, P., M. Meerson-Aksenov, and B. Schragin (compilers) *Samosoznaniye* (*Insights*) (Khronika Press, New York, 1976)

Marshall, Richard, Thomas Bird, and Andrew Blane (eds) *Aspects of Religion in the Soviet Union* (University of Chicago Press, Chicago and London, 1971)

Matthews, Mervyn *Privilege in the Soviet Union* (Allen & Unwin, London, 1978)

Meerson-Aksenov, Michael, and Boris Schragin *The Political, Social and Religious Thought of Russian Samizdat* (Nordland Publishing Company, Belmont, Mass., 1977)

Mezentsev, V. A. *Otvety veruyushchim* (*Answers to Believers*) (Politicheskaya Literatura, Moscow, third edition 1971)

The Moscow Patriarchate 1917–1977 (The Moscow Patriarchate, Moscow, 1978)

Neerskov, Hans *The Land of Closed Churches* (Danish European Mission, Søborg, n.d.)

Novikov, M. P. *Pravoslaviye i sovremmenost* (*Orthodoxy and the Modern World*) (Izd. Moskovskogo Universiteta, Moscow, 1965)

Ogryzko, I. I. *Deti i religiya* (*Chilren and Religion*) (Lenizdat, Leningrad, 1970)

Pascal, Pierre *The Religion of the Russian People* (Mowbrays, London and Oxford, 1976)

Paxton, John (ed.) *The Statesman's Year Book* (Macmillan, London, 1980)

Pitirim, Archbishop of Volokolamsk, *The Orthodox Church in Russia* (Thames & Hudson, London, 1982)

Pospielovsky, Dimitri *The Russian Orthodox Church Under the Soviet Regime 1917–1982* (St Vladimir's Seminary Press, Crestwood, New York, 1984)

Puzin, Alexei *Religion in the USSR* (Novosti Press Agency Publishing House, Moscow, 1967)

Razrushennye i oskvernyonnye khramy (*Destroyed and Profaned Churches*) (Posev, Frankfurt/Main, 1980)

Regelson, Lev *Tragediya russkoi tserkvi 1917–1945* (*The Tragedy of the Russian Church 1917–1945*) (YMCA Press, Paris 1977; English translation (of Part 1 only) in KC archive)

Romanyuk, Vasyl *A Voice in the Wilderness*, translated and edited by Jurij Dobczansky (Society for the Study of Religion under Communism, Wheaton, Illinois, 1980)

The Russian Orthodox Church (Progress Publishers, Moscow, 1980)

The Russian Orthodox Church. Organization, Situation, Activity (The Moscow Patriarchate, Moscow, 1958)

Sbornik zakonov SSSR 1938–1975 (*Collection of Soviet Laws 1938–1975*) (Izdaniye 'Izvestiya Sovetov Deputatov Trudyashchikhsya SSR', Moscow, 1975)

Scarfe, Alan (ed.) *The CCDBR Documents: Christian Committee for the Defense of Believers' Rights in the USSR*, translated by Maria Belaeffa (Door of Hope Press and Society for the Study of Religion under Communism, Glendale/Orange, California, 1982)

Shafarevich, I. R. *Zakonodatelstvo o religii v SSSR* (*Legislation on Religion in the USSR*) (YMCA Press, Paris, 1973; unpublished English translation in KC archive)

Simon, Gerhard *Church, State and Opposition*, translated from German by Kathleen Matchett (C. Hurst & Company, London, 1974)

Soloukhin, Vladimir 'Chernye Doski' ('Black Boards'), in *A Winter's Day* (Moscow, 1969); translated as *Searching for Icons in Russia* (Harvill Press, London, 1971)

Solzhenitsyn, Alexander *Letter to Soviet Leaders* (Index on Censorship and Fontana Books, London, 1974)

——— (ed.) *Iz-pod glyb* (YMCA Press, Paris, 1974); translated into English as *From Under the Rubble* (Collins & Harvill Press, London, 1975)

——— *Bodalsya telyonok s dubom*, translated into English by Harry Willetts as *The Oak and the Calf* (Harper & Row, New York, 1979)

Soviet Christian Prisoner List 1981 (Society for the Study of Religion under Communism, Orange, California, 1981)

Spravochnik agitatora i propagandista (*The Propagandist's and Agitator's Handbook*) (Moscow, 1966)

Stroyen, William B. *Communist Russia and the Russian Orthodox Church 1943–62* (The Catholic University of America Press Inc., Washington DC, 1967)

Struve, Nikita *Christians in Contemporary Russia* (The Harvill Press, London, 1967)

——— (ed.) *Rapport secret au comité centrale sur l'état de l'église en URSS* (Seuil, Paris, 1980)

Tancher, V. K. *Osnovy ateizma* (*The Foundations of Atheism*) (Kiev, 1961)

Ugrinovich, D. M. *Vvedeniye v teoreticheskoye religiovedeniye* (*Introduction to Theoretical Religious Studies*) (Mysl, Moscow, 1973)

Uspenskaya pochayevskaya lavra (*The Pochayev Lavra of the Dormition*) (Izd. Moskovskoi Patriarkhii, Moscow, 1983)

Voslensky, Michael *Nomenklatura. The Soviet Ruling Class: An Insider's Report* (Doubleday, New York, 1984)

Ware, Timothy *The Orthodox Church* (Penguin Books, Harmondsworth, Middlesex, 1963, revised 1964)

Yakunin, Father Gleb, and Lev Regelson *Letters from Moscow*, edited by Jane Ellis (Keston College and H. S. Dakin Company, San Francisco, 1978)

Yanov, Alexander *The Russian New Right* (Institute of International Studies, University of California, Berkeley, 1978)

Yudin, I. N. *Pravda o Peterburgskikh svyatinyakh* (*The Truth about the Petersburg Shrines*) (Leningrad, 1972)

Zhenshchina i Rossiya, 10 December 1979 (S) (Des Femmes, Paris, 1980); English translation, *Woman and Russia* (Sheba Feminist Publishers, London, 1980)

Articles
(also *Chapters, Reports, Interviews*, Samizdat *Articles, Films*)

Agursky, Mikhail 'Mezhdunarodoye znacheniye "Pisma k vozhdyam" A. Solzhenitsyna' ('The International Significance of A. Solzhenitsyn's *Letter to Soviet Leaders*') (S), 9 June 1974, *AS*, no. 1965

—— 'The Intensification of Neo-Nazi Dangers in the Soviet Union' (S), in Meerson-Aksenov and Shragin *The Political, Social and Religious Thought of Russian Samizdat*, 1977

—— 'The Attitude to Religion in the New Russian Literature', *RCL*, vol. 10, no. 2 (1982)

Alexius of Tallin and Estonia (Metropolitan) 'Excerpts from Listeners' Letters Programme', Radio Moscow 26 February 1977, *Summary of World Broadcasts*, SU/5459/B/1, 10 March 1977

Altayev, O. 'Dvoinoye soznaniye intelligentsii i psevdo-kultura' ('The Dual Consciousness of the Intelligentsia and Pseudo-Culture') (S), *Vestnik RSKhD*, no. 97 (1970)

Anon. 'O perspektivakh khristianstva sredi yevreyev' ('On the Perspectives for Christianity Among the Jews') 13 June 1974, *Moskovsky sbornik* (S), Moscow; KC archive

Anon. 'Fr Dimitri Dudko: An Eye-Witness Account', *RCL*, vol. 4, no. 2 (1976)

Antic, Oxana 'The Condition of the Kiev Monastery of the Caves', *Radio Liberty Research*, RL42/79, 7 February 1979

—— 'Taxation of Clergy in the USSR', *Radio Liberty Research*, RL254/81, 24 June 1981

Arranz, Fr Miguel SJ 'Inside the Russian Church — by a Jesuit at Work in Leningrad', interview in *Catholic Herald*, 28 March 1980

'Atheist Convictions for Youth', editorial, *Pravda*, 18 October 1984

Barabanov, Yevgeni 'The Schism Between the Church and the World', in Solzhenitsyn (ed.) *From Under the Rubble*, 1974

—— 'Pravda gumanizma' ('The Truth of Humanism'), 1975, in Litvinov (ed.) *Samosoznaniye*, 1976

—— 'Zabyty spor' ('A Forgotten Argument') (S), *Vestnik RKhD*, no. 118 (1976)

'"Bezobidny" kompromiss?' ('A "Harmless" Compromise?'), *Komsomolskaya pravda*, 10 September 1980

Binns, Christopher A. P. 'Soviet Secular Ritual: Atheist Propaganda or Spiritual Consumerism?', *RCL*, vol. 10, no. 3 (1982)

Binyon, Michael 'Latvian Diary', *The Times*, 28 March 1980

—— 'Tax Cuts and Social Benefits for Soviet Clergy', *The Times*, 4 November 1980

—— 'Moscow Opens Lavish Bible Centre', *The Times*, 6 October 1981

—— 'Salving the Soul of Russia', *Sunday Times* colour supplement, 8 January 1983

Bociurkiw, Bohdan R. 'The Orthodox Church and the Soviet Regime in the Ukraine, 1953–1971', *Canadian Slavonic Papers*, vol. XIV, no. 2 (1972)

—— 'Religious Dissent and the Soviet State', in Bociurkiw and Strong *Religion and Atheism in the USSR and Eastern Europe*, 1975

Bogolepov, Alexander A. 'The Legal Position of the Russian Orthodox Church', in Marshall, Bird and Blane *Aspects of Religion in the Soviet Union*, 1971

Borodin, L. 'Mersi — ili volosy dybom' ('Merci! or Hair on End'), in *Moskovsky sbornik* (S), Moscow, 1974

Bourdeaux, Michael 'How Soviet State Kept Control of Church Council', *Church Times*,

17 March 1972

———— 'Pilgrimage to Siberia', *Christianity Today*, 7 September 1979

———— 'The Black Quinquennium: The Russian Orthodox Church 1959–1964', *RCL*, vol. 9, nos 1–2 (1981)

Bourdeaux, Michael, and Kathleen Matchett 'The Russian Orthodox Church in Council 1945–1971', in Bociurkiw and Strong *Religion and Atheism in the USSR and Eastern Europe*, 1975

Candle in the Wind, television documentary film, Pacem Productions, California; typescript in KC archive. Interviews recorded 1982; film completed 1984

Chartres, Richard 'The Moscow Peace Conference, May 1982', *RCL*, vol. 10, no. 3 (1982)

Chelnov, M. 'Kak byt?' ('How To Be?') (S), *Vestnik RSKhD*, no. 97, (1970)

'The Church of the Russians', Part II, an NBC Religious Program, in association with the National Council of Churches of Christ, original broadcast 17 July 1983; typescript in KC archive

Clement, Olivier, and Nicolas Lossky '"L'Aveu" et le martyre: a propos du P. Doudko', *La Croix*, 20–21 July 1980

Dubrov, Andrei 'Documents: Anatoli Levitin', *RCL*, vol. 2, no. 2 (1974)

Dudko, Father Dimitri 'Kreshcheniye na Rusi' ('Baptism in Russia') (S), *Vestnik RKhD*, no. 117 (1976)

———— 'O chem propovedovat?' ('What Should We Preach About?') (S), *Russkoye vozrozhdeniye*, no. 2 (1978)

———— 'Zapad ishchet sensatsii . . .' ('The West is Seeking Sensations . . .'), interview in *Izvestiya*, 21 June 1980

———— 'Pritcha o nepravednom domopravitele: tragediya-monolog' ('The Parable of the Unjust Steward: a Tragic Monologue') (S), 1980–81?; typescript in KC archive

———— 'Khozhdeniye po krugam . . .' ('A Passage through the Circles [of Hell]') (S) 31 July 1980; typescript in KC archive

Duluman, Ye. 'Narusheniye pravoporyadka i koshchunstvo' ('Violation of Law and Order and Blasphemy'), *Pravda Ukrainy*, 11 March 1973

Dunlop, John 'The Eleventh Hour', *Frontier*, vol. 18, no. 2 (1975)

Ellis, Jane 'Father Dudko: The Flower of Russia's "Religious Spring"', *The Times*, 29 January 1980

———— 'USSR: The Christian Seminar', *RCL*, vol. 8, no. 2 (1980)

———— 'The Christian Committee for the Defence of Believers' Rights in the USSR', *RCL*, vol. 8. no. 4 (1980)

'*L'eremo dello "starets" Tavrion*' ('The Hermitage of *Starets* Tavrion'), *Russia Cristiana*, no. 168 (1979)

Fielding-Clarke, Rev. O., and Mrs X. 'The Other Side of the Penny: Impressions of Six Weeks with the Russian Church', April–June 1973, Derby; typescript in KC archive

Filaret, Metropolitan of Minsk and Belorussia, Untitled talk in the Moscow Patriarchate cathedral in London, November 1980, *KNS*, no. 112 (29 November 1980)

Final Act of the Conference on Security and Cooperation in Europe, Helsinki, 1 August 1975 (HMSO, London, 1975)

Fletcher, William C. 'Religion and Soviet Foreign Policy: A Functional Survey', in Bociurkiw and Strong *Religion and Atheism in the USSR and Eastern Europe*, 1975

———— 'Backwards from Reactionism', in Dennis J. Dunn (ed.) *Religion and Modernization in the Soviet Union*, 1977

Florovsky, Georges 'The Elements of Liturgy in the Orthodox Church', *One Church*, vol. XIII, nos 1–2 (1959)

Furov, V. Lecture to staff members working on the *Great Soviet Encyclopaedia*, May 1975; *Chronicle of Current Events*, no. 41 (Khronika Press, New York, 1976)

'Garantirovano vsem' ('Guaranteed to Everyone'), *Golos rodiny*, no. 1 (1980)

Giryayev, Ye. 'Religiozno-filosofsky seminar v Leningrade' ('The Religio-Philosophical Seminar in Leningrad') (S), *Vestnik RKhD*, no. 123 (1977)

Goricheva, Tatyana 'Paradoksy zhenskoi emansipatsii' (Paradoxes of Female Emancipation'), *37* (S), Leningrad; typescript in KC archive

———— 'Lettere a un Fratello spirituale' ('Letters to a Spiritual Brother'), January–June 1979, *Russia Cristiana*, no. 6 (1982); German translation in Tatiana Goricheva *Die Rettung*

der Verlorenen, 1982
—— 'Religious Revival', *Light in the East*, vol. 4, no. 1 (January 1981)
—— 'Gli Occhi di Fede di una Donna Russa' ('A Russian Woman's Eyes of Faith'), *Litterae Communionis*, no. 6 (June 1981)
Goricheva, Tatyana and Natalya Malakhovskaya, Interview, *Guardian*, 31 July 1980
Gorsky, V. 'Russky messianizm i novoye natsionalnoye soznaniye' ('Russian Messianism and the New National Consciousness') (S), *Vestnik RSKhD*, no. 97 (1970)
Harries, Rev. Richard 'Assessing Soviet Peace Rhetoric', unpublished typescript in KC archive
Ivanov, L. 'Outspoken Priest Nearly Killed in Road "Accident" ', *The Guardian of Liberty*, May–June 1975
Kelly, David 'Nairobi: A Door Opened', *RCL*, vol. 4, no. 1 (1976)
Klochkov, V. 'Zakon i svoboda sovesti' ('Law and Freedom of Conscience'), *Pravda*, 10 September 1982
—— 'Teoreticheskiye voprosy' ('Questions of Theory'), *Pravda*, 25 May 1984
Kolosov, L. 'Komu sluzhil "otets" Gleb?' ('Whom did "Father" Gleb Serve?'), *Trud*, 2 September 1980
Kondryatev, Ye. D. 'Kritika pravoslavnykh teologicheskikh kontseptsii "primireniya" nauki i religii' ('Criticism of Orthodox Theological Concepts of the "Reconciliation" of Science and Religion'), *Voprosy nauchnogo ateizma*, no. 19 (1976)
Kornel, R. and Yu. Nekrasov 'Khameleon' ('The Chameleon'), *Moskovsky komsomolets*, 11 April 1959; and 'More on the Chameleon', ibid., 13 October 1959
Krasikov, N. 'Posle pomestnogo sobora' ('After the Local Council'), *Nauka i religiya*, no. 12, 1975
Krasnov, A. (pseudonym of Anatoli Levitin-Krasnov) 'O dvukh yumoristicheskikh statyakh i odnom ochen seryoznom dele' ('On Two Humorous Articles and One Very Serious Matter') (S), 1959, in *Dialog s tserkovnoi Rossiei*, 1967
—— 'Otvet G. Gerodniku' ('Reply to G. Gerodnik') (S), 1963; English translation in Bourdeaux *Patriarch and Prophets*, 1975
—— 'Golosuyet serdtse' ('The Heart Votes') (S), 12 March 1963; typescript in KC archive
—— 'Bolnaya tserkov' ('The Ailing Church') (S), 27 August 1965, *AS*, no. 886
—— 'Kaplya pod mikroskopom' ('A Drop under the Microscope') (S), December 1966, *Vestnik RSKhD*, no. 83 (1967); English (abridged) in Bourdeaux *Patriarch and Prophets*, 1975
—— 'V chas rassveta' ('At the Hour of the Dawn') (S), *Posev*, May 1968
—— 'Zemlya dybom' ('The Earth Turned Upside Down') (S), Moscow, 1974; *AS*, no. 1876
Kuroyedov, Vladimir 'Sovetsky zakon i svoboda sovesti' ('Soviet Law and Freedom of Conscience'), *Izvestiya*, 31 January 1976; English translation in *RCL*, vol. 4, no. 2 (1976)
—— 'O svobode sovesti podlinnoi i mnimoi' ('On Freedom of Conscience, both Real and Imaginary'), *Izvestiya*, 28 January 1978; English translation (abridged) in *RCL*, vol. 6, no. 4 (1978)
—— 'Ravny pered zakonom?' ('Equal before the Law?'), *Literaturnaya gazeta*, 7 July 1982
Kuznetsov, Anatoli 'Zakrytaya dver avtobusa' ('The Closed Door of a Bus'), *Religiya i ateizm v SSSR*, no. 5 (104) (April 1976)
Levitin-Krasnov, Anatoli 'Otets Dimitri Dudko' ('Father Dimitri Dudko') (S), Moscow, May 1974, *AS*, no. 1975
—— 'Tserkov v Sovetskom Soyuze' ('The Church in the Soviet Union'), interview, *Russkaya mysl*, 5 December 1974
—— 'Le KGB et les jeunes seminaristes russes', *Catacombes*, October 1975
—— 'Save these Honest People', *Novoye russkoye slovo*, 7 May 1977; English translation in Yakunin and Regelson *Letters from Moscow*
—— 'Censorship and Freedom of Speech', *Radio Liberty Research*, RS 85/79, 25 May 1979
—— 'Religion and Soviet Youth', *RCL*, vol. 7, no. 4 (1979)
Lowrie, Donald A., and William C. Fletcher 'Krushchev's Religious Policy', in Marshall, Bird and Blane *Aspects of Religion in the Soviet Union*, 1971
Mashkov, Yu. T. 'Golos s rodiny' ('A Voice from the Homeland'), *Russkoye vozrozhdeniye*, no. 4 (1978)
Masson, Paul *La Libre Belgique*, 10–12 October 1979
Meerson-Aksyonov, Mikhail 'L'Eglise en URSS', *Etudes*, June 1973

———— 'Rozhdeniye novoi intelligentsii' ('The Birth of a New Intelligentsia') in Litvinov *et al.* *Samosoznaniye*, 1976

———— 'La Chiesa ortodossa en lo Stato ateo', *Russia Cristiana*, no. 169 (November–December 1979)

———— 'The Russian Orthodox Church 1965–1980', *RCL*, vol. 9, nos 3–4 (1981)

Modesto, Pietro 'The "Confession of Guilt" of the Orthodox Priest Father Dudko', *Informationsdienst*, Kirche in Not/Ostpriesterhilfe, 79/169-B2, 28 November 1980

Moskvitin, V. 'Pastyr vo khmelyu' ('The Tipsy Pastor'), in an unnamed, undated local Soviet newspaper; *DCCDBR*, vol. 7, p. 844

Moss, James 'The Remnants of Orthodox Monasticism', *Chelsea Journal*, September–October 1976

Nichols, Alan 'Documentary Record on the Australian Anglican Delegation's Visit to the Soviet Union, Poland and Yugoslavia', 14 June–4 July 1976; typescript in KC archive

Nikodim, Metropolitan of Leningrad 'Izmenyayushchi syamir' ('The Changing World'), *JMP*, no. 10 (1975)

Nikon (Yakimov), Hieromonk 'Vpechatleniya ochevidtsa' ('Impressions of an Eyewitness'), *Vestnik RKhD*, no. 132 (1980)

Okulov, A. F. and D. M. Ugrinovich 'Problemy filosofii religii na XIV Mezhdunarodnom filosofskom kongresse v Vene' ('Problems of the Philosophy of Religion at the XIVth International Philosophical Congress in Vienna'), *Voprosy nauchnogo ateizma*, no. 7 (1969)

Oppenheim, Raymond 'Russian Orthodox Theological Education in the Soviet Union', *RCL*, vol. 2, no. 3 (1974)

Osipov, Vladimir 'Tri otnosheniya k Rodine' ('Three Attitudes towards the Motherland') (S), 25 March–2 April 1970, *Vestnik RSKhD*, no. 103 (1972)

———— 'Berdyaevsky kruzhok v Leningrade' ('The Berdyaev Circle in Leningrad') (S), January 1972, *Vestnik RSKhD*, nos 104–5 (1972)

———— 'Otkrytoye pismo Gennadiyu Shimanovu' ('Open Letter to Gennadi Shimanov') (S), 29 April 1973, *AS*, no. 1732

———— 'Pyat vozrazhenii Sakharovu' ('Five Objections to Sakharov') (S), April 1974, *AS*, no. 1696

———— 'K voprosu o tseli i metodakh legalnoi oppositsii' ('On the Question of the Goals and Methods of Legal Opposition') (S), May 1974, *AS*, no. 1760

Ostrozhinsky, V. 'Vrazhdebnaya ideologiya' ('The Alien Ideology'), *Pravda*, 25 May 1984

Posdeef, Helene 'Geneva: The Defence of Believers' Rights', *RCL*, vol. 4, no. 4 (1976)

Pospielovsky, Dimitri 'Metropolitan Nikodim Remembered', *RCL*, vol. 6, no. 4 (1978)

Potapov, Father Vladimir 'Pravoslavnoye inakomysliye v SSSR' ('Orthodox Nonconformism in the USSR'), *Russkoye vozrozhdeniye*, nos 7–8 (1979)

Pozdeeva, Elena (alias Posdeef, Helen, qv) 'The Report Card of the Moscow Patriarchate's Delegation in Nairobi', *Radio Liberty Research*, 23 February 1976, RL 104/76

Pozner, Vladimir, Radio Moscow, 24 April 1976, *Summary of World Broadcasts*, SU/5193/A1/5, 27 April 1976

———— ' "Unexpected" Reason for Ban on Bible Imports', Radio Moscow, 21 January 1978; *Summary of World Broadcasts*, 26 January 1978, SU/5723/A1/6

'Problemy sovremennogo khristianstva (Iz lichnoi perepiski)' ('Problems of Contemporary Christianity (From Personal Correspondence)'), *Vestnik RKhD*, nos 115 (1975), and 118 ʹ(1976)

Pronin, Viktor 'Chuzhaki' ('Aliens'), *Ogonyok*, 23 and 30 August 1981

Rahr, Gleb 'Combien d'Orthodoxes y-a-t-il en Russie?' ('How Many Orthodox Are There in Russia?'), *Catacombes*, February 1973

———— 'Skolko v Rossii pravoslavnykh khramov?' ('How Many Orthodox Churches Are There in Russia?'), *Posev*, January 1974

Roshchin, Boris 'Svoboda religii i klevetniki' ('Freedom of Religion and the Slanderers'), *Literaturnaya gazeta*, 13 April 1977

Rozenbaum, Yu. 'Takoi zakon yest' ('There Is Such a Law'), *Nauka i religiya*, no. 4 (1964)

'Russian Believers Plead', *International Herald Tribune*, 4 September 1977

Sabant, Philippe 'Religion in Russia Today', *Tablet*, 19 January 1980

Safronov, Yu. 'Avtoritet ateista' ('The Authority of the Atheist'), *Izvestiya*, 12 November 1971

Samuil, Archimandrite, and Metropolitan Filaret of Kiev 'Reuter Concoction Refuted by Church Leader', interview with Novosti Press Agency, *Soviet News*, 12 March 1974
Sapiets, Marite 'Monasticism in the Soviet Union', *RCL*, vol. 4, no. 1 (1976)
Sawatsky, Walter 'Bibles in Eastern Europe Since 1945', *RCL*, vol. 3, no. 6 (1975)
—— 'The New Soviet Law on Religion', *RCL*, vol. 4, no. 2 (1976)
—— 'Secret Soviet Lawbook on Religion', *RCL*, vol. 4, no. 4 (1976)
Scarfe, Alan 'Dismantling a Human Rights Movement: A Romanian Solution', *RCL*, vol. 7, no. 3 (1979)
Serapion, Bishop of Irkutsk, Interview, Novosti Press Agency, 25 April 1978
Shevelev, V., 'Neprostaya arifmetika' ('Not Simple Arithmetic'), *Nauka i religiya*, no. 2 (1973)
Shimanov, Gennadi 'Zapiski iz krasnogo doma' (S); translated into English as *Notes from the Red House* (Diane Books, Glendale, California, second edition 1972)
—— 'Kak otnositsya k sovetskoi vlasti' ('How to Relate to Soviet Power') (S), Moscow, 2 June 1974; KC archive
—— 'Idealnoye gosudarstvo' ('The Ideal State') (S), Moscow, 29 May 1975; KC archive
—— 'Protiv techeniya' ('Against the Current') (S), Moscow, 1975; KC archive
—— 'Otvety voprosam korrespondenta zhurnala *Yevrei v SSSR*' ('Answers to Questions of a Correspondent of *Jews in the USSR*') (S), Moscow, 13 May 1976; KC archive
Shimanov, Gennadi, Felix Karelin and L. Ibragimov 'Priglasheniye k dialogu' ('Invitation to a Dialogue') (S), Moscow, 1978; KC archive
Shirshov, B. 'Ubezhdat faktami' ('Convince by Facts'), *Meditsinskaya gazeta*, 24 March 1970
'Shkola molodogo ateista' ('School of the Young Atheist'), *Molodyozh Moldavii*, 28 March 1981
Steele, Jonathan 'Churches Are Seen But Not Heard', *Guardian*, 20 November 1979
—— 'A Useful Opium for the State?', *Guardian*, 21 November 1979
Sukharev, A., Deputy Minister of Justice of the USSR, Interview, *New Times*, 4 January 1976
Sysyn, Frank E. 'The Ukrainian Orthodox Question in the USSR', *RCL*, vol. 11, no. 3 (1983)
Teodorovich, Nadezhda 'The Rejuvenation of the Russian Clergy', in Fletcher and Strover *Religion and the Search for New Ideals in the USSR*, 1967
Teplyakov, M. K. 'Sostoyanie religioznosti naseleniya i otkhod veruyushchikh ot religii v Voronezhskoi oblasti (1961–1964gg)' ('The Situation of the Religiousness of the Population and the Departure of Believers from Religion in Voronezh Region (1961–1964)'), in Krasnikov *Voprosy preodoleniya religionznykh perezhitkov v SSSR*, 1966
'Threats to Peace', World Council of Churches Executive Committee, Liebfrauenberg, Woerth, France, 11–15 February 1980, Document no. 19 (revised)
Udodov, A. 'Skolko pravoslavnykh v Rossii?' ('How Many Orthodox Are There in Russia?'), *Posev*, February 1976
Ukhov, Ye. 'Klyuchi Sviyazhska' ('The Keys of Sviyazhsk'), *Trud*, 18 August 1981
'Unseparate Church and State', *Time*, 23 June 1980
Vasili (Krivoshein), Archbishop 'Arkhiyepiskop Veniamin (Novitsky)' ('Archbishop Veniamin (Novitsky)'), *Vestnik RKhD*, no. 120 (1977)
Viktorov, A. 'Spasat etot unikalny pamyatnik' ('Save this Unique Monument'), *Dekorativnoye iskusstvo SSSR*, no. 6 (1982)
Vladimirov, V. 'Dokhodnoye mesto' ('A Lucrative Place'), *Kommunist Tadzhikistana*, 3 April 1977
Voort, Theo Van Der 'Ich war Student der Leningrader Geistlichen Akademie' ('I was a Student at the Leningrad Theological Academy'), *Religiya i ateizm v SSSR*, no. 131 (June 1978); untitled, undated English version in KC archive
Vsevolodov, A. 'Sovetsky fond mira' ('The Soviet Peace Fund'), *Sovetskaya yustitsiya*, no. 9 (1970)
Walters, Philip 'A New Creed for Russians?', *RCL*, vol. 4, no. 3 (1976)
—— 'Vladimir Osipov: Loyal Opposition?', *RCL*, vol. 5, no. 4 (1977)
—— 'The Ideas of the Christian Seminar', *RCL*, vol. 9, nos 3–4 (1981)
'Warum Dudko wiederrief' ('Why Dudko Recanted'), *Menschenrechte*, September–October 1980
Woodrow, Alain 'La Vie Religieuse en URSS' ('Religious Life in the USSR'), *Le Monde*, 7 September 1978

Yachnik, Ye. 'Vot tebe i "Bozhi slugi" ' ('So Much for the "servants of God" '), *Sovetskaya Kirgiziya*, 5 February 1976

Yakunin, Father Gleb 'Moskovskaya Patriarkhiya i "kult lichnosti" Stalina' ('The Moscow Patriarchate and "The Cult of Personality" of Stalin'), *Russkoye vozrohdeniye*, no. 1 (1978)

Yershov, I 'Sotsial'na aktivnist' osobi i relihiino-modernists'ky kontseptsiyi' ('The Social Activity of the Individual and Modernist Religious Conceptions'), *Lyudina i svit*, no. 4 (1977)

Zholkovskaya-Ginzburg, Irina 'Testimony on the Russian Orthodox Church before the Commission on Security and Cooperation in Europe' (in Washington DC), 21 May 1980; KC archive

Periodicals

ABN (Anti-Bolshevik Bloc of Nations) *Correspondence*, Munich
Agitator, Moscow
Bakinsky rabochi (*Baku Worker*), Baku
Baptist Times, London
Baptist World Alliance News Service, Washington DC
Bratsky vestnik (*Fraternal Herald*) (official Baptist publication), Moscow
Cahiers du Samizdat, Brussels
Calendar of the Russian Orthodox Church, Moscow
Canadian Slavonic Papers, Toronto
Catacombes, Paris
Catholic Herald, London
Chelsea Journal, Chelsea, London
Christian Science Monitor, Boston
Christianity Today, Carol Stream, Illinois
Chronicle of Current Events, Amnesty International, London (translation of *Khronika tekushchikh sobytii*, Khronika Press, New York)
Chronicle of the Lithuanian Catholic Church, New York
Church Times, London
Contacts: revue française de l'Orthodoxie, Paris
La Croix, Paris
CSCE (Conference on Security and Cooperation in Europe) *Weekly Review*, Washington DC
Current Abstracts and Annotations, Radio Liberty, Munich
Daily Courier News, Elgin, Illinois
Daily Telegraph, London
Eastern Churches Review, London
Ecumenical Press Service, Geneva
Episkepsis, Geneva
Etudes, Paris
Frankfurter Allgemeine Zeitung, Frankfurt-am-Main
Frontier, London (discontinued 1975)
Gésu, Milan
Glaube in der 2. Welt, Zurich
Golos Rodiny (*Voice of the Motherland*) (Soviet newspaper for émigrés), Moscow
Guardian, London
Guardian of Liberty, Munich
Idea, Wetzlar, West Germany
Information Bulletin of the Department of External Church Relations of the Moscow Patriarchate, Moscow
Information Bulletin of the Working Commission to Investigate the Use of Psychiatry for Political Purposes, London

Informationsdienst G2W (Glaube in der 2. Welt), Zurich
Informationsdienst Kirche in Not, Königstein, West Germany
International Herald Tribune, London
Izvestiya (Soviet Government newspaper), Moscow
Journal of the Moscow Patriarchate, Moscow
Keston News Service (*KNS*), Keston, Kent, England
Komsomolskaya pravda (Soviet Young Communist newspaper), Moscow
Kommunist Tadzhikistana (Tadzhikistan republic newspaper), Dushanbe
Licht im Osten, Stuttgart
Literaturnaya gazeta (leading Soviet literary weekly), Moscow
Litterae Communionis, Milan
Lyudina i svit (*Man and the World*) (Soviet Ukrainian atheist monthly), Kiev
Mariya (S) (feminist journal), Leningrad
Mariya (*Émigré* continuation of above), Frankfurt-am-Main
Meditsinskaya gazeta (*Medical Gazette*), Moscow
Menschenrechte, Frankfurt-am-Main
Molodyozh Moldavii (*Youth of Moldavia*), Kishinyov
Le Monde, Paris
Moscow News, Moscow
New Times, Moscow
Nash sovremennik (*Our Contemporary*), Moscow
Nauka i religiya (*Science and Religion*) (leading Soviet atheist journal), Moscow
Novosti Press Agency, Moscow
Novoye russkoye slovo (*New Russian Word*), New York
Novy mir (*New World*) (leading Soviet literary monthly), Moscow
Ogonyok (*Little Fire*) (Soviet satirical magazine), Moscow
One Church, Youngstown, Ohio
One World, the WCC, Geneva
Orthodox Monitor, New York
Ostkirchliche Information, Hanover
Posev, Frankfurt-am-Main
Pravda, Moscow
Pravda Ukrainy (*Truth of Ukraine*), Kiev
Pravda Vostoka (*Truth of the East*), Tashkent
Radio Liberty Research, Radio Liberty, Munich
Religion in Communist-dominated Areas, New York
Religion in Communist Lands (*RCL*), Keston, Kent, England
Religiya i ateizm v SSR (also published as *Religion und Atheismus in der UdSSR*) (*Religion and Atheism in the USSR*), Munich
Review of Socialist Law, Leyden, The Netherlands
Romanian Orthodox Church News, Bucharest
Russia Cristiana, Milan
Russkaya mysl (*La Pensée russe*), Paris
Russkaya zhizn (*Russian Life*), San Francisco
Russkoye vozrozhdeniye (*Russian Revival*), New York
Russland und Wir (*Russia and Us*), Bad Homburg, West Germany
SGOIS, Newsletter of the Saint George Information Service, London
Samizdat Bulletin, San Mateo, California
Service Orthodoxe de Presse, Courbevoie, France
SMOT (Free Interprofessional Association of Workers) *Information Bulletin* (S), *Arkhiv samizdata*, Munich
Le Soir, Brussels
Southern Cross, Sydney
Sovetskaya Belorussiya (*Soviet Belorussia*), Minsk
Sovetskaya Kirgiziya (*Soviet Kirgizia*), Frunze
Sovetskaya Moldaviya (*Soviet Moldavia*), Kishinyov
Sovetskaya Rossiya (*Soviet Russia*), Moscow
Sovetskaya yustitsiya (*Soviet Justice*), Moscow

Soviet News, London
Suchasnist, Munich
Summary of World Broadcasts, Caversham, England
Tablet, London
Time magazine, New York
The Times, London
Trud (*Labour*) (Soviet trade-union newspaper), Moscow
UBS (United Bible Societies) *World Report*, London
Ukrainian Review, London
Vedomosti verkhovnogo soveta (*Annals of the Supreme Soviet*), Moscow
Vesti iz SSSR (*USSR News Brief*), Munich
Vestnik RKhD (Russkogo Khristianskogo Dvizheniya) (*Herald of the Russian Christian Movement*), Paris. Until 1974 this journal was known as
Vestnik RSKhD, the 'S' standing for Studencheskogo (*Student*)
Volnoye slovo (*Free Word*), Frankfurt-am-Main
Voprosy nauchnogo ateizma (*Questions of Scientific Atheism*), Moscow
Vstrechi, Frankfurt-am-Main
Zarya vostoka (*Dawn of the East*), Tbilisi

Samizdat (selected)

Anon. 'Arkhiyereisky sobor 1961' ('The Council of Bishops 1961'), unsigned and undated, 35 pp., *AS* no. 701; typescript in KC archive
Christian Committee *Dokumenty khristianskogo komiteta zashchity prav veruyushchikh v SSSR* (*Documents of the Christian Committee for the Defense of Believers' Rights in the USSR*) (Washington Research Center, San Francisco), vols 1–13, 19, 77–9. (See Introduction, note 2, for details.) Cited as *DCCDBR*
Eshliman, Father Nikolai, and Father Gleb Yakunin 'Zayavleniye predsedatelyu presidiuma verkhovnogo soveta SSSR' ('Declaration to the Chairman of the Presidium of the Supreme Soviet of the USSR'), 21 November 1965; English translation in Bourdeaux, *Patriarch and Prophets*
Furov, V. 'Izvlecheniya iz informatsonnykh otchetov Soveta po delam religii pri Soviete Ministrov SSSR Tsentralnomu Komitetu KPSS (za 1968–1974gg)' ('Extracts from Informational Reports of the Council of Religious Affairs under the Council of Ministers of the USSR to the Central Committee of the CPSU'), 1968, 1970, and 1974; typescript in KC archive. (See Introduction, note 1, for further publication details.) Cited as the CRA Report
Moskovsky sbornik (*Moscow Miscellany*), Moscow, September 1974; bound typescript in KC archive
Obshchina (*Community*), no. 2, Moscow, 1978; typescript in KC archive
Rusak, Deacon Vladimir 'Tipograficheskaya problema' ('The Problem of Printing'), Moscow, 1980; typescript in KC archive. This is a section of Rusak's long *samizdat* history of the Russian Orthodox Church: Stepanov, Vladimir (pseudonym) *Svidetelstvo obvineniya. Tserkov i gosudarstvo v Sovetskom Soyuze* (*Testimony of the Prosecution. Church and State in the Soviet Union*), Moscow, 1980, 3 vols; photocopy in KC archive; reproduced by Institut Glaube in der 2. Welt, Küsnacht, Switzerland
37, Leningrad, 1975–81; some issues in KC archive
Veche, nos 1–10, Moscow, 1971–74; KC archive
V svete preobrazheniya (*In the Light of the Transfiguration*), Grebnevo, Moscow, September 1978–; some copies in KC archive
Yakunin, Father Gleb and Lev Regelson 'Obrashcheniye k delegatam v assambleya Vsemirnogo Soveta Tserkvei ('Appeal to the Delegates of the Fifth Assembly of the World Council of Churches'), Moscow, 16 October 1975; English translation in *RCL*, vol. 4, no. 1 (1976), reprinted in Yakunin and Regelson *Letters from Moscow*
Yakunin, Father Gleb, and Leve Regelson 'Generalnomu Sekretaryu Vsemirnogo Soveta Tserkvei Filippu Potteru' ('To the General Secretary of the World Council of Churches,

Philip Potter'), Moscow, 6 March 1976; English translation in Yakunin and Regelson *Letters from Moscow*, and Bourdeaux *et al. Religious Liberty in the Soviet Union*

Yakunin, Father Gleb *'Doklad svyashchennika Gleba Yakunina Khristianskomu komitetu zashchity prav veruyushchikh v SSSR o sovremennom polozhenii Russkoi Pravoslavnoi Tserkvi i o perspektivakh religioznogo vozrozhdeniya v Rossii'* ('Report of Father Gleb Yakunin to the Christian Committee for the Defence of Believers' Rights in the USSR on the Current Situation of the Russian Orthodox Church and the Prospects for a Religious Renaissance in Russia'), Moscow, 15 August 1979; *DCCDBR*, vol. 11. Cited as The Yakunin Report

Zemlya (*Earth* or *Land*), Moscow, no. 1 (1 August 1974), *AS*, no. 1909; no. 2 (25 December 1974), *AS*, no. 2060

Legislation

Konstitutsiya (Osnovnoi zakon) Soyuza Sovetskikh Sotialisticheskikh Respublik (Constitution (Fundamental Law) of the Union of Soviet Socialist Republics) (Yuridicheskaya literatura, Moscow, 1983)

Postanovleniye o religioznykh obyedineniyakh (Resolution on Religious Associations) of the All-Union Central Executive Committee and the Council of People's Commissars of 8 April 1929, as amended by the Edict of the Presidium of the Supreme Soviet of the RSFSR of 23 June 1975; *Vedomosti Verkhovnogo Soveta* (*Annals of the Supreme Soviet*), no. 27 (873) (3 July 1975); English translation in *The Review of Socialist Law*, vol. 1 (September 1975)

Ugolovny kodeks RSFSR (Criminal Code of the RSFSR), Ministry of Justice of the USSR (Yuridicheskaya literatura, Moscow, 1983)

Archives

Arkhiv samizdata (*AS*) (Samizdat Archive), Radio Liberty, Oettinger Strasse 67, Munich
Keston College (KC) archive, Keston College, Heathfield Road, Keston, Kent, England

INDEX

Abramkin, Valeri 330, 419–20
Adventists, Seventh-Day 369, 374
aesthetic appeal of Orthodox worship 288
Afghanistan, Soviet invasion 273, 398, 422
Agursky, Mikhail 300, 324, 331, 339, 406
  Christian Seminar, lecture to 384
  on nationalism 324–5
Akhmatova, Anna 317
Akinfiev, Archpriest Dimitri 208
Aksyonov see Meerson-Aksyonov
Alexander, Archimandrite; Bishop of Dimitrov 118, 248
Alexenko, Fr Leonid Demyanovich 98
Alexi, Archbishop of Kalinin 94
Alexi, Metropolitan of Tallinn and Estonia 130, 143, 207, 208
  Council for Religious Affairs 225
  Local Council 234
  offices held 9n1, 119, 248
  supports official views 208–9, 216, 426
  theological training 205
Alexi, Patriarch 197, 224, 263, 272
  Council of Bishops (1961) 56–8, 63, 64, 66–7
Alimpi, Archimandrite 140
Alipi, Archimandrite (Voronov) 141
All-Russian Social Christian Union for the Liberation of the People (VSKhSON) 292, 388
All-Russian Society for the Preservation of Historical and Cultural Monuments 30
All-Union Church of True and Free Adventists 369
American Council of Churches (National Council of Churches of the USA) 267
Amvrosi, Fr 140
Andropov, Yuri 454
Anthony (Antoni), Metropolitan of Sourozh 320, 425
anti-religious campaign (1959–1964) 4, 5, 14, 270–1
  baptism registration 197
  Council of Bishops 57
  monasteries 125, 139–41
  seminaries 100
anti-religious literature 5, 251, 406
  conversion through reading 115
  on clergy corruption 88–90
anti-semitism 7, 300, 345, 345n9, 450, 452

anti-Soviet agitation and propaganda (Article 70) 439, 442
anti-Soviet slander 316–17, 408, 445
anti-Western attitudes 348
Antioch, Patriarch of 206
Antoni, Archbishop of Chernigov 216
Antoni, Archbishop of Vilnius 89
Antoni, Metropolitan of Leningrad 154, 205, 207, 210, 217
Apelli, hegumen 140
archives, Soviet, inaccessibility 399
area deans 93
Argentina, diocese 206, 249
Argentov, Alexander 388, 413–14
Arkhangelsk diocese 17
Armenian Apostolic Church 176
Asino 21, 22
Astrakhan, Tony 327
atheism 188, 251
  anti-religious 5, 88–90, 251, 406
  constitution 255
  eradication of religion 251–5
  propaganda 260
  proselytisation 31
Athos, Mount 125
authoritarianism, political 319
Averyanov, Alexei 111

Balashokva (Rovno region) 26
Balkhash (Kazakhstan) 21
baptisms
  numbers 177–8
  records and registration 173, 178, 195–8
  secret 90, 198
Baptist Churches 369, 374
  churches 17
  membership 17, 176, 186
  unregistered meetings 32
Baptists
  samizdat 295
  '37' Seminar 391, 393
Barabanov, Yevgeni 320, 331, 371, 405
  articles 332–3, 346–7
  international publicity 316–18
Begun, Iosif 378
Belgrade Conference (1978), appeal to 25, 25n71
belief see renaissance, religious
believers
  congregations 39–40, 75
  numbers 173–81

520